D1247509

Psychotherapeutic Agents

New Roles for Nonprofessionals, Parents, and Teachers

Edited with commentaries by
BERNARD G. GUERNEY, JR.
Rutgers—The State University

HOLT, RINEHART AND WINSTON, INC.
New York Chicago San Francisco Atlanta
Dallas Toronto Montreal London Sydney

To my mother and father

Library of Congress Catalog Card Number: 69-12829
03-075365-1
Printed in the United States of America
1 2 3 4 5 6 7 8 9

PREFACE

The education of those difficult to educate, the prevention of delinquency, and the betterment of mental health—these are among the most pressing needs in the nation today, and a sense of commitment leads professionals in education, medicine, and the social and behavioral sciences to be deeply concerned with selecting the appropriate strategies for dealing with these pressing needs. The primary focus of the present work is on a strategy for meeting mental health needs, rather than education or delinquency. However, the problems of mental health in today's world are inextricably intertwined with problems of education and the promotion of constructive social functioning. New methods for dealing with these latter problems are implicit in all the readings presented in this book, and explicit or central in several of them.

It is now becoming evident to many of those concerned with finding solutions to problems in all of these areas that, with traditional methods and any foreseeable increase in manpower, progress will remain unsatisfactory. The attempt at solution presented in this book is the development of new methods, which use professional personnel[1] in such a manner as to increase vastly the impact that they can have on the masses in need of their help. This solution requires the use of others who are naturally significant to those in need of help, or who can be made to be significant as intermediaries, as aides, or as agents of the professionals.

The design of this book is also influenced by a substrategy within the general strategy of using nonprofessionals. This substrategy is to concentrate resources most heavily on improving the social and psychological welfare of *children*. Nicholas Hobbs has suggested (see p. 23) that the *only* way to make substantial changes in the mental health of the adult population a generation from now is to devote at least 75 percent of our resources to the mental health problems of children. In choosing and organizing the selections for this book, this substrategy was followed, and emphasis was given to programs designed for children. The four central parts of the book, wherein specific treatment programs are outlined, have, in fact,

[1]The word "professional" in the book is meant to be synonymous with "mental-health professional," and the word "nonprofessional" means "mental-health nonprofessional."

been limited to descriptions of work with children. (When applicable, references to work with adults may be found in the Suggested Additional Readings following each part.) The other three parts of the book—which deal with mental health needs and new directions (Part 1), with training (Part 2), and with research on the use of nonprofessionals (Part 7)—are more general in nature, and do contain selections devoted to adults. Fortunately, from the point of view of those who agree with Hobbs, systematic utilization of volunteers and other nonprofessionals seems to be developing most rapidly and extensively in programs that are geared to young children and adolescents.

One purpose of this book is to present the reader with some of the historical developments and factual considerations which underlie the strategy of using nonprofessionals as therapeutic agents. The major purpose, however, is to present specifically and in some detail remedial methods and procedures based on this strategy. There is no other book at present which attempts a general coverage of such efforts. Although programs based on this strategy seem to be developing very rapidly now, it has proved possible—because of the relative recency of the whole movement—to present a fairly comprehensive picture of such developments up to this point in time in this single volume. The Suggested Additional Readings at the end of each part direct the reader to work which is similar to that appearing in the text, or which has not yet been reported in sufficient detail to warrant inclusion. Following the Introduction a few additional references are also provided to sources which go into greater theoretical depth.

In preparing this book, I had in mind those groups of people who are in a position to participate at various levels in the types of remedial psychosocial efforts which the book describes. Since the strategy on which these efforts are based is specifically designed to draw upon the efforts of a population which is quite large in comparison to that which is involved in traditional methods, these potential participants represent a wide range of groups. One group would be professionals in the field of mental health who want to determine whether they do or do not wish to adopt, adapt, or devise methods based on the use of nonprofessionals. This group includes psychiatrists, psychologists, social workers, psychiatric nurses, and teachers—particularly teachers in special education. Administrators and policy-making personnel of public schools, special schools, mental health clinics, child guidance centers, reformatories, and residential treatment centers for children represent other groups which certainly should be directly interested in the programs outlined in this work.

Some of those prominently concerned with the probable course of development of the roles of mental health professionals predict that the training and supervision of others, largely nonprofessionals, will replace one-to-one direct service as the major service role of professionals. If such methods receive even extensive *trial* in the coming decade, those teaching advanced students in the fields of mental health and in special education and psychiatric nursing may well wish to use this book for supplementary reading. Undergraduates in the social and behavioral sciences are considered to be prime candidates for becoming significant others to maladjusted children because of the training value to themselves, and because they are so often willing and able to offer their services. College teachers interested in encouraging projects of this nature with undergraduates should find the projects described here stimulating to their students.

The selections have been drawn from a wide variety of journals, as well as from papers recently presented at scientific and professional meetings. For this reason, very few of our intended readers have easy access to more than a small sample of them. By bringing together this widely dispersed material, as well as through the introductory comments to each part, the reader, it is hoped, has been provided with sufficient background to support his own creative thinking along similar lines.

Any merit of a work of this nature derives, of course, primarily from the authors of the selections themselves, and grateful acknowledgments are hereby extended to them. We also wish to thank the publishers —specifically acknowledged on the first page of each selection—who allowed us to reprint those articles which originally appeared elsewhere. Due appreciation is also expressed to the National Institute of Mental Health, which, through Grant No.MH02506, has provided great encouragement for our own particular endeavors in the type of work to which the book is devoted. It is a great pleasure, also, to acknowledge the help, encouragement, and counsel of Dr. Michael P. Andronico, Dr. Lillian Stover, Dr. G. Franklin Stover, Dr. Gary Stollak, Mrs. Louise Clempner, Mrs. Miriam Schlosser, and my wife, Dr. Louise F. Guerney.

Bernard G. Guerney, Jr.

New Brunswick, N. J.
February 1969

CONTENTS

PART 7: *Research on the Use of Symbionts and Nonprofessionals* 471

INTRODUCTION: Why Try Nonprofessionals?

It is now acknowledged that professional manpower cannot meet the mental health needs of the population through the use of present methods, and that there is no reasonable hope that such manpower can be increased sufficiently to do so in the future. But the same statement could have been made twenty years ago. Psychoanalysis, as an extremely time-consuming and costly process with an uncertain outcome, is now under widespread attack. But, like an ego with its superego, psychoanalysis throughout its history could scarcely be defined without reference to its appendant severe critics.

Why, then, does one now sense that there is ferment in the mental health field, why is there an unmistakable aura of change, of germination? Without doubt, the civil rights struggle and the war-on-poverty have had much to do with the professional's current heightened awareness of unmet mental health needs and with his commitment to do something about them.

An equally important ingredient of this recognition and desire, however, is the feeling, now, that something *can* be done. There is a feeling that innovations may be at hand which may be able to meet the need. For one thing, the mental health field, at this point in its development, already has a record of some success in attempting to increase its therapeutic effectiveness and to make more efficient use of its personnel. The development of group therapy represented a major breakthrough in that regard. Doubtless, the success of group therapy procedures facilitated the conception and initiation of family therapy, which has grown very rapidly in the last decade. Like group therapy, it also offers considerable economy of professional effort. It has been clear in both of these developments that this economy was not achieved at the expense of effectiveness. Such methods were based on theoretical expectations that the processes involved would, with appropriate cases and circumstances, offer certain advantages which would more than compensate for any disadvantages due to the lack of a more personal and private relationship to the therapist. This view, held by few at first, is now almost universally accepted; and group therapy and family therapy are viewed as extremely valuable additions to the therapist's armamentarium.

There are other developments which also seem to have paved the way for a higher level of public participation in the psychotherapeutic and rehabilitative processes. These have to do not with the question of whether psychotherapy could proceed effectively in a group instead of an individual context, but with the question of whether, even in individual psychotherapy, it was necessary to have an intellectual-emotional understanding of the genesis of one's problems in order to overcome them. The view that this was necessary came from the psychoanalytic tradition. As long as this assumption prevailed, truly significant expansion of psychotherapeutic effectiveness via the inclusion of large segments of the population in the rehabilitative effort remained blocked.

Clearly, it is a most difficult task to guide an individual on a Dantesque voyage through the black labyrinth of unwanted childhood memories and to succeed in uncovering and emerging with those which, brought into the light of day, would free him to respond more appropriately to present circumstances.

But more recent developments in theory have altered the conception of the psychotherapeutic task: genetic intrapsychic introspection is no longer the *sine qua non* of psychotherapy. In addition to J. L. Moreno, S. R. Slavson, and other pioneers in group therapy, the neo-Freudians, especially Karen Horney and Harry Stack Sullivan, have prepared us theoretically to recognize just how significant *interpersonal interactions* and *social-psychological forces* are in understanding and treating emotional disorders—how very significant "significant others" are. This was another step necessary to bring us to the threshold of expansion at which we now stand. More recently, and most significantly, the views of Carl Rogers and of B. F. Skinner (foremost among several learning theorists) helped the therapist to break out of this self-imposed handicap of demanding near-omnipotence of himself. They did so by offering alternative approaches, which were mainly *ahistorical.*

Neither of their approaches requires a therapist to play Virgil for the patient. The techniques which adherents of their views employ, while they call for personal qualities certainly not found in everyone, do not by any means call for the very special attributes and training of therapists following a psychoanalytic model. Both of these more recent approaches do require a reasonably adequate intellect, patience, interpersonal sensitivity, self-control, and a strong motivation to help others. These qualities alone are not sufficient for a person to become a professional person or a scientist. But given an individual with these qualities, or even the potential for developing these qualities, it is possible for a follower of Rogers or of Skinner to consider training him, in a reasonable period of time, to begin helping others with their problems of psychosocial adjustment.

Although client-centered therapy and the behavior modification techniques espoused by those following learning theory differ greatly, this should not be allowed to mask the fact that they share certain common elements, and that both can be incorporated into a larger concept of the rehabilitative task. We cannot enter into this in any detail here, except to emphasize that both methods: a) have an ahistorical approach to this task; b) have a set of basic principles which are not so numerous, complicated, intricate, or foreign to everyday experience that they cannot be grasped by the great majority of persons; and c) rely upon patterns of therapeutic behavior which can be specified, taught, and measured with relative ease and reliability.

Because of the work of such leading thinkers and their followers, and the acknowledged success of group therapy and family therapy, psychotherapists and others concerned with social rehabilitation have become more hopeful about applying their aid to more people, and to a wider range of problems. It appears that with theoretical reformulation, with hope fostered by the above-mentioned historical developments, and with recognition of the tremendous need, mental health professionals are now ready to experiment in an attempt to offer service at an entirely new level. Borrowing a phrase used by physicists, we may speak of this level as offering a service increase "an order of magnitude" greater than previous approaches—a difference comparable to that between the tin lizzie and the airplane in the field of transportation. If the experiment is, on the whole, successful, it can bring psychosocial rehabilitative services in line with needs in the foreseeable future. The strategy underlying such experimentation appears to be the only one now visible which offers the hope of accomplishing this.

We refer, of course, to the use by the professional of others—nonprofessionals—to implement his plans; to his use of others who can, for a specific task at hand, learn those facets of the professional's knowledge and skills which would enable them, with his help, to serve their common ends, as if they were ten or one hundred more of him.

This, naturally, is an oversimplification, as they will certainly not be replicas of the professional even in the circumscribed areas in which they are trained. And here lies the tantalizing, the fascinating, core of the experiment: will these rehabilitative agents turn out to be pale carbons of the professional, hardly replacing the energy expended by professionals to train them, or—at the other extreme—once given the specified skills, will their unique qualities be such as to enhance or strengthen the rehabilitative effects beyond the level which professionals themselves could achieve even if professionals were in adequate supply? Of course, we have made great progress if the answer lies anywhere but at the lowest end of the two extremes.[1]

Allowances must be made for the enthusiasm of the experimenter, both with respect to its effect on his objectivity and the additional impetus it may afford to the people he is trying to help. As techniques become more widespread, their effects often tend to become less dramatic. Nevertheless, the apparent effectiveness of the high-leverage methods described in this volume is quite impressive, all the more so when one realizes that these are but first steps in uncharted territory, and that, as we gain experience, we can expect to learn a great deal more about how to select and use therapeutic agents more effectively. Much of the promising benefit of this strategy must be considered solely in terms of the increased manpower made available through special training at less than the professional level. In psychosocial rehabilitation, if a trainee is not already a significant person in the life of the individual being helped, this may involve teaching the trainee ways to make himself a "significant other" to that individual. Such efforts are represented in this work in the selections describing the training of nonprofessionals and the varieties of programs using nonprofessionals. It is an approach with great promise for helping persons in need of help for social and emotional problems.

But what makes this high-leverage approach even more encouraging is that initial efforts in this direction suggest that the nonprofessionals, at least in certain instances, seem to provide therapeutic effectiveness *beyond* that which would be achieved by professionals. The instances in which this may be most likely to occur are those in which the therapeutic agents

[1]One might question whether the extremes are fairly drawn. There is, after all, the possibility that these agents may actually do harm. But it is felt that this possibility is very minimal in comparison to the damage being done by present practices, albeit this damage may be due to sins of omission (because of lack of personnel) rather than commission. Potential harm stemming from the use of nonprofessionals is minimal for two other reasons: first, because efforts toward using therapeutic agents are likely to be much more closely watched than existing practices, since they are by nature much more public and open to scrutiny; and secondly, because they are likely to take place in the context of evaluative research, since they must prove themselves relative to established practices and practitioners. Those experiments which do not work could be promptly discontinued, before they can be of significant harm.

are "naturally significant others" or "symbionts"[2] to the persons being helped. With respect to children, three categories predominate this field: parents, teachers, and peers. Traditionally, these naturally significant others have not been thought of as very promising rehabilitative agents; first, because they were not trained to provide such help, and secondly, because their other responsibilities or types of relationships with the child or both seemed to preclude the objectivity and orientations necessary to the rehabilitative task. The theoretical developments and therapeutic techniques mentioned above now permit these assumptions to be challenged. Once they are challenged, the advantages of using such persons directly for rehabilitation cease to be invisible.

These groups, by virtue of their natural role in his environment, have an *emotional significance* for the child which a professional person could hope to duplicate only after months or years of intensive effort—and then only if he were very skilled and if other circumstances (created largely by the symbionts!) were just right. To be sure, the consequences of this emotional significance can be either good or bad; in fact, for the children with whom we are here concerned, the influences of one or more of these groups has probably been bad in at least some of their aspects, or the child would not have a problem. The question is whether the therapist has a better chance of correcting the difficulties largely through his own intensive efforts with the child, or through enlisting a member of these significant groups as his agent for effecting change.

As the reader will see later on, the early indications are that the powerful emotional significance of these naturally significant others *can* be harnessed and used for therapeutic purposes. But leave aside now the question of emotional significance, and consider merely the amount of *time* the child spends with these groups in comparison to the professional therapist, and it will be seen that given appropriate skills, these figures loom large as potential influencers. Leave aside both emotional significance and time, and consider only the effects that training groups of parents, teachers, and of children in therapeutic principles can have on the *prevention* of psychosocial problems for *all* the children with whom these groups have contact. The conclusion seems obvious: the use of significant others, and especially symbionts, as agents for the psychosocial rehabilitation of children (and adults) deserves intensive and extensive trial, with accompanying research and evaluation.

This volume will acquaint mental health professionals and educators with the various methods being developed by those who see the use of nonprofessionals as remedial agents as a major avenue toward the goal of adequate mental health services. In addition to informing them, hopefully

[2]See page 246 for a discussion of this term.

this volume will also encourage them to try these methods for themselves; or, more importantly, to apply the general strategy and principles involved in this approach in new ways which will be most appropriate to the remedial goals and special populations with which they are particularly concerned. There is much room for such further innovation in this particular aspect of mental health's third revolution.

SUGGESTED ADDITIONAL READINGS

Ferster, C. B. Reinforcement and punishment in the control of human behavior by social agencies. *Psychiatric Research Reports*, 1958, Vol. 10, 101–118.

Morrice, J. K. W. The community as therapist. *Journal of the Fort Logan Mental Health Center*, 1967, Vol. 4, No. 3, 125–147.

Rogers, Carl. *Client-centered therapy*. Boston: Houghton Mifflin Company, 1951.

Rogers, Carl. The necessary and sufficient conditions of therapeutic personality change. *Journal of Consulting Psychology*, 1957, Vol. 21, No. 2, 95–103.

Rogers, Carl. *On becoming a person*. Boston: Houghton Mifflin Company, 1961.

Skinner, B. F. *Science and human behavior*. New York: Crowell-Collier and Macmillan, Inc., 1953.

Ullmann, Leonard P., and Krasner, Leonard (Eds.) *Case studies in behavior modification*. New York: Holt, Rinehart and Winston, Inc., 1966. Introduction, pp. 1–65.

Werry, John S., and Wollersheim, Janet P. Behavior therapy with children: A broad overview. *Journal of the American Academy of Child Psychiatry*, 1967, Vol. 6, No. 2, 346–370.

PART 1

Mental Health Needs and Directions of Change

Introduction

IF the mental health movement may be regarded as entering a revolutionary phase, the first selection, by Hobbs, may be considered its manifesto. His nine objectives for the training of mental health workers represent both a platform and a challenge for the mental health professions. Many of these objectives bear directly on the theme of this book. Hobbs stresses the widely recognized but largely unmet need for concentrating our efforts on the problems of children, recommending that 75 percent of mental health resources be directed to such work. He calls traditional individual therapy a "dead-end" and urges new goals in the training of professionals, emphasizing innovation and an orientation toward working through other persons who can multiply the professional's efforts.

I would place added emphasis on the role that *primary* prevention should play in this revolution—the actual prevention of problems as opposed to early case recognition and treatment. This requires broad-based educational and training programs that are nonexistent today. One of the great advantages inherent in training nonprofessionals is that this process can be bidirectional; that is, it can yield intimate knowledge about the attitudes, abilities, and deficiencies of ordinary individuals; knowledge which the professional must have if he wishes to launch effective primary preventive programs in mental health. We need to know much more about the present practices, conceptions, misconceptions, and attitudes covering interpersonal relationships held by workingmen, businessmen, parents, teachers, and even children. We need to know much more about which methods will prove practical and effective in changing attitudes and practices which require modification. The attempt to employ nonprofessionals and significant others as therapeutic agents should teach us a great deal along those lines. In the process of learning more about what attitudes we need to change in others, and how they can be changed, we may find out which of our own preconceptions and attitudes as professionals also need changing.

The article by Smith and Hobbs shows how many of the objectives described in the first article might be applied to the movement now under way, supported in part by the Federal government, to establish community mental health centers throughout the country. The emphasis this program puts on consultation and public education—for example, the possibility of training programs for managers and teachers—coincides with the theme of this volume. Smith and Hobbs also point out the opportunity the comprehensive community mental health center affords for developing nonprofessional roles for "indigenous" persons to bridge cultural gaps between the professional and the person he seeks to help.

The word "indigenous" is most appropriately used with respect to members of a culture or inhabitants of a region—in this instance, the culture of poverty and the inner city. However, the underlying concept also seems valid with respect to the desirability of training parents as representatives of a particular "family subculture," and teachers as representatives of the "school subculture." These subcultures often can be about as unfamiliar to a mental health professional as the culture of poverty. The professional could well benefit in very similar ways here by having a representative of the special culture aiding him in his work. Whether broadly or narrowly interpreted, the use of indigenous others is highly consonant with the concept of employing naturally significant others as therapeutic agents. The consonance of the viewpoint of Smith and Hobbs with that of this volume also applies to the view that community mental health centers should not be limited to programs deriving from an "illness" model, but should innovate, should consider cost factors, experiment with new services, experiment with new divisions of labor among those providing services, and tap the "great reserves of human talent among educated Americans who want to contribute their time and efforts to a significant enterprise".

The selection by Fidler, Guerney, Andronico, and Guerney presents a more detailed consideration than Hobbs and Smith permitted themselves, of some of the historical changes in theoretical orientation toward psychotherapy which have prepared the way for this "third revolution." This paper makes many of the same points made in the Smith and Hobbs article, but centers them around the illustration provided by one new method—filial therapy. In the context of this method, the authors present the changing of focus in the psychotherapeutic endeavor away from the isolated individual and an "illness" model, and toward the consideration of community and social psychological problems such as cost factors in treatment, the importance of adequate communication, and the need to consider change of an individual within the context of his subculture—and the way this is facilitated by using a member of that subculture as an agent of change.

Gordon's article on Project Cause also uses a specific program to help focus on more general issues. The article makes it clear, through reasoning and documentation, that, as stated in the Preface to this book, problems in the areas of education, juvenile delinquency, and psychological adjustment are inextricably intertwined, and that together they constitute a "powder keg" difficult to defuse. He makes it clear that to defuse it, professionals working in the problem areas must revise their methods of functioning to include the nonprofessional. Only this approach seems to offer a realistic cost factor and a chance to reach over barriers imposed by differing subcultures. This requires, Gordon continues, that the professional's role be modified to include, among other things, a training and supervisory function vis-a-vis the nonprofessional. That such changes are not easy to make is made clear in his realistic discussion of the problems and challenges such changes pose for professionals, for programs, and for agencies.

Rioch discusses with great insight the difficulty of achieving the necessary acceptance by professionals of the idea of using nonprofessionals as psychotherapeutic agents, and suggests that a greater identification of the professional with the goal of advancing knowledge, as opposed to practicing a craft or an art, would facilitate the necessary changes. It is not easy for a professional to give up some of the deep personal satisfaction that comes from the direct one-to-one intensive helping relationship. But it seems clear from both Gordon's and Rioch's presentations that some changes in this direction are inevitable, and that the professional should prepare to guide them, rather than fight them.

Blum's paper documents the need for such change as it applies to the social work profession and social welfare. Rather than base practices on the way in which professional social workers have conceived of their task and role in the past, he proposes a rethinking of the problem in terms of the multifaceted needs of clients, and a division of labor based on such an analysis. The professional social worker could occupy key decision-making positions, and would remain the person accountable for the services provided. However, instead of one worker trying to be all things to all people, as is currently the practice, a differentiation of tasks could encourage the maximum use of the special strengths each worker brings to an agency, and permit the development of sufficient personnel to meet the existing need for services.

Probably the strongest and most general objection of professionals to the use of nonprofessionals, and especially to the use of indigenous and inherently significant others, is their belief that the deficiencies and biases the nonprofessional may have in common with the person to be helped might make him ineffective as an agent of change. Riessman, in the final article of this section, does not deny the legitimacy of this concern. However—although he does not put it precisely in this way—he makes the point that if such persons do share these deficiencies and these biases, then they, too, are in need of help. And, contrary to the old saw about the blind leading the blind, some evidence is beginning to accumulate—some of which will be found later in this book—suggesting that being an agent of change can help not only the target person, but the agent himself. Professional therapists are quite fond of talking about how their professional work has led to their personal growth. Teachers are fond of saying that the best way to learn is to teach. Riessman's observations about the helper-therapy principle may well stimulate further research into the underlying causes of such phenomena. Meanwhile, is it fair not to admit the possibility that nonprofessionals can benefit others while benefiting themselves, in much the same way as psychotherapists and teachers benefit themselves while helping others? While there is no denying the possible pitfalls which Riessman also points out, it is possible that some of the most efficient change programs of the future will rely on just such a double-change phenomenon.

Mental Health's Third Revolution

NICHOLAS HOBBS

There have been three mental health revolutions. Pinel led the first, bringing humane concern for the mentally ill; Freud led the second, bringing passionate attention to the intrapsychic life of man. The third revolution, now in the making, is appropriately a corporate effort without an eponym as yet. Mental health, always a public health problem, is finally adopting public health strategies, with strong support from some quarters and resistance from others.

The exciting thing for me about this session on movement and resistance to change in the mental health professions is the assumption that professional people have a responsibility for the management of innovation. The implication is that the mature profession does not simply respond to the needs of society but claims a role in determining what society should need and how social institutions, as well as individual professional careers, can be shaped to the service of an emerging social order. The responsible professional person becomes the architect of social change.

This paper was presented at the 1964 Annual Meeting of The American Orthopsychiatric Association, Inc. It is reprinted with permission from *The American Journal of Orthopsychiatry*, 1964, Vol. XXXIV, No. 5, 822–833, Copyright 1964, The American Orthopsychiatric Association, Inc., and with permission of the author.

AN OVERVIEW

I see a two-phase process: the invention phase and the engineering phase. The invention phase is what we are about in this session; the engineering phase invokes, among other things, the development of new training programs and the building of new institutions. I propose to talk about the third mental health revolution, the inventions it requires and their implications for training programs.

The first mental health revolution may be identified with the names of Philippe Pinel in France, William Tuke in England, and Benjamin Rush and Dorothea Lynde Dix in America. It was based on the heretical notion that the insane are people and should be treated with kindness and dignity. Though 170 years old, this revolution has, unhappily, not yet been consummated. Its ideals may not yet be taken for granted and must therefore be given a major emphasis in training programs at all levels. You will recall that the central thesis of *Action for Mental Health*, its story line, is that the mentally ill do not get adequate care because they are unconsciously rejected by family, neighbor and professional alike. I regard this as an oversimplification, but the fact that there are still practices to support the argument of the Joint Commission's report may remind us that the work of Pinel is not yet done.

The second revolution was born in Vienna—its charismatic leader, Sigmund Freud. Its agents were the wearers of Freud's ring and other disciples who carried his ideas, making a few adjustments of their own, throughout the Western world. Freud was a giant, a companion of Darwin, Marx and Einstein in shaping our culture, our beliefs about man. It is impossible not to include Freud in a training program today, for if his ideas were to be omitted from the syllabus they would be brought in, as the clothes they wear, by every participant who has been exposed to novels, plays, poetry, television, the jokes of the day and even to *Infant and Child Care*, the most popular publication of the United States Government Printing Office.

Revolutions generally tend to excess and Freud's is no exception. A counter-revolution is required to restore balance and common sense. Freud has led us to a preoccupation with the intrapsychic life of man. No, I think "obsession" is a better word to suggest the passionate commitment we have to the world inside a man's skull, to the unconscious, the phenomenal, the stuff that dreams are made of. Everyone must become a therapist, probing the argument of insidious intent, stalking ragged claws scuttling over the bottoms of silent seas. The psychiatrist forgets Adolph Meyer and can no longer give a physical examination. The psychologist lays down his diagnostic tools, forgets research and gets behind a desk to listen. The social worker goes inside and waits for the patient to come. The preacher takes to his study and the teacher to the case conference. The most thoroughly trained person of all, the psychiatrist who has completed psychoanalytic training, becomes a monument of Veblenian inutility, able to treat maybe a hundred patients in his entire professional career. We owe a tremendous debt to Freud, as a son to a wise and insightful father, but to use our heritage we must break with him and discover our own, authentic idiom. The pendulum is already swinging back, and I am here trying to give it a little push.

The third mental health revolution, the one we are now challenged to further, is not readily identified with the name of a person but is evident in the common theme that runs through many seemingly disparate innovations of the last 15 years.

The therapeutic community, the open hospital, the increased interest in children, the growth of social psychiatry, the broadened base of professional responsibility for mental health programs, the search for new sources of manpower, the quickened concern for the mentally retarded, the proposed comprehensive community mental health centers, these developments are evidences of a deep-running change, indicative of this: *The concepts of public health have finally penetrated the field of mental health.* Up to the last decade the mental health effort was developed on a clinical model; now we are committing ourselves to a new and more promising public health model and are seeking specific ways to make it work in practice.

Mental health used to mean its opposite, mental disease; now it means not just health but human well-being. The revolution of our time is manifested not only in changed practices but more consequentially in changing assumptions about the basic character of mental disorders and of mental health. A great stride forward was made when aberrant behavior was recognized not as madness, lunacy or possession by a devil but as an illness to be treated like other illnesses; a perhaps even greater stride forward may result from the growing recognition that mental illness is not the private organic misery of an individual but a social, ethical and moral problem, a responsibility of the total community.

By an accident of history the problem of mental retardation is being brought into prominence, with a clear demand that the mental health professions no longer shirk their responsibility for the mentally handicapped individual. Thus the scope of the mental health field is broadening at the same time that its basic character is undergoing change. Mental retardation is also being redefined to recognize the preponderant involvement of social and educational influences in the over-all problem.

It is a paradox that the care of the mentally ill has always been largely a public responsibility but that the concepts of public health, of early detection, of prophilaxis and prevention, of adequate treatment of all regardless of wealth or social position, have never had much influence. Toward the end of the Eighteenth Century, the *maisons de santé* in Paris did give humane treatment to the insane, but these facilities were expensive and thus not available to the great masses of the afflicted. In America moral and humane treatment was established in a few of the better early institutions, such as the Friends Asylum in Philadelphia, but the indigent insane continued to be neglected, to be housed in overcrowded and filthy quarters, to be bound in camisoles and forgotten. The chains that Pinel had struck off were simply turned to leather. It was in the interest of the indigent insane that Dorothea Dix launched her crusade. Of course, the situation today is much better, but the dominant theme of advantage for the well-to-do and relative neglect for those without substantial means remains depressingly evident. In June 1963, The National Institute of Labor Education presented a report, "Issues in the New National Mental Health Program Relating to Labor and Low Income Groups," in which the following observations are central to the argument: "While in principle the state hospital is available to the community at large, in practice its population is overwhelmingly drawn from lower income groups. To bring about a reduction in state mental hospital populations, therefore, requires that treatment and rehabilitation services be created in the community which can effectively reach lower socioeconomic groups. . . . To a larger extent, the orientation and treatment methods of existing community facilities have been based on services to middle and upper class individuals. They have neither attracted blue collar workers nor found them to be suitable clients when and if they presented themselves for help."

Two contemporary books seem to me to present in boldest relief the character of the public health, mental health problem today. One is by Hollingshead and Redlich and the other is by George Albee.

The former, *Social Class and Mental Illness*, is often quoted but not for its main point, a point so startling and so revealing of the character of much of our current mental health effort that one suspects its neglect can only be due to professional embarrassment and consequent repression of the disturbing facts. Hollingshead and Redlich studied all persons receiving psychiatric treatment in New Haven, Connecticut, during a specific period, to find out what determined the kind of treatment they received. One would normally make the simple-minded assumption that diagnosis would determine treatment, that what was done for a patient would be based on what was the matter with him. The investigators found no relationship between diagnosis and treatment. They studied other variables such as age and sex, and found these unrelated to treatment. The one variable related to type of treatment received was the socioeconomic status of the patient. If he were from the lowest socioeconomic group, he received some kind of mechanical, inexpensive and quick therapy such as electric shock. If he were from a high socioeconomic group, he received extended, expensive, talking-type psychotherapy. If the patient were not only affluent but also a member of an old, prestigious family, so situated in life that he bestowed honor on his helper, he received extended talking-type psychotherapy, but at a discount. The relationship between socio-economic status and type of treatment received was not manifested in private practice alone but was also evident in the treatment provided by clinics and other public supported agencies. Thus all the mental health professions are involved.

The second pivotal book is George Albee's. I regard his monograph *Mental Health Manpower Trends,* prepared for the Joint Commission on Mental Illness and Health, as a most important and instructive book for the shaping of a national mental health program as well as for the development of curricula for the training of psychiatrists, psychologists, social workers and other mental health specialists. The book requires, it seems to me, a fundamental shift in strategy in providing mental health services to the people of this nation.

Albee's main thesis can be stated simply: The prospective supply of people for training in the mental health professions is limited, demands for services will continue to grow more rapidly than the population of the country, and there will not be in the forseeable future enough mental health personnel to meet demands for service.

It is widely and I think erroneously assumed that the personnel shortages so much with us everywhere are a local and a temporary phenomenon. We assume that it is a matter of waiting a year or so for the training programs to catch up. Albee's point is that they will not catch up. We can't solve the problem in the way we are trying to solve it.

Keep these two disturbing books in mind and then consider: (1) the geographical distribution of psychiatrists and (2) the growth of private practice in clinical psychology. Most psychiatrists are concentrated in urban centers in proportions much higher than the relative concentration of population. Over 50 per cent of the psychiatrists trained under NIMH grants go into private practice. Mental health services flow in the direction of money and sophistication. The most vigorous development in clinical psychology today is the extension of private practice, following the model of psychiatry, which has followed the model of the private practice of medicine. Psychologists in private practice are a major power group in the American Psychological Association. Several universities are working toward the establishment of professional schools for the training of psychological practitioners.

Now there is nothing wrong with the private practice of psychiatry or psychology except that it does not provide a sound base for the development of a national mental health program. The one-to-one relationship, the fifty-minute hour, are a dead-end, except perhaps for the two participants or as a source of new knowledge. This mode of offering service consumes far too much manpower for the benefit of a far too limited segment of society. We must find a more efficient way of deploying our limited resources of mental health manpower.

These two books, more than any I know, tell us what the third mental health revolution must accomplish. We must find new ways of deploying our resources of manpower and of knowledge to the end that effective mental health services, for prevention, for diagnosis, for treatment, for rehabilitation, can be made available to all of the people. Furthermore, we now have two other books that provide us with guidelines to action. They are *Action for Mental Health*, the report of the Joint Commission on Mental Illness and Health, and *National Action to Combat Mental Retardation*, the report of the President's Panel on Mental Retardation.

IMPLICATIONS FOR TRAINING PROGRAMS

To prescribe the content of professional curricula is hazardous at all times and downright foolhardy in a time of revolution. The most useful and productive thing to do is to keep up a lively debate on educational objectives for mental health professions and to leave it to local initiative, to the faculties of graduate and professional schools and to directors of inservice training programs, to determine what to teach and how to teach it. As a contribution to the debate on goals, I would identify nine objectives that should guide the development of educational programs for social work, nursing, psychiatry, medicine in general, clinical psychology and the various adjunctive disciplines.

1. The changing conception of the nature of mental illness and mental retardation will require that the mental health specialist be a person of broad scientific and humanistic education, a person prepared to help make decisions not only about the welfare of an individual but also about the kind of society that must be developed to nurture the greatest human fulfillment.

I am, frankly, gravely concerned about the proposed comprehensive community mental health centers. Here is a bold and imaginative proposal that may fail because top-level mental health personnel may not be prepared to discharge the responsibilities of a comprehensive community mental health program. When the great state hospitals were built across this country in the Nineteenth Century, someone must have thought them the last word, the best way to care for the mentally ill. There is a chance that the new mental health centers will be nothing more than a product of the general urbanization of America, a movement from country to city. Twenty years from now, people may moan not over bricks and mortar but over glass and steel; there is a real danger that we shall succeed in changing only the location and the architecture of the state hospital. If the new centers turn inward toward the hospital, they too will be monuments to failure. If they turn outward to the community, as some of the testimony before the Congress said they should, who among us will know what to do? Psychiatrists, social workers, nurses and psychologists have been trained primarily as clinicians, as intrapsychic diagnosticians, as listeners with the third ear; we are clinicians, not public health, mental health experts. Who among us knows enough about schools, courts, churches, welfare programs, recreation, effects of automation, cultural deprivation, population mobility, delinquency, family life, city planning and human ecology in general to presume to serve on the staff of a comprehensive community mental health center? The first training program we should plan should be for ourselves. We have nothing more urgent to do.

2. The concept of the responsibility of the doctor for patient, case worker for client, so appropriately honored in traditional educational programs for the physician, social worker and clinical psychologist, must be reconceptualized to define the responsibilities of these specialists as workers with other professionals who can contribute to the development of social institutions that promote effective functioning in people.

The psychiatrist might have limited himself to the treatment of the hospitalized psychotic or the acutely debilitated neurotic, leaving lesser problems of adjustment to teachers, clergymen and counselors of various types. With respect to the mentally retarded he might have limited himself to those so handicapped as to require institutionalization, defining the rest as slow learners and thus the responsibility not of medicine but of education. Psychiatry has, wisely I think, chosen not to take this constricted course but to concern itself with a broad spectrum of problems that are also the historical concerns of other professional groups. Most of the mental health effort, as we now define it, overlaps substantially with the domains of education, religion, welfare, correction, and even recreation, communication, architecture and city planning. There is nothing in most mental health training programs to provide either content or method for dealing collaboratively with other professional groups to solve the problems legitimately defined as both mental health and something else. Indeed, there is much in the education of the doctor, the psychologist and the social worker that actually militates against effective collaboration in these areas of overlapping concern. For example, the honorable concept of the physician's responsibility for his patient, so carefully and appropriately nurtured in medical training, gets extended unconsciously to relationships with other professional people and becomes an issue not of responsibility but of hegemony. What the physician sees as being responsible, his colleague sees as being arrogant. The physician always seems surprised and hurt by this incongruity in role perception, this seemingly unwarranted misunderstanding of his intent. The more thorough his clinical training, the less well prepared he may be for public health responsibilities. Somehow, without sacrifice of clinical competence, the psychiatrist must be trained to meet role requirements of truly co-operative enterprises involving a variety of professional people. Is there anywhere an approved residency program in psychiatry that explicitly trains for this concept of professional responsibility?

Clinical psychology is equally vulnerable to charges of incompetence in collaborative skills. Its arrogance is not that of responsibility but of detachment, a product perhaps of professional timidity and defensiveness, coupled with the platitudinous allegation that we need more research before we can contribute to social action programs. Perhaps only the social worker, before the advent of the sit-behind-the-desk-and-do-therapy era, is prepared for public health, mental health responsibilities.

3. The mental health specialist must be trained in ways to multiply his effectiveness by working through other less extensively and expensively trained people. The one-to-one model of much current practice does not provide a sound basis for a public health, mental health program.

The most promising approach to this problem at the present time is to use the extensively trained, expensive, and scarce mental health specialists to guide the work of other carefully selected persons with limited training. Such manpower is available, even in abundance, and its effective use depends on the ingenuity of the mental health specialist and his willingness to extend himself by working through other people. I would cite the work of Margaret Rioch in training carefully selected housewives to do psychotherapy under supervision; the use of college student volunteers in mental hospitals, and our Project Re-ED in Tennessee and North Carolina in which carefully selected teachers are working with disturbed children with the support of mental health and educational specialists. The place to start is in the universities, medical schools, residency centers and inservice training programs. The challenge to the mental health specialist in training should be, after establishing his own basic clinical competence, to work out ways in which he can multiply his effectiveness, say by a factor of six, by discovering means of working through other people.

4. Current developments will require that mental health training programs be revised to give attention to mental retardation commensurate with the degree of responsibility that the mental health professions have already assumed for the retarded. Since mental retardation is a much broader problem than it is usually considered to be in those few medical,

social work and psychological training programs that have given it attention, the inclusion of mental retardation in these curricula will require a substantial extension of their conceptual underpinnings. Slums are more consequential than galactosemia or phenylketonuria.

I surmise that few things could so radically alter the character of education in medicine, psychiatry, psychology and social work as a serious commitment to doing something about the problem of mental retardation. The health professions have laid claim to much of the problem; at least three of the institutes of the National Institutes of Health are involved; a substantial portion of every state's mental health program is devoted to the retarded. Yet in most training programs it receives peripheral attention.

For one thing, mental retardation is not a disease entity. It is a host of conditions manifested in impaired intellectual and social competence. It is due to chromosomal aberrations, intrauterine trauma, prematurity, metabolic disorders, accidents, cultural deprivation, inadequate opportunities to learn and acute emotional disturbances. Mental retardation is widely regarded as a hopeless condition; yet it is hard to think of a human affliction as amenable to productive intervention. But again, a radical reconceptualization of the problem is required. When it is in our interest to make the problem of mental retardation loom large, we cite the figure of 5,400,000 retarded in the country. Yet the major emphasis of most of our programs is on the 400,000 who have some apparent physical anomaly, to the neglect of the 5,000,000 who are primarily a challenge to the adequacy of our social institutions. We are more intrigued by galactosemia than challenged by slums and poor schools. We presume to claim the finest medical care in the world but stand eleventh among nations in infant mortality, evidence of widespread inadequate prenatal care that also produces prematurity and much mental retardation. Assumption of responsibility for the retarded will require that our major professional groups make as their cause equal access to medical services and educational opportunity for all people without regard to means or social status.

5. Curriculum constructors in social work, psychiatry and psychology must come to terms with the issue of the relationship between science and practice. Are the scientist and the practitioner to be one or are their functions separable? Just at the time when psychologists seem ready to back off a bit from their insistence that the two functions should go together, there is an opposite trend developing in medical education. The issue is absolutely basic and must be clearly resolved before the content of training programs can be discerned.

6. The main source of nourishment for the mental health professions has been clinical practice leavened and limited by research. The shift

toward a public health emphasis in mental health programs will require that the mental health specialist work through social institutions. He must acquire an appreciation of how disparate groups of people organize to achieve common goals and he must know how to encourage this process. He will need to be adept at institution building, at social invention, at the ordering of individual and community resources in the interest of mental health. I have found instructive a study by Harland Cleveland of the successful foreign service officer, who is in a position very much like that of the public health, mental health officer. He is confronted with a tremendous problem, his resources are limited, his staff is inadequate and he is expected to make a difference in the lives of a substantial number of people. Cleveland found that the highly effective foreign service officer had, among other attributes, a strong institutional sense, a sense of the ways in which social groups invent institutions to serve their ends and a notion of how this process can be furthered in the interest of his concerns. It seems to me that the public health, mental health specialist must develop a comparable sensitivity and skill.

7. An increased public health emphasis in mental health programs will accentuate the need for prevention and thus lead to a greater emphasis in professional training on problems of children, on childhood disorders and early indications of later difficulties and, especially, on normal patterns of development.

I would urge that we invest approximately 25 per cent of our resources to mount a holding action against the mental health problems of the adult, devoting the major portion, at least 75 per cent, of our resources to the mental health problems of children. This is the only way to make substantial changes in the mental health of our adult population a generation from now. I have made this suggestion on a number of occasions and no one ever takes exception to the substance of the argument. But, alas, children are unprofitable clients and, furthermore, they don't vote, so I expect they will continue to be neglected unless the public health challenge grips the mental health professions.

8. The new curricula should paradoxically reinstate an age-old study, that of morals and ethics, not professional ethics but classical ethics. There are two reasons for this. First, the therapeutic relationship, whether between two people or in a broader social effort, is at heart an ethical enterprise, with respect to both method and outcome. Second, we face the awesome prospect of becoming efficient in our efforts to influence human behavior. With increasing effectiveness we must become increasingly concerned with the consequences of our work. We cannot responsibly remain satisfied with vague definitions of what we mean by mental health.

9. Educational programs for mental health specialists should anticipate

an increasing obsolescence rate for knowledge and build habits of continuing scholarship and independent study. The more productive we are in mental health research, the more ingenious in the development of new social institutions, the more quickly will training programs become obsolete. The mental health specialist must be a continuing learner; training for independent learning must be a major commitment of mental health educational programs. National conferences are pleasant but they can only suggest new directions for study. Learning is ultimately a lonely enterprise.

From these nine considerations, these nine objectives for the training of mental health workers, there is instruction perhaps for the improvement of training programs, but there is a more insistent challenge that we re-examine the total structure of our mental health program to test its adequacy to get done the tremendous task that confronts us.

I thus come to a potentially distressing point. There is a possibility that the improvement of training is not our problem at all. I see little profit, from a public health viewpoint, in the following:

To train better and better psychotherapists to treat fewer and fewer people.

To improve the training of nurses to take care of increasing numbers of hospitalized old people who are no longer ill.

To hone to a fine edge the group work skills of an attendant who must watch more than 80 mentally retarded adults in a cyclone fence compound.

To improve the skills of the obstetrician in providing prenatal care to the poor in big cities when his contact with the mother is limited to 30 minutes before the arrival of the baby.

To train for exquisite precision in diagnosis when differentiated treatments are not available for differential diagnoses.

And so on for the social worker, the recreational worker, the occupational therapist, the community volunteer.

I come back to the possibility that we may not be able to solve the problem the way we are trying to do it, no matter how adequate our training. We must pay attention to the organizational structures for providing services, to the more effective deployment of our limited resources of highly trained people, to invention of new patterns for the provision of mental health services. These new patterns of organization may then have more influence on training than any other single consideration. Indeed perhaps a major goal of all inservice training programs today should be to train for the invention of new and more efficient forms for providing service, and then for skill in the diffusion of innovation.

A CASE STUDY IN INNOVATION

I should like, in conclusion, to present a case study in social innovation, to illustrate the thesis that it will be of no moment simply to train ourselves to do better what we are already doing. There must be invention of new forms for the provision of mental health services, forms that will treat realistically the problems of cost, of limited resources of highly trained talent, and of the necessity of extending mental health services to all of the people and not to a privileged few. Actually I might cite many new inventions, for the necessity of building public health concepts into mental health programs has already commanded attention and stimulated innovation, but I shall limit myself to one example simply because I know it well and can describe it fairly. I refer to our Project Re-ED, which is a compressed way of saying "a project for the Re-education of Emotionally Disturbed Children."

Project Re-ED was deliberately planned to meet a pressing social need that had been identified some eight years ago by a study of mental health resources in the South conducted by the Southern Regional Education Board. That study revealed an acute shortage in the region of specialized services for emotionally disturbed children. There were a few hospital units but most children in trouble were placed in detention homes, in institutions for the retarded, on wards with psychotic adults, or were left at home to fester there, occasionally seen by an itinerant teacher. The specialized services of all 16 states would not meet the requirements of the least populous state. While the situation has improved in recent years the problem remains acute. Furthermore, it is nationwide. The problem promises to be chronic, for we aspire to apply the clinical model to all disturbed children, and this simply can't be done because of limitations on the supply of personnel—even if it were desirable, which I question. We must turn to a public health, mental health model if we are to make any substantial headway at all. Re-ED is one such approach; there could of course be many others.

Two residential schools for emotionally disturbed children have been established, one in Nashville, Tennessee, the other in Durham, North Carolina. Each school will serve 40 children between the ages of six and 12, who are too disturbed or disturbing to be retained in a public school and who come from families that are too disrupted for the child to benefit from day care. The schools are staffed entirely by carefully selected young college graduates who have skills in teaching, recreation, camping, physical education, crafts and so on. They have been given nine months of specialized training for their work, and are called Teacher-Counselors. There is one social worker to mobilize community resources in the interest of the child and his family and one liaison teacher to co-ordinate a Re-ED school with the child's regular school. The Teacher-Counselors are backed by consultants: psychiatrists, psychologists, social workers, pediatricians and curriculum specialists. This is a sketch of the basic plan.

Now let us look at some of the principles that guide the program and warrant, I believe, the use of Re-ED as an example of a deliberate turning away from a clinical model toward a public health, mental health model for the provision of services to emotionally disturbed children.

1. The program draws on a source of manpower that is in reasonably good supply and does not compromise on the quality of the person who works with the child 24 hours a day.
2. Re-ED is basically a plan by which highly trained mental health specialists can multiply their effectiveness by working through other less well-trained people. If we could get most mental health specialists thinking along these lines, and then if we could invent the institutions to support them, the mental health personnel problem might be solved.
3. Re-ED concentrates on children from six to 12, hoping to prevent more serious later difficulties by early intervention. This is the mental health analog to the public health strategy of early case finding.
4. The program in Re-ED is organized around ecological rather than intrapsychic concepts. The task is not to "cure" the child (a clinical goal) but to get into reasonably functioning order the circumscribed social system of which the child is an essential part (a public health goal). The effort is to get the child, the family, the school, the neighborhood and the community just above threshold with respect to the requirements of each with respect to the other. When it is judged that the system has reached a level of functioning so that the probability of its successful operation exceeds the probability of failure, the child is returned home. A little improvement in all components or a dramatic improvement in any one component may make the system operational for the child. With this concept, it makes sense to plan for an average length of stay for a child in a Re-ED school of from four to six months.
5. A public health effort must have a public vocabulary. All of the theory of Re-ED, the objectives of the program and the processes by which these objectives are furthered, have been put into a simple vocabulary using English words as English words are commonly used.
6. A public health effort must be economically feasible. We think Re-ED is. The existing clinical model for the residential care of disturbed children costs from $25 to $80 a day, with an average of around $50. We think that Re-ED schools can be operated for around $12 to $15 per day. More important than the daily cost is the cost per child returned to his family and school as described above.

I describe Project Re-ED not as a solution to the problem of the emotionally disturbed child. It obviously is not that. An array of services will be required—as in any good public health program—to do the job, including hospitals and better public school programs for the disturbed child. I see it, rather, as one social invention that can make a difference. For an effective public health, mental health program in America, we need similar innovations in a number of fields: in the prevention of mental retardation due to inadequate prenatal care and to acute cultural deprivation; in the care of the chronic schizophrenic, the alcoholic, the drug addict; in programs to arrest deterioration in the aged and for the care of hospitalized oldsters who are no longer ill. By such innovations the concept of public health can come to the field of mental health.

The Community and the Community Mental Health Center[1]

M. BREWSTER SMITH
NICHOLAS HOBBS

Throughout the country, states and communities are readying themselves to try the "bold new approach" called for by President John F. Kennedy to help the mentally ill and, hopefully, to reduce the frequency of mental disorders. The core of the plan is this: to move the care and treatment of the mentally ill back into the community so as to avoid the needless disruption of normal patterns of living, and the estrangement from these patterns, that often come from distant and prolonged hospitalization; to make the full range of help that the community has to offer readily available to the person in trouble; to increase the likelihood that trouble can be spotted and help provided early when it can do the most good; and to strengthen the resources of the community for the prevention of mental disorder.

The community-based approach to mental illness and health attracted national attention as a result of the findings of the Joint Commission on Mental Illness and Health that was established by Congress under the Mental Health Study Act of 1955. After 5 years of careful study of the nation's problems of mental illness, the Commission recommended that an end be put to the construction of large mental hospitals, and that a

Reprinted with permission from *American Psychologist*, 1966, Vol. 21, No. 6, 499–509, Copyright 1966 by the American Psychological Association, and with the permission of the authors.

[1]This statement was adopted on March 12, 1966, by the Council of Representatives as an official position paper of the American Psychological Association.

flexible array of services be provided for the mentally ill in settings that disrupt as little as possible the patient's social relations in his community. The idea of the comprehensive community mental health center was a logical sequel.

In 1962, Congress appropriated funds to assist states in studying their needs and resources as a basis for developing comprehensive plans for mental health programs. Subsequently, in 1963, it authorized a substantial Federal contribution toward the cost of constructing community mental health centers proposed within the framework of state mental health plans. It appropriated $35,000,000 for use during fiscal year 1965. The authorization for 1966 is $50,000,000 and for 1967 $65,000,000. Recently, in 1965, it passed legislation to pay part of the cost of staffing the centers for an initial period of 5 years. In the meantime, 50 states and 3 territories have been drafting programs to meet the challenge of this imaginative sequence of Federal legislation.

In all the states and territories, psychologists have joined with other professionals, and with nonprofessional people concerned with mental health, to work out plans that hold promise of mitigating the serious national problems in the area of human well-being and effectiveness. In their participation in this planning, psychologists have contributed to the medley of ideas and proposals for translating the concept of comprehensive community mental health centers into specific programs. Some of the proposals seem likely to repeat past mistakes. Others are fresh, creative, stimulating innovations that exemplify the "bold new approach" that is needed.

Since the meaning of a "comprehensive community mental health center" is far from selfevident, the responsible citizen needs some guidelines or principles to help him assess the adequacy of the planning that may be underway in his own community, and in which he may perhaps participate. The guidelines and discussion that are offered here are addressed to community leaders who face the problem of deciding how their communities should respond to the opportunities that are opened by the new Federal and state programs. In drafting what follows, many sources have been drawn upon: the monographs and final report of the Joint Commission, testimony presented to Congress during the consideration of relevant legislation, official brochures of the National Institute of Mental Health, publications of the American Psychiatric Association, and recommendations from members of the American Psychological Association who have been involved in planning at local, state, and national levels.

The community mental health center, 1966 model, cannot be looked to for a unique or final solution to mental health problems: Varied patterns will need to be tried, plans revised in the light of evaluated experience, fossilized rigidity avoided. Even as plans are being drawn for the first comprehensive centers under the present Federal legislation, still other bold approaches to the fostering of human effectiveness are being promulgated under the egis of education and of economic opportunity programs. A single blueprint is bound to be inadequate and out of date at the moment it is sketched. The general approach underlying these guidelines may, it is hoped, have somewhat more enduring relevance.

Throughout, the comprehensive community mental health center is considered from the point of view of members of a community who are seeking good programs and are ultimately responsible for the kind of programs they get. The mental health professions are not to be regarded as guardians of mental health, but as agents of the community—among others—in developing and conserving its human resources and in restoring to more effective functioning people whose performance has been impaired. Professional people are valuable allies in the community's quest for the health and well-being of its members, but the responsibility for setting goals and major policies cannot be wisely delegated.

COMMUNITY INVOLVEMENT AND COMMUNITY CONTROL

For the comprehensive community mental health center to become an effective agency of the community, community control of center policy is essential.

The comprehensive community mental health center represents a fundamental shift in strategy in handling mental disorders. Historically, and still too much today, the preferred solution has been to separate the mentally ill person from society, to put him out of sight and mind, until, if he is lucky, he is restored to normal functioning. According to the old way, the community abandoned its responsibility for the "mental patient" to the distant mental hospital. According to the new way, the community accepts responsibility to come to the aid of the citizen who is in trouble. In the proposed new pattern, the person would remain in his own community, often not even leaving his home, close to family, to friends, and to the array of professional people he needs to help him. Nor would the center wait for serious psychological problems to develop and be referred. Its program of prevention, detection, and early intervention would involve it in many aspects of community life and in many institutions not normally considered as mental health agencies: the schools, churches, playgrounds, welfare agencies, the police, industry, the courts, and community councils.

This spread of professional commitment reflects in part a new conception of what constitutes mental illness. The new concept questions the appropriateness of the term "illness" in his context, in spite of recognition that much was gained from a humanitarian viewpoint in adopting the term. Mental disorders are in significant ways different from physical illnesses. Certainly mental disorder is not the private misery of an individual; it often grows out of and usually contributes to the breakdown of normal sources of social support and understanding, especially the family. It is not just an individual who has faltered; the social systems in which he is embedded through family, school, or job, through religious affiliation or through friendship, have failed to sustain him as an effective participant.

From this view of mental disorder as rooted in the social systems in which the troubled person participates, it follows that the objective of the center staff should be to help the various social systems of which the community is composed to function in ways that develop and sustain the effectiveness of the individuals who take part in them, and to help these community systems regroup their forces to support the person who runs into trouble. The community is not just a "catchment area" from which patients are drawn; the task of a community mental health center goes far beyond that of purveying professional services to disordered people on a local basis.

The more closely the proposed centers become integrated with the life and institutions of their communities, the less the community can afford to turn over to mental health professionals its responsibility for guiding the center's policies. Professional standards need to be established for the centers by Federal and state authorities, but goals and basic policies are a matter for local control. A broadly based responsible board of informed leaders should help to ensure that the center serves in deed, not just in name, as a focus of the community's varied efforts on behalf of the greater effectiveness and fulfillment of all its residents.

RANGE OF SERVICES

The community mental health center is "comprehensive" in the sense that it offers, probably not under one roof, a wide range of services, including both direct care of troubled people and consultative, educational, and preventive services to the community.

According to the administrative regulations issued by the Public Health Service, a center must offer five "essential" services to qualify for Federal funds under the Community Mental Health Centers Act of 1963: (*a*) *inpatient care* for people who need intensive care or treatment around the clock; (*b*) *outpatient care* for adults, children, and families; (*c*) *partial hospitalization*, at least day care and treatment for patients able to return home evenings and weekends, perhaps also night care for patients able to work but needing limited support or lacking suitable home arrangements; (*d*) *emergency care* on a 24-hour basis by one of the three services just listed; and (*e*) *consultation and education* to community agencies and professional personnel. The regulations also specify five additional services which, together with the five "essential" ones, "complete" the comprehensive community mental health program: (*f*) *diagnostic service;* (*g*) *rehabilitative service* including both social and vocational rehabilitation; (*h*) *precare and aftercare*, including screening of patients prior to hospital admission and home visiting or halfway houses after hospitalization; (*i*) *training* for all types of mental health personnel; and (*j*) *research and evaluation* concerning the effectiveness of programs and the problems of mental illness and its treatment.

That the five essential services revolve around the medically traditional inpatient-outpatient core may emphasize the more traditional component of the comprehensive center idea somewhat at the expense of full justice to the new conceptions of what is crucial in community mental health. Partial hospitalization and emergency care represent highly desirable, indeed essential, extensions of the traditional clinical services in the direction of greater flexibility and less disruption in patterns of living. Yet the newer approach to community mental health through the social systems in which people are embedded (family, school, neighborhood, factory, etc.) has further implications. For the disturbed person, the goal of community mental health programs should be to help him and the social systems of which he is a member to function together as harmoniously and productively as possible. Such a goal is more practical, and more readily specified, than the elusive concept of "cure," which misses the point that for much mental disorder the trouble lies not within the skin of the individual but in the interpersonal systems through which he is related to others. The emphasis in the regulations upon consultation and public education goes beyond the extension of direct patient services to open wide vistas for imaginative experimentation.

The vanguard of the community approach to mental health seeks ways in which aspects of people's social environment can be changed in order to improve mental health significantly through impact on large groups. Just as a modern police or fire department tries to prevent the problems it must cure, so a good mental health center would look for ways of reducing the strains and troubles out of which much disorder arises. The center might conduct surveys and studies to locate the sources of these strains; it might conduct training programs for managers, for teachers, for ministers to help them deal with the problems that come to light. By providing consultation on mental health to the governing agencies of the community, to schools, courts, churches, to business and industry, the staff of the center can bring their special knowledge to bear in improving the quality of community and family life for all citizens. Consultation can also be provided to the state mental hospitals to which the community sends patients, to assist these relics of the older dispensation in finding a constructive place in the new approach to mental health. Preferably, revitalized state hospitals will become integral parts of the comprehensive service to nearby communities.

In performing this important and difficult consultative role, the mental health professionals of the center staff do not make the presumptuous and foolish claim that they "know best" how the institutions of a community should operate. Rather, they contribute a special perspective and special competencies that can help the agencies and institutions of community life—the agencies and institutions through which people normally sustain and realize themselves—find ways in which to perform their functions more adequately. In this endeavor, the center staff needs to work in close cooperation with other key agencies that share a concern with community betterment but from different vantage points: councils of social agencies, poverty program councils, labor groups, business organizations, and the like. To promote coordination, representatives of such groups should normally be included in the board responsible for the center's policies.

Communities may find that they want and need to provide for a variety of services not specifically listed among the "additional services" in the regulations issued by the Public Health Service: for example, a special service for the aged, or a camping program, or, unfortunately, residences for people who do not respond to the best we can do for them. The regulations are permissive with respect to additional services, and communities will have to give close and realistic attention to their own needs and priorities. For many rural areas, on the other hand, and for communities in which existing mental health services are so grossly inadequate that the components of a comprehensive program must be assembled from scratch, the present regulations in regard to essential services may prove unduly restrictive. Communities without traditions of strong mental health services may need to start with something short of the full prescribed package. So long as their plan provides for both direct and indirect services, goes beyond the traditional inpatient-outpatient facility, and involves commitment to movement in the direction of greater comprehensiveness, the intent of the legislation might be regarded as fulfilled.

Many of the services that are relevant to mental health will naturally be developed under auspices other than the comprehensive center. That is desirable. Even the most comprehensive center will have a program that is more narrowly circumscribed than the community's full effort to promote human effectiveness. What is important is that the staff of the center be in good communication with related community efforts, and plan the center's own undertakings so as to strengthen the totality of the community's investment in the human effectiveness of its members.

FACILITIES

Facilities should be planned to fit a program and not vice versa.

The comprehensive community mental health center should not be thought of as a place, building, or collection of buildings—an easy misconception—but as a people-serving organization. New physical facilities will necessarily be required, but the mistake of constructing large, congregate institutions should not be repeated. The danger here is that new treatment facilities established in medical centers may only shift the old mental hospital from country to town, its architecture changed from stone and brick to glass and steel. New conceptions are needed even more than new facilities.

Small units of diverse design reflecting specific functions and located near users or near other services (such as a school or community center) might be indicated, and can often be constructed at a lesser cost than a centralized unit linked to a hospital. For example, most emotionally disturbed children who require residential treatment can be effectively served in small residential units in a neighborhood setting removed from the hospital center. Indeed, there is the possibility that the hospital with its tense and antiseptic atmosphere may confirm the child's worst fears about himself and set his deviant behavior.

Each community should work out the pattern of services and related facilities that reflects its own problems, resources, and solutions. The needs and resources of rural areas will differ radically from those of urban ones. Every state in the nation has its huge mental hospitals, grim monuments to what was once the latest word in treatment of the mentally ill, and a major force in shaping treatment programs ever since. It should not be necessary to build new monuments.

CONTINUITY OF CONCERN

Effective community action for mental health requires continuity of concern for the troubled individual in his involvements with society, regardless of awkward jurisdictional boundaries of agencies, institutions, and professions.

A major barrier to effective mental health programing is the historical precedent of separating mental health services from other people-serving agencies—schools, courts, welfare agencies, recreational programs, etc. This is partly a product of the way of thinking that follows from defining the problem as one of illness and thus establishing the place of treatment and the professional qualifications required to "treat" it. There are thus immense gaps in responsibility for giving help to people in trouble. Agencies tend to work in ignorance of each other's programs, or at cross purposes. For example, hospital programs for emotionally disturbed children often are operated with little contact with the child's school; a destitute alcoholic who would be hospitalized by one community agency is jailed by another.

Current recommendations that a person in trouble be admitted to the total mental health system and not to one component of it only fall short of coming to grips with the problem. The laudable aim of these recommendations is to facilitate movement of a person from one component to another—from hospital to outpatient clinic, for example, with minimum red tape and maximum communication among the professional people involved. Such freedom of movement and of communication within the mental health system is much to be desired. But freedom of movement and of communication between systems is quite as important as it is within a system.

No one system can comprise the range of mental health concerns to which we are committed in America, extending from serious neurological disorders to include the whole fabric of human experience from which serious—and not so serious—disorders of living may spring. Mental health is everyone's business, and no profession or family of professions has sufficient competence to deal with it whole. Nor can a mental health center, however comprehensive, encompass it. The center staff can and should engage in joint programing with the various other systems with whom "patients" and people on the verge of trouble are significantly involved—school, welfare, industry, justice, and the rest. For such joint programing to reflect the continuity of concern for the individual that is needed, information must flow freely among all agencies and "systems." The staff of the center can play a crucial role in monitoring this flow to see to it that the walls that typically restrict communication between social agencies are broken down.

REACHING THOSE WHO MOST NEED HELP

Programs must be designed to reach the people who are hardly touched by our best current efforts, for it is actually those who present the major problems of mental health in America.

The programs of comprehensive community mental health centers must be deliberately designed to reach all of the people who need them. Yet the forces generated by professional orthodoxies and by the balance of public initiative or apathy in different segments of the community—forces that have shaped current "model" community mental health programs—will tend unless strenuously counteracted to restrict services to a favored few in the community. The poor, the dispossessed, the uneducated, the "poor treatment risk," will get less service—and less appropriate service—than their representation in the community warrants, and much, much less service than their disproportionate contribution to the bedrock problem of serious mental illness would demand.

The more advanced mental health services have tended to be a middle-class luxury; chronic mental hospital custody a lower-class horror. The relationship between the mental health helper and the helped has been governed by an affinity of the clean for the clean, the educated for the educated, the affluent for the affluent. Most of our therapeutic talent, often trained at public expense, has been invested not in solving our hard-core mental health problem—the psychotic of marginal competence and social status—but in treating the relatively well-to-do educated neurotic, usually in an urban center. Research has shown that if a person is poor, he is given some form of brief, mechanical, or chemical treatment; if his social, economic, and educational position is more favored, he is given long-term conversational psychotherapy. This disturbing state of affairs exists whether the patient is treated privately or in a community facility, or by a psychiatrist, psychologist, or other professional person. If the community representatives who take responsibility for policy in the new community mental health centers are indignant at this inequity, their indignation would seem to be justified on the reasonable assumption that mental health services provided at public expense ought to reach the people who most need help. Although regulations stipulate that people will not be barred from service because of inability to pay, the greatest threat to the integrity and usefulness of the proposed comprehensive centers is that they will nonetheless neglect the poor and disadvantaged, and that they will simply provide at public expense services that are now privately available to people of means.

Yet indignation and good will backed with power to set policy will not in themselves suffice to bring about a just apportionment of mental health services. Inventiveness and research will also be indispensable. Even when special efforts are made to bring psychotherapy to the disturbed poor, it appears that they tend not to understand it, to want it, or to benefit from it. They tend not to conceive of their difficulties in psychological terms or to realize that talk can be a "treatment" that can help. Vigorous experimentation is needed to discover ways of reaching the people whose mental health problems are most serious. Present indications suggest that methods hold most promise which emphasize actions rather than words, deal directly with the problems of living rather than with fantasies, and meet emergencies when they arise without interposing a waiting list. Much more attention should also be given to the development of nonprofessional roles for selected "indigenous" persons, who in numerous ways could help to bridge the gulf between the world of the mental health professional and that of the poor and uneducated where help is particularly needed.

INNOVATION

Since current patterns of mental health service are intrinsically and logistically inadequate to the task, responsible programing for the comprehensive community mental health center must emphasize and reward innovation.

What can the mental health specialist do to help people who are in trouble? A recent survey of 11 most advanced mental health centers, chosen to suggest what centers-in-planning might become, reveals that the treatment of choice remains individual psychotherapy, the 50-minute hour on a one-to-one basis. Yet 3 minutes with a sharp pencil will show that this cannot conceivably provide a realistic basis for a national mental health program. There simply are not enough therapists—nor will there ever be—to go around, nor are there enough hours, nor is the method suited to the people who constitute the bulk of the problem—the uneducated, the inarticulate. Given the bias of existing facilities toward serving a middle-class clientele, stubborn adherence to individual psychotherapy when a community can find and afford the staff to do it would still be understandable if there were clear-cut evidence of the superior effectiveness of the method with those who find it attractive or acceptable. But such evidence does not exist. The habits and traditions of the mental health professions are not a good enough reason for the prominence of one-to-one psychotherapy, whether by psychiatrists, psychologists, or social workers, in current practice and programing.

Innovations are clearly required. One possibility with which there has been considerable experience is group therapy; here the therapist multiplies his talents by a factor of six or eight. Another is crisis consultation: a few hours spent in active intervention when a person reaches the end of his own resources and the normal sources of support run out. A particularly imaginative instance of crisis consultation in which psychologists have pioneered is the suicide-prevention facility. Another very promising innovation is the use under professional direction of people without professional training to provide needed interpersonal contact and communication. Still other innovations, more radical in departure from the individual clinical approach, will be required if the major institutional settings of youth and adult life—school and job—are to be modified in ways that promote the constructive handling of life stresses on the part of large numbers of people.

Innovation will flourish when we accept the character of our national mental health problem and when lay and professional people recognize and reward creative attempts to solve it. Responsible encouragement of innovation, of course, implies commitment to and investment in evaluation and research to appraise the merit of new practices.

CHILDREN

In contrast with current practice, major emphasis in the new comprehensive centers should go to services for children.

Mental health programs tend to neglect children, and the first plans submitted by states were conspicuous in their failure to provide a range of services to children. The 11 present community programs described as models were largely adult oriented. A recent (1965) conference to review progress in planning touched occasionally and lightly on problems of children. The Joint Commission on Mental Illness and Health by-passed the issue; currently a new Joint Commission on Mental Health of Children is about to embark upon its studies under Congressional auspices.

Most psychiatric and psychological training programs concentrate on adults. Individual psychotherapy through talk, the favored method in most mental health programs, is best suited to adults. What to do with an enraged child on a playground is not normally included in curricula for training mental health specialists. It would seem that our plans and programs are shaped more by our methods and predilections than by the problems to be solved.

Yet an analysis of the age profile of most communities—in conjunction with this relative neglect—would call for a radically different allocation of money, facilities, and mental health professionals. We do not know that early intervention with childhood problems can reduce later mental disorder, but it is a reasonable hypothesis, and we do know that the problems of children are receiving scant attention. Sound strategy would concentrate our innovative efforts upon the young, in programs for children and youth, for parents, and for teachers and others who work directly with children.

The less than encouraging experience of the child guidance clinic movement a generation and more ago should be a stimulus to new effort, not an occasion for turning away from services to children. The old clinics were small ventures, middle-class oriented, suffering from most of the deficiencies of therapeutic approach and outreach that have been touched upon above. A fresh approach to the problems of children is urgently needed.

We feel that fully half of our mental health resources—money, facilities, people—should be invested in programs for children and youth, for parents of young children, and for teachers and others who work directly with children. This would be the preferable course even if the remaining 50% were to permit only a holding action with respect to problems of adults. But our resources are such that if we care enough we can move forward on both fronts simultaneously.

The proposal to place the major investment of our mental health resources in programs for children will be resisted, however much sense it may make, for it will require a thoroughgoing reorientation of the mental health establishment. New facilities, new skills, new kinds of professional people, new patterns for the development of manpower will be required. And new and more effective ways must be found to reach and help children where they are—in families and schools—and to assist these critically important social systems in fostering the good development of children and in coming to the child's support when the developmental course goes astray. This is one reason why community leaders and other nonprofessionals concerned with the welfare and development of people should be centrally involved in establishing the goals of community mental health centers. They can and should demand that the character of the new centers be determined not by the present habits and skills of professional people but by the nature of the problem to be solved and the full range of resources available for its solution.

PLANNING FOR PROBLEM GROUPS THAT NOBODY WANTS

As a focus for community planning for mental health, the comprehensive center should assure that provision is made to deal with the mental health component in the problems of various difficult groups that are likely to "fall between the stools" of current programs.

Just as good community programing for mental health requires continuity of concern for the troubled individual, across the many agencies and services that are involved with him, so good programing also requires that no problem groups be excluded from attention just because their problems do not fit neatly into prevalent categories of professional interest, or because they are hard to treat.

There are a number of such groups of people, among whom problems of human ineffectiveness are obvious, yet whose difficulties cannot accurately or helpfully be described as mainly psychological: for example, addicts, alcholics, the aging, delinquents, the mentally retarded. It would be presumptuous folly for mental health professionals to claim responsibility for solving the difficult social and biological problems that are implicated in these types of ineffectiveness. But it would also be irresponsible on the part of persons who are planning community mental health programs not to give explicit attention to the adequacy of services being provided to these difficult groups and to the adequacy of the attack that the community is making on those aspects of their problems that are accessible to community action.

Recently, and belatedly, national attention has been focused on the mentally retarded. This substantial handicapped group is likely to be provided for outside the framework of the mental health program as such, but a good community mental health plan should assure that adequate provision is in fact made for them, and the comprehensive center should accept responsibility for serving the mental health needs of the retarded and their families.

Some of the other problem groups just mentioned—e.g., the addicts and alcoholics—tend to get left out partly because treatment by psychiatric or psychological methods has been relatively unproductive. Naturally, the comprehensive center cannot be expected to achieve magical solutions where other agencies have failed. But if it takes the approach advocated here—that of focusing on the social systems in which problem behavior is embedded—it has an opportunity to contribute toward a rational attack on these problems. The skills that are required may be more those of the social scientist and community change agent than those of the clinician or therapist.

In planning its role with respect to such difficult groups, the staff of the center might bear two considerations in mind: In the network of community agencies, is humanly decent care being provided under one or another set of auspices? And does the system-focused approach of the center have a distinctive contribution to make toward collaborative community action on the underlying problems?

MANPOWER

The present and future shortage of trained mental health professionals requires experimentation with new approaches to mental health services and with new divisions of labor in providing these services.

The national effort to improve the quality of life for every individual—to alleviate poverty, to improve educational opportunities, to combat mental disorders—will tax our resources of professional manpower to the limit. In spite of expanded training efforts, mental health programs will face growing shortages of social workers, nurses, psychiatrists, psychologists, and other specialists. The new legislation to provide Federal assistance for the staffing of community mental health centers will not increase the supply of manpower but perhaps may result in some minor redistribution of personnel. If adequate pay and opportunities for part-time participation are provided, it is possible that some psychiatrists and psychologists now in private practice may join the public effort, adding to the services available to people without reference to their economic resources.

The manpower shortage must be faced realistically and with readiness for invention, for creative solutions. Officially recommended staffing patterns for community mental health centers (which projected nationally would require far more professionals than are being trained) should not be taken as setting rigid limitations. Pediatricians, general medical practitioners, social workers other than psychiatric ones, psychological and other technicians at nondoctoral levels should be drawn into the work of the center. Specific tasks sometimes assigned to highly trained professionals (such as administrative duties, follow-up contacts, or tutoring for a disturbed child) may be assigned to carefully selected adults with little or no technical training. Effective communication across barriers of education, social class, and race can be aided by the creation of new roles for specially talented members of deprived groups. New and important roles must be found for teachers, recreation workers, lawyers, clergymen. Consultation, in-service training, staff conferences, and supervision are all devices that can be used to extend resources without sacrificing the quality of service.

Mental health centers should find ways of using responsible, paid volunteers, with limited or extended periods of service. There is a great reservoir of human talent among educated Americans who want to contribute their time and efforts to a significant enterprise. The Peace Corps, the Vista program, Project Head-Start have demonstrated to a previously skeptical public that high-level, dependable service can be rendered by this new-style volunteer. The contributions of unpaid volunteers—students, housewives, the retired—can be put to effective use as well.

PROFESSIONAL RESPONSIBILITY

Responsibility in the comprehensive community mental health center should depend upon competence in the jobs to be done.

The issue of who is to be responsible for mental health programs is complex, and not to be solved in the context of professional rivalries. The broad conception of mental health to which we have committed ourselves in America requires that responsibility for mental health programs be broadly shared. With good will, intelligence, and a willingness to minimize presumed prerogatives, professional people and lay board members can find ways of distributing responsibility that will substantially increase the effectiveness of a center's program. The tradition, of course, is that the director of a mental health center must be a psychiatrist. This is often the best solution, but other solutions may often be equally sensible or more so. A social worker, a psychologist, a pediatrician, a nurse, a public health administrator might be a more competent director for a particular center.

The issue of "clinical responsibility" is more complex but the principle is the same: Competence rather than professional identification should be the governing concern. The administration of drugs is clearly a competence-linked responsibility of a physician. Diagnostic testing is normally a competence-linked responsibility of a psychologist; however, there may be situations in which a psychiatrist or a social worker may have the competence to get the job done well. Responsibility for psychotherapy may be assumed by a social worker, psychiatrist, psychologist, or other trained person. The director of training or of research could reasonably come from one of a number of disciplines. The responsible community member, to whom these guidelines are addressed, should assure himself that there is a functional relationship in each instance between individual competence and the job to be done.

This issue has been given explicit and responsible attention by the Congress of the United States in its debates and hearings on the bill that authorizes funds for staffing community mental health centers. The intent of Congress is clear. As the Senate Committee on Labor and Public Welfare states in its report on the bill (Report No. 366, to accompany H.R. 2985, submitted June 24, 1965):

> There is no intent in any way in this bill to discriminate against any mental health professional group from carrying out its full potential within the realm of its recognized competence. Even further it is hoped that new and innovative tasks and roles will evolve from the broadly based concept of the community mental health services. Specifically, overall leadership of a community mental health center program may be carried out by any one of the major mental health professions. Many professions have vital roles to play in the prevention, treatment and rehabilitation of patients with mental illnesses.

Similar legislative intent was established in the debate on the measure in the House of Representatives.

Community members responsible for mental health centers should not countenance absentee directorships by which the fiction of responsibility is sustained while actual responsibility and initiative are dissipated. This is a device for the serving of professions, not of people.

TRAINING

The comprehensive community mental health center should provide a formal training program.

The need for centers to innovate in the development or reallocation of professional and subprofessional roles, which has been stressed above in line with Congressional intent, requires in every center an active and imaginative training program in which staff members can gain competence in their new roles. The larger centers will also have the self-interested obligation to participate in the training of other professionals. Well-supervised professional trainees not only contribute to the services of a center; their presence and the center's training responsibilities to them promote a desirable atmosphere of self-examination and openness to new ideas.

There should be a director of training who would be responsible for: (*a*) in-service training of the staff of the center, in the minimum case; and, in the larger centers, (*b*) center-sponsored training programs for a range of professional groups and including internships, field placements, postdoctoral fellowships, and partial or complete residency programs; and (c) university-sponsored training programs that require the facilities of the center to give their students practical experience. Between 5% and 10% of the center's budget should be explicitly allocated to training.

PROGRAM EVALUATION AND RESEARCH

The comprehensive community mental health center should devote an explicit portion of its budget to program evaluation. All centers should inculcate in their staff attention and respect for research findings; the larger centers have an obligation to set a high priority on basic research and to give formal recognition to research as a legitimate part of the duties of staff members.

In the 11 "model" community programs that have been cited previously, both program evaluation and basic research are rarities; staff members are commonly overburdened by their service obligations. That their mental health services continue to emphasize one-to-one psychotherapy with middle-class adults may partly result from the small attention that their programs give to the evaluative study of program effectiveness. The programs of social agencies are seldom evaluated systematically and tend to continue in operation simply because they exist and no one has data to demonstrate whether they are useful or not. In this respect the "model" programs seem to be no better.

The whole burden of the preceding recommendations, with their emphasis on innovation and experimentation, cries out for substantial investment in program evaluation. Only through explicit appraisal of program effects can worthy approaches be retained and refined, ineffective ones dropped. Evaluative monitoring of program achievements may vary, of course, from the relatively informal to the systematic and quantitative, depending on the importance of the issue, the availability of resources, and the willingness of those responsible to take the risks of substituting informed judgment for evidence.

One approach to program evaluation that has been much neglected is hard-headed cost analysis. Alternative programs should be compared not only in terms of their effects, but of what they cost. Since almost any approach to service is likely to produce some good effects, mental health professionals may be too prone to use methods that they find most satisfying rather than those that yield the greatest return per dollar.

All community mental health centers need to plan for program evaluation; the larger ones should also engage in basic research on the nature and causes of mental disorder and on the processes of diagnosis, treatment, and prevention. The center that is fully integrated with its community setting will have unique opportunities to study aspects of these problems that elude investigation in traditional clinic and hospital settings. That a major investment be made in basic research on mental health problems was the recommendation to which the Joint Commission on Mental Illness and Health gave topmost priority.

The demands of service and of research are bound to be competitive. Because research skills, too, are scarce, it is not realistic to expect every community mental health center to have a staff equipped to undertake basic research. At the very least, however, the leadership in each center should inculcate in its training program an attitude of attentiveness to research findings and of readiness to use them to innovate and change the center's practices.

The larger centers, especially those that can establish affiliation with universities, have an obligation to contribute to fundamental knowledge in the area of their program operations. Such centers will normally have a director of research, and a substantial budget allocation in support of research, to be supplemented by grants from foundations and governmental agencies. By encouraging their staff members to engage in basic studies (and they must be sedulously protected from encroaching service obligations if they are to do so), these centers can make an appropriate return to the common fund of scientific and professional knowledge upon which they draw; they also serve their own more immediate interests in attracting and retaining top quality staff and in maintaining an atmosphere in which creativeness can thrive. As a rough yardstick, every center should devote between 5% and 10% of its budget to program evaluation and research.

VARIETY, FLEXIBILITY, AND REALISM

Since the plan for a comprehensive community mental health center must allocate scarce resources according to carefully considered priorities tailored to the unique situation of the particular community, wide variation among plans is to be expected and is desirable. Since decisions are fallible and community needs and opportunities change, provision should be made for flexibility and change in programs, including periodic review of policies and operations.

In spite of the stress in these guidelines on ideal requirements as touchstones against which particular plans can be appraised, no single comprehensive center can be all things to all men. Planning must be done in a realistic context of limited resources and imperfect human talent as well as of carefully evaluated community needs, and many hard decisions will have to be made in setting priorities. In rural areas, especially, major alterations in the current blueprint would seem to be called for if needed services are to be provided. As a result, the comprehensive community mental health centers that emerge should be as unique as the communities to whose needs and opportunities they are responsive. This is all to the good, for as it has been repeatedly emphasized, there is no well-tested and prefabricated model to be put into automatic operation. Variety among centers is required for suitability to local situations; it is desirable also for the richer experience that it should yield for the guidance of future programing.

The need for innovation has been stressed; the other side of the same coin is the need for adaptability to the lessons of experience and to changing requirements of the community. Flexibility and adaptiveness as a characteristic of social agencies does not "just happen"; it must be planned for. The natural course of events is for organizations to maintain themselves with as little change as possible, and there is no one more conservative than the proponent of an established, once-radical departure. Plans for the new centers should therefore provide for the periodic self-review of policies and operations, with participation by staff at all levels, and by outside consultants if possible. To the extent that active program evaluation is built intrinsically into the functioning of the center, the review process should be facilitated, and intelligent flexibility of policy promoted. Self-review by the center staff should feed into general review by the responsible board of community leaders, in which the board satisfies itself concerning the adequacy with which the policies that it has set have been carried out.

This final recommendation returns once more to the theme, introduced at the outset, that has been implicit in the entire discussion: the responsibility of the community for the quality and adequacy of the mental health services that it gets. The opportunities are now open for communities to employ the mechanism of the comprehensive mental health center to take major strides toward more intelligent, humane, and effective provision for their people. If communities rise to this opportunity, the implications for the national problem of mental health and for the quality of American life are immense.

The following people read an early draft of this statement and made suggestions for its improvement. Their assistance is gratefully acknowledged. They in no way share responsibility, of course, for errors of fact or judgment that may be in the paper.

George W. Albee
Roger Bibace
Arthur J. Bindman
Hedda Bolgar
Joseph E. Brewer
Mortimer Brown
John D. Cambareri
Robert C. Challman
Emory L. Cowen
Joseph J. DeLucia
Gordon F. Derner
Morton Deutsch
Paul R. Dingman
Herbert Dörken
Henry Dupont
J. Wilbert Edgerton
John C. Glidewell
Leonard D. Goodstein
Lee Gurel
Robert A. Harper
Ira Iscoe
Nelson C. Jackson
James G. Kelly
Oliver J. B. Kerner
Barbara A. Kirk
Lewis B. Klebanoff
Sheldon J. Korchin
Maurice Kott
Harry Levinson
John J. McMillan
Harry V. McNeill
Sherman E. Nelson
J. R. Newbrough
Nancy Orlinsky
Thomas F. A. Plaut
David B. Ray
Sheldon R. Roen
Joseph Samler
Bernard Saper
Guy Scott
Saleem A. Shah
Edwin S. Shneidman
Franklin C. Shontz
George A. Silver
Hans Strupp
Donald E. Super
Harold C. Taylor
Forrest B. Tyler
Mrs. Bernard Werthan
Stanley F. Yolles
Alvin Zander

Filial Therapy as a Logical Extension of Current Trends in Psychotherapy

JAY W. FIDLER
BERNARD G. GUERNEY, JR.
MICHAEL P. ANDRONICO
LOUISE GUERNEY

As the concepts and preoccupations of psychiatry have shifted from intrapsychic pathology to social and cultural pathology, so the therapeutic techniques have proliferated and been modified. As in all fields of endeavor, changes occasionally follow the development of new concepts while, at other times, new concepts follow after a practice or technique has been found effective. Rapid changes in concepts as with Freud's theory and rapid changes in practice as with the tranquillizers have a revolutionary impact. Other changes such as the drift of psychiatrists into private practice and the development of modified psychotherapeutic techniques have been rather gradual and relatively unnoticed. This is comparable to the evolutionary process in nature and political systems. The technique of filial therapy, the use of the parent as a direct therapeutic agent, is one such development in technique which brings our current trends of change into focus.

Filial therapy involves the training of parents of emotionally disturbed youngsters up to ten years of age to conduct play sessions with their own children with a set of very specific guidelines and controls (1). The children themselves are not seen in therapy; rather, their parents are relied upon to effect changes with the support of the therapist and a group of other parents involved in the same process.

This selection is based on a paper presented at the Sixth International Congress of Psychotherapy, London, 1964, and is presented with the permission of the authors.

Several aspects of recent changes in psychotherapeutic practice are brought into focus by this procedure. Each has some relevance to the understanding of the place of this technique in the evolutionary process of therapeutic practices. The frame of reference of the psychotherapist, the limits within which he is conceived to work is one of these aspects. Many writers note that the work of Freud was related to the stage of science, politics, and culture of his time. This helped bring his focus upon the internal compartments of the mind in a way that seems to reflect the cellular pathology that preoccupied medicine. This frame of reference included an attempt to isolate the patient, reflected in the procedural method of having the patient not look at the therapist, and thus study him in a state of isolation as complete as was possible. As befitted this frame of reference, the descriptions were of units within the person and of the methods whereby these units interacted with each other.

Once the investigators of this method became comfortable with the concepts and procedures, they became increasingly aware of the attention they were giving to the interaction of the patient with his family at earlier stages of development. This being an important part of the concept of how the internal pathology came to develop, it brought into focus the interaction of the individual with the people in his environment and a study of how this induced change. The focus of psychotherapy at the time might be viewed as having expanded somewhat so that it not only included the individual and the mechanisms within, but also the relationship to the family of origin.

Conceptually, the next step might be viewed as the development of ego psychology, in which the attention was paid to the current interactions of the individual and the important people in his environment as a present-day extension of the historical developmental interactions. This, once again, extended the frame of reference so that it now included the patient and his internal mechanisms, plus his interactions with the significant people in his environment, past and present, but not including the treatment relationship itself. This last relationship was seen rather as a transference representation of other real and fantasied relationships.

The development of interpersonal theory, with a very special emphasis upon the reality as well as the fantasy components in the relationship between therapist and patient, brought a greater breadth and scope to the treatment situation and had a major impact on changing the procedure to include face-to-face confrontation as well as the realization that some of the patient's reactions to the therapist could have a so-called "reality basis" and not necessarily be comprehensible in terms of transference. This again enlarged the area to which the therapist attended. One of its very natural sequelae was the focus upon countertransference as an elaboration of the observation that the therapist as a very real person has an impact upon the treatment process, and that treatment is indeed an interpersonal transaction involving all these many facets that have been enumerated, regardless of whether we choose to include them in our frame of reference and pay attention to them, or whether we choose to ignore some of them.

Presumably, under the pressure of war and of the need for extensive psychotherapeutic services, a number of therapists proceeded to develop group psychotherapy, which altered the immediate treatment situation so that it now included several people simultaneously in a treatment as well as a real life confrontation. The comfort with interpersonal theory helped make this transition comprehensible and workable for a large number of therapists. This expansion of the area of focus that was considered legitimate for the psychotherapist then followed two different trends. One might be viewed as the institutional sequel to group psychotherapy and the other viewed as the outpatient or private practice sequel to it.

In the institutional pattern, we can see the use of group psychotherapy, in many instances, involving a high proportion, if not all, of the patient population. The subject matter introduced by the patients under these circumstances includes more elements of awareness of the institution itself and of its administrative practices, and of the patient-to-patient interactions as well as the staff-to-staff interactions. This awareness is present in such developments as the therapeutic community and milieu therapy, which take into account the present treatment reality of the patient and its relationship to the patient's pathology.

In the outpatient area, the use of group psychotherapy has been followed by increasing attention to current reality at home and the institution of family therapy as a way of coping with and modifying this aspect of the patient's life. The increasing awareness of community factors in the production of psychiatric illness is now encouraging the development of community psychiatry, which brings into the frame of reference of the psychotherapist the entire communication network of the community insofar as these communications aid or retard the mental health of the citizens.

Inherent in this description of changes in the frame of reference of the psychotherapists has been an awareness of a change in role and function as well. At this point we might turn our attention specifically to the role assumed by the therapist of a child in treatment. In the beginning of intensive psychotherapy of children, the practice of isolating child and therapist was taken over from adult psychotherapy. During the therapy session itself, the therapist was a de facto substitute parent as well as professional. Parents themselves were either avoided completely or were contacted on the basis of non-treatment issues only. The folklore of psychiatry pictured the parent as a competitor with a largely negative influence on the object of mutual concern—the child.

This stage was rapidly followed by enlarging the scope to include one or both parents, although each was seen individually. One or several psychotherapists acted as change agents for each of the individuals in a family with the intention of getting them to integrate in a new manner. Later, the whole family was brought together with one or more therapists into the same setting, thereby insuring that any change perceived or initiated by one member of the family would be more readily and rapidly understood by the others. The effect of this was to introduce indirect therapeutic efforts via the parents and to take a step toward working as an ally of the parent rather than as competitor.

In the filial therapy approach, developed by the second author, there is a different kind of integration involved, in that the *agent* of change as well as the person being changed are members of the same family constellation. The treatment situation is, therefore, not so readily dissociated from other life experiences. The therapist must see himself as an ally of the parent or he would be unable to carry out his professional function. The parent also loses any of his covert satisfaction in therapeutic failure which appeared as part of his competition with the therapist in earlier practices.

The implication of having the child taken over into a somewhat secret relationship was that if the parents were better parents, the child would not be sick. Regardless of the truth of such assumptions, the parent who felt excluded was clearly subject to guilt and hostility as a reaction. Tension would also occur when therapeutic changes in the child went beyond the symptom itself. For instance, if a child had a headache because of his inability to express hostility and treatment relieved him of his headache, the parents would be gratified. On the other hand, if he simultaneously learned how to be overtly aggressive, the parent would find a great deal of difficulty in adapting to this changed mode of behavior. To the extent that the parent feels unrelated to the changes which have occurred, he will feel more and more alienated by them. The efforts of the filial therapist afford the opportunity to avoid some of these negative reactions. Displacement of the parent does not occur and he is very likely to appreciate any changes in behavior as relevant to the symptomatic manifestations.

Displacement does not occur because the parent—through the play sessions he conducts with the child—is himself the immediate worker of changes. The model for the manner in which the parents are trained to conduct their play sessions with the child is that of the client-centered play therapist. The goals of the play sessions are as follows: (a) to help the child change his perceptions or misperceptions of the parent's feelings, attitudes, and behavior; (b) to allow the child—through the medium of play—to communicate thoughts, needs, and feelings to his parents that he had previously kept from them and often from his own awareness, or in other terms, to lift repressions and resolve anxiety-producing internalized conflicts; and, finally (c), to bring the child a greater feeling of self-respect, self-worth, and confidence.

Throughout the parents' training, it is emphasized that the techniques are relatively meaningless if they are applied only mechanically and not as an attempt at genuine empathic understanding. When a parent and the therapist feel he is ready, usually after six to eight weeks, the parent begins play sessions at home with his child for thirty minutes once weekly. This may later be increased, as desired, up to forty-five minutes and two or more times a week. It is important to note that there is no pressure on the parent to apply the therapeutic principles outside the sessions; he is allowed to make such generalization when he is ready to do so.

In the beginning, the orientation of the parents' own weekly group meetings which continue throughout the course of the therapy is toward learning the method and is so oriented partly in order to maximize motivation and minimize resistance. While technique remains a pertinent area for discussion throughout, the emphasis may go more and more in the direction of exploring the parents' own attitudes and problems in relation to their children, especially as these are illustrated by their reactions and observations of the children's actions in the play sessions. The therapist is then behaving as does a supervisor with student therapists. He learns about the child largely through the parents' reports, and he encounters the countertransference reactions of the parent who tries to act within the constraints of the treatment requirements.

In the filial therapy approach, the parent is actively ego involved in any changes which take place and is almost unavoidably made aware of the relationship between one aspect of change and another. Thus distress and confusion as well as the resulting resentment are greatly diminished and the parent does not set up the same kinds of resentment of the therapist for taking over his own relationship to the child.

Not only is the family tempted into a given set of attitudes toward the therapist by the characteristics of the treatment relationship, but the same is true of the therapist in his attitudes toward the family. To return once again to the model of the therapist dealing exclusively with a child and conceiving of his frame of reference as involving only the internal psychic structure of that child, it has been common to hear complaints that the family does not understand the child nor psychotherapy and that the child would be doing fine if only the family would change in behavior. Likewise, it frequently gets stressed that the family is to blame for the symptomatology with the stress on the judgmental aspect to the extent that it occasionally beclouds the issue of just how family behavior did produce the pathological phenomena under question. This is especially true in institutional practice if it can be demonstrated that within the institution the child is asymptomatic.

The use of filial therapy puts the therapist in a different position so that he is now very much interested in gaining the understanding and cooperation of the parent, and, therefore, is less likely to be involved in expressing his blame and resentments and more likely involved in comprehending the mechanisms which have led to the symptomatic picture.

Parallel difficulties exist for the child in traditional treatment. If we assume that a child in dealing with a therapist learns how to accommodate to a different set of standards and communicative practices, we can contend that, in a way, this is like making an adjustment to a new culture. Then at home he is confronted with trying to work with his new cultural adaptation in his old cultural framework. In filial therapy, the child and parent are involved together in establishing and working out the times, places, and circumstances for new and old behavioral practices, which may help to minimize such stress and confusion. This aspect of patient life undoubtedly also affects many adults who are institutionalized and who find in an institutional culture the tools for a good adjustment only to learn with dismay when they are discharged that the same tools are not available and a symptomatic pattern returns. We are often inclined to blame this on society or blame it on the patient rather than to simply acknowledge that adaptation to our micro-society is not necessarily adequate preparation for adaptation to the larger community. In the case of filial therapy, whatever changes are made include the parents at the same time and thereby largely avoid issues of translation of therapeutic impact or completely relearning mechanisms of adjustment. As a result, the therapist is less likely to feel himself identified with the child although he will still be very much focused on the issue of changing that child. He is less likely to conclude that the child is right and the parent wrong in an altercation and more likely to try to understand that altercation in a fully rounded manner.

The basic concept of disease is involved in the practice of psychiatry and the changes in this concept have paralleled the changes in practice. The notion that treatment was aimed at removing a symptom or a disease was congenial with the basic practice of isolating the patient or of paying attention to single mental mechanisms which were considered the cause of the symptom. As the basic frame of reference changed, the concept of pathology was accepted as being a difficulty in adaptation to the physical and interpersonal environment. Treatment was then seen as the readaptation of the maladapted individual. This change in focus extended the efforts at socializing patients within hospitals and within the groups of group therapy.

As the emphasis on psychiatric disorder has drifted toward the social phenomena, the patient is seen more as a scapegoat of his family or other group situation, and treatment is visualized as a process of reintegration within the group. This notion is more congenial to family therapy and most especially to filial therapy.

The trend away from viewing pathology in the general framework of cellular pathology has been paralled by several other changes in practice. Hospitals themselves became more like "real life" with the inclusion of many community activities. Half-way houses continued the trend into the community, while the establishment of psychiatric units in community hospitals carries this even further. Some few places have even been able to bring the whole family into the institution, having their counterparts in obstetrics and pediatrics, where family units have been held closer together in acute medical emergencies. Filial therapy also produces an incease in the parent-child interaction in contrast to the enforced separation that characterizes most other approaches to the psychiatric care of children. This, too, is a treatment which more closely resembles "real life."

The style of communication in psychotherapy is also influenced by the concepts of communication. At the beginning of the century the assumption was commonly accepted that it was not possible to communicate with psychotics. Since then a number of psychotherapists became convinced that it was possible to communicate with the schizophrenic. They discovered that if you learned the language and established rapport through it you could then enable the psychotic to begin to use conventional language. This modification in treatment approach brought about an important change in attitude toward the significance of the patient-therapist relationship. Under this new treatment process, it was no longer possible to achieve or even reasonably attempt to be a detached, objective, uninvolved therapist. The process of empathy so central to this new approach to understanding the schizophrenic was found to be a definite contribution to the treatment of all psychiatric disorders. Once again the advance was in the direction of involving the therapist and patient in total or as stated earlier in a more lifelike manner.

In filial therapy, the role of empathy in communication is given very great weight. Rather than being concerned with these qualities in the therapist vis-a-vis the child, one attempts to develop these attributes in the parent. Rather than being involved with the secondary phenomena of transference and countertransference, one is involved in the direct attempt to increase empathy and understanding in the current life relationship itself. Insofar as the psychopathology is generated out of the distorted and faulty communication between child and parent, it should be more effective and more enduring to improve that dyadic or triadic unit than to effect change via the substitutive transferential relationship to a professional person.

The theme of economy of action which is opened by this last observation is also worth some serious consideration as related to current trends in psychiatry. We are currently preoccupied with efforts to make medical and mental health services more available to the general population rather than only to the wealthier classes. Even in terms of our present practices there are personnel shortages. Further expansion necessitates the development of greater leverage in the use of the professional person's time, to make an hour of his time useful to more people without, of course, sacrificing the quality of treatment.

Filial therapy allows for treatment of six to eight parents and their respective children using only one office and one-and-a-half to two hours of professional time. We do not yet know how the filial therapy method compares in effectiveness to other methods appropriate to this population. Nor do we know what types of disturbed parent-child relationships or what social classes are most responsive to it. However, if our initial impressions of its general effectiveness are valid, it does indeed increase the leverage of professional time and physical resources with respect to the population with whom it is currently being employed. And we feel that further study might suggest that the essentials of the technique could be applicable to other ages and types of population.

With this approach there is less chance for the treatment situation to be isolated from real life, as happens on many occasions with individual psychotherapy. In the parent's relationship with the child, he must become involved with the totality of that relationship in contrast to the possibility of reporting only a portion of his interchanges with the child when dealing with the therapist. The advantage to the child is that he experiences acceptance directly from the parent rather than first a therapist with the intention of transplanting that experience to his own family. It is also recognized as a more powerful experience when the child works through his emotional turmoil with the parent rather than with the parent surrogate.

With the initiation of any new technique there may be reactions to its mere newness which can be expected to be manifested by resistance on the part of professionals. There are likely to be anxieties about fulfilling their responsibilities when they do not have continued contact directly with the child. There is also the specter of opening up a Pandora's box of potential for evil if the parent is given additional "weapons" against the child. As with all therapies these issues will have to be answered by accumulation of experience and later, if necessary, by appropriate modifications in method or by case selection. This present report is made because of the very challenge to assumptions and practices inherent in this recently conceived treatment technique. It may be a stimulus for other innovations as well in addition to being a justification for this technique.

REFERENCE

Guerney, B., Jr., Filial Therapy: description and rationale. *J. Consult. Psychol.*, 1964, 28, No. 4, 304–310.

Project Cause, The Federal Anti-Poverty Program, and Some Implications of Subprofessional Training

JESSE E. GORDON

The Federal Anti-Poverty Program has brought home an awareness of a developing problem in our national life, that of youth unemployment. The magnitude of the problem can be sensed from the following statistics. The rate of unemployment for those in the age range of 16 to 21 years is approximately 15%, three times the national average of 5.7%. There were 1.2 million jobless youth in 1963, not counting those who were in school. This unemployment is not evenly distributed over all youth; it is heaviest among nonwhites. Twenty-seven percent of nonwhite youths within the 16- to 21-year age range are jobless. This is double the rate of unemployment for white youth. Further, the unemployment rate for nonwhites is rising twice as fast as the rate for whites, a trend which has existed at least since 1955. That these differences between whites and nonwhites in unemployment are not only a product of differences in educational attainment is indicated by the fact that when education is comparable (i.e., comparing nonwhites with high school diplomas with high school graduated whites), the unemployment rate for the nonwhites is still twice that of the whites.

These problems will further multiply in the immediate future. Between 1964 and the end of this decade, 17 million youth will reach labor market

Reprinted with permission from *American Psychologist*, 1965, Vol 20, No. 5, 334–343.

age. Current estimates indicate that 7 million will have quit school before the twelfth grade. These 7 million are very likely to include the 3.5 million young people growing up in poverty families (i.e., families earning less than $3,000 a year) containing five or more children to be supported by this inadequate income.

We know what tends to happen to out-of-work and out-of-school youth. They concentrate in slums where they can find "something" to do—as reflected in crime statistics. Eighty-eight percent of all car thefts are committed by people under 25 years of age. For crimes of homicide, rape, robbery, burglary, aggravated assault, larceny, and auto theft, 46% of all arrests are of young people 18 years or younger.

To make mattters worse, the national trends are for an increasing loss of entry level jobs. While there are increasing needs for older, skilled technical personnel, farm employment which has functioned as an introduction to the world of work for young people has declined. Automation tends to displace the least skilled, the least trained, the least educated, the youngest workers.

The evolution of societies and cultures is highly coordinated with the kinds of economic situations within which the societies and cultures exist. Linton and Kardiner (1952) showed us how the culture of Tanala-Betsileo changed in response to the change from dry to wet rice cultivation. It is no less true that the subculture of America in which unemployment has been most chronic, and indeed, has become hereditary, has made its adaptations. Where work has traditionally not existed, there is little achievement motivation. Where opportunity does not exist, there is disbelief in the rewards for work. We thus have a growing group of young people who do not value work, who do not believe in the rewards of work, and who therefore have no skills appropriate to the labor market. Even if they would, they do not know how to apply for a job, they do not know how to behave in the social role of an employee, and thus they do not know how to keep a job. As this group grows in size, it will constitute an ever-increasing danger to the larger society; the irony of it is that the subculture of chronically unemployed youth has evolved to the point at which even the availability of work is insufficient by itself to end the unemployment. Making jobs available to people who have little interest in work, little belief in its rewards, and no skills, produces the paradox of continued unemployment together with labor shortage. We are thus in the unfortunate position of sitting on a powder keg and not knowing how to defuse it. If the availability of jobs is no longer sufficient to solve the problem, then perhaps job availability plus vocational counseling, guidance, and employability development is what is needed. Indeed, it seems to be the only possible solution and it is the one which forms the organizing principle for several aspects of the Federal Economic Opportunity

Program. But in many ways this may seem to be a most unpromising solution. The very existence of masses of chronically unemployed and unemployable youth testifies to the continued failure of counseling and guidance as professions and as a body of social institutions to meet the need. And this failure is as deeply rooted and structural as is the problem of chronic unemployment. I would like to discuss quite briefly some of the dynamics which have prevented counseling and guidance, psychology, and social work from dealing effectively with this problem in the past. Much of what follows may be generalized from the field of vocational counseling to other aspects of the helping professions which may be involved in the several antipoverty programs, such as teaching, casework and group work, family counseling, child guidance, programs for the aging, etc.

PROFESSIONAL UNPREPAREDNESS

1. Lack of Techniques

The counseling process and its array of associated techniques as represented in the standard textbooks and educational curricula is one which has been evolved through decades of practical experience and research with middle-class clients and subjects, most in both categories being students. The techniques which have been developed are therefore specifically appropriate to well-motivated applicant-clients who are verbally expressive and quite accepting of middle-class values relative to work and achievement. They are accustomed to accepting the kind of role assigned to a student-client vis-à-vis a counselor, social worker, or psychologist, and to working within that role.

While some experimental and demonstration agencies in recent years have tried various new procedures for making contact with disadvantaged youth, for motivating them, counseling them, and training them, these techniques have not yet been collected into a coherent body of principles and methods, they have not been adequately communicated to the profession, and they have not found their ways into university programs of counselor preparation, into textbooks, and into the repertories of counseling agencies by and large. Some idea of the inappropriateness of the standard techniques can be gathered from the difficulties faced by the Selective Service Rehabilitant Program. The program was started last February 17 to help disadvantaged youth, mostly school dropouts and unemployed, to find employment and a place in society. The program hoped to do this by guiding draft rejectees into state employment offices for interviews, counseling, and job placement, in the traditional model of vocational counseling.

Underemployed and unemployed rejectees were invited by letter to visit employment service counselors in their offices to talk about jobs and career planning. Of the 234,000 rejectees so invited, of whom 78,000 were unemployed, only 42,000 showed up for interviews, and of these 32,000 were unemployed or underemployed. Thus the majority of the unemployed and underemployed who received letters—46,000—failed to respond. And of the 42,000 who did respond, fewer than 13,000 were referred to jobs; fewer than 7,000 of these hired, and some for only a few days. One-third of these invited Selective Service rejectees had less than an elementary education; 80% were school dropouts. It is apparent from this experience that arranging for an office appointment for counseling services is an unsuccessful way of making counseling services available to these youth, and that the services available for those who do respond are inappropriate and relatively nonproductive. The United States Employment Service recognizes this now, and has begun a program of stationing Employment Service personnel in the induction centers themselves; they are going to where the clients are instead of waiting for these unemployed to come to them.

2. Class Bias in Recruitment and Training of Professionals

Whether it is cause or effect of the middle-class orientation of counseling techniques and procedures, it is true that counselor education, and even more so, clinical psychology, devotes almost all its resources to the preparation of counselors and psychologists for middle-class secondary schools, middle-class agencies, and for universities, thus missing entirely the body of needy, out-of-school non-middle-class people. The result has been that almost 90% of the graduates of counseling and guidance training programs find employment in schools and universities. The figures for psychology are comparable in indicating an overwhelming orientation toward serving the educational and counseling needs of the middle class. A number of factors contribute to this state of affairs:

a. Students of counseling and guidance, psychology, and social work typically come from marginal middle-class backgrounds. Their need to confirm and enhance their social status leads them to a preference for the accoutrements of a professional identity, such as office work, the use of verbal and conceptual skills, connection with solidly respectable social institutions such as schools, job security, and a public identity which, if not outright prestigeful, is at least considered respectable. They prefer to work with people who will enhance their identities, and they tend to feel threatened by association with the milieu from which the marginal middle class is so anxious to separate itself. Thus social psychological factors within the personnel available for the helping professions incline them towards school counseling with college-bound youth.

b. When such candidates for training find themselves in a professional training program, their inclinations are reinforced. The prestigeful role models most available to them are their professors, the conditions of whose employment (teaching and research, publish or perish) result in staff selection factors which emphasize research, theorizing, scholarship, verbal-conceptual skills, and the enjoyment of theoretical and academic discussion with peers. These available role models thus omit reference to actual counseling, to actual contact and involvement with disadvantaged youth, to familiarity with the culture of poverty, and with lower-class orientations and values. Within such a faculty, processes take place which maximize the rewards of grades, honors, and scholarships for those students who most completely incorporate the characteristics of their models. These are the students who are most highly recommended for the most prestigeful job placements upon completion of training. These organizational factors within the university thus operate to further move students away from work with disadvantaged youth. The university community thus tends to further attract students whose interests and attitudes are consonant with the university ethos and which are therefore inappropriate for work with disadvantaged youth, and to repel the action oriented who thus do not gain access to the profession. While these action oriented may possess some of the skills and characteristics necessary for counseling with disadvantaged youth, they may not possess the skills and characteristics most frequently rewarded in training programs ostensibly designed to prepare them for service work. This is a reflection of a situation in which the skills required for successful completion of training are different from, and perhaps even negatively correlated with, the skills needed for successful performance on the job.

It is worth noting here that those professionals who rise to the top of their professions are often those who best exemplify some of the factors described above. These are the people who constitute the professional leadership and who help to define the profession for the public and for potential recruits to it.

3. Inappropriateness of the Model for Personal Help

Another related factor which has rendered the helping professions inappropriate for meeting the problems of current youth unemployment is in the nature of the professional model for helping work which has been developed and amplified through the course of the class-restricted history of the helping professions. This model is one in which a fully qualified professional person takes all responsibility for the counseling. He carries out personally all aspects of the process, including public information, motivating of clients, intake, testing and diagnosis, interviewing, referral, and follow-up and evaluation. A fully qualified professional practices in all areas. As new knowledge has been created concerning each of these functions, there is a press to increase the length of training and preparation to acquire more and more information about all of these aspects, and no one may be graduated with a professional degree who has not mastered all of them. This lengthening of the training process further restricts and limits the supply of professional counseling personnel, and so further intensifies the self-selection of lower middle-class students and increases the time in which the conformity pressures within the training institution can operate.

This model of the professional as the "compleat clinician" and the implied model of the helping process are based on implicit acceptance of the transference hypothesis which sees personal counseling as evolving and moving forward only in the context of a continued personal and intimate relationship between client and counselor. It is assumed that the intimate concerns and life activities of a client can only be exposed where there is an intimate personal relationship. I would like to suggest the possibility that this assumption is valid for the middle class, but may not be valid in lower-class culture. Middle-class children are raised within an ethic of modesty. They are taught that there are spheres of their own activities, mostly those involving biological functions of toileting, eating, and sexuality, which may not be shared or made public to anyone outside of the immediate family, and may even be entirely private within the family. The possibilities for such privacy hardly exist in crowded tenements in which several families live together and share inadequate facilities. I suspect that one of the results of these living conditions is a reduction in the demand for intimacy as a precondition for "exposing" personal matters. Furthermore, the dynamic bases for transference are attenuated in lower-class culture in which children are brought up by a variety of other people, a shifting group of adults, neighbors, temporary parents-consorts, and whatever siblings happen to be around at the moment. There is thus less investment of affect in a single reliable person, and there may also, therefore, be a greater readiness to relate to the *roles* of others rather than to the individual characteristics of the individuals filling those roles. For these reasons I suggest that there is less need for a transference relationship as a precondition of counseling, less readiness to develop transference attitudes, and a smaller demand for intimacy with a particular counselor, in lower-class culture. Thus the professional model of counseling as a one-to-one relationship may not be necessary or even desirable for working with disadvantaged youth.

One consequence of the primacy of this "transference model" of counseling is that it makes no room for subprofessionals, and it therefore makes no demand for professionals to be skilled in supervision of subprofessional roles or in training people for subprofessional roles. I shall return to this point in another section of this paper.

4. Shortage of Professionals

Even without these social and psychological dynamics, the helping professionals are ill fit to cope with the problems of youth unemployment by the severe shortage of trained professional workers. The current demand for psychologists, social workers, and counselors far exceeds the supply, and the demand is growing at a much greater rate than the student bodies in these professions. For years we have been telling ourselves that we were not turning out enough qualified professionals to meet the social needs, and some of the leading universities have even abdicated from any attempt to meet the needs by concentrating their efforts on turning out theoreticians and researchers and leaving others to turn out practitioners. The others, of course, attempt to emulate the leaders, and in the scramble for academic prestige few concern themselves with whether anybody has picked up the responsibilities of which the leaders have divested themselves.

TWO SOLUTIONS

Two solutions to the problem of providing services to the disadvantaged have been offered. The first is akin to the phenomenon studied by Festinger (1956) in his *When Prophecy Fails.* If the existing structuring of the professions is failing to meet the need, then increase the dosage. Thus pleas are made for more Federal aid for faculty and for student support so that more professionals can be trained. But, of course, if the middle-class orientation of the professions is not altered, or the structural or dynamic factors responsible for this orientation are left undisturbed, there is no reason to think that an increased supply of professionals would result in more effective counseling with the disadvantaged, or a greater quantity of such counseling, particularly as middle-class affluence grows and makes it increasingly capable of absorbing more of the services of the trained professionals being produced. This is, then, a solution which does not solve anything except the problem of enhancing and protecting the traditional identities of the professions which have evolved, by a total preservation of the models on which their activities are based.

Until recently, this was the only solution offered by the helping professions, and as the problems of youth employment grew, it remained for the Federal Government to step in and take political action. The

Department of Labor's Project CAUSE was one of the actions taken. In the summer of 1964, Project CAUSE recruited almost 1,900 people for intensive 8- to 10-week training courses conducted by 27 universities around the country, designed to prepare these recruits for subprofessional roles in Youth Opportunity Centers, conceived of as specialized branches of existing employment services.

Despite intensive intraprofessional discussions about subprofessional training in the recent past, the major thrusts have been away from terminal MA training in psychology, from a 1-year MA to a 2-year MA in counseling and guidance, and to the 2-year MSW as a minimum requirement in social work. Thus none of the helping professions have made room for subprofessional roles of the kind for which Project CAUSE recruits were to be trained. This led inevitably to ambiguity and uncertainty regarding the roles for which they were being trained. Nevertheless, the character of the training made it clear that the successful trainees, designated as Counselor Aides and Youth Advisors to discriminate them from the fully qualified professionals, would be some kind of a cross between social workers and vocational counselors, and would work under the supervision of qualified professionals. Thus the solution to the problem of the shortage of professional personnel who can deal with disadvantaged youth posed by Project CAUSE is one in which a new subprofession has been created by Federal action. The recruitment, selection, and training, as described by Kranz (1964), were intended to create a subprofession which would be particularly appropriate for the needs of disadvantaged youth. Project CAUSE, while the largest, is just one of many programs designed to produce subprofessionals, such as pilot projects in training retirees to supervise sheltered workshops, training of tutors for literacy training projects, psychiatric aide training, job retraining counselors, and many others.

The helping professions are thus faced with a fait accompli, and they are unprepared for it. In the absence of any other viable solution to the shortage of counselors for disadvantaged youth, the professions must either adapt to this new subprofession and include it within their structures, or leave the field of counseling with the disadvantaged to an entirely independent and potentially rivalrous subprofession.[1]

[1]Many of the projects with vocational orientations which have excited the most interest, because of their inventiveness and willingness to break out of traditional molds—projects such as Mobilization for Youth, JOIN, JOBS, Haryouth-Act, the Los Angeles Youth Opportunity Board—are heavily staffed by social workers, with almost minimal participation by professionals in vocational counseling and guidance. These agencies make extensive use of personnel with varieties of academic and special training, but without specific professional identities (in the sense of having the usual degrees); they are "home grown" to meet the specific needs of the projects, have developed exceptional competence, and have made some of the most original contributions to the field.

I believe that subprofessional training can be a most appropriate and effective solution to the problems described above, and that Project CAUSE presages a new and exciting day of development and revision in the helping professions which will add considerable vitality to them. It poses some challenges which, if met, will involve exciting growth and development in the helping professions which have had so much success in meeting other challenges in the past. The consequences of not meeting the challenges include the further restriction of psychology, counseling, and social work to more and more limited ranges of activities, to increasing concentration on minutia and esoterica, and to an early senescence.[2]

IMPLICATIONS FOR THE PROFESSIONS

I see the challenges posed by Project CAUSE as falling into five general areas:

1. How can the counseling process be subdivided into roles which can be filled by subprofessionals operating in a team under the direction of qualified professional?
2. How are subprofessionals to be supervised, and how can students in professional training programs be trained for supervision?
3. If some part of subprofessional training is to take place in service agencies, how can the professional staffs of these agencies develop skills in training methods and techniques?
4. If much of the service work is done by subprofessionals, shall they be administered by a professional person who does not provide direct service to clients, or should agencies be administered only by those who are intimately and experientially familiar with the services to be provided by the agency?
5. Given the already overburdened staffs of university departments, where is subprofessional training to be located and by whom conducted?

I would like to make some brief comments about each of these challenges in the remainder of this paper.

1. Job Specifications and the Counseling Team

The most important challenge faced by the helping professions today is that of attempting to break down the professional role into subprofes-

[2]In one leading graduate department, almost all the students in clinical psychology receive the bulk of their training in agencies serving moderately disturbed outpatient middle-class adults. Few of the students are interested in hospitalized people; none are interested in lower-class youth.

sional classifications or subroles, each of which may be filled by people with less than complete professional training and whose training is specific to the roles. I must admit that I cannot think of how this might be done; however, I have no doubt that it can be done. I can conceive of a team, operating under the direction of a professional, in which each member of the team bears a responsibility for one part of the total helping process. Thus one might be an outreach person whose job it is to make contact with the youths to be served. A second might specialize in dealing with other community agencies. A third might play a "big brother" role in such matters as teaching a young man how to fill out an application, or going with him to his first job interview. Still another member of the team might be the one who specializes in home visits, and yet another might be the test administrator. Intensive psychological interviewing can probably only be done by a professional person, but intake work could well be done by a subprofessional, which in many agencies would be an improvement over the secretary-receptionist who fulfills this function.

Thus far, such a breakdown into subroles has not been developed, except in medicine, which makes use of practical nurses, nurses aides, nurses, laboratory technicians, and medical technologists, all of whom can be trained at less than the BA level. It was the absence of such a breakdown which produced the ambiguity and confusion concerning the job specifications for Counselor Aides and Youth Advisors in Project CAUSE, and may pose similar difficulties for the VISTA volunteers and the staffs of Job Corps Centers and Camps, Neighborhood Youth Corps, and other such eleemosynary programs. Without such job specifications which can fit the subprofessional into a structure for providing appropriate and high quality services, and which can make the training of the subprofessionals specific to their roles, the training programs must opt for a generalized introduction to the professional field, thus turning out junior professionals who know a little bit about everything the professional knows a lot about, and who therefore can be expected to do a little bit of everything the professional does. With the continued shortage of personnel, it is no wonder that agencies rapidly come to use their subprofessionals as if they were fully qualified, thus producing lowering of professional standards. But the fault for such a development lies not with the concept of subprofessional training, or with the Governmental agencies which are specifically responsible for taking action in the interests of the public welfare; the fault lies with the professions which, lacking a clear mechanism which requires responsiveness to the needs of the public, have done little to meet the needs, and have not prepared themselves to use and incorporate subprofessionals in their structures. It is no use to demand that subprofessionals trained by the Government must be supervised, and must not simply be ill-trained junior professionals, if the professions take no steps to develop valid subprofessional roles, and to train their members for using and supervising those who fill the roles adequately and appropriately. In brief, the lowering of standards which the professions fear so much as a consequence of subprofessional training is more likely to occur as a result of the professions' unpreparedness than it is a necessary consequence of the use of subprofessionals. And each restrictive step taken by the professions to protect and enhance standards increases the pressures which lead to Government action in creating subprofessionals who must then operate without clearly defined roles and without appropriate supervision, thus ultimately further threatening the professional standards. We recognize such self-defeating defensive reactions to perceived threat as neurotic in clients. The cure lies in making adaptations of the needs, skills, and goals of the professions to the realities; such an adaptation can be much more enhancing than blind resistance, defense, and denial.

There are some attractive advantages to a team model. The specialized training for each of the roles can probably be done in short intensive training programs which could probably recruit from indigenous personnel and from other groups such as the early retired, married women, etc., for whom long-term academic work is either inappropriate, unavailable, or unwanted. Thus the helping professions can tap a much larger pool of potential workers who can be trained fairly rapidly and with much less expense than is required for full professionals. The fully qualified professional can probably head up two or more such teams, since he would be spending much less time in activities which can be handled by the subprofessionals. Thus each professional person could service a greater number of clients, effecting a needed economy in the use of scarce professional resources.

For example, the problems of the Selective Service Rehabilitant Program, described above, indicate that counseling with disadvantaged youth requires that steps be taken actively to contact clients, rather than waiting for the clients to come to the agency. Counseling personnel cannot sit in an office and wait; they must go out to where the clients are. Further, counseling with such clients poses some additional problems which require that counseling personnel work directly in the living environment of the clients. Relatively nonverbal, nonexpressive, and educationally disadvantaged clients, unlike the middle-class patients in psychotherapy which forms the model for counseling services, cannot reproduce verbally within an interview all of the factors and events which exist in their life spaces. Nor can they carry back to their home environments the processes and events which took place during the interviewing and counseling and translate them into actions in their homes and neighborhoods by converting the verbal dialogue into appropriate specific actions. In dealing with this population, the professional must go to the client's home and talk to him there; he must meet him at work; he must hold family conferences in the client's home; he may have to meet with the client and his peers in the neighborhood gathering places. He may have to visit the client's school, his employer, the police, and other social agencies. Such visits outside the agency office are essential, but they are also incredibly costly of time and money. Considering the present and future shortage of fully qualified professionals, I do not see how they can justify the time and money which will be eaten up in city traffic jams, in public transportation systems; a counselor with a 2-year master's degree who spends 2 or more hours a day between here and there is far too expensive. Out-of-office work may be essential, but much of it can be done by subprofessionals who may even be stationed in the communities and neighborhoods being served.

A second major advantage of the helping team is that it may include workers from the same milieu as the clients served by the team, and these workers could well be much more successful than the fully qualified professional in making contact with potential clients, in motivating them, and in interpreting the agency to the client. Where they have been well trained and well supervised, indigenous leaders have made important contributions which cannot be made by anyone else. There are dimensions of expression, voice inflection, gesture, body language, which are almost instantly recognizable as signs of class and ethnic origin. The indigenous leader can communicate instantly to the suspicious and distrustful client, avoiding noblesse oblige, in a way that many middle-class professionals cannot do when dealing with disaffected, hostile, anomic youths who see the middle-class agency worker as part of the system against which he is fighting. In the long run, disparities between the class castes of counselor and client might make no difference in the outcome of the counseling, if the long run is long enough and the counseling approaches psychotherapy in its depth and intensiveness. But the kind of work which will be most common in the various phases of the Anti-Poverty Program is not likely to use the long run, and, in brief contacts, first impressions can be all important in determining whether the client will be relaxed and receptive, or on his guard and defensive. Indigenous personnel who "speak the client's language" can form an extremely effective bridge between the milieu of the client and the milieu of agency; they can make important contributions to the counseling team in contacting the clients to be served, in maintaining them through their agency contacts, and may be particularly effective in follow-up work with the clients in their home, community, and on the job. A client is more likely to be able to report continuing difficulties, after his counseling contacts, to an indigenous worker, than he is to the professional interviewer toward whom the ethic of mutual cooperation and courtesy requires that he affirm the success of the counseling and deny continued problems.

2. Supervision

If we are going into subprofessional training, perhaps using a team concept such as that suggested above, then the second challenge to the helping professions involves training for supervision. In the current model of counseling, the worker "on the line" requires no skills in supervision, since there is no one present to supervise. In graduate training programs it is generally assumed that as the recent graduate acquires more and more experience, he will begin to move up in the organizational hierarchy. He will gradually take on supervisory responsibilities and will develop his skills in supervision by emulating those who supervise him. Even with the current model of counseling, this assumption is false. Many graduates find that their very first job is that of head of an agency or a service. They are immediately expected to supervise, with no prior training in supervision. Typically, they fall back on the kinds of supervision they experienced as graduate students. But this kind of supervision is specifically appropriate to highly verbal, academic, intelligent, professionally trained personnel. It is not appropriate for subprofessionals. But if a counseling team is going to work effectively, much will depend on the quality and competence of the supervision it receives, supervision which is designed for subprofessional roles. Recognition of this important function in professional training is long overdue, and the renewed recognition of the importance of supervision which was stimulated by Project CAUSE and similar programs may be listed as among the achievements of these programs. It is of no use for the professions to seek guarantees that subprofessionals will be given adequate supervision if the professions do not produce people who are trained to provide it.

3. Training Skills

A third challenge posed by subprofessional training is concerned with training methods. While subprofessionals might be trained for varying periods of time in academic settings, it seems likely that such training will serve best as a prologue or introduction to the professional field, while the major portion of the skill training for the specific roles to be filled by the subprofessionals can best be handled by representative agencies in which the subprofessionals will be employed. The local community agency is likely to be the best place in which to train indigenous leaders, but the task of providing such in-house training for subprofessionals is a large one, and is one for which most agencies are ill equipped. When the notion of using indigenous personnel was first developed in the lower East Side of New York, the very first problem which had to be faced was that of providing suitable training within the agency, and with the only available models of training being those derived from academic education, the burden for innovation and creativity fell on the training agencies. When asked to do training, many agencies automatically fall back on the patterns established by their own professional training, and so they institute workshops, lectures, and seminars. Such procedures, as imitations of university education, can just as well be done at a university which is experienced with them. They fail to capitalize on the distinctive contributions which can be made by an operating social agency. It is the agency's work setting which must be involved if the agency is to do the kind of training for which it is best suited.

Training of residents and interns has been a standard part of the tasks of many agencies for years. However, there is a certain amount of arrogance implied by the fact that despite this traditional role, little or no training in methods of education is given to the students in the profession who man these training agencies. Is our level of insight into human behavior so complete and deep that we have nothing to learn from the specific studies and skills of educators? Thus I suggest that increased demand for agencies to do role-specific training implies a recognition of training functions as part of the role of a fully qualified professional person. This recognition further implies the building into professional training of courses in training methods and procedures.

4. Who Shall Administer?

The picture which emerges from the above discussion is that of a fully qualified professional person more highly trained in supervision and in training methods than in the past; he heads a team or teams of subprofessionals, trains people for the team, and supervises the activities of the team members. In brief, the professional person functions as an administrator. But where is he to learn agency administration? If he is a social worker, he may have learned it in the course of his graduate training. If he is a vocational counselor or a clinical psychologist, he will have learned it only by imitation of university professors who operate captive agencies which function very differently from those serving the disadvantaged poor. This indicates still another implication of subprofessional training.

I think it worth noting that there are some psychological factors which impinge on supervision and administration in the helping professions. It seems to me as if people in the helping professions as a group are reluctant to supervise and administer. They seem to dislike being in superior-subordinate relationships. This may be connected with the antiauthoritarianism which is so characteristic of those in the helping professions, or it may come from a variety of other sources about which one could speculate. The point is simply that there does seem to be an avoidance or reluctance, which must be overcome if supervision and administration are to be institutionalized as part of the professional's function and as elements in his training.

One problem in connection with administration should be mentioned. The age-old question involved here is of whether an agency ought to be run by people specifically trained in supervision, or whether it should be run by professionals who are completely experienced in the function being administered. If the fully qualified member of the team devotes himself to administration, supervision, and training, there is the danger that he will become so far removed from the realities of actual work with the clients as performed by the subprofessionals that his supervision and administration may become unrealistic. This problem has not been solved in the schools, in the universities, in business, or in Government; it is unlikely to find its completely adequate solution in the helping professions. Nevertheless, it is a problem which needs to be recognized, and it is part of the challenge posed by the broadening of counseling to include subprofessionals.

5. Who Shall Train?

The last problem I would like to discuss here concerns the locus of subprofessional recruitment and training. In Project CAUSE, the training was located in universities and was dominated by academic instruction. As indicated earlier, the success of such instruction rests heavily on the academic skills and the verbal-conceptual orientation of the trainees. It was also suggested earlier that these skills may be different from those which are required for successful performance in subprofessional roles. One is not likely to find many indigenous leaders, for example, who will be able to fit themselves into the academic mold even for brief, intensive training. Furthermore, the very concept of an indigenous leader is destroyed when one thinks of sending such a person to a university distant from his neighborhood, and away from his milieu. On the other hand, there are no other institutions which can marshal the intellectual and professional resources for providing such training. It is possible that local community colleges and junior colleges may be able to play a role in subprofessional training, especially if they are able to make use of personnel from higher institutions and community agencies.

Such training will demand an interdisciplinary approach, if it is specifically designed for workers with the disadvantaged. Skill and technique instruction will have to come from experienced clinicians, workers, and/or counselors, but the limitations in their experience to middle-class populations will require supplementation from sociologists, economists, criminologists, housing authorities, community action specialists, jurists, and others who have devoted their attentions to problems of the poor. It was the experience of many of the universities which participated in Project CAUSE training that contact with these other fields proved to be a source of renewed excitement and stimulation to the members of the counseling and guidance departments. Continued interaction of this sort can do much to invigorate counseling and guidance both as a profession and as a field of scholarship.

To recapitulate: There are overwhelming social needs requiring increased professional attention. There is a shortage of professional personnel, and the models which underlie the structures of the professions as presently constituted are inappropriate for meeting the social needs. One solution to these problems lies in subprofessional training, to implement a team concept which may provide services more appropriate to the population needing them and which can compensate for the shortage of fully qualified professionals. The establishment of subprofessional training requires attention to ways in which helping work can be subdivided into subprofessional roles which are effective and economical, the development of techniques for supervision, the training of professionals in supervision, attention to methods of in-service training and the development of training skills in professional personnel, the use of the fully qualified professional person as an administrator of services, and attention to the location and institutionalization of subprofessional training. The helping professions must attend to these problems if they are to remain responsive to the changing nature of the social needs, and if they are to continue to make the kind of contributions to society for which they are the most appropriate social institutions currently available. Failure to meet these challenges through a rigid clinging to methods no longer appropriate to the needs could render these professions so inappropriate that new ones may have to arise to fill the gap.

PROFESSIONAL STANDARDS AND RESISTANCE TO CHANGE

I would like to make a final comment about professional standards. As I see it, the development of subprofessional roles involves both a lowering and a raising of traditional standards. The establishment of specific subprofessional roles affords an economy of training which many will see as a lowering of professional standards (Odgers, 1964). On the other hand, the inclusion of these roles within the professional structures, as suggested above, requires that the fully qualified professional develop new and more advanced skills than those which are currently included in his repertoire. In this sense, we have a call for higher standards. There are those who criticize Project CAUSE and other similar programs as an attack on professional standards. I believe this to be a short-sighted view which implies a refusal on the part of the professions to adapt to the current needs, with the standards-enhancing implication of such an adaptation. The appeal to standards is traditionally the socially accepted defense against disturbance of the established status quo. Segregation in the neighborhoods has been defended by reference to standards of neighborhood care and upkeep; the exclusiveness and hegemony of medieval guilds was defended by reference to craftsmanship standards; the segregation of school children has similarly been justified. I see little use for high and restrictive standards for professional treatment if, because of those standards, treatment is completely denied to those needing it. And the data clearly indicate that effective and appropriate treatment is being denied to the disadvantaged youth of today. While such denial may not be willful or intended, its reality testifies that opposition to an expansion of appropriate services in the service of a defense of standards is in the interests of maintenance of the Establishment rather than in the interests of those needing help.

REFERENCES

FESTINGER, L. *When prophecy fails.* Minneapolis: Univer. Minnesota Press, 1956.

KRANZ, H. A crash program to aid disadvantaged youth. *Guidepost*, 1964, 6, 3–6.

LINTON, R., & KARDINER, A. The change from dry to wet rice cultivation in Tanala-Betsileo. In G. E. Swanson, T. M. Newcomb, & E. L. Hartley (Eds.), *Readings in social psychology.* New York: Holt, Rinehart & Winston, Inc., 1952. Pp. 222–230.

ODGERS, J. Cause for concern. *Counselor Education and Supervision*, 1964, 6, 17–20.

Changing Concepts in the Training of Therapists

MARGARET J. RIOCH

Many professionals in the mental health field recognize the ability of nontraditional workers with relatively little training to produce good therapeutic results. The question is raised and discussed as to why the guardians of our present system are slow to use fully new resources the effectiveness of which have been demonstrated. The suggestion is made that professionals with long traditional training should identify themselves with the advancement of knowledge and leave more of the practice of crafts to new categories of workers.

One criterion for valuable research is that it stimulates other research. By this criterion, Poser's study has already succeeded, even in the prepublication stage.[1] Having read the paper I felt impelled to conduct an informal experiment among my friends and acquaintances. I described the study to them briefly, but before telling them the results, I asked how they thought it turned out. About half of them said they thought there would be no difference between the professional and lay therapists, and the other half said they throught the lay therapists would come out ahead.

Reprinted with permission from *Journal of Consulting Psychology*, 1966, Vol. 30, No. 4, 290–292, Copyright 1966 by the American Psychological Association and with the permission of the author.

[1]Poser's study is included in the last section of this book. He found that: "by comparison to an untreated control group . . . lay therapists achieved slightly better results than psychiatrists and psychiatric social workers doing group therapy with similar patients."

The objection may well be raised that my sample was skewed in directions which people are too polite to mention. Nevertheless this bit of informal "research" does demonstrate that some experienced and chronologically mature mental health professionals expect to find that they and their colleagues do not achieve any better results than nonprofessionals, at least in measurable ways, on a short-term basis, in group therapy, with hospitalized schizophrenics. The only surprise manifested in my sample was over the fact that there were any significant differences at all.

I think it is relevant to report that I found a similar phenomenon when my colleagues and I were working on our National Institute of Mental Health (NIMH) Pilot Project in Training Mental Health Counselors (Rioch, Elkes, Flint, Usdansky, Newman, & Silber). It was easy to find distinguished psychiatrists and psychologists who said they had no doubt that our mature women trained in 2 years, part-time, would do as well as the regular professionals functioning as therapists for neurotics. This was stated before we had any demonstrable results. I do not mean to say that there was no opposition to this program and no skepticism about it. Of course, both were and are present. I do mean to say that there is a fairly large group of mental health professionals who believe that long years of academic and professional training are not essential for much of the actual practical work which needs to be done in this field. We are engaged in an area in which rigorous proof of "who does best" or even of "who does what" is practically impossible. But it is possible to demonstrate that our old notions about what training is essential are based on prejudice, or at least on preconceptions, and not on facts. It is possible to raise more than a shadow of doubt about whether the training programs into which our main efforts and financial support are being thrown are really the most effective and most efficient ones for the tasks that need to be performed. It seems to me that the importance of Poser's study lies just in this.

Psychologists, who are interested in understanding human behavior and who also would like to do something about human suffering, might perhaps turn their interest to themselves and their fellow professionals in an effort to understand why they move so slowly if at all in using some of the new ways of alleviating the manpower shortage in the mental health field which have been shown to have at the very least a good chance of success. There are, of course, the flaws in the experimental designs in the studies which purport to carve out new paths. These, however, are surely not the reason why the studies have not been repeated on a large scale and with improved design. We are faced with a serious situation of huge numbers of mentally ill people, including or excluding delinquents, dropouts, criminals, and just plain troubled citizens, and a shortage of the professionals who claim to have some knowledge of how to cure, prevent, or deal with such problems. Experimental programs have now shown a number of new ways of dealing with these problems which can be used either along with or instead of traditional ones. Additional manpower can be recruited from segments of the population not yet adequately exploited. These include students, as shown in the present study, dropouts, mature married women, and various kinds of indigenous helpers, including the poor, the hospitalized, and the incarcerated offenders. The intelligent use of machines too can save professional hours and produce positive results. More important even than the saving of traditional professional time, these new workers have a double advantage. They bring fresh points of view, flexible attitudes, and sometimes new methods into the field. They also solve their own problems in helping to solve the problems of others. They become constructive, better integrated citizens themselves, which is the most important thing of all, for in so doing they add to the community's pool of good will, rather than to its pool of discontent and suspicion.

If this is the case, why are we so slow in making use of these new tools which lie close at hand ready and waiting to be used? Why do we bring out all the regulations of academia and bureaucracy to make the hiring of people trained in nontraditional programs difficult and the setting up of such programs frustrating? It seems reasonable to suppose, given what we know of human behavior, that we are impelled not only by good and humanitarian motives to solve the problems of the mentally ill. We are concerned also with ourselves, our security, and our prestige. If we think that our only task is to do the best we can for the unfortunate patients, we blind ourselves to our other task, which is to do the best we can for ourselves. We too are patients who need care. Unless the mental health professional finds that nontraditional programs are in some way or other in his own interest as well as in the interest of the traditional patients, he cannot be expected to be in favor of them. It is unreasonable for any of us to expect psychologists and psychiatrists to act only for altruistic reasons while we are understanding and sympathetic about the egotism of the problem children in our society. We are all problem children. If we have invested long years of hard work in achieving a high professional status, including many courses that were dull and many examinations that were nerve wracking, and we are told that some young bit of a girl with no training can do the job as well as or better than we can, it is natural that we should try to find some objections.

Why then did psychologists and psychiatrists, who expressed themselves both about Poser's study and about the work of my colleagues and myself at NIMH, have no objections? Perhaps it was because they had already recognized in their own clinical work that their effectiveness was not a result of the courses and the examinations. They had found this an interesting psychological phenomenon and had begun to study it in their own ways, though not necessarily systematically. They had found that it added interest and challenge to their work to wonder about the value of the tradition in which they had been trained and to try out new ways, so that for them it was a confirmation of themselves to hear that a respectable scientific study was finding something similar. Furthermore, they had begun to redefine their own task. No matter what their official job description, they were actually engaged not simply in treatment of the mentally ill, but in pushing back the frontier of knowledge. In this task they could use all the help they could get from experimental programs and nontraditional workers. They did not either think or feel that such programs were inimical to their own interests. Surely we know enough about depth psychology to know that how we feel about a program is as important to our actions as how we consciously and intellectually think.

We are part of the same society which produced our patients. By hook or by crook or by good management, we have got the keys in our pockets, not in theirs. To preserve our own mental health we have to keep the keys in some form or other, and it is natural enough to want to hold the larger and better keys. It is even arguable that it is in the interest of the patients to distribute the keys according to an established hierarchical system. But systems change inevitably. If our mental health system is to change in an orderly, evolutionary manner rather than a chaotic, revolutionary one, I suggest that the professionals would benefit if they would identify themselves with the advancement of knowledge rather than with the practice of a craft, or if you prefer, of an art. This would leave some very large keys for them and at the same time make it possible for them to unlock the doors for many others.

With regard to Poser's study, I agree whole-heartedly that we need to differentiate a great deal more clearly the questions we are asking. Questions concerning what factors produce what kind of changes have not been answered in this study, but if the study were carried out on a larger scale, over a longer period of time, some of them might be approached. It is clear that what works in a small way in a first experiment will not necessarily continue to work if the method becomes general. This has been the fate of many treatment innovations in mental hospitals which is all the more reason to use them while they are new. My own prediction would be that if the same college girls who were so successful in their first venture were used again in the same way for five succeeding summers, their effectiveness would taper off. This does not mean that we should not use personnel of this kind. In fact it would be both interesting and important to find out when they do reach their peak usefulness and if and when they do taper off.

One question which I should like to raise has to do with Poser's statement that the patients were unaware of the distinction between the professionals and the untrained college students. I suppose this means that the patients were unsophisticated and that they were not informed. I do wonder, however, whether even very poorly educated patients would not be aware of the subtle as well as the obvious differences in the institutional hierarchy. Would not the attendant who brought the patients to the group meetings address the visiting doctors differently from the way he addressed the young girls? In any case, there was an obvious difference in the average age of the professionals and the nonprofessionals. The thing I am suggesting is that one possible factor in the positive results obtained by the nonprofessionals was that the patients cooperated more readily with people who were felt to be closer to themselves in the social hierarchy, that is, close to the bottom of the ladder. This would fit with the fact that two patients who functioned as therapists obtained good cooperation. It seems to be an almost universal finding in experiments of this kind, that whatever good or bad or indifferent effects come to pass upon the "objects" of the help given, the helpers themselves are sure to profit.

Another question which interests me very much but which may be quite unanswerable has to do with the attitudes of the psychiatrists, social workers, and occupational therapists in this study toward the experiment. Were they aware of how the study was being carried on? And what did they think of the results? If any of them were like the subjects of my informal experiment, they would take pleasure in the findings, but perhaps they were not. I raise the question because it is possible that some of the factors we have to look for in trying to explain the results of the study lie in the attitude of the various therapists, both professional and nonprofessional, toward the experiment itself.

REFERENCE

RIOCH, M. J., ELKES, C., FLINT, A. A., USDANSKY, B. S., NEWMAN, R. G., & SILBER, E. National Institute of Mental Health pilot study in training mental health counselors. *American Journal of Orthopsychiatry*, 1963, 33, 678–689.

Differential Use of Manpower in Public Welfare

ARTHUR BLUM

Manpower shortages in social welfare necessitate basic changes in organizational structure and manpower utilization. These changes must be based on how best to serve client needs, not on present professional role definitions and organizational patterns.

Social work as a profession is rapidly approaching a critical period, demanding far-reaching and crucial decisions in the area of manpower utilization. The pressures of expanding social welfare services, concentration on long-neglected client populations, and the development of new knowledge are only a few of the factors contributing to the increasing need to reassess social work's practices. The profession must engage the accusations that it has become so imbedded with tradition and bureaucratic structures that innovation and creativity are strangled.

It is no longer possible to ignore the fact that fewer than one out of four social welfare workers have two years or more of graduate education and only one out of twenty public assistance workers has achieved this level of education.[1] Nor can increased recruitment efforts by graduate

This paper was delivered at the Thirteenth Annual Meeting of the Council on Social Work Education, Denver, Colorado, January 1965. It is reprinted with permission of the National Association of Social Workers, from *Social Work*, Vol. 11, No. 1 (January 1966), pp. 16–21, and with the permission of the author. A brief biography of the author has been omitted.

[1]*Salaries and Working Conditions of Social Welfare Manpower in 1960* (Washington, D.C.: U.S. Department of Labor, Bureau of Labor Statistics, 1960).

schools of social work be offered as a potential solution in light of the 1963 total enrollment in graduate schools in the United States of 6,592.[2] Even if enrollments were doubled, this would not begin to meet the needs that presently exist or the increasing demands for staff resulting from the mammoth antidelinquency and antipoverty programs. New programs, adequately financed, are still faced with problems of staff shortages. Today manpower has become more of a problem than money.

Social workers are being held accountable for the lacks in services offered to such client populations as slum-dwellers, delinquents, and the unemployed. Questions are being raised even in communities that recognize and sympathize with the financial limitations under which social work has labored as to whether the best use is being made of financial and manpower resources. There is need for critical self-examination of the profession's practices and services while it is still in control of its own destiny and direction of growth. The profession has not been willing to evaluate critically where it is or where it is going, but has instead spent the bulk of its energies refining where it has been.

DIFFERENTIATION OF TASKS

The first step in analyzing the problems in the utilization of manpower is to differentiate between the tasks that can be performed by the professional social worker and those that can be performed by the social welfare worker or the worker without a master's degree in social work. It is essential that these tasks be differentiated in relation to the needs of the client to be served and not solely from a professional definition of the role.[3]

Reflected in the admission procedures and course requirements in graduate schools of social work is the assumption that what the professional social worker does is different from what the social welfare worker does. A student applying for admission who has had experience as an employee of a social welfare agency is not differentiated from the student with no experience, nor are the curriculum requirements essentially different. He is required to take a series of related courses, and the failure

[2]*Statistics on Social Work Education* (New York: Council on Social Work Education, 1963).

[3]Bertram M. Beck, "Wanted Now: Social Work Associates," *The Social Welfare Forum, 1963* (New York: Columbia University Press, 1963), pp. 195–205; Richard A. Cloward, "Social Class and Private Social Agencies," *Education for Social Work, 1963* (New York: Council on Social Work Education, 1963), pp. 123–137; Willard C. Richan, "A Theoretical Scheme for Determining Roles of Professional and Nonprofessional Personnel," *Social Work*, Vol. 6, No. 4 (October 1961), pp. 22–28; Frank Riessman, "The Revolution in Social Work," *Trans-action,* Vol. 2, No. 1 (November/December 1964), pp. 12–17.

to complete any one of these courses denies him access to the professional degree. The inference is that this entire combination of academic experiences, together with supervised field work, is necessary to equip him to undertake the professional practice of social work. Further, criteria for admission to most schools of social work require that the student demonstrate, prior to admission, an ability to relate to people. The focus in professional training is on how the worker consciously *uses* this ability to relate in order to enable the client to change. The point at which professional training really begins is when the student says, "I've got a 'good' relationship with the client, now what do I do with it?"

The inference underlying this thinking appears to be that the social welfare worker may have the ability to relate but is not able to use his relationship in a conscious way toward a specific goal until he has an integrated knowledge base resulting from graduate education. Logically, it could be said that although the goals of the social welfare worker may be similar to those of the professional social worker, the means he uses in striving toward these goals should be different. The conscious use of the worker-client relationship is not available to the social welfare worker. He must, therefore, rely heavily on other tools in his work with the client, among which may be the provision of maintenance payments, the finding of a job, or the protection of the client from exploitation by community institutions.

In order to maximize the social welfare worker's utilization of the tools and techniques available to him, it follows logically that the structure of the social welfare agency, the job description, and the conditions for delivery of service (size and type of caseload and so on) should differ in relation to the worker. Have such adjustments been seriously considered or made?

During the Depression of the 1930s the task and responsibility of providing income-maintenance payments was shifted from the family service agency to the public assistance agency. The rationale for the shift included the philosophical question of government responsibility, the overwhelming need as a result of the Depression, and, later, a redefinition of the role and function of the professional social worker in the family service agency. But not only did the public assistance agency assume responsibility for this task, it also incorporated the model and structure of the family service agency as the most effective framework to facilitate the maximum utilization of this tool. Basic to the structure and consistent with its underlying assumptions were the conditions of one worker to one client and small enough case loads to permit intimacy. The worker was to minister to the total needs of the client and to assume full responsibility for all aspects of the case. This procedure was seen as essential for the establishment of a relationship and provided the necessary conditions for the conscious use of that relationship. Since it has been possible neither to staff this structure with workers who can make professional use of the relationship nor to meet the requirements of small case loads, it becomes necessary to assess this model critically as to its utility and desirability.

INSTITUTIONAL TREATMENT MODEL

Other models of services are available, such as the institutional treatment model. The arrangement of services in the institution includes a single worker who has major responsibility for the case but whose job includes the co-ordination and use of a team of specialists. The needs of the client are assessed and the entire range of manpower resources are available to minister and administer for the welfare of the client. Thus it is possible to define the function of the cottage staff, recreation worker, teacher, tutor, Big Brother and Big Sister, institution director, nurse, group worker, caseworker, and any other needed staff as they relate to the needs of the client. Different cases demand different utilizations of this staff and as a specific case progresses shifts in emphasis and services can be made. Jobs can be defined in more functional terms and staff with differential educational backgrounds can be mobilized and utilized effectively. Essential to this structure is the diagnostic function and the co-ordination of services for the benefit of the client. This structure provides the flexibility that is essential for the client and further makes it feasible and desirable to employ a range of persons with varied backgrounds and skills. It gives direction, also, for the training of skilled specialists who can function effectively under the direction of the generalist.

Not only does this type of model provide greater latitude for manpower utilization, it may provide better service to the client. Experiments in the use of trained social workers as cottage parents have demonstrated the futility of this approach, because (1) the social worker found it difficult to concentrate on the management problems in the cottage (making beds, supervising the brushing of teeth, seeing that the children kept appointments) and (2) good cottage parents had something to offer the child emotionally that was different from but as crucial as the equipment of trained social workers. There is evidence also that this type of multifunctional arrangement does not create confusion for the client as long as the staff members are clear about their roles within the organization.[4]

[4]Arthur Blum and Norman A. Polansky, "Effect of Staff Role on Children's Verbal Accessibility," *Social Work*, Vol. 6, No. 1 (January 1961), pp. 29–37.

NEEDS OF THE CLIENT

As stated earlier, any plan for the utilization of manpower must begin with the needs of the clients and progress in relation to how best to meet these needs. Too often the tasks of the social welfare worker have been defined in relation to what a professional social worker would do if he occupied the position or in relation to what is now being done.[5] Yet there is little research evidence to support the assumption that what is presently being done is successful. Rather, there is increasing evidence that given the best of what the present system demands adequate services would still not be provided for whole populations of clients, such as the victims of poverty.[6] We have been more willing to define the problem in relation to where the profession of social work is than where the client is.

Even a cursory inventory of some of the needs of the public assistance client would include provision of income-maintenance payments given in such a way as to maintain the dignity of the individual; provision of health services; protection against exploitation by the community and its institutions (whether this is done by protecting the client or by teaching him how and providing the opportunities for him to protect himself); education on household management, budgeting, shopping skills, and the like; preparation for future functioning including, when necessary, job preparation and job-finding; establishment of an institution (the agency) that is on the client's side and helps to defeat his feelings of alienation and helplessness; a worker who will treat the client like a human being and who can help repair past emotional damage if needed. It is this combination of client needs that must become the base from which services are derived, manpower needs defined, and manpower utilization decided. It must also serve as the basis for agency structure and the design for the delivery of services.

MULTIFUNCTIONAL APPROACH

As these needs are addressed, it becomes obvious that many of them can best be met by persons who do not necessarily have graduate training in social work and that a variety of technicians, specialists, and emotionally empathic persons, properly coordinated, is needed to do the job. It is

[5]Willard C. Richan, "Occupational Restructuring: A Challenge to Social Work Research." Paper delivered at the Institute on Research Approaches to Manpower Problems in Social Welfare Services to Children and Families, National Association of Social Workers, Duluth, Minn., August 23–26, 1964. (Mimeographed.)

[6]Henry J. Meyer, Edgar F. Borgatta, and Wyatt C. Jones, *Girls at Vocational High* (New York: Russell Sage Foundation, 1965).

unlikely that one worker can do the total job, although the client may well need a single individual to whom he can relate and who will act as a mediator for these services. It is also likely that the role of this worker will change over time as the client is more able to function independently in relation to other staff. At present, the one-to-one model recreates the mother-child relationship and does not encourage the growth process involved in extending that relationship to father, siblings, peers, and other adults. Is social work guilty of developing a structure designed to start where the client is and keep him there?

A multifunctional approach of this kind offers other advantages as well. It would no longer be necessary to engage in ongoing debates over whether there should be social work aides, technicians, associates, and so on; it would be necessary to create a series of job categories essential to the services offered.[7] Jobs could be created that do not require graduate training, are not designed specifically as recruitment devices for schools of social work, permit promotion and career aspirations to be fulfilled, and have respectability.[8] Employment could begin within the categories that demand routine services or are dependent primarily on what the worker brings with him to the job. The worker could progressively advance to jobs whose tasks require additional skills and knowledge.

Training in such a setting could become much more specific and job oriented. All workers would need to become sensitized to the needs of their client groups. Beyond this, however, job-specific training could be undertaken, which could include many present training methods but could go even further in providing apprenticeship experiences, team

[7]For a review of beginning attempts in job differentiation see *A Study of the Use of the Social Work Assistant in the Veterans Administration* (Washington, D.C.: Department of Medicine and Surgery, Veterans Administration, July 1965); Roger Cumming, "Effective Use of Social Work Services," *Personnel Information*, Vol. 6, No. 2 (March 1963); James R. Dumpson and Lawrence Podell, "Alternative Deployment of Public Assistance and Trained Casework Personnel" (New York: Department of Welfare of the City of New York, 1964) (mimeographed); Laura Epstein, "Differential Use of Staff: A Method to Expand Social Services," *Social Work*, Vol. 7, No. 4 (October 1962), pp. 66–72; Marcella Farrar and Mary L. Hemmy, "Use of Nonprofessional Staff in Work with the Aged," *Social Work*, Vol. 8, No. 3 (July 1963), pp. 44–50; Margaret M. Heyman, "A Study of Effective Utilization of Social Workers in a Hospital Setting," *Social Work*, Vol. 6, No. 2 (April 1961), pp. 36–43; "Use of Personnel Without Professional Training in Social Service Departments" (New York: Medical Social Work Section, National Association of Social Workers, May 1959); *Utilization of Personnel in Social Work: Those With Full Professional Education and Those Without* (New York: National Association of Social Workers, 1962); Verne Weed and William H. Denham, "Toward More Effective Use of the Nonprofessional Worker: A Recent Experiment," *Social Work*, Vol. 6, No. 4 (October 1961), pp. 29–36; Ernest F. Witte, "Training Social Work Associates," *Education for Social Work, 1963* (New York: Council on Social Work Education, 1963), pp. 12–23; Corinne H. Wolfe, "Improving Services by Better Utilization of Staff," *Journal of the American Public Welfare Association*, Vol. 19, No. 2 (April 1961).

[8]Arthur Pearl and Frank Riessman, *New Careers for the Poor* (New York: Free Press, 1965).

supervision, and the like. As the worker progresses in his ability to assume greater responsibility he could be trained to undertake more complex functions. The trainer, however, would be able to build on successful experiences with simpler tasks. This would necessitate moving away from the model of graduate school social work training and developing new training approaches that are more appropriate for social welfare workers. The tendency has been to train social welfare workers in the same way as professional social workers without recognizing the fact that they are being trained to undertake different tasks and functions and not to become amateur social workers.

BUILD ON WORKER'S STRENGTHS

This differentiation of tasks and use of a team approach would also provide the opportunity to build on the strengths the worker brings to the agency and make it possible to compensate for all people. One worker would not be expected to be all things to all people. In Project CAUSE, an eight-week training program for students with some college education sponsored by the U.S. Department of Labor and administered at Western Reserve University through the Youth Development Training Center, it became obvious that different students displayed different talents and potential that could be utilized in an agency offering a range of services. It was necessary to establish a minimum base of expected functioning, but beyond this minimum a wide range of functioning could be utilized effectively in the agency's operation.

Five students stand out vividly. All were from slum areas in New York City and all demonstrated areas of personality dysfunction in their behavior, in individual assessment interviews, and on psychological tests. In each case there was a strong need to over-identify with the clients and an inability to sustain a long-term intimate relationship in which the worker could continue to identify that it was the client who had the problem and needed help. However, each of these students had exceptional ability to reach out and establish initial contacts with clients whom professional social workers were unable to reach. They were able to use this talent in their field work experiences to facilitate contact between the client and ongoing workers and involve the clients in available services—a feat that existing agency staff members had been unable to accomplish. The crucial element that needs to be stressed is that these same students would have had difficulty had they been expected to assume total responsibility for these clients on a long-term basis.

Other students showed ability to execute routines and to provide concrete services to clients with empathy and feelings that supported the clients' dignity and self-concept. Some of these same students, however, became frightened, authoritarian, and ineffective in worker-client situations that were totally dependent on giving through the relationship. As can be expected, others functioned well in the relationship but could not tolerate routines and forms. Yet each of these different types of students could perform a useful function in an agency whose structure provided for a range of talent utilization rather than trying to fit these students into the mold of generalist or professional social worker.

The role of the professional social worker in this type of multifunctional structure would relate primarily to decision-making. This would include diagnosis, case assignment, supervision, consultation, administration, and co-ordination of the service team. The professional social worker would occupy key decision-making positions and maintain the responsibility of accountability for the service. In assuming this function of accountability, it may become necessary for the supervisor periodically to schedule an interview with the client to assess progress and service directions—to use his diagnostic ability in direct relationship with the client and not become totally dependent on the workers' records. Certain difficult and crucial decisions, such as placement, may need to be implemented by the supervisor himself through interviews with the client or joint interviews involving the supervisor, worker, and client. Within the context of a team approach and fresh interpretations of the meaning of the relationship, as it relates to the client's view of the relationship, these procedures could be acceptable and of great benefit to the client and part of the in-service training experience of the worker.

IDENTIFICATION WITH AGENCY, NOT WORKER

Returning again to the needs of the clients, one of the crucial needs is the knowledge that an agency, staffed by a variety of workers, exists to offer as immediate and appropriate help with problems as possible. Accepting this need of the client to know that an agency—and not just a single worker—is there to help, the workers might become more free to minister to this need. It is difficult to understand why there has not been a move toward the development of "crisis teams." Such a team would be on twenty-four-hour call and would be composed of specialists who know procedures and whom to call in the event of a variety of emergencies. Workers would not have to drop everything to handle emergencies, and at the same time the client would receive the necessary immediate assistance from the agency.

An assumption is made here that the client must be helped to identify with the agency and not with a single worker in the agency. Questions have been raised as to whether a client can identify with an abstraction. There is considerable evidence in the social science literature that individuals can and in fact do identify with larger collectives. An institution can itself offer support and security that goes beyond the individual relationship, which is needed badly by clients. The structure of the agency and the utilization of staff must be related to fulfilling this need. This is especially important in agencies with high staff turnover.

CONCLUSIONS

The issues that have been raised thus far in relation to social welfare agencies apply equally well to other types of agencies. Client needs must be assessed as to which of these needs are best met by different levels of worker, under what conditions, and within what type of agency structure. The literature on utilization of manpower reflects that too often the starting point is what the professional social worker is now doing that he thinks he should not be doing or that can be done by someone else, rather than with the needs of the client groups.

The problem of manpower utilization in our changing society presents a bold challenge to the social work profession today. Solutions will not be found in wishful thinking but will require major changes in practice, institutional arrangements, and methods for delivery of services.

The "Helper" Therapy Principle

FRANK RIESSMAN

An age-old therapeutic approach is the use of people with a problem to help other people who have the same problem in more severe form (e.g., Alcoholics Anonymous). But in the use of this approach—and there is a marked current increase in this tendency—it may be that emphasis is being placed on the wrong person in centering attention on the individual receiving help. More attention might well be given the individual who needs the help less, that is, the person who is providing the assistance, because frequently it is he who improves!

While it may be uncertain that people *receiving* help are always benefited, it seems more likely that the people *giving* help are profiting from their role. This appears to be the case in a wide variety of self-help "therapies," including Synanon (for drug addicts), Recovery Incorporated (for psychologically disturbed people), and Alcoholics Anonymous. Mowrer notes that there are over 265 groups of this kind listed in a directory, *Their Brother's Keepers.*[1] The American Conference of Therapeutic Self-Help Clubs publishes an official magazine, *Action*, describing some of the functions of these groups.

Reprinted from *Social Work*, 1965, Vol. 10, No. 2, 27–32, with the permission of the National Association of Social Workers and the author. A brief biography of the author has been omitted.

[1]O. Hobart Mowrer, *The New Group Therapy* (Princeton, N.J.: D. Van Nostrand Co., 1964), p. iv.

While there is still a need for firm research evidence that these programs are effective, various reports (many of them admittedly impressionistic) point to improvement in the givers of help rather than the recipients. Careful research evaluating these programs is needed, because there are numerous contaminating factors that may be contributing to their success, such as the leadership of the therapist, selection of subjects, and the newness or novelty of the program.

Although much of the evidence for the helper principle is observational and uncontrolled, there is one experimental investigation that provides at least indirect verification or support of the principle. In a study by King and Janis in which role-playing was used, it was found that subjects who had to improvise a speech supporting a specific point of view tended to change their opinions in the direction of this view more than subjects who merely read the speech for an equivalent amount of time.[2] They describe this effect in terms of "self-persuasion through persuading others."

Volkman and Cressey formulate this principle as one of their five social-psychological principles for the rehabilitation of criminals:

> The most effective mechanism for exerting group pressure on members will be found in groups so organized that criminals are induced to join with noncriminals for the purpose of changing other criminals. A group in which criminal "A" joins with some non-criminals to change criminal "B" is probably most effective in changing criminal "A", not "B" . . . .[3]

Perhaps, then, social work's strategy ought to be to devise ways of creating more helpers! Or, to be more exact, to find ways to transform *recipients* of help into *dispensers* of help, thus reversing their roles, and to structure the situation so that recipients of help will be placed in roles requiring the giving of assistance.

In most of the programs mentioned thus far the helpers and the helped have had essentially the same problem or symptom. The approach is carried one step further in Recovery Incorporated, in which emotionally disturbed people help each other even though their symptoms may differ.

A somewhat more indirect expression of the principle is found in the sociotherapeutic approach reported by Wittenberg some years ago.[4] Wittenberg found that participation in a neighborhood block committee formed to help other people in the neighborhood led to marked person-

[2]B. T. King and I. L. Janis, "Comparison of the Effectiveness of Improvised Versus Non-Improvised Role Playing in Producing Opinion Changes," *Human Relations*, Vol. 1 (1956), pp. 177–186.

[3]Rita Volkman and Donald R. Cressey, "Differential Association and the Rehabilitation of Drug Addicts," *American Journal of Sociology*, Vol. 69, No. 2 (February 1963), p. 139

[4]Rudolph M. Wittenberg, "Personality Adjustment Through Social Action," *American Journal of Orthopsychiatry*, Vol. 18, No. 2 (March 1958), pp. 207–221.

ality development and growth in a woman who had been receiving public assistance and who also had considerable personality difficulty.

WORK OF NONPROFESSIONALS

Another variant of this principle is found in the work of indigenous nonprofessionals employed as homemakers, community organizers, youth workers, recreation aides, and the like. Some of these people have had serious problems in the recent past. Some are former delinquents. It has been observed, however, that in the course of their work, their own problems diminished greatly.[5] One of the important premises of the HARYOU program is that "indigenous personnel will solve their own problems while attempting to help others."[6]

The helper therapy principle has at least two important implications for the nonprofessional of lower socioeconomic background: (1) Since many of the nonprofessionals to be recruited are former delinquents, addicts, AFDC mothers, and the like, it seems quite likely that placing them in a helping role can be rehabilitative for them. (2) As the nonprofessionals benefit from their new helping roles, they may actually become more effective workers and thus provide more help to others at a new level.

Thus, what is presented here may be a positive upward spiral in contrast to the better-known downward trend. That is, the initial helping role may be furnishing minimal help to the recipient, but may be highly beneficial to the helper, who in turn becomes more efficient, better motivated, and reaches a new stage in helping skill.

THERAPY FOR THE POOR

The helper principle probably has universal therapeutic application, but may be especially useful in low-income treatment projects for these two reasons:

1. It may circumvent the special inter-class role distance difficulties that arise from the middle-class-oriented therapy (and therapist) being at odds with the low-income clients' expectations and style; the alienation that many low-income clients feel toward professional treatment agents

[5]*See* Gertrude Goldberg, "The Use of Untrained Neighborhood Workers in a Homemaker Program," an unpublished report of Mobilization For Youth, New York, N.Y., 1963; and *Experiment in Culture Expansion* (Sacramento, Calif.: State of California Department of Corrections, 1963).

[6]*Youth in the Ghetto* (New York: Harlem Youth Opportunities Unlimited, 1964), p. 609.

and the concomitant rapport difficulties may be greatly reduced by utilizing the low-income person himself as the helper-therapist.

For the same reason much wider employment of neighborhood-based nonprofessionals in hospitals and social agencies as aides or social service technicians is recommended. Like the helper-therapist, they are likely to have considerably less role distance from the low-income client than does the professional.

2. It may be a principle that is especially attuned to the co-operative trends in lower socioeconomic groups and cultures. In this sense it may be beneficial to both the helper (the model) and the helped.

STUDENTS AS HELPERS

In Flint, Michigan, a group of fourth-grade pupils with reading problems was assigned to the tutelage of sixth-grade pupils who were also experiencing reading difficulties. It is interesting to note that while the fourth graders made significant progress, the sixth graders also learned from the experience.[7] Mobilization For Youth has used homework helpers with a fair amount of success, in that the recipients of the help showed some measurable academic improvement.[8] It may be that even more significant changes are taking place in the high school youngsters who are being used as tutors. Not only is it possible that their school performance is improving, but as a result of their new role these youngsters may begin to perceive the possibility of embarking on a teaching career.

Schneider reports on a small study in which youngsters with varying levels of reading ability were asked to read an "easy" book as practice for reading to younger children. She observes:

> For the child who could read well, this was a good experience. For the child who could not read well it was an even better experience. He was reading material on a level within his competence and he could read it with pleasure. Ordinary books on his level of interest were too difficult for him to read easily and so he did not read books for pleasure. Reading for him was hard, hard work; often it left him feeling stupid and helpless. This time it was different . . . he would be a giver; he would share his gift with little children just as a parent or teacher does.[9]

[7]Frank B. W. Hawkinshire, "Training Needs for Offenders Working in Community Treatment Programs," *Experiment in Culture Expansion* (Sacramento, Calif.: State of California Department of Corrections, 1963), pp. 27–36.

[8]"Progress Report" (New York: Mobilization For Youth, July 1964).

[9]Gussie Albert Schneider, "Reading of the Children, By the Children, For the Children." Unpublished manuscript, 1964. (Mimeographed.)

In a sense these children were role-playing the helper role in this experience, as they were reading aloud to adults in anticipation of later reading to small children.

The classroom situation illustrates an interesting offshoot of the helper principle. Some children, when removed from a class in which they are below average and placed in a new group in which they are in the upper half of the class, manifest many new qualities and are in turn responded to more positively by the teacher. This can occur independently of whether or not they play a helper role. But some of the same underlying mechanisms are operative as in the direct helper situations: the pupil in the new group is responded to more, he stands out more, more is expected of him, and generally he responds in turn and demands more of himself. Even though he may not be in the helper role as such, similar forces are at work in both cases, stimulating more active responses. (Unfortunately, this principle may be counteracted if the teacher treats the entire group as a "lower" or poorer group and this image is absorbed in an undifferentiated manner by all the members of the class.)

A connected issue worthy of mention is that in the new situations in the schools, where (hopefully) integration will be taking place, youngsters coming from segregated backgrounds will need help in catching up, in terms of reading skills and the like. It is generally argued that the white middle-class children who do not need this extra assistance will suffer. Their parents want these youngsters to be in a class with advanced pupils and not to be "held back" by youngsters who are behind.

However, in terms of the helper principle, it may very well be that the more advanced youngsters can benefit in new ways from playing a teaching role. Not all fast, bright youngsters like to be in a class with similar children. We have been led to believe that if one is fast and bright he will want to be with others who are fast and bright and this will act as a stimulus to his growth. It does for some people, but for others it most certainly does not. Some people find they do better in a group in which there is a great range of ability, in which they can stand out more, and, finally—and this is the point of the helper principle—in situations in which they can help other youngsters in the classroom. In other words, some children develop intellectually not by being challenged by someone ahead of them, but by helping somebody behind them, by being put into the tutor-helper role.

As any teacher can report, there is nothing like learning through teaching. By having to explain something to someone else one's attention is focused more sharply. This premise seems to have tremendous potentiality that social workers have left unused.

LEADERSHIP DEVELOPMENT

Carried one step further, the helper principle allows for the development of leadership in community organizations and the like. It has been found, for example, in tenant groups, that an individual might be relatively inactive at meetings in his own building, but display quite different characteristics when helping to organize another building. In the new situation, forced to play the helper role, leadership begins to emerge. The character of the new group, in which the individual is in a more advanced position vis-à-vis the remainder of the group, contributes toward the emergence of new leadership behavior. This is simply another way of saying that leadership develops through the act of leading. The art of leadership training may lie in providing just the right roles to stimulate the emergence of more and more leadership.

While some individuals fall more naturally into the helper or leader role (in certain groups), this role can be distributed more widely by careful planning with regard to the sociometry and composition of the group. When the group is fluid, the introduction of new members often encourages older members who were formerly in the follower role to assume a more active helping role.

Following King and Janis' lead, role-playing can be utilized to have a person who formerly was the recipient of help in the group now play a helper role, thus aiding him to persuade himself through persuading others.[10] Many similar group dynamic approaches can be used in order to utilize most fully the potentialities of the helper principle. Seating arrangements can be altered, individuals can be placed in key positions—for example, chairing small committees—and temporary classroom groupings can be formed in which pupils previously submerged by more advanced classmates are now allowed to become helpers or models for less advanced youngsters. The essential idea in all of this is to structure and restructure the groups so that different group members play the helper role at different times.

HELPER THERAPY MECHANISMS

It may be of value to speculate briefly regarding the various possible mechanisms whereby the helper benefits from his helping role. Brager notes the improved self-image that probably results from the fact that a person is doing something worthwhile in helping someone in need.[11]

[10] *Op cit.*

[11] George Brager, "The Indigenous Worker: A New Approach to the Social Work Technician," *Social Work,* 1965, Vol. 10, no. 2, pp. 33–40.

The King-Janis study suggests that becoming committed to a position through advocating it ("self-persuasion through persuading others") may be an important dimension associated with the helper role. Pearl notes that many helpers (such as the homeworker helpers) are "given a stake or concern in a system" and this contributes to their becoming "committed to the task in a way that brings about especially meaningful development of their own abilities."[12]

There is undoubtedly a great variety of other mechanisms that will be clarified by further research. Probably also the mechanisms vary depending on the setting and task of the helper. Thus helpers, functioning in a therapeutic context, whether as professional therapeutic agents or as nonprofessional "peer therapists," may benefit from the importance and status associated with this role. They also receive support from the implicit thesis "I must be well if I help others." People who themselves have problems (e.g., alcoholics, drug addicts, unwed mothers) should derive benefit from this formulation. Moreover, their new helper roles as such may function as a major (distracting) source of involvement, thus diverting them from their problem and general self-concern. There is no question also that individual differences are important so that some people receive much greater satisfaction from "giving," "helping," "leading," "controlling," "co-operating," "persuading," and "mothering."

Helpers operating in a teaching context, again both as professionals and nonprofessionals, may profit more from the cognitive mechanisms associated with learning through teaching. They need to learn the material better in order to teach it and more generalized academic sets may emerge from the teacher role. Finally, the status and prestige dimensions attached to the teacher role may accrue unforeseen benefits to them.

The helper in the leader role may benefit from some of the same factors related to the teacher and therapist roles as well as the "self-persuasion through persuading others" mechanism and their "stake in the system." In essence, then, it would seem that the gains are related to the actual demands of the specific helper role (whether it is teacher, leader, or therapist), plus the new feelings associated with the meaning and prestige of the role and the way the helper is treated because of the new role.

CAUTIONS AND CONDITIONS

In a sense, the helper principle seems counter to the widely accepted psychological dictum that warns against therapist projection. The well-

[12]Arthur Pearl, "Youth in Lower Class Settings," p. 6. Paper presented at the fifth Symposium on Social Psychology, Norman, Okla., 1964.

known danger, called to our attention by all of psychoanalytic theory and practice, indicates that a therapist with a specific problem may, unless he has understanding and control of this problem, project it to the person he is treating. Of course, in many of the cases cited this situation does not arise because both the treater and the treated suffer from the same malady. But in other cases when rehabilitated nonprofessional workers are hired to work with people who either have no specific problem or do not have the problems of the helper, the possibility of projection as well as psychological contagion has to be considered.

Two controlling devices are suggested to guard against the potential risk: (1) the helper should not be involved in any intensive treatment function unless he has considerable awareness of his problem and the projection issue, and (2) professional supervision is absolutely necessary; perhaps one of the difficulties of the amateur therapeutic self-help programs is the antiprofessionalism that frequently characterizes them.

There is another potential danger residing in the helper therapy principle, especially if it is to be applied on a large scale. Much of the intrinsic value of the technique may depend on it operating in a relatively subconscious fashion. Once people know they are being placed in certain helping roles in order to be helped themselves, some of the power of the principle deriving from feelings of self-importance and the like may be reduced. That this is not entirely true is evident from role-playing situations in which the subjects know the object of the game but still are affected. Nevertheless, the question of large-scale manipulation of the principle, with the increased likelihood of mechanical and arbitrary application, does hold some danger that only careful observation and research can accurately evaluate.

IMPLICATIONS

The helper principle may have wide application in hospital groups (both in- and outpatient), prisons, correctional institutions, and so forth. Scheidlinger suggests that the principle may have powerful implications for social work's understanding of the therapeutic process in all group therapy. Not only are individual group members aided through helping other members in the group, but the group as a whole may be greatly strengthened in manifold ways as it continually offers assistance to individual group members.[13]

Levine suggests that in a variety of types of habit change, such as efforts

[13]Conversation with Saul Scheidlinger, Community Service Society, New York, N.Y., January 18, 1964.

to curtail cigarette smoking, the helper principle may have considerable validity. Smokers who are cast in the role of persuading other smokers to stop smoking have themselves been found to benefit from their commitment to the new antismoking prescription.[14]

The helper principle does not really require that only the helper profit or even that he benefit more than the person receiving help. Thus it is seen in the Flint, Michigan, study that the fourth graders receiving help benefited at least as much as the givers of help.[15] The helper principle only calls attention to the aid the helper receives from being in the helper role.

The helper principle has been utilized with varying degrees of awareness in many group situations. What we are calling for is more explicit use of this principle in an organized manner. Conscious planning directed toward the structuring of groups for the widest possible distribution of the helper role may be a decisive therapeutic intervention, a significant leadership training principle, and an important teaching device. It is probably no accident that it is often said that one of the best ways to learn is to teach. Perhaps also psychiatrists, social workers, and others in the helping professions are helping themselves more than is generally recognized!

[14]Conversation with Sol Levine, Harvard University School of Public Health, Cambridge, Mass., January 12, 1964.

[15]Hawkinshire, *op. cit.*

SUGGESTED ADDITIONAL READINGS

Action for Mental Health. Report of the Joint Commission on Mental Illness and Health. New York: Basic Books, Inc., 1961.

Albie, George W. *Mental health manpower needs.* New York: Basic Books, Inc., 1959.

Albie, George W. Conceptual models and manpower requirements in psychology. *American Psychologist,* 1968, Vol. 23, No. 5, 317–320.

Arnhoff, Franklyn N. Reassessment of the trilogy: Need, supply, and demand. *American Psychologist,* 1968, Vol. 23, No. 5, 312–316.

Benjamin, Judith G., Freedman, Marcia K., and Lynton, Edith F. Pros and cons: New roles for nonprofessionals in Corrections. United States Department of Health, Education, and Welfare, Office of Juvenile Delinquency and Youth Development. Washington, D. C.: Government Printing Office, 1966.

Carkhuff, Robert R. Training in the counseling and therapeutic practices: Requiem or reveille? *Journal of Counseling Psychology,* 1966, Vol. 13, No. 3, 360–367.

Colarelli, Nick (sic) J., and Siegel, Saul M. *Ward H: An adventure in innovation.* Princeton: D. Van Nostrand Company, Inc., 1966.

Cowen, Emory L., Gardner, Elmer A., and Zax, Melvin (Eds.). *Emergent approaches to mental health problems.* New York: Appleton-Century-Crofts, 1968.

Duhl, Leonard J. The changing face of mental health. In *The urban condition,* Duhl, Leonard J. (Ed.) New York: Basic Books, Inc., 1963, Pp. 59–75.

Fairweather, George W. *Methods for experimental social innovation.* New York: John Wiley & Sons, Inc., 1967.

Jones, Maxwell, Baker, A., Freeman, Thomas, Merry, Julius, Pomryn, B. A., Sandler, Joseph, and Tuxford, Joy. *The therapeutic community: A new treatment method in psychiatry.* New York: Basic Books, Inc., 1953.

Lief, Harold I. Subprofessional training in mental health. *Archives of General Psychiatry,* 1966, Vol. 15, 660–664.

MacLennan, Beryce W., Fishman, Jacob R., Klein, William L., Denham, William H., Walker, Walter L., and Mitchell, Lonnie E. The implications of the nonprofessional in community mental health. Paper presented at the meeting of the American Orthopsychiatric Association, San Francisco, April, 1966.

McGee, Richard K. The suicide prevention center as a model for community mental health programs. *Community Mental Health Journal,* 1965, Vol. 1, No. 2, 162–171.

Pearl, Arthur, and Riessman, Frank. *New careers for the poor.* New York: The Free Press, 1965.

Peck, Harris B., Levin, Tom, and Roman, Melvin. The Health Careers Institute. A mental health strategy for an urban community. Paper presented at the Annual Meeting of the American Psychiatric Association, May, 1967.

Pratt, Steve. Statement of the philosophy and program of the Jacksonville State Hospital. Mimeographed document, Jacksonville State Hospital, Jacksonville, Illinois, August, 1966.

Pratt, Steve, and Tooley, Jay. Contract psychology and training contracts. Brief summary of some of the material prepared for presentation as part of the Symposium, The Role of Psychologists in Training the Nonprofessional. In *Proceedings*: 15th Conference of Psychology Program Directors and Consultants in State, Federal and Territorial Mental Health Programs, Chicago, September, 1965, Pp. 21–26.

Rapoport, Robert N. *Community as doctor: New perspectives on a therapeutic community.* London: Travistock Publications; and Springfield, Illinois: Charles C. Thomas, 1960.

Reiff, Robert. Mental health manpower and institutional change. *American Psychologist*, 1966, Vol. 21, 540–548.

Riessman, Frank, and Hallowitz, Emanuel. The neighborhood service center—an innovation in preventive psychiatry. Paper presented at the American Psychiatric Association Meetings, Atlantic City, New Jersey, May, 1966.

Sanders, Richard. New manpower for mental hospital service. Paper presented at the University of Rochester Conference on Emergent Approaches to Mental Health Problems, June, 1965.

Shaevitz, Morton H. Student involvement in action programs and implications for clinical training. Paper presented at the Annual Meeting of the American Psychological Association, New York, September, 1966.

Vail, David J., and Karlins, Miriam. A decade of volunteer services: History and social significance. *International Journal of Social Psychiatry*, 1965, Vol. 11, No. 2, 105–109.

Werry, J. S. Psychotherapy—a medical procedure? *Canadian Psychiatric Association Journal*, 1965, Vol. 10, No. 4, 278–282.

PART 2

Selection, Determination of Roles, Problems, and Methods in Training Nonprofessionals

Introduction

THE selections included in this part direct the reader's attention specifically to methods and problems in selection, role assignment and training of nonprofessionals, and to administrative aspects of such programs.

Richan employs the concept of organizational (externally imposed) controls as opposed to professional (self-imposed or internalized) controls, specificity versus generality of skills, and client vulnerability to clarify some of the administrative and ethical considerations involved in utilizing and training nonprofessionals.

The Jewish Board of Guardians has been making extensive use of volunteers for many years. The Big Brother (and Sister) movement, engaging adult volunteers to help youngsters, represents a pioneer program in the use of nonprofessionals as psychotherapeutic agents, lending special interest to the article by Lichtenberg. Among other interesting observations, Lichtenberg points out that the care necessary in screening should probably be inversely related to the amount of training and supervision an agency is able to provide, and that it is advisable during the indoctrination period to prepare volunteers for the worst of the experiences that they may encounter in the course of their efforts to be of help to others. Favorable experience with the Big Brother program leads Lichtenberg to suggest active exploration of programs—"volunteer-friends" for example—wherein the volunteer may serve as the "chief instrument" of the helping process.

Goodman's article describes a program which is making use of nonprofessionals as "chief instruments." The companionship therapy program is aimed at helping fifth and sixth grade boys. The article is included in this particular section because it describes highly inventive group methods used for the selection and training of the college students who help the youngsters. This highly heuristic program involves systematic training and mutual evaluations among the trainees. The initial goal is to foster understanding and also "self-disclosures and emotional risk taking." These behaviors are regarded as the "baby steps of honesty and courage" which in turn are seen as major components of the helping relationship. The training process itself affords self-screening and also provides quantitative information used for selection purposes by the administrators of the program. Goodman sees this procedure as yielding a high percentage of students with therapeutic potential. It would seem desirable to give serious consideration to an initial-job-performance, or role-playing selection model, such as this project illustrates, wherever it is feasible to do so in screening applicants for new programs.

Many of the problems involved in motivating and preparing a volunteer to work with a child are naturally different from those encountered when the helping agent is a parent and therefore already emotionally involved, and in constant interaction, with the person he is to help. The selection by Andronico *et al.* deals with the problems faced by the professional who must try to balance the role of teacher with certain aspects of the traditional role of psychotherapist. The attention that must be given to the training of skills per se, versus the recognition of the feelings and emotional needs of the trainee, varies from person to person and with respect to the stage of the treatment process. The authors explain their view that the advantages accruing to the unusual mixture of roles—for therapist and client alike—greatly outweigh the disadvantages.

A very different set of problems from those encountered in the training of highly motivated persons such as parents or conscientious volunteers is elucidated by MacLennan. Some supplemental information (from another article) will be illuminating to the reader with respect to MacLennan's paper. The criteria that the Center for Youth and Community Studies at Howard University used to *select* Human Service Aides were ones that traditionalists unfamiliar with the helper-theory principles or with the idea of using "products of the system to meet some of the system's needs" might have wished to use to *exclude* candidates. The trainees had to be young (16 to 21) and from a high delinquency area. The first ten were unemployed school dropouts. Most of the boys were delinquents, and most of the girls had out-of-wedlock babies. The training here began with such down-to-earth matters as spelling, why one needed supervision and how it was used, and, indeed, why it was necessary to get to work on time, and to stay at work in the face of frustrations. The training advances to the study of human behavior, growth and development, interpersonal relations, and cultural structure and values.

One of the major administrative problems in the program described by MacLennan was developing the necessary job opportunities and educational channels that would allow for continued career development of the trainees. Indeed, at this point in time, despite the tremendous need, finding adequate employment and adequate stepping stones for future career development are among the greatest problems facing the general movement toward the use of nonprofessionals as therapeutic agents. It is highly significant that, despite all these obstacles, all but two of the first 38 trainees found employment, and only two have had further difficulties with the law. The trainees are now serving, for example, as mental health therapists, recreational aides, classroom aides, and counselor aides in Department of Welfare Institutional programs. (See Suggested Additional Readings, MacLennan, 1966.)

Hawkinshire, too, considers the issues of selection, training, and administration when dealing with members of a group who are generally considered even more unpromising as rehabilitative agents; that is, former prisoners. He raises the question of whether a change agent should always be selected on the basis of being "different" from the person to be changed, and stresses the potentials for using persons of similar background and disposition. With respect to training, he points out, among other things, the relevance of specific skills; "anticipatory practice"; the immediate availability of feedback and support from a supervisor and peers; and on-the-job follow-up. With respect to administrative considerations, he explains why—in innovative programs such as these—it is mandatory: (a) to convince the general community that its needs and wishes will be respected, (b) to offer continuing support to trainees, and (c) to evaluate continuously the effects of the program.

Riessman's work with disadvantaged indigenous nonprofessionals now permits him to make specific and detailed suggestions concerning the selection and training of the indigenous nonprofessional. He finds the group interview a valuable technique in selection. Training, among other things, should be in an informal setting, should allow the expression of competitive feelings, be flexible and provide for self-direction, and should provide a basis for identification with professionals and employed nonprofessionals.

Jackson's work with this sort of trainee provides additional specific suggestions for training, and demonstrates the many mental health roles that may be filled by this group.

A Theoretical Scheme for Determining Roles of Professional and Nonprofessional Personnel

WILLARD C. RICHAN

For many years it has been a truism of social work that there are not enough of us to go around. The problem is brought home to us by statistics showing that the vast majority of positions in social welfare programs are filled by nonprofessional workers.[1] Recently there has been renewed interest in this problem, with a somewhat different slant: rather than simply trying to recruit more people into the profession—a laudable objective, to be sure—groups are now looking for better ways of using nonprofessional workers. Thus the field seems readier to face the fact that, given our present structure of service, we are unlikely in the foreseeable future to attract and educate anywhere near the number of social workers required to fill every "social work" position. Consequently, attention has shifted to the nonprofessional, or at least to a dual interest in both professionals and nonprofessionals.[2]

This article is based partly on the writer's work as a consultant to the Subcommittee on Utilization of Personnel, Commission on Social Work Practice of NASW, as a representative of the firm of Laurin Hyde Associates. Although he is indebted to both the subcommittee and commission members, he takes full responsibility for the article's contents. It is reprinted from *Social Work*, 1961, Vol. 6, No. 4, 22–28, with the permission of the National Association of Social Workers and the author. A brief biography of the author has been omitted.

[1]The most recent manpower study reports that 1 out of 4 social welfare workers hold graduate degrees, with 18 percent reporting a master's degree from a graduate school of social work. *Salaries and Working Conditions of Social Welfare Manpower in 1960* (New York: National Social Welfare Assembly, 1961), pp. 1, 42.

[2]The great and growing interest of social workers in this problem can be seen in the number of studies and articles on the subject. *See*, for example, Margaret M. Heyman's

The following material represents one approach to the question of how best to use graduate social workers and other agency personnel. In effect, what has been done here is to look at the provision of social welfare services with the implied question, "Why do we need professional social workers at all?" In other words, there are certain functions that need to be fulfilled; to what extent do they call for professional workers, and to what extent are there alternatives in the service situation? Presumably there are points at which one can determine a greater or lesser need for the trained worker, depending on other factors.

NEED FOR ASSURANCES[3]

Social workers, by and large, operate in agency settings, so it is not surprising that our ways of giving service have many attributes associated with formal organizations or bureaucracies.[4] It is no accident that the same historical era has witnessed a vast increase in both formal organizations and organized professions, for both share much in common. Both reflect a high degree of job specialization and division of labor. They emphasize science rather than intuition as a basis of decision and action. Recruitment and career success in both are based on competence and adherence to behavioral standards rather than on such devices as personal popularity and heredity. Yet, as we shall see, their differences are as significant as their similarities.

Do these similarities and differences just happen? It is a basic premise here that they do not. Rather, they are necessary for the effective provision of services. In essence, these characteristics reflect mechanisms by which professions and formal organizations assure that adequate standards

---

article in the April 1961 issue of *Social Work*, "A Study of Effective Utilization of Social Workers in a Hospital Setting" (Vol. 6, No. 2, pp. 36–43). Other reports include the following: Edwin J. Thomas and Donna L. McLeod, *In-Service Training and Reduced Workloads* (New York: Russell Sage Foundation, 1960); Fergus T. Monahan, *A Study of Non-Professional Personnel in Social Work* (Washington, D.C.: Catholic University Press, 1960). Projects recently completed or now in progress include a four-year study by the Advisory Committee on Social Welfare Education, Liaison Committee of the Regents of the University of California, and the State Board of Education; the Bureau of Public Assistance Educational Standards Project; and a co-operative study by the University of Chicago School of Social Service Administration and the Cook County Department of Public Aid.

[3]In this section the writer has drawn upon the following materials: H. L. Wilensky and C. N. Lebeaux, *Industrial Society and Social Welfare* (New York: Russell Sage Foundation, 1958); Lloyd E. Ohlin, "Conformity in American Society," *Social Work,* Vol. 3, No. 2 (April 1958), pp. 58–66; Robert D. Vinter, "The Social Structure of Service," in Alfred J. Kahn, ed., *Issues in American Social Work* (New York: Columbia University Press, 1959), pp. 242-269; and Talcott Parsons, *The Social System* (New York: The Free Press, 1952), Chap. 10.

[4]For a more thorough treatment of bureaucracies and their characteristics, *see* Robert K. Merton, ed., *Reader in Bureaucracy* (New York: The Free Press, 1952).

of performance will be maintained. Assurance of standards is important. If an agency could not give such assurances, it would lose its clientele, potential clientele, and sources of financial support. Likewise, a profession which could not assure a certain level of practice by its members would soon lose public confidence. Thus, agencies and professions develop controls over the behavior of workers. There are, of course, important variations in the need for such controls; very often the nature of the clientele is such that it compensates for the lack of some controls.

A distinction will be drawn in the ensuing discussion between so-called "organizational controls" and "professional controls." In simplest terms, the difference lies in the location of such safeguards. Organizational controls reside in the structure of the agency itself. Professional controls are internalized by the practitioner. This is to state the distinction in extreme terms. One important characteristic of social work is that, being an organization-based profession, its controls are of both types. But discussion of the extremes will help to clarify the distinction. For example, at one end of the scale, decision-making responsibility would rest in the organization, embodied in detailed rules and regulations. At the other, the educated judgment of the worker would be given maximum latitude.

One may cite various differences between the two kinds of controls, again focusing on the extremes. Under the organizational system, correct actions are spelled out for the worker in large numbers of concrete instructions. The scope of any worker's responsibility is narrowed, thus allowing him to master the great volume of specific rules and procedures. Ethical behavior is reinforced by direct observation of the worker by his superiors, frequent and detailed reports on his activities, administrative reviews, and similar devices. If he fails to do his job properly, he may be punished by not being promoted or, in serious cases, by being fired.

The "pure" professional is controlled in very different ways. Instead of minute regulations, competence is based upon a generalized body of knowledge and generalized skills assimilated over an extended training period. Thus, the worker can apply his knowledge to a greater variety of situations than is possible under concrete instructions, and can use himself more flexibly. The professional person comes to identify with ethical standards during his professional education. These are reinforced continually by pressures within the professional community, the professional literature, and (sometimes) legal sanctions. In effect, ethics become part of the practitioner. There is also considerable difference in the recruitment, selection, and screening of candidates for the two kinds of roles.

As already suggested, social work is a very "organizational" profession. Thus, for example, we rely on supervision and recording to a greater extent than such fields as medicine and law. At the same time, even in the social agencies considered most bureaucratic, there is constant emphasis on being professional, and workers are in fact relatively unbureaucratic. For example, the public assistance worker, with all his detailed procedures and administrative controls, is asked to be sensitive, alert to the unexpected, and guided by high inner ethical standards.

Other things being equal, it would be cheaper and easier to rely mainly on organizational and not professional training and controls. The point is, of course, that other things are not usually equal. The problems we deal with; the need for confidentiality; client contacts that even the supervisor does not see; the fact that human beings, our central concern, do not fit readily into neat categories—all these factors make social welfare a field in which organizational controls are frequently ineffective and can be damaging. Yet within this field there are appreciable differences in the degree to which situations call for organizational or professional controls, or indeed the extent to which either kind of control is needed at all.

From these considerations two key variables emerge. It is suggested that they serve as criteria for the types of personnel needed in various aspects of social welfare programs. They are *client vulnerability* and *worker autonomy*.

Client vulnerability refers to the susceptibility of people we serve to damage or exploitation stemming from incompetent or unethical behavior by agency personnel. This vulnerability may be something the client brings with him or may actually result from the kind of service being provided by the agency. In effect, client vulnerability indicates the extent to which controls *as such* are required, whether organizational or professional. The more vulnerable client needs greater assurance that standards of competent and responsible behavior are being maintained.[5]

Worker autonomy is related to the relative appropriateness of organizational as opposed to professional controls. As externally provided formulas and directives are lacking and as external enforcement of standards becomes more difficult, the worker is more autonomous, more dependent on internal controls. In other words, there is a greater need for professional knowledge, skill, and discipline.

CLIENT VULNERABILITY

Client vulnerability can be subdivided into two types: that resulting from the nature of the client and his situation and that arising from the nature of the service.

[5]For a somewhat different treatment of client vulnerability, *see* Elliot Studt's discussion of "Worker-Client Authority Relationships in Social Work," *Social Work*, Vol. 4, No. 1 (January 1959), pp. 23–24.

Nature of Client Situation. The people who use the services of formal organizations vary widely in their susceptibility to damage from failure to provide skilled and responsible service. As an example of a person who is not very susceptible, one might consider the experienced builder who patronizes a lumber yard. He is sophisticated about the product he is buying, and if dissatisfied he simply goes to another lumber yard. He may bring pressure on the lumber dealer by talking to other builders. Even if he receives inferior merchandise, his life is probably not upset unduly. At the other end of the spectrum, there is the foster child with adjustment problems. He cannot "shop" for service, and mishandling may be devastating to him. Social agency clientele in general tend to be at this more vulnerable end of the continuum. Our case loads are often peopled by social outcasts and those poorly equipped to protect themselves. And within social welfare programs there are appreciable variations in the degree of client vulnerability. In public assistance, for example, the retired person getting supplementary aid for medical needs is ordinarily less vulnerable than the kind of client getting Aid to Dependent Children. Even within ADC, there is a difference between the vulnerability of the disabled father and the unwed mother.

Nature of Service. The initial vulnerability that the client brings to the organization is modified by the kind of service offered and the way it is given. A disturbed mother may receive the wrong advice about baking a cake and be upset only temporarily by the result. If the same mother receives wrong counsel about her marriage or her children, however, we have a far different situation. Here again, social agency clientele tend to be highly vulnerable. By being able to give or withhold important benefits, workers have much power over their clients; this power is sometimes reinforced by legal authority. We invade the privacy of individuals and concern ourselves with their total functioning.

But again, there are important differences within social welfare services. Miller points out that group members are less dependent than casework clients on the worker's integrity and competence because of greater power in relation to the worker.[6] In a single community center a teen-ager may have only superficial contact with a volunteer running a dance, but be highly involved with his club adviser, seeking all manner of crucial advice from the latter. Even the same worker can have varying impact on the same client by choosing to focus on or bypass certain areas of the client's life. Thus, the way the agency defines its goals and service can affect client vulnerability. The intensity of relationship between worker and client also affects the vulnerability of the latter, for there is introduced a greater risk of harmful unconscious involvement.

[6]Irving Miller, "Distinctive Characteristics of Supervision in Group Work," *Social Work*, Vol. 5, No. 1 (January 1960), pp. 72–73.

So far we have considered the relative need for assurances of some kind but have not gone into the relative merits of organizational and professional assurances. Theoretically, either would be equally appropriate if client vulnerability were the only factor involved. Let us now turn to other factors that do affect the appropriateness of these two types of controls.

WORKER AUTONOMY

Worker autonomy can be subdivided into three categories: (1) lack of explicit and concrete guides, requiring the exercise of discretionary judgment by the worker; (2) low visibility, and thus lack of external control, of what the worker is doing; and (3) lack of support for professional standards in the agency itself.

Lack of Explicit Guides. The use of rules, routines, and regulations in the right place can lead to speed, efficiency, and productivity. The concrete formula, which is still there and still valid even though a particular worker drops out of the picture, can act as a reliable assurance of a certain kind of performance. But in a field like social work such a device can seriously hamper operations. We in social work are concerned with the subtleties of human personality in social situations. We are oriented toward change. Even when an agency limits its function to a narrow area of the client's life, the worker is often expected to understand his total functioning. Under such circumstances, concrete rules and formulas tend to break down. It is impossible to cover in any manual of procedures the infinite variety of material with which we deal. Only another type of knowledge—general principles that cover situations never anticipated, and skill in applying them selectively—can possibly cope with many of the problems social agencies deal with. Workers must have a chance to use disciplined discretion. Frequent approval from higher-ups may help insure that they are acting in the best interests of their clients. But when decisions have to be made on the spot and situations change within the course of an interview, such constant checking is too cumbersome and may hamper the worker-client relationship. In such a case, the organization has to rely on the inner knowledge and standards of the worker.

Once again, however, the need for such flexibility of the worker is not uniform. Establishing eligibility for public assistance may lend itself to specific regulations, but establishing eligibility for adoption of a child does not. Even with the same clientele, an agency may be able to depend on organizational controls for workers doing telephone intake but require professional controls in the continuing contacts between a worker and a client.

Low Visibility of Practice. Confidentiality and privacy of worker-client contacts are generally thought of as protections for the client. And so they are. But this "hidden" aspect of social work practice also carries with it certain hazards for the client. If only the worker and the client know what goes on in the interview, direct agency controls over the worker are lessened. The factory bureaucrat may be under the direct observation of his superior, and the results of his work are there, in the form of production charts, for all to see. Not so the social caseworker, who meets his client behind closed doors, with the supervisor's knowledge limited to what the worker includes in his recording.

Again, there are wide differences in social welfare programs. Miller cites a distinction between group work and casework. Speaking of group work, he says,

> Supervisors will often assert that they just know, or can sense or "smell," what is really going on in the agency and how members feel about each other and the worker, without reading records or discussing it. . . . They know by walking through halls, "covering" the building, dropping into the lounge or game room, being friendly with members, and even occasionally being invited into group meetings.[7]

Not only the supervisor, but board members of group work agencies may "see for themselves" by sitting in on worker-client contacts—something strictly taboo in casework. Even among programs where worker-client contacts are private, there are differences in visibility. The public assistance supervisor has a more reliable measure of what his worker is doing than does the supervisor in a psychiatric setting; the recommended grant for the recipient is concrete and either is or is not supported in material submitted by the worker. When the organizational control of direct scrutiny breaks down, it has to be replaced by the professional knowledge, skill, and responsibility of the trained practitioner. A special instance of low visibility is employment of workers away from "home base," as in the use of group workers with street gangs.[8]

Lack of Organizational Support for Social Work Standards. Lack of support for social work standards occurs when workers are situated in so-called host settings or where there is no agency structure, as in private practice. Among traditional social agencies there are wide variations in the degree of commitment to professional standards. The profession as a profession must assure certain standards, regardless of the extent to which the organization is guided by them. Organizational controls are intended to support the organization's goals and its survival; such controls may be irrelevant or even contrary to the goals of the profession. In extreme

[7] *Ibid.*, p. 72.
[8] *See* Ohlin, *op. cit.*

cases of disparate goals, the profession might oppose having its members participate, of course.

Professions characterized by private practice tend to have very exacting codes of ethics and tests of competence, usually supported by legal regulation. These stringent standards and the devices for enforcing them substitute for the organizational supports found in organization-based practice.

COMBINING THE TWO MAJOR VARIABLES[9]

By putting together these two major variables, *client vulnerability* and *worker autonomy*, we are able to distinguish a number of different worker roles, each with appropriate functions, educational preparation, and career lines. The combinations are shown below schematically.

CLIENT VULNERABILITY		Worker Autonomy	
		High	Low
	High	1. The Professional	2. The Specialist
	Low	3. The Subprofessional	4. The Aide

When both client vulnerability and worker autonomy are high, the greatest professional knowledge, skill, and discipline are needed. When clients are highly vulnerable but set procedures and external controls are appropriate, the specialist—with technical training around specifics—can be used. When an operation essentially like that of the professional, yet with less vulnerable clientele, is called for, the person with a "preprofessional" kind of education is indicated. Finally, when external guidelines and controls are available and clients are least vulnerable, use can be made of lay persons with only brief in-service training around specifics. We thus come out with the following typology:

The Professional. This role involves high client vulnerability and high worker autonomy. Therefore, full professional education in a university setting is needed. This is the "ultimate" career line in social welfare programs.

The Specialist. This worker does tasks which can be routinized and controlled externally without detracting from the service to the client, but may work with highly vulnerable clientele. His education is technical

[9]What follows has not been included in material prepared for the Subcommittee on Personnel Utilization.

and geared to the specific skills and knowledge he will need. It could be appropriately given in agency-operated schools or community college settings. This position would provide a career in itself and would not be seen primarily as a steppingstone to full professional status.

The Subprofessional. This person would perform the same kinds of tasks as the professional worker, but with less vulnerable clients. Thus this position would provide an opportunity to develop experience under more protected circumstances than would be available to the full professional worker. Undergraduate education, broadly focused on social welfare principles, similar to that suggested in the Curriculum Study of the Council on Social Work Education, would prepare the individual for this role. Unlike the *specialist*, the *subprofessional* would be considered "incomplete" and would be oriented toward eventual completion of graduate training. Likewise, if he stopped his training at the undergraduate level, he would not achieve the status and rewards accorded to the *specialist.*

The Aide.[10] This low man on the totem pole would have only the most limited responsibilities, with the least vulnerable clientele. Volunteers now frequently fulfill this role in social agencies. But since many proficient—and professional—persons volunteer their services in some programs, the term *aide* seems most appropriate. As is implied, this individual would probably aid a regular worker; in other words, he would not work alone. He could be trained quickly, through brief in-service orientation courses. This position would allow persons interested in the field to get a taste of social work before investing in formal education or training.

A final word should be added regarding this classification. It is clearly a projection into the future, especially with respect to educational standards. This scheme is proposed as a way out of the existing confusion and disagreement regarding the appropriate education and utilization of nonprofessional workers in social welfare programs.

SUMMARY

Faced with tremendous personnel shortages, the field of social work is turning its attention to establishing standards for appropriate utilization of professional workers and other personnel in social welfare programs. What is proposed here is a theoretical scheme for determining various worker roles. Agencies and professional groups need to assure their

[10]It should be stated emphatically that the role projected here is not the one usually meant by the term "case aide," which combines aspects of the specialist and the subprofessional, although probably leaning in the direction of the latter.

clientele and others that competent and responsible practice, based on social work principles, will be maintained. Two characteristic means of providing such assurances are so-called organizational (or external) and professional (or internal) controls. In the former, workers have routines and other concrete guidelines to action and are kept from deviating by external supervision. The "pure" professional has generalized knowledge and skills which can be applied to an infinite variety of situations, and he internalizes professional ethics so that they become part of him.

As client vulnerability increases, there is a greater need for assurances by the agency that standards of competence and ethics will be maintained. As worker autonomy increases—that is, when the worker must rely more upon inner knowledge and inner discipline—the so-called organizational controls become less appropriate and professional controls are needed. Client vulnerability and worker autonomy, then, become key factors in determining the amount and kinds of controls needed. These two factors can be broken down into subcategories. When they are combined, we have four worker roles: the *professional*, the *specialist*, the *subprofessional*, and the *aide*. Appropriate education and functions have been proposed for each of these roles.

On the Selection and Preparation of the Big Brother Volunteer

BEN LICHTENBERG

Social workers are giving a good deal of attention to the possibilities for increased service to client groups through the use of volunteers. There is greater recognition that, even if unlimited numbers of specialists in the fields of human relations were available, they still could not meet all the needs of people who are in trouble. The creative use of the large group of citizens, stable but untrained, who would like to lend a hand to their fellowmen may provide one answer to the problem of offering more help to those who are emotionally disturbed or are drifting without direction. We are beginning to understand more fully than ever that it is our responsibility to relate to the total person—to his ego strengths, capacities, and everyday needs—as well as to his pathology. Moreover, it is clear that distressed individuals draw help in meeting their problems from many sources—from relationships with their friends and associates, as well as from their more formal contacts with social workers, physicians, clergymen, or educators.

The use of the social worker's professional skills can be extended if they are employed to a greater extent than is now true in the selection and preparation of volunteers who, in turn, can render a direct service to a large number of clients. In doing this, the worker utilizes his psychosocial diagnostic skills in understanding both the individual client and the

Reprinted from *Social Casework*, 1956, Vol. 137, No. 8, 396-400, with the permission of Family Service Association of America and author. A brief biography of the author has been omitted.

individual volunteer, and in guiding the service the volunteer is giving.

PURPOSE OF BIG BROTHER PROGRAM

This paper deals primarily with the selection and preparation of volunteers in the Jewish Big Brothers, a service arm of the Jewish Board of Guardians. It is based on almost three years of experience with Big Brothers assigned to boys served in the out-patient clinic, during which the writer has processed more than forty potential Big Brothers, and in eleven cases has served either as consultant to the worker who supervised the volunteer, or directly as supervisor of the volunteer assigned to a boy who was no longer in therapy. In an additional case, there was supervision of a Big Brother assigned to a boy whom the writer was treating.

The purpose of the Big Brother program is to provide friends for those boys who are deprived, in their natural environment, of a relationship with a mature adult male. The relationship with the Big Brother is a "substitute" for the relationship that a boy normally has with his father, an older brother, an uncle, a grandfather, or even a particularly friendly neighbor. It may enable the boy to form more adequate identifications, to have an opportunity to imitate a mature adult, and to develop an association that can broaden his activity horizons. In other words, the Big Brother, in addition to providing a human object for identification, also can give the boy an opportunity to enrich his non-human object relationships. The latter purpose may be achieved through a visit to an airport, attendance at a symphony, playing ball, making furniture, and so on. Stating the matter in psychoanalytic terms, the Big Brother volunteer provides opportunity for further ego development—including the internalization of more adequate ego ideals—and for the healthier evolution of the superego. The belief that these processes are to some degree still amenable to external, nonpsychotherapeutic influences during latency and adolescence is implicit in this work. The Big Brother is assigned, therefore, to offer the boy enriched opportunities for growth and maturation.

Very little research has as yet been undertaken to determine the factors involved in the decision to assign a Big Brother to a boy in therapy. At this point it can be reported only that the variables in question pertain not only to psychosocial diagnosis, but also to such factors as the personal and theoretical views of the members of the clinic team on such matters as: the place and value of environmental manipulation, the motivations of volunteers, the benefit to the client in relation to the investment of time in supervising the volunteer.

SELECTION OF VOLUNTEERS

If the goals of the Big Brother project are to be fully achieved, the selection and the supervision of the volunteers are of primary importance. So far it has not been possible to work out simple, and at the same time truly valid, criteria for the selection of Big Brothers. Certainly, we want men who are mature. But this statement does not tell us *how* mature the man should be, or in what *areas*. The matter is further complicated by considerations of supply and demand at any given time. It is possible to be more "choosy" during those periods when the number of available men exceeds the number of boys who are awaiting Big Brothers.

Let us say, for example, that we have a request for a Big Brother for a boy, David, aged 11, who had lost his father six months previously, and who has no interested male relatives or other suitable adult males in his environment. His mother, who was upset while the father lived, is now seriously disturbed. (Her request for David to have a Big Brother may be, on another level, a request for a second husband.) David's already burdened personality is being subjected to still greater stresses, and he reacts with anger to his mother's increased need for closeness. She, in turn, feels he is getting out of hand and tries more and more to control him. The only Big Brother available, Mr. D, is a man who seems to function well in his work but who impresses the interviewer as being overly guarded when it comes to examining his own personal relationships. He appears to have a genuine liking for boys and to be interested in activities that David would enjoy. Shall we attempt to set up this friendship, or wait until we have a Big Brother about whom our impressions are still more positive? Will the kind of support Mr. D can offer David *now* be of more help in the long run than the aid of a more "ideal" Big Brother assigned in perhaps a few weeks or months? Will the burdens that David must carry along while awaiting a more suitable Big Brother inflict too much damage upon both David and his mother? These are the kinds of questions that must be raised and for which we do not always have the answers.

The main generalizations one can make are related primarily to the kinds of men one would *not* use as volunteers. As a rule, we would not use a man who is in the midst of a serious personal crisis, is not responsible and honest, is severely disturbed, has a strong feminine component in his personality, whose main motivation is to prove paternal adequacy, or cannot accept guidance in his relationship with the boy. In other words, we avoid using individuals whose personal difficulties indicate it is unlikely that they have much to offer a boy or that they can really focus on the boy's needs.

Leaving aside, for the moment, the fact that the Big Brother's preparation for his assignment to friendship begins in his own childhood years, the immediate preparation of the volunteer is initiated when he is asked, usually by an active Big Brother, to participate in the Big Brother movement. It is generally easier to screen the volunteer if, having been interested by someone else, he takes the initial step in arranging the appointment. No "selling" is then necessary and we are not put in the position, when a potential Big Brother is not suitable, of having to turn him down after we have sought his services. Although some workers in a few agencies set no conditions around the first interview with a potential Big Brother, it is my experience that the work proceeds more smoothly if the interview is held in the office. Hence, I turn down requests that we meet for lunch or in some other casual manner. I explain that we shall need to spend at least an hour together and that privacy is important. The time and place of subsequent meetings should be geared to an understanding of the individual volunteer, and flexibility on the part of the professional worker is important. Although the professional worker is the supervisor, it need hardly be stated that the relationship is not one of supervisor-student, therapist-patient, or employer-employee. In working with the lay person, one cannot simply be a human relations specialist who is there for consultation; one must also be a motivator and a giver of inspiration.

THE SCREENING INTERVIEW

The frank but sensitive handling of the screening interview is, in itself, an important part of preparation. When the interview begins with the worker's obtaining simple factual data such as the volunteer's age, education, marital status, occupation, religious interests, recreational interests, and organization memberships, these matters may serve as departure points for the more personal details of his life. If, during the interview, the worker's respect for him has been communicated, if the worker has been able understandingly to deal with the volunteer's exposition of his own strengths and weaknesses, and if they have together attempted to explore why this particular man wants at this particular time to help a boy, the tone has been set for the subsequent relationship not only to the agency but also, to some extent, to the boy. Since a great deal may be learned from the queries made by the potential volunteer, the man who does not spontaneously raise questions is urged to do so.

It is generally also possible to arrive at an understanding of where the interviewee sees himself at this particular point in his life. The very process of obtaining this picture emphasizes, for the potential Big Brother, the personal and individual nature of the work upon which he is about to embark. It is important to stress this, since the very process helps to counteract one of the cultural trends prevalent today—the trend toward conformity, uniformity, and denial of individual differences. In turn, his work with the boy is thereby strengthened. In addition, the investigation suggests to the volunteer that his understanding of himself is important in helping the boy.

It is usually advisable to ask the man something about his brothers and sisters, his parents, his marriage, and his immediate family. From these data we can gain an understanding of some of the patterns of relationships in his own family—patterns that inevitably will be reproduced, to some extent, in his relationship with a youngster. Again, the very discussion of these matters suggests to the volunteer that the relationships that he has experienced are relevant to his work with a boy. The potential volunteer who confides that it always used to bother him when his father preferred to play ball with his younger brother may, perhaps, be told that it is likely that some of the feelings that he has had toward his own younger brother may come up in his relationship with the boy to whom he is assigned. If he anticipates these reactions, it may be easier for him to handle them.

A cardinal principle in preparing a volunteer to serve as a Big Brother is that the preparation must be done in relation to our understanding of the man himself—of his own feelings, background, and family relationships, and of his expectations about the friendship. It should perhaps be stressed here that we do not rule out working with the Big Brother who is not able to verbalize his feelings about relationships. The Big Brother must also understand that the relationship on which he is about to embark is one that may continue for many years.

FURTHER PREPARATION

A boy who needs a Big Brother is, by definition, a deprived boy. He is having some difficulty that is related to the fact that there is no suitable father or other adult male in his family or immediate environment who can help him with normal growth and development. Whether or not the boy is offered psychotherapy or counseling, he is suffering from an emotional disturbance. This point is stressed since there is sometimes a tendency to think either that only boys who are receiving psychotherapeutic treatment are emotionally disturbed, or that because a boy is suffering from an emotional disturbance, psychotherapy is the only remedy. All boys need friends, whether or not they have, or need, psychotherapy.

The volunteer should be prepared for the fact that the boys whom we serve are, at best, rather difficult. Having suffered deprivations, they are often demanding and angry. In many instances the volunteer, having begun his friendship with a boy, begins to wonder whether it is worth while. Many of these boys cannot easily show the appreciation of the volunteer's friendship which, on some level, they may genuinely feel. They tend to deny feelings of gratitude by an overly casual attitude, or sometimes by direct provocativeness. There are also many boys who find it necessary to vent, in one way or another, all their anger about their deprivations on the person who is now filling the gap. The boy without a real father often has a fantasied father about whom he has unconscious feelings of love and hate—hate because he has been deserted. A child who has no father often imagines that his father left him out of anger because the child was bad. Some boys fantasy that their mothers got rid of their fathers and may, therefore, get rid of them, too. Since they see the world egocentrically, they frequently cannot conceive that the fathers who are absent could have left for reasons that have little connection with the sons.

Thus it is important to anticipate with the volunteer rough spots that may develop in the relationship and to be ready to help smooth them over. It is often wise to prepare the volunteer for the worst. He can be told that it is quite possible that the boy will not seem to like him particularly. He is warned that it is usually best for him to take the initiative in making each appointment with this boy, since if it is left up to the boy, his own feelings of worthlessness or inadequacy will often interfere with his making this proposal. Also the boy may well interpret as a rejection the fact that the Big Brother himself does not say, "Suppose we get together at such-and-such a time on such-and-such a day." The very busy Big Brother has to be warned that although occasionally appointments can be left open, it is best not to tell the boy that he will call him later about the time of the next appointment. Particularly in the first six months of a relationship, this kind of flexibility is too much of a threat for many of these boys. Meetings between the boy and the volunteer should occur on a minimum of once a week. Our Big Brothers are prepared to confer with professional staff immediately after the first and second contacts and then at least once a month for the first few months. Thereafter, the frequency of supervisory contacts can be diminished as long as the written reports are submitted after each contact.

Another phase of preparation relates to the individual boy to whom the volunteer will be assigned. For example, the volunteer who is working with a boy who is incapable of uttering even the smallest personal remark about himself is advised to encourage confidences from the boy. We do not suggest to the volunteer that he probe and thus inhibit such confidences, but rather suggest that he be prepared, so that when they do come he shows real interest and respect for them and doesn't do anything to dam them up again. On the other hand, with the youngster who tends to talk obsessively about his intimate problems, the volunteer is advised not to encourage such verbalization. He is warned not to deprecate these remarks but simply, when it is tactfully possible, to change the subject or focus on something away from the boy's own inner problems. Thus, the preparation of the Big Brother is also dependent upon how much we know about the boy, his patterns of behavior, and his needs.

The most important preparatory work is done with the volunteer prior to his contact with the boy and in the early stages. Later work with the Big Brother is not so critical, although it is certainly also of great importance. For example, the 11-year-old boy who is in latency is not the same boy four years later at 15. The man who has established a comfortable relationship with Johnny, aged 11, who is eager to imitate him, may be quite stunned when Johnny, at 15, begins suggesting that the Big Brother's judgments and ideas are not "one thousand per cent correct." The Big Brother, at this time, may need help in handling his own responses to this changed relationship so that they can be constructive for both individuals. In general, one encourages the Big Brother in his relationship by occasionally helping him to see the importance of his work with the boy. Even the most gifted untrained person often has difficulty in assessing the value of his effort.

OTHER CONSIDERATIONS

This discussion has centered on the preparation of the individual volunteer. It is important for the individual Big Brother to meet from time to time with men who are giving the same kind of service. It is important for him to have an opportunity to exchange his views and feelings, his disappointments and successes, with other men who are in this work. It is also important for him to participate occasionally in a group session led by a professional worker on further understanding of boys in general. Talks by experts on healthy family relations can also be helpful.

The preparation of the volunteer in Big Brother work is, in many ways, similar to preparation of any human being for any kind of living situation or specific task. We need to begin with someone who has a potential for adequate performance. Our best preparation is never complete. The amount of time, effort, and personnel which can be devoted to preparation is dependent not only upon the amount of time the volunteer has available but also upon the size of the resources of the individual agency. Perhaps in those agencies where much time cannot be spent in preparing the Big Brother it is important that a greater amount of time and care be spent in screening, so that only the most suitable men are used.

Although some of the less obvious pitfalls and difficulties in this work, such as the worker's personal reaction to the volunteer (a kind of "counter-transference"), have not been discussed, they are nevertheless of major importance and warrant further consideration.

The program that has been discussed in this paper is one in which the volunteer has been used as an auxiliary service. At present there are a number of areas, particularly in institutional programs, in which volunteers are used to supplement the services of the professional staff. To my knowledge, there are few undertakings in the social work field in which the volunteer serves as the chief instrument of the helping process. It may be that an exploration, approached in a creative spirit, of further possibilities for the use of the volunteer as the "chief instrument" will result in making available far more aid to such groups as patients discharged from mental institutions who have no relatives or friends to assist them in finding suitable living quarters, jobs, or recreational activities. Also, exploration may reveal a number of instances in the family service agency's case load in which the "volunteer-friend" can be of real and enduring help. This is not a proposal that the volunteer substitute for the caseworker in situations in which the client needs psychotherapy or casework therapy. Rather, it is my belief that there are a number of important services which can be performed as well, or better, by an appropriate lay person, and that the "helping potential" of the social work profession can be increased if we make greater use of our knowledge and skills in the direction of organizing and guiding such enterprises.

An Experiment with Companionship Therapy: College Students and Troubled Boys — Assumptions, Selection, and Design

GERALD GOODMAN

Nontraditional programs for helping troubled people are cropping up all over the country. They can be a cause of concern to nearby professionals and the community at large. They are also subject to polemical evaluation by those sure of their values or dangers. Few serious researchers seem attracted by these programs. Thus, we know little about how to study them and less about their effectiveness and most about their adventures in getting off the ground. I would like to skip over the adventure story of how we started and what the implications of our work might be in favor of an outline of our project's structure, selection procedure, and research design. I also do not have enough time to detail our primary assumptions, except to say that client-centered theory and research have been a major influence. We think people can help themselves with other people's honesty and courage. The baby-steps of honesty and courage in the helping relationship are self-disclosure and emotional risk-taking. For us, these are the critical interpersonal modes that in combination produce qualities that are helping. The relationship of these qualities to age, training, and theoretical orientation are still a mystery. Therefore, we are quite con-

The Interpersonal Relations Project is financed by the National Institute of Mental Health (MH–00992) and sponsored by Stiles Hall-University YMCA. This paper was presented before the Mental Health Section of the American Public Health Association at the Ninety-Fourth Annual Meeting in San Francisco, Calif., November 2, 1966. It is reprinted from *American Journal of Public Health*, 1967, Vol. 57, No. 10, 1772–1777, with the permission of the American Public Health Association, Inc. and the author. A brief biography of the author has been omitted.

fused except for our unhappy lack of confidence in most traditional orientations toward psychotherapy—especially their tendency to cling to a medical model of the helping relationship using professional distance and patient management. To me, professional distance and patient management seem to foster the type of therapist role-taking that generates concealment, expedient manipulation, and an ineffective type of responsibility toward troubled people. In short, our project is—in part—a reaction to the one-way intimacy that shapes most current professional therapy environments. We try not to let our bias and attendant assumptions compromise the rigor of our research or the freedom of our questions.

SELECTION OF PARTICIPANTS

Our nontraditional helpers are male college students. Their clients are troubled boys. They are brought together with instructions to meet twice a week over the school year and do what they please. We do not ask them to talk about problems. Half of the students (we call them counselors) attend weekly training sessions. All of the counselors attend an initial workshop based on client-centered principles and take a short two-person teaching machine course on interpersonal relations. We study the entire program—boys, counselors, and training—using systematic observations from our participants' peers, from participants themselves, and from the boys' parents and teachers. We try not to let the research interfere with the program itself. The major research questions point at the process of the relationship, boy and counselor change, counselor training, and the matching of counselor and boy. For example, we want to know if positive change in the boy is related to his counselor's personality type, or the topics of conversation and activities pursued during the relationship, or the training of counselors. Unfortunately, questions such as these require large quantities of data, especially since we use a multiobserver, multiinstrument design. Good answers for most of the questions will not be ready until 1968.

This is the procedure we use for selecting our clients—the boys. A neater job seemed possible by concentrating on preadolescent boys. Each year the program starts by collecting systematic observations on all 1,500 of Berkeley's fifth and sixth grade public school boys. Children describe their classmates on Wiggins' and Winder's "Peer Nominations Inventory" and teachers describe their pupils on a parallel form generating dimensions such as hostility, isolation, and likeability.

Next, we send an announcement to all parents and their boys openly describing the project and inviting application for boys who are having distinct problems getting along with people. When the combined systematic descriptions of parents, teachers, and classmates indicate that a boy is having real problems, we place him in a pool of potential participants. The pool is carefully searched for 50 highly matched pairs of boys. Twenty-five of the matched pairs have problems with isolation, withdrawal, depression, and the like. For simplicity we call these boys "Quiets." The remaining 25 are designated "Outgoings" and evidence problems with aggression, hostility, and so forth. One of each pair is randomly selected to participate and the other to serve in a nonparticipating control group. In this way we end up with 50 participating boys and their 50 individually matched controls—both groups evenly divided as evidencing "quiet" and "outgoing" problems. A group of 200 random stratified boys were also selected for study.

Now to the counselors. We invite applications from students through campus-wide advertisement at the University of California at Berkeley. The job offers $1.40 an hour, including report-writing and training sessions. Applicants describe themselves on the "Adjective Check List," Wrightsman's "Philosophy of Human Nature" questionnaire, Jourard's "Self-Disclosure Questionnaire"; and they take Chapin's "Social Insight Test." After that, students are scheduled to attend our group assessment sessions. Each session is attended by eight applicants and three staff members. These sessions provide the major source of our selection information. As a warm-up, the group is asked to do the following task: one applicant asks the group a personal question without knowing who will answer it. Anyone feeling comfortable with the question is encouraged to respond briefly (a minute or less) and directly. When the first two-person exchange is complete, the procedure rather automatically begins again as another person throws out a question. Anyone who has not answered a question can respond. The procedure continues around the group until everyone has both asked and answered one question.

At that point the group receives new instructions. Each member is given a card and asked to fill it out with a description of one of his interpersonal concerns that can eventually be read to the group. These descriptions are most often about problems with a girl friend, parents, roommates, and involve concerns about guilt, giving and taking, control, concealment, esteem, and general problems of relating to people. An applicant, chosen at random, is asked to read his card to the group. We call him the "discloser." Any other applicant can make an effort to understand how the discloser feels about the problem read to the group by engaging him in a five-minute dialogue. We call the second person the "understander." Understanders are instructed not to give advice or interpret and to avoid asking many questions. Thus, one person is attempting to solve the problem of how to disclose or to be genuine in a manufactured group situation, while the other is attempting to solve the problem of how to listen—how to understand spontaneously. Of course, the task is made more difficult because of the observers, but students have a go at it with great spirit. They often complain that we cut off the dialogues too quickly. At any rate, we assume that the conditions are roughly equal for all applicants, and that the procedure may offer some index of an applicant's potential to understand and disclose in a dyad.

The procedure continues around the group, as in the warm-up round, and everyone tries each task once. At the end, all applicants rate each other, and the three staff members rate the applicants. Ratings are done on a sociometric type instrument, with items such as "He really seemed to understand what the other person meant" with six-point scales ranging from "much like him" to "not like him." Items cover the areas of warmth, self-disclosure, empathy, rigidity, surgency, and so on. We have discovered a tendency for strong rating agreements between individuals. Correlations between the ratings of applicants and staff were generally strong, with the exception of the disclosure item. It seems our professionals have special standards for the act of emotional self-disclosure. Applicants and staff produced very similar ratings on items describing mildness, dominance, depression, tension, and good potential for working with troubled boys. Moderate agreement was observed for rigidity, understanding, and warmth items.

Various patterns of group assessment scores were developed as criteria for accepting applicants into the program. For example, any applicant not seen as warm, self-disclosing, and understanding by a majority of the combined student and staff raters, was rejected. Thus far, we have been accepting about 65 per cent of the applicants who get as far as our group assessment procedure. Many applicants screen themselves out before getting to that point, so an estimate would be that we hire fewer than 50 per cent of those students asking for an application. I am becoming convinced that this group assessment selection procedure yields a high percentage of students with therapeutic potential. It certainly appears superior to our old method of using judgments and ratings from two individual interviews with professionals, combined with self-ratings and test scores. We began using the group assessment method during our third year of operation. All three of our group trainers were individually impressed by the change in the quality of counselors for that year. Our office staff noticed the difference too. It is too early to tell if these counselors are better able to help troubled boys because we are in the midst of analyzing third-year outcome data. Just one more thing about this assessment technic—it seems to generate descriptions that can be externally validated. Certain self-description scales correlate with the group scores in a meaningful way—especially in the quiet-outgoing areas. It was also surprising to find that a student's performance on the old Chapin "Social Insight Test" was strongly correlated with the group assessment item on understanding. Several counselors who were accepted as borderline on the group assessment criteria turned out to be poor counselors, in our estimation, as the year progressed. We have not completed refining and studying this method, but it is reasonable to guess that it can be useful in detecting good mental health counselors in wide applications utilizing little professional manpower.

After counselors are selected, they are reliably divided into a "Quiet" group and an "Outgoing" group on the basis of the group assessment ratings and several self-description sources. Counselors are then matched to boys in the following way: half of the quiet counselors are paired with boys evidencing quiet problems, and the other half of the quiet counselors are paired with boys having outgoing problems. The same procedure is followed for the group of outgoing counselors. This matching system gave us four dyad types: quiet counselors with outgoing problem boys, outgoings with quiets, and so on. Boys and counselors were matched on social class. A balanced half of counselors from each of the four dyad types were then selected for group training. This type of balancing allows us to assess the effects of training with a more rigorous design.

COUNSELOR TRAINING

Thus far our selection procedures for boys, and their counselors, and their matching into dyads have been outlined. Now I shall briefly sketch out the training of counselors. Before the actual companion relationships begin, all of the counselors attend two half-day experimental workshops on helping relationships. The workshops include lectures, structured small group interaction, listening to bits of therapy tapes, and some procedural orientation. Counselors must have also taken at least three lessons of programed instruction on interpersonal relations. The ten-lesson course we use was developed by Berlin and Wykoff, and contains many role-playing experiments. Counselors take the course in pairs.

Half of the counselors received additional inservice training by meeting weekly in discussion groups of eight all through the year. The training is essentially self-exploration, with professional leaders functioning primarily as facilitators of communication. Often a counselor's behavior in the group is related to his behavior with his boy. I suppose the most common thing discussed and demonstrated in the groups is emotional self-disclosure. At the end of each group session, counselors describe each other on warmth, understanding, and disclosure scales. Mean ratings for each counselor are placed on a flow chart that is returned to the group before the next session. Counselors attend about 25 two-hour sessions over the academic year.

This past program year has been the first capable of yielding meaningful findings. Since it has just been completed, there are only a few scattered results available. Our research design and variables are geared to study the various subgroups such as "quiet" or "outgoing" subjects, "trained" or "untrained" counselors, and so on. It appears that the measured gains of quiet and outgoing boys tend to cancel each other out when combined. Therefore, we do not expect any dramatic differences in gain between participating boys—grouped as a whole—and their nonparticipating controls. Tentative findings from our second year suggest that boys with quiet problems gain the most from participating, and that boys with group-trained counselors gain more than boys with untrained counselors. So far, the raw third-year data look as though they will produce the same pattern—even though some of the research methods have changed. However, it is still too early to say what type of boy gains most with what type of counselor. It is certainly possible that our final results might suggest that group-trained college students can be of significant help when paired with isolated, depressed, or withdrawn boys. It may be that hostile acting-out boys only gain significantly when paired with group-trained counselors. A quick look at the third-year data suggests that possibility. A clearer picture of how effective student counselors are in helping troubled boys should emerge in several months.

We are also studying changes that may occur in the student counselors as a result of participating. A group of nonparticipating matched students are assessed at the beginning and end of the school year on most of the same instruments. The early results fit our expectations, based on investigations of programs using college students as companions to mental hospital patients (Holzberg and Cambridge-Radcliffe Program). So far, our counselors show dramatically heightened interest in the behavior of children, in working with troubled people, and in the way they interact with friends. Differences between counselors and controls are very significant. Group-trained counselors gain a bit more than untrained counselors. An item concerned with interest change in political issues was inserted to test acquiescence set. It showed no difference between counselors and controls.

Counselors feel they relate to friends better as a result of participating. This finding generates one of the strongest differences between the counselors and controls. Without going into detail, I can say that we have evidence suggesting that counselors do not tend to offer spurious claims to change. Experience over the past three years has convinced us that counselors find it easy to be self-critical and conservative in their appraisal of their effectiveness. Some additional miscellaneous second-order findings follow. Counselors tend to feel that psychotherapy helps people much of the time. This may be a reflection of their faith in the psychologically helping relationship. Most of the group-trained counselors were positively impressed with the groups. Many gave convincing details on how the training created important changes in their lives. The two-person teaching machine received negative comments from about half of the counselors. However, they claimed it taught them something despite its redundancy and condescending flavor. We are planning to change it. It also seems our counselors tend to be higher self-disclosers than the average student and, at the project's end, they tended to disclose significantly more personal feeling concerning their personalities and school work than did the controls. Counselors also reported that they disclosed much more to their male friends at the end of the program than did controls. Outgoing counselors tend to disclose a bit more than quiet counselors. Untrained counselors showed more discrepancy between what they "would tell" their boys and what they "did tell" their boys during the project. Perhaps group training helped counselors discuss things that they wanted to disclose with their boys. These odds and ends of information suggest that we may eventually find working with troubled boys changes students in important ways.

Some other questions about counselors that we hope to answer soon follow. Does the group assessment method produce patterns of scores that predict effective counselors? More specifically, will ratings of counselors' self-disclosure, warmth, ability to understand, depression, rigidity, and surgency predict measures of change in boys from observations of parents, peers, and teachers? Are quiet or outgoing counselors more effective with quiet or outgoing boys? Are variables such as age, vocational goal, quality of school work, and attitude toward human nature related to effectiveness? Is the counselor's measured effectiveness predicted by his previous experience working with children? His training in the project? His having received psychotherapy? His expressed motive for joining the project? His perception of the boy during visits? The types of things he tells his boy? And so on. Finally, can patterns or clusters of these variables help us locate students who can help troubled boys the most?

We will ask this set of questions separately of counselors with several different types of boys. As we have indicated, we are trying to find out which students work best with which boys under what conditions. A few small but solid answers should make us happy. We also want to know how many boys get worse, and whether enough get better to make the entire enterprise worthwhile. If the research eventually shows that the program fails, we will advertise our errors so that others will not repeat them. If it succeeds, we will prepare a cookbook for distribution to the many communities throughout the country who want to start their own programs.

BIBLIOGRAPHY

Berlin, Jerome I., and Wycoff, L. Benjamin. Human Relations Training Through Dyadic Programmed Instruction. American Personnel and Guidance Association Convention, 1964. (Mimeo.) Atlanta, Ga.: Human Development Institute.

Chapin, F. Stuart. Preliminary Standardization of a Social Insight Scale. *Am. Sociol. Rev.* 7: 211–225, 1942.

Gough, Harrison G., and Heilbrun, Alfred B. Jr. *The Adjective Check List Manual.* Palo Alto, Calif.: Consulting Psychologist Press, 1965.

Holzberg, Jules D., Gewirtz, Herbert, and Ebner, Eugene. Changes in Moral Judgment and Self-Acceptance in College Students as a Function of Companionship with Hospitalized Mental Patients. *J. Consulting Psychol.* XXVIII, 4: 299–303 (Aug.), 1964.

Jourard, Sidney M. *The Transparent Self.* New York: Van Nostrand, 1964.

Umbarger, C. C., Dalsimer, J. S., Morrison, A. P., and Breggin, P. R., *College Students in a Mental Hospital.* New York: Grune & Stratton, 1962.

Wiggins, Jerry S., and Winder, C. I. The Peer Nominations Inventory: An Empirically Derived Sociometric Measure of Adjustment in Preadolescent Boys. *Psychol. Rep.* 91643 677 Mon. Supp. 5V8, 1961.

Wrightsman, Lawrence S., Jr. Measurement of Philosophies of Human Nature Scale (July), 1966, (mimeo.).

The Combination of Didactic and Dynamic Elements in Filial Therapy

MICHAEL P. ANDRONICO
JAY FIDLER
BERNARD GUERNEY, JR.,
LOUISE F. GUERNEY

Many innovations have been made in the quest for more efficient methods of therapy. Various group methods such as group therapy and group counseling employ either dynamic or didactic methods in their approaches. Filial therapy, as developed by Guerney (1964), employs both didactic and dynamic elements. It is a method of teaching parents of emotionally disturbed children to relate empathically to their children for prescribed periods of time. After the initial diagnostic interviews, the children are not themselves seen in therapy; instead, they have "play periods" at home with one or both parents. The goal of the play periods is to enable the child to work through his emotional problems via play in the therapeutic atmosphere of parental empathy. The parents are seen in groups of six to eight members which meet on a weekly basis. During the first eight to ten group meetings, they learn to master the techniques of the play periods, which are closely tailored after those of client-centered play therapy.

In the first session or two, the major principles are explained to the parents, as follows: (a) the child should be completely free to determine the use he makes of the time and materials, i.e., the child leads and the parent follows without making suggestions or asking questions; (b) the

Reprinted from *International Journal of Group Psychotherapy*, 1967, Vol. 17, No. 1, 10–17, with the permission of the International Universities Press, Inc. and the authors. This paper is based on experience in a filial therapy research project supported in part by Public Health Service Grant MH 08653–01 from the National Institutes of Health.

parent's major task is to empathize with the child, to understand the intent of his actions, and his thoughts and feelings; (c) the parent's next task is to communicate this understanding to the child by appropriate comments, particularly, whenever possible, by verbalizing the *feelings* that the child is actively experiencing; and (d) the parent is instructed to be clear and firm about the few "limits" that are placed on the child, e.g., time limits, not breaking specified toys, and not physically hurting the parent. In later group sessions, the therapist gives a demonstration with one of the group members' children. Two demonstrations by the therapist, one with a girl and one with a boy, usually suffice for this purpose. The time before the half-hour demonstration sessions is spent briefly reviewing the principles, and the time after them is spent discussing the principles the group saw demonstrated.

A questionnaire which the group members will later use to report on their own sessions at home is distributed at the demonstration sessions. This outline is as follows: "1. (a) What, if any, difficulties did you have in actually following your role during this session? (b) What, if anything, do you think went particularly well as far as your role in the session is concerned? 2. (a) What, if any, difficulty did you feel the child had in accepting the nature of the session? (b) What, if any, special satisfactions do you think the child gained because of the nature of the session? 3. What needs and/or feelings do you think the child showed during this session? For example, a desire to depend on others, a desire for independence, for attention, for belonging, affection, admiration, etc. Or, feelings such as enjoyment, aggression, guilt, jealousy, anger, affection, pride in accomplishment, etc. Cite the words or behavior which suggested the presence of these needs or feelings to you. 4. Make any other comments you might wish to make about this session." Group members discuss the therapist's demonstration along these lines in preparation for the time they will discuss their own sessions.

In the following weeks, group members work with their own child or with each other's children to test their ability to perform what they have learned and seen. This gives the therapist the opportunity to supervise, and it provides him with ideas about what to look for once the parents have started the home play periods. For example, if a parent allows a child additional time at the end of a demonstration session to finish a game, both the therapist and the other members of the group have an opportunity to discuss this with the parent. In addition to giving a didactic explanation of the importance of the time limit as an aid to the development of a child's internal controls, the therapist can also explore the possibility of the child's attempting to manipulate the parent and the parent's responsiveness to such attempts.

At about the eight or ten-week mark, those parents who have demonstrated successfully and feel ready purchase a standardized group of toys and start the home play periods. To help make the play periods a special situation, the toys are never used outside the play periods. The toys are those usually found in play therapy, such as clay, Tinkertoys, crayons and paper, a hand-puppet family, rubber knife, toy pistol, a baby bottle, a family of small plastic dolls, a dollhouse made from a cardboard carton with plastic tape designating the "rooms," etc. The sessions are held in whatever room the parent feels offers the fewest distractions to the child and the greatest freedom from worry about breaking things or making a mess; this may be a basement area, a family room, a bedroom, or a kitchen. The times are set aside regularly and in advance, and the play period is regarded as inviolate; it is kept free from such distractions as phone calls and interruptions by siblings. The children are instructed that they are having these sessions because the parents are interested in learning how to play with them in a different, "special" way than they ordinarily do. They are also told that the parents attend sessions at the hospital or clinic because they are interested in learning how to play this special way at these certain times. The first play periods are on a weekly basis for a half hour, and then are increased to forty-five minutes two or more times weekly. The home play periods and ways of improving the parents' performance of their role continue to be discussed in group meetings. Although there is lecturing in the parent sessions, emphasis is laid upon the solution of problems through group discussion.

PARENTS' GROUP SESSIONS

This paper will concern itself primarily with the parents' group rather than the play sessions. However, it is important to note that the home sessions are intended to be genuinely therapeutic for the child and that experience has borne out this expectation. A rationale for the effectiveness of the sessions has been presented in another paper (Guerney, 1964). The point we wish to make here is that the home sessions are not an elaborate pretext to lure the parents into exploring their own feelings. The teaching element that we have described is considered an essential function in its own right. On the other hand, it is not possible to instruct parents on how to interact with their children for even a limited amount of time without coming face to face with the emotional life and problems of the parents as these affect and have affected the parent-child interaction. In a conventional group therapy situation, the focus is upon dynamic intra- and interpersonal elements, and any didactic elements are viewed as clearly secondary. In the filial therapy situation, the therapeutic "contract" is enlarged to include teaching as well as exploration of dynamics, with the didactic element in fact providing a framework for the entire therapeutic process.

The parents are told that it is expected that, in the course of learning how to conduct the play periods with their children, they will also explore their own feelings. The therapist uses his clinical judgment to determine when to shift from didactic to dynamic elements. Concentration on the parents' feelings may occur, for example, when it becomes obvious that a particular parent is unable either to understand or to follow through behaviorally with a concept because of his own emotional problems. Some parents, for instance, experience difficulty in being able to enforce the therapeutic limits that have been set for the child, as is required by the technique. It can be made clear that this problem is not shared by all of the parents and thus represents an individual motivational or emotional deviation. Another parent may find that she can be permissive except when it comes to listening to dirty words, and will wonder why this should be so difficult for her when it is not for others.

One parent, in structuring for the initial session at home, said, "You can do anything you want to here—except be mean to Mommy," the last phrase having slipped out before she was aware of it. In reporting it, knowing that it was completely in opposition to the required role, she realized for the first time how fearful she was that her unaggressive, phobic child harbored deep resentments toward her. Often, the group is able to handle such material without any interpretation by the therapist, and once the emotional problem is worked through, the process may return to a didactic discussion of play periods. The handling of the parent group sessions is similar to that of group supervision sessions with psychotherapists in training. Although the focus is usually upon the play sessions with the children, any obvious problem that a parent has turns the focus upon the parent and his difficulty in handling whatever area of the child's behavior is causing difficulty. For example, one father eagerly anticipated hostility and active acting-out in his son's sessions, comparable to the delinquent and rebellious behavior his son was displaying in the home and in the community. After several home sessions, the father blurted out his disappointment and anger that his son was "only drawing pictures of flowers!" Although the father's feelings were initially discussed in conjunction with the idea that expression of positive feelings in the sessions could also be therapeutic, in the course of several months the father was helped by the therapist and the group to realize that his anger was related to his doubts of his own masculinity and his resentment toward his wife for "always trying to wear the pants in the family."

Since all members of the group have been trained to conduct play periods in the same way, the play periods provide a standardized situation in which every group member can meaningfully and quickly compare himself and his child with other members and their children. Since most parents play the expected role remarkably well most of the time, any exceptions to this rule are highly significant. When dynamic and emotional elements do enter the picture, they often do so in such a way that their inner-determined and emotional basis is easy for all to see. Because the parent has accepted the goal of behaving in a certain way, but then at times finds a specific aspect of his behavior contrary to his own conscious desires and goals, he is often highly motivated to uncover the emotional nuances or expectations underlying his reactions. These may involve relationships with other family members as well as the particular child in question.

The didactic elements of filial therapy also allow the parents to observe their children's behavior in a standardized situation. Countless everyday situational variables such as different teachers and playmates are not present to confound the parent's picture of the child's behavior or to offer convenient opportunity for distorted interpretations of it. Similarly, the parent's perception of the child is more accurate because the parent is temporarily removed from the usual daily pressures. One mother, for example, reported that her daughter was spending several sessions in vehement attacks upon the bop bag with the alligator puppet and the rubber knife. The mother said, "You know, I never realized this before, but Carolyn has a tremendous amount of anger in her. My husband and I used to think she was our sweet angel, with not even one angry thought. He still thinks so, but I'm beginning to see differently." From this point on, the mother related instances of increasing assertiveness by her daugher, accompanied by her own more comfortable tolerance of it.

Because the home play periods involve a limited period of time, the parents are able to react to these situations and their own insights with less threat to their egos than would be the case if they felt obligated to change immediately and permanently. In this situation, they are only required to behave in an empathic manner for certain periods of time. What usually occurs, however, is that many parents spontaneously experiment with the reflective, empathic principles outside the play periods, and begin to realize that these principles have application in ordinary situations as well.

DISCUSSION

We have had experience to date with nine such groups, two of which have ended, while the other seven are in various stages. (Selection of cases was made by screening all children between the ages of four and ten referred by schools, physicians, etc. Those who were diagnosed by the clinic or hospital as having emotional problems were included in the study, while those who were diagnosed as being mentally retarded, brain-damaged, or schizophrenic were omitted. Presenting problems ranged from academic underachieving to stealing, the typical kinds of referrals encountered in child guidance facilities.) Because of our limited amount of experience with this method, we are not in a position to give definitive answers to questions that might logically arise about a new treatment approach. On the basis of our experience so far, we feel that the same characteristics that seem to raise or lower probability of success in more traditional therapies, e.g., ability or inability to explore one's own and others' feelings, also tend to do so in this form of therapy. We expect to learn more about how specific types of problems and personalities react to this particular method as we continue our research. At present, we exclude no one except on the basis of the disabilities mentioned. We feel that a number of parents benefited from this form of therapy who, according to our initial diagnostic impression, would not have accepted the idea of more traditional therapies or would have dropped out early in therapy. Such parents could accept the initial task-orientation aspects of this program and work gradually into more personal explorations, whereas they were not likely to have tolerated traditional, non-task-oriented approaches.

Some parents attempt to focus entirely on learning of the method, tending to shy away from discussions of feelings and to concentrate on the specific subject matter of the home play periods. Despite this, all groups that have been in existence for any length of time have become involved to a significant extent in discussing the feelings of group members about themselves and other important people in their lives.

Perhaps as a result of the initial tutorial role of the therapist, at first the group tends to look to the therapist for "right" or "wrong" answers to questions more properly dealt with by self-exploration and consideration of internal feelings and motivations. However, it has not proved very difficult for the therapist to establish different expectations from group members with respect to questions of techniques versus dynamic considerations. And the groups have seemed fully capable of accepting this differential behavior on the part of the therapist.

It has been our experience that the didactic component of this approach tends to provide entrée into emotionally and dynamically significant areas more than it tends to inhibit discussion of same. For the therapist, when to limit himself to tutorial goals and when to encourage exploration in depth is not always an easy decision to make. However, it is not a decision that is qualitatively different from decisions that interpretive therapists frequently make in deciding how far to explore a given issue.

Some of the unique advantages of the approach appear to be directly traceable to the blending of didactic and dynamic elements. The dynamic element provides an opportunity for the parents to discuss their feelings in the group sessions. The teaching of a role that inhibits negative responses on the part of the parents within the play periods does not result in the parent's denial or repression of feelings in the group sessions. And expression of these feelings and exploration of their underlying dynamics presumably helps to prevent conflicts building up and being expressed in the home.

The didactic element, in addition to its other contributions, places the treatment of parents on a different plane than is usually the case. Training parents to help in the treatment of their children provides them with a sense of useful and active participation. This seems to reduce resistance to change and serves as a strong motivating force. Experience thus far has shown that parents attend their sessions with regularity and do not tend to terminate prematurely.

Assuming that future groups corroborate our initial experience, the advantages of filial therapy are several. It has so far been found to be effective by the traditional clinical and qualitatively evaluated criteria of reduction of physical and behavioral symptoms, increased harmony between parents and children, and improved academic performance. This being the case, the number of patients which a single therapist can treat is significantly increased, along with a significant decrease in the amount of physical space required in a clinic. One therapist can see six to eight mothers in one room for an hour and a half, and have each mother see at least one child at home. Since parents are encouraged to include most, if not all, of their children in this method, often as many as three or four children receive these home play periods. In addition to the obvious increase in number of people who are thus exposed to a therapeutic setting without increasing the amount of professional time involved, the element of preventive mental health is introduced, hopefully decreasing the probability of future referrals from "problem families."

REFERENCE

Guerney, B., Jr. (1964), Filial Therapy: Description and Rationale. *J. Consult. Psychol.,* 28:304–310.

Special Problems in Training the Non-professional

BERYCE W. MACLENNAN

In this paper I plan to outline briefly some of the special problems which we, at the Institute for Youth Studies, Howard University (originally the Center for Youth and Community Studies[1]) have encountered in the training of socially disadvantaged youth with limited education and often irregular work histories to work as non-professional aides in a variety of human services such as health, recreation, education, social research, mental health and welfare institutional care, and community organization (Center for Youth, 1965; MacLennan, 1966a, 1966b; Felsenfeld, 1966). Although we were primarily concerned with youth I believe that some of the difficulties which we had to deal with, are typically present in the training and utilization of the indigenous non-professionals who live in our large urban slums.

Training for such New Careers involved not only the recruitment and training of youth but also the development of jobs and channels for advancement, training trainers and supervisors and ensuring adequate resources for remedial and higher education (MacLennan, 1966a, 1966b; Klein et al, 1966).

Many of the youth with whom we worked had long histories of poor

This paper was presented at the Seventy-Fourth Annual Convention of the American Psychological Association, New York, September, 1966. It is reprinted with the permission of the author.

[1]Projects funded by N.I.H., O.J.D.Y.C, Labor Department, O.E.

functioning; getting into difficulty with the law, dropping out of school and giving no indication of their potential ability We found it impossible to predict at the beginning of training who would excel and who would find it hard to complete the course In general, our population was characterized by:

1. A low self concept.
2. A wide gap between their life aspirations and their expectations and consequently a reluctance to mobilize themselves to sustained effort and a difficulty in enduring frustration related to work or learning.
3. A tendency to act out impulsively and a stereotyped range of methods for handling difficulties.
4. A very limited knowledge of possible work roles and of the rationale for institutional structures.

Immediate program needs were, therefore, to arouse the hope and interest of the youth in the possibility of a career and to make very clear that we respected them and had confidence that they could realize their aspirations if they were prepared to make the efforts; to create jobs and possibilities for career advancement and to design a training situation with sufficient structure to sustain the youth through beginning difficulties. To this end we devised a three-part training program which included a part-time supervised work experience, skill workshops and a daily small group meeting which served as a medium for counseling and for the transmission of general background information and discussion of social issues (MacLennan & Klein, 1965).

On the job, we found that the youth exhibited predictable problems; coming late, absenteeism, goofing off, lack of know-how in getting help when anything went wrong. With close liaison between trainers and supervisors (they met or telephoned three to five times a week) we were able to feed these problems back into the training group and to face the youth with the consequences of their behavior for the agency, the client and themselves. We challenged the "street" code of not squealing on and covering up for each other as unfunctional in this situation where we were fostering the attitude that everyone should help each other succeed. With mounting confidence and the realization that the kind of human services which they were able to perform had real meaning to others the youth became extremely enthusiastic and their attitudes changed from a desire to exploit to a willingness to put even more into their job than was demanded of them.

Similarly in the training sessions. At first, the youths' behavior was not of a quality which would be accepted by or from professionals. Some boys and girls became restless during the discussion. They would whisper to each other, engage in diversionary argument or even go to sleep or walk out. Initially, while pointing out that this kind of behavior did not serve the youth's purposes of successfully completing training and embarking on a career, our major emphasis was on demonstrating that the youth had something to contribute to the discussions. As time went on the aides themselves developed more esprit de corps and began to disapprove and challenge disruptive behavior to the point where the group was able to maintain its own control and to engage in well focused discussion.

As the youth began to change and to see themselves as respectable members of a social service hierarchy, to work regularly and to give up some of their old anti-social behaviors, their concepts of themselves began to change and they could no longer see themselves as failures, social outcasts or delinquents. They began to find that they were growing away from their old friends on the "street" and even in some cases from their families. If they wanted to keep out of trouble they could no longer associate with their friends. Because they were working regularly and not hanging around they could not really belong with their old group. Because they had a regular salary, they had less need to perform delinquent acts. This created a conflict for the youth and a very few could not face the separation, failed to work out an adjustment, gave up their attempt for a new career and reverted to their old ways. The majority, however, were able to make the change. In the long run, however, beyond the training period with its many supports, there may be others who find the new life too hard and lonely. To counteract this, we advocated but did not succeed in establishing a human service aide social club which would provide both social supports and mutual assistance. This problem of sustaining the youth beyond the training period has also been experienced in other youth programs such as the Job Corps and the Neighborhood Youth Corps.

As the youth begin to feel differently about themselves, the problem now arises as to what kind of person they wish to be and what kind of new life should they lead. Merely to emulate the professional is not always functional for the special advantage of the human service aide is that he knows intimately the life of his clients or patients and can be accepted as one of them. Over time, however, if the individual advances, it seems inevitable that he will become less closely connected to the poor and that this will be compensated for by a wider range of competence. For some, however, the experience of poverty has been so painful that, as they become more affluent, poverty and the poor are no longer accepted by them. For these, some alternative career may have to be devised, for it is impossible to serve adequately those whom we reject.

However, as the youth become aware of the life which the middle class live, they also find this less than satisfying. They compare the serial common-law relationships of the poor to the multiple marriages of the more affluent and do not find a great difference. They examine critically the tendency of some middle class workers to sacrifice human relations and the family to the demands of the job and material advantage. With characteristically youthful idealism they sometimes begin to demand a new and different world which contains more humanity and warmth.

A further conflict arises out of the imperfections of the agencies within which the youth must work. While in our training we attempt to inculcate a sense of integrity into the youth and to teach them to care for and to respect their charges, the youth do not always have the opportunity to work under supervisors who are respectful and knowledgeable. In a few instances, the youth have been required by their supervisors to mishandle others as when a youth was forced to beat a child who could not control his bladder. In other situations, the aides, some of them struggling to overcome their delinquent tendencies, have been pressed to break the rules of the agency by their supervisors as when teachers insisted that the aides join them for a cigarette in the basement against the regulations of the school.

If the youth are expected to confront and examine their mistakes and to learn from their errors, it is essential that trainers and supervisors strive to be equally undefensive. If they insist on protecting themselves and each other, the youth will consider them to be phony and have no further respect for them. In a Job Corps staff training program a counselor asked what he should do when a corpsman criticized another staff member. He felt he had to support and protect the staff thus creating the institutional dichotomy so clearly described by Goffman (1961) and others. Professionals have often been unwilling to admit the youth to their staff meetings, to accept them as full staff members and to discuss their difficulties in front of them.

Essentially it has to be recognized that the introduction of the indigenous non-professional into an agency puts a demand on all to change not only in terms of the reorganization of task and job but also through a need to review values and to reach out to each other so that good communication can be established. In such a situation some conflict is inevitable and it is only through a willingness to respect each other and to examine differences that these problems can be satisfactorily resolved.

REFERENCES

Center for Youth and Community Studies. Training for New Careers. *OJDYC*, D. C. 1965.

MacLennan, B. W. et al. Training for New Careers. *Community Mental Health Journal*, June 1966.

Felsenfeld, N. et al. *The Training of Neighborhood Workers.* Institute for Youth Studies, D. C. 1966.

MacLennan, B. W. The Human Service Aide. *Children*, September 1966.

Klein, W. et al. *The Training of Youth Counselors.* Institute for Youth Studies, D. C. 1966.

MacLennan, B. W. and Klein, W. Utilization of Groups in Job Training, *Int. J. Gp. Psychother.* October 1965.

Goffman, Erving *Asylums.* New York: Doubleday-Anchor #A277, 1961.

Training Procedures for Offenders Working In Community Treatment Programs

FRANK B. W. HAWKINSHIRE, V

A Retrospective View of Negative Social Interaction

The fact that this conference has been called to discuss the use of the offender as a therapeutic agent smacks of rank heresy. This is such a daring break with history that I feel somewhat compelled to raise the spectre of the past so that we can recognize just how heretical we are Make no mistake, some of the very same issues which we have been reflecting on, and will continue to think about, were raised over one hundred years ago. These issues were fought most bitterly and the evidence offered for each position was seen as compelling I am speaking, of course, of the arguments raging at the turn of the 19th Century over the decisions to adopt the Auburn or Pennsylvania system. Rehabilitation, or reform, was the most salient issue and the merits of each system were touted with exaggerated claims.

We should bear in mind the fact that the elaborate prisons built at the start of the 19th Century were devoted to certain theories of rehabilitation which placed heavy stress on separation, solitude, and close

Reprinted, with the permission of the author, from *Experiment in Culture Expansion,* Proceedings of a Conference on "The use of products of a social problem in coping with the problem," held at the California Rehabilitation Center, Norco, California, 1963; Carol Spencer (Ed.). Sponsored by The National Institute of Mental Health, U. S. Department of Health, Education and Welfare.

confinement, the exact antithesis of what we are advocating now, about 140 years later.

Let us look at one claim offered by a supporter of the Pennsylvania system dedicated to silent, solitary confinement. Mrs. Basil Hall, a noted Scottish traveler interested in prisons stated:

> . . . the principal (jailor) concerned, condemns the system pursued at Auburn, Sing Sing and similar establishments and is all for solitary confinement by day as well as by night unaccompanied by an occupation except a Bible in each cell. I cannot enter into his views in this particular and think that the good old copy line, "Idleness is the parent of mischief," may hold good in a prison as well as out of it, and although the culprits may be shut out from the power of doing evil with their hands, their minds must run to still greater waste than before. . . . (Written during a 14 months' sojourn in America, 1827–1828, published in a collection of papers edited by Una Pope Hennessy, London, 1931, p. 136).

Even though this good soul was of the opinion that labor should be permitted in prisons, she was not about to have conversation or socializing of any sort. There was, of course, another view

In spite of the prevalent zeal for the solitary system, some denounced it roundly as likely to cause mental disease and imbecility To this charge there were ready replies from those who strongly advocated the Pennsylvania system Inspectors of the Western Penitentiary made some very interesting statements justifying their position in the annual report of 1854:

> Shut out from a tumultuous world, and separated from those equally guilty with himself, he can indulge his remorse unseen, and find ample opportunity for reflection and reformation. His daily intercourse is with good men, who in administering to his necessities, animate his crushed hopes, and pour into his ear the oil of joy and consolation. Thus provided, and anxiously cared for by the officers of the prison, he is in a better condition than many beyond the walls guiltless of crime. (*Journal of Prison Discipline and Philanthropy,* January, 1862, p. 26.)

To the leading prison authorities it was clear that keeping prisoners *incommunicado* was a most salutary thing. They felt sure that negative socialization of the neophyte would come about from word of mouth information, from hardened criminals. Seldom was there any feeling that communication between prisoners could *become* worthwhile, if not inherently so, under proper guidance and supervision of staff. Some of our most enlightened prison administrators and penologists of that day seemed committed to the notion that prisons were inherently "breeding grounds of crime", "factories of corruption", and "finishing schools for mobsters". Stemming directly from this belief came the practice of separating prisoners from one another once they were released from the institution on parole. This practice continued the axiomatic assumption that prisoners in association with one another only spelled trouble. There was a great deal of truth to these assumptions but like all sweeping generalizations the case was somewhat overstated.

A Contemporary View of Effective Social Interaction

In contradistinction to the past, I would now like to present a model of a project which might indicate ways of maintaing *effective* collaboration among former inmates so as to support socially sanctioned behavior in the community rather than anti-social behavior. This model implies an assumption on my part that there is something that can be done to manipulate the peer culture to support positively sanctioned collaborations among former prisoners. It also implies that negative collaborations will be faced realistically and dealt with so as to minimize any negative impact on the community I can add little evidence for these assumptions but can share some experiences which, if you accept my assumptions, could be the basis for effective guidelines in exploring this issue. Toward this end let me briefly describe some of our work with the Flint Youth Study.

The Flint Youth Study has taken the community as its locus of operation. We envision the community as a type of factory which is charged with the unique function of building new units to replace existing ones now in use. Like the quality control engineer we see some real value in taking the "finished" product right off the assembly line and examining it to find out what could have been done during the manufacturing process to have made a better product. We have found out some interesting things. Like the quality control engineer we have also sampled products during various stages of development for the insights which they can give, or we can gather, about their experiences through our mythical factory. Here again we have gained some interesting data. We have concluded that many things can be done by the products of the system to correct or improve current operations if we listen to their excellent advice! We have just started several programs utilizing products as teachers, helpers, and demonstration agents in their former setting. Let us examine the workings of our cross-age project, which I like to call PLOY (Peggy Lippitt-Olders with Youngers) to see an example of a product working within the system.*

> Two years ago pupils of a sixth grade class from the University laboratory school were assigned as helpers in the junior kindergarten with four year olds. First, we administered a sociometric test to the sixth graders to determine the power structure and then the class was divided into two main groups consisting of equal numbers of high and low status members. Only those wishing

*This project is about to be published with tapes and instructional materials.

to participate in the project were included. They were told that they were needed to help out with the junior kindergarten during the year and that they would be given some training so that they could do a better job. Second, they were allowed to go to the experimental room in pairs to "observe the way four-year olds play." We wanted them to have a clear picture of what this age group looked like and what they did when they attended school in order to make the training program more concrete and interesting for them. After they all had a chance to visit and participate with the kindergarteners they met in a seminar (we used that very adult sounding term) to discuss what they "might do" when they came down to "help out." Such topics as "helping them to be self-reliant," and "offering them alternative ways of behaving other than hitting and fighting" were some of the subjects covered in seminar.

Training Issues

The real problem with any training program of this type comes in making it vivid enough so that those experiencing the training will have a feeling of competence to deal with the problems they will face in the real situation. Giving the trainees a chance to try out their learned skills becomes important to any training venture of this kind. Towards this end role playing of actual situations which might be encountered were used in order to provide "try-out" opportunities. It was amazing to see 11 and 12 year olds become involved in these situations and how creative they became when they had clear guidelines for their behavior. It is important to structure the situation with clear role prescriptions or they become manipulative, domineering, aggressive, or even give up their status position and "act like four year olds" when they enter the junior kindergarten.

One example of a seminar training problem, taken from the actual classroom situation, involved one of the youngest and smallest girls in her room.

> Jane was very much afraid of saying no to anybody. She came from a large family and everybody was older and larger than she. One day she came to school with a stuffed hippopotamus and went around pretending she was going to bite everybody with her animal. She went up to one of the helpers (as they are called) and said, "I am a hippopotamus and I am going to eat you up." We asked the helpers what they would do under the circumstances. One boy said that he would have said, "I am a lion who is king of beasts. Wouldn't you like to be my friend?" Another girl offered, "I am a baby hippopotamus and you can be my mother and take care of me."

The possibilities for utilizing this type of teacher program are widespread. We recently received a report from the Chicago school system reporting that 300 different classrooms each day are without supervision because there are no teachers to fill the vacancies. Approximately 50 sixth graders are now helping to fill the breach. We know nothing about the training which these "teaching assistants" are receiving or might have received in the past. *No training, or poor training, is a real danger in such a program.*

This program is just one example of how a system's products can be used to meet some of the system's needs. We can get very excited about this project because of the highly creative examples which can be devised to meet various demands. There are, however, some real areas of exploration beyond the mere excitement of creativity and innovation which must be charted most carefully to make sure that these exciting ideas don't founder on the rocks of reality. I raise these issues so that we can bring careful evaluation to the picture rather than resorting to spirited, but partisan, debate to carry forth our zeal.

WHO SHOULD BE THE CHANGE AGENT

One of the most crucial issues in choosing a change agent is the problem of "same vs. different". Is the change agent going to be exactly the same as the one he is attempting to help or should he be different? Let us examine what we mean by "same". Same refers to the total life situation of the change agent rather than just a common label, such as prisoner, or the like. It is true that this common label may be a shared feature but the degree of involvement in the criminal subculture, wealth of criminal experience, etc., may be very different. Bearing this distinction in mind, many would answer almost intuitively that being the same would of course not be helpful. We would caution against this assumption. There are some excellent examples of "same" helping "same."

First, Maxwell Jones uses psychiatric patients as helpers of one another in his therapeutic communities. The staff makes no effort to decide who can be helpful to whom. The whole spirit of the community compels everyone to get into the helping process. Second, the National Training Laboratories have experimented with "helping pairs." Delegates to the laboratory are paired off, without regard as to their "helping" expertise, in order to provide feedback to each other. In both of these situations equals help each other. In a sense it is the bond of "common shared fate" which seems to motivate the diadic relationship and proves beneficial to both parties. We would suspect that the proximity to failure is real for both parties so that real involvement can be obtained. A reality check is provided the helping pair by having A help B, B help C, C help D, and D help A. Each person has a chance to be a help-giver as well as a help-receiver. The opportunity to share each role, I think, brings about increased involvement and a heightened reality to the relationship. In the therapeutic community the staff provides a reality check. Third, the sixth grade kindergarten project uses some sixth graders who are behavior problems. We have found these older problem children to be excellent in working with younger children who, in many ways, are expressing some of the *same* behavioral symptoms. Focusing the training issues on the younger children allows the older ones to work through some of their own problems without threat to their self-esteem, or the necessity for a long supporting relationship before being ready to broach sensitive areas. In short, it would appear that "same" may be a very meaningful and creative way of handling the change agent role. There are other considerations beyond the dimension of sameness, one being trainability.

Trainability of Change Agent

The question of trainability should be resolved in making a final decision as to what group to include as change agents. We have found that some of the helpers were not able to handle the actual situation even though they were intellectually capable of understanding the problems. One of these was a pressured child who reflected this condition in her own behavior. When she was first sent to help out she was, unfortunately, assigned to the gym. When the younger children arrived, they ran wild, yelling and screaming all over the room. This was too tempting a situation for the older girl and she immediately joined in, leading them out of control rather than helping gain control. She seemed to become seduced by the situation and lost her own sense of control. Expression of her own impulses was too strong for her to be effective in controlling others. She was dropped from the program.

Role Definition

It is important that the role of the change agent be clearly defined. In the helping pairs it was important to establish who was helping whom. Without this clarification, mutual sharing of discontents or "disease" was the *modus vivendi* with nobody taking responsibility for the change efforts. In the Stanford Therapeutic Community, where I worked, the patients had to be reassured constantly that it was their responsibility to help one another and not tattle to staff or ignore situations. It was important to tell the sixth graders that the younger children could and would look up to them as friends and models, whereas they often felt adults were bossy and mean.

The helping pairs resisted clarification of the roles and we found that the helpers wanted to work with children much younger than themselves. It became clear that younger children gave more positive feedback, providing more ego gratification to their helpers. It was also apparent that there was much more mutual learning when the sixth graders served as helpers to the fourth graders than when they were helpers to the kindergarten group. Some of the preference for the younger group may be explained in terms of competence. When the tasks are more remote from the current learnings of the helpers they have a chance to develop greater competence and feel in better control. In the sixth-fourth grade project there was more "shared fate" because the helpers had just recently mastered the skills groped for by the fourth grader. He had a more recent picture of his own experiences in mastering a new task and could be more empathic with the younger child. Of course, he became more personally involved thus experiencing the positive and negative situations more acutely.

PROBLEMS

I am sure that all of us have experienced some of the excitement that comes from working on a creative program. I would, however, like to share with you some of the problem issues which must be faced in order to have a program which represents the quality level that we originally envisioned when the project was on the drawing boards. These are just some issues which were salient to us with the PLOY project. Many of these issues represent generic problems which should be faced. There is no special priority implied in my list:

1. Training program should be aimed at what we call *anticipatory practice.* When the trainee can see the relevance of his training, he is able to become more involved in the projects. Observations of the actual work situation and type of people the trainee will be working with was a technique used with the helpers. This served to heighten the reality of the practice situations and removed some of the elements of artificiality which often stigmatize the training cases.
2. *At-the-elbow support* is needed for the trainee. In setting up the program, an opportunity for try-out of newly acquired skills is essential. With the trainer at the elbow, correction, exploration of consequences, and systematic review of what has taken place can go forward as a natural part of the learning situation The trainee acquires added confidence in knowing that he is able to receive help if it is needed. This can be important aid in speeding up the training process. Increasing degrees of freedom from the direct supervision of the trainer should be built into this role relationship to prevent overdependence.
3. *Feedback* was found to be an important aspect of the helping process in our project. The National Training Laboratories utilized feedback

as the main task of the helping pairs. Adequate feedback can be a powerful device to bring the actual performance of the learner in line with his own expectations. The effective use of feedback is often lacking in training programs where communication of information, one way, seems to be the only real purpose of the training events. This condition often blocks the learner from expressing feelings of anxiety. If these feelings were dealt with, the effectiveness of the training process would be increased sevenfold. Dealing with the trainees' anxiety reactions to the work situations does not mean giving platitudinous reassurances, rather it means working through the specific issues as if they were real problems for the trainee. From his perspective they are very real.

4. A *support group* for the change agents is needed in any program. We have found that trios make better working groups than duos or singles. The support groups can serve as a source of critique and new ideas. The work load can often become simpler for each individual member when the group can learn to work together as an effective unit. The support group prevents the isolation of the change agent from new ideas and colleague evaluations. Interaction with a continuous group will permit the loss of identity with the primary task of the agency in favor of totally accepting the needs of the client.

5. The *total content* of the work situation must be included in the training program Focusing on attitudes or skills alone is not enough. At least three different areas must be included under content to make an effective training program. These are: (a) the goals of the program, (b) the skills which need to be acquired to carry out the tasks, and (c) the human relations issues which must support the change agent-client interaction Traditionally we deal quite effectively with the first two areas but usually ignore the third. The success or failure of community programs may rest on how the trainer deals with this last area.

6. *Realistic case material* should be prepared so that the trainees can try out their skills in the type of situations which they might face. Role playing provides a chance to become sensitive to some of the problems as well as to develop specific, rather than general, methods of approach which can be transferred realistically and effectively to the actual situation. There will be pressures from the trainees to have techniques on hand, often foreclosing effective innovation of their own. Prepackaged solutions can be avoided if the trainee gets in the habit of working out solutions from a springboard situation provided in role playing. This will tend to increase the trainee's confidence in handling situations that arise spontaneously in the work process.

7. *Continuous training* must be seen as an important part of the program. Initial training is crucial but on-the-job and follow-up training sessions are important to keep the original spirit and openness typical of experi-

mental programs. As the change agents become settled in their jobs they tend to adopt standard solutions "that worked in the past". The fact that certain procedures are seen as "standard methods" rather than a specific measure for a particular issue is evidence that the procedure may have become obsolete Repeated opportunities to innovate, within the protection of a tryout situation, will help keep the program moving towards greater creativity and improving quality output.

These are some of the issues which we have found to be important in our projects, *regardless* of the target of application. Let us now turn to the specific target of the community and mention briefly some of the possible issues which might be faced in this venture.

Community Action for Change

First, there is the need to be aware of the dangers that are involved in working in the community. Mistrust of the agency and the motives of the change agents is common. Some of the problems resulting from mistrust of the various groups attempting to move into communities' programs have been so traumatic that withdrawal of effort has become an unfortunate but typical pattern. Seeing the venture as one of convincing the community that its needs and wishes will be respected, insofar as they are realistic, is absolutely mandatory to deal with this mistrust. If and when issues are raised by community members which are not realistic, then the community action program must mobilize its resources to work through the issues with the community rather than "bull dozing" them with flowery statements about the program's "benefits to the community" or the "expertise of the staff". These techniques are bound to produce failure in the long run. Members of the community should be included in the decision making structure of the program through an Advisory Board. Citizen board members can sometimes alleviate some of the distrust that comes from the community. Representation from all relevant areas, not just the politically expedient, should be the guiding principle in selecting membership for an advisory group.

Second, the change agents in the action program should not be cut loose in the community without real backing and tie-in to an agency structure. Detachment of the change agents from the mainstream of professional experiences moves them too close to the situation so that they are not always able to make effective use of community supports nor deal with important feedback from the community. Frequent in-service and workshop training sessions and trio work groups are means to combat this problem. Meetings with the advisory board and other members of the total agency will help keep the change agents "in touch".

Third, continuous evaluation of the project is essential to deal with problems of quality control and reformulation of goals. Evaluation calls for action research, not just basic research. Basic research can be a part of the project but it will not answer the questions, "How are we doing?" and "Where should we be going?" For the program to have validity and spread potential it must have solid answers to these questions and not just rely on the enthusiasm of the "converts to spread the word." Regular reports on the project can help force these two issues out into the open and will provide helpful records of experiences for spread to other communities. The write-up should include information as to what went wrong, as well as what worked out best. Pinpointing skill needs and human relations issues represents part of the material which must be included for increased spread potential.

Fourth, the project staff should examine repeatedly the question, "Is our message getting through?" We often accept, without question, the fact that what we have said is what people now believe. This is far from true and the differences of opinion become most salient during periods of crisis. This is not the time to try to clarify the message for the community.

Summary

In conclusion let me briefly mention my major points. First, the decision to use "peers" as the change agents seems to have more validity than traditional approaches would indicate. Second, the degree of trainability may not be best assessed in terms of how much success the former product had in getting through the system. His success may make him intolerant of those who are having difficulty, or he may be too willing to resort to solving externally the client's problems rather than allowing the client to work through the situation on his own. Third, clear role definition must be given to the total project as well as to individual change agents so that everybody can see what goals are and measure the success achieved in locomoting towards these goals. Fourth, the training program must have several components to make it potent and useful to the trainees. Some of the issues to be included are: (a) anticipatory role practice for the trainees; (b) at-the-elbow support of the trainee once he moves into the actual working situation; (c) feedback to the trainee as to how he is doing, both from the object of his work as well as from his trainer; (d) an effective support group for the trainee to help orient him toward the total situation—trios represent a rather optimal size; (e) clarity as to the total picture required to function in the job—goals of the program, skill needs, and human relations issues; (f) realistic case material, role playing, and observation periods of experienced workers make the training program meaningful and salient to the trainees' later experiences; and (g) continuous training is a basic part of the program.

Strategies and Suggestions for Training Nonprofessionals

FRANK RIESSMAN

Problems related to the introduction and training of nonprofessionals in various structures (neighborhood service centers, service agencies, etc.) are presented. New approaches to phased, on-the-job training and the coordination of training and supervision are proposed. Problems related to the role ambiguity of the nonprofessional are discussed. Ten recommendations are offered relating to the group interview in the selecting of aides, the formation of nonprofessional groups and unions, the development of career lines, the new participation ideology of indigenous nonprofessionals (distinguishing them from traditional nonprofessionals, e.g., psychiatric aides), the limitations of traditional T groups (sensitivity groups), etc.

Approximately one hundred and fifty thousand nonprofessional positions have been established in the United States as a result of the antipoverty and related legislation If the nonprofessional revolution is to create more than jobs, if it is to develop genuine careers for the poor, moving them up the ladder, step by step, authentic training is the key (Pearl & Riessman, 1965). Trainers must be trained in how to evaluate nonprofessionals; how to encourage participation; how to listen; how to supervise in new ways; how to provide functional on-the-job learning.

Reprinted from *Community Mental Health Journal*, 1967, Vol. 3, No. 2, 103–110, with the permission of the Columbia University Press and the author. A brief biography of the author has been omitted.

Nonprofessionals are being utilized in a number of different structures. One major model is the neighborhood service center. This may be a storefront, employing 5 to 10 nonprofessionals with one or two supervisors, which was the pattern at the Lincoln Project (Hallowitz & Riessman, 1966), or the larger multiservice neighborhood centers, which may include anywhere from 30 to 200 nonprofessionals with a professional staff of 5 to 30 supervisors.

This model is characterized by a high ratio of nonprofessionals to professionals and a base of operation in the community, on the "home turf," so to speak, of the nonprofessional. The character of the involvement of the NP is likely to be quite different from the second model. Here the NP is attached to a service agency, such as the Welfare Department or the Health Department. He is not in the majority and his base of operations is not in the community but rather in the agency itself. Some of these agencies may be committed to an ideology emphasizing the value and significant new role of the nonprofessional, but in other cases they may simply be utilizing the new manpower because of the assistance it provides to professionals or because funding was available for NP positions.

Thus the variables to be considered are: the ratio of professionals to nonprofessionals; the base of operation, whether it be in the community or in the traditional agency; and the ideology or lack of it connected to the utilization of this new type of personnel. Training and supervisory staff should consider these three dimensions as they have implications for training methodology and supervision and for the development of the nonprofessional, the role he can play, his participation, and his power.

In the Lincoln setting it is interesting to note that nonprofessionals function both in neighborhood-based centers, where they are in the majority, and in a multipurpose clinic, where they are in the minority. At joint staff meetings the professionals have the opportunity to observe all the nonprofessionals (16–32) functioning at a meeting in which there are approximately 25 professionals present. Initially, these meetings included only 5 nonprofessionals. Marked differences in participation took place at the point where the percentage of nonprofessionals significantly increased.

Frequently, professionals assume that NP's identify with the poor and possess great warmth and feeling for the neighborhood of their origin. While many NP's exhibit some of these characteristics, they simultaneously possess a number of other characteristics. Often, they see themselves as quite different from the other members of the poor community, whom they may view with pity, annoyance, or anger. Moreover, there are many different "types" of nonprofessional: some are earthy, some are tough, some are angry, some are surprisingly articulate, some are slick, clever wheeler-dealers, and nearly all are greatly concerned about their new roles and their relationship to professionals.

It is most important to note then that NP's are frequently quite competitive with professionals. In essence, many NP's think they are different from the poor and would be more effective than professionals if they had a chance. Many are aware of the new ideology regarding nonprofessionals that calls attention to the special properties (style, etc.) that enable the NP to communicate with the low-income community in an effective manner. They feel this gives them something of an edge over professionals, and when combined with the training and knowledge they are acquiring in the professional structure, they will be "double smart."

While nonprofessionals may be selected because of certain characteristics they possess, such as informality, humor, earthiness, neighborliness—in other words some of the "positive" characteristics of the resident population—the other side of the coin cannot be ignored. That is, they may possess characteristics of low-income populations that interfere with effective helper roles. For example, they may possess considerable moral indignation, punitiveness, suspicion, or they may be so open and friendly on occasion that the significance of confidentiality escapes them. Thus, while the training staff will want to build on their positive helping traits and potential skills, to some extent there must be an effort to either train out or control some of these other negative characteristics (negative in playing the helping role in a social service framework).

ROLE AMBIGUITY: WHO AM I?

One of the greatest problems experienced by the nonprofessional is role ambiguity or lack of role identity: He does not know who he is or who he is becoming. He is no longer a simple member of the community—if he ever was one—nor is he a professional. Actually, he is a highly marginal person, just as the new community action programs he frequently represents are also highly marginal and lacking in a clear identity

"Nonprofessional" describes what he is *not*, but does not clearly indicate what he is. He is not simply a citizen nor a volunteer participating in the organization, although the desire to have him represent the feelings of the neighborhood produces some similiarity with the citizen advisory board role of the local resident. He is not the traditional kind of employee because his participation, neighborhood know-how, and advice are sought; yet he is also an employee. He is not a professional, even though he does represent the agency and many people in the community may see the aide as a new kind of social worker. He is not a political action organizer, even though he does develop groups in the community concerned with various types of change. He is an amalgam of all these various roles, and his trainers and the leaders of the community action programs must understand and try to clarify this new role. But to repeat, the role itself has strains and contradictions, and the nonprofessional must be assisted to live within the framework of these dilemmas. He is the new marginal man. He must be selected with this in mind, trained and supervised in this fashion, and assisted in forging this new role. Perhaps he will become the new integrated man for the "Other America."

Finally, the ambiguity is also related to the unclarity of goals and programs in the rapidly developing community action programs. The newness of the programs, the vagueness of many of the goals, and the fact that the tasks for nonprofessionals are only beginning to be defined contribute to the total atmosphere of amorphousness and produce confusion and anxiety. The programs are new, the jobs are new, and the personnel are new. Clearly, flexible and innovative supervisors and trainers are required to function in this difficult, rapidly evolving situation. All staff members, supervisory and nonprofessional, should be made honestly aware of the character of the situation; that is, the fact that it is rapidly changing and not highly structured and traditional. Some tolerance has to be built up for this climate and some structure has to be provided as quickly as possible. To some extent, structure can be achieved by attempting to define as specifically as possible the job function, and the description of it should be provided in as much detail as possible without sounding overwhelming.

PHASED TRAINING

The relationship of training to job performance for the nonprofessional is different than it is for other types of employees. Perhaps the main reason for this is the general lack of skill possessed by the nonprofessional and, more particularly, the lack of certain requisite skills for the new jobs (e.g., recordkeeping).

The traditional principle that long periods of training are necessary before an individual can be employed must be reversed; the motto should be "Jobs First—Training Built In."

It has become axiomatic that most of the training of the nonprofessional will take place on the job itself This requires that job functions be phased in slowly and that the NP's receive ample time to master the required tasks at each stage before going on to more advanced tasks.

Prejob training (to be distinguished from core training or the training in basic knowledge which can take place throughout the program) should be oriented primarily to enabling the NP to perform the simplest entry features of the job in a fairly adequate fashion. Moreover, the job itself must be broken down and phased in, so that in the initial stage the nonprofessional will be required to perform only limited aspects of the job itself. Further skills will be learned on the job itself, through on-the-job training and systematic inservice training.

The preservice period should be short lest anxiety be built up and the aide become threatened by the anticipated job. The learning should be active; the aide should be doing things, and knowledge and concepts should be brought in around the discussion of his activities.

As quickly as possible the aide should be placed on the job itself for a part of the day under close professional supervision. The sooner the aides can get their feet wet, the better they will feel. Thus, in the Lincoln Project, the aides were placed on the job in the Neighborhood Service Center for one-half a day in this prejob period (after a three-week period spent in job simulation, practice, etc.). The half day in which they were not working was utilized to discuss the specific experiences they were having.

Beyond this point, the really significant training and learning will occur on the job itself and in carefully planned discussion about the work they are doing. It is not to be assumed, unlike many other positions, that the NP knows his job when he begins it. Rather, in the early stages of this on-the-job experience, he is actually involved in continuous training, and the first job operations are to be considered preliminary aspects of the position that he will ultimately fulfill. He is really still in training on the job itself.

ON-THE-JOB TRAINING

On-the-job training, then, becomes decisive, and different types of on-the-job training should be considered. The aides will learn from simply performing some of the tasks—that is, they will learn from their own experience; the aides will learn from each other (utilizing peer learning and the helper principle); the aides will learn from their supervisor, who will support them and correct their mistakes and provide assistance at any time on request. The aides will also learn from a special series of group meetings that can be held. One such group can be concerned with systematic training introducing, for example, further skills in interviewing. There can also be group discussions about general problems being experienced: on-the-job problems with professionals, problems with other agencies, problems about their own marginality, problems stemming from competition with each other or annoyance with the type of supervision they are receiving. These discussions should be task centered, with personality and individual components coming in as relevant (the traditional sensitivity training—T group—experience seems to require considerable modification if it is to be used with the nonprofessional population).

Another very significant type of informal training can be developed as the program of the agency moves forward. In the Lincoln NSC program the initial phase was concerned with providing and expediting service. After a number of months, the program moved toward the development of groups, committees, community action, campaigns (voter registration, etc.). At this point the program had to be discussed with the aides, and this provided an excellent opportunity for the introduction of new training with regard to concepts and skills. Thus, in order to involve clients in a community meeting, it was necessary to discuss with the aides plans for calling such a meeting, how to conduct the meeting, how to bring the client population to the meeting, how to develop committees, and so on.

The discussion, which was program centered for the most part, brought in training in what might be described as an informal but highly functional fashion. But it is exactly in this fashion that the aides seemed to learn best. They needed to know how to conduct a meeting, develop participation in committees, and the like, and consequently their motivation was high and the learning was sensitive and highly directed. Moreover, issues about how fast can we move, what kinds of action can we take, what is our relationship to the community became commonplace discussion, and the concepts and goals of the program were easily introduced in this context. For example, one of the aides asked why we couldn't use an Alinsky-type TWO program approach. Other aides suggested that if we did, we wouldn't have our jobs long. The leader indicated that there were target populations among the poor whom the Alinsky groups did not influence easily but that our agency, because of its legitimacy, might be able to work with and involve in various types of nonmilitant activity. A great deal of excited discussion took place and apparently much concrete understanding regarding the agency's viewpoint emerged.

To take another example: At one of the community meetings that was called, where over 100 people from the neighborhood attended, the combined enthusiasm of the aides who led the meeting and the client-citizens who attended it went into the formation of eight different committees. In a discussion after the meeting the aides were able to understand fairly easily that they had really run ahead of themselves; that they had taken on more work than the agency could handle. Various methods for consolidating the committees and developing volunteers were then discussed in a highly meaningful fashion. Thus the fact that the programs of the new neighborhood service centers are not fully developed can be used to good advantage in the phasing of the training of the nonprofessionals. As these programs develop, new training appropriate to the program phase can be introduced, and this is a most meaningful way for the aides to learn.

The Howard Community Apprentice Program provides another illustration of functional learning. Initially the functionally illiterate research aides in the Howard Program interviewed each other with a tape recorder and learned only the simplest principles of interviewing in order to perform this task. Before long, they recognized that they needed to know something about how to record this information and categorize it, and later they needed some statistics in order to analyze it appropriately. As each of these needs became apparent, the appropriate training was introduced to develop the requisite skills. This can be done either formally or informally, through systematic inservice training and/or through informal discussions related to the problem.

HOW TO UNIFY TRAINING AND SUPERVISION

When possible, it seems useful to have one person responsible for selecting the aide (interviewing him either individually or in a group), training him, and supervising him in the actual program. This was the model developed by Mary Dowery at the Mobilization for Youth Parent Education Program. It allowed for identification by the aides with one person and prevented the confusion that develops when there are multiple leaders. The limitations in this type of model relate to the fact that one person cannot encompass all the required skills that are to be imparted to the NP's. This difficulty can, to some degree, be minimized by introducing a number of different consultants as assistants to the trainer at various points. However, the trainer has to utilize this information selectively and interpret to the aides what the consultant is offering. The consultant does not become the leader.

However, in the larger agency model, it will not be as easy for one person to play the multiple roles of selector, trainer, and supervisor. For this model a number of adaptations are recommended.

NP's can be introduced in a circumscribed sphere of the agency—in one department, for example, where the selection, training, and supervisory responsibilities are delegated to one person or to a team of two or three individuals working closely together.

Another possibility is to permit professionals in the larger agency to volunteer to select and work with a nonprofessional assistant, in a sense, functioning as selector, trainer, and supervisor. While some general suggestions can be offered as to how the professionals might use the nonprofessionals, in general it would seem best at this stage to permit the professionals to define the assignments and working relationships. Some professionals will want the NP's, at least at first, to do fairly menial tasks, simply serving as assistants. Others may suggest fairly early that nonprofessionals perform new and meaningful assignments, really discussing things with clients, for example, rather than merely serving as translators. It should be especially valuable for the nonprofessional to work with the professional on a one-to-one basis initially, rather than being involved in a team in which the professionals are the majority.

The professionals who self-select themselves might meet together from time to time with an individual in the organization or a consultant who has responsibility for the development of the use of nonprofessionals — this could be a trainer or other program developer In these discussions, some of the experiences of the professionals would be exchanged and discussed, problems would be raised, and the specialist or consultant would offer advice, bring in experience from other settings, suggest problems that might arise, indicate different roles that nonprofessionals could play.

This way of involving professionals might be an excellent way in which to introduce the nonprofessionals into a particular institution and establish the tradition of using NP's. The resistance on the part of the professionals who did not self-select themselves for working with nonprofessionals might be dissipated after they observed some of the initial (hopefully) positive experiences of the professionals who volunteered.

In the multiservice centers where large numbers of NP's are to be employed, it will not be possible to integrate the selection, training, and supervisory functions in one individual or small team. To obtain a more full and systematic training product, it is probably best to have the training done by a special training agency. Even though a large part of the training will have to be on the job itself, the training organization can dispatch its senior trainers to the service agency in order to provide the initial on-the-job training. (The training institution can provide prejob training at its own base.) The training agency will, of course, have to work very closely with the service organization and plan to phase out its own role, leaving in its place a training and supervisory capability.

RECOMMENDATIONS

1. Trainers should not expect or demand deep identification with the poor on the part of nonprofessionals, and they should anticipate competitive feelings toward professionals (often professionals other than themselves, but not always).

2. Constant support and assistance must be provided; supervisors should be available for assistance at all times, and it should be clear to the NP that he can request help without any negative implications regarding his evaluation. (Frequently NP's confuse supervisors with factory foremen.) On the other hand, opportunity for considerable initiative and flexibility on the part of the NP must be established. He wants both the flexibility and the support. He is a new kind of employee, and reflecting the developing antipoverty ideology, he wants more of a say, or at least wants to be consulted, regarding the operation of various programs and rules.

3. The process of obtaining the job must be made as simple and short as possible. Every effort should be made to reduce the competitive feelings that the recruits may develop in relation to other candidates for the position. Long delays between the original time of the job application and later interviews are likely to produce considerable anxiety for the candidate. This attitude may be carried over in the training and on the job itself, thus producing competitive difficulties with other aides and anger toward the program and the staff.

4. The group interview can be used very successfully in selecting applicants. Aside from the fact that it is economical in time, the group process permits the selector to observe how the candidates relate to other people in a group; who influences whom; who listens; who is sensitive; who is overwhelmed by group pressure; who has leadership potential, etc. It is also possible to produce an excellent group atmosphere and develop the beginnings of later camaraderie, *esprit de corps*, group feeling, teamwork, etc. The danger, however, lies in the competitive setting in which the applicants observe that they have to compete against others for a limited number of jobs.

The competitive troubles can be reduced by establishing an informal, friendly setting; coffee and cake should be supplied from the beginning, even before the group forms and starts to talk. A leisurely pace of discussion can be established by the leader or the co-leader. Everybody should be introduced. Plenty of time for warming up should be available. The group should be no larger than 10 people and should be sitting fairly close together in a circle or around a table. But the selectors must make perfectly clear that evaluation is taking place and that it will be difficult to assess people unless they participate and have something to say. Otherwise "quiet ones" will be penalized by this group selection process. The group session itself should stress interaction and not go around the circle having each person announce his interests or goals.

5. Nonprofessionals frequently expect magic from the training process; that is, they expect to learn how to do everything they are supposed to do quite perfectly. To the degree that this is not achieved, they blame the training process. To some extent this reflects a naive view about training, education, and learning. The training staff should be aware that it probably will receive this reaction and insofar as possible should try to explain to the trainees that many dimensions of the job will take some time to learn fully in practice. Fundamentally, of course, the trainees' reaction reflects their anxiety about the new job and role and this has to be dealt with in other ways as indicated below. Trainers also sometimes expect too much from the training; sometimes their expectations of nonprofessionals are initially too high and their appraisal of adequate progress is based on experience with more experienced professional learners. While NP's have some surprising knowledge and understanding of a variety of issues, there are areas of their knowledge that are unbelievably remiss. They often have great gaps in their knowledge or know-how about the system—how to fill out forms, how to make outlines, how to take tests, how to read effectively. Because they are frequently very sensitive and bright in their understanding of people and the neighborhood, the tendency (in halo fashion) is to assume that their understanding is equally good in areas removed from their previous experience. Thus, it is a shock to discover that a nonprofessional who has conducted an excellent interview with a client records the interview inadequately. Constant training and emphasis must be built in to improve report-writing skills, etc.

6. Nonprofessionals have quickly learned that part of the ideology of the antipoverty movement is directed toward developing, not merely jobs for nonprofessionals, but career lines as well. It is therefore extremely important that the agency establish these lines so that there can be aides, assistants, associates, supervisory positions, and possibly assistant neighborhood service center director positions available to the nonprofessional through career development and education. The training staff must clarify these career lines, indicating the relationship of education to them and further indicating the time involved before individuals can expect to "move up." If this is not done appropriately, aspirations may develop very rapidly and may outstrip possibilities.

7. Nonprofessionals should be encouraged as soon as possible to form their own groups or unions. (We would predict that organization and

unionization of the aides will progress fairly rapidly in the coming period.) Aides at Harlem Hospital have been encouraged to meet by themselves, but these meetings have been recorded and utilized by the research staff there. The Lincoln aides meet independently at an "aides-only" meeting, not under the surveillance of their professional supervisors. These groups are very important in developing the power of the aides and a feeling of identification as a group and should contribute greatly to the formation of role identity and job identity. In the Lincoln Project, aides also met off the job on their own time. These meetings led to the development of leadership among the aides, to powerful group identity vis-à-vis the professionals on the staff, and to the raising of a number of highly significant demands: the demand for greater participation in certain aspects of decision making of the organization (this was not an unlimited demand for participation on all decisions); the demand for closer supervision and periodic discussions with the leaders of the program; the curtailment of T groups (sensitivity training groups, which were highly unpopular among the aides); the demand for career lines to be developed so that nonprofesssionals could move up the ladder—the associated demand for education to be provided by the Yeshiva University, of which the Lincoln Project is a part; the demand that if volunteers were to be used, they should be carefully trained; the demand for a greater voice in the selection of delegates to the local Anti-Poverty Community Convention, the request for the aides-only meeting.

8. While much emphasis has been placed on the use of group procedures in training, it should be noted that a great deal of deep learning develops on a one-to-one identification basis. Bank Street College's summer experiment, in which each teacher worked one hour per day with one student, found this one of the most effective learning devices. And Mobilization for Youth's homework helper program, in which one high school youngster worked individually with one elementary school youngster, also supports the value of the one-to-one relationship. This principle can be utilized at a number of points in the training design. As noted above, individual aides can be assigned to professionals in the agency who select themselves for this purpose and volunteer to develop a nonprofessional assistant. We have also found that it is possible to use experienced, trained nonprofessionals to assist in one-to-one work with new trainees; that is, for a period during the day a new trainee can be assigned to work alongside of an experienced nonprofessional. This has to be done selectively or else we will have the "blind leading the blind." But when it is supervised thoroughly, there exists the possibility of utilizing the full advantages of peer learning. Peers learn from each other in very different ways and sometimes more fully than they learn from "superior" teachers. The "helper principle" notes that the peer teacher

(that is, the more advanced aide) learns enormously from imparting information to the trainee; he learns from teaching (Riessman, 1965).

9. While a certain degree of anxiety is useful in stimulating learning, the NP is probably faced by far too much anxiety due to his role ambiguity. Hence, every effort should be made to reduce the anxiety level. This can be achieved by phasing of tasks (not demanding too much too fast), defining the job as carefully as possible, developing group support, providing specific training and evaluation (positive performance should be commended in as detailed a fashion as are weaknesses), providing constant supervisory support and assistance, and holding frank discussions of program and role difficulties. We suspect that the NP's anxiety tolerance is not high and that a learning style that utilizes anxiety stimulation is not characteristic of this population.

10. Many professionals express great concern about nonprofessionals losing their community ties, their feeling for the neighborhood, and their identification with "the people." This is based on the obvious fact that nonprofessionals are no longer simply members of the community but are now employed by an agency. Moreover, since career lines may develop, the NP's can anticipate moving up the ladder and, in some cases, becoming professional.

The issue is not whether the NP identifies with the poor or not, but rather whether he remains committed to them. (Many professionals are committed to the poor without in any way identifying with this population.) What the Anti-Poverty Program needs from the indigenous nonprofessional is his knowledge, his ability to communicate with the poor, and his commitment. It does not need his identification with the poor.

Actually, it generally takes people a long time to lose their knowledge and understanding of the ways, traditions, style, and language of their origin. And if they initially have some commitment, this concern will not fall away overnight. Thus, the commitment and knowledge can remain even if immediate identification diminishes. Moreover, commitment can be maintained by the reinforcement of it by the agency and the training staff. In other words, to the extent that the agency reflects the developing antipoverty ideology, it can reinforce and reward at every turn the nonprofessional's concern for his neighborhood and the poor. The training staff can be critical of any tendency on the part of the nonprofessionals to lose this commitment as they come to identify with the agency or with professionals. In other words, it is possible for nonprofessionals to develop new identifications, at the same time maintaining traditional commitments. In fact, these commitments can be deepened by new systematic understanding regarding the nature of poverty. It is in this context that continuous training can perhaps provide its greatest contribution to the nonprofessional and the antipoverty program.

REFERENCES

HALLOWITZ, E., & RIESSMAN, F. The role of the indigenous nonprofessional in a community mental health neighborhood service center program. Paper presented at the American Orthopsychiatric Association, San Francisco, April 15, 1966

PEARL, A., & RIESSMAN, F. *New careers for the poor.* New York: Free Press, 1965.

RIESSMAN, F. The "helper" therapy principle. *Soc. Wk,* April 1965, 10 (2), 27–31.

Group Methods in Training and Practice: Nonprofessional Mental Health Personnel in a Deprived Community

JUNE JACKSON CHRISTMAS

Currently efforts are being directed toward developing mental health services which are therapeutically useful to disadvantaged persons. A program, staffed in large part by persons from deprived backgrounds, is presented. A model for group training of such nonprofessionals for their new roles is described.

Experience in the Group Therapy Program of the Department of Psychiatry, Harlem Hospital, has led us to conclude that nonprofessional mental health personnel, trained and used in certain settings, can provide an added therapeutic dimension of particular significance to deprived patients. Moreover, they are a source of added manpower.[10,11] Use of indigenous aides, mainly from the patients' own socioeconomic groups (working class or lower socioeconomic class) in varied mental health roles not only provides new types of mental health services, but also makes possible identification of the effect of these new roles on patient progress, family, community and professional attitudes. Such information may well be applicable to programs in need of new sources of manpower for effective social welfare and health services.[1]

This paper was presented at the 1965 annual meeting of the American Orthopsychiatric Association, New York, New York. It is reprinted with permission from *American Journal of Orthopsychiatry*, 1966, Vol. XXXVI, No. 3, 410–419, Copyright 1966, the American Orthopsychiatric Association, Inc., and with the permission of the author. The superscripts throughout this article pertain to the list of references given at the end of the article.

Mental health aides, men and women of all ages, have been recruited through clubs, churches and community agencies as well as through aides already active. Others have been recruited through such programs as the Harlem Domestic Peace Corps and Vista. Because the patient of lower socioeconomic status generally identifies more easily with the nonprofessional of his own social class than with the middle-class or upper middle-class professional, he has more readily used the nonprofessional as a role model. Ease of communication in the language of the deprived community and knowledge of reality factors in the lives of the patients have supplemented such identifications.

Emphasis on the advantages of using persons from the same socioeconomic groups as the patients has not led us to overlook the assets of the middle-class aide. With supervision and development, the middle-class aide can use his greater ease in dominant culture verbalization and conceptual thinking to advantage. The talents and skills which may have come from advanced education and employment may help patients (and other nonprofessionals) to develop their skills. Since most adult urban middle-class Negroes are at the most a generation or two removed from the working class, those who are relatively free of conflicts around their current status in society may use this background for greater understanding of the patients. Many working-class Negroes express middle-class values, particularly in reference to child-rearing practices and life goals,[9] but they feel incapable of achieving these goals or of integrating these values and practices with the values of the ghetto. Middle-class aides have assisted such patients and families in the process of integration and translation into effective behavior. Aware of broad issues, the middle-class mental health worker has served as a link to the predominantly middle-class community leadership. At the same time the worker has assisted the development of potential leaders from more deprived groups.

In the selection of persons for work with psychiatric patients, the objectives of education described by Levine[8] are particularly relevant: the development of compassion, commitment and competence. Persons have been sought who indicate the ability to develop these qualities. Of prime importance is the ability to develop compassionate understanding of the patient, his strength and his weakness, his inner life and his outer world. Next in importance is the capacity for commitment to work and thus to the attainment of satisfaction from a job done well. Of third importance is competence in specific aspects of the work assignment. The personality of the applicant, his feeling for people and his potential for commitment should receive greater attention than previous training, work skills or formal education. In the presence of compassion and commitment, the acquisition of specific skills may be put to more productive use in the service of the patient and in the growth and development of the mental health worker.

A variety of positions have been filled by nonprofessional aides in this department. They include mental health aide, activities aide, educational aide, family service aide, casework aide, training aide, rehabilitation aide, expediter, and research aide.

SUITABILITY OF NONPROFESSIONAL GROUP APPROACHES WITH THE DISADVANTAGED

Group methods recently have been in wider use with disadvantaged persons in health and welfare services.[6] Certain features of group techniques suggest their appropriateness for this patient population as well as the usefulness of training groups as one approach to staff from the same background.

The democratic and cooperative aspects of groups prove useful to persons who have had disturbing life experiences with authority and who may perceive the therapist in a one-to-one relationship as an inevitably malevolent authority figure. The opportunity for concrete direction and group problem-solving, the use of a social action process rather than a verbal process, and the use of multiple therapeutic figures are additional enabling features. Because therapeutic groups allow the concept of causality to be dealt with, there can be movement away from the life adaptation of living only in the moment often seen in deprived persons.

Reference has been made elsewhere to several factors of significance in planning mental health services for a deprived Negro community.[2] They include the historical determinants of certain aspects of present-day Negro life; the social reality, values, and norms of that life, and the psychological effects of poverty, segregation, discrimination and deprivation.

The historical facts of slavery, namely, deprivation of freedom, separation from the culture of the past and enforced disruption of families through slave-holding practices, are seen as related to current problems and self-attitudes of the deprived Negro, perhaps of the deprived Negro patient to an even greater degree. These include feelings of hopelessness and helplessness, unproductive anger and self-hate, problems in identity and a pattern of unstable family relationships. The creative use of nonprofessional mental health workers indigenous to the community can help patients identify and deal with a number of these factors, provide much needed human services and have a significant effect upon the social structure of the community.

Situational and environmental pressures play a great part in the emotional problems of Negro patients and their families. As the most disadvantaged economic group in our society, Negroes have fewer material resources to aid them in their parenting tasks, fewer opportunities to develop skills, and a narrower repertory of socially productive roles which can be successfully filled.[4]

The effects of severe and longstanding social and economic deprivation, ghetto life, racial prejudice and discrimination upon personality development and mental health are not well understood and deserve further study. The relationship between such external stresses and recovery from mental illness warrants investigation as well. Nonprofessional staff, with their ability to communicate in the language of the patient, can play a vital role as research aides in such studies. Moreover, since patients and nonprofessionals come from social and economic backgrounds which are similar in many respects, there can be opportunity to identify factors responsible for successful functioning in the deprived community, and to use this information in treating those who have shown lack of success, whether by the development of psychosis, delinquency, or the more usual apathy, self-hate, and despair.[3]

Moreover, the fact that Negroes by and large have maintained a belief in the democratic ideal, may be a positive factor in their ability to benefit from the egalitarian aspects of groups.[2]

GROUP PSYCHIATRIC SERVICES WITH NONPROFESSIONAL PERSONNEL

Since October, 1964, we have provided a day treatment program for a small number of chronic, psychotic, posthospital patients. Goals include a decrease in individual psychopathology, improved socialization, constructive use of leisure time and prevocational motivation and training.

An essential feature of this half-day program, based in a community center near the hospital, has been the use of nonprofessionals as aides in casework, rehabilitation and family service. Working continuously with a group of 20 patients, two full-time and four part-time aides fill both the traditional roles of service and assistance and a newer therapeutic relationship role.

Professional direction is provided by the chief of the group therapy program, a psychiatrist. Other professional staff includes a psychiatrist with special interest in chronic psychosis and in drug therapy, a psychiatric nurse and a supervisor of social service. All provide part-time service. Nonprofessional training is conducted by the psychiatric director, nurse and social service supervisor. Consultation is provided by divisions with which its program is coordinated, e.g., day hospital, inpatient service; community psychiatry, and mental hygiene clinic.

PATIENT GROUP MEETINGS

1. *Group Psychotherapy*. Weekly group psychotherapy is led by a psychiatrist. The nonprofessional aides begin by acting as observers, then observer-recorders and finally cotherapists and recorders. They use their observations and the professional's interpretation of group interaction to understand efforts of patients to cope with inner conflicts. They relate these efforts to recover from mental illness to behavioral patterns illustrated in other parts of the program in which they play more active roles.

2. *Medication Group*. Once a month a group meeting is held for the prescription and control of medication. Led by a psychiatrist, discussion takes place concerning indications for and reactions to drug therapy. The nurse coordinates this and nonclinical parts of the program. The nonprofessional aides take part in the group discussion, enriching it through their knowledge of the patients' behavior in other settings. Attention is paid to the general physical condition of patients. The aides expedite indicated services in other clinics. They gain knowledge of patient responses and attitudes to medication. As the patients derive emotional support from the group discussion, they are able to use medication with greater regularity and more effectiveness.

3. *Therapeutic Community Meeting*. Weekly the patients, aides and professional staff meet to discuss matters of community concern in a democratic manner, using the interactional method. Through patient and staff participation, patients have an opportunity to increase their ability to cope with reality, to advise, to plan and with staff support to begin to make decisions for themselves. With time, the nonprofessional aides generally become active participants. The meeting serves both a therapeutic function for patients and a training function for staff in group techniques.

4. *Workshop*. A weekly "higher horizons" discussion is led by the psychiatric nurse with other appropriate professional staff (social worker, vocational counseling consultant). Designed to provide educational and cultural enrichment, to aid in resocialization and to stimulate prevocational motivation, it focuses on life-situation solutions. The nonprofessional aides bring their own experiences in coping successfully, their knowledge of the strengths and potentials for enrichment in the ghetto and their ability to communicate in the language of the patient. Profes-

sional staff bring their experience in counselling and their knowledge of the demands of the wider city. Community participation is encouraged (e.g. arts, civic affairs, employment, education).

5. *Member-Peer Discussion Group.* A weekly discussion group of nonprofessional staff and patients has proved extremely useful in developing patient leadership and self-help. Identification with the nonprofessional group leaders as role models and the opportunity for freedom of expression have led to growth on the part of both aides and patients. The meetings have become a prototype for other informal discussions on a range of subjects, some of which would not have been dealt with as readily, as easily, or with as much patient autonomy in a meeting with professional staff.

PATIENT GROUP ACTIVITIES

The group spends its day in various activities which encourage patient self-help. These include communal self-help activities, occupational therapy, recreational therapy and prevocational training.

The aides work with the whole group, subgroups or individuals according to a program planned for each patient. During the period under consideration the patients' products have become less craft-like and increasingly marketable as the group has moved nearer the stage of readiness for work in a sheltered workshop. A few individuals have returned to the job market. A few have sought vocational rehabilitation for which they had been previously unprepared. Most have used the program for improved personal, familial and social adjustment.

OTHER SERVICES BY NONPROFESSIONAL STAFF

Each full-time aide is responsible for *case service* to specific patients. Individual assistance to patients in dealing with social and reality issues is supplemented by patient-aide group discussion of problems, possible solutions and their relationship to patients' attempts to develop more successful adaptive behaviors. In this way the handling of one person's problems in such areas as securing better housing, passing voter literacy tests, finding employment, or seeking welfare stipends becomes an enabling process for other patients.

Aides collect basic social history data and elicit information related to the patients' backgrounds of which they have useful knowledge. They assist patients with applications, phone calls and contacts with those agencies which play major roles in the lives of the poor. Social casework requiring professional skill is under the direction of the supervisor who, through supervision of the aides, has become acquainted with the history of all the patients. Even in the instances requiring professional casework, appropriate and complementary service is provided by the nonprofessionals.

Limited *family service* has been given by aides, not only in relation to patients, but also to assist with those social and mental health problems which are of indirect relationship.

The *home interview*, one or a series, is used at some point with all patients. In some instances the psychiatrist or other professional (nurse, social worker) along with the case aide assigned to the patient meets with the patient and his family at their home with all participating in the interview. In other instances, home interviews are conducted by the nonprofessional aides alone. The home interview serves one or more functions: a diagnostic tool for the study of patterns of family interaction, a therapeutic process for the individual and/or family, a technique to increase involvement of the hard-to-reach patients, a method of handling a crisis situation, or a way of gaining a therapeutically useful view of part of the patient's social reality generally unknown to the psychiatrist.

An informal *survey* of the social, recreational and rehabilitation needs of certain aftercare patients in the mental hygiene clinic was developed and administered by aides. The survey led to the formation of this program. More recently aides have collected data relevant to patients' work interests and skills in order to further prepare the group for vocational rehabilitation.

Experienced and skillful nonprofessionals have been used in *community mental health education* to make more effective contact with their peers than has been accomplished by the use of professionals alone. The community setting and the staff of indigenous workers have fostered those positive aspects of the deprived culture which are supportive of patients' growth toward mental health. Aware of the total city, aides make selective and therapeutic use of positive aspects of the wider city in order to counteract constrictive aspects of ghetto life and widen the emotional and cognitive experience of the patients.

GROUP METHODS OF TRAINING NONPROFESSIONAL MENTAL HEALTH PERSONNEL

1. *Orientation and Observation.* A short orientation period of no more than two to three weeks provides an opportunity for acquiring general information about personality development, human relations, social issues, emotional disorders and health services. Approaches are used

which stimulate questions and discussion. Orientation begins with short, focused, nondidactic lectures in easily understood language by the person with continuing responsibility for nonprofessional training. It proceeds to the use of audiovisual aids, acquaintance with the institution and hypothetical case material. Later, when patterns of questioning and discussion have been established by the aides, others from this program and related programs in the hospital and from the community lead the discussion. The subject matter moves from the general to the specific, from mental health problems to mental health services and ways of providing them in this setting. "Learning about" and "hearing about" are soon supplemented by seeing others in work situations. This observation period allows gradual work involvement with the observers assisting others in tasks related to those projected for them, but less complex and less directly patient-related.

2. *On-the-Job-Training.* Action-oriented nonprofessionals have proved able to use the work as a learning experience. Graduated tasks, shared responsibility and appropriate supervision encourage questions, observations and participation in conferences, rounds and therapeutic activities. In-service training continues throughout the period of work.

3. *Continuous Training Group Experience.* A continuous group experience for the nonprofessionals is led by the training psychiatrist. The goals of the transactional process are increased awareness of those unconscious attitudes which can be antitherapeutic as well as of those which aid patient improvement and staff morale, increased understanding of patient behavior, improved learning and problem solving, and a better ability to translate self-understanding and knowledge into effective work behavior.

These weekly 90-minute meetings are basically unstructured with group discussion and group interaction predominating. However, role playing and role training also take place. Through observation of the interaction within the training experience itself and the use of the social process, problems in interpersonal relationships are worked through with emphasis on those which are work-related. Group support and group reinforcement contribute to improved intrastaff communication; the aim is to transfer this knowledge and improved communication to patient-staff interaction and to patient services.

At this point there are indications that an effective group can contain six to eight persons, that heterogeneity in style of action, speech and manner gives an increased opportunity for a variety of interactions and that regularity of participation is important. Variations in educational level are not necessarily negative factors; the commonality of exposure to some kind of social and economic deprivation seems a universalizing factor. Leaders develop and role differentiation takes place in an atmosphere that is goal-oriented. The group task changes but can be identified at all times. Individual and group movement toward a solution takes place with movement away from leader orientation to peer orientation.

The phases in such a group might be described as those of clarification, observation and evaluation and finally that of autonomous problem solution.

One effect of this type of training is related to the prejudices common in our society. The group experience helps the aides identify blind spots concerning social class and race. In working with deprived minority patients, it has been found therapeutically advantageous for the helping persons to have minimal distortions in such areas. For example, patient conflicts around identity, dependency, sexuality and aggression can thus be better dealt with. Similarly, attitudes of hostility, self-hate and group hate were recognized and handled in this experience.

4. *Nonprofessional Staff Meetings.* A weekly meeting of nonprofessionals alone is another valuable training technique, for the teaching of specific skills and for general staff development. The aides rotate the task of reporter for these conference records. Such a meeting cannot take place until the group has become cohesive, begun to use the continuous training sessions and had some successful work experiences.

Nonprofessional staff meetings begin with the expression of preference for a structured meeting with a topic, move to the phase of ventilation or "bull session," and then to the third most productive phase in which autonomous problem solving is the focus. In these meetings there is less interpretation of interaction and more emphasis on content than in the continuous training groups. It would appear that such issues as peer communication, autonomy and independence, initiative, leadership, roles, values and decision-making can be effectively dealt with by nonprofessional group discussion in the framework described.

The most effective leaders appear to be those who can create a work atmosphere within the meeting, to allow varied expressions of opinion, and to appreciate the different styles of work and skills of their peers. There is a need for research, particularly in the areas of the development of leadership among working-class people. Other studies[5,7] have dealt with a different population and setting. Controlled evaluation of similar types of meetings should be particularly useful in programs using indigenous persons as leaders.

5. *Preparation of Reports.* Daily observations made by the aides concerning individual patients and group atmosphere, group interaction, manifest and latent content become a valuable part of the clinical records. Since many nonprofessionals have greater ease in speaking in their own "in-language" than in writing or in using professional terminology, they should be encouraged to make tapes or to dictate reports.

For instances in which handwritten records are essential, outlined forms at the beginning provide a structure helpful to persons not at ease in writing. Both oral and written anecdotal reports are useful, not only for keeping an ongoing record of patient progress but for developing communication and observation skills.

6. *Staff Enrichment and Development.* Efforts which broaden the horizons of the nonprofessionals lead to increased self-esteem and improved functioning in their job roles. Selected reading, trips, participation in community programs and respected work relationships with other staff and patients all help the helper. As Riessman[12] has pointed out, placing such people in a helper role is often highly therapeutic for them; moreover:

> . . . as the nonprofessionals benefit personally from their helping roles they should become more effective as workers. . . . Such a cycle could be an important positive force in a depressed community.

7. *Individual and Group Supervision.* In the beginning, aides need weekly structured, individual supervision, often with one supervisor only. With experience they may rely more on group supervision at weekly intervals and on informal, spontaneous consultation with various professionals or other nonprofessionals with whom they come in contact in the course of a day's work. In all instances it is important for nonprofessionals to know that there is someone to whom problems may be brought who is readily available to encourage the finding of solutions and to offer support.

8. *Participation in Over-all Departmental Program.* At first professionally led conferences of nonprofessionals alone from their particular program will be likely to facilitate greater participation on their part than will groups of professionals and nonprofessionals from the institution as a whole.[1] As nonprofessionals become less inhibited by the greater verbal ease of professionals and the status differences and more familiar with others in the total program, they will gain awareness of the value to themselves and others of discussing their observations in such meetings. They should be encouraged to participate gradually and in their own mode and language. Thus their ideas and experience may be more widely used by other staff and their own knowledge broadened.

Some generalizations emerging from our experience in training may be made.

1. The main training focus should be continuous work experience which uses institution and community as the field for training.
2. The effectiveness of action-oriented approaches[11] and social processes in training is demonstrable.
3. The relationship of concept to practice and of theory to content should be made explicit.

4. Group training methods can lead to increased learning, greater self-awareness and improved functioning on the part of aides.

5. The need for clear role definition is marked. Attention should be paid to role expectations. In many instances competition between professionals and nonprofessionals, overidentification with professionals or with patients, or the relegation of nonprofessionals to positions of "lower" rather than "different" value can be dealt with or prevented. It is often desirable that aides be trained to function in more than one position. For this reason a combination of structure of tasks, role definition and role flexibility is essential.

6. Clarity of intrastaff communications and productive staff transactions should be goals for professional and nonprofessional staff.

7. In order to teach (and work with) nonprofessional personnel with greater success, professionals need knowledge of factors which may influence work attitudes, values and behavior of persons from deprived backgrounds.

8. Respectful openness on the part of professionals to the development of new training methods which nonprofessionals themselves evolve as appropriate to their needs can contribute to general staff development and morale and to patient service.

9. Career development and further training can afford certain aides the opportunity and incentive to move into related fields as nonprofessionals (e.g. child care, education, work with the aged), to move ahead as nonprofessional supervisors or to become trainers of others.

10. Major responsibility for training and supervision should be vested in someone with a positive and accepting attitude toward working with staff with varying types of skills, professional and nonprofessional.

11. With new roles for nonprofessionals, the future of professionals as supervisors, trainees or consultants presents a significant challenge.

IMPLICATIONS

Consideration must be given to the wider implications of new methods and new careers for the field of mental health and for human relations.[2]

There are at present many long overdue efforts to provide more effective mental health services for the poor.[13] As Harlem Hospital and similar institutions further develop such programs, with the addition of controlled evaluations we shall gain increased understanding of the relationship between the course of recovery from mental illness and sociocultural factors. Even further, such programs will provide the opportunity for knowledge of the effect on personality development of the stresses of poverty, segregation and discrimination.

New methods of psychiatric service, which use the social process as a therapeutic vehicle, may prove applicable to other programs in need of techniques more therapeutically useful to deprived persons.

Similarly, new training methods, which use group interaction and group reinforcement, have proven useful for nonprofessional mental health aides. They have used this training to develop a sense of identity and of value in their work, to be better able to communicate with patients and with other staff and to translate understanding and knowledge into effective therapeutic behaviors. This, too, has implications for other programs in need of new sources of manpower.

Finally, we turn to the social implications of these new approaches. The need for human services for the people of economically disadvantaged communities is marked, particularly in health, education and social welfare. With unemployment disproportionately high, the need for work is even greater. The use of a previously untapped sector of the community for necessary work in mental health thus serves two desperate needs.

REFERENCES

[1]CHRISTMAS, J. J. **1965.** Psychiatric rehabilitation with nonprofessional aides. Unpublished report.

[2]CHIRSTMAS, J. J., AND E. B. DAVIS. **1965.** Group therapy programs with the socially deprived in community psychiatry. Int. J. Grp. Psychother. 15 (4): 464.

[3](a) DAVIS, E. B. Psychiatric perspectives on the current racial crisis. Paper delivered at Amer. Psych. Assn., Los Angeles, May 1964.

[4](b) DAVIS, E. B. From family membership to personal and social identity. The Negro Family Paper delivered at University of California, Berkeley, November, 1964.

[5]FELDMAN, L. J., AND N. E. ZINBERG. **1964.** Application of group methods in college teaching Int. J. Grp. Psychother 14: 344–359.

[6]FENTON, N., AND K. WILTSE. **1963.** Group Methods in the Public Welfare Program. Pacific Books. Palo Alto, California.

[7]GRUEN, W. Variations in leadership as determinants of group processes in therapy-oriented training groups. Paper presented at Am. Grp. Psychother. Assn., San Francisco, January, 1965.

[8]LEVINE, L. S. Overreactions to dissent: a threat to survival of the democratic ideal. Paper delivered at San Francisco Humanist Assn., San Francisco, May, 1964.

[9]LEWIS, H. Poverty and the behavior of low-income families. Paper delivered at Amer. Orthopsychiatric Assn., Chicago, March, 1964.

[10]REIFF, R., AND F. RIESSMAN. 1964. The Indigenous Nonprofessional: A Strategy of Change in Community Action and Community Mental Health. National Institute of Labor Education. New York, N.Y.

[11](a) RIESSMAN, F. 1964. New Approaches to Mental Health Treatment for Labor and Low Income Groups. National Institute of Labor Education, New York, N.Y.

[12](b) RIESSMAN, F. Training of nonprofessionals. Paper delivered at Howard University Center for Youth and Community Studies, Washington, D.C., April, 1964.

[13]RIESSMAN, F., J. COHEN AND A. PEARL, eds. 1964. Mental Health of the Poor. Free Press of Glencoe. New York, N.Y.

SUGGESTED ADDITIONAL READINGS

Avrunin, William. The volunteer in case work treatment. *The Family,* 1944, Vol. 25, No. 4, 137–143.

Barker, Robert L., and Briggs, Thomas L. *Trends in the utilization of social work personnel: An evaluative research of the literature.* Research Report Number Two, Utilization of Social Work Personnel in Mental Hospitals Project (mimeographed), NIMH Grant MH-1420. National Association of Social Workers, Inc., 2 Park Avenue, New York, N.Y., 10016, June, 1966.

Barr, Sherman. Some observations on the practice of indigenous nonprofessional workers. Paper presented at the Council on Social Work Education, 14th Annual Program Meeting, New York, January, 1966.

Berenson, Bernard G., Carkhuff, Robert R., and Myrus, Pamela. The interpersonal functioning and training of college students. *Journal of Counseling Psychology*, 1966, Vol. 13, No. 4, 441–446.

Berlin, Jerome I., and Wyckoff, L. Benjamin. *General relationship improvement program*, 4th ed. Atlanta, Georgia: Human Development Institute, Inc., 1964.

Brennen, Earl C. College students and mental health programs for children. *American Journal of Public Health*, 1967, Vol. 57, No. 10, 1767–1771.

Burmeister, Eva E. Child-care worker in residential treatment—professional or nonprofessional? Paper presented at the meeting of the American Orthopsychiatric Association, Washington, D. C., March, 1967.

Carkhuff, Robert R., and Truax, Charles B. Training in counseling and psychotherapy: an evaluation of an integrated didactic and experiential approach. *Journal of Consulting Psychology*, 1965, Vol. 29, No. 4, 333–336.

Chambers, Guinevere S., and Foster, Genevieve W. Toward improved competence in child-care workers. 2. A two-level training program. *Children*, 1966, Vol. 13, No. 5, 185–189.

Chaplan, Abraham A., Price, Jr., John M., Zuckerman, Isadore, and Ek, Jon. The role of volunteers in community mental health programs. *Community Mental Health Journal*, 1966, Vol. 2, No. 3, 255–258.

Curriculum Outline, Chicago State Hospital Pilot Program for Mental Health Aide Training in Collaboration with the Manpower Development Training Act. Mimeographed document, 1967. Available from Engandela, Victor, J., Director Mental Health Aide Training

Program, Chicago State Hospital, 6500 West Irving Park Road, Chicago, Ill. 60634.

Davison, Gerald C. The training of undergraduates as social reinforcers for autistic children. In Ullmann, Leonard P., and Krasner, Leonard (Eds.) *Case studies in behavior modification.* New York: Holt, Rinehart and Winston, Inc., 1966. Pp. 146–148.

Deane, William N., and Ansbacher, Heinz I. Attendant-patient commonality as a psychotherapeutic factor. *Journal of Individual Psychology,* 1962, Vol. 18, 157–167.

Eisdorfer, Carl, and Golann, Stuart E. Principles for the training of "new professionals" in mental health. *Community Mental Health Journal,* in press.

Ewalt, Patricia (Ed.). *Mental Hospital Volunteers.* Charles C. Thomas, 1967.

Fellows, Lloyd, and Wolpin, Milton. High school psychology trainees in a mental hospital. Paper presented at the California State Psychological Association Convention, 1966.

Fisher, Harriet, and Sternberg, Sydney. Social work technicians—a manpower answer. Paper presented at American Association of Psychiatric Clinics for Children Meeting, San Francisco, 1966.

Frechtman, Bernice Wolf. Education for and by volunteers—The psychiatric social worker's role. *Journal of Psychiatric Social Work,* 1951–1952, Vol. 21, No. 4, 177–180.

Frechtman, Bernice Wolf. The utilization of volunteers in sociodynamic psychotherapy. In Pollak, Otto, and collaborators, *Social science and psychotherapy for children.* New York: Russell Sage Foundation, 1952, pp. 170–199.

Glasser, William. *Reality therapy.* New York: Harper & Row, 1965.

Golann, Stuart E. Initial findings of the follow-up study of child development counselors. *American Journal of Public Health and the Nation's Health,* 1967, Vol. 57, No. 10, 1759–1765.

Gorlich, Elizabeth H. Volunteers in institutions for delinquents. *Children,* 1967, Vol. 14, No. 4, 147–151.

Hallowitz, Emanuel, and Riessman, Frank. The role of the indigenous nonprofessional in a community mental health neighborhood service center program. Paper presented at American Orthopsychiatry Association Meetings, San Francisco, April, 1966.

Houtz, Fanny. Volunteers in treatment. *Survey,* 1944, Vol. 80, No. 10, 285–287.

Hromadka, Van G. Toward improved competence in child-care workers. 1. A look at what they do. *Children,* 1966, Vol. 13, No. 5, 181–184.

Hunter, G. F., Goldman, Arnold R., and Smith, Robert S. *Mental health workers—Selection, training, and evaluation of recent college graduates serving as therapeutic technicians.* Philadelphia State Hospital, Philadelphia, Pa. Mimeographed report.

Karowe, Harris E. How volunteers can help disadvantaged children. *Children*, 1967, Vol. 14, No. 4, 151–156.

Kennedy, Emery G., and Strowig, R. Wray. Support personnel for the counselor: Their technical and non-technical roles and preparation. *Guidance Journal*, 1967, Vol. 45, 857–861.

Korson, Selig M., and Hayes, Winifred L. Empathic relationship therapy utilizing student nurses: A five-year pilot study. *American Journal of Psychiatry*, 1966, Vol. 123, No. 2, 213–218.

Lourie, Reginald S., Rioch, Margaret J., and Schwartz, Samuel. The concept of a training program for child development counselors. *American Journal of Public Health*, 1967, Vol. 57, No. 10, 1754–1758.

MacLennan, Beryce W. New careers as human service aides. *Children*, 1966, Vol. 13, No. 5, 190–194.

Mann, Lester, Wright, Thomas S., Hilsendager, Donald R., and Jack, Harold K. A pilot training program to develop physical recreation leaders for work with emotionally disturbed children. *Community Mental Health Journal*, 1967, Vol. 3, No. 2, 159–162.

McGee, Richard K. A New program for training psychological assistants. Paper presented at the annual meeting of the American Psychological Association, New York, September, 1966.

Meyer, Carol H. *Staff development in public welfare agencies.* New York: Columbia University Press, 1966.

Mitchell, William E. Amicatherapy: Theoretical perspectives and an example of practice. *Community Mental Health Journal*, 1966, Vol. 2, No. 4, 307–314.

Patterson, Cecil H. Subprofessional functions and short-term training. *Counselor Education and Supervision*, 1965, Vol. 4, 144–146.

Pierce, Richard, Carkhuff, Robert R., and Berensen, Bernard G. The differential effects of high and low functioning counselors upon counselors-in-training. *Journal of Clinical Psychology*, 1967, Vol. 23, No. 2, 212–215.

Reding, Georges R., and Goldsmith, Ethel F. The nonprofessional hospital volunteer as a member of the psychiatric consultation team. *Community Mental Health Journal*, 1967, Vol. 3, No. 3, 267–272.

Reiff, Robert, and Riessman, Frank. The indigenous nonprofessional. *Community Mental Health Journal*, 1965, Monograph No. 1.

Reinherz, Helen. Leadership of student volunteers. *Mental Hospitals*, 1962, Vol. 13, No. 11. 600–603.

Riessman, Frank. The revolution in social work: The new nonprofessional. *Trans-Action*, 1964, Vol. 2, No. 1, 12–17.

Riessman, Frank. Strategies and suggestions for training nonprofessionals. Mimeographed paper. Department of Psychiatry, Albert Einstein College of Medicine, New York.

Sanders, Richard. New manpower for mental hospital service. Paper presented at the University of Rochester Conference on "Emergent Approaches to Mental Health Problems," June, 1965.

Schlossberg, Nancy K. Sub-professionals: To be or not to be. *Counselor Education and Supervision*, 1967, Vol. 6, 108–113.

Siegel, Benjamin. Students as professional aides in direct patient relationships in a state hospital. Paper presented at the annual meeting of the American Psychological Association, New York, September, 1966.

Siegel, Saul M., and Colarelli, Nick J. Gaining more from research experiences. *Mental Hospitals*, 1964, Vol. 15, 666–670.

Spergel, Irving. Role behavior and supervision of the untrained group worker. *Social Work*, 1962, Vol. 7, No. 3, 69–76.

Tharp, Roland G., Wetzel, Ralph J., and Thorne, Gaylord L. The natural environment: Challenge and opportunity. *Welfare in Review*, in press.

Walker, C. Eugene. The development and evaluation of a psychology practicum program for undergraduate students. Paper presented at the California State Psychological Association Convention, 1966.

Warme, G. E. Consulting with aide-therapists. *Archives of General Psychiatry*, 1965, Vol. 13, 432–438.

Yeager, Wayne, Sowder, Wilson T., and Hardy, Albert V. The mental health worker: A new public health professional. *American Journal of Public Health*, 1962, Vol. 52, No. 10, 1625–1630.

SOME TRAINING PROGRAMS

Materials describing pioneer formal training programs leading to what has been called "preprofessional," "semiprofessional," or "subprofessional" status in mental health and related fields may be obtained from the following sources.[1]

[1]The editor is grateful to Dr. Sam Silverstein, Chief, Utilization & Development Section, Experimental and Special Training Branch, Division of Manpower and Training Programs, National Institute of Mental Health, Chevy Chase, Maryland, for his help in locating these projects.

"Associate Degree in Mental Health Technology." Louise M. Atty, Department of Nursing, Daytona Beach Junior College, P. O. Box 1111, Daytona Beach, Florida 32015.

"Graduate Program in Child Care and Child Development." Dr. Guinevere S. Chambers, Training Program Director, Western Psychiatric Institute and Clinic, University of Pennsylvania, Pittsburgh, Pennsylvania.

"Training Mature Women as Mental Health Rehabilitation Workers." Dr. Ida F. Davidoff, Department of Psychiatry, Albert Einstein College of Medicine, Eastchester Road and Morris Park Avenue, Bronx, New York 10461.

"Associate Leader and Case Aid Training Program." Dr. Victor A. Gelineau, Director of Case Aid Program, Boston State Hospital, 74 Fenwood Road, Boston, Mass. 02115.

"Two-year Program for the Training of Mental Health Workers." Dr. John Hadley, Department of General and Applied Studies, Purdue University, Fort Wayne, Indiana.

"Undergraduate Education of Child Care Specialists." Dr. Robert S. Harper, Professor, Department of Psychology, Knox College, Galesburg, Illinois.

"Psychiatric Technician Training Program." Dr. Alan Kraft, Director of Fort Logan Mental Health Center, Fort Logan, Colorado.

"Training Program for Child Development Counselors." Dr. Reginald S. Lourie, Director, Department of Psychiatry, Children's Hospital of D. C., Washington, D. C.

"Training Manpower for Health and Mental Health Services in New York City." Dr. Harris B. Peck, Associate Professor of Psychiatry, Lincoln Hospital, Albert Einstein College of Medicine, 333 Southern Boulevard, Bronx, New York 10454.

"A Multidisciplinary Training Program for Houseparents." Dr. Henry Platt, Director, Psychological Training, The Devereux Foundation, Devon, Pa.

"Training New Workers for Social Interaction Therapy." Dr. Richard

Sanders, Director of Psychological Services, Research and Development, Philadelphia State Hospital, Philadelphia, Pa.

"Educational Program for Alcoholism Counselors." Dr. Abraham M. Schneidmuhl, Director, Alcoholism Clinic, Baltimore City Health Department, 900 American Building, Baltimore and South Streets, Baltimore, Maryland 21202.

PART 3

Varieties of Programs Using Nonprofessionals

Introduction

THE papers in this Part were chosen to demonstrate the wide variety of settings in which nonprofessionals can be utilized to help children, the range of problems that may be alleviated by this approach, the many types of persons used in such programs, and the numerous ways in which these people can be transformed from strangers into highly significant others to troubled children. The physical settings described include public schools during or after school hours, a religious community center, a special day school for autistic children, the children's unit of a mental hospital, a residential cottage setting, an institute for temporary group care of children on welfare, and a child's own home.

As implied by the settings mentioned above, the types of cases involved also run the gamut from the underachiever, the neglected, the withdrawn and phobic, through the acting-out child, to the organic and psychotic. In fact, in the majority of cases reported, the difficulties are quite severe. Probably the desperation felt by people who want to help such severely disturbed children, plus the feeling in certain cases that nothing else has worked, promotes the inventiveness and courage required to undertake innovative treatment methods.

A glimpse is also provided in this chapter of the great variety of groups with potential for providing psychotherapeutic and remedial agents. They include mothers selected from the community, the elderly, and the college student.

How do these nonprofessionals become significant others to disturbed children—how do they become meaningful enough to the child to promote his social-psychological well-being? As befits an innovative movement, the ways to bring this about show great variety. None of the projects described here was extremely restrictive in selecting the nonprofessionals. But some projects relied rather heavily upon finding the right person. Thus, Nichtern relied on knowledge and personal contacts rather than publicity to recruit "teacher moms" who would be empathic, realistic, and warm; and Johnston informally observed the behavior of potential applicants when they came in contact with children to help her select the applicants she thought would be most naturally suited to be effective foster grandparents. Cowen, Zax, and Laird relied on the natural enthusiasm they could expect to find among students in elementary education and psychology, and tried to eliminate only those few who would be obviously unfit.

The primary reliance is thus placed on the training or supervisory experience which the professionals, or, as in Cowen et al., professionals-in-training, provide. Obviously, further weeding out by nature and design can take place during the early phases of this process. In fact, however, even these informal selective procedures provided people who usually met all of the professional's expectations. Johnston particularly reports many of the fears that are easily aroused in professionals about using nonprofessionals, and describes how these fears were laid to rest by the actual results.

In most projects there was some, but not much, advance training given concerning theory and practice. The natural enthusiasm and personableness of the selected nonprofessionals is relied upon to get things started. But, always, a good deal of opportunity is offered the nonprofessional to report on his observations and experiences, and to receive supervision of his work. The behaviorally oriented programs do provide more structure and specific training for their nonprofessionals; no doubt because the procedures they use are more clearly specifiable and more easily taught than, say, warmth or empathy; but later in this book the reader will find projects teaching even behaviors such as these.

That the workers did become significant others to the children, often with little in the way of formal instruction, is attested to by the positive reports about the children's reactions, and the effectiveness of the programs in helping the children. Some also report positive effects on the nonprofessionals—notably, Cowen, Zax, and Laird, who felt their volunteers acquired more realistic attitudes toward professionals and more accepting attitudes toward disturbed children. Johnston not only found the work of significant benefit to the children and her nonprofessional workers, but also described what is only implicit in the remaining articles—that benefits also may accrue to the professionals and to the agency itself.

A College Student Volunteer Program in the Elementary School Setting

EMORY L. COWEN
MELVIN ZAX
JAMES D. LAIRD*

A college student, afterschool, day-care volunteer program for primary grade children with manifest or incipient emotional problems is reported. Attitudes differentiating volunteers from nonvolunteers and changes in volunteer attitudes following participation in the program are identified. A description of the program itself, including objective process data and evaluation of outcome indices is presented. Interrelations among various process measures, among the several outcome measures, and, finally, between process and outcome measures are summarized.

Increasingly in recent years, it has become apparent that existing resources within the mental health helping professions are insufficient to meet social needs. Such an awareness encourages consideration of new

Reprinted from *Community Mental Health Journal*, 1966, Vol. 2, No. 4, 319–328, with the permission of the Columbia University Press and the authors. Brief biographies of the authors have been omitted.

*The present research was carried out as part of a grant from the National Institutes of Mental Health, CSRB Branch (MH 01500-01). This support is gratefully acknowledged. The authors express their sincere appreciation to David Beach and Joanne Traum for their participation in the classroom observation and data analysis phases of the project. Miss Traum's participation was made possible by her appointment to an NSF undergraduate research fellowship. The cooperation of Joseph Merenda, Principal; Louis D. Izzo, Project Psychologist; and Mary Ann Trost, Project Social Worker, in making necessary arrangements at the school is also gratefully acknowledged. And finally, we acknowledge the participation of Robert Pierce and Philip Miller as group leaders.

approaches for the resolution of real and pressing social problems. Whether one thinks in terms of shoring up present helping structures, of developing techniques better suited for the large masses who are seemingly unreached by present methods, or of considering models that emphasize early detection and prevention, one is led to question long-standing assumptions concerning the necessity of advanced, high-level professional training as a prerequisite for *all* those involved in mental health-type "helping" interactions.

One practical result has been the increased use, in a variety of mental health settings, of two types of nonprofessional personnel. One group, the subprofessionals, is characteristically paid and is given specific, focused, and time-limited training designed to fit them to some particular role and task (Project Re-Ed, 1964; Sanders, 1967). Another group of nonprofessionals is the volunteers, most often college students (Umbarger, Dalsimer, Morrison, & Breggin, 1962; Holzberg & Knapp, 1965), who receive little training and no pay.

While there has certainly been a proliferation of subprofessional and volunteer programs in the mental health sphere in recent years, such programs have, understandably, been primarily service oriented. If a sounder basis for reshaping mental health helping services is to be developed and if volunteer and subprofessional manpower is to have an increasingly important and extensive role in this "hypothetical new order," it becomes essential that such emergent programs be carefully researched in their multiple facets. Two notable exceptions to the general absence of research on these programs have been Kantor's (1962) evaluation of the effectiveness of the Harvard program, for the patients, and Holzberg's extensive program of research on the effects of participation in his program on the student volunteers themselves (Holzberg & Gewirtz, 1963; Holzberg, Gewirtz, & Ebner, 1964; Holzberg & Knapp, 1965; Knapp & Holzberg, 1964).

The program to be described in the present report involved college undergraduates working in the school setting with emotionally disturbed youngsters referred by teachers and other school personnel. The program was a relatively modest one, which operated for a very short period of time, and was set up primarily as a first step in evolving a model for this type of activity that might be effectively integrated with a long-range program for early detection and prevention of emotional disorders in the school setting. Despite these limitations of size and duration, preliminary research evaluations of the following issues were undertaken: (a) What types of students volunteer for a program of this type and in what ways are they differentiable from their nonvolunteer peers? (b) What types of changes, if any, take place in volunteers as a function of participation in this program? (c) What is the general nature of the program itself, descriptively, including some estimate of range transactions that may take place between volunteer and child in this type of setting, i.e., process analysis? (d) What relationships may be found between types of volunteer-child interactions and any one of several outcome measures available for the child? (e) What changes in behavior and evaluation of the children who are exposed to the program take place following such participation?

METHOD

Recruitment of Volunteers

The prospective program was viewed as one specific, feasible model for early secondary prevention in the school setting. Its purpose was to provide a meaningful relationship and beneficial experience for emotionally disturbed children by pairing them with active, enthusiastic, ego-involved college student volunteers. The possibility that the projected program might also contribute to primary prevention through its effects on the attitudes of the volunteers was also considered. To maximize the possibility, attempts were made to recruit volunteers from among elementary education majors. If these students, who were themselves about to become teachers, could get to know, work with, and learn about children experiencing psychological difficulties, perhaps they could acquire an increment in "gut" understanding, which would have beneficial effects throughout their subsequent teaching careers.

With cooperation from the staff of the School of Education, 8 elementary education majors were recruited as volunteers for the program; there were 15 additional volunteers from an abnormal psychology class. Each of these 23 candidates was interviewed by one of three advanced clinical psychology graduate students who were to be affiliated with the program. No attempt was made to select volunteers on the basis of a set of preconceived positive personality attributes; rather the simple goal was to weed out the several students who seemed either flagrantly maladjusted or grossly unsuited for the purposes of the program. All 8 education student volunteers were accepted for the program. Of the 15 psychology students interviewed, 3 were dropped for personal reasons and another 3 because their schedule of free hours did not match those required for the program; thus there remained a total of 17 acceptable volunteers—8 from education and 9 from psychology.

Evaluation of Volunteers

A group-testing session was set up before the program got under way. It was made clear to the volunteers that the data to be collected were not, in any way, to be used for selection purposes (which they were not) but rather were part of a research appraisal of the overall program.

The instrument used to evaluate volunteer attitudes and change in such attitudes following participation in the program was an adaptation of the semantic differential (SD) (Osgood, Suci, & Tannenbaum, 1957) designed for this purpose. For our use, the instrument included nine critical concepts, related to schools and mental health, each of which was rated in terms of 17 polar scales, mostly of the evaluative type.

This instrument was administered about one week before the program started and again about one week after it ended, thus providing some basis for a pre-post comparison of attitudes. A control group of eight education and nine psychology students comparable to the volunteers, except for the fact that they did not actually volunteer for the program, was also evaluated with this measure. It was only possible to test this latter group once; hence they are controls only for the "pre"-point in our sequence.

Instruction and Training for Volunteers

A brief effort at orientation of volunteers was carried out before the program got under way. A fairly lengthy meeting was held at the university to discuss such issues as mental health problems in modern society, professional manpower shortages, the need for work in early detection and prevention of emotional problems, the philosophy of the present program, its objectives, and the place of the volunteers in it. At that time some possible ways in which the program might operate were considered. However, this remained relatively unstructured, and it was stressed that the volunteer would have considerable freedom and latitude. Indeed, the project was described as an exploratory one, and volunteers were encouraged to follow their natural reflexes and to feel free to try out new ideas and to follow up hunches, viewing themselves neither as therapists nor as intellectualized analyzers of personality. Rather, we attempted to foster a spontaneous, warm, "friend" relationship with the child.

In still another preprogram meeting, the volunteer group was taken to the school where the principal, as well as the social worker and psychologist attached to the basic early detection and prevention project being conducted there (Zax & Cowen, 1967), met and spoke with them. The volunteers were given the opportunity to go through the building, to become acquainted with the equipment and facilities that would be at their disposal and to meet and talk with other key school personnel.

Selection and Evaluation of Children

The program was housed in a single elementary school in Rochester, New York, in which was located the broader program for early detection and prevention of emotional disorders (Zax & Cowen, 1967). The school, although a relatively small one, covered a fairly large geographic area and included children ranging socioeconomically from lower-lower class to upper-middle class. The contemplated afterschool activities program was described to the teaching staff of the primary grades, and teachers and project personnel were asked to refer those youngsters who they considered might profit from it. Thirty-four primary grade children were referred, and for each, the classroom teacher submitted three types of referral materials. The first of these was a teachers' behavior rating scale, adapted from our earlier work

(Cowen, Izzo, Miles, Telschow, Trost, & Zax, 1963), including 25 negative behavioral characteristics (e.g., "is dependent on others," "is upset by criticism," "is disobedient," "is critical of others," etc.). The teacher was asked to check those items which described the behavior of the child being rated and to provide an intensity rating along a three-point scale for each characteristic so designated. In addition the teacher made a single overall adjustment rating for the child based on a five-point scale. The second measure used was a 34-item Adjective Check-List (ACL), divided equally into positive and negative items (trait-descriptive adjectives). The teacher was asked to check all relevant descriptive terms, using S and V, respectively, to designate "somewhat" and "very." The final teacher-submitted item was a prose referral statement indicating the specific nature of the child's principal problem(s) as she perceived them.

Although the majority of the 34 referrals were initiated by the teachers, a certain number were also referred by project personnel. The latter included several youngsters who had not yet manifested overt problems, but who were judged by the mental health clinical services (MHCS) team, on the basis of social work interview, psychological evaluation, and/or actual observation of behavior (Cowen, *et al.*, 1963), to have a high probability for showing such behavior in the near future. The total pool of 34 youngsters reflected, in the main, three major classes of problems: acting-out; shyness, timidity, and withdrawal behavior; and problems of failure in educational achievement.

To establish some crude basis for preliminary evaluation, half of the youngsters were included in the afterschool activities program and became an experimental (E) group. The other half, matched roughly in terms of age, sex, grade, and judged overall severity of problem, became a control (C) group.

Parents of the experimental children were contacted via form letter over the signatures of the school principal and the MHCS team. In this letter the program was described as a recreational one, which would be made available to certain primary graders who might be expected to profit from and to enjoy such an experience. All parents so contacted agreed to have their youngsters participate, and our final E group included 11 boys and 6 girls.

The several teachers' forms were submitted for all E and C youngsters about one week before the program got under way. The same forms were done a second time and resubmitted for all 34 children about one month after the program ended, shortly before the end of the school year. In each case the relevant observation period was defined as the two-week time block immediately preceding the ratings.

Since it was evident that the postproject ratings by the teachers might well have been contaminated by their awareness of the child's assignment to the E or C group, an attempt was made to obtain independent observation and evaluation of these youngsters by naive judges.

To this end, an 18-item behavior rating scale was developed for use in the actual classroom situations. Twelve of these items consisted of full seven-point scales ranging from a theoretically positive extreme, +3 (e.g., "responds pleasantly when approached") to a theoretically negative extreme, −3 (e.g., "rebuffs others when approached"). The remaining six items were "half-items," reflecting only the negative extreme of the continuum (from 0 to −3), e.g., "disrupts class" (−3) or "seeks attention from teacher" (−3). There was a clear-cut preference for items to reflect actual, ongoing, observable behavior rather than inferences about the child.

In a prior reliability study two naive observers, one an advanced undergraduate psychology major and the other a second-year social psychology graduate student, observed the behavior of a sample of 15 primary grade youngsters in another school. An obtained inter-judge $r = .79$, based on total scale scores, suggested that this instrument was sufficiently reliable for use in the evaluation of the afterschool activities program.

Accordingly, the judges then observed all E and C youngsters in the actual classroom setting over two 45-minute observation periods. Eight presumably healthy, well-adjusted, symptom-free children were intermixed in the observational groups, thereby providing an opportunity for a small validity assessment of the instrument. The mean behavioral rating for the combined E and C groups was 7.7, while the comparable figure for the eight normal "extras" was 16.0 ($t = 2.10, p > .05$), indicating that seemingly well-adjusted youngsters can indeed be differentiated from children with problems on this behavioral index.

Course of the School Program

Volunteers were assigned to the children on a one-to-one basis, although in practice, during the course of the program, they often formed small and, usually, loosely structured groups. As it turned out there were 3 male volunteers and 14 female, which did not match very closely the referral pattern of 11 boys and 6 girls. The 3 male volunteers were assigned to 3 boys for whom a male identification model was considered to be strongly indicated. All other assignments were made on a random basis. Three groups of from 5 to 7 volunteers were set up, each under the direct supervision of an advanced clinical psychology graduate student. The latter were themselves under the supervision of the clinical psychologist directing the program. Each volunteer group went to the school twice a week. The volunteers arrived at the end of the school day, at 3:30 p.m., met their children, and engaged in whatever the day's activities were to be for about 70 minutes.

Virtually the entire resources of the school were placed at the disposal of the group. This included the gymnasium, auditorium, playground, music room, arts and craft shop, home economics room, game room, several kindergartens, etc. Our belief was that a variety of activities and settings within the school building, emphasizing expression, recreation, and cathartic activity could provide potentially suitable vehicles through which the undergraduate volunteer and child might interact.

In order to arrive at some clearer picture of the nature of the modal volunteer-child transaction, a form was developed to assess the amount of time devoted to varying activities. This form included a series of descriptive categories that appeared to encompass the full range of possible activities by the child. The categories used, each defined in several sentences for the volunteer, included: *running, semi-organized physical play, organized play, exploring, competitive table games, co-operative and constructive table activities, artistic activities,* and *talking.* A generalized *other* category was also provided. This encompassed *reading, school-type activities, food-making,* and several others with negligible frequencies. The volunteer also provided an estimate of the percentage of total time spent by the child with others, either children or volunteers (i.e., contacts other than the specific one-to-one volunteer-child interaction).

Each volunteer submitted "process" data three times during the course of the program: at the conclusion of each third of the total program period. At these same intervals, the volunteer also submitted S-D ratings for the following two concepts: *the child that you are working with* and *the type of relationship you have had with your child.* For each set of ratings a single summed evaluative score, reflecting perceived goodness of the child and perceived adequacy of the relationship, was derived, and for convenience of data analysis, these measures were considered together with the basic process indices.

The afterschool program got under way the first week in March and lasted, on a prearranged basis, until the second week in May. It was broken twice by one week, nonoverlapping vacations once for the school children and once for the volunteers; hence, a maximum of about 14 or 15 meetings in the school setting was possible during the planned program period.

The volunteers brought considerable enthusiasm to the program and, indeed, embellished it in ways not anticipated beforehand. They would often provide certain "extras" that they felt might be helpful or interesting to their child. Illustratively, they might bring special toys or games "borrowed" from a younger sibling, relative, or friend or even purchased on their own. Several of the girls brought construction materials to fabricate toys or objects and, on quite a few occasions, brought along food to be prepared (e.g., eggs to be boiled and made into egg salad sandwiches, or brownie and other cake mixes to be baked and consumed during the activity period). Many volunteers soon began to feel the need to "do more" for the child than could be accomplished during the limited meeting periods. Several correspondences between volunteers and children sprang up during vacation periods, and a rash of special outside activities, both on individual-pair and small-group bases, sprang up. In the final weeks of the program, for example, many volunteers brought their youngsters up to the university to see the campus and to have dinner with them. Some were taken to see a baseball game or other type of athletic event. Trips were arranged to the downtown area, to an animal shelter, to the local zoo, and for picnicking. Though none of the foregoing activities were preplanned as part of the program, they reflect well the interest and dedication of the volunteers.

Volunteer Discussion Groups

One of the fundamental aims of the program was to provide the volunteer an opportunity to think about, talk about, and integrate his actual contact experiences, primarily with the child but perhaps also with the parents or teachers with whom he might be in touch. We wished also to provide the opportunity for advanced graduate students in clinical psychology to acquire experience in a supervisory, consultative, and resource role vis-à-vis less well-trained subprofessional manpower, acting in mental health-related roles in a community setting. To further these objectives, at the very end of each afternoon's activity in the school, the volunteer group and the graduate student leader returned to the campus, as a unit, for a post-mortem discussion session, generally lasting about an hour, from 5 to 6 p.m. At these meetings, volunteers discussed specific children and the problems they presented, critical incidents that they had experienced, issues of understanding children's behavior, some of their own anxieties and concerns, and specific problems of technique, handling, and intervention. These sessions appeared to provide the volunteer a useful opportunity to learn around the vehicle of the very recent, quite vivid, concrete, and emotionally impactful experiences they had had. The experience suggests that the close temporal contiguity between activity and discussion period and maintenance of continuous group contact furthered these objectives.

Most of these sessions were recorded and were discussed weekly by the graduate student group with the clinical psychologist in charge of the program. The focus of these latter meetings was on the handling of the student discussion sessions rather than on the children themselves. Over a period of time, it became increasingly clear that the optimal role of the leader was not the "spinal cord" therapist's role, an easy and logical one for clinicians to slip into. Rather, it was one of being an issue-centered, discussion-oriented, contributing member of the group. The model was that of a teacher–discussion leader, always striving to bring relevant issues closer to the surface, paced so as to allow for the considerable perceptivity and diagnostic acumen of the volunteer. In many instances, with careful leads and transitional observations, the leader could create a situation that allowed the volunteer group, following some struggling, groping, and pursuit of blind alleys, to come to some meaningful and acceptable understandings of children's behavior, their own attitudes and behavior, and the interaction of the two. More concrete illustrations of this process in action have been presented elsewhere (Zax & Cowen, 1967).

RESULTS

Attributes of Volunteers

In order to determine the pattern, if any, of differentiating attributes of volunteers, direct comparisons of the volunteer and control groups, based on t ratios, were undertaken for the S-D responses. A substantial number of significant differences were observed. These are summarized in Table 1. With 9 concepts and 17 scales included in the present form, a total of 153 comparisons were made between E and C group members. The 32 significant differences at $p = .05$ or beyond exceed chance expectancy and manifest an internal consistency suggestive of genuine differences between the two groups.

Changes in Volunteers Following Participation

In order to identify the nature of attitude changes in volunteers, if any, following participation in the afterschool program, comparisons of pre- and postexperience responses to the S-D were carried out. In this case, since two testing of the same group of 17 S's were being compared, a matched-pair t test was used for the analysis.

Once again, a substantial number of significant attitude changes were found when comparing pre- vs. postexperience attitudes of the volunteers.

TABLE 1

Semantic Differential Comparisons of Volunteers (V) and Controls (C)

Concepts and Scales	Mean V	Mean C	t
Elementary Schools			
cooperative-uncooperative	2.24	3.35	2.88**
interesting-boring	2.18	3.35	2.46*
active-passive	1.88	3.47	3.63**
tense-relaxed	5.11	4.00	2.47*
good-bad	1.82	2.65	2.14*
strong-weak	2.88	3.94	2.56*
Emotionally Disturbed Children			
helpful-harmful	3.41	4.53	2.90**
worthless-valuable	5.71	4.41	2.39*
Mental Health			
unfriendly-friendly	5.59	4.71	2.44*
cooperative-uncooperative	2.53	3.47	2.72*
good-bad	1.59	2.59	2.16*
active-passive	2.35	3.35	2.39*
unpredictable-predictable	5.06	3.94	2.56*
Mental Health Workers			
cooperative-uncooperative	1.53	2.12	2.07*
pleasant-unpleasant	1.53	2.12	2.07*
cold-warm	6.06	5.35	2.25*
Myself			
pleasant-unpleasant	1.88	2.47	2.07*
Profession of Teaching			
strong-weak	2.41	3.24	2.36*
School Principal			
effective-ineffective	2.12	3.24	2.25*
fair-unfair	1.88	2.88	2.85**
cooperative-uncooperative	2.00	3.00	3.23**
unfriendly-friendly	5.82	4.94	2.68*
cold-warm	5.24	4.18	3.11**
helpful-harmful	1.94	2.94	3.12**
excitable-calm	5.71	4.71	2.96**
pleasant-unpleasant	2.18	3.41	3.46**
good-bad	1.88	3.00	3.78**
interesting-boring	1.82	3.24	2.97**
Teachers			
cooperative-uncooperative	1.94	2.59	2.75**
strong-weak	2.24	2.94	2.13*
effective-ineffective	1.82	2.65	2.25*
fair-unfair	1.76	2.71	3.27**

Note.—Each scale in the table is listed so that the adjective to the left corresponds to 1 and the adjective to the right corresponds to 7 on the actual rating forms used by *Ss*.

*Denotes significance at the .05 level.

**Denotes significance at the .01 level.

TABLE 2

Pre- and Postprogram Comparisons in Semantic Differential Responses of Volunteers

CONCEPTS AND SCALES	MEAN PRE	MEAN POST	t
Children			
active-passive	1.29	1.17	3.11**
tense-relaxed	5.41	4.41	2.38**
Elementary Schools			
interesting-boring	2.18	2.71	3.50**
active-passive	1.88	2.71	4.20**
tense-relaxed	5.12	4.35	2.62*
unfriendly-friendly	5.71	5.29	3.35**
pleasant-unpleasant	2.35	2.82	3.11**
Emotionally Disturbed Children			
effective-ineffective	5.00	4.12	2.99**
active-passive	3.71	2.41	3.39**
cold-warm	4.06	5.18	3.08**
cooperative-uncooperative	4.94	4.06	2.37*
unfriendly-friendly	4.12	5.41	4.07**
Mental Health			
cold-warm	4.94	5.47	2.73*
Mental Health Workers			
pleasant-unpleasant	1.53	2.00	2.43*
unfriendly-friendly	6.41	6.12	2.58*
Myself			
pleasant-unpleasant	1.88	2.41	3.50**
good-bad	2.06	2.29	2.22*
Profession of Teaching			
unfriendly-friendly	6.24	5.76	3.77**
interesting-boring	1.29	1.65	2.40*
School Principal			
interesting-boring	1.82	2.59	2.34*
Teachers			
unfriendly-friendly	6.18	5.88	2.58*
excitable-calm	5.24	4.53	2.22*

Note.—Each scale in the table is listed so that the adjective to the left corresponds to 1 and the adjective to the right corresponds to 7 on the actual rating forms used by *Ss* to evaluate concepts.

*Denotes significance at the .05 level.

**Denotes significance at the .01 level.

These significant differences are summarized in Table 2. With the total number of comparisons again coming to 153, the 22 observed significant differences exceed expectancy, and their patterning is an interpretable and internally consistent one.

The Nature of the Volunteer-Student Interaction. The process forms submitted by the volunteers after each third of the total experience were used as the basis for arriving at a descriptive summary of the children's activities during the total program. Table 3 presents means and sigmas for the several activity categories, based on the three individual summaries submitted and their total. It may be noted that there is considerable variability across volunteer-child pairs for all categories and that there appear to be generalized changes in category frequencies, over time.

Interrelationships Among Process and Outcome Measures

Outcome Measures. Three indices were derived for use as outcome measures, each of which was based on some comparison of a preprogram and postprogram evaluation of youngsters in both E and C groups. The first of these, Teachers Behavior Discrepancy Score, was based on the difference between the summed preprogram behavioral ratings of the child by the teacher and her summed postprogram behavioral ratings. The second, a Teachers ACL Discrepancy Score, reflected differences in the pre- and postprogram ACL forms submitted by the teacher. The third measure, Teachers Pre-Behavior vs. Observers Post-Behavior Index, was designed to introduce some independence of observations and was somewhat more complicated than the first two. In this instance, based on the combined E + C groups, the teachers' summed behavior score, pretest, was converted to a standard score. Similarly the postexperience judges' behavior observation scores of all 34 youngsters were converted to standard scores, and a difference score between the two sets of standard scores was derived. The intercorrelations among these three criterion measures were all moderately positive, ranging from +.35 to +.50, and significant. Comparison of E and C groups on the three criterion change score measures indicated that there were no significant differences between them on any measure.

Process Measures. For purposes of the analysis, various of the single process categories were pooled, both on logical grounds as well as to yield more stable frequencies. *Running* was a sufficiently high-frequency category so as to stand alone. *Semi-organized play, organized play,* and *exploring* were combined and the amalgam was labeled *physical games and exploring.* Similarly, *competitive table games, cooperative and constructive table activities,* and *artistic activities* were lumped together, the new fused category being labeled *table games* and *artistic activities. Talking*, which represented a totally different type of interaction from any of the others, was allowed to remain intact. This, in effect, yielded four substantive process categories. Percentage of time spent with others was a fifth measure used, and the sixth and seventh were the summed semantic differential evaluative ratings of the child and of the relationship. An intercorrelation matrix for these seven basic process and process-related indices was

TABLE 3

Summary of Process Measures, by Percentage of Time Spent in Various Activities

Activity	First Mean	Third SD	Second Mean	Third SD	Third Mean	Third SD	Total Mean	SD
Running	17.1	15.6	15.3	13.8	11.5	12.2	14.6	9.4
Semi-organized physical play	15.3	8.7	11.9	9.4	13.8	8.2	13.9	13.9
Organized physical games	8.5	9.5	6.8	12.1	9.7	16.4	8.3	11.3
Exploring	7.9	6.4	3.5	6.6	8.9	12.0	6.8	9.4
Competitive table games	14.6	11.6	6.5	6.0	5.2	8.9	8.7	9.7
Constructive table activities	10.6	12.1	15.9	13.7	17.9	18.8	14.6	16.2
Artistic activities	9.7	11.3	10.3	14.1	7.5	9.8	9.2	12.2
Talking	6.9	7.0	13.5	14.4	14.1	10.8	11.5	9.2
Other: includes food-making, reading, music, and other school-type activities	9.4	7.8	16.3	12.7	11.4	9.7	12.0	13.9

computed, based on sum score in each category for the total period. The principal substantive relations emerging from this analysis were the strong positive relation between frequency for the category *talking* and *conversation* and goodness of estimate of the relationship ($r = .58$) and the strong negative relation between actual percentage of time spent with others and both talking ($r = -.55$) and goodness of estimate of the relation ($r = -.55$).

Process vs. Outcome Measures. In order to determine whether any relationships existed between process and outcome measures, the seven process measures were each separately correlated with the three outcome measures. Although these interrelations were not strong, measures of positive-rated change related positively to frequency of *talking* and *conversation* ($r = .57$) and generally negatively with the process measure of *running*.

DISCUSSION

Discussion deals both with specific issues raised at the outset of this investigation as well as with a general evaluation of the program and with both empirical data and clinical impressions and appraisals accreted during the conduct of the program itself.

Who Volunteers? The findings suggest that our volunteers were indeed differentiable, attitude-wise, from nonvolunteer controls. It should be borne in mind that the volunteer group was essentially an unscreened one, only 3 of 23 interviewed students having been dropped because they seemed, to the interviewers, to be clearly unsuited for the job to be done. Comparisons of the volunteer and the control groups on the semantic differential index reveal a clear-cut and internally consistent pattern of differences. Thus, the volunteers rated a whole series of concepts, particularly "institutional" ones such as *elementary school, mental health, mental workers,* the *school principal,* and *teachers*, as significantly more favorable than did the controls. In the main, the volunteers' scale responses gravitated to the extreme positive end of the evaluative continuum on these concepts, whereas the controls gave much more reserved and neutral evaluations. One gets the impression here that the volunteers represented, initially, an enthusiastic, overidealistic, "see-no-evil" group and that they viewed institutional concepts in a stereotypically positive way.

Results of studies by Holzberg and his associates on a similar college student volunteer program can be interpreted as showing a similar pattern. Compared to controls, their volunteers are more extreme in their moral judgements (Holzberg, *et al.,* 1964), more interested in religion and social values as measured by the Allport-Vernon-Lindzey Scale of Values, and more nurturant and introceptive as measured by the Edwards Personality Pattern Inventory (Knapp & Holzberg, 1964), all of which can be seen as stereotypically positive responses. They also found no differences between volunteers and controls in attitudes toward mental illness (Holzberg & Gewirtz, 1963), a finding paralleled here in the essential absence of initial differences between volunteers and controls on the concept *emotionally disturbed child.*

Changes in Volunteers. A second basic area of concern to us pertains to changes in volunteers following participation in the program. The semantic differential change scores for the volunteers were not only internally consistent but also fell into line nicely with the pre-experience semantic differential analyses reported above. In the main, two types of changes were observed. The first of these, a generalized one, involved a diminution of the idealized image of institutional concepts held by this group before their contact experience. For example, following participation, *elementary schools* were seen as less interesting, less active, less relaxed, less friendly, and less pleasant. This is not to say that they were seen as passive, tense, unfriendly, etc.; rather the change was from an extreme positive response to a moderately positive one. It might thus be said that the postexperience ratings of institutional concepts by the volunteers were more healthily realistic. At first blush, one might argue that such a change could be viewed as a simple down-shift in response style, implicating an avoidance of extreme scores on the posttest. Data based on still another, very critical, concept, *emotionally disturbed children,* would refute that argument. For this concept, the pattern of significant scale changes was from an initially neutral position to a final positive one wherein such youngsters were seen as less ineffective, more active, warmer, more cooperative, and more friendly. Here, apparently, exposure to, and interaction with, youngsters experiencing emotional difficulties constituted a basis for more positive and accepting attitudes toward them. The general pattern of postexperience change for the volunteers, then, appears to have been a salutary one. Similar changes, to more positive attitudes toward mental illness, have been found to result from participation in Holzberg's program (Holzberg & Gewirtz, 1963) as well as movement toward more realistic moral judgments and greater self-acceptance (Holzberg, *et al.*, 1964).

The Nature of the Process

A reasonably clear modal picture of how volunteers and children actually spent their time, granting the very considerable variability across pairs, may be gleaned from the process summary data presented in Table 3. Although this table reflects a fairly accurate normative picture of how volunteers and children actually spent their time together, certain aspects of the data remain hidden. For one thing, the group profile ill fits any single relationship, and substantial variability of volunteer-child patterns of interaction appear to have been the order of the day.

Formal statistical analyses of these data have not been undertaken, primarily because of the very small *N*s and highly variable categories being dealt with. The aim here was simply to provide a rough profile of activities. Perhaps the most salient substantive inferences that can be made pertain to the initial relatively high frequency and systematic drop over time in the largely disjunctive, disharmonious, cathartive categories of *running, semi-organized physical play* (including fighting and wrestling), and *competitive table games* and to the parallel initial low frequency and increase over time in the cooperative, relational functions of *constructive table games* and *talking* and *conversation.* Perhaps this configuration hints at the operation of a type of challenge and testing of limits at the beginning of the relationship between volunteer and child, which slowly gave way to more congenial, "together" types of activities. It might be hoped that for the child the provision of a warm, interested, adult friend is facilitative in this shifting process.

Process-Outcome Relationships. Intercorrelations among the three change-score outcome measures for children are all low to moderately positive and significant, suggesting that although they are indeed measuring something in common, there remain substantial areas of nonoverlap of measurement.

The failure of these outcome measures to discriminate between E and C groups is no doubt attributable to a variety of factors. In the first place, the group *N*s of 17 each were extremely small and were governed by practical expedience rather than by ideal research conditions. Second, the program itself was set up as a short-range model and "de-bugging operation." It was in effect for just over two months, broken on two separate occasions by one-week school vacations, first for the volunteers and then for the children. One of the persistent observations (indeed concerns) of the volunteers throughtout the course of the program was that the total number of contacts with the child was much too few. One might expect that benefits and satisfactions to the volunteers would derive largely from *initial* exposure to, and participation in, the program and would reach an asymptote in time. For the children, however, a longer-range, more continuous process in which beneficial effects assume an additive quality over time, seems more realistic, even in the ideal. Finally, it should be noted that our control group was a particularly harsh one, in the sense that its members were simultaneously exposed to the everyday experience of another program also aimed at early secondary prevention. The latter, involving housewives working as teacher aides with emotionally disturbed children in the actual classroom situation (Zax & Cowen, 1967), though it was manifested in a very different form, shared a common set of aims and objectives with the afterschool volunteer program.

Interrelationships among the several process-type measures are limited. Apparently, in the volunteer's eyes, time spent talking with the child was seen as perhaps the most desirable form of interaction that spoke a good relationship between the two. Where the child was occupied to a considerable extent by others, the relationship tended to be viewed unfavorably.

With respect to process-outcome relationships, the major significant finding was the strong positive relationship between talking and improvement as measured by the D score between teachers' prebehavior rating and observers' postbehavior rating. In general, the process-outcome correlation matrix was hampered by the limited *N*, which required substantial correlation for statistical significance. It is therefore of some interest to note that the process measure of *talking*, previously described as a cooperative, harmonious type of activity, showed a directionally positive correlation with all three outcome measures, whereas the dysjunctive process category of *running* showed a directionally negative relationship to the same three criterion indices. Obviously, our *N*s were not sufficiently ample here to allow for strong speculation. However, the present analysis offers one or two interesting leads and constitutes a model that may ultimately help us to achieve a better understanding of helpful, as opposed to inert, interactions and interventions.

Implications

The volunteer program described in the present report is one that seems, in principle, to combine many potential virtues, including: furthering of the development of community-based field programs in early secondary prevention; recruitment, training, and supervision of new sources of subprofessional manpower, and modification of graduate training in the helping professions. At a clinical and experiential level, the program appears to have gone a long way toward furthering those objectives. It was certainly well received by those who were touched by it, including parents of participating youngsters, teachers and other school personnel, the volunteers, the graduate student supervisors, and finally the youngsters themselves. On more than one occasion, for example, children who took sick in school on a program day were unwilling to be sent home, because they did not wish to miss out on this highly valued experience.

Efforts at formal research evaluation, admittedly crude and restricted because of the very limited size and duration of the program, at least provided some preliminary information and hunches with respect to several issues of primary concern. For example, we know of the original idealistic attitudes of volunteers, how these tone down as a result of participation in the program, paralleled by a significantly more favorable set of attitudes toward the target clinical group—in this case, emotionally disturbed children. We have arrived at a fair understanding of the nature of volunteer-child process interactions—preferred ones, limited-frequency ones, and those that change over time—with some preliminary estimates as to the whys behind these facts. Indeed, there are even several suggestions as to which may be helpful as opposed to inert or negative types of interactions.

The assumptions underlying the present project, hopefully, have fairly widespread implications. Certainly the school is one very important and very logical institution for fostering work in the early detection and prevention of emotional disorders. Moreover, it seems desirable to study further the effectiveness of the basic model, concretely modified as indicated, with other groups and in other settings.

REFERENCES

COWEN, E. L., IZZO, L. D., MILES, H., TELSCHOW, E. F., TROST, M. A., & ZAX, M. A mental health program in the school setting: description and evaluation. *J. Psychol.,* 1963, **56** (part 2), 307–356.

HOLZBERG, J. D., & KNAPP, R. H. The social interaction of college students and chronically ill mental patients. *Amer. J. Orthopsychiat.*, 1965, **35**, 487–492.

HOLZBERG, J. D., & GEWIRTZ, H. A method of altering attitudes toward mental illness. *Psychiat. Q. Suppl.*, 1963, **37**, 56–61.

HOLZBERG, J. D., GERWITZ, H., & EBNER, E. Changes in moral judgment and self acceptance as a function of companionship with hospitalized mental patients. *J. Consult. Psychol.*, 1964, **28**, 299–303.

KANTOR, D. Impact of college students on chronic mental patients and on the organization of the mental hospital. *Proceedings of the College Student Companion Program Conference.* Stratford, Conn.: Conn. State Dept. of Mental Health, 1962.

KNAPP, R. H., & HOLZBERG, J.D. Characteristics of college students volunteering for service to mental patients. *J. Consult. Psychol.*, 1964, **28**, 82–85.

OSGOOD, C. E., SUCI, G. J., & TANNENBAUM, P. H. *The measurement of meaning.* Urbana, Ill.: University of Illinois Press, 1957.

PROJECT RE-ED. *A demonstration project for the re-education of emotionally disturbed children.* Nashville, Tenn.: Peabody College, 1964. (mimeo)

SANDERS, R. New manpower for mental hospital service. In E. L. Cowen, E. A. Gardner, & M. Zax (Eds.), *Emergent approaches to mental health problems.* New York: Appleton-Century-Crofts, 1967.

UMBARGER, C. C., DALSIMER, J. S., MORRISON, A. P., & BREGGIN, P. R. *College students in a mental hospital.* New York: Grune and Stratton, 1962.

ZAX, M., & COWEN, E. L. Early identification and prevention of emotional disturbance in a public school. In E. L. Cowen, E. A. Gardner, & M. Zax (Eds), *Emergent approaches to mental health problems.* New York: Appleton-Century-Crofts, 1967.

A Community Educational Program For the Emotionally Disturbed Child

SOL NICHTERN
GEORGE T. DONAHUE
JOAN O'SHEA
MARY MARANS
MARGARET CURTIS
CHARLES BRODY

A special educational program for severely emotionally disturbed children was established within the existing school system of a community, to probe individual training based on the therapeutic principle of the "teaching mother." Through the individual approach, optimum relationship and elimination of the need to isolate the child from the community or family, this program emerged as a therapeutic process with dramatic effects on the progress of the children and the community's awareness of mental health.

Seriously emotionally disturbed children frequently present extensive problems in training and education. Their intrinsic distortions in personality often serve to interfere with the normal learning process so that many of them develop severe educational disabilities. This disruption makes their education in the normal setting extremely difficult and may lead to their exclusion from the established educational facilities within the community. Thus, the natural difficulties of these children in integrating into their social milieu and peer group are compounded by their segregation and isolation. At the same time, providing the necessary

This paper was presented at the 1961 Annual Meeting of the American Orthopsychiatric Association, Inc. It is reprinted with permission from the *American Journal of Orthopsychiatry*, Vol. XXXIV, No. 4, July 1964, 705–713, Copyright, 1964, the American Orthopsychiatric Association, Inc. and with the permission of the authors. Brief biographies of the authors have been omitted.

specialized facility and services for their education and training becomes costly. The expense of such a program is usually so great that many of these children are denied the opportunity of obtaining an education based on their capacities and needs because neither the community nor the family is able to provide the appropriate service.

Accumulating experience with these severely disturbed children suggests that the therapeutic milieu can be of great importance to their achievement of some degree of maturity. Many present such serious problems in personality integration that the elements of relationship loom large in making possible the learning process. If this learning process can be influenced successfully, then the relationship of the disturbed child to himself and others improves. This cycle compounds itself and frequently plays a critical role in the ultimate level of intellectual, emotional and social development achieved by the child.

Recognizing these factors and faced with the problem of an ever present group of seriously disturbed children who could not be adequately handled in the regular classroom, the Elmont, New York, Elementary School District set about to create a specialized program within the established educational framework of the community. The general objectives were to provide each of these seriously disturbed children with an individual education and training program based on identifiable needs.

These children are the little people described in the *Saturday Evening Post* as "attic" children.* They are childhood schizophrenics, in some instances giving evidence of "organicity" or brain damage. They range in age from five to nine. They display the extremes in behavioral patterning. They run the gamut from withdrawal with autistic overtones to the exceedingly aggressive, hostile, disruptive child. They are atypical to a high degree. In most, there are poor biological patterning and serious maturational lags. In some cases there is evidence of diffuse damage to the central nervous system with visuomotor deficits. Most have either fine or gross motor coordination difficulties. Some have both. They are hyperactive and clinging. All have problems of impulse control. Time and spatial orientation are poor. They view the world as frightening and overwhelming. Their environmental awareness varies markedly. Some are hypersensitive to auditory or visual stimuli. All have some distortions in basic life concepts. There appears to be insular development of skills and achievements. All have some degree of distractibility, unpredictability, rigidity, perseveration, anxiety, disorganization and resistance to authority.

On a social level, most experience poor peer relationships. They are

*Congdon, T. B., Jr. 1960. The "attic children" go to school. The Saturday Evening Post. October 1:38.

unaware of social standards, have isolationist tendencies and display disruptive and destructive attitudes toward others.

It is apparent that the intelligence testing completed with these youngsters cannot be reliable because of the variables involved. However, it would appear that with one exception these children fall within a normal to superior range.

The literature is scanty concerning the "how" of dealing with these children. In fact, some of it is discouraging in the sense that it includes little description of what has succeeded educationally with them. Certainly not enough has been achieved for these youngsters by public education around the country. As a consequence, this group represents an appalling waste of human resources, the need for the conservation of which is today receiving national attention. If it is believed, as it is in Elmont, that public education has a responsibility to educate all the educable children of all the people, then these children must cease to be excluded from school. But how to work with them?

They have been characterized as distractible. Then any program must be structured to reduce distractibility to a minimum. This meant to Elmont no more than two children to a classroom. Some of them are hyperactive. This meant increasing the amount of adult supervision. This, coupled with the fact that these children are laden with anxiety, poorly oriented in space and time, suffering from intrinsic personality distortions, complicated oftentimes by segregation and isolation and sometimes by parental lack of understanding, strongly indicates the need for a one-to-one relationship with a teacher. Not just any one-to-one relationship—but a relationship of great warmth, acceptance and understanding—of love. This kind of teacher, in addition, must be able to help these children operate within identifiable and acceptable limits and to enforce such limits without destroying the basic relationship in the process. Teaching materials need to include more tactile devices than for other children. Teaching methods must be completely flexible with only one criterion—if it works, use it; if not, discard it and try some alternate approach. Finally, some group activities must be included.

To structure a program that would include all of these elements was a staggering administrative problem, the more so, because Elmont is not an economically favored community. The task then became one of finding five classrooms, teachers for nine children on a one-to-one basis, educational supplies of an unusual nature, professional direction and a sponsoring organization. Why a sponsoring organization? Because the State of New York, like most states, has been slow in providing the communities with the financial support and leadership needed to work intelligently with the seriously emotionally disturbed child of school age.

The ultimate goal of the educational program was individualized training through optimum relationship and final reintroduction of the child to the regular classroom setting without ever totally separating the child from the family or community structure. By providing the necessary specialized program within the context of a one-to-one relationship and preventing the child's exclusion from the community, it was felt that the educational program itself could become therapeutic to the child. A basic premise of this approach is that proper education and training can be a therapeutic process. If accomplished within the established framework of the family and community, the disruptive effects of separation anxiety can be eliminated. And, if successful, perhaps these children can the sooner be returned to regular classrooms, able to function in a group and not handicapped by educational deficits serious enough to constitute a barrier to their adjustment in the normal educational setting.

In casting about for a possible solution, it seemed that all the resources needed were at hand in the community but were either unorganized or under jurisdictions apart from the Board of Education. Since space could not be provided in the schools—there are 6,000 children in buildings with a rated capacity of 4,800—space would have to be provided, and free of charge. As in almost all communities, there were areas not normally used during school hours, for example, church halls and basements, fire department meeting halls, an American Legion dugout and the like. A neighbor, the Elmont Jewish Center, was just completing a building with eight or ten classrooms, an arts and crafts room, kitchen, playground and even an outdoor swimming pool. This seemed ideal. Permission was asked and received to use six classrooms during the mornings and any of the other facilities the program needed. The Rabbi was understanding enough to suggest that, if the children caused some damage, his Board would understand.

The Board of Education agreed to supply transportation for the children and was understanding about a number of other matters.

The Elmont Kiwanis Club agreed to sponsor the project and provide financial support. For instance, the Club paid the premiums to insure the Temple and the staff from suits, should a youngster be injured and his parents sue. The Club has provided about $600 for special equipment needed such as the two-sided easels and flannel boards used for each child, electric answer boards, large locked steel cabinets in which to store and secure gear and equipment and the milk and cookies provided for each child daily during snack time.

This provided an almost ideal place and financial and sponsoring support. What about staff?

Obviously, the school psychologists and the head school physician would help—they were employees of the School District and dedicated people. The psychiatric director was associated with the West Nassau

Mental Health Center. When approached, he undertook to convince his Board of Directors that he should be allowed a reasonable flexibility in his schedule, so as to assist with the professional direction of the enterprise, and at no charge to the program. He knew the children because the Mental Health Center was providing guidance for most of them, or their parents, or both.

The most difficult problem, however, was how to procure a teaching staff sufficient to accommodate a one-to-one relationship. Few school districts, least of all Elmont, can afford one teacher to one pupil. Furthermore, the kind of people needed—warm, empathic, mature, emotionally stable and dedicated—are difficult enough to find, even when salary is available. There were in Elmont, as in most communities, women of this kind who have done a good job with their own children and who were in a position to contribute some of their time to community activities. From among such women came the volunteer teachers. No broadcast appeal was made for these volunteers, which eliminated the necessity for refusing the help of people not suited to working with these children. By personal contact, a number of mothers were invited to contribute two mornings each week to working with a child—the work to be done under the supervision of the professional educational staff and the psychiatric director. These mothers were interviewed by the educational administrator and the psychologists. Every effort was made to discourage them by painting a black picture of what they were about to get into. These interviews also provided a good opportunity for the professionals to get some insights with regard to each of the volunteers. It was felt that if two mothers were teamed and assigned to a particular child two mornings a week, this would come close to resolving the problem of a one-to-one relationship. There was no trouble in securing the original 12 volunteer teachers to start with six children—now expanded to 18 working with nine children.

The teams were thoroughly briefed by the professional staff concerning the child with whom each would be working. They were given educational materials appropriate for their child and a sketchy introduction to teaching methodology, and the enterprise was under way. An early elementary teacher was detailed to the project to assist the volunteers as needed, to supervise, and to coordinate the details of supply, transportation and the like. The School District's psychologists, head school physician, and psychiatric consultant worked closely with the volunteers as they began to feel their way in assisting these children toward personality integration and educational development.

This individual teaching had to be merged with a group activity program. At the outset, group activities consisted of morning exercises, including salute to the flag, Regent's prayer, and a "show and tell" period. In addition, one other group activity of about 20 minutes was provided toward the middle of the morning; this included arts and crafts, music, physical education and story time. The other group experiences included a daily snack of milk and cookies and the children's experience in riding together in the School District's station wagon bus to and from school. Every child's birthday was celebrated by a simple party during snack time. The volunteer teachers supervised these group activities on a rotating basis, usually two or three to an activity. Increasing use is being made of the playground facilities for free play and it seems to work reasonably well.

Another facet of instruction is worthy of note. Music lessons for some of the children seem to be worth-while. One organic schizophrenic eight-year-old boy, for instance, who constantly fiddled with anything he could get his hands on, has been found to have perfect pitch and is progressing quite nicely on the piano.

The key to progress appears to be the one-to-one relationship, and the physical contact provided thereby. The volunteer teachers soothe the children with their hands, shelter them with their arms and mollify them by holding them on their laps when necessary. This physical contact has proved to be the strongest teaching aid used. Not solely because of the physical contact, but because the volunteers are the kind of people who, in this manner, communicate a genuine warmth and affection to children not always lovable. In the process, they absorb the children's anxiety. Important is the fact that, because of this one-to-one relationship, the need of the child can be fulfilled at once, with no delay. Therefore, it is unusual to see any of these children in the tantrums characteristic of such children.

Another successful technique, not unique but uniquely used through the one-to-one ratio, was to call upon the visual, auditory and tactile senses simultaneously for learning. When a child can't learn a word or letter by just seeing it, he hears it, and, using block letters and the individual flannel board easels, can feel it and trace it with his fingers. This seemed to facilitate considerable educational progress with the children.

What are the outcomes of this program after a year and six months of operation? First, for the children, three of the original six children are now in school in regular programs on a half-day basis. They are:

> D. C., male, 7 years, 5 months. His diagnosis was schizophrenic reaction of childhood. His situation was complicated by considerable pathology in the total family situation. His mother has been hospitalized for mental illness and his father was also disturbed. The child developed much better controls, a longer attention span, real enthusiasm for the work and learning situation and a positive relationship to his volunteer teachers and some of the other children. His hyperactivity was greatly reduced and coordination showed marked improvement. He is now functioning in a regular first grade of 30 children.

B. T., female, 7 years, 7 months. Her diagnosis was mild cerebral palsy and mental retardation, with poor coordination, short attention span, little interest in other children, poor hand-eye coordination, distractibility and hyperactivity. She progressed so that she could handle a pencil and produce basic forms. Her attention span increased. Her interests broadened. She acquired some impulse control, completed the readiness program, learned to identify and write her name, developed arithmetical concepts of most-least, first-last, sequence, bigger-smaller and so on, and left-to-right progression. She is now successfully functioning in one of the District's classes for the educable, mentally retarded.

J. A., male, 8 years, 8 months. His diagnosis was schizophrenic reaction of childhood with the severe regressive symptom of soiling. He was hyperactive, harmful to others and disruptive so that he could not be contained in the regular classroom. There was considerable family pathology. His parents would not co-operate with the therapeutic proposals offered by the local mental health center. When placed in the educational-therapeutic milieu, this child progressed rapidly, academically and socially. His soiling ceased. His relationships at home improved. He began to relate well to the other children in the program. He is functioning at present in regular third grade on a half-time program.

Three more children are in the process of being weaned away from the special program and reabsorbed into the regular classroom. They are:

C. M., female, 8 years, 1 month—an aphasic child with organic involvement and extensive emotional problems. This child was known to many clinics in New York City as well as some local mental health facilities, who advised that she was completely hopeless and should be totally exempted from school. She was a completely withdrawn child. She now enjoys physical contact. She has improved impulse control, and in appearance is a happy, normal, attractive little girl who plays with others and occasionally assumes leadership. She is reading at the second grade level, is anxious to learn and writes and spells adequately for an eight-year-old. Most important of all, she speaks—in fact, at times, is a chatterbox—not always easy to understand, but has a sizable vocabularly and is anxious to communicate. She is doing nicely in second grade and is in the middle group in reading in her class.

R. L., male, 8 years, 1 month—a schizophrenic child with bizarre behavior, violent at times, who hurt other children, did not participate with group, did not respond to reasoning and was egocentric, autistic-like, immature, demanding and given to extreme temper tantrums and sulking. He was physically large and poorly coordinated. He now has positive relationships with his peers, particularly with adults. His coordination is improving. He has lost much of his impoliteness and is receptive to suggestions and authority. He tries to play successfully with other children and sometimes shares willingly and voluntarily. He has a high degree of academic ability, particularly in mathematics and science. In mathematics he can solve problems mentally that most of us need pencil and paper to figure. His resistance to reading has been overcome and he is reading on grade level. He is performing well in fourth grade.

C.C., male, 8 years, 9 months—a schizophrenic child who seemed superficially to be a severe behavior problem. He demonstrated gross distortions in conceptualization, visuomotor perceptualization and extreme unevenness of performance. His deficits inhibited his adjustment in all areas. When entered in the special program, it was found necessary to start his academic program at the beginning. He needed much repetition and variety of approach. He advanced again to the second grade level and is now functioning with competence in a regular second grade; this despite a family with much pathology, including severe marital discord and extreme inconsistencies in the handling of the child.

It is believed that all the other children, in time, will progress to the point where they, too, will be able to function within acceptable limits in regular classrooms.

As to the impact of the program on the volunteer teachers, they have persisted. During the second year of operation only three of the original 18 had to be replaced—one for reasons of pregnancy, one with a complicated family situation and one who just did not want to continue but agreed to act as a substitute when needed. It is thought they are deriving a good deal of personal satisfaction from the contribution they are making directly to the children. In addition, they have achieved a certain status in the community because of their generosity, which has been recognized by testimonial dinners and some publicity. Perhaps the socializing with the other women, too, has helped reduce the separation rate. They have been treated by the professionals working in connection with these children as professionals, and undoubtedly have profited in terms of developing keener insights into some of their own problems, and in understanding their own children better. Although they were untrained when they started, they have, over the months, acquired a good deal of training in an unorganized way, which, when coupled with their own intrinsic characteristics, has greatly increased their stature.

It has taken its toll, however. A transference mechanism has resulted at times in the volunteers' identifying with their pupil too closely. Progress with these children has been slow and long-term. Sometimes the volunteers were discouraged and unable to see the gains being made. Accordingly, the professionals had to be alert to this and, through group discussions and individual consultations with the volunteers, absorb some of their anxieties and avoid having the impact of their experience influence their own families and personal lives in an undesirable way.

At times the volunteer teachers have become somewhat competitive in their zeal to make academic progress with their pupils. This is both desirable and undesirable. It is important that the volunteers be cognizant of the children's need for academic progress and, concomitantly, their need for more adequate integrative personality processes. Here the psychologists were useful in their constant supervision of the individual programs.

The program has had a catalytic impact on the community, both within and beyond the school. A greater awareness has developed on the part of principals and some teachers that adaptations to the individual needs of children are profitable and satisfying investments of imagination, time and effort. There has been a great expansion of their efforts in grouping children so that this or that child is placed with the teacher who, by personality, will provide the optimal conditions for the child's total growth. Some children with problems are now being accommodated by part-time programs weighted with more art, or music or physical education. Some are being given a good deal more individual instruction. In general, the resources of the School District are being mobilized and adapted for accommodating to children's individual needs. Teachers are developing not only an awareness but also some skill in identifying children who are in need of specialized help—and at an earlier age. Most important of all, the professional educators are undergoing a subtle improvement of attitude, brought about perhaps by greater knowledge, which has led to understanding of children, acceptance of them as they are and, as a result, adaptation to their needs.

The school children themselves, while not familiar with the project for emotionally disturbed children, are nonetheless developing the same kind of awareness in connection with mental health as with cerebral palsy, the heart fund, Red Cross, Boy Scouts, Girl Scouts and the like. They included a $400 donation to the local mental health center in their children's community chest last year and again this year.

The community itself is developing a similar awareness and understanding. This is an important step forward in its education in connection with the whole mental health problem. It feels some pride too, and comfortable, now that all of its exceptional children, not just the physically handicapped, are in organized programs of education. This, in turn, is the finest kind of public relations for the school system and could be helpful at budget time when citizens are asked to vote on school expenditures.

The impact of the program on the parents of these children and their families is difficult to estimate. The psychologists, of course, keep in touch with the parents by telephone and home visits. It seems apparent to them that in some instances the children's progress has had a salutary and stabilizing influence on the total home situation. In some others, there seems to be neither awareness nor understanding of what is operative with the child and what the community is contributing. With several, the only preoccupation is that of when the child will be in regular school. No attempt has been made to develop any relationship between the volunteer teachers and the parents. In fact, the children's parents have been discouraged from making contact with the volunteers, to prevent exposing the volunteers to these parents, who, because they are often somewhat disturbed, should be handled only by professionally trained people. One group meeting of the parents was attempted some time ago for the purpose of exploring the establishment of regular meetings, on the theory that they might gain some support and some insights from regular association with parents of children like their own. This meeting produced absolutely nothing constructive, and no further attempt has been made to bring the parents together.

This whole enterprise, of course, is informative and simultaneously raises some questions. It suggests first, that one of the primary requisites for success in handling the seriously emotionally disturbed child is a one-to-one relationship with a particular kind of teacher. The needs of these children are so diverse and can change so from day to day, hour to hour, and even moment to moment, that individualized supervision and teaching is a *sine qua non* for successful treatment and educational development, at least during the years of their greatest disorganization. It suggests too, that the educative process is in itself therapeutic and, when conducted in an atmosphere impregnated with therapeutic principles, can become the vehicle for great progress with these children.

It further suggests that the resources for working successfully with the seriously disturbed child are at hand in most communities and need only to be mobilized and channeled. Without minimizing a bit the need for state and federal support for programs for such children, it demonstrates that great strides can be taken by determined communities without relying on government for solutions, or the public for fund drives. It seems to imply, too, that untrained personnel of the right kind can make enormous contributions to the well-being of such children when carefully selected, oriented and guided. This perhaps is most important because, even if all the funds needed were made available, it would not be possible to train personnel in adequate numbers in the immediate future. Then too, some professionals might not achieve the success of the volunteer teachers, since to them it would be a career and in some instances not the labor of love it is to the volunteers.

The questions it raises are many, but the two most important are, first, that of identification procedures and, second, that of whose responsibility these children are, the educator's or the mental health department's. Sometimes it was found that diagnoses conflicted even in terminology, let alone work-up procedures. Perhaps the question is best resolved by asking another: "Is this the kind of child who needs this kind of program and can profit from it?" If the answer is yes, maybe this is the only criterion that needs to be applied until there is more agreement among the professionals concerning diagnostic procedures and terminology.

Educators and mental health people have been debating for years over whose responsibility these children are. Meanwhile, not enough of a constructive nature is being done for these children and their bewildered parents. Perhaps a part of the answer lies in what Elmont has demonstrated in a small but significant way—a decent joining of forces by the two, so that each contributes from its own discipline. When this is done, it should make an unbeatable combination professionally, and in the meantime society can get on with the job of rehabilitating these unfortunate children.

The Therapeutic Use of Student Volunteers

HELEN REINHERZ

One of the vital questions being discussed in almost every service field today is whether the scope of services can be extended by the use of semitrained persons under the supervision of highly trained professionals.[1] As yet, however, there has been little experience in the planned use of individual volunteer-patient relationships to bring about therapeutic change in mentally ill children.[2] One such program was, however, operated in Massachusetts for 4 years (1959–63), and has been discontinued only temporarily because of the difficulty of finding a supervisor. The volunteers were college students from Radcliffe and Harvard who were members of Harvard's Phillips Brooks House; the setting, the Massachusetts State Hospital at Waltham. Two years of experience with this program as its first supervisor has convinced the writer of its value both to the child patients and to the young volunteers involved.

The program actually had its beginnings as far back as 1954, when members of Phillips Brooks House organized a mental hospital volunteer program through which 200 students participated in recreational and

Reprinted from *Children*, 1964, Vol. II, No. 4, 137–142, with the permission of the U.S. Department of Health, Education, and Welfare, Welfare Administration, Children's Bureau, and the author. Photographs have been omitted.

[1]Eliasoph, Eugene: The use of case aides in a treatment setting. *Social Casework*, March 1959.

[2]Joint Commission on Mental Illness and Health: Action for mental health. Basic Books, New York. 1961.

social activities with adult patients on both a group and an individual basis and in group activities for children. In 1959, when a grant from the National Institutes of Health was received by the Harvard University Study of Student Volunteers for a demonstration and research project (Public Health Service Grant No. O. M. 233), the first "case-aide group" for individual work with children was initiated at the hospital.

This first volunteer case-aide group for children was set up on an experimental basis with five students—two boys and three girls—assigned to work individually with a single child. The children were chosen by the staff on the basis of the following criteria: They had not been selected by professional therapists for treatment; they would be in the hospital during the coming year; and they did not have severe behavior problems.

Previously, in spite of the persistent requests of the students, the professional staff of the children's unit had been reluctant to have students work on an intensive individual basis with child patients. Some staff members expressed the fear that young nonprofessionals would get over-involved in a nontherapeutic way. Some members were afraid that the volunteers, wishing to give, would be too permissive and that therefore they would have difficulty in setting the limits on behavior which are needed by disturbed children.

Because of this reluctance, the experiment was introduced only after considerable staff discussion and not until cooperation from the majority of the staff was assured. The keys to acceptance were systematic communication with staff members, from attendants to clinical director; the volunteers' demonstration of responsible performance and maturity; and the promise of careful supervision by the program's leader, a professional social worker.[3] By the beginning of the second year the program seemed to be well accepted in the unit.

EVOLUTION OF THE VOLUNTEER'S ROLE

The students spent one afternoon a week with the children, meeting with the supervisor for 15 minutes ahead of time to be briefed on any progress or problems which the children had exhibited since their last visit. They also met with the supervisor an hour and a half afterward to discuss their experiences, the meaning of children's behavior, the norms of child development, and the concepts of mental health. Their role with the children evolved as a natural outgrowth of their experiences with their patients, plus some of the supervisor's ideas of what contributions these

[3]Reinherz, Helen: Group leadership of student volunteers in a mental hospital. *Mental Hospitals*, November 1962.

young adults with relatively healthy egos, strong motivation, and dedication could make to the children.

In the entire course of the students' work with the children, emphasis was placed on the value of a well-chosen activity in helping to give the children a satisfactory experience in mastery, as well as in building student-patient relationships. Activities ranged from model building, frog hunting, bike riding, shopping, reading, even shoelace tying, to walks and more walks to the local pond, park, sandwich shop, or even to a restaurant or a museum. Each activity was planned for the need of the particular patient.

The students first thought of themselves as socializing influences, bringing the outside world to children from severely deprived backgrounds and bringing the children out into the world. They also saw one of their major functions as providing individualized activities for patients who were unable to fit into organized hospital groups.

As the program continued, however, the students tried to define the exact nature of their role. Were they friend, uncle, big brother or sister, or parent to the patient? After the program had been going for a while, some professional staff members referred to the students as "therapists." This created much consternation among the students and some searching reevaluation of their function. As a monograph written by several of the students indicated,[4] the volunteers found it easier to assume the socially validated role of big brother or sister than a more parental or professional role.

Near the end of the first year, the students redefined their role in a report presented at a hospital staff meeting. They said they would still maintain the important function of the volunteer in representing the outside world as a friendly place to the patient; but that they felt having a relationship in depth with each child had even greater value. With the supervisor's help they defined the case-aide role as ego-supportive, educative in the broadest sense of the word, and parental in that it brought the child healthy relationships and activities that are a part of the normal experiences of childhood.

CLARIFYING GOALS

At the beginning of the first year, both students and supervisor had very limited goals. We did not hope for fundamental changes in the patient's total functioning. We hoped only to support and to strengthen the intact areas of the patient's personality which enabled him to function to some

[4]Umbarger, Carter et al.: College students in a mental hospital. Grune and Stratton, New York. 1962.

extent. Only a few months after the program was initiated, however, two of the children who had been most deprived of steady adult support, and who had been unable to trust adults, began to show striking changes in ability to relate to people—at first with their volunteers and then with other adults in the hospital. Goals of the students and supervisor gradually became more ambitious and clear.

For example, two statements on goals written by one student, Ellie, at different times of the year showed maturation on both her own and her patient's part. The patient was a 9-year-old boy who had been admitted to the hospital after uncontrolled attacks on children and animals. He had been diagnosed as borderline psychotic with possible organic brain damage. In the hospital his behavior had been withdrawn and babyish, a "too good" reversal of his former aggressive behavior.

In October after first seeing this young patient, Ellie wrote:

> I want to give Billy a true friend. I hope to give Billy self-confidence to help himself to the extent that he doesn't feel he must seek attention or love by asking people to do things for him that he can really do for himself.

In May, Ellie described her role and goals in different terms:

> I wanted him to be able to use me as an example of a stable, loving, female figure which he had never known, to use his experience with me in his relationships in the future. . . . I wanted him to feel that he could talk to me or express himself in actions without evoking harsh judgments or retaliation, whatever he did. It is only by expressing his feelings in words, as he is beginning to do, that he will learn inner controls and only in this way will he gain confidence in himself, other people, and his ability to sustain meaningful relationships.

She added: "In the last 3 months I have had success," and she had indeed. Her patient's new maturity and confidence were noted by members of the hospital staff. He was talking more and holding his own with his more aggressive peers. In his relationship with his volunteer, he was able, at last, to express his own ideas in choosing activities and to tell her some of his fears of aggression and retaliation. Billy's progress was so apparent that the decision was made to discharge him at the end of the year.

In the first 2 years of the program 12 college students took part in this volunteer case-aide program. Their general goals fell into the following seven categories. (The examples give an indication of their plans and accomplishments.)

1. Teaching that Loving People Is Not Dangerous. The forming of relationships with parental figures in the early weeks and months of life plays an overwhelmingly important role in ego development.[5] Many of

[5]Gerard, Margaret Wilson: The emotionally disturbed child. Child Welfare League of America, New York. 1957.

our child patients had suffered pathogenic experiences with significant adults due to illness, accident, or their parents' lack of capacity to furnish love. Because of early disappointments, reinforced in many instances by later separations, the children were fearful of placing trust in people or of investing emotionally in the experience of loving others.

Richard, an 8-year-old boy, was diagnosed as psychotic. He showed little emotion or feeling even on separation from his parents. Much of his day was spent in fantasies of space and rockets. He identified himself with the most powerful objects and said he "liked nothing in this world."

Early in the year, Nancy, the student who worked with Richard, said she hoped—

> to form a relationship that would have meaning for both of us and to use it to help him decide to want to live in this world.

In describing her relationship with him at the end of the year, she said:

> We love each other. Our relationship is a blend of mother-child; friends; older sister and younger brother. The best way to describe it is to say he is my child and I am his volunteer. In the beginning he seemed not to know how to understand and accept love. Now human emotions and feeling have real meaning for him. He can express and receive affection.

The ward psychiatrist noted the enthusiasm with which Richard waited for the coming of his volunteer. She also noted that at the end of the year he was showing a response to other adults and even a sense of humor. He said to his volunteer, "I have got 'real' feelings, you know." It was true.

Lewis, age 10, had been diagnosed by the staff as having a "schizophrenic reaction." His mother, who was both educationally and emotionally deprived, had been deserted by his father. She had turned to Lewis to fulfill her emotional needs and was overtly seductive with him. At the same time she was terrified of his attempts to seem grown up.

Lewis was always confused about whether he was a little boy or a grown man. He began to show signs of great emotional disorganization about the time he entered school. He was hallucinating and had a rich fantasy life with delusions of destructive nature. He also showed paranoid traits and seemed unable to form relationships. However, his outward appearance was deceptively one of maturity, adequacy, and independence.

Ruth, his volunteer case aide, described her goals with Lewis:

> My primary aim was to provide Lewis with a nonseductive relationship with a female. When I realized that he had problems about dependence, denying his need for it and trying to control the relationship, I tried to encourage him to share control with me and to rely on me for some things. . . . I wanted him to feel he could trust me.

At the end of the year, she said:

> I found with all the goals I set I was able to help Lewis accomplish some things. . . . I felt I was able to give Lewis a chance to see some of the facets of possible healthy human relationships and experience them with me. . . .

Ruth was able to have a nonsexualized relationship with this child, a pal relationship which he had not achieved with any other adult. She used his interest in scientific matters, closely allied with his previous exclusive interest in human anatomy, as a means of finding a socially acceptable sublimated outlet. The two worked on nature projects associated with insect life, went on several frog hunting expeditions, and built puppets together. At relaxed moments, Lewis, a virtual nonreader, could even read a bit with Ruth.

2. Helping Patients Achieve a Sense of Self-Identity and Self-Esteem. Peggy, a student volunteer, set as one of her prime goals with Mike, her patient, the hope that she could help him feel valuable and important to someone. Mike was a child twice rejected: first, by his natural parents; then, by his adoptive parents. He was of illegitimate birth and mixed Oriental and Caucasian ancestry. Mike had been accused of aggressive assaults and fire-setting by his adoptive parents. However, he did not misbehave at the hospital, where he was observed to be a basically depressed child with a placid exterior. He refused to relate to anyone more than superficially.

Peggy, a warm and perceptive girl with much experience with children, said, "I felt he was worth while. I tried to show him this so he would believe in himself again." Mike responded rapidly to Peggy and began to respond to other adults in the hospital as well as to show improvement in all his functioning. After 9 months the hospital staff, which had despaired of placing him outside the hospital, decided to place him in a foster home, where he has adjusted successfully.

Chris, another student, tried to formulate realistic goals with 11-year-old Georgie, who was said in staff conference to be "in and out of psychosis." Known as "Fatso" on the ward, Georgie was described by the staff consulting psychiatrist as an "empty container with a facade of secondary identification." Chris wished to give him a firmer sense of self-identity, a greater feeling of self-sufficiency: "He must learn what sort of person he is and have a greater sense of being a real, whole person."

Toward the end of the year Chris took Georgie on a visit to the local zoo. While there Georgie talked about what it would be like to be the various birds and animals he saw, but finally sighed, "It's always better to be yourself."

3. Providing Auxiliary Ego and Superego in Times of Stress. One important function of the student volunteer case aides is to lend the support of a healthy ego to the child and to serve as his superego, thereby helping the child achieve a more accurate perception of reality.

Peggy's second patient was Hilda, an adolescent girl of 14 who was mute and withdrawn in her first weeks at the hospital. At first she was thought to be schizophrenic, but psychological tests and her subsequent behavior indicated that she had probably been in a depressive reaction precipitated by the hospitalization of a psychotic older sister. Hilda's depression gradually lifted, aided, perhaps, by the attempts of Peggy and the ward personnel to entice her into enjoyable activity.

Soon, however, Hilda began to make aggressive sexual overtures to the younger boys in the hospital and to engage in other delinquencies. Through these crises, Peggy attempted to give her young charge the feeling of self-esteem, at the same time indicating strong disapproval of her asocial acts. The ward personnel spoke of Peggy as the one person close enough to Hilda to be able to stand by her during her difficulties and not to feel irritated by her misbehavior and her many demands. At the end of the year, Hilda, although somewhat flighty and overtalkative, at times seemed aware of her problems, aware of the world, and anxious to find her place in it.

4. *Providing Corrective Emotional Experiences with an Adult.* We should never minimize the importance of identification with the healthy characteristics of an adult as a mechanism providing tremendous impetus for growth in young children, particularly children who have had faulty models in their early lives. The students' youth and their deep emotional commitment to the children assigned to them made identification with the volunteer a striking feature of most of these volunteer-child relationships.

We have already referred to Nancy's loving and truly selfless relationship with Richard. After many months of experiencing this, Richard began to show some concern for Nancy's feelings. When he kept her waiting, he said, "I'm sorry to do that to you." In the last several meetings, he began to show awareness, interest, and loving concern for other children whom he previously had ignored. The gentle words he used to express his concern for the wishes of these children were duplicates of phrases he often heard from his volunteer.

Georgie, who had learning difficulties, pointed proudly to the Harvard shirt Chris had given him and said, "I'll wear this to my test tomorrow. I'm a Harvard. I'm Chris." A happy sequel was that he passed his test with room to spare and graduated to the next grade.

Mike, on leaving the hospital, said to his volunteer, "I'm going to take you away with me here," pointing to the area of his small middle. How many professionals can claim such a testimonial from a satisfied client?

5. *Helping to Establish Inner Controls.* The controls of disturbed children are always poor. Necessary for almost all our children was the setting of firm limits to aggressive behavior and to emotional and ma-

terial demands. We hoped that the children would incorporate some of these outside controls and make them a solid part of their functioning. In testing how far they could go with the volunteers, the children often seemed to be asking, "Can you control me as well as love me?"

One of the volunteers learned dramatically that her patient was much happier when she imposed limits on his acting-out behavior. Once she allowed him to attack her physically, and so much anxiety was aroused in both that it was evident in their relationship for many weeks. Both volunteer and supervisor had to work hard on ways of handling this.

6. *Teaching that There May Be Ways to Handle Old Problems.* The children could also be taught new methods of securing some of the emotional rewards of love and attention, status and achievement. Billy learned from his volunteer that achievement in doing things for himself, even tying a bow, brought more positive attention than did helpless babyishness. Georgie learned new ways to approach the "kids" on the ward. Chris, his volunteer, accompanied him in spirit through his tortuous odyssey from ward scapegoat, through placation and identification with aggressors to, at last, holding his own as a member of ward society. Georgie's social worker said with surprise, "Georgie just stopped being the ward pushover."

The students also tried to redirect some of the children's socially unacceptable expression of impulses into more acceptable channels. Many of the planned activities, from bowling for Billy, who feared his own and others' aggression, to science projects for Lewis, had sublimating aims.

7. *Strengthening Healthy Aspects of the Patient's Functioning.* The students encouraged those of their patients' interests and modes of functioning that were clearly healthy. Hilda had some real intellectual ability and loved to read. Peggy used this to interest her in serious reading projects. She also encouraged her to write.

Chris used Georgie's interest in animals and nature to teach him about some aspects of human relationships. Ruth drew on Lewis's executive ability in helping him carry on a puppet project designed to win him respect from his peers.

UNIQUE CONTRIBUTIONS

Students and supervisor tried to factor out together the elements that made the case-aide contribution to the children different from the contribution of the professionally trained therapist and of the semitrained, paid attendant counselor, often also a student with background courses in psychology and sociology. They identified the following unique elements in the volunteer-patient relationship:

1. The Patient Looked on the Volunteer as a Representative of the Community Outside the Hospital. The case-aide volunteers of the children's unit took the children off the hospital grounds as often as possible, trying to give them the kind of experience available to normal children. Usually they spoke with pride of their patient's good behavior in restaurants and museums, behavior which often was exactly opposite the child's usual behavior in the hospital. Moreover, in taking the children into the community they had an opportunity to witness many of the difficulties the children had in dealing with the world outside the hospital—from unrealistic fears to not knowing how to behave in various situations. Such difficulties were handled on the spot by the students, often with therapeutic results.

2. The Case-Aide Relationship Was Activity Oriented. The activities not only had great ego building values in themselves, but also provided an easier way for children who had much difficulty in verbalization to build a relationship. For some of the children in the hospital, the relationship with the volunteer case aide provided the impetus for giving up a deep distrust of adults. Through the case-aide program, which was less threatening to the children than the traditional forms of therapy, once unreachable children developed the ability to relate meaningfully to adults and so became receptive to other forms of psychological help.

3. The Volunteers' Youth Made Them Highly Suitable as Figures for Identification. In two cases of preadolescent boys, identification with male volunteers was especially marked. Both these boys had undergone several years of psychotherapy but neither had matured so rapidly and noticeably as he did in the 9 months of "case-aide therapy." One boy who had been in the hospital for 3 years was ready for discharge at the end of the year. The other was allowed to go home for an extended visit for the first time in several years.

Some of the successes that college students have had in working with emotionally disturbed children may also be related to the fact that college students have just resolved or are in the process of resolving many basic issues of maturation. In late adolescence identity problems, particularly those associated with sexual role and career choice, are among the most pressing issues besetting the individual, and their successful resolution spells the difference between a productive and an unfruitful adult role. Since the emotionally disturbed child is also grappling with many problems of identity, though on a different level, the college student is in a position to be particularly sensitive to many of his struggles and needs. In many cases the supervisor observed that as the student aided the child in working out the problems of self and maturity, the student too seemed to be achieving a definitive solution for himself.

The role of the supervisor required much thought and continuous reappraisal.[3] The goal was always to retain the volunteer's asset of nonprofessional spontaneity and, at the same time, to sensitize him to the meaning of the patient's behavior and to ways of handling it. The professional always had to assume responsibility for judging and balancing the interests of patients, volunteers, and hospital program.

In noting the progress of the patients who were involved in this program some other factors besides the volunteers' services must be kept in mind—especially improvements which were taking place in the hospital milieu, the ratio of staff to patients, and general staff morale. Nevertheless, assessment of the program has to rely on the clinical judgment of the hospital staff, who can note changes in behavior and symptomatology. After the first year of the program, the ward psychiatrists, who have the greatest formal responsibility for the total planning for the patient, reported that three out of four children in the program the entire year showed improvement in functioning. In the second year, when patient selection had the advantage of some experience, the ward physicians reported change and progress in all seven patients. In several cases psychological tests confirmed positive growth. At the end of the first year, two of the five patients were discharged. At the end of the second year, two of the seven patients were ready for discharge, and a third had gone home on extended leave.

The experience of this program indicated that college student volunteers have much to offer in the therapeutic armamentarium of a State hospital for children. Students, supervisor, hospital staff, and patients, by their own statements, were united in this belief.

College Students in a Behavior Therapy Program With Hospitalized Emotionally Disturbed Children

S. F. KREITZER

It is becoming more widely recognized that there is an insufficient supply of professional people to meet the needs of those who have been hospitalized for serious behavioral or emotional disorders. The likely continuation of this unfortunate situation demands ventures into creative therapeutic programming and the search for new sources of therapeutic personnel. This paper describes and evaluates such a program, a *Behavior Therapy Program* in which 21 college students after a minimum of training and experience, provided an intense therapy experience for seven seriously disturbed, hospitalized children.[1]

Behavior therapy is an approach oriented toward changing observable behavior. In principle it is quite simple: help an individual to behave in the "desired" way and see to it that this behavior is rewarded. Because it does not require an understanding of complex causes and intricate psychodynamics, it is particularly suitable for use by nonprofessional, minimally trained personnel. Davison (1965), for example, after a simpler,

This paper was presented at the California State Psychological Association Convention, January, 1966.

[1]The author wishes to acknowledge the cooperation of Norbert I. Rieger, M.D., Assistant Superintendent, Children's Division, Camarillo State Hospital, and the encouragement of Ivar Lovaas, PhD, Psychology Department, U. C. L. A., who provided the students for the program.

smaller program of this kind, concluded that ". . . intelligent, highly-motivated students can be trained in a very short time to execute a behavior-control program that requires the application of learning principles to the manipulation of psychotic behavior in children."

DESCRIPTION OF THE PROGRAM

The "student-therapists" in this program were, for the most part, psychology majors in their senior year who were receiving course credit for this experience: two-thirds of them were female. Each student had completed a course oriented toward behavioral analyses of psychopathology. During the program, they met with the author in a weekly two-hour group supervision session. In addition, they wrote and reviewed each other's session-by-session therapy reports. The students' enthusiasm also brought about frequent sharing of problems and ideas with one another and with the author.

The patients that were selected for this program were active, free of overly offensive behavior, not dangerous to the student-therapists, and readily influenced by the therapists' approval and disapproval. Four young boys and three adolescent girls were selected; their ages ranged from 5 to 15. Each child had been in the hospital for at least six months and none was in individual or group therapy at the time of the program.

Included were Keith, a five year old mute boy; Robert, a fetching, fearful boy of five who spoke only rarely; Larry, an emotionally labile boy of five who was easily upset into destructive tantrums and whose speech was largely inappropriate; Harry, a seven year old boy who yelled and screamed, but could not talk; Barbara, a large 13 year old girl who giggled and talked to herself a great deal of the time about matters of idiosyncratic meaning; Dee, a so-called "hallucinating," bizarre-behaving girl of 13; and Elizabeth, a very quiet, chronically depressed 15 year old.

Three, four, or five distinct "target" behaviors (behaviors to be acquired or eliminated) were then outlined for each of the children. Each of these target behaviors was directly related to some behavior of the child which led people to see him as "strange" or "bizarre." These target behaviors were quite varied, ranging from helping a child to produce particular speech sounds, to the elimination of "silly," or inappropriate behavior, to the teaching of appropriate interpersonal behaviors like answering questions and maintaining eye-contact when talking with someone. For every child, interestingly enough, we found some aspect of speech—its presence, quality, or content—important enough to be chosen as a target behavior.

The scheduling of the patient-therapist contacts represented a radical departure from the more traditional "one-to-one" relationship. It was a novel plan designed to provide each patient with frequent therapy contacts in spite of the fact that each therapist could appear at the hospital only one-half day a week. One-third of the therapists (seven) came on Mondays; another third came on Wednesdays; and the last third came on Fridays. During the three hours that each therapist was at the hospital he saw two patients for approximately 45 minutes each. Each of the seven patients in this program, therefore, had two different therapists on Mondays, another two therapists on Wednesdays, and another two therapists on Fridays. A given patient, then, had six different therapy sessions during the week with six different student-therapists. The schedule of patient-therapist remained the same for each of the six weeks of the program.

PROGRAM EVALUATION

While there were some exceptions, the general findings was that the target behaviors of the children in this program were seen as improved. This was ascertained at the end of the program by asking a number of the staff members to rate changes, if any, in the target behaviors of the children they knew in the program. All the children were rated by the cottage psychiatric technicians and by the student-therapists; some of the children were also rated by teachers and cottage physician. Many of the target behaviors for the children for whom there were teachers' ratings involved the elimination of socially offensive (or inappropriate) behaviors and the establishment of more appropriate behaviors. There was an interesting finding here: The teachers and student-therapist reported more improvement than the technicians reported. One of the most provocative explanations of this difference is that the children have learned to act more appropriately in the presence of those people who "demand" this "better" behavior. In other words, the teachers and student-therapists were least tolerant of "silly" or so-called "sick" behavior and (therefore?) reported seeing the least of it.

The general effectiveness of the program and the observation that the children seem to learn to behave in accordance with the *sanctioned* expectations of the people with whom they interact, is supportive of the idea that a behaviorally oriented program can be quite effective in altering the so-called pathological behavior of hospitalized children. That is to say, when dealing with target behaviors that are to be eliminated or target behaviors that are to be strengthened, the simple principle of *consistent* reward for the behavior to be strengthened and *consistent* punishment for the behavior to be eliminated may be a quite effective means for helping many children to act in different and more desirable ways. This in no way minimizes the importance of the behavior therapist in choosing and/or structuring situations that facilitate the initial occurrence of the new way of behaving, i.e., so that it may be rewarded. It appears that systematic sanction seems to be effective, even when implemented by a sequence of therapists with these children; in fact, it might even be *more* effective when more of the child's social environment responds consistently to the way he behaves. Two limitations, though, must be mentioned with respect to this idea. First, the idea of "many therapists" trained as these people were trained does not seem to be equally effective for all kinds of target behaviors. These therapists were *least* effective in teaching new and/or complex behaviors that the child could not easily produce. Second, learning theory predicts, and relevant research has shown, that punishment is usually not effective in eliminating undesirable behavior in those causes where the individual has alternate means for achieving the same end as the undesirable behavior achieves.

This experience for the students was a rewarding one; they entered the program in an energetic and enthusiastic way and their motivation remained high throughout the period of the program. Some of the students requested the continuation or expansion of the program and a few students even called this the "highlight of their college experience." Parenthetically, it seems that what was "rewarding" in the theoretical sense, for these students was the experience of confronting a challenging situation that was so structured that they were able to meet it successfully.

The importance of this program was (1) the demonstration of the suitability of a behaviorally oriented therapy approach for the behavior problems of hospitalized, disturbed children and (2) the feasibility of using (part-time) nonprofessional personnel as therapists in such a program.

You might be interested to know where we have gone from here. We have embarked on an intensive training program which has as one of its main objectives to teach nonprofessional hospital employees how to teach speech to essentially mute children. So far, the technicians involved in this training are learning behavior therapeutic techniques suitable for speech teaching and the children involved are slowly but surely learning how to talk.

REFERENCE

Davison, G.C. The training of undergraduates as social reinforcers for autistic children. In L. Ullmann and L. Krasner (Eds.) *Case studies in behavior modification.* New York: Holt, Rinehart and Winston, Inc., 1965, pp. 146–148.

Some Casework Aspects of Using Foster Grandparents for Emotionally Disturbed Children

RUTH JOHNSTON

They wait at the gate to greet their foster grandparents. Eager, impatient children wait for equally eager foster grandparents who will take them out of the group-care unit of the county child welfare agency to the privacy of a vacant sitting room, office, niche in the hall, or spot under a shade tree on the institution's grounds.

All are children being cared for by the Medical and Emotional Treatment Service Unit of the Summit County (Ohio) Child Welfare Board, known by the staff as the METS. Most of them are of preschool age, and most of them have physical, mental, or emotional handicaps, or a combination of these problems. All are under the county's care as dependent and neglected children.

The foster grandparents come to the children for 4 hours a day through the Foster Grandparents Project, a demonstration project to give employment to needy persons who are over the age of 60, sponsored by the Office of Economic Opportunity (OEO) and the Administration on Aging of the U.S. Department of Health, Education, and Welfare. The chief interest of the Summit County Child Welfare Board in participating in the project, however, has been in tapping the potential of foster grandparents as treatment agents in its social casework efforts to help the children to a happier life.

Reprinted from *Children*, 1967, Vol. 14, No. 2, 46–52, with the permission of the U.S. Department of Health, Education, and Welfare, Welfare Administration, Children's Bureau, and the author. A brief biography of the author has been omitted; as have photographs.

Through its METS unit, the Summit County Child Welfare Board provides temporary group care for some young children who must be removed from their homes for their protection—and sometimes their very survival—and for whom no other arrangement is immediately available. Many children arrive at the agency with such aggravated behavioral problems that even the most experienced and capable foster parents could not cope with them. Even some very young children seem so damaged by their experiences that they need the kinds of control that can be provided only in group living before they can form the kinds of relationships with other human beings that are prerequisite to a successful foster home experience.

Like most child-care agencies, however, our agency has realized that its child-care workers could not give individual children enough attention to provide them with the necessary ego-building experiences. Such children, we felt, needed the kind of loving, personal attention that a foster grandparent might be able to give them.

Our agency was one of the first 21 agencies chosen by the Administration on Aging to participate in the Foster Grandparents Project. Planning took place in 1965. It was agreed that each participating agency would adapt its program to the needs of the children under its care within the framework of policies established by the Administration on Aging and OEO. The agencies would choose the grandparents, train them for their work, and assign them to specific children.

The staff for the Summit County Foster Grandparents Project consists of a part-time director from the agency's social service staff, a part-time supervisor hired especially for this position, and a part-time consultant and a full-time field supervisor from the agency's institutional child-care staff. In addition, a five-member advisory committee, representing senior citizens groups, labor unions, the Summit County Child Welfare Board, and the local community action council, meets together regularly to review the program's policies.

SELECTION AND ORIENTATION

The actual hiring of grandparents began in January 1966. Ten grandparents were accepted at that time from 75 applicants. Later, the agency employed two other groups of foster grandparents—10 in each group. Of the 30 foster grandparents employed, 23 are still in the project—18 grandmothers and 5 grandfathers.

For acceptance to the program, the applicants had to meet the OEO criteria of having no more than $1,800 per year income (since lowered to $1,500) and of being over 60 years of age. They also had to have their physician's approval and had to be able to hear and see well, to move around easily, to pick up small children, to climb stairs, to sit on the floor, and to play games.

Other criteria called for the subjective judgments of agency staff members made on the basis of personal interviews and of study of the foster grandparents' written applications: functional literacy; reasonably good grooming; pleasant appearance; ability to listen and ability to express meaning; and some indication of having had enjoyable experiences with children, their own or other people's.

In our selection process, we sought evidence of satisfactory life experiences; adequate adjustment to age and financial status; an interest in people, especially children; a wish to be of service to someone; and an ability to understand and accept the agency's policies. We tried to find clues to these qualities during the application process and through observation of the applicants as they were shown through the METS unit. One crucial test was the "touch test"—a literal reaching out to children followed by a spontaneous and positive response from the children.

Before the orientation program began, we had wondered whether older people not used to an academic approach would be able to accept and benefit from an orientation program. We had wondered how approachable they would be in respect to the staff and one another and how adaptable they would be to the routine and policies of the agency. We were pleasantly surprised to find that the foster grandparents immediately saw themselves as a "group" and began at once to participate in the discussions. They seemed to have the wisdom that comes with age and genuine interest in the project.

The orientation began with an overall description of the agency, its plant, staff plan, and major policies regarding child care. But, the chief focus was on helping the foster grandparents understand the children and how to work with them. When we outlined the ways in which children normally develop, we found the foster grandparents were interested from two standpoints: (1) As a new way of looking at child-rearing practices, since most of them had never before considered child rearing from a theoretical point of view; and (2) as an opportunity to tell of their experiences with their own children and grandchildren.

After discussing theory, we focused our attention on the particular children with whom the grandparents would be working. Again we were pleasantly surprised at the general openmindedness and flexibility shown in these discussions. However, we found out later that all the foster grandparents had not understood all of what was said and were not actually prepared for the situations they would face. But, in spite of some difficulties with the children, they stood pat in their determination to help the children assigned to them.

We tried to help the foster grandparents understand that these children would not be like their own grandchildren and that as foster grandparents they would have different obligations and responsibilities than as grandparents. We told them that a major goal of the project was to meet each child's needs and help him solve his problems.

During the orientation week, we discerned many kinds of strength in the foster grandparents—sincerity, security, self-esteem, flexibility, warmth, and stamina—that we hoped would be passed on to our children. We also found weaknesses in these areas. However, by appraising each individual, we attempted to match grandparent and child so that their strengths and weaknesses would complement one another's. The goal was to provide the child with a person to whom he could relate and in whom he would see the qualities he needed most.

By the end of the orientation week, everybody was eagerly anticipating the climax—the assignment of particular children to particular grandparents. We arrived at these assignments on the basis of information received from the agency's child-care workers and the children's social workers. While these workers were usually in general agreement about the child's needs, the child-care workers tended to emphasize behavioral problems and the social workers to emphasize inner conflicts. Where it seemed necessary, we had conferences with the workers on particular children before coming to a decision. In all assignments, the child's needs were given first priority. No consideration was given to race or age of grandparents or child.

AGENCY TEAM MEMBERS

The first foster grandparents received their assignments on January 28, 1966. On that day, the foster grandparents, all of whom had been introduced to all the children previously, were literally sitting on the edge of their chairs in their eagerness to find out which ones they would get. Without exception they accepted the children selected for them. Subsequently, either the director or supervisor talked with the grandparent, giving him information about his particular child that would help him in working with the child. The grandparent was frankly told about the child's present problems and what the agency's long-term goal for him was, given suggestions for dealing with the child, and encouraged to do "what comes naturally" within the framework of the agency's rules and the child's special needs.

Each foster grandparent and child were assigned a place where they could be alone together and were supplied with a bag full of toys selected for that particular child and used by him only when he was with his foster grandparent.

The foster grandparents showed a surprising ability to understand and accept the basic policies of the agency with regard to the development of children and to help us implement them. In fact, one of our staff members has used the term "intuitive casework" to describe what some of the foster grandparents have done.

We feel, and let the grandparents know we do, that they are a part of an agency team caring for children. They keep a record of their work with the children and are encouraged to report both the good days and bad days and to express their own thoughts about the child, his problems, and his progress. These records are shared with the child-care and social work staffs. The entire staff has been pleased to see how pertinent they are.

Warm relationships between the foster grandparents and their assigned children began developing immediately, and the grandparents soon learned at first hand about the children's problems.

One grandmother wrote after a short time:

> Johnny was so glad to see me. They told me he could hardly wait until I came. We got our toys and went to our room. I noticed he was nervous and shy. All at once he began to open up to me and tell me how his mommy had come and brought him some toys, and he asked me to please help him grow up so he could whip his daddy for beating up his mommy. It broke my heart to see him in this attitude. I think parents' troubles shouldn't be pushed on the child, especially at this age. Johnny is very smart and understands more than most children his age.

This grandmother has said that Johnny's show of feeling came as a shock to her even though she had been warned. However, a warm relationship has developed between them.

In this early period a foster grandfather wrote of a very disturbed little boy:

> He is to me the greatest because he is my grandson. He is not what I would call a bad, bad boy. Sometimes he is nice as he can be, otherwise is real mean, but I hope to help to make a good boy out of him. There are times I think I see a big change. I hope every day I can find some way to cope with him.

The grandfather has found a way to cope, and the change in the child is almost unbelievable.

One woman was assigned a little girl who was so withdrawn that she went for days without speaking. After a while this foster grandmother wrote:

> I have noticed a change in her personal pride. Now she will ask me to comb her hair, give her a bath, put her in a dress instead of pants. These are things she did not even notice when I got her, and to me this is a marked improvement, for as long as you can keep a child's personal pride up and keep it feeling someone else cares you have a chance of their trying to build a life.

In general, the foster grandparents have been most willing to share their impressions with other staff members. However, as they get to know a child they tend to become increasingly protective of him and have to be reminded from time to time that their job is not to protect the child from criticism, but to work with everyone else toward helping him overcome his problems.

Some foster grandparents have been remarkably acute in their observations. One recorded:

> Every day I understand him better and treat him as an individual. He seems to be searching for something he can't quite find, and to be inwardly at war with himself, which makes him resentful and rebellious.

SOME BYPRODUCTS

After nearly a year we are able to appreciate the program from the standpoint of the agency, the social work staff, the child-care staff, the foster grandparents, and of course the children.

Agency Benefits. In addition to what the program has done for our children, it has resulted in increased community good will toward the agency. The 30 foster grandparents and 5 advisory committee members who have taken the orientation course and the community agencies that have referred prospective foster grandparents to the agency now have a better understanding of the agency and its program. And the agency has been called to the attention of the public at large through favorable news and magazine stories focused on the opportunity it has given older people to work with children.

Casework Benefits. The agency's social workers probably had both the greatest hope and the most misgivings of all the staff members about the Foster Grandparents Project. They realized that the children would benefit from a one-to-one relationship that the child-care workers could not provide. They recognized that one or two visits a week from a caseworker was not enough to sustain a very young, disturbed child. However, their training and experience had taught them the value of skilled casework based on investigation, diagnosis and treatment, and they wondered how foster grandparents with no professional education could fit into a casework plan.

The social workers also wondered how, with the restrictions on age and income set by the Office of Economic Opportunity, foster grandparents could be found who were not too physically, culturally, and educationally limited to be able to give the children what they needed. They also wondered whether the children would be faced with conflicts in loyalty between caseworkers and foster grandparents or between foster grandparents and the child's own parents and relatives. They wondered whether the foster grandparents would have enough understanding and stamina to bear up under the child's expressions of hostility or whether they would get enough satisfaction out of the job themselves to be able to give anything of value to the child.

Almost without exception, the social workers' fears have been laid to rest and their hopes fulfilled. Moreover, they have often found information gained from the grandparents useful in furthering their own understanding of the children in their caseloads. For example, a grandparent wrote of a child:

> We went for a walk today and she opened up a bit by talking of her mother, whom she mentions quite often, but more than her mother she speaks of her father. Sally asked me why doesn't her daddy get well. I did not know what or how to answer her but I tried to make her feel better. . . .

Sally had not previously revealed her deep concern about her father. Learning of it through the foster grandparent, the social worker could help the little girl deal with it.

During the past year, among the children who were assigned foster grandparents, nine have been returned to their own homes and nine have been placed in foster family homes. While the foster grandparents cannot be given the entire credit for the emotional progress that enabled these children to go into a family setting, in each case a foster grandparent made a definite contribution toward it. The social workers helped the child use the relationship with his foster grandparent to find the strength for these moves.

While the grandparents have felt sad at the loss of the children, in each case they gave them real support in moving on. One foster grandmother wrote to a once extremely withdrawn child:

> This is from your dear grandmama, and I must say that I have enjoyed you so very much since I have had you in my care, and I did my best to bring you up to here with a secret prayer. Wherever you go, or wherever you be, I pray that the good Lord will be there.

Another foster grandmother who had helped a very aggressive child establish control recorded:

> Bill has been informed he is going to a foster home where he will have a mommy and daddy. He is strong willed sometimes, slow to obey, but, if let alone, he will change his attitude. I am very happy that he has a mother and daddy plus a good home because that is what every child needs to develop a strong character and become a good citizen. I really am reluctant to give him up, but it is for a better way to develop finer character. I keep telling him he is leaving his foster grandmother for a real foster mother plus a home of his own and so much else to make him feel free and happy.

Some of the social workers have reported that the children in their caseloads are more approachable since they have had foster grandparents, that they talk more to the social workers, listen better, are more able to bear the separation from their parents, and generally have a better feeling about people, particularly the adults in their lives. One grandparent wrote a little boy who 3 months earlier had had great difficulties in personal relationships:

> It has been a pleasure working with Dan, also a real challenge at times, but it has been rewarding just to see him grow in size, disposition, and temperament. He has changed from the sulky, disobedient little fellow I met on May 3. I feel my time and effort have been well spent.

Child-Care Benefits. The foster grandparent program has meant that some children are out of the child-care unit for 4 hours a day, thus giving the child-care workers more time to spend with the children who do not have foster grandparents. As a result, the children in group care are happier, more relaxed, and more controllable.

The houseparents tell us that having a foster grandparent is a "status symbol" among the children. They also report that the children who have foster grandparents play better, eat better, sleep better, and look better than the other children.

Children in METS who do not have grandparents are those who are in temporary care, who are too young, or whose particular needs could not be met by any foster grandparent who is available for assignment at the time.

Some minor difficulties have occurred in the METS unit since the initiation of the foster grandparent program. Child-care workers and foster grandparents sometimes meet head on with conflicting ideas, often involving housekeeping problems, and occasionally resulting in bruised feelings. However, since foster grandparents and child-care staff alike have genuine concern for the welfare of the children, none of these minor difficulties have amounted to anything that poses any real problem. There is generally a friendly, satisfying give and take between foster grandparent and houseparent. If any real difficulty should arise between them, however, the supervisor of the child-care staff would be responsible for dealing with it.

Grandparent Benefits. The foster grandparents themselves all seem to enjoy a feeling of being of use. One foster grandfather said recently that it gives him a reason for getting up in the morning.

When the foster grandparents are asked what the experience has meant to them, they nearly always cite the progress they see in the development of the children assigned to them and their pride in their accomplishments. One grandparent reported:

> Fred was very good and played good and was in an unusual good mood all morning. He did not bite or try to bite me or anyone.

In spite of being bit, hit, kicked, spit on, cursed, run away from, berated, yelled at, and disobeyed, the foster grandparents have kept perspective and have often seen the deeper meaning of the child's behavior and even the humor in it. One seriously disturbed child suddenly hit his grandmother with a knife handle and then complained because she bled. Three months later the same child accidentally kicked the grandmother while playing and was most solicitous and concerned. The foster grandmother reported both incidents, the second with pride, even though it had resulted in a black eye for her.

There has been almost no absenteeism among the foster grandparents except for illness. They have come to the agency through cold and heat and on holidays. They have gone with their children on all-day picnics, hikes in the woods, walks in the park, visits to the circus; they have gone wading with them to help them catch tadpoles; in short they have gone wherever the children have gone, without question and apparently with pleasure.

THE CHILDREN

The *raison d'être* of our program is, of course, the children—what they have needed, what they have received, and what they have become. For them the experience has been a positive one physically, mentally, and emotionally. We have followed Erikson's eight stages of man[1] in classifying the development that has taken place in the children during this period. Some children have made remarkable progress; others, very little. However, in every case some progress is evident.

Sense of Trust. For many of our children the relationship with their foster grandparent is the first positive relationship they have had with an adult. It starts, whether the child is age 2 or 8, with having a lap to sit on and involves being cuddled and comforted. It moves on to confidence that the foster grandparent will do what he says he will do.

Before coming to us many of our children have been given little in their own homes except the bare essentials. Yet after a child's placement away from home, his parents often try to make up for their own hurt and that of the child by bringing him gifts. To the child these seem only a superficial token of love. We try to restore the proper balance by having the foster grandparents give the children much attention and warmth but little in a material way. The foster grandparent and the child take a walk together to enjoy one another and the outdoors rather than to get an ice

[1]Erik H. Erikson, *Childhood and Society.* New York: W. W. Norton & Co., 1950.

cream cone. However, if occasionally the grandparent combines the two purposes, we do not object.

Autonomy. Through their genuine feeling for the children, the foster grandparents have helped absolve some of the shame and doubt brought on the children by the loss of their parents.

We believe that the grandparents, using their own experience, interest, initiative, and imagination, have helped develop the children's personalities in a more personal and intimate way than could have been done by a social worker or child-care worker. They have helped children develop a feeling of worth by offering them warm affection, and this affection has deepened as the children have begun to return it. They have demonstrated their sense of the child's worth by doing things for him—bathing, dressing, combing hair, tying shoes, pulling up socks, putting on mittens and cap. Through words, expressions, and gestures, they have shown appreciation of the child himself and their pleasure in the way he looks, behaves, and achieves. With very young children, they have done this unconsciously through simple games such as "Show me your nose."

The fact that the foster grandparent "belongs" to the child adds to the child's sense of worth. Children have shown their need and their appreciation of this by being very possessive of their grandparents and very jealous of their attention.

Initiative. The grandparent not only encourages the use of the creative toys provided for the child; he also participates in imaginative play with them, thus helping the child learn to use initiative and imagination. Showing his appreciation of the child's creative efforts, he encourages the child to experiment not only with what he can do with his own mind and body but also with how he can control outside things.

Many of our children have insufficient ability to express themselves in words. Not having been encouraged to talk in their own homes, they tend to act out rather than talk out their feelings. Because of this we have urged the foster grandparents to read aloud to the children, to tell them stories, and above all to talk to them and to encourage them to respond. As a result, many of the children have learned to talk not only about the things they see around them but also about their thoughts and feelings.

Industry. We have encouraged the foster grandparents not only to do things for the children but also to expect the children to do things for them and eventually for other adults and other children. Children willingly run errands for grandparents, help them pick up toys, and do other things because "Grandmother asks you to," and they seem to derive a sense of satisfaction from it.

Foster grandparents have also taught children how to greet people, how to eat properly, and how to take care of themselves and their clothing. Many of our children have had no previous opportunity to learn about such social amenities. Feeling comfortable in these areas increases the child's self-assurance, thus releasing energy for further growth.

Foster grandparents have also helped some children prepare to enter school. By showing their appreciation of the children's efforts they have made learning easier for the children.

One determined foster grandparent helped a physically handicapped little girl who had spent most of her time in a wheelchair progress first to a walker and then to crutches. There were numerous clashes of will, sometimes ending in a draw, but most often in the grandparent's maintaining control and in turning the experience into a positive one for the child.

Sense of Identity. The foster grandparents have helped children establish a sense of identity by each transmitting to his child his feeling that the child is special, through helping him know what he can do, and through helping him accept controls. Many of our children before coming to us were controlled too harshly or not at all. The foster grandparents are making a great contribution in helping the children respect both their own rights and the rights of others by establishing a benign control.

The foster grandparents have also helped children learn to share—for example, to take turns on a tricycle. The grandparent is obviously proud when his particular child awaits his turn, especially when the child thinks of something interesting to do while waiting.

The grandparents have also helped the children become conscious of the world around them. We have encouraged them to take their children walking and to call attention to the sunlight, fresh air, green grass, birds, insects, and pebbles. Last spring METS was ablaze with dandelions in peanut butter glasses. Last summer it housed large collections of tadpoles, bugs, and pebbles. Last fall, red and yellow leaves lined the walls.

We believe that the very fact of being taken out of the group physically for a period of quiet and relaxation with only one other person has been of great benefit to the child. It has not only allowed him the satisfaction of a one-to-one relationship but has also given him an opportunity to become acquainted with himself and to learn about his own areas of strength and limitation by experimenting on an accepting adult.

Obviously, we feel that this experiment has been a success.

SUGGESTED ADDITIONAL READINGS

Andronico, Michael P., and Guerney, Jr., Bernard G. The use of a child psychotherapeutic aid in a Head Start Program. Unpublished report, 1967.

Avrunin, William. The volunteer in case work treatment. *The Family*, 1944, Vol. 25, No. 4, 137–143.

Bard, Morton, and Berkowitz, Bernard. Training police as specialists in family crisis intervention: A community psychology action program. *Community Mental Health Journal*, 1967, Vol. 3, No. 4, 315–317.

Barthol, Richard P., Groot, Henriette, and Tomlinson, T. M. Variations of the theme of group interaction: The use of student volunteers as role models for psychiatric patients in a quasi-sensitivity training (Peanut Cluster) laboratory. Paper presented at the American Psychological Association Conference, New York, 1966.

Benjamin, Judith G., Freedman, Marcia K., and Lynton, Edith F. *Pros and cons: New roles for nonprofessionals in Corrections.* United States Department of Health, Education, and Welfare, Office of Juvenile Delinquency and Youth Development. Washington, D.C.: Government Printing Office, 1966.

Big Brothers, Inc. Big Brothers, Inc.; what it is, what it does, how it does it. Mimeographed brochure. New York: Big Brothers, Inc.

Bijou, Sidney W. Experimental studies of child behavior, normal and deviant. In Krasner, Leonard, and Ullmann, Leonard P. (Eds.) *Research in behavior modification.* New York: Holt, Rinehart and Winston, Inc., 1965, Pp. 56–71.

Brennen, Earl C. College students and mental health programs for children. *American Journal of Public Health*, 1967, Vol. 57, 1767–1771.

Burchard, John D. Systematic socialization: A programmed environment for the habilitation of antisocial retardates. *Psychological Record*, in press.

Burchard, John, and Tyler, Jr., Vernon. The modification of delinquent behaviour through operant conditioning. *Behaviour Research & Therapy*, 1965, Vol. 2, 245–250.

Christmas, June J. Sociopsychiatric treatment of disadvantaged psychotic adults. *American Journal of Orthopsychiatry*, 1967, Vol. 37, No. 1, 93–100.

Davison, Gerald C. A social learning therapy programme with an autistic child. *Behaviour Research & Therapy*, 1964, Vol. 2, 149–159.

Davison, Gerald C. The training of undergraduates as social reinforcers for autistic children. In Ullmann, Leonard P., and Krasner, Leonard

(Eds.) *Case studies in behavior modification.* New York: Holt, Rinehart and Winston, Inc., 1966. Pp. 146–148.

Dinsmoor, James A. Comments on Wetzel's treatment of a case of compulsive stealing. *Journal of Consulting Psychology*, 1966, Vol. 30, No. 5, 378–380.

Donahue, George T., and Nichtern, Sol. *Teaching the troubled child.* New York: The Free Press, 1965.

Feder, Bud. Consultation with guidance personnel in crisis situations. Paper presented at the 37th Annual Meeting of Eastern Psychological Association, New York, 1966.

Fellows, Lloyd, and Wolpin, Milton. High school psychology trainees in a mental hospital. Paper presented at the California State Psychological Association Convention, 1966.

Field, Lewis W. An ego-programmed group treatment approach with emotionally disturbed boys. *Psychological Reports*, 1966, 18, 47–50.

Foster Grandparents Project. Mimeographed reports of OEO Demonstration Project. Available from J. Iverson Riddle, M.D., Superintendent, Western Carolina Center, Morgantown, North Carolina.

Garvey, W. P., and Hegrenes, Jack R. Desensitization techniques in the treatment of school phobia. *American Journal of Orthopsychiatry*, 1966, Vol. 36, 147–152.

Goodman, Gerald. Companionship as therapy: the use of nonprofessional talent. In Hart, J. T., and Tomlinson, T. M. (Eds.) *New directions in client-centered psychotherapy.* Boston: Houghton Mifflin Company, 1969.

Graziano, Anthony M. Programmed psychotherapy: a behavioral approach to emotionally disturbed children. Paper presented at the 38th Annual Meeting of Eastern Psychological Association, Boston, 1967.

Greenblatt, Milton, and Kantor, David. Student volunteer movement and the manpower shortage. *American Journal of Psychiatry*, 1962, Vol. 118, 809–814.

Harvey, L. V. The use of non-professional auxiliary counsellors in staffing a [marital] counselling service. *Journal of Counseling Psychology*, 1964, Vol. 11, No. 4, 348–351.

Heilig, S. M., Farberow, N. L., and Litman, R. E. The role of nonprofessional volunteers in a suicide prevention center. *Community Mental Health Journal*, 1968, in press.

Holzberg, Jules D. The companion program: Implementing the manpower recommendations of the joint commission on mental illness and health. *American Psychologist*, 1963, Vol. 18, No. 4, 224–226.

Holzberg, Jules D., Whiting, Harry S., and Lowy, David G. Chronic patients and a college companion program. *Mental Hospitals*, 1964, Vol. 15, 152–158.

Lang, Peter J. The transfer of treatment. *Journal of Consulting Psychology*, 1966, Vol. 30, No. 5, 375–378.

Lawton, M. Powell, and Lipton, Mortimer B. Student-employees become companions to patients. *Mental Hospitals*, 1963, 14, 550–556.

May, Dorothy C. The use of volunteers in conjunction with psychotherapy. Masters thesis, Smith College School for Social Work, 1949.

Roche Report: Frontiers of Hospital Psychiatry. Nonprofessionals: Key workers in "attitude therapy." Vol. 5, No. 10, May, 1968.

Skeels, Howard M. Adult status of children with contrasting early life experiences. *Monographs of the Society for Research in Child Development*, 1966, Vol. 31, No. 3.

Spingarn, Natalie D. (Ed.) *The volunteer and the psychiatric patient.* Washington, D.C.: American Psychiatric Association, 1959.

Umbarger, Carter C., Dalsimer, James S., Morrison, Andrew T., and Breggin, Peter R., assisted and with an introduction by Kantor, David, and Greenblatt, Milton. *College students in a mental hospital.* New York: Grune and Stratton, 1962.

Walker, C. Eugene. The development and evaluation of a psychology practicum program for undergraduate students. Paper presented at the California State Psychological Association Convention, 1966.

Wetzel, Ralph. Use of behavioral techniques in a case of compulsive stealing. *Journal of Consulting Psychology*, 1966, Vol. 30, No. 5, 367–374.

PART 4

Peers as Therapeutic Agents

Introduction

IN the preceding commentary we have referred to parents, peers, and teachers as being naturally significant others, and spoken of volunteers becoming significant others to children by virtue of the role assigned to them. The phrase "significant others" is one used mainly in the context of the interpersonal theories of Harry Stack Sullivan. As it is usually employed, a significant other may be important to an individual's current life in a psychological sense only, rather than in terms of physical interaction. The influence of a significant other may be a function of past rather than present interaction, and often refers to a one-way process.

In the lives of children, there are several groups of significant others with whom the child lives a sizable portion of his life. They form a very special subgroup of significant others. These individuals not only influence the development of the child's self-concept, his concepts of others, and the development of his behavioral patterns, but *they* in turn are intimately affected and influenced by the youngster himself. Paramount among such groups are parents, teachers, and peers. In unusual settings, other groups play a similar role; for example, psychiatric aides and attendants in residential institutions. Such individuals interact with the child during a large part of his day, hold a position of influence or power over him, and, knowingly or unwittingly, respond in a meaningful way to almost everything the child does. Even a failure of response in such a person in certain instances is a very significant act. Their responses are often "reflexive" to the child's, in the sense of being immediate and unthinking; their behavior is in large measure shaped by his. In turn, his future patterns of interaction are being molded or "trained" by their responses.

It bears repeating that persons in such a position vis-a-vis the child may be those with the greatest potential for beneficial influence upon the child's psychosocial adjustment. This potential arises first from the fact that large numbers of such people are available who have some inherent motivation for training. Second, by virtue of their roles, such individuals meet or fail to meet the physical and psychosocial needs of the child. Third, such persons provide models or identification figures for the child. Thus, the nature of their everyday interaction with the child puts them in a position of great influence with respect to the child's personality development.

Because of the important role and the great potential of such figures as therapeutic agents, it seems convenient and desirable to designate them by a special term, and the word "symbiont" is suggested. A dictionary definition of symbiosis in biology is "the living together of two species of organisms . . . usually restricted to cases in which the union of the two animals or plants is not disadvantageous to either, or is advantageous or necessary to both."[1] Symbion is Greek for living together and, in biology, the word symbiont applies to organisms living in a state of symbiosis.

Those in the mental health professions already have used the term symbiosis to refer to interaction among humans. Margaret Mahler[2] has referred to the relationship of an infant and mother as "social symbiosis" or simply "symbiosis," and to one type of psychotic child as the symbiotic child. (Overwhelming separation anxiety does not allow this type of child to develop an ego independent from that of its mother.) Generally speaking, the use of the word symbiosis to designate a mutally helpful relationship is as appropriate, or more appropriate, than its use to designate a pathological relationship.

The term seems to do justice to the type of relationship which exists between people whose actions are inherently significant to one another's adjustment. The fact that the term can be used to refer both to the person being changed and the change agent is viewed as an advantage. Such duality is very consistent with the basic underlying assumption involved in using this type of nonprofessional as change agent; these assumptions are that (a) the attempt to change another almost inevitably involves a change in the nature of a *relationship*, and (b) the helper is often himself changed for the better as a consequence of his efforts. In this sort of therapeutic endeavor, the line between the changer and the one changed often

[1]*The American College Dictionary*. New York: Random House, Inc., 1947.

[2]Mahler, Margaret S. On child psychosis and schizophrenia. *Psychoanalytic study of the child*, Vol. VII. New York: International Universities Press, 1952. Pp. 286–306.

is not nearly so clear as in traditional treatment approaches, and it is appropriate that the word used to describe the participants reflects that fact.

The study by Buehler, Patterson, and Furniss shows that in the institutional setting for delinquent children which they studied, transactions between the children were more frequent than those between the children and staff. They feel it reasonable to hypothesize that "the inmate behavioral system not only shapes and controls its own numbers, but also . . . shapes and controls the behavior of the staff." It seems clear that the question the reader should ask himself is not whether it is appropriate to encourage peers to influence the behavior of others, since this is obviously occurring anyway, but whether ways can be found to structure the interpersonal environment so that this influence is beneficial rather than detrimental to the group and the individuals comprising it. This study poses that question, and the other studies in this section are tentative first steps toward answering it. A prediction is ventured here that there will be many more clinical studies dealing with this question in the future.

The utilization of companionship between young children and volunteer teenagers to meet some of the important psychosocial needs of both is illustrated in the carefully thought out program of Perlmutter and Durham. Another program using high school students was intended to be more directly psychotherapeutic. Fellows and Wolpin engaged their teenagers with adolescents and preadolescents in a mental hospital in "group therapy . . . counseling and tutoring . . . and . . . pilot conditioning programs" in addition to various social activities. They conclude that the program was of considerable value, and pose many interesting questions concerning the direction and dimensions which future projects of this nature might explore.

As was also the case in the studies just discussed, the peer participants in Gittelman's studies are not symbionts; they do not spend a sizable portion of their lives together. In comparison to the previously mentioned projects they are, however, closer in age (12 to 14) and status, and they share a common background of having been referred to a county mental health clinic for help. In this project, perhaps more than in any other in this section, the peers are deliberately and systematically used as psychotherapeutic agents, in the sense that they are given clearly defined psychotherapeutic roles to play. Moreover, as they played roles toward the child which allowed him to practice desirable behaviors, and as they rated the adequacy of his responses, they were fully cognizant of their status as therapeutic agents for one another. Such awareness may be one important element in facilitating secondary positive effects expected due to the helper-therapy principle. Gittelman's work may well be a major breakthrough in the use of peers as therapeutic agents, and of child group therapy in general.

The use of peers who *are* symbionts is illustrated in the remaining selections. Some of these studies tend to involve highly specific role training for the symbionts, others attempt to arrange the motivations and social system of the groups in such a way that the symbionts tend to move toward the desired behavior in the natural course of events. Some are interested only in changing the "target" children, others clearly rely on the helper-therapy principle and mutual change.

In the study by Patterson, Jones, Whittier, and Wright, peers were involved only in a very general way by sharing in the "reinforcements" given to one boy to reduce his hyperactivity. Observations and comparison with similar studies, however, led the experimenter to hypothesize that "the importance of any change in behavior lies in the effect which it produces upon the reaction of the social culture" and that "a change in status in the peer group implies peer reinforcement for socially acceptable behavior patterns of a wide variety . . . in addition to those which are specifically being conditioned by the experimenter." This hypothesis led Straughan, Potter, and Hamilton to record certain types of peer activities presumed to be helpful in getting an elective mute to respond verbally in a classroom situation. Their findings were consonant with the assumption that the peer influence was salutary. Both of these studies relied upon a structuring of the environment to bring about the desired responses by peers (rewards available to the total group contingent upon the target child's improved behavior).

The remaining selections are also of exceptional significance in that the individuals used to effect psychosocial change in their peers are symbionts. Also, these projects rely a great deal on the helper therapy principle. It is probably not coincidental that delinquents should be so heavily represented in this Part, since it has long been observed that delinquents as a group tend to be notoriously unresponsive to adult authorities, while being acutely sensitive to social acceptance or rejection by their peers.

The project to teach learning skills to disturbed delinquent children, described by Minuchin, Chamberlain, and Graubard, made use of one of the techniques also employed by Gittelman: the peers took turns in judging the appropriateness of one another's behavior in a given set of circumstances and with specified criteria for making judgments. The authors describe how the "judging functions seemed to have significant effects on the behavior and in the process of self-observation in the children," these effects being of a positive nature. This project dealt with an "educational" problem rather than with the "emotional" problems of these children, but the conclusion can hardly be escaped, upon reading this article, that each of these two sets of problems feeds on the other, and that the processes involved in dealing with one cannot help but work on the other, that the progress achieved in either one will usually result in at least some progress in the other, and that the same techniques might be employed to deal with nonclassroom behavior. The gains achieved in this project did not generalize very much, but the authors point out that even these restricted gains may be considered encouraging for a pilot project lasting only five weeks. The problem of encouraging generalization from behaviors achieved in the circumscribed therapeutic situation to other, more natural, circumstances is one faced by all therapists.

The last selection in this part is the Essexfields research program described by Pilnick, Elias, and Clapp. The setting here is outside the child's home community, to which he returns every night. But a great deal of attention is given in this project toward maintaining a natural kind of peer interaction between the participants. "The same pressure to conform which affects delinquents in the community through a delinquent peer group is applied at Essexfields by a peer group ascribing to conventional norms." The descriptions of cultural "seeding" and other methods of cultural transformation represent a major contribution to the therapeutic use of peers. As the authors point out, the potentiality of peer group approaches has hardly been tapped. Their approach—which skillfully blends natural peer processes, unobtrusive teaching of appropriate role behaviors to status members of the group who then pass them on to their peers, and the application of institution social controls—offers much food for thought with respect to the problems of achieving therapeutic generalization and of tapping the therapeutic potential of the peer group.

The Reinforcement of Behavior in Institutional Settings

R. E. BUEHLER
G. R. PATTERSON
J. M. FURNISS

Three studies are reported which identified and measured social reinforcers occurring among inmates and staff in institutions for delinquent children. Observation and coding procedures were derived from interpersonal communication and operant conditioning research. Results indicate that the social living system of a correctional institution tends to reinforce delinquent responses and to punish socially conforming responses, and the delinquency reinforcing responses tend to occur on nonverbal levels of communication. Implications for rescheduling reinforcers within the social system are discussed.

INTRODUCTION

The importance of the peer group in shaping and controlling behavior has been stressed by both socio-cultural and psychological theorists. The present report summarizes a series of pilot studies which identify some of the behavioral processes associated with shaping and controlling behavior within a peer group of delinquent adolescents.

The assumptions implicit in these studies are derived from recent literature on social learning and interpersonal communications behavior.

Reprinted with permission from *Behaviour Research & Therapy*, 1966, Vol. 4, 157–167, Copyright 1966, Pergamon Press, Inc., and with the permission of the authors. These studies were supported in part by research grants from the Office of the Institution Research Coordinator, Board of Control, State of Oregon, Salem, Oregon.

Specifically, it is assumed that the interpersonal communication transactions within a peer group function as reinforcers. When put in terms of a reinforcement paradigm this means that in the peer group situation behavior operates upon the social environment. The nature of the environmental response(s) (which often is not a single act but multifarious movements on the part of several persons) influences the future probabilities of the recurrence of the behavior. If the environmental response is rewarding to the actor, the act will tend to be repeated. If the response is aversive the act tends not to recur. Within this general framework, outlined initially by Skinner (1953), we are suggesting that the delinquent peer group provides massive schedules of positive reinforcement for deviant behavior and negative reinforcement or punishment for socially conforming behavior. If these hypotheses are correct, it would appear that settings which provide prolonged interpersonal transactions among delinquent adolescents might be expected to provide an excellent opportunity for maintaining existing deviant behavior and, for the "novice", an opportunity to acquire new sets of deviant behavior. We would hypothesize too that within the institutional setting, the majority of social reinforcers are provided by the peer group rather than by the staff. The institutional setting thus would be seen as a "teaching machine" programmed for the maintenance and acquisition of deviant behavior rather than for retraining the child to more socially adaptive behavior.

STUDY NUMBER ONE

A pilot study by Patterson (1963) provided a preliminary test for these hypotheses. Fifteen 2-hr observations were made in a detention home for delinquent children. The observer sampled most of her observations from a small group of delinquent girls. After observing for a period of time, the observer would withdraw and write a descriptive account of each episode in which either a delinquent response or a response which was obviously conforming to social norms occurred. Each behavioral description also outlined the consequences of these responses; e.g. Roberta: "She is sickening" (referring to the housemother); Steve: "Not very smart either". Karen laughs. This direct criticism of an adult authority figure is reinforced immediately by two different members of the peer group. The various delinquent responses were classified into responses reflecting delinquent value systems; i.e. deviant sex behaviors, breaking rules, any form of rejection of adult authority, aggressive talk and expressing ideas consistent with delinquent behavior. The other major category of responses consisted of behavior corresponding to societal norms; i.e. talking of going to college, admission of feelings of guilt and regret for having indulged in delinquent acts, expressions of expectations regarding avoidance of delinquent behavior, saying they liked someone on the staff, and expressions of cooperation with the treatment program etc.

The consequences of this behavior were classified in two general categories: "positive reinforcement" and "punishment". Under the heading of positive reinforcement were included such peer reactions as: approval, agreement, interest, attention, laughing, smiling, imitating the speaker, etc. Under the heading of punishment were categorized such behaviors as: disagreeing, threatening, frowning, ignoring, sneering, etc.

The data were clear in showing overwhelming positive reinforcement (70 per cent) for such behavior as rule breaking, criticisms of adults and adult rules, aggressive behavior, and "kicks". In keeping with the hypotheses the peer group was most likely to disapprove when the behavior in question deviated from the delinquent norms. These data, of course, represented a limited sample obtained by one observer from one group in a single institutional setting. Although the results obtained were in keeping with the general predictions made, it was necessary to carry out an extensive replication before placing any confidence in the conclusions. Such a replication was carried out in Study Number Two which is reported in more detail below.

STUDY NUMBER TWO

The methodology in a study conducted by Furniss (1964) was derived from the social reinforcement model utilized by Patterson and an interpersonal communications behavior analysis method developed by Buehler and Richmond (1963). These two methodologies were combined because it appeared to the writers that each set of procedures would contribute something unique to our understanding of delinquent behavior. Social learning research has tended to simply classify communication behavior as verbal or non-verbal, without identifying the specific communication behavior which is utilized by members of particular sub-groups of the population. Since socio-cultural studies have long indicated that there are wide variations among people in the use of interpersonal communication behavior, it follows that there are no standard reinforcement contingencies which cross all age, sex, and cultural sub-groups. As a means for obtaining more precise measures of peer group social reinforcement behavior in an institutional setting Furniss combined the interpersonal communication behavior analysis method and the social reinforcement method utilized previously by Patterson.

The interpersonal communication analysis method is a method for observing and measuring interpersonal communication behavior in terms of four postulated levels of communication (Richmond and Buehler, 1962; Buehler and Richmond, 1963 a and b). This method, developed within a transactional rather than a self-action or interactional frame of reference (as defined by Dewey and Bentley, 1949) is based upon the postulate that all interpersonal behavior is communication and that this behavior occurs on four primary levels. These levels are: (1) bio-chemical; (2) motor movement; (3) speech and (4) technology. Each of the four levels or categories has sub-categories which are defined operationally in terms of observable movement on the part of a person during interpersonal transactional episodes. The unit of measure is a time interval of 2.5 sec. All behavior which occurs in any category is scored once in each interval. Meaning, intent, effects, etc. are rigorously excluded from scoring system as these are seen as observer's subjective interpretations of the observed behavior and should be derived, if necessary, from analyses of the sequences of ongoing behavior rather than imputed to the behavior by the observer.

It was predicted that the combination of these two methods and their implicit coding systems would result in a more powerful instrument for measuring the specific reinforcement processes within a peer group. Furniss' study was done in a State institution for girls who had been committed by Juvenile Courts for a variety of socially maladaptive behavior.

METHODS

Observations were made during students' leisure time hours on the cottages. The observer would note all interaction episodes on the part of the subject or subjects being observed at the time and write, immediately after, a detailed list of all behavior which she observed. These lists were later coded independently by two judges for: level of communication on which each observed act occurred; whether the act was in accordance with delinquent or socially appropriate norms; and the peer response(s) (reinforcements). Responses were categorized as positive reinforcements if there was an indication of attention or approval given the subject by a peer or peers, and as punishments if the peer response was disinterest or disapproval. The criteria used in classifying behavior as delinquent or nondelinquent were derived from the Girl's Handbook of the institution which listed the institution's expectations regarding inmate behavior. The congruence between the social norms expressed in the Handbook and those operant in the culture of the communities from which the girls came has never been validated empirically, but was accepted tentatively for purposes of the study.

It was hypothesized that the peer group would provide more social approval than disapproval for delinquent behavior. Second, it was hypothesized that the schedule of rewards for delinquent behavior and the amount of delinquent behavior would not vary as a function of the differences in the social living situations (cottages) within the institution. Third, it was hypothesized that the reinforcing behavior would be significantly more frequent on the non-verbal than the verbal levels of communication.*

Six subjects were randomly selected in each of two "open" (less restricted, presumably less delinquent girls) and two "closed" (more restricted, presumably more delinquent girls) cottages, or a total of twenty-four subjects. The subjects' age range was 13.5 – 18 yr. Length of institutionalization varied from 2 to 30 months. Prior institutionalization was not checked. On each of the four cottages the groups were heterogenous with respect to age, length of residence in the institution, and behavior which led to commitment by the Courts.

Each subject's interpersonal transactions with peers were observed for a total of 50 min, composed of two 25-min periods on two different days. The order of subject observations was random on each cottage and observations were distributed equally, over time, on all cottages.

RESULTS

Analysis of the data yielded the following results:

1. In peer reinforcement of delinquent behavior, the non-verbal levels of communications were used in 82 per cent of the reinforcing responses, while verbal reinforcement was used in only 18 per cent of the responses, on all sample cottages.
2. In peer reinforcement of socially conforming behavior, 36 per cent of the reinforcers occurred on the level of speech and 64 per cent occurred on the non-verbal levels.
3. The frequency of delinquent responses did not differ with respect to "open" versus "closed" cottages. Consequently, "open" as compared to "closed" cottage status did not signify any significant difference in the frequency of delinquent behavior within the peer group.
4. Delinquent behavior was rewarded by the peer group on the open cottages as frequently as it was rewarded on the closed cottages.
5. On all sample cottages (four of the institution's eight) the reinforcement of delinquent responses by peers occurred significantly more often ($P<.001$) than the punishment of delinquent responses.
6. On all sample cottages the peer group punished socially conforming

*This hypothesis was not stated in Miss Furniss' original research design but was added by Buehler and Patterson in analyzing her data.

behavior more frequently ($P<.01$) than they rewarded such behavior.

These results are extremely suggestive as to what learning takes place within the inmate social system in an institution and what is involved in altering behavior in treatment institutions. In the main, *delinquent behavior* on the part of the peer group and its members *occurs* and is *reinforced* on the *non-verbal level of behavior.* In other words, the bulk of the teaching among the girls is non-verbal. This corresponds with well-known postulates regarding communication behavior as articulated by Mead (1934), Hall (1959) and others.

In terms of treatment processes, it becomes obvious that the continuous peer group reinforcement of behavior by non-verbal communications must be taken into account and dealt with. It is clear that verbal behavior among peers does not alone accurately represent the teaching process which actually takes place within peer groups. Furthermore the data from the closed cottages suggest that institutional criteria for "improved behavior" may be related simply to "security" (more or less locked doors) and other maintenance variables rather than to *changed social attitudes and behavior.* In actual ratio of punishment versus reward for delinquent or nondelinquent behavior, Furniss' data agree essentially with those previously obtained (in a smaller institution) by Patterson, namely, in 132 responses to delinquent behavior, 116 (88 per cent) were rewarding and 16 (12 per cent) were punishing. Thus, regardless of institution size, the peer group communication transactions tend to maintain the very attitudes and behavior which led to institutionalization.

STUDY NUMBER THREE

The next in this series of pilot studies consisted of efforts to test some methods for developing a specific behavioral analysis for each individual member of a delinquent peer group in an institution, to refine the methods for determining the peer group reinforcement contingencies, and to develop procedures for determining schedules of reinforcement to be administered initially by the staff and eventually by the peer group itself.

The two previous pilot studies, while focusing for empirical purposes only upon the peer group, did nevertheless lead to the definite impression that staff members in both settings tended to reward and punish indiscriminately. The focus of attention in the third study was upon the peer group behavior and the reinforcement contingencies dispensed by the immediate staff members.

The assumption in this study was borrowed directly from current social reinforcement literature. This assumption involves both the interpersonal communication and the social reinforcement paradigms discussed previously. An analysis of current literature indicates that: first, the behavior which needs to be either reinforced or extinguished must be identified specifically; second, the environmental response (reinforcing agent) must be on the same level of communication as the act which is to be reinforced. There are exceptions to this, of course, but this is assumed to be a general rule: e.g. smiling or frowning is a more spontaneous response to a smile than is a verbal statement such as "I am glad to see you smile" or "stop your smiling". In an official communication system such as presented by a school, a verbal punishment or reward may be used by the teacher in response to a non-verbal act on the part of the student, but within the peer group itself, as Furniss' data indicated, there is a high level of congruence between the level of communication utilized by the actor and the peer group respondents. We would speculate that this congruence in levels of communication through which reinforcements are continuously dispensed in ongoing peer group transactions may be one reason why the peer group is so effective in shaping and controlling behavior.

These considerations, among others, suggested to Buehler and Patterson that the field of investigation should be enlarged to include the reinforcing behavior operant in the total social system of one residential cottage in the institution for delinquent girls which was utilized in Furniss' study. This involved refining the methods for identifying the schedules of reinforcement within the peer group of girls and the reinforcing behavior of the staff members with reference to the girls' behavior.

METHODS

Behavioral observations were made by an observer equipped with a small portable dictation machine with a microphone inserted in a rubber mask which covered the observer's mouth. As a means for obtaining a maximum amount of data on individual girls, a sample of six subjects was selected randomly for daily observations. The observer went on the cottage at 4 p.m. on five days a week and remained until the girls' bedtime at 9 p.m. The observations included two 1-hr group meetings each week which were conducted by the senior author. Two cottage supervisors (housemothers) and a staff social worker attended the group meetings along with the twenty-four resident girls.

The observer focused her attention on the interpersonal transactions on the part of the six subjects, including their transactions with staff members. The tapes were transcribed each day and separate sheets were extracted for each of the six subjects and each staff member. These individual behavioral protocols were coded in terms of communication and reinforcement categories.

BEHAVIORAL DIAGNOSES

The behavioral protocols obtained in the manner described above were utilized along with behavioral data in the subject's case folder in developing a specific behavioral diagnosis for each subject. The following data presents in some detail a sample of a behavioral diagnosis and a reinforcement prescription for one subject:

> *Personal history.* I.Q. 124. Father inconsistent in his reinforcing behavior, ranging from over-indulgence to physical cruelty. Mother indulged in frequent outbursts of anger and unreasonable accusations. The unreasonable demands made upon the subject by her parents led to a cruelty petition against the home by the Juvenile Court. Subject was committed to the institution after several unsatisfactory foster home placements. Intake information indicated that the subject defied family authority, had few friends, considerable heterosexual activity with a variety of partners, AWOL from foster homes. She alternated between affectionate and hostile behavior with reference to adults. When she felt rejected, she became immature and demanding. Adults generally found her annoying and troublesome and rejected her. Her response to adult rejection was to act out as described above. She had one illegitimate child and refused to give it up. The child was being cared for by the subject's mother and this led to constant friction between the subject and her mother. Subject wanted to live away from her family and care for her child.

The institutional staff reported of the same ambivalent pattern toward adults. The subject appeared to the staff to be eager to please, demanded much attention, manipulated adults and peers, refused to obey rules, tended to be loud, noisy, disruptive and coercive. The staff saw her as acting in a superior manner toward her peers, attempting to boss them, and as being generally rejected by her peers.

The subject's interpersonal transactional behavior was observed at intervals over a period of 5 days. The kind of reinforcements she was being given by her peer group and by the staff and her responses are presented in Table 1.

These behavioral data indicate that the peer group punished the subject for identifying with social norms in a ratio of almost three to one, while the staff rewarded her in a ratio of nine to one. However, the frequency of the reinforcements that were dispensed by the peers greatly outnumbered those dispensed by the staff. Furthermore, when she was hostile toward her peers they rewarded her in a greater than two to one ratio and when she was hostile toward adults, the adults punished her more or less consistently. She tended to punish her peers when they made social gestures toward her, although she rewarded adults for doing the same thing. The peer group's persistent punishment when the subject verbalized identifications with social norms is very clear. She expressed thirty-seven such identifications and the peer group punished her twenty-seven times and rewarded her ten times. The staff, on the other hand, rewarded her eighteen out of twenty times that she identified with social norms in their presence.

Table 1

	Reward for Subject's Behavior				Subject's Reward to Others			
	From Peers		From Adults		To Peers		To Adults	
Behavior	No. Observed	Reinforcement	No. Observed	Reinforcement	No. Observed	Reinforcement	No. Observed	Reinforcement
Social	29	12+ 17−	23	16+ 7−	8	3+ 5−	5	5+ 0−
Hostility	19	13+ 6−	5	0+ 5−	2	0+ 2−	0	
Coercive	9	1+ 8−	3	0+ 3−	5	1+ 4−	1	0+ 1−
Identification with Delinquency	1	0+ 1−	1	1+ 0−	0		0	
Identification with Social Norms	37	10+ 27−	20	18+ 2−	2	1+ 1−	0	

+positive reward.
−punishment.

These observations indicate that the reinforcement system for the subject tended to be very inconsistent. Her peers tended to reward her for being a delinquent and to punish her whenever she made moves toward socially appropriate behavior, while the staff would alternately reward her and punish her for the same acts.

In the group sessions the subject behaved as would be predicted from the reports and observations shown above. She would verbally identify herself with social norms (getting a job and taking care of her child, staying out of further trouble with Juvenile Court, etc.) and was persistently punished by her peers for these identifications. She would retaliate and some of her peers would counter-retaliate. This intra-group conflict would rise in intensity as long as the group discussion leader played a non-directive role. When the leader's role shifted to identifying the group's behavior (i.e. "S is trying to say that she wants to leave this institution, get a job, etc. and some of you girls are punishing her for wanting to do these things"), the girls who silently approved S's behavior would begin to reward her.

It was noticeable in the group meetings that the more aggressive, dominating and coercive girls tended to punish those girls who attempted to show some socially conforming attitudes, expectations, and behavior.

This was particularly true of another subject who was the leader of an informal sub-group of girls on the cottage. This girl saw the group meetings as a distinct threat to her control over her domineering "gang". A previous group leader had given in to the two rival informal groups on the cottage and was meeting separately with each of them. Under the former leader's non-directive leadership the two rival gangs remained intact and in daily conflict for control of the communal life on the cottage. When this gang behavior was pointed up in meetings of all the girls and the staff, the two gang leaders would aggressively punish every girl who in one way or another supported the discussion leader's efforts to elicit cooperation in seeking solutions to the intra-cottage problems. This behavior strengthened the authors' assumption that if schedules of reinforcement within the peer group are to be changed in the direction of socially appropriate behavior, something other than "non-directive" evocative therapy is required.

The behavioral analyses described above suggested that the initial treatment prescription for the subject may be as follows:

Reward

(1) Every socially appropriate approach to an adult;
(2) all of the subject's references to her maternal role and her maternal role responsibilities;
(3) give the subject much attention and praise when she engages in socially responsible acts toward her peers;
(4) reward the subject's peers when they reward her socially appropriate acts, and
(5) reward the subject's peers when they resist being coerced by the subject.

Punish

(1) Ignore the subject's loud, boisterous, coercive and bossy behavior, and
(2) confront, and in any other appropriate way, punish the subject's peers when they punish her for her efforts to conform to socially appropriate norms.

Each of the six subjects' behavior was observed and analyzed in the manner described above. The specific behavioral categories for each girl varied, however. Such categories as: isolation from peers, passive resistance, or physical aggression were also used in order to tailor-make the descriptive system for each girl. One subject in particular, a very attractive girl who was a strong leader among her peers, showed thirteen coercive acts towards her peers for which she was rewarded nine times and punished only four times. She also showed fourteen coercive acts towards adults and was rewarded seven times and punished seven times by adults. She showed hostility towards adults in the presence of her peers a total of twenty-six times and was rewarded by her peers twelve times and punished fourteen times. For the same behavior she was rewarded three times and punished twenty-three times by adults. This suggested how she was being taught by her peer group to be an aggressive, coercive leader and to continue to be hostile and defiant toward adults.

The observed transactions between the staff and the girls were not as frequent as were the transactions among the peers because the adult staff members showed a tendency to remain in their offices or to sit on the periphery of the social group. However, the observed adult behavior of six staff members who at one time or the other were on the cottage over a period of a week, is summarized in Table 2.

Table 2

Behavior of Six Staff Members in the Cottage, One Week of Observation

	Reinforcement Given to Girls		Reinforcement Received from Girls	
Behavior	No. Observed	Ratio	No. Observed	Ratio
Social	18	11+ 7−	19	10+ 9−
Coercive	20	11+ 9−	14	11+ 3−
Hostile	1	1+ 0−	16	8+ 8−
Information Giving	3	1+ 2−	4	3+ 1−
Information Asked	5	3+ 2−		
Usurping Role of Student	5	3+ 2−		
Coping with Problems			4	1+ 3−
Not Coping			12	3+ 9−
Decision Making: self			15	10+ 5−
refer decision to girl			7	4+ 3−
refer decision to group			7	1+ 6−
refer decision to administrator			11	3+ 8−

These data support the impression obtained in the preceding studies, namely, that staff members tended to reinforce and to punish indiscriminately. Such vacillating schedules of reinforcement would tend, we assume, to reduce severely the effectiveness of the staff in influencing inmate behavior in any direction. In the two classes of behavior with the greatest frequency, social and coercive, the staff response was approximately equal in punishment and in reward. It is interesting to note too that the girls reinforced and punished the staff in an equally inconsistent manner. The peer group's response to coping behavior on the part of the staff is particularly interesting in view of the traditions of staff authority and responsibility in penal institutions. When the staff failed to cope with problems they were punished in a three to one ratio. When staff referred problems back to the group for group action and/or decision the staff was punished by the peer group in a ratio of six to one. Also, when staff referred problems to the administration the peer group punished them consistently (8:3). The implications of these data for further research and theory construction with reference to therapeutic and/or educational social systems are challenging indeed.

DISCUSSION

The persistence of delinquent behavior in institutions where the official aim is to "correct" such behavior has been documented repeatedly in long and melancholy "recidivism" lists. Of equal note is the fact, frequently mentioned in the literature, that during the process of institutionalization many cases of adolescent deviation (e.g. truancy, running away from home, etc.) are converted into severe criminal offenders. The "peer group culture" has been blamed for these reversals of official intentions, but *how* the peer group achieves these effects has not been identified or described in *behavioral* terms. Nor has the staff behavior which contributes to these effects been documented. The data in the three studies reviewed above identify two separate behavioral systems within a single peer group and the other is operated by the staff. While no data were obtained in these pilot studies on the relative effects of the two behavioral systems, other data on peer group phenomena (Patterson, 1963; Schrag, 1961; and others) permit us to hypothesize that it is the peer group behavioral system which has the predominating effects. In fact, it is reasonable to hypothesize that the inmate behavioral system not only shapes and controls its own members but also it shapes and controls the behavior of the staff.

The problem as we see it is to identify and to establish controls over the behavior occurring in peer groups which keeps the group resistant to institutional treatment objectives. We emphasize the term "treatment objective" because these data suggest that while the objective of the institutions in which the data were obtained was to "correct" the delinquency, the behavioral operations of the staff tended to reward or punish delinquent behavior indiscriminately. There is ample evidence in social reinforcement research that when reinforcements are inconsistent the reinforcing agent has no effect.

These data suggest that a social reinforcement approach to behavioral diagnosis and treatment planning and operations is feasible. The impressive data on behavior modification which has been summarized in part by Krasner and Ullmann (1965) and by Bandura and Walters (1963), as well as in a wide range of scientific journals, suggest that this may be a promising approach to treatment operations in a "correctional" setting.

As an initial step to modifying delinquent schedules of reinforcement within a peer group, we assume that a rigorous behavioral approach needs to be adopted by the staff. It was noted by the authors in informal conversations with staff members that they had a marked tendency to attach moral labels to the inmates and would respond to the label rather than to specific behavior of the labeled girl; e.g. Mary is "good" therefore she will be rewarded persistently regardless of her behavior, Susie is "bad" therefore she will be punished persistently regardless of whatever moves she makes toward socially conforming behavior. Once a behavioral frame of reference is adopted, the next step in this paradigm would be to adopt a rigorous observational system for identifying the specific behaviors and reinforcing contingencies within the inmate peer groups. The method of observing the behavior as described above is simple, requires no instruments and can be adopted easily by relatively untrained persons (the Research Assistant in Study No. 3 was a college sophomore). The final steps would be to tailor-make a schedule of reinforcement to fit each separate inmate and the group as a whole, and to teach the staff how to use their own interpersonal communication behavior as a source of reinforcement.

REFERENCES

BANDURA A. and WALTERS R. H. (1963) *Social Learning and Personality Development.* Holt, Rinehart and Winston, Inc., New York.

BUEHLER R. E. and RICHMOND J. F. (1963a) Interpersonal communication behavior analysis: a research method. *J. Commun.* **XIII**, No. 3.

BUEHLER R. E. and RICHMOND J. F. (1963b) Pilot study on interpersonal communication behavior analysis method. *Research Report*, Board of Control, Salem, Oregon.

DEWEY J. and BENTLEY A. F. (1949) *Knowing and the Known.* Beacon Press, Boston.

FURNISS JEAN (1964) *Peer Reinforcement of Behavior in an Institution for Delinquent Girls.* Unpublished Master's Thesis, Oregon State University.

HALL E. T. (1959) *The Silent Language.* Doubleday, New York.

KRASNER L. and ULLMANN L. P. (1965) *Case Studies in Behavior Modification.* Holt, Rinehart and Winston, Inc., New York.

MEAD G. H. (1934) *Mind, Self and Society.* University of Chicago Press, Chicago.

PATTERSON G. R. (1963) *The Peer Group as Delinquency Reinforcement Agent.* Unpublished Research Report, Child Research Laboratory, University of Oregon, Eugene, Oregon.

PATTERSON G. R. and ANDERSON D. (1964) Peers as reinforcers. *Child Dev.* **35**, 951–960.

RICHMOND J. F. and BUEHLER R. E. (1962) Interpersonal communication: a theoretical formation. *J. Commun.* **XII**, No. 1.

SCHRAG C. (1961) Some foundations for a theory of corrections. *Cressey, The Prison.* Holt, Rinehart and Winston, Inc., New York.

SKINNER B. F. (1953) *Science and Human Behavior.* Crowell-Collier-Macmillan, New York.

Using Teen-agers To Supplement Casework Service

FELICE PERLMUTTER
DOROTHY DURHAM

In a variety of settings, current social work practice reflects the effective use of untrained personnel to help professional agencies implement their services. These untrained workers are frequently full-time employees who have undergraduate degrees.[1] Thus, volunteers who are used usually are mature adults with experience and/or training.

However, in Champaign, Illinois, a joint agency project, co-sponsored by a teen-age youth council and a school social work department, conducted an experimental program, using teen-agers to supplement casework service.[2] Superficially the program was similar to "Big Brother" programs known in many communities, but in Champaign it was the teen-ager who served as a "Pal" to a youngster. This program, however, was developed as part of a professional social work service, and the goals and structure were carefully defined using fundamentals of social work practice.

Reprinted from *Social Work*, 1965, Vol. 10, No. 2, 41–46, with the permission of the National Association of Social Workers and the authors. Brief biographies of the authors have been omitted.

[1]Verne Weed and William H. Denham, "Toward More Effective Use of the Nonprofessional Worker: A Recent Experiment," *Social Work*, Vol. 6, No. 4 (October 1961), pp. 29–36; Marcella Farrar and Mary L. Hemmy, "Use of Nonprofessional Staff in Work with the Aged," *Social Work*, Vol. 8, No. 3 (July 1963), pp. 44–50.

[2]"A Community Program of Intergroup Activity for Youth." This project is being supported by a National Institute of Mental Health grant. The grantee institution is the Human Relations Commission, City of Champaign, Illinois.

The protection of the client and the maintenance of professional standards are of great importance in all social work agencies and, in defining the role of the non-professional, the conscious differentiation between "organizational controls" and "professional controls" is crucial. Organizational controls are those which are defined by—and occur within—the structure of the agency. The professional controls, which rest with the practitioner, are the product of professional training and experience.[3]

Thus, in working with volunteers—especially teen-agers—since professional controls are not highly developed, organizational controls must be carefully defined to the fullest extent to offer a framework for effective operation. This carefully defined structure will offer support, both tangible and intangible, in the more subtle and unstructured areas where professional controls must operate, since some professional controls are always necessary to cope with the flexible decisions that must be made and that the organizational rules cannot predict. Through supervision and the spelling out of the organizational controls, the professional worker must simultaneously attempt to give the volunteer an understanding of his role as a worker as well as the goals of a professional social work service.

This orientation will enable the volunteer to grow in his role in the helping process as he develops a more conscious and flexible use of self in relation to the service offered. Reliance on external, organizational controls alone would prevent the individualized approach that is necessary to handle particular situations.

To clarify further the appropriate areas in which nonprofessionals can effectively offer service, Richan discusses combining the variables of worker autonomy and client vulnerability: the more vulnerable the client, the more professional the worker must be.[4] Thus, in a program using teen-agers as part of the therapeutic process, the teen-ager would operate with minimal autonomy, and the children serving as clients would be selected on the basis of low vulnerability or low susceptibility to damage from a relationship with a nonprofessional.

BENEFIT TO TEEN-AGERS

A basic assumption of the Pal Program was that the teen-ager would benefit from the program as much as the child client. The opportunity to fulfill an important social role by meeting the needs of a child dependent

[3]Willard C. Richan, "A Theoretical Scheme for Determining Roles of Professional and Nonprofessional Personnel," *Social Work*, Vol. 6, No. 4 (October 1961), pp. 22–28.
[4]*Ibid.*

on him would serve to support the teen-ager's quest for a sense of uniqueness and personal identity. The experience of serving as a Pal would be independent of his parents' sphere of influence, would focus on giving rather than receiving, and would offer an "object interest" outside of self, thus providing important steps in the development of emotional maturity.[5]

In a society where man is alienated from others, the involvement in a giving and meaningful relationship would further serve to give the teen-ager a sense of relatedness, which is especially difficult to achieve in a world of casual encounters.[6] Fromm attempts to define the art of loving; he suggests that of primary importance are focusing on others, overcoming narcissism, and the necessity of viewing people objectively.[7] These opportunities are available in the Pal relationship, which focuses primarily on the child's needs and helps the teen-ager move from fulfilling his own gratifications to a new orientation of give-and-take in relation to another person.

The teen-ager, as opposed to the adult, has the unique advantage of being closer in age to the child, and is, therefore, more likely to participate informally and unselfconsciously in activities related to the child's interests (e.g., skating, bicycle riding). Since the child may perceive the teen-ager as a combination of peer and adult and thus less identified with the adult world of parental authority, his needs may be met on various levels.

The opportunity for orientation and introduction to the field of social work for the teen-ager facing college and vocational choices cannot be underestimated. The active participation in a social work program can fulfill this purpose more effectively than the more casual chance encounter with the profession through high school career day programs. Because of the nature of the social work profession, unless one is in need of service, there is little opportunity for direct experience with social work practice.[8]

A final important point regarding the unique opportunity in working with teenagers is related to the idea of a "peace corps," which offers meaningful experience with diverse socioeconomic problems for the participant. In contemporary society, suburban living isolates people from encounters with members of other socioeconomic strata, and automation has reduced the opportunity for a meaningful and necessary work experi-

[5]Leon Saul, MD, *Emotional Maturity* (Philadelphia: J. B. Lippincott Co., 1947), pp. 7–12.

[6]Erich Fromm, *The Sane Society* (New York: Holt, Rinehart and Winston, Inc., 1955).

[7]Erich Fromm, *The Art of Loving* (New York: Harper & Row, 1956), p. 118.

[8]The field of group work is probably an exception and illustrates the importance of direct contact, since many practitioners have entered the field through their experience with group workers in settlement houses and camps and similiar settings.

ence for the teen-ager. Local programs must be developed that can broaden and enrich the teen-ager's development.[9]

PAL PROGRAM

The School Social Work Department in Champaign recognized the need of supplementing its services for elementary school children who were either receiving intensive casework from professional staff social workers, or, although not necessarily in need of casework, who could benefit from satisfying relationships with interested older persons. Therefore, the Champaign Youth Council was approached with the request that it sponsor a program to provide "Pals" for these children.

The Youth Council is a citywide, representative group composed of twenty-six teen-age organizations. Since one of its objectives is to broaden the teen-ager's awareness of current social problems, the Pal Program was enthusiastically accepted; member groups felt that participation would provide an opportunity for meaningful service.

The program was carefully defined by the directors of both co-operating agencies. Since this was the first attempt to involve teen-agers in the therapeutic process, the initial group selected to participate numbered only eight individuals to allow for close supervision of the teen-ager as well as interagency contact. A second basic decision was to limit the age of the clients to children between 6 and 10 years of age (first through fourth grade), thus setting up an organizational control by having an age differential that would serve as an added protection to the situation. Pals had to be 16 years old or over.

Teen-age participants were selected through a formal application procedure that involved their mailing in an application form on which references and standard personal data were given. During a personal interview, it was explained that participation in the program required attendance at monthly group-training sessions.[10]

The Pals met regularly with their youngsters, one half-day weekly. They were encouraged to involve the children in planning for the next session, but it was recognized that the children might not be ready to be involved in this manner, so the Pals were responsible for being prepared with several varied suggestions. Among others, the activities included

[9]Paul Goodman, *Growing Up Absurd* (New York: Random House, 1956).

[10]Twenty-two teen-agers submitted their names to the Youth Council office, and formal applications were mailed to them, requesting that completed forms be mailed back to the office. This step was taken deliberately, since many teen-agers will enthusiastically sign up for a program but not follow through with the ongoing responsibility. Only eight of the teen-agers were accepted into the program.

window-shopping, ice-skating, and visits to the libraries and museums.

Since a careful process of matching children to teen-agers was not feasible, children were selected on the basis of a positive prognosis in relation to what the Pal Program offered. Children with behavior problems were not chosen, since the teen-ager was not prepared or qualified to handle "acting-out" or aggressive behavior.

Children selected for the program were recommended by the social worker, or as a result of a staff conference composed of teacher, principal, psychologist, and social worker. These children were in need of an adult with whom to identify and an experience outside of a family constellation that fostered extreme dependency, cultural stimulation, and community contact.

The following record briefly describes the background of a child referred to the Pal Program and—through supervision—the help offered to the teen-ager:

> Larry H is a 9-year-old boy. His parents are in the process of divorcing, and he has little contact with his father. Mrs. H is a very anxious person, almost overwhelmed by her many problems. There is intense sibling rivalry between Larry and his 5-year-old sister. Larry is extremely nonverbal and does not communicate with his caseworker or teachers. His Pal Jack is thus an important figure in Larry's life. He is a warm, sensitive teen-ager who accepted the child and his problems. While Jack was threatened by Larry's noncommunicativeness, the support and interpretations offered through supervision have helped him work effectively with the boy. Jack was concerned that Larry wished to go bowling repeatedly. He felt that he did not know how to introduce a variety of activities because of the boy's intense desire only to go bowling. The meaning of bowling was discussed in terms of Larry's needs for success through the development of masculine activities, skill in the sport, and the security offered via the regularity of the activity. Jack found this meaningful and was able to relax his expectations of program variety. However, in view of the cost of bowling, it was decided that bowling could be alternated with other activities, and Larry was involved in understanding the activity's limits, imposed by its cost.

The financial arrangements for the program varied in each case. The caseworker discussed with the parent how much he could contribute to the cost of the child's activities. In most cases, the parent paid for the child's carfare and a coke. Money from home could not be provided for three children, and their Pals decided to handle this situation themselves by personally biking the children, seeking out free activities, or paying for a special treat. The teen-agers were told that a $20 group fund, donated to meet their expenses, existed, and they were encouraged not to use their own money. (It is interesting to note that the $20 was not used.) All Pals were encouraged to plan free or inexpensive activities with the purpose of exposing the children to resources they could subsequently use on their own.

SUPERVISING THE VOLUNTEERS

The reality of the staff situation—namely, that the volunteers were high school students with extremely limited free time—demanded a specific and selective use of supervision. Monthly group meetings were deemed the most appropriate vehicle, although teen-agers were also encouraged to call the supervisor any time between group sessions if the need arose.

The first meeting was an orientation session; its basic purpose was to help the Pals recognize the professional level of the program. Each Pal received a folder with material that was used as a discussion stimulant, not for take-home reading. The first half of the meeting focused on the behavior characteristics of children in relation to age and socieconomic background as well as the possible feelings of the various participants in the program, including the child client, his parents, and the teen-age Pal himself. After discussing the anxiety the children might be experiencing, the Pals were able to discuss their own apprehension. This background material was consciously used by the supervisor as a fundamental approach to the problem of professional control and orientation.

The second half of the orientation meeting handled material in the sphere of organizational controls. In addition to discussing specific program suggestions, structural matters—such as frequency and regularity of Pal outings, length of time of each, and steps in the initial contact with the child and his parents—were handled.

The monthly meetings were important to the teen-agers and there were few absences. Written report forms, which were sent to the supervisor by the Pal before each monthly meeting, described his sessions and enabled the supervisor to prepare specific points to be raised in the meetings.

The following discussion was the result of an incident described in one Pal's record:

> Martha's child had a bike which was too large for him, and she did not feel it was safe for traffic. Since they frequently went to a park near her home, she lent him her sister's smaller bike, which he rode very well. The group's response was that this was not a good idea, since the bike was not his and only emphasized the inadequacy of his own bike. Martha explained that the bike was certainly in as poor condition as his bike but just fit him better. The supervisor interpreted the meaning of the bike to the child as unrelated to its condition, and more related to the satisfactory experiences he was deriving from it. Thus, when the relationship would end, not only would he be minus a Pal but his bike would seem all the less desirable. Martha understood the point made.

The group meetings served the important purpose of allowing each Pal the opportunity to discuss his own questions, problems, and reactions to the program. Each teen-ager derived great satisfaction from detailing his monthly experiences, even if they did not differ at all from those described by the others. This seemed to relieve his tension, and to support him in his efforts as a Pal. Meaningful material was frequently raised at this time that further strengthened his ability to act sensitively in individualized situations calling for unique responses (professional control area). For instance:

> The child asked if the Pal would be with her forever, and the teen-ager interpreted this as mature foresight, and viewed the question from an intellectual framework. This child had just moved into the community, her parents were divorced, and a sibling had died. The supervisor helped the group explore the meaning of loss of relationships to this child, and the teen-ager was then able to see this question as an expression of anxiety and fear, rather than intellectual maturity.

Although some discussions were related to individual children and their needs, others were of general group concern:

> Many of the Pals wanted to take the children to their homes for visits, and raised the question of the advisability in the group meeting. The worker asked the group to discuss this matter, and Ralph commented that if there was a specific reason to take the youngster home, it would be OK, but a visit without a purpose did not seem appropriate. After exploring the needs on the part of both teen-ager and child for this visit, the worker interpreted the caseworker's response to this matter, namely, that visits to the Pals' homes were not recommended. However, if a specific occasion arose which seemed appropriate, such a visit could first be cleared with the supervisor.

A professional decision thus became an organizational control in this carefully structured situation.

PALS AND CASEWORKERS

The relationship between the caseworkers and the Pals was carefully defined. The teen-agers were never directly in contact with the caseworkers, and all interagency discussion was handled between the casework supervisor and the group work supervisor. However, the caseworkers did write brief monthly reports for their client's Pal, with comments about the program and any relevant material that could be helpful to him. Of great importance to the Pals, these reports served as support and recognition from the caseworkers, thus giving the teen-agers a feeling of direct participation with the casework process. In turn, the records written by the Pals were shared with the caseworkers and incorporated into the casework folders at the end of the year. The teen-agers were not viewed as "therapists," and this separation further helped to prevent confusion regarding their function.

Other organizational controls served to protect both the teen-ager and the child. The program was structured on an annual basis; new Pal assignments were to be made yearly to prevent the relationship from becoming too emotionally involved. Since the teen-agers did not have the professional competence to handle possible complications in the relationship, this was considered a realistic limitation.

Futhermore, the Pal Program ended in June, to coincide with the school social work departmental calendar, and since casework service was terminated for the summer, the Pal Program, as an adjunct to casework, was discontinued for this period of time, too. While the supervisor worked with the teen-agers in their group meeting to help prepare for termination, the caseworkers simultaneously worked with the children and their parents.

In their evaluation of the program at the final group meeting, the teen-agers agreed that they themselves had benefited as much as the children. They stated that since their life experiences were restricted to their immediate home and school environments this program gave them an opportunity to broaden their vistas. Not only were some of the socio-economic backgrounds different, but the intrafamily problems encountered offered contrasts, stimulating thought about their own background. Thus the experience of providing a unique service was gratifying and important in developing ego-identity.

THE PROGRAM'S SIGNIFICANCE

On the basis of this experimental program, the authors have found that the use of teen-agers in the therapeutic process not only serves an important purpose from the client's point of view but is also deeply significant for the participating teen-ager. The development of emotional maturity, the ability to establish meaningful relationships, the capacity to give to others, as well as an introduction to the profession of social work are several values to be derived from a program of this kind.

However, such a program must be carefully designed, with the teen-age volunteer operating with minimal autonomy with children of low vulnerability whose needs can be met through a nonprofessional relationship.

The professional staff must be aware of the controls, both organizational and professional, that are called into play. Thus, the organizational controls must be developed to a maximum, while the more independent professional controls are used minimally. Accordingly, the structure developed for the Pal Program was designed to maximize the help available automatically in the situation:

1. Monthly group meetings were held for general supervisory purposes, but the teen-agers were encouraged to call the supervisor any time the need arose.
2. The size of the group was kept to eight members to assure full participation.
3. An age differential was established to minimize problems of identification and confusion between the teen-ager and the child. The teen-ager had to be 16 or over, while the child client was between 6 and 10 years of age.
4. A turnover of Pals was planned annually to protect the teen-ager from over-involvement with the child's problems.
5. The program stopped during the summer, coinciding with the casework schedule.
6. Pals did not communicate directly with the casework staff, because this might be confusing for them. Rather, the supervisory staff served as a liaison between the Pals and the children's caseworkers.

In this industrialized, impersonal society, in which the opportunities for meaningful relationships have diminished as the need for emotional contacts has increased, the teen-age population can be involved in social service programs in a variety of ways. This involvement should not be viewed merely as appropriate for successful, achieving teen-agers, but rather as a challenge to involve teen-agers from various backgrounds. Perhaps even the potential high school dropout, who has been helped to finish school, might be chosen to work with a younger child with similar problems.

The vistas are broad, and social work agencies—both public and private—have the opportunity and challenge of involving teen-agers creatively in the implementation of their services.

High School Psychology Trainees in a Mental Hospital

LLOYD FELLOWS
MILTON WOLPIN

The program to be described in this paper grew rather naturally out of the experiences we had had with college students, as described by Dr. Walker in the previous paper. It seemed fairly clear that hospital staff, in all areas, for many reasons, including a very active volunteer program, was open and receptive to the kind of possibility we were considering, and that they were, in fact, reasonably sophisticated. Thus, to a very large extent, any success in our program with high school students was clearly a consequence of a highly favorable atmosphere at the hospital, in which innovation is encouraged to the extent that our plans fit in readily with the zeitgeist.

Thus in the spring of 1965 we contacted a local high school, detailed the experience we had had working with students at the college level, and asked if they were interested in developing a pilot program for high school students for the approaching summer. Cooperation at all levels at the high school was very good.

We aimed for, and developed, a small group of top-notch upper-classmen, three seniors and a junior, boys who were excelling academically and in a wide range of extra-curricular activities.

These youngsters were required to spend four full days a week for eight weeks at the hospital, where they were assigned to work with the

This paper was presented at the California State Psychological Association Convention, January 1966. It is reprinted with the permission of the authors.

adolescent and pre-adolescent boys' units. They were paid $50 a month for the two months. There was some question whether any payment should be involved, and it was decided that their expenses should be reimbursed on a par with domestic peace corps type work. We expected and received strong commitment in time and energy to the training program.

Following an initial week of orientation to the hospital, its various programs, and discussion of the elements of psychology which applied, the trainees began to work on the adolescent male unit. The first two weeks required almost the full time of the one psychologist involved in the program. It was the most demanding time for the supervisor. The third and following weeks required a diminishing amount of time, so that by the end of the first month the teen age trainees were fairly well on their own except for the planning and discussion of their experiences, an hour a day, with their supervisor. The permissive discussion hour was an important part of the program in that it allowed the students to ventilate their feelings concerning various experiences, and to learn from the supervisor additional behavioral dynamics. Initially the supervisor needed to suggest programs and activities which might be carried out by the trainees. As they became familiar with the types of activities which were considered as being helpful, they planned for themselves and became adept at implementing their plans, despite the administrative complexities of a large mental hospital.

The trainees were involved with patients both individually and in groups. They conducted group therapy with a leave-planning group, did counseling and tutoring in basic skills with academically retarded adolescents, and engaged in pilot conditioning procedures. They organized and supervised various social activities and outings such as beach parties, camp-outs, social dances, hikes and swimming. They ran sports events including baseball, basketball, volleyball and football.

A typical day included running a club group therapy session, taking a group swimming, eating with some boys in the patients' dining hall, tutoring at the school, and reading on their own subjects that interested them in the professional library.

In order to familiarize the trainees with the range of resources of the community, field trips to mental health facilities were included in the program. They saw the juvenile court and juvenile hall, a boys' group home, and a foster home. To encourage the involvement of the local community in the program, various friends of the trainees were invited to participate in activities with the patients, both at the hospital and on outings.

The high school trainees attended various lectures at the hospital along with staff members. They attended also psychiatric interviews, staffings, and team meetings on the adolescent unit. Their supervised involvement as subprofessionals enabled them to study the relationship between diagnosis, social and medical history and the current behavior of their new friends.

Their effect upon the patients was particularly notable with one dorm of 13 boys with whom they concentrated. Many of the boys idealized the trainees and sought to copy whatever they did. The trainees were held in a kind of "big brother" high respect. In the months since the summer program closed, a number of the boys from the dormitory have been placed in foster or group homes where they seem to be adjusting well, having learned some aspects of effective behavior from the trainees.

This sort of program seems to be an effective means of overcoming some of the problems in mental hospitals, at least it seems to work with adolescents.

Intensive inquiry with staff, patients and students has failed to elicit negative comments of any consequence. On the contrary there is much enthusiasm, on the part of all concerned, for a larger project this coming summer. The students routinely report having gained invaluable experience, with recent reports, from some who are now in undergraduate school, indicating that it has clearly seemed to enrich their course work, giving them a very meaningful background for classes, especially in psychology.

In the face of this, it seems that in many ways the program, similar to formal research often-times, has raised many more questions than it answered. We worked in a good tradition, that of many other programs, indicating that volunteers have a great deal to offer, plus some of the more recent emphasis, in formal psychotherapy, of playing down the value of insight and interpretive procedures, while emphasizing instead appropriate models and both explicit and implicit expectations that one was far more capable than might previously have been allowed. Our procedures were certainly consistent with work such as Bandura's on social imitation and modeling, as well as Harlow's, whose animal work clearly points to the major importance of successful experience with peers.

Where, however, do we stop? What is the lower age limit for success in ventures such as these? Sixteen? Fourteen? Four? Can youngsters bring a breath of fresh air and hope into the lives of the older, and somewhat infirm? Would a similar approach work in reform schools, jails and clinics? Would it work with a population of persons in acute distress, as compared to those we know best in state hospitals, the chronic? Must we rely on youngsters who are clearly among the more adequate and capable or can juvenile delinquents, for example, be deliberately introduced into such a setting, by coming over daily from their own institution, with the explicit expectation that they have something to offer and can help others? Would deliberately fostering such expectations result in a positive experience on both sides?

Our experience certainly suggests that non-professionals can be of considerable value. In addition, by reaching students early, we may be able to enrich curricula, maybe even at the grade school level, all the while conceivably developing potential psychology graduate students.

We also need to ask ourselves, however, about the possibility of developing systems that do not have to reach outside themselves to maintain and enhance the well-being of its members. Gerald Patterson, at the University of Oregon, is beginning to suggest that peers in a school system, as a group, may be far more powerful and efficient in these regards, than introducing the professional, one to one, operant conditioners. We may want to consider the teacher or psychologist learning to serve as consultant to any group—e.g.—a school classroom, to help those directly and immediately involved, to learn how to function in continuously effective communication with their peers. Thus one's therapists finally may really become those whom one encounters daily, in the classroom, on the job, or in the hospital. These latter suggestions while clearly at some substantial remove from our immediate experience, would seem to be basically consistent with the growing data indicating the marked value of the non-professional. At the very least they seem worthy of some investigation.

Behavior Rehearsal as a Technique in Child Treatment

MARTIN GITTELMAN

INTRODUCTION

Since its inception, behavior therapy has been characterized by the development and innovation of a wide range of technical strategies. Beginning with the earliest work of Jones (1924), and Rayner and Watson (1920), new approaches based on learning theory have continued to proliferate, providing the therapist with a considerable armamentarium in the treatment of neurosis. However, as Rachman (1962) has pointed out, the focus in the investigation and treatment of behavior disorders has been on work with adults, and relatively less in the area of children's disturbances. Rachman ascribes this disparate advance to the difference in the nature of disturbances in children and adults. Whereas adults manifest behavior patterns which are unadaptive and must be broken down, children are more often seen for their inadequate or inappropriate development of desired behavior. While this is often the case, children are frequently seen who require help in breaking down behavior patterns, as well as those who need to adopt developmentally appropriate behavior.

This is particularly so with children whose primary disturbance is manifested in the expression of inappropriate aggression and hostility towards their peers, parents, or other authority figures (most often teach-

Reprinted with permission from *Journal of Child Psychology and Psychiatry*, 1965, Vol. 6, 251–255, ers). Such children are readily provoked into rage and 'acting out' by minimal instigation. While the roots of such behavior are often traceable to parental practices (Bandura, Ross and Ross, 1963; Schaefer and Bayley, 1963; Sears, Maccoby and Levin, 1957) and can often be modified by parent counselling, more immediate intervention is frequently required, particularly with older children. As is well known with such children, efforts to point out the unadaptive nature of their responses are met with little or only temporary success. Even when the child states that he knows he has nothing to gain by expressing anger, he often feels powerless to resist striking out against real or imagined provocation. This paper is a report of an attempt to apply learning theory principles to the treatment of such children. Since children on the whole appear to have difficulty in deliberately producing the vivid visual images necessary for desensitization therapy, a method which more closely approximates the elements of the instigatory situation is required. The method, as it has developed, involves the use of role-playing or behavioral rehearsal, whereby various instigatory situations are played out by the child and, in the case of group therapy, by various members of the group.

METHOD

While there are many variations of the technique, that which has proved to be clinically most useful requires the elicitation from the child of various situations which in the past have provoked him to aggression or defiance. These situations are then presented, through acting, in a hierarchical manner, with the mildest situation presented initially. As a child develops tolerance for these mild situations, those of a higher instigatory valence are gradually introduced. An arbitrary point score is constructed and the child's responses to instigation are rated by other group members and by the therapist.

An example of such a scoring system is: Two minus points for overt expression of aggression, e.g. striking out; one minus point for an 'emotional' response, e.g. flushing, clenching fists, tightening of the facial musculature, etc. No points are given for a neutral response. On the positive side, one point is scored for a passive reaction, as for example when the child goes 'limp' as he is lifted or pushed. Finally, two points are given for a reaction involving a verbal response which in some way serves to disarm or mollify the instigator. The point system, as noted, is an arbitrary one and can doubtless be improved. However, in practice it serves to quickly differentiate for the child which behaviors are acceptable, and which are not. Moreover, the points received by the child, and possibly more important, the approval he wins from the group for particularly ingenious responses, may be conceptualized as a form of social reinforcement.

The procedure is one which children find enjoyable—often, of course, because (for the instigator) it serves as a way of expressing aggression, albeit a socially acceptable one. That is, the instigator is helping the other child to inhibit his own aggression, and as such is functioning in a therapeutic manner. Even the child who is provoked finds his role bearable, since it will be his turn next to play the part of the instigator. Even extremely passive children, who fear aggression, gradually find behavior rehearsal is not threatening in the context of the protective therapy setting.

Other variants of the technique can be used with children who are not physically aggressive, but who, for example, are having school difficulties because of 'clowning' or who express hostility or defiance by facial or gestural cues. Of course such behavior is often based on underlying difficulties, which can be helped by insight therapy. However, one is impressed by how often a child appears to have obtained genuine insight into the basis of his behavior, and yet finds it difficult to change an established pattern. In such cases, behavior rehearsal would seem to be a valuable adjunct.

In practice, the method draws upon the techniques of psychodrama (Moreno, 1959), that described by Wolpe (1958) in establishing assertive responses, and to training given to civil rights workers in passive resistance (Belfrage, 1965). Recently, young Negro children have been prepared for entry into desegregated schools by subjecting them to sorts of abuse they might expect upon entering the school. Because such preparation is often traumatic for young children, the attrition rate prior to entry has reportedly been high, and it has been suggested that gradual introduction to a hierarchy of provocation would be less traumatic (Gittelman, 1964).

CASE ILLUSTRATION

To illustrate behavior rehearsal with children, a case is described. The context of the treatment was in a group of seven boys ranging from 12–14 years of age who met for 2 hours each week as outpatients at a community mental health clinic. The group was mixed, in the sense that three of the boys presented varying degrees of 'acting out' behavior, one child was extremely constricted and fearful of aggression, and the remaining three showed a variety of problems. Most of the children were having learning difficulties as well as problems in the home.

One of the group members, Ralph, a 13-year-old whose parents were divorced and who lived with his mother, presented the greatest problems in the expression of aggression. His temper outbursts had proved so violent that he had been expelled from one school and was threatened with expulsion from his new school. The boy was extremely small in stature, giving the impression of a child some 2 or 3 years younger. It is likely that this was due to the fact that he had been a premature infant, weighing only 2 pounds 10 ounces (1·19 kg) at birth. Despite his prematurity and a slow rate of physical growth for the first 6 months, development had proceeded within normal limits and no signs suggestive of cerebral dysfunction could be inferred from his developmental course. Intelligence testing as well as clinical impression indicated that his intellectual functioning was in the high average range. While he was extremely small in size, he was physically agile and an excellent fighter, feared by many of his peers and, most likely, by some of his teachers.

Ralph's pattern of response to stress was generally as follows: The slightest stimulus would cause him to feel singled out and provoked. Another child who might brush his shoulder in passing, or a teacher's criticism of his work, would cause him to become enraged. Under these conditions, he would respond impulsively, striking out at the other child without waiting for an apology or explanation. During his first session with the group, Ralph provided an example of how easy he was to provoke. While presenting the group with his background and school difficulties, one of the group members asked him whether he was a 'good fighter'. Ralph turned quickly to the boy, his eyes narrowed in anger, and said "You want to try me?" With his teachers he could not resist answering back and was at all times prepared to strike out. In discussing these incidents in the group, he reported feeling that unless he responded aggressively others would think him weak and he would face even greater provocation. Ralph's difficulties had approached a crisis point when he threatened to kill his mother's boy friend with a knife. Following this incident, Ralph said that he understood his reaction was inappropriate and that he felt anxious and guilty, but felt powerless to inhibit his immediate uncontrolled reaction.

Treatment with Ralph proceeded along lines previously described. Behavior rehearsal was initiated after four 2-hr. weekly sessions. Ralph was first asked to describe, in as great detail as possible, situations which aroused unadaptive affective responses. Subsequently several of the situations were acted out with Ralph and the therapist, or another group member, alternating roles. This was done to provide a more detailed picture of Ralph's behavior, but was also incidentally found to be useful in suggesting alternative modes of behavior to him. Following this procedure, the group members alternately acted out instigating and provocative situations. Initially only the largest group members were used, since

Ralph found himself unable to refrain from striking out. A hierarchy of provocative situations was then constructed and individual group members each acted out one. In practice it was not possible to follow the usual formal course of desensitization, proceeding from the least to increasingly provoking situations, since the group members differed in their ability to make 'real' the instigatory situation. However, a gradient of provocative situations was generally adhered to, and ratings made of Ralph's reactions. Illustrations of some of the instigatory situations presented to Ralph, as well as his initial response, included: (1) Being approached and 'accidentally' bumped, with an immediate apology made by the instigator (low intensity reaction). After Ralph was able to tolerate this provocation, the situation was modified by having the instigator follow the 'accidental' brushing with an attempt to provoke Ralph to fight. This was done initially by verbal provocation (e.g. implying that Ralph was cowardly for not responding). Still later, physical instigation was used such as pushing, stepping on his toes, and lifting him. (2) Another situation presented to Ralph involved the enactment of a robbery (high intensity reaction). In this situation the aggressor asked Ralph to empty his pockets, remove his tie and jacket. As the situation was enacted, Ralph was constantly rated by the group. For example, when he slowly complied with the demands to empty his pockets, he was given one negative point. In contrast, he was given two plus points when, as the instigator carefully folded Ralph's tie and placed it in his pocket, he commented that he (the instigator) was welcome to it and did he also need a wristwatch? (3) With two group members acting as classmates and one playing the role of teacher, Ralph was subjected to a number of instigatory situations. Following a pre-arranged plan, developed while Ralph waited outside the room, the boy sitting next to him asked him a question. The 'teacher', who pretended to be writing on the blackboard, turned to Ralph and asked him to be quiet. One plus point was given him when he did not proclaim his innocence. While Ralph was initially unable to inhibit aggression in the early scenes, he was gradually able to avert rage, but still showed signs of anger, clenching his fists, flushing, etc. Still later, following his chance to provoke several of the other boys, he was noticeably able to tolerate increasingly instigative acts. After the formal aspects of the game, the group was encouraged to discuss their subjective reactions to the roles they had played.

After four group sessions in which behavior rehearsal was employed, Ralph reported a considerable improvement in his behavior out of the group. At that point he had completed eight weekly two-hour sessions over approximately a two and a half month period. He said that while he often felt angry and provoked by many situations, he now felt much more able to inhibit aggressive responses. While he continued to have difficulties in school, involving learning problems, his school guidance counselor reported much diminution of his aggressiveness, which had previously been almost a daily occurrence. Follow-up lasted four months after therapy was initiated, with consistent absence of any major 'flare-ups'. Post-treatment follow-up and direct examinations were precluded when he stopped treatment on moving to another city, after having attended some 12 group-meetings. However, contact with Ralph's mother nine months after termination revealed that he continued to show progress in his school work and had not shown a further outbreak of impulsive or aggressive behavior.

Conceptually, behavior rehearsal with children may be viewed as an attempt to intervene in, or inhibit, unadaptive responses and provide and reinforce more socially acceptable alternative responses. In children who exhibit impulsive and aggressive behavior and who are motivated to change, the technique may serve a useful therapeutic role.

SUMMARY

This paper describes a technique in the treatment of aggressive, 'acting-out' children in an out-patient group setting. The method involves the use of role-playing or behavior rehearsal, whereby various instigatory situations are played out by the child and other group members. While the technique is similar in many respects to psychodrama, an effort has been made to introduce certain learning theory concepts, particularly that of desensitization. A case illustrating the technique is presented.

REFERENCES

BANDURA, A., ROSS, D. and ROSS, S. A. (1963) Vicarious reinforcement and imitative learning. *J. Abnorm. Soc. Psychol.* **67**, 601–607.

BELFRAGE, S. (1965) *Freedom summer.* Viking Press, New York.

GITTELMAN, M. (1964) Report on the Work of the Medical Committee for Human Rights in Mississippi. Paper read at Albert Einstein College of Medicine in New York, November 25.

JONES, M. C. (1924) A laboratory study of fear: the case of Peter. *Pedag. Semin.* **31**, 308–315.

MORENO, J. L. (1959) Ch. 68: Psychodrama. *American Handbook of Psychiatry.* Edited by Arieti, S. Basic Books, New York.

RACHMAN, S. (1962) Learning theory and child psychology: therapeutic possibilities. *J. Child Psychol. Psychiat.* **3**, 149–163.

RAYNER, R. and WATSON, J. B. (1920) Conditioned emotional reactions. *J. Exp. Psychol.* **3**, 1–14.

SCHAEFER, E. S. and BAYLEY, N. (1963) Maternal behavior, child behavior, and their intercorrelations from infancy through adolescence. *Monogr. Soc. Res. Child Dev.* **28,** 1–127.

SEARS, R. R., MACCOBY, E. E. and LEVIN, H. (1957) *Patterns of child rearing.* Harper & Row, New York.

WOLPE, J. (1958) *Psychotherapy by reciprocal inhibition.* Stanford University Press, Stanford, California.

A Behaviour Modification Technique for the Hyperactive Child

G. R. PATTERSON
R. JONES
J. WHITTIER
MARY A. WRIGHT

This paper describes a procedure for the conditioning of attending behaviour in a brain-injured hyperactive boy.

Observations of the behaviour of two hyperactive children were made in the classroom setting. These observations were made from an observation booth adjoining the classroom and provided data on the frequency of occurrence of the following high rate responses: walking, talking, distraction, "wiggling". Each child was observed for a minimum of ten minutes a day, four days a week. Following several weeks of baseline observation, the conditioning procedure was begun with the experimental subject. The conditioning trials took place in the classroom setting. During each time interval in which one of the high rate responses did not occur, S received an auditory stimulus (secondary reinforcer). This auditory stimulus had previously been paired with the delivery of candy and pennies. The stimulus was dispensed by a radio device which activated an earphone worn by the subject. At the end of each conditioning trial, S received whatever candy or pennies he had "earned".

The data show that the control subject showed no significant change in the frequency of occurrence of the high rate responses during the three month period. The experimental subject showed a significant decrease in non-attending behaviour. This reduction in rate was maintained over a four week extinction period.

Reprinted with permission from *Behaviour Research & Therapy*, 1965, Vol. 2, 217–226,

This report describes a procedure for the conditioning of attending behavior in a brain injured hyperactive boy. The data from the experimental and control subject show that it is possible to condition this behaviour in a classroom setting and that the effects generalize from the conditioning period. Follow-up data show that these effects persist over at least a four week period of time.

Taken together, the incidental findings from a large number of empirical studies would suggest that the activity level of the child is a critical variable in the socialization process. In the normal child, high activity levels are associated with a more frequent occurrence of a wide range of social behaviour, e.g. dependency and aggression (Sears *et al.*, 1953; Hinsey, Patterson and Sonoda, 1961) and acceptance by peers (Tuddenham, 1951). Data from the longitudinal study by Bayley and Schaefer (1963) showed that differences in activity level in infancy relate to a wide variety of adolescent behavior patterns such as friendliness, boldness, irritability, and distractibility. In this study, the correlations between activity level and these types of social behaviour were all positive. Factor analyses of the behaviour of normal children are consistent in showing an "activity" dimension (Walker, 1962; Baldwin, 1948).

It is evident that *very* high rates of behaviour are aversive to adults. Data collected by Patterson (1956) from four child clinics showed that "hyperactivity" was one of the most common problems for which children were referred to child clinics. Factor analyses of the behaviour of "disturbed" children by Patterson (1964) and Dreger and Dreger (1962) showed "hyperactivity" as a factor dimension in both studies.

The antecedents for this behaviour are poorly understood. Studies with animals are consistent in showing a relation between emotional and or deprivational states and activity levels (Campbell and Sheffield, 1953; Hill, 1958). There are also a series of studies with human subjects which strongly suggest constitutional factors (unspecified) as additional determinants.

The research of Irwin (1930) and Balint (1948) showed wide individual differences in activity level at birth. The data presented by Jones and Bayley (1950) and by Walker (1962) offer some support for a hypothesis regarding constitutional differences in activity level in older children. A third, well-documented antecedent for variations in activity level was found in the relation between anoxic conditions at birth and later activity levels of the child (Parmellee, 1962; Graham, Ernhart, Thurston and Croft, 1962).

Whatever the antecedents for this behaviour, the empirical findings suggest an interesting hypothesis which has directed the attention of this research group to the problem of "controlling" so-called "hyperactive" behaviour. The general hypothesis is that there is a curvilinear relationship between activity level of the child and the acquisition of socially acceptable behaviour. Up to moderately high levels of activity, the child's behaviour will elicit an increasing number of reactions from peers and adults. Assuming that these reactions are, by and large, positive, this should imply that the very active child will acquire social skills at a faster rate than the less active child. It is further assumed that *extremely high* rates of behaviour are aversive for other people; hence, the reactions from the culture are more likely to be punitive. In this situation, the child operating at high activity levels may very well be punished *even* when he is displaying socially acceptable behaviour, e.g. "friendliness".

This higher ratio of punishment to reinforced behaviour for the hyperactive child should result in his developing social behaviour at a slower rate.

The *specific responses* emitted by the hyperactive child must be conditioned as a result of the social rewards and punishments provided by parents, teachers, and peers. This being the case, it should be possible to create a procedure for conditioning more appropriate behaviour in the hyperactive child. Patterson (1964) used a conditioning procedure to increase the frequency of attending behaviour in a hyperactive boy. This pilot study was carried out in a classroom setting using non-social reinforcers to shape this behaviour in a series of fifteen conditioning trials. James (1963) programmed the teacher's behaviour so that social reinforcers were made contingent upon the occurrence of socially acceptable behaviour in a group of hyperactive children. Over a twenty month period, this arrangement seemed to produce dramatic changes in five of the children.

The present report described a modified, and improved, technique for controlling the behaviour of the hyperactive child. Observational data on the frequency of the occurrence of "non-attending" behaviour in the classroom constitute the data testing the effects of the conditioning procedure. These data were collected for both an experimental and a control subject. It was assumed that the classroom setting had been conditioning a variety of behaviour patterns which competed with successful academic performance, e.g. such responses as looking out the window, walking about the room. In the conditioning procedure, immediate reinforcement was provided for brief intervals of responding in which *only* attending behaviour occurred. It was predicted that this procedure would result in a decrease in occurrence of non-attending behaviour during the conditioning sessions. Furthermore, it was predicted that these effects would generalize to occasions when the conditioning apparatus was not being used. Because the conditioning trials actually occurred in the classroom setting, it was expected that over a series of trials, many of the stimuli in the classroom would become conditioned to elicit attending rather than non-attending behaviour. Because of the complexity of the matrix of stimuli found in the classroom setting, the conditioning of attending behaviour may very well be "slower" than would be the case if the conditioning occurred in a more controlled laboratory setting. However, the classroom procedure should result in greater generalization of effects than would be obtained by conditioning in the more controlled laboratory setting.

The third hypothesis was that the effects would persist over a four week extinction period. This "prediction" was based upon the subjective findings from the earlier study by Patterson (1964) in which parents and teachers reported effects which persisted over at least a six month period. This apparent resistance to extinction seemed to be a function of a change in the reinforcement schedules provided by the peers and by the teacher. It was assumed that a similar situation would occur in the present case; a change in the child's aversive behaviour should increase the ratio of positive reinforcement provided by peers and by the teacher. It is the change in the peer and teacher programme of reinforcement which maintains the conditioning effects. Although the present report is concerned only with demonstrating the persistence of the conditioning effects, a study recently completed by Straughan (in preparation) shows that the peer group is in fact re-programmed by a procedure similar to the one described in this report.

PROCEDURES

The Experimental Subject (ES)

Ten years of age, Raymond had been exposed to a series of foster and adoptive homes. Although the medical records described him as a full term baby, he weighed only three and one half pounds at birth. At the age of nine months his first adoptive parents returned him to the agency with the complaint that he never moved his left arm and leg. A craniotomy performed at that time revealed almost complete atrophy of the right cerebral hemisphere. Somewhat later in his development, the effects were manifested in the hemiplegic carriage and gait, increased tendon reflexes and positive Babinski. The movements of the tongue were also impaired, resulting in a moderate to severe articulation defect.

Until adopted at the age of five, Raymond had been placed in a total of nine different homes. His intellectual ability generally varied within the range of educable but retarded. At the age of six, he obtained an IQ of 59; more recently, he obtained an IQ of 65 on the verbal scale of the WISC and 86 on the performance scale.

Two years prior to the experiment, he was admitted to the Children's

Hospital School, a day care center for physically handicapped children. While in residence at the school he has been placed in a foster home (the same home in which the control subject resided). Immediately following his admission to the school, his teacher described him as having a short attention span, and as being aggressive to the younger children. All teacher evaluations which followed described him as being very hyperactive.

The Control Subject (CS)

Ricky was a ten-and-a-half year old boy who sustained a severe head injury at the age of six in an automobile accident. The head injury involved a skull fracture over the left parietal region and resulted in his being in a coma for five months. The skull fracture was lifted surgically and he was discharged from the hospital with the diagnosis of traumatic hemiplegia. The injury resulted in spastic functioning of the left arm and leg. Although he had good visual, tactile and auditory functioning, there was a marked impairment of motor functioning in lips, tongue, and perhaps the larynx. As a consequence he had no speech. On a variety of tests including the Peabody Picture Vocabulary and Raven Matrices given over a three year period, his scores ranged from the eighties to the low nineties.

Ricky's parents had arranged for him to stay in a foster home while in residence at the Children's Hospital School. Observations of his classroom behaviour indicated that most of the time he displayed non-attending behaviour, e.g. walking about the room, staring into space, almost continuous movement of arms or legs.

Observation Procedures

Both subjects were observed in the classroom setting over a period of two weeks in order to determine the specific characteristics of their non-attending behaviour. The general impression was that neither of them devoted much time to school work but were instead in almost constant motion. After several try-outs a check-list was devised such that sixty ten-second observations in sequence could be taken on a given child, for a total of ten minutes per check-list. There were seven categories of non-attending behaviour which characterized these two subjects. Each of these categories had sixty observation cells following it.

A tape recording announced the beginning of each ten-second interval to the observer, who watched from behind a one-way screen. If a particular category of non-attending behaviour occurred during a given ten-second period, a check mark was placed in the appropriate cell, and that behaviour was ignored for the rest of that interval; if other forms of non-attending behaviour occurred during that interval, check marks were placed in the appropriate cells, and they, too, were then ignored until the next ten-second interval began.

It was also recorded on the check-list whether the child being observed was (1) working alone, (2) in a classroom activity (e.g. story-telling, singing), or (3) receiving personal attention from an adult, during any given set of ten-second observation periods. Total scores for each of the categories of interfering behaviour, and a grand total, were recorded for each ten-minute period.

The types of behaviour observed in the final form of the check-list are described below:

1. Movements directed toward the body: e.g. wringing of hands, rubbing eyes, swinging arms, leaning forward in the chair, scratching, or stretching.
2. Movements in chair: e.g. shuffling of chair, sliding back and forth in chair, twisting of body in chair, or leaning clear out of chair so that buttocks no longer rested on it.
3. Distraction: e.g. looking over toward a noise, toward someone who has just entered the room (unless teacher also looks up), out of the window, or off into space.
4. Gross movements of legs and feet: e.g. pumping of leg, wiggling of feet, or crossing of legs, or other shift of their position.
5. Fiddling: Arm and hand movements directed toward objects: activities of the hand(s) that interfered with schoolwork or assigned activities, e.g. stroking the desk, fingering the box of colour crayons.
6. Communicative or quasi-communicative activity interfering with schoolwork, e.g. talking to self, pointing, laughing, attempting to attract someone's attention, talking to someone without permission.
7. Walking or standing that was not encouraged or subsequently approved of by the teacher.

Each child was observed for a minimum of ten minutes a day, four days a week. Four observers collected the data; each observer was responsible for one set of data per week. Three days of observations were made in the morning during a time when the children were working at independent projects at their desks. One of the observations was made during the afternoon in which the classroom setting tended to vary over a wide range of group activities.

After one week's practice in using the check-list, two pairs of observers were checked for agreement in data collecting. The total frequency of non-attending behaviour patterns were summed for eight ten-minute intervals for each pair who had been observing the experimental subject. When using *total* frequency of occurrence on non-attending behaviour the correlation between one pair of observers was 0·90 and the correlation between a second pair was 0·91.

The two subjects were seated close together in the class. The data presented in a later section of the paper show that the two subjects displayed about the same total frequency of non-attending behaviour at the beginning of the experiment. They did, however, differ somewhat in the kind of non-attending behaviour displayed. The control subject showed about three times the number of leg movements, about half the number of distraction responses and chair movements, and twice as much "walking" as did the experimental subject.

Conditioning Procedure

Baseline data were collected for both subjects during the period 1 November through 19 November. The data were collected on eleven days during this interval.

Between 20 November and 10 December, data were collected on nine days on the classroom behaviour of both subjects. The experimental subject was taken out of the room for a brief period each day and adapted to the conditioning procedure and apparatus. The observation data were collected prior to the experimental subject's being taken from the classroom.

During this adaption phase, *ES* was taken out of the classroom for approximately ten minutes each trial. He was told that the apparatus was being used in an effort to teach him to sit still so that he could study better. He was taken into a small room containing two chairs and a desk. After being seated at the table a pair of suspenders were snapped in place holding the small radio receiving unit on his back. After the earphone had been adjusted he was told to open his workbook and complete the homework assignment given him by the teacher. He was told that the buzz which he would hear indicated that he had earned a piece of candy. During the next few minutes, *E* activated the earphone and dropped candy into a small cup in front of him for each ten-second period in which he did not display any non-attending behaviour. At the end of a trial, he was given his pieces of candy and returned to the classroom.

A third phase lasted from 11 December through 15 January. Data were collected for both subjects on eight days during this interval. Following the observation period on each of these days, *ES* was conditioned in the classroom for periods ranging from five to eighteen minutes.

On the first trial, the following announcement was made to the class:

> Raymond has some trouble with sitting still and this makes it hard for him to learn things. This little earphone which he is wearing will tell him when he is sitting still. When he sits still, he earns candy for himself and for the rest of you. When he is finished, we will take the earphone off and give him

> the candy that he has earned. He can pass it out to the rest of you at the end of the class period.

During the conditioning trial, *E* was in a one-way observation room (which contained a speaker) adjoining the classroom. Using a radio transmitter device, a signal was sent for each ten-second interval in which none of the non-attending responses occurred. This fixed interval schedule was maintained for the first four conditioning trials and candy was used for rewards. The first conditioning trial lasted seven minutes, and the trials were increased by one to three minutes each day until twenty-minute trials were reached.

On the fifth and all preceding trials, a variable interval schedule was used, the units consisting of: 2, 5, 10, 15, 20 and 30 seconds. To counteract possible satiation, pennies were used on alternate days for reinforcing stimuli. After interviewing the teacher, plastic soldiers (a special preference of Raymond's) were also included in his "earnings". It was agreed that Raymond would keep all plastic soldiers for his own. The total number of reinforcers for a given trial ranged from fifteen to seventy.

Between 17 January and 21 February nine follow-up observations were made. These data constitute the extinction plans of the experiment.

RESULTS

The data in Fig. 1 present the mean frequency per minute of the total for non-attending behaviour for both subjects in all three phases of the study. The points on the graph represent the mean number of responses per minute for each trial in which observations were made for *both* the experimental and control subjects in each of the four phases.

When examining these data, it is well to keep in mind that the observation data were *not* collected *during* the conditioning period but rather in the ten-or twenty-minute period immediately prior to each trial. In effect, each day's observation data for the experimental subject represented the cumulative effects of conditioning on preceding days. For the experimental subject, the data presented here are generalization data for the effects of conditioning.

In analysing these data, the sign test was used to compare the total frequency scores obtained on the same days for the two subjects. The analysis shows that although the *ES* tended to show a higher frequency of non-attending behaviour during the baseline phase of the experiment, this difference was not significant. During the adaptation period, this trend is reversed; but again, the two subjects are not significantly different from each other. During the conditioning phase, the experimental subject

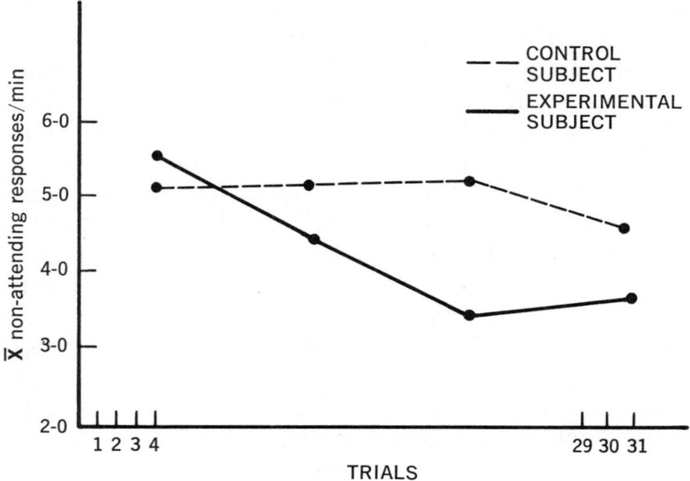

Fig. 1. Effect of behaviour manipulation.

shows significantly fewer non-attending responses than does the control subject (*P* less than 0·06). This difference is maintained during the extinction phase (*P* less than 0·03).

These findings are in keeping with the main hypothesis that the procedure would significantly modify the behaviour of the experimental subject. The data also support the prediction that the effects of the conditioning would generalize to occasions when the apparatus was not being used to control behaviour. This latter finding is of particular importance when considering the practical implications of this procedure. The prediction that the effects would persist over a four week period was also supported by the data.

The unexpected but interesting finding from the study is the fact that the control subject showed a drop of about 13 per cent in the occurrence of non-attending behaviour from the conditioning to the follow-up phase. Because of the limited number of observations involved for this single subject, it was not feasible to test for the significance of this decrease. However, in a study by Anderson (in preparation) using similar subjects and a design in which observations were made for a control subject in the *same classroom*, a similar decrease of 11 per cent was obtained. Furthermore, the drop also occurred during the period following the *termination* of the conditioning study. Although both sets of findings may be coincidental they suggest the possibility that other children in the classroom are affected by the procedure and the resulting change in the behaviour of the experimental subject. In any case, these findings would suggest that in future studies, the control subjects should be observed in classrooms in which conditioning procedures are not introduced.

Because of the possibility that the different types of non-attending behaviour might be differentially affected, the frequency of occurrence for each of these responses was plotted separately for the *ES*. An inspection of these graphs showed that there were in fact differences in effects. The responses "fiddling" and "distraction" (the most frequent responses) were similarly affected in that both of them showed a small decrement during adaptation and a marked decrement during conditioning which continued to drop during the follow-up phase. However, "leg movements", "chair movements", and "arm movements" were similar in that all of them showed a marked drop during conditioning but a rapid increase during the extinction period. It is evident that these motor movements were only temporarily affected by the procedure. Inspection of the data relevant to the response "walking" indicates that it was not affected by the procedure. These findings suggest that the conditioning of attending behaviour has differential implications for the "fate" of the various non-attending responses with which they are in competition.

DISCUSSION

These data offer strong support for the efficacy of behaviour modification techniques for the control of the hyperactive child. The findings are in agreement with the earlier pilot study by Patterson (1964) and the more recent study by Anderson (1964).

Although the effects were significant in all three studies, there are some qualitative differences among the findings which would have implications for future studies of this type. In both the pilot study and the Anderson (1964) study the effects seemed to be more "dramatic"; in these studies, the improvements in behaviour were apparent to even the casual observer. These differences have led to the *ad hoc* assumption that the conditioning procedure initiated a chain of events which, although by-products, were probably of greater social significance than the decrease in non-attending behaviour.

The one variable which seems to account for the difference among studies is the greater involvement of the peer group in the Anderson study and the pilot study. In the pilot study, for example, there were loud cheers and clapping at the end of a trial and frequent social reinforcement by individuals in the classroom both during and following a trial. In these studies there seemed to be a change of status for *ES* within the peer group. Before the conditioning trials, both *ES* s had been barely tolerated or rejected. Following conditioning they were more accepted by the other children.

In the present study, however, the general atmosphere of the Hospital School is very much oriented towards the individual child, e.g. occupational therapy, speech therapy, individual tutoring in the class; it is our impression that this group of children is the least cohesive group we have observed to date and has an extremely high tolerance for deviant behaviour. Perhaps it was this lack of involvement by the peer group which accounts for the minimal change in the present instance. At this time, the functional importance of the reaction of the peer group or the teacher to decreases in high rate responses is an untested hypothesis. However, a recent study by Straughan (in preparation) shows that the peer group reactions do change and that they can be programmed to become contingent upon the socially adaptive behaviour of the experimental subject. These findings would suggest that the development of techniques for reprogramming schedules of reward and punishment on the part of the parents and peer group could be of critical importance. Certainly, this type of programming deserves far more attention than it has received in behaviour modification studies carried out thus far.

Our hypothesis at this point is that the importance of any change in behaviour lies in the effect which it produces upon the reactions of the social culture. If, for example, a small decrement in the rate of aversive behaviour is immediately followed by approval of the peer group or the teacher, this should accelerate the acquisition of new behaviour. As these new behaviour patterns are acquired, they should in turn lead to an even greater reaction from the peer culture. Under these conditions the change in behaviour could be dramatic, even if the focus of observation is limited to the decrease in non-attending behaviour. The hypothesis would suggest, however, that the observational data should be expanded to include two vital types of information. On the one hand it would be imperative to collect data on the *kind of reactions* being elicited from the peer group and the *kind* of *ES* behaviour which elicits these reactions. Second, it should also include the occurrence of social behaviour which would be secondarily affected by an increase in positive reactions from the peer group, e.g. friendly behaviour, frequency of participation in group activities during recess. The assumption is that a change in status in the peer group implies peer reinforcement for socially acceptable behaviour patterns of a wide variety. This should be reflected in a rapid increase in adaptive behaviour, in addition to those which are specifically being conditioned by the experimenter.

This would suggest in turn* that in the planning of behaviour modification programmes it would be important to arrange a hierarchy of responses which would lead to the child being ignored or punished by the social culture. A change in the rate of such behaviour—and "hyperactivity"

*This hypothesis was offered by J. Straughan.

might be such a response—would produce the greatest generalized effects in terms of a wide range of social responses. The question, of course, as to the nature of such a hierarchy is an empirical one, but it would seem to be of prime importance to collect these kinds of data as quickly as possible. The implication is that it will not be necessary to devise a conditioning procedure to extinguish each of the child's behaviour singly and separately.

There seem to be enormous day-to-day fluctuations in the rate of occurence of the non-attending behaviour. During the baseline period, for example, the experimental subject on one day showed an average of 9·4 non-attending responses per minute. This was a day on which a visiting teacher had taken over the class. Periods immediately preceding holidays also seemed associated with high rates of non-attending behaviour. Various daily activities within the classroom also seemed to have differential effects, e.g. data obtained during a group reading period showed the rate of non-attending behaviour to be only 3·3 responses per minute. It would be expected that to some extent these variations in situations would have a similar effect upon both the experimental and control subject; however, the data offer only limited support for this hypothesis. The correlation between total frequency of non-attending behaviour over the first six weeks for the *ES* and *CS* was only 0·25.

In spite of the extensive efforts made to collect data which accurately reflect the effects of the behaviour modification technique used here, there is one respect in which adequate controls were lacking. This involves the potential lack of control over the behaviour of the observer. Due to the fact that each observer also functioned as an experimenter in the conditioning trials, it is possible that a consistent bias is present in the data. This possibility would indicate the need for using observers who do not know which subject is the experimental and which is the control. This arrangement is being followed in studies now under way.

Acknowledgments—The writers gratefully acknowledge the financial assistance provided by MH grant 08009–01 in purchasing the equipment used in this study. The writers are also indebted to the support and critical thinking provided by the informal seminar on Behavior Modification sponsored by the University Psychology Clinic. The writers also wish to thank Byron Krog and his teaching staff at the Children's Hospital School for allowing us to invade the privacy of the classroom.

REFERENCES

ANDERSON D. (1964) Application of a behavior modification technique to the control of a hyperactive child. Unpublished M. A. Thesis, University of Oregon.

BALDWIN A. L. (1948) Socilization and the parent child relationship. *Child Develpm.* **19**, 127–136.

BALINT M. (1948) Individual differences of behavior in early infancy: an objective method for recording. *J. Genet. Psychol.* **73**, 57–79.

BAYLEY NANCY AND SCHAEFER E. S. (1963) Maternal behavior, child behavior, and their intercorrelations from infancy through adolescence. *Monogr. Soc. Res. Child Develpm.* **28**, 3.

CAMPBELL B. A. AND SHEFFIELD F. D. (1953) Relation of random activity to food deprivation. *J. Comp. Physiol. Psychol.* **46**, 320–322.

DREGER R. AND DREGER GEORGIA E. (1962) Behavior classification project: Report 1.

GRAHAM FRANCES, ERNHART CLARIE, THURSTON D. and CROFT MARGUERITE (1962) Organic development three years after pre-natal anoxia and other potentially damaging newborn experience. *Psychol. Monogr.* **76**, 53.

HILL W. F. (1958) The effect of long confinement on voluntary wheel running by rats. *J. Comp. Physiol. Psychol.* **51**, 770–773.

HINSEY C., PATTERSON R. and SONODA BEVERLY (1961) Validation of a technique for conditioning aggression in children. Paper read at Western Psychol. Conv.

IRWIN O. C. (1930) The amount and nature of activity of new born infants during the first ten days of life. *Genet. Psychol. Monogr.* **8**, 1–92.

JAMES C. E. (1963) Operant conditioning in the management and behavior of hyperactive children: five case studies. Unpublished manuscript, Orange State College.

JONES MARY C. and BAYLEY NANCY (1950) Physical maturing among boys as related to behavior. *J. Educ. Psychol.* **41**, 129–148.

PARMELLEE A. (1962) European neurological studies of the newborn. *Child Develpm.* **33**, 169–180.

PATTERSON G. R. (1964) An application of conditioning techniques to the control of a hyperactive child. *Case Studies in Behavior Modification* (L. P. Ullmann and L. Krasner). Holt, Rinehart and Winston, Inc., New York.

PATTERSON G. R. (1955) A tentative approach to the classification of children's behavior problems. Unpublished doctoral dissertation. University of Minnesota.

PATTERSON G. R. (1964) An empirical approach to the classification of disturbed children. *J. Clin. Psychol.* **20**, 326–337.

SEARS R. R., WHITING J. W., NOWLES V. and SEARS P. (1963) Some child rearing antecedents of aggression and dependency in young children. *Genet. Psychol. Monogr.* **47**, 135–236.

STRAUSS A. A. and LEHTINEN LAURA (1950) *Psychopathology and Education of the Brain Injured Child.* Grune & Stratton, New York.

TUDDENHAM R. D. (1951) Studies in reputation: I. Sex and grade difference in school children's evaluation of their peers. II. The diagnosis of social maladjustment. *Psychol. Monogr.* **66,** (1) 58.

WALKER R. (1962) Body build and behavior in young children. *Monogr. Soc. Res. Child Develpm.* 27, 3.

The Behavioral Treatment of an Elective Mute

JAMES H. STRAUGHAN
WARREN K. POTTER, JR.
STEPHEN H. HAMILTON, JR.

This report describes a new application of a technique originally designed for modifying hyperactive behavior in the classroom (Patterson, 1964). In addition data are presented which help to clarify the social consequences of the technique. In Patterson's procedure a small signal light and a counter of the odometer type are placed on the hyperactive child's desk to serve as a secondary reinforcer for periods during which hyperactive behavior does not occur. Another reinforcer, e.g. candy or pennies, is given each day at the end of the training period. The child is told or taught beforehand that each activation of the signal light and counter means an additional penny or piece of candy at the end of the period. According to the study cited above and to later studies (Patterson *et al.,* 1964; Anderson, 1964), the technique is effective in treating hyperactivity, but apparently the social instigating and reinforcing behaviors of the peers are an important variable. Such changes in peer behavior were readily apparent to the observer but were not recorded in any of the original studies. In the case study reported here, a record was kept of that verbal behavior of the peers which was directed towards the subject.

The case presented in this report differed from those previously reported in that the disorder was elective mutism in the classroom. Reed (1964) has commented on the difficulty of treatment with these cases and

Reprinted with permission from *Journal of Child Psychology and Psychiatry*, 1965, Vol. 6, 125–130, Copyright 1965, Pergamon Press, Inc., and with the permission of the authors.

also summarized some of their diagnostic characteristics. The present case showed such characteristics as (*a*) remaining silent except with intimate friends, (*b*) showing unusual timidity and shyness, (*c*) having no known neurological deficiencies, (*d*) reported mute from his entrance in school at age six, (*e*) doing unsatisfactory academic work, and (*f*) scoring in the defective range on intelligence tests.

CASE HISTORY

Gene was a 14-year-old boy in a school for the mentally retarded. He had been transferred to the special school from the public schools at the age of eight. At that time, as at the time he was seen for treatment, two important symptoms were (*a*) an apparent inability to do satisfactory academic work and (*b*) a lack of verbal responsiveness. His I.Q. as measured by the Leiter International Performance Scale (Leiter, 1948) in 1964 was 52. Several earlier tests with the W.I.S.C. and Stanford-Binet had indicated I.Q.'s of from 60 to 65.

Gene's academic and social progress during the five years preceding treatment had fluctuated considerably showing frequent regressions. For example, he learned how to add and subtract to the number five on one day, but had apparently forgotten this skill on the following day. It was observed that he responded better to women, and made more academic progress during a year when a woman volunteer worked with him at least once a week.

His teacher reported that Gene's behavior at the beginning of this school year was consistent with his previous school years. During the first two weeks of classes Gene did not utter one word in the classroom, not even when asked to do so. It was reported that he made a few vocal responses to some of his peers on the playground and on the schoolbus. Some of his peers explained for him that he would not talk. Gene would appear to "tighten up" physically by crossing his arms, holding his breath, and looking away from the questioner. On the other hand, if he was asked to perform a motor task such as opening a window, turning on the lights, or throwing away a piece of paper he would immediately do so.

Gene's teacher made considerable efforts to increase his responsiveness during the months before experimental treatment began. The results were discouraging. The teacher tried such tactics as repeated and persistent encouragement, mild coercion, and immediate praise for any signs of response. On one occasion Gene was told that if he did not respond, no one would eat lunch, and he could not go to school the next day. The task was to read aloud a sentence from the text after hearing the teacher say the same sentence. Gene stammered, made a series of facial gestures, and blurted out a reasonable approximation to the stimulus words. After this, in the teacher's opinion, Gene was somewhat more responsive to requests and social prodding from the class and teacher.

During the months preceding treatment Gene's behavior outside the classroom contrasted with his non-communicativeness within. For example, he would lead the students on short hikes, keep them in line, show them alternative routes, and assume responsibility for the group. Upon returning to the classroom, he would resume his mute role. There was ample other evidence indicating that Gene was capable of talking and performing on a relatively adequate level for an adolescent boy.

Because it appeared as though Gene's refusal to talk was directed particularly against the teacher, he attempted to find additional ways of establishing a relationship with the boy. In January he took him to a local pet shop, because he had indicated an interest in animals. Gene was shy and nervous while alone with his teacher away from school, yet his interest was obvious. A few days later the entire class visited the pet shop, and Gene conducted a tour, including a demonstration of how to make the Mynah bird talk.

Gene's academic work, arithmetic, reading, and writing, was done poorly or not at all. A similar pattern had been reported for other years. His teacher and other observers reported that the impression conveyed is not so much that Gene could not perform but that he would not.

TREATMENT PROCEDURES

The work with Gene was divided into four phases: (1) preliminary observation, (2) systematic observation, (3) treatment, and (4) post-treatment observation.

The first phase, preliminary observation, began with the beginning of the school year in September. Gene's behavior in the classroom was observed from time to time by several persons, and informal reports were made to a study group every other week or so. His teacher was a member of this group. During this time initial attempts were made to formulate Gene's problem in terms of observable behavior (or lack of it). The teacher was encouraged to continue attempts to treat him. By January when the group was formed for the purpose of treating Gene, the problem had been formulated as social non-responsiveness, particularly verbal non-responsiveness, directed largely towards the teacher, but generally noticeable in the classroom. In order to systematize record keeping, a list of Gene's more prominent responses to another person was prepared and coded for ease of scoring. These typical behaviors were: looking at the other person, smiling at the other person, responding by some motor activity, no response, or talking in response. Although the last response was rarely observed, it was included because its absence was considered the most important sign of his pathology.

During the second phase (systematic observation) Gene's behavior was carefully recorded for 21 days, 20 minutes a day. All occurrences of the five responses listed above were recorded during the 20-minute period. In addition, a record was kept of who directed the question or other eliciting stimulus at Gene, whether instructor, volunteer, or peer. Where Gene made more than one response, his responses were recorded in order of their appearance. Systematic observation, treatment, and post-treatment observation were all begun at the same hour of the day, 11 o'clock or a few minutes after, during what was usually an arithmetic class for the children.

Patterson *et al.* (1964) report correlations between pairs of observers for total frequencies of non-attending behaviors of 0·90 and 0·91. In the present study observer reliability was not systematically checked and there is reason to suppose that where observers worked together their observations were not entirely independent. However, frequencies of talking recorded by two observers who worked together for five days correlated 0·95.

The third or treatment phase lasted for 18 days, 30 minutes a day. During the first 10 minutes Gene's behavior was observed and recorded with no reinforcement being given. During the remaining 20 minutes reinforcement was given as described below. The reinforcing apparatus was as described by Patterson (1964)—a small box containing an electric counter, with a light bulb on top. For the treatment of Gene this box was placed in front of the room where all of the class could see it. Light and counter could be controlled by a member of the treatment team who sat in an observation booth at the rear of the classroom. Members of the class were already somewhat familiar with this apparatus because it had been used in the room during the fall and early winter for the treatment of a hyperactive retarded boy (Anderson, 1964).

On the first treatment day one of us explained to the class what was happening somewhat as follows:

> This is a magic box which we are going to use to help Gene. Gene has trouble answering when the teacher or someone else speaks to him. It is very important to Gene that he learns to talk in the classroom when asked. Also, by talking Gene will earn a party for the class. Each time he talks when asked, this light will go on. We will count up how many times he has talked each day and mark it on this chart. When the chart is full, Gene will have earned a party for the class. You can help Gene earn the party for you by helping him to talk. Now we will show you how the magic box works.

The teacher then approached Gene and asked him a simple question. After some stuttering Gene was able to come up with an answer (incorrect), the bulb lighted, and the counter buzzed and clicked. Following two more demonstrations of the apparatus the class was continued as usual.

A reinforcement was given each time that Gene responded vocally to some appropriate instigation of another individual—usually a question or request from the teacher. Responses of more than one word were given triple reinforcements. Although Gene's behavior was highly variable, and the classroom activities were not always appropriate for eliciting responses, he was generally reinforced between 80 and 100 times during the 20 minute session. At this rate the chart was filled in and he earned the classroom party after nine days, and the party was held on the tenth day.

Until the party was earned, the only reinforcements were from the light, counter, and chart. Progress was entered on the chart in front of the class immediately following each day's conditioning session. Following the party, small candies (M & M's) were used as reinforcers and distributed to the class following each treatment period.

During the post-treatment observation Gene was observed for 9 consecutive school days for 30 minutes a day. The purpose of this was to determine if the effects of the treatment continued after reinforcement was discontinued.

PROGRESS

The total amount of talking done by Gene is shown in Table 1.

Table 1

Frequency of Talking

	Total Observation Time	Frequency of Talking	Frequency Per Ten Min
Before Treatment	420 min	97	2·31
During Treatment	180 min	493	27·39
After Treatment	270 min	852	31·56

$x^2 = 1008{\cdot}16 \quad P < 0{\cdot}001 \quad df = 2$

These figures are based upon the observation of clear, meaningful vocalizations consisting of one word or longer. Before treatment Gene's vocalizations in the classroom were almost entirely monosyllabic. By the 12th day of the reinforcement period it became clear to the observers that much of Gene's talking consisted of sentences or longer utterances, therefore utterances of more than one word were recorded separately. As recorded from the 12th day of reinforcement to the end of the post-treatment observation, 34·2 per cent of Gene's utterances consisted of more than one word. To the best of our recollection prior to reinforcement, all of his statements were monosyllabic.

A chi-square analysis of the data in Table 1 was done by basing the expected frequencies upon the total amount of observation time within each phase of the study. The chi-square analysis shows that the frequencies within the different phases are significantly different from one another ($p < 0 \cdot 001$). Analyses of individual pairs show that talking during each phase is significantly increased over the preceding phase.

The frequency of Gene's vocal responses to the instructor is shown in Table 2. Analysis was done by basing expected frequencies upon the number of instructor's questions or other promptings. The chi-square analysis shows that the frequencies within the different phases are significantly different from one another ($p < 0 \cdot 001$). Analyses of individual pairs show that the significant difference is between the frequency of talking in phase 1 and the other two phases.

The frequency of peer vocal approaches to Gene is shown in Table 3. The overall analysis indicates that there were significant effects ($p < 0 \cdot 001$), and analyses of individual pairs show that peer approaches to Gene increased significantly during each phase of the study.

Table 2

Talking in Response to Instructor

	No. of Instructor's Questions	No. of Vocal Responses	Proportion of Vocal Responses
Before Treatment	311	35	0·11
During Treatment	195	105	0·54
After Treatment	292	178	0·61

$x^2 = 106.62 \quad P < 0.001 \quad df = 2$

Table 3

Peer Vocal Approaches to Gene

	Total Observation Time	Number of Approaches	Number Per Ten Min
Before Treatment	420 min	15	0.36
During Treatment	180 min	28	1.56
After Treatment	270 min	139	5.15

$x^2 = 183.93 \quad P < 0.001 \quad df = 2$

DISCUSSION

These data offer strong support for the hypothesis that Patterson's technique for manipulating classroom behavior was effective in changing the patient's elective mutism. Within the time period of the study there is no doubt that Gene's vocal responsiveness increased markedly and that peer vocalizations directed towards him also increased. Not recorded in this study were the peer comments, gestures, and other forms of encouragement and pressure for which no particular vocal response was demanded of Gene. The observers were convinced that such demonstrations of peer interest increased from near zero, prior to reinforcement, to a high level during and following reinforcement, corresponding to the recorded increase in peer vocalization. The recorded data are compatible with the hypothesis that peer reactions play a role in maintaining the reinforced behavior after the experimental reinforcements are stopped. There is no reason, however, to believe that other effects of the new behavior are not also influential, and the question of how long the new behavior is likely to be maintained is not answered.*

It was anticipated that Gene's classwork would improve with his increased vocal responsiveness, although no measures were planned to record such a change. However, Gene's teacher was impressed by the change in his scholastic output. He reported toward the end of the experiment that since the reinforcement phase of the experiment had begun, Gene had completed two full workbooks at a rate of about one workbook in two weeks. This compared with what the teacher described as a prior production of one or two pages in the workbook per week, or perhaps somewhat more than one workbook completed in a year.

The success of this method with other cases of elective mutism awaits further trials. The case reported was the only school-age child known to us with this disorder. It seems to us that the usual criteria applicable in the operant conditioning of human behavior are applicable here, i.e. the operant rate must be greater than zero, and an effective reinforcing operation must be available. Where speech never under any circumstances occurs in the classroom, then it may be necessary to place the elective mute in a situation where speech will occur, and make this situation more and more like the classroom, after the rate of vocalization has increased. Reed (1963) presents a method somewhat like this, but used as reinforcement only whatever personal influence and rapport the therapist had with the child. Presumably peers are much more reinforcing than therapists.

*Upon inquiry during February of the following school year, the school's director reported that some of Gene's gains had been maintained but that his responsiveness was not at the same level as immediately following treatment.

SUMMARY

A reinforcement procedure is described which has been used in the classroom for the modification of hyperactive behavior. The reinforcement consists of flashing a signal light which means that a reward such as candy or points towards a party has been earned. The application of this procedure to a case of elective mutism is described. Significant increase in talking occurred. Data are presented suggesting that changes in peer behavior are an important part of the procedure.

Acknowledgements—The writers gratefully acknowledge the co-operation of the director, Mrs. Elizabeth Waechter, and the staff of Pearl Buck School for encouraging our work with their children. Clarification of procedures and collection of data were aided by Lyn Williams, Carl Jacobsen, and Herb Gunderson. Dr. G. R. Patterson contributed much to the value of our discussion.

REFERENCES

ANDERSON, D. (1964) *Application of a behavior modification technique to the control of a hyperactive child.* Unpublished M. A. Thesis, University of Oregon.

LEITER, R. G. (1948) *Manual for the* 1948 *Revision of the Leiter International Performance Scale: Part I.* C. H. Stoelting, Chicago, Illinois.

PATTERSON, G. R. (1964) An application of conditioning techniques to the control of a hyperactive child. L. P. Ullman and L. Krasner (Eds.), *Case studies in behavior modification.* Holt, Rinehart and Winston, Inc., New York.

PATTERSON, G. R., JONES, R., WHITTIER, J. and WRIGHT, MARY A. (1964) *A behavior modification technique for the hyperactive child.* Unpublished manuscript.

REED, G. R. (1963) Elective mutism in children: A re-appraisal. *J. Child Psychol. Psychiat.* 4, 99–107.

A Project to Teach Learning Skills To Disturbed, Delinquent Children

SALVADOR MINUCHIN
PAMELA CHAMBERLAIN
PAUL GRAUBARD

Patterns of communication in low socioeconomic families which produce acting-out children were analyzed, implications for learning discussed, and an experimental "game" curriculum for teaching formal elements of communication was designed and tested in ten sessions over the five weeks with six disturbed, delinquent children.

This paper will describe a pilot project conducted at the Floyd Patterson House, a community residential treatment center for juvenile delinquents. The project was designed to explore certain hunches and experiences of the authors after extensive work with multiproblem lower-class families.

It has been our experience that the psychological disturbance of the children in such families almost always is accompanied by lack of achievement in school and academic subjects, despite individual intelligence tests showing that some children are of normal or superior intelligence. It was felt that an exploration of the learning style of the disturbed

This paper was presented at the 1966 annual meeting of the American Orthopsychiatric Association, San Francisco, California. It is reprinted, with permission, from *American Journal of Orthopsychiatry*, 1967, Vol. 37, 558–567, Copyright 1967, the American Orthopsychiatric Association, Inc., and with the permission of the authors. Brief biographies of the authors have been omitted. Pamela Chamberlain is now Pamela Chamberlain Dollarhide.

delinquent not only would help us discover ways of teaching the disturbed child, but also might bring to light evidence about ways of teaching his psychologically healthier but equally nonachieving siblings and peers.

The authors of this paper also were interested in exploring the feasibility of a model of interdisciplinary collaboration between clinician and educator. In this project the clinician, whose background and orientation included work in social psychiatry and family therapy, developed a profile of the cognitive-affective style of the children of disorganized low socioeconomic families. This profile was developed in such a way that it helped the educators in the project develop an intervention or repairing curriculum which made it feasible to teach these children.[1] This paper will, therefore, be organized in two sections. The first section will present an overview of (1) socialization processes in the disorganized low socioeconomic family as gathered through the psychiatrist's tools and (2) some of the assumptions about the influence of these processes on the learning style of the child and his encounters with school. The second part will describe the intervention curriculum and the pilot project which was developed to explore ways of enabling these children to learn.

SOCIALIZATION PROCESSES IN THE DISORGANIZED LOW SOCIOECONOMIC FAMILY[2]

We will (1) summarize certain family interactions that contribute to disturbances in focal attention of the child and (2) delineate characteristics of the communication patterns in the child.

1. Parents' responses to children's behavior are global and erratic and, therefore, deficient in conveying rules which can be internalized. The parental emphasis is on the control and inhibition of behavior rather than on guiding and developing responses. The unpredictability of parental controlling signals handicaps the child's development of rules. Since the child cannot determine what part of his behavior is inappropriate, he learns to search out the limits of permissible behavior through inspection of the parents' mood responses. He learns that the rules of behavior are directly related to the power or pain of an authoritarian figure.

Lacking norms to regulate behavior, and caught in experiences which

[1]For a review of the literature, see the December, 1965 issue of the *Review of Educational Research*, Vol. 35, 5.

[2]This section has been elaborated further in a paper entitled *Psychoanalytic Therapies and the Low Socio-Economic Population*, by S. Minuchin, M. D.

hinge on immediate interpersonal control, the children need continuous parental participation to organize interpersonal transactions. Because of the undifferentiated qualities of the parent-child style of contact, these transactions are generally ineffective and perpetuate a situation in which an overtaxed mother responds erratically to a confused child. The child then behaves in ways which will reorganize his "known" environment: controlling contact by the mother. Thus, the child learns to search the immediate reaction of others for clues to the solution of conflict situations, and remains relatively unexercised in the use of focal attention for observing himself as causal in a situation, or in learning how to differentiate the specific characteristics of a situation.

2. In the disorganized low socioeconomic family there is a deficit of communication of information through words and the attendant rules which regulate the communicational flow. In the overcrowded and overburdened living conditions of these large families the adults pay little attention to the requests and needs of individual children. The children in turn accept the fact that their words by themselves will not be heard. In the development of the necessary techniques for making their needs known, the children discover that intensity of action or sound is more effective than the power or cogency of an argument.

Transactions involving power operations occupy a large part of family interaction, and the ranking of each other can occur around an infinite variety of subjects. The attempt is made to resolve conflict by a series of escalated threats and counterthreats. The conflict itself is unresolved and will appear and reappear in other contexts.

Diffuse affect is communicated through kinetic modifiers such as pitch and intensity of voice tone, grimaces and body movements. In the resolution of conflict it often seems that it is unnecessary to hear the content of what is being transacted. Specific subject matter rarely is carried to a conclusion. It is unusual for more than two family members to participate in an interaction around a specific point. A topic usually is interrupted by a disconnected intervention of another family member. Since interactions usually revolve around issues of interpersonal accommodation, the "subject matter" can shift abruptly without changing the nature of the interpersonal conflict that is being negotiated.

The end result is a style of communication in which people do not expect to be heard and, therefore, assert themselves by yelling. There is a lack of training in elaboration of questions to gather information or garner the nuances of degree. There is also lack of training in developing themes to their logical conclusion, and there is no closure on conflicts. This communication style can be entirely adequate for the transactions of gross power and nurturing relationships, but it is insufficient to deal with chronic and subtle conflicts requiring the search for, ordering of, and sharing of different or new information.

There is an interaction effect (1) between the style of control exercised by the parents, which consists primarily of immediate but erratic reactions and, (2) the characteristics of the communication process in the family. Consequently, the child is trained to pay attention to the person with whom he is dealing rather than to the verbal content of the message.[1] Because the child is trained to focus on the hierarchical organization of the social relationships in the family, he is less free to take in the more autonomous aspects of the transaction or the specific content. Numerous observations of both classroom and clinical sessions bear out this conclusion: in this population it is the prevailing practice to allow the constant defining of interrelatedness of people to outweigh the meaning of the content of all but the most dramatic content messages.

Being trained in this communication and control system prepares the child to clash with the demands of the school because the style violates certain schoolheld assumptions about the characteristics of learners. School emphasis is on the recruitment of focal attention to the service of abstract content and on the use of this content for symbolic exploration of the world.* These expectations violate the child's orientation and methodology of processing data. The child copes with the cognitive anxiety aroused by school demands by eliciting from the teacher that which is most familiar to the child in relating to people—proximal control. Thus, much of the "acting out" or disruptive behavior in the classroom is an attempt to repair relations with an important figure, and recreate a "familiar environment." The teacher usually perceives such behavior as an aggressive act and responds with removal of the child from the school.

We suggest, therefore, that the child's difficulty in school behavior and learning is related to: (1) difficulty in focusing attention; (2) a communications style that handicaps the child in the enlistment and ordering of new information, and (3) the child's search for a solution to conflicts in interaction with the teacher.

Within this context an intervention curriculum was designed to initiate children into the methods of learning in schools. The goal was to instruct them in the communications system used in school and to train them in observation of others as well as in self-observation.

*Dr. Alan B. Wilson, during the discussion of this paper, reminded us that public schools in general do not encourage and reward attention to abstract content, and the exploration, ordering, and conceptualization of the world, but on the contrary, many schools with culturally deprived children encourage "mechanical reasoning" and docility.

SUBJECTS

The subjects were six children in residential treatment at the Floyd Patterson House, a unit of the Wiltwyck School for Boys. All of the children had been remanded to the treatment center for aggressive and dissocial behavior. They belonged to the lowest social class, as defined by Warner,[2] and it had been impossible to contain them either at home, at school or in the community. All but one had been in residential treatment for at least a year. The children comprised one full special class for emotionally disturbed children which was run by the Board of Education and housed in a regular public school. The children carried various psychiatric diagnoses, but no child was diagnosed as psychotic or organically impaired.

PROCEDURE

Class sessions were conducted at the residential center during school hours by a remedial educator. The children were told that they were going to receive remedial lessons at the center during school time and that they were required to attend. The goals of the program were made explicit. In fact, the keynote of the entire project was explicitness, and every step of the curriculum process was spelled out.

The children were told that they were going to be taught a curriculum which would help them do well in school even if the teacher did not like them.*

The children also were told that if they could master the communications curriculum, they could probably leave the special education class and begin learning in regular public school classes because of what they would bring to the situation.

A room with a one-way mirror and an observation booth with sound equipment were used. A procedure was initiated in which the children assumed alternate roles as participants and observers. Two children rotated in the role of observers behind the one-way mirror. The family therapist and educational director trained the children in the process of rating the other children's ability to respond to the teaching, and in specifically enumerating behaviors which enhanced or interfered with learning.

The emphasis in judging was on performance in relation to learning,

*Teachers' liking them, or not liking them, was the primary way that children saw things happen in school. They got a good mark on a spelling test because the teacher liked them, or they were suspended because the teacher did not like them.

rather than on conforming or being well behaved. At the end of each session, the "judges" would tell the children their rating and the specific reasons for each point lost or earned. A small monetary reward was given for each point by the educational director. The "judges" were also rated and given points and a monetary reward by the educational director and therapist.

CURRICULUM

The 10 sessions focused specifically on communication and unraveling the process and mysteries of the classroom to the children. Lessons were sequentially built around the following skills: listening, the implications of noise, staying on a topic, taking turns and sharing in communication, telling a simple story, building up a longer story, asking relative and cogent questions, categorizing and classifying information, and role playing.

Each session was structured in the form of games.* It was felt that the use of games where the processes could be labelled by the teacher was the most efficacious way of teaching skills. The selection of games was made from activities designed for teaching listening skills to kindergarten or primary-age children. The teacher felt that the children functioned at approximately a five-year developmental level in terms of communication skill—even though their chronological age averaged 10 and their mental age was only slightly lower.

The teacher relied on her knowledge of the daily life of the children in school and the treatment center to introduce familiar elements in the stories and games. It seemed much simpler to involve them in focusing attention on a story in which the names were familiar, for example, than on a story about a fictional character.

The first topic introduced was *listening*, and the first game played was Simon Says, a game the children already enjoyed and felt safe with. It was spelled out that winners in this game were people who knew how to listen and pay attention.

In the game that followed, the children listened to messages read over the telephone and then attempted to repeat them exactly. The difference between guessing and careful listening then was made explicit, and the results were contrasted.

The strength of the children in reading faces and expressions was

*Many of the games were adapted from or suggested by *Listening Aids Through the Grades* by David and Mary Russell, and *The Preliminary Perceptual Training Handbook*, published by the Union Free School District in the Town of Hempstead, Uniondale, New York. The teacher kept as her own reference point the section on *Education of the Senses* in the *Montessori Method* by Maria Montessori.

discussed. It was explained that in the games played in these sessions it would be more useful to listen to the words than to try to feel out the speaker, since winning would depend on skill at the former exercise.

Number games also were played. The children had to listen to a series of digits and report a certain one. There was discussion around what it is like to wait to respond, to hold directions in mind, to concentrate, and other experiences common to classroom learning.

Since the children were making too much noise at the outset of these sessions, *noise* was a natural topic for the next lesson. A game was designed in which a child would tell a story and the others would begin, one at a time, to make such sounds as knee-thumping, seat-tapping, key-jangling, and the sorts of extraneous noises the children introduced during classroom discussions. One of the children increased the volume of his voice until he silenced the noisemakers and could finish his story, although at considerable expense to his vocal cords. Another child helplessly repeated the same words until he felt himself defeated, and joined in the noisemaking. Dialogue was developed on the effect on the speaker and the listener when such noise was going on, and this was related to its implications for classroom learning.

Since children had difficulty starting one at a time to make their noises and stopping them on cue, the next topic which evolved in the group was *taking turns*. Simple, well known nursery rhymes were divided up, with each child taking his part in turn. Discussion centered on the difficulties of listening for one's own part, talking in turn, waiting for the other person to speak. Again, it was seen that the familiarity of the material was reassuring to the children and disposed them to thinking they could win the games.

In a later session, an unfamiliar story, made up by the teacher, was told and all the children participated. They had to listen for their own parts, decide when to come in, and let the others know when they were finished speaking.

At this point, it was possible to initiate discussion of the *logic in stories and then in conversations*. In a later session, the children cued each other in on "getting off the topic."

After the first five sessions, the mechanics began to become incorporated and the sessions turned to conceptual skills. Moreover, as the children began to experience hearing and being heard, *judging and being judged in positive terms*, and winning money and praise for explicit achievements, they seemed to join the teacher in wanting to understand the games and to win them.

This response was noticeable in the reduction of noise level in the room, in the questions about process from the children, and in their beginning attempts to regulate their own behavior in the direction of school expectations. At the same time, the children began to anticipate verbally what they would win or how they had lost. Outside the classroom they talked about what they would do with their winnings.

In the sixth and seventh sessions, the teacher engaged the children in games which involved skills such as *categorizing*. From a start with "I Spy," involving objects in the room, the children were able to move to variations of 20 Questions. The latter involved asking questions so they could order their universe.

The children became actively involved in problems about which questions helped another person to guess the answer, and why some questions were irrelevant. They displayed growth in framing especially good questions and recognizing what made them useful. Excitement in the group was high as success grew.

After the children had had some experience in concentration on formal aspects of communication, the teacher turned to *role playing* to help them discover how attention to these skills could assist them in the classroom. She and the children took turns playing out situations in which a child "won" in an interaction with a teacher because of attention to the words being said, by asking good questions instead of blowing up, or by waiting his turn, etc.

Although they were later able to analyze what they had done, the children in the heat of role playing would be so overcome with indignation that they could not prevent themselves from flaring up and attacking the speaker.

They took the roles they felt they played with adults and authority figures. Although playing those parts involved much farce, there was also empathy by now with what the adult was experiencing. A child playing the part of a guidance counselor said to another child, "I'm willing to listen to you, and I expect you to let me finish."

It was obvious that the role playing brought the usefulness of the tools they were learning to a level where children could reach out and label their own actions accurately. In the final summarizing session, the adults and the children played roles in situations demanding various skills which had been the focus of the project, with children alternating in back of the mirror as judges.

Both the "judges" and the children in the group were quick to pick up and label "mistakes" purposefully incurred by the adults as getting off the topic or "asking irrelevant questions." More impressive, children within the group displayed an ability to help each other in these areas. Their increased self-awareness and their pleasure in their mastery of new skills caused the project to end on the note where adults and children were engaged in mutual pleasurable recall of the learning that had occurred.

OBSERVATION

Beyond the one-way mirror, the two rotating "judges" were trained in the process of rating the performances of their peers. The rating was done on a continuum from 0 to 5. At first children seemed only to feel that they were being judges when they were giving out zeros, an interesting commentary on their previous experience of being judged. After the lesson, the "judges" came into the classroom and reported the rating of each child in the group. They needed to describe the reason for each evaluation. In this way the "judges" were being trained for differentiated observation and reporting. After the first lessons, the children accepted the peer evaluation with very little questioning.

From early notions of, "Give me all five, or I'll mess you up afterward," or "I'm going to give both of them 0's because I lost last week," the children moved to statements such as, "Really, you don't give points because you like somebody, but for good listening."

As they began to get the idea of judging performance rather than behavior, they also began to differentiate in their ratings between 0 and 5, giving a 3 for a response that was "good, but not so good," or a 4 for a point that was "almost right, but not quite." At the same time, they began to say, "When you were cursing (banging your seat down on the floor, etc.) you weren't listening to the teacher," instead of, "I gave you a 0 because you messed up."

The alternating in the "judging" functions seemed to have significant effects on the behavior and in the process of self-observation in the children. They were conscious of being observed and therefore observed their own behavior. A child stopped himself in the beginning of a fight, looked at the mirror, and put his hands in his pockets; children would apologize to the one-way mirror, etc.*

THE TEACHER

In this project the teacher and the children were working within an explicit mutuality of goals. The children were trying to move to a regular classroom and to learn how to learn; the teachers were attempting to teach the children a program that would facilitate their own goals.

The teacher introduced familiar topics, was explicit in her expectation, geared the introduction of new themes to the children's level of readi-

*We have elaborated elsewhere that we consider this process of self-observation and self-control due to increased awareness of an observing other as an intermediate step in the development of introspection in the acting-out child.

ness, shifted from abstract to concrete demands depending on their level of cognitive anxiety, focused continuously on the learning task, and de-emphasized her role as a controller, or as a provider or rewarder. The rewards given were for performance, and the teacher reminded the children that the "judges" were their peers and, by implication, themselves. In general, the teacher's self-expectation was to present herself to the children as a benign and highly differentiated adult related to them through the complementation of their task.

In the beginning the program focused the children's attention on discrete elements of communication, listening, taking turns, labelling, etc. But to the extent that the mechanical aspect of communication was mastered, the teacher introduced the idea of the *relationship* of the discrete pieces of information. She taught "how to ask questions that will give you the best information for the solution to your problem." In role playing the relationship between personal behavior and interpersonal outcome was underscored.

RESULTS AND DISCUSSION

The results of this pilot project are based on clinical observations of the children's behavior in and out of the sessions, and verbal reports by the counselors. We decided to rely on observations of the process to gather information for a more systematic study. We are well aware, that the conclusions of this paper are quite limited, but we hope to extend our research in an area that appears quite promising. Within this scope, we shall discuss our observations.

Attention. There was a marked increase in the children's ability to maintain focal attention for increased lengths of time. In the beginning, children were disruptive and unable to pay attention. From the fifth session on, however, the disruptive behavior and the noise diminished, and the concentration on achievement became central. The increased ability for differentiated attention was clearly seen in the behavior of the "judges." From initial emphasis on rating only "all or nothing" patterns (5 or 0), they were later focusing on gradients of behavior and after the session were able to remember the why's of their rating, organize their data and report on the behavior of their peers and also of the teacher.

In the sessions the division line between attention and disruptive behavior was very frequently criss-crossed by the children. When the teacher made an assumption that the children had greater ability than they had, or she moved too quickly for them, the structure they had been able to maintain broke down and their old maladaptive functioning reappeared.

Hyperactivity and diffuse disorganized behavior seemed to accompany lack of explicitness in the teacher's expectation about goals and the means of attaining them. We think that the children coped with situations of cognitive anxiety by an adaptation that has been proved successful at home: search for the controlling interpersonal contact with the teacher.

Style of Communication and Cognition. From initial reliance on speed of response and intensity of sound and activity, the children moved to increased use of verbal responses within the context of "the rules of the game." They listened, took turns, and searched for the best questions. In their search for the right words, they slowed their tempo considerably *

In the last sessions, when children were playing 20 Questions and later role playing, their language was not only improved in the "mechanics" of dialogue, but they were using a more differentiated and conceptual style. This was very evident in the 20 Questions game in which the child needs to organize and shrink the universe to find the correct answer. Their ability to improve very rapidly in this game in one session from "random and very concrete questions" to categories and system "questions" would seem to indicate the *availability* in these children of a more conceptual style of thinking and reporting that is generally not used in the classroom or in their daily life. This untapped capacity is *available* under certain conditions and not in others. As a matter of fact, at the end of each period when the rules were over and the "judges" became peers, the children's self-monitoring evaporated and their diffuse hyperactive "bumping" on things and each other reappeared. The seesawing from a "restricted" to an "elaborated" cognitive-communicational style according to the conditions of the field raises interesting theoretical considerations. It suggests (1) that between the ages of 10 and 12 the cognitive-communicational style of these children could be reversible, (2) that educational remedial intervention with this population could be carried successfully with children much older than four years and (3) that we should study changes over a period of time before assuming that they are integrated in the child's new way of learning.

Children's learning in the project was manifested in their life at the institution and in the classroom. For example, one child observing two adults talking at the dining-room table said to them: "I like to see the way you are talking." This same child in a family therapy session "rated" the members in his own family for performance in the therapeutic task and told them the reasons for his rating.

A rather withdrawn and silent boy told his remedial teacher, "I could tell you the names of the things on this table and we could play a game with them." He then invited her to play a 20 Questions game.

*This self-editing process seems similar to Bernstein's description of the "hesitation phenomena" in middle-class children.

Children were heard by the counselors *planning* strategies of how to win the money in the session and what they would do with it. In informal talks with peers and in group therapy children would monitor each other: "You are talking out of the subject," "Do not interrupt, he is talking," etc. They would even correct the counselor for "not hearing" or "talking out of turn."

The General Consideration. The intervention curriculum and teaching methodology appeared to be quite effective in changing the learning behavior of the children during the length of the project. This change was achieved by focusing not on behavior, but on cognitive growth. We think that with these children, as in the general field of learning disabilities, the underlying correlates of the disability must be remediated before successful teaching of the *skill per se* can be accomplished.

In our population, but also perhaps in the group of disadvantaged children, they must master a curriculum which develops an ability to (1) focus attention and (2) use communication rules in ways that facilitate gathering and ordering of information. These tasks must be learned before they can master meaningful academic skill.

While the teacher emphasized in the beginning discrete skill in listening and simple learning labelling, the children moved very quickly (10 lessons) to complex and formal operations: categorizing and role playing. The proper balance of concrete and abstract ingredients seem necessary in the curriculum for development of the capacity to move ahead in learning. It was surprising to the authors that so much change in the children could be achieved in such a short time. We attribute this phenomenon to the favorable effect on this program of the therapeutic milieu in Patterson House.

It seemed natural that most of the children regressed to previous patterns of contact and communication when the conditions of the field changed. We couldn't expect internalization of new behavior patterns in five weeks. But we finished the project with an optimistic sense that the road is worthwhile.

REFERENCES

1. BERNSTEIN, B. 1961. Social structure, language and learning. Educational Research. 3 (June).
2. WARNER, L., *et al.* 1960. Social Class in America. Harper Torchbooks, New York.

The Essexfields Concept: A New Approach to the Social Treatment of Juvenile Delinquents

SAUL PILNICK
ALBERT ELIAS
NEALE W. CLAPP

Rehabilitation of the delinquent adolescent requires the utilization of concepts developing out of the various social sciences. The Essexfields program in Newark, New Jersey, has attempted to design a "social system" which encompasses certain knowledge related to the impact of peer group experience upon delinquent adolescents. Its promise lies in its ability to alter deviant "street norms" and to create, through the group experience, new norms which are "prosocial" in nature. In addition, Essexfields has attempted to recognize the need for a meaningful transitionary period as boys return to full-time community living and continues to utilize the graduate peer group to aid this development. The total Essexfields process is being evaluated through a research program designed to examine its effectiveness as a treatment agent as well as its internal processes. Finally, this paper points to the potential applications of the Highfields-Essexfields approach, particularly within the classroom setting.

Individual behavior is only partly determined by one's personal history. Except for the extraordinary person, people do not usually surpass the limitations of the culture into which they are born. By and large the societies in which we live are mediated for us through units called primary groups, which are characterized by a high degree of informality. The

Reprinted from *The Journal of Applied Behavioral Science*, 1966, Vol. 2, No. 1, 109–125, with the permission of National Training Laboratories, National Education Association, and authors.

family is the best example of such a primary group found in every culture.

Primary groups have considerable face-to-face interaction and a considerable degree of ingroup cohesion. These small groups are often more crucial in shaping individual standards than the school or the institution in which they are embedded. Mannheim (1955) writes:

> Where pilfering is practiced by an influential section of the workers, those who do not take part will be not only unpopular as nonconformists but even suspect as traitors, with all the unpleasant consequences which this entails.

The individual finds his niche and commits himself to a set of values in primary groups (familial, occupational, ethnic, peer, and neighborhood). His identity is largely shaped by these emotionally charged relationships.

Much of what is termed "delinquency" consists of behavior patterns which are socially proscribed and which have evolved out of experiences in peer groups and in the community. The group character of delinquency has attracted increasing attention from various research and action programs both in the community and in correctional facilities. In social work, Breckenridge and Abbott (1912) many years ago called attention to the group nature of delinquency. In psychology, Aichhorn (1935), Healy and Bronner (1936), and Redl and Wineman (1951), among others, have recognized that effective preventive work with delinquents must take into account the empirical evidence that many delinquent acts have a distinct social character. Slavson's (1954) emphasis upon the education of the delinquent through a corrective experience in democratic community living recognized the group nature of much antisocial behavior. The research efforts of sociologists, particularly Shaw and McKay (1931) in their classic studies of urban delinquency, have highlighted the crucial role of the group factor as the context for a considerable amount of delinquent behavior. The work done by McCorkle and Korn (1954) and Ohlin and Lawrence (1959) has been instrumental in focusing attention upon the role of the inmate social system in neutralizing the treatment programs in our correctional institutions. It has been suggested that current treatment programs be reorganized and oriented toward group objectives rather than predominantly toward individual needs, as is now generally practiced in clinical therapy groups. This suggestion is based upon the assumption that the delinquent's behavior is due in large part to the internalization of a set of norms and values which are obtained from a "subcultural" life which is in conflict and is deviant from our major cultural values.

The delinquent's meaningfully real world is extended beyond the family constellation. Contemporary knowledge of the psychological forces impinging upon the adolescent enables us to begin to understand the full meaning and impact of peer group affiliations for the adolescent. The need of adolescents to conform to peer group norms and values has often been witnessed by youth workers as well as parents. When one refers to the "tyranny of adolescents," one is expressing an awesome appreciation of the powerful energies and pressures generated by this strange social configuration called the peer group. A careful examination of the life of a "gang" or the life of delinquent "crowds" often reveals certain norms and values which are desperately upheld by each peer group member. Norms and values are not necessarily a part of the deep psychological equipment of the individual delinquent, but often—and this is crucial—these norms and values are adopted as modes of behavior primarily because through the dynamic process of the group interaction (involving coercion and conformity) these values have been so designated to each member. In delinquent groups, conformity to "street" norms contains the opportunity for status as well as masculine identification. Cloward and Ohlin (1960) have pointed out the significance of opportunity structures as related to delinquent behavior.

> Since discrepancies between aspiration and opportunity are likely to be experienced more intensely at some social positions than at others, persons in status locations where the discrepancy is most acute may develop a common perception and sense of indignation about their disadvantages as contrasted with the advantages of others. Interaction among those sharing the same problem may provide encouragement for the withdrawal of sentiments in support of the established system of norms. Once freed of allegiance to the existing set of rules, such persons may devise or adopt delinquent means of achieving success.

THE ESSEXFIELDS PROGRAM

A treatment approach founded upon these assumptions would attempt to reduce conformity to delinquent peer-determined norms and would encourage the development of new behavior patterns which are "prosocial" in nature. This can be accomplished within the context of a treatment environment which provides the *opportunity* for delinquent adolescents to make responsible choices among a variety of possible alternatives and which makes it possible for the adolescent to transfer his peer group allegiances to a more prosocial group whose values are nondelinquently oriented. In 1961, under a grant from The Ford Foundation, the Department of Institutions and Agencies in the State of New Jersey established a group rehabilitation center in the heart of Newark. This program is designed to rehabilitate sixteen- and seventeen-year-old delinquent boys who are referred by the Essex County Juvenile Court. The criteria for admission to the program are that the boys not be severely disturbed, not be homosexual, and not have had a previous institutional experience. The type of boy Essexfields seeks is the individual whose participation in delinquent activities is usually accompanied by peer group affiliations. The "lone wolf" type of boy is excluded from this program. The average stay in the program is approximately four months, although this varies from boy to boy. A boy is released from the program when his Essexfields peers feel he is ready to resume his place in the community.

This program design was patterned after the Highfields Residential Group Center in Hopewell, New Jersey. For the past 15 years, the Highfields program has been notably successful in working with a similar group of boys in a residential setting (McCorkle, Elias, & Bixby, 1958). The Essexfields program differs from this design in that the boys return to their homes every evening and are at home during the weekend.

The program is housed in an old three-story building located in an area of high delinquency in Newark. Twenty boys participate at any one time and thereby maintain the necessary intimacy of interpersonal relationships. The boys meet in the building each weekday morning at 7:30 a.m. Under the supervision of a (nonprofessional) work supervisor, they are transported by bus to the grounds of a nearby county mental hospital. At 8:30 a.m., they begin their workday, for which they are paid $1.00 per day. They are assigned to various duties such as chopping wood, weeding, cutting hedges, trimming and edging grass, and snow removal in the wintertime. The boys eat their lunch and supper at the hospital with hospital employees in the employees' cafeteria. At 5:30 p.m., they are transported back to the facility in Newark.

The Essexfields work situation is an essential ingredient in the program, since it provides a primary opportunity for the boys to get to know one another intimately. Almost all boys who come to Essexfields initially express a dislike for work. Nevertheless, there is something about work which tends to reveal a boy's behavior for all to see. As a result, Essexfields boys, while at work, deal with one another in an atmosphere filled with tension, gratification, success, and failure. In addition, the boys travel on the Essexfields bus together for 1½ hours a day, eat two meals together for 1½ hours a day, have recreation together for 2½ hours a day, and work as a group for 6½ hours a day. After returning to the building in Newark, the boys relax, play cards or ping-pong until 7:00 p.m., at which time the guided group interaction sessions begin, under the direction of two professional group therapists. Two group meetings are held, each lasting 1½ hours and each consisting of ten boys. At 10:00 p.m., the boys return to their homes, to report back again the following morning. This procedure is followed five days per week.

THE ESSEXFIELDS SOCIAL SYSTEM

Essexfields is basically a self-contained social system with its own subculture. Norms, traditions, language, and conceptions of deviancy have developed which are indigenous to the system. Since only about five boys are admitted to the program each month and the same number released, it is possible for the program always to have "old" boys and "new" boys interacting concurrently, which enables the peculiarities of the culture to be transmitted at all times. It is believed that through exposure to this experience the adolescent offender can assume "conventional" or "law-abiding" norms as he discards delinquent norms. The same pressure to conform which afflicts delinquents in the community through a delinquent peer group is applied at Essexfields by a peer group ascribing to conventional norms.

However, intrinsic to the "new" norms built into the Essexfields experience is an emphasis upon a freedom of choice. Delinquents, not unlike other adolescents, present a pattern of rigidity of behavior. Alternative forms of reacting to life situations are rarely considered by the delinquent adolescent. Consequently, the effort at Essexfields is to create a social system which, through the utilization of group pressures, results in a greater freedom of behavioral choices. It might be stated that Essexfields establishes a process of interaction which creates a "conformity to freedom."

The social system at Essexfields was initiated by transferring boys from the already-existing Highfields project in Hopewell, New Jersey. Ten boys, transferred over a period of two months, provided the norms necessary for the establishment of the Essexfields "culture." This system of "seeding" has since been utilized in establishing the Collegefields project and other youth-serving programs in the New Jersey area. However, it is obvious that a method depending upon this form of seeding cannot have wide application. Other methods have therefore been developed. Getting a culture started is largely dependent upon the skill of the "therapist" or group leader. He must be "culture" conscious and highly aware of the subtlety and nature of the existing norms which each delinquent brings into the new group experience. His role initially is that of the "gatekeeper" of the norms. All prodelinquent norms need to be commented upon as being dysfunctional; otherwise the group would interpret the leader's passivity as implying support of the "old" norms. At the same time the leader must be cautious not to allow himself to do battle with the total group's delinquent norms. Allies need to be gathered and group support developed for the prosocial norms. The initial phase of developing a culture can be time-consuming, but is obviously crucial. The establishment of a prosocial culture enables the marshaling of powerful group pressures toward a group evaluation of deviant behavior.

Representative of the pressure which the peer group can apply to a deviant member is this excerpt from a recent group meeting:

> Carl took on a very sorrowful expression and then started to explain why he found it necessary to defend people. He started out, "I just can't help it. I feel sorry for people. I want to help them."
> Fred: Help them? You defend against help. Why can't you see it?
> Allen: You ain't trying to help. You're just sponging and you know it. That's why the hell you don't bust cliques. (reveal other boys' deviances)
> Fred: You're messing up our lives.
> Carl: I didn't want to see people get busted. (arrested)
> Allen: You realize you messed up our lives. Why did you continue?
> At this point even the boys that don't usually say much started getting on Carl. Carl cringed before this onslaught and then confessed. "Now I realize. Now I'm scared for the boys. I didn't take things in before. I still saw it my way. This program was a lot of bull to me."
> The circle closed in and the entire meeting fired questions from all directions.
> Carl: When the pressure is on me I had to bust cliques. I wasn't involved before.
> Gary: You're supposed to be involved with everything that goes on at Essexfields. You just wanted to sponge.
> Carl: I accept that now. I see it now.
> Allen: Admit it, Carl. You don't give a damn for this program, do you?
> Carl: Yes I do. Why would I bust my cliques if I didn't care about the program?
> The meeting replies in unison, as if it has been rehearsed: "To save your own skin."
> Allen, Frank, and Fred continued on Carl. Frank was very good—strong and perceptive. Allen supported him admirably.
> Gary: Tell us the real reason you busted those cliques.
> Carl pretended he didn't know at first, but Fred pointed out that Carl feared going to jail and had only busted his and other cliques to impress rather than help.
> Frank: You are helping yourself and you didn't care about us. Who do you care about? Tell the truth. Who in the hell do you really care about?
> Carl: Myself! Myself! Myself! I cared about me. I see it all now. I realize now.
> Allen: When did you realize? Right now? Right this moment?
> Carl: Yes. Now. Tonight.
> The entire meeting was on Carl now.
> Frank: Do you mean to tell us you played a role until right now?

Not only does the group apply pressure but in so doing enables the deviant to re-examine his behavior and find suitable alternatives.

> Ed began his meeting by explaining how when he first came to Essexfields he would take the bus to East Orange with Roger and then turn around and take it back to Newark. When he was caught doing this he gave it up and began to stay at his aunt's house. He admitted that he had been sneaky and had tried every possible excuse to remain in Newark. He did not tell of this past weekend incident until I reminded him, and then he admitted that he had left

> East Orange after his aunt had squabbled with him, had come to Newark, and called Dr. P. When Dr. P. had advised him to return to East Orange to sleep, Ed had agreed but then had remained in Newark anyway. The meeting began to show Ed several alternative procedures which he might have followed. They asked him if he had requested his father to give his aunt some money for his weekend meals and also asked if he could not use part of his pay for subsistence in East Orange. They suggested that he do his own laundry as long as his aunt seemed to object to his using her soap and water and in general showed good sense of purpose for an immature meeting. Most active in this respect were Bob and Roger, with Sam and Dan making occasional contributions. The boy grew more sincere as the meeting continued. The boys drew parallels to Ed's behavior in this situation with his behavior at Essexfields, and Ed listened carefully. On one occasion Roger said, "How come you could only stand listening to your aunt for two hours on Saturday night, yet you can take the boys' getting on you from 7:30 in the morning until 10:00 at night, six days a week?" Ed gave the "right" response by saying that he could take the boys' criticism because they were trying to help him, but his aunt obviously was not.

Hopefully, the loyalty of the delinquent will be transferred from his peer group in the community to the peer group at Essexfields. If this can be accomplished, alternatives to delinquent behavior can be evaluated by each boy and utilized, and the adolescent can find satisfaction in conforming to law-abiding values. Through the Essexfields process, the culture becomes so ingrained, yet dynamic, that the individual involvement and commitment to this new peer group creates an untenable anxiety which seems to result in a gradual shift in loyalties. Initially, a "new" boy is unable to accept Essexfields as a legitimate alternative to his delinquent associates and often continues to involve himself in delinquent behavior. However, his deviancy when visible is condemned by his new peer group. Hoping to achieve status among this new group, the individual begins a process of examining the validity of his previous behavior patterns as well as the new "norms" he is exposed to. When the process of emotional commitment to the new group begins to occur, delinquent behavior seems to diminish. Simultaneously, ties to neighborhood peer groups also tend to diminish. This process seems to occur quite unconsciously and often to the surprise of the boy himself.

FORMAL STRUCTURE

Some of the aspects of the culture as perceived by Essexfields boys are most vividly described in their terms. For the new boy, Essexfields becomes a *task* which he must solve. He is expected by his peers first to tell his "story." This consists of relating to the other boys the details concerning all of the "trouble" he has ever been in. The "how" and the "what" of his behavior are stressed. He then "gets his problems." Usually, these problems consist of those deviancies easily recognized by the conventional community, supplemented by those attitudinal deviancies as perceived by other Essexfields boys. In other words, while a boy might receive a "light finger" problem for stealing, he may also receive a "cold-hearted" problem or an "easily influenced" problem. While these characteristics as such would not result in an appearance before juvenile authorities, they are related to the underlying causes for the boy's delinquencies and constitute possible sources of delinquency for the boy in the future. Thereafter, in order to achieve acceptance, the new Essexfields boy devotes himself to overcoming these "problems" by utilizing the aid, the suggestions, and insight of his peers and the Essexfields staff. The ability to perceive the underlying causes of a boy's problems at Essexfields is known as "going deep" and being able to ask "why" questions. This trait is well esteemed in the hierarchy of Essexfields values.

INFORMAL STRUCTURE

Although occasionally many of the informal norms of the program achieved the status of formal norms, at Essexfields this process has been accomplished by the boys rather than through the direction or intent of the staff. The jargon, or language, of Essexfields is accepted by all boys, and as it becomes part of the pattern, the definition of terms occasionally becomes more rigid.

Most of the jargon reflects deviancies as perceived by Essexfields boys. The alliance of two or more boys to conceal a deviancy from the group is termed "cliquing." A boy may be accused of "cliquing with himself" if he fails to reveal his own misdemeanors. "Playing a role" is considered a major deviancy, as it conceals a boy's "true feelings." Without the revelation of these "true feelings," a boy cannot be "helped." Of course, both of these techniques are used by almost all Essexfields boys in an effort to sustain themselves within the program during the early stages. These "adaptive" mechanisms are similar to the ones utilized by Essexfields boys at school and at home prior to their involvement with the Essexfields "treatment community." Nevertheless, there is a blanket condemnation of this procedure, and gradually a boy will learn to adapt himself to the program without the use of these defenses. Frequently, this is done through assuming responsibility and status within the program, which allows a boy to become respected by the peer group in such a manner that it is not necessary for him to protect himself from their criticism. Frequently, the so-called stronger, more "sophisticated" boys master the group techniques in such a manner that they become virtually unassailable. This method of coping with the Essexfields system must also result in failure, as the boy is reminded that unless he allows himself to be criticized and have his deviancies exposed he cannot be "helped."

Through the three years of operation of this program, certain traditions have been established by the boys. Some of the boys have carved their names and the dates of their attendance on an old plank of wood which they found in the basement of the building. Others take pride in "changing their pin" on a map in the office which shows the location of all Essexfields boys past and present, with a color key. Among the less obvious traditions are the responsibilities which an older boy is expected to assume, such as "checking up" on other younger boys on weekends and delegating "hours" to be worked off. Boys will "check" themselves if they suddenly become aware of their own deviant behavior or they will admonish other boys to "check" themselves.

THE CULTURE OF SOCIAL CONTROL

The function and purpose of social control at Essexfields is flexible, nonpunitive, and essentially nonpredictable and noninstitutional. Basically, those measures employed are intended to arouse individual and group responses, create certain anxieties, and cause the individual and the group to reflect upon the nature of the deviancy and the need to alter behavior.

Among those sanctions which are present at Essexfields are the following:

1. *Hours:* A boy is given hours by the staff or the group as a result of those infractions which endanger his status in the program. Normally, it would include such actions as arriving at the program late, purposeful or accidental avoidance of responsibility, stealing, fighting, or difficulty in adjusting to the program.
2. *On Report:* A boy is put on report, which means a loss of a day's pay, as the result of behavior problems at the work situation or while at the facility.
3. *Keeping a Boy Back:* Occasionally a boy is not allowed to accompany the group to the work situation. Kept at the center, he is expected to ponder his deviancies. This is done less frequently and implies a more serious problem of adjustment to the program.
4. *Bringing a Boy Back:* Much in the manner that a boy is kept at the house, a boy may be picked up at the work situation by the staff and returned to the center. The purpose of this action is similar in nature and severity to the aforementioned policy.
5. *Extra Duty:* Extra duty is imposed by the work supervisor at the

work situation for minor deviancies there. "Extra duty" results in the loss of certain privileges enjoyed by the boys at work, such as a short break for smoking.

6. *Returning a Boy to Court:* The ultimate sanction imposed at Essexfields is to return a boy to court. This measure is utilized only when a boy is regarded as being unsuitable for the program. Occasionally, the members of the group themselves urge this action and, in the meetings, may give opinions as to whether they feel a boy can be "helped" or not. This final sanction is known as "giving up on a boy." Frequently, one or two boys will attempt to "save" the individual. Sometimes this is accomplished by "taking responsibility" for the boy. (In this case, all efforts are exerted to "help" the boy in question.)

In essence, a variety of strains have gone into the development of the conceptual framework of Essexfields. The offender must be made aware of the fact that (a) he has been defined as a delinquent by conventional society and (b) he must take account of this conception of himself if he is to change. Frequently, offenders—particularly those of middle-class origin—do not see themselves as delinquents but rather as unfortunate victims of an irrational system of social justice. To paraphrase Tannenbaum, their evil has not been dramatized sufficiently to permit the development of a delinquent self-conception (1938).

Opportunities must be provided for the delinquent to experiment with a fairly wide range and variety of social roles and relationships. The social world of the delinquent does not allow for exploration of too many interactions outside the prescribed ones, especially those with a conventional tinge, without imposing severe sanctions.

The peer group must be seen as a medium of change and a source of influence over its members. In this way, plans and efforts to change can be accepted and supported by the group. In other words, change, as an end in itself, must be legitimized by the group as proper conduct for its members.

A setting must be provided for the peer group to develop a system for assigning status to its members on the basis of prosocial patterns of interaction that is independent of the system for allocating status within the delinquent social world. All too frequently delinquents are evaluated in terms of surface conformity to institutional norms. This procedure serves only to encourage the emergence and maintenance of therapeutic parasites.

ALUMNI

Essexfields graduates frequently return on visits. In some instances specific help is requested, such as information re obtaining a driver's license or enlistment in the Armed Services. In other instances, personal problems at home or at school result in a visit. Little of the "street" culture's reluctance to admit "weakness" or the need for help is visible in the Essexfields graduate. On occasion, a graduate will obtain a job for an Essexfields boy or aid in the resolution of a family problem. "Alumni" meetings are held every Saturday morning to provide assistance for boys currently in the program who are having difficulty adjusting to the conventional norms.

FAMILY CONTACT

Experience has indicated that severe pressures at home can impede a boy's attempt at accepting and adjusting to the peer group's new expectations of him. Parents who do not have a full understanding of the purposes of the program tend to subvert its efforts. Many parents distrust governmental agencies. Consequently, parental interviews take place with the parents of all boys shortly after their admission to the program. For the most part, experience has revealed a desire on the part of the parents to support the prosocial norms of the peer group culture, although continued contact through home visits is often necessary.

TRANSITION TO THE COMMUNITY

Presumably, when an Essexfields boy leaves the program his interpersonal sensitivity and his self-insight have increased and his motivation to engage in new behavior patterns in the community has been heightened. Near the end of his stay at Essexfields, a boy concerns himself in his discussions with his peers and with the staff about his future plans. The following summary written by a boy upon leaving Essexfields gives some indication of the degree of insight gained in Essexfields and also reveals the way in which a boy approaches the transition to the community:

> When I first came to Essexfields I thought it was a nut house. I figured I would survive four or five months and that was it. When I went downtown when I wasn't supposed to, I figured it would be best not to say anything. When I confessed, I did so only because I was tricked into it by one of the boys. I still cliqued after that because I was afraid to have the boys get on me. After my second month I started to take the program as a place to help me and not to hurt me. I started understanding some of my problems, and then the program became interesting and I wanted to understand more about myself.
>
> All through the program I had a hard time getting along with the boys because of the way I carried myself and the manner in which I impressed to get in good with the boys, which I tried to do all my life. I didn't know how

> to deal with boys. Then one helped meeting brought this out, but at first I thought they just said that because they didn't like me. I kept it on my mind all that weekend and then I saw it in myself. Then my real self came to light and my role was left behind. Also it was seen that I didn't have enough self-confidence in myself as a person and seemed to belittle myself and impressed to bring up my own standings to myself. I still have not gained all my self-confidence in myself, but I can see myself, and I looked back on myself to see my good points. It wasn't hard to look at my good points, but it was hard to gain self-confidence. The way I have to do this is by completing goals and accomplishing things.

Occasionally an "early release" is recommended by the peer group. This enables a boy to look for a job or return to school while still in the program. In this manner, a boy with severe problems focusing around work and school can utilize the evening group meetings to develop further insight regarding his behavior. An employment opportunity committee has been established with the aid of a number of employers in the area. The primary purpose of this committee is to develop job contacts for Essexfields graduates. In addition, Essexfields alumni have provided "job leads" for boys who are leaving the program. In some instances, the transition to the community has been facilitated by a referral to a child guidance clinic or to a family agency, if the need arose. Nevertheless, it has been our experience that a job market that is unable to absorb the unskilled, poorly educated "exdelinquent" tends to create severe problems even for the highly motivated youngster.

MODIFICATIONS AND PROGRAM IMPLICATIONS OF THE ESSEXFIELDS APPROACH

The utilization of the peer group as an effective treatment agent for the adolescent has many implications beyond the field of correction. Recently, through a grant from the President's Committee on Juvenile Delinquency, Department of Health, Education, and Welfare, a modification of the Essexfields program was initiated in the New Jersey area. Collegefields is a nonresidential treatment center for fourteen- and fifteen-year-old boys. As in the case of the Essexfields program, Collegefields provides a daily experience in quided group interaction. However, instead of the work experience which exists in the Essexfields situation, Collegefields provides an intensive educational experience which is designed to assist potential school dropouts in developing sufficient skills and motivations to want to remain in school after release from the Collegefields program. Consequently, an attempt is being made through this new program to deal with educational limitations as well as delinquent patterns.

More recently, the Kilmer Job Corps Training Center in Edison, New

Jersey, has adopted a modification of the Highfields-Essexfields approach in their work with culturally disadvantaged youngsters, ages 16 through 21. At this writing, the plan is to develop approximately 200 peer groups within the total Kilmer setting. Using the guided group interaction approach, it is hoped that norms can be developed within these groups which will make it possible to redirect and reorient the culturally disadvantaged children who will arrive from all sections of the United States.

Other illustrations are beginning to abound in work with adolescents. Child guidance clinics and family service agencies are beginning to re-examine their more traditional approaches to the treatment of the adolescent. It would appear that the potentiality of peer group approaches has hardly been tapped. With a little creativity and imagination, one can easily begin to envision the implications of this approach within school systems themselves. Educators have neglected for many years the group implications of the experience of children in school systems. Hopefully, the Highfields-Essexfields experience may point toward these new directions.

RESEARCH DESIGN

An important part of the Essexfields experiment is an evaluation of the project extending over a period of several years. The evaluation includes three aspects: (1) the recidivism study; (2) analysis of the treatment process in the program; and (3) an examination of the experiences and problems encountered by the administration in the course of its brief history.

Research is still under way and data are presently being collected for analysis. These findings will be presented in a later paper. However, the results have been encouraging. During the four years of the operation of the Essexfields program, 246 boys were admitted. Fifty boys, or approximately 20 per cent, were found to be unsuitable while in the program and were returned to the Juvenile Court for further disposition. In many of these instances, the boys involved refused to participate in the program, leaving the Essexfields staff no alternative. In some instances, severe psychiatric problems prevented participation, and in only a few instances were boys apprehended while in the program for committing a new offense in the community. Of the remaining 196 boys who successfully completed the program, only 24 boys, or 12 per cent, were committed to a correctional institution after their release from Essexfields. This is a remarkable figure as compared with reported recidivist statistics ranging anywhere from 50 to 75 per cent elsewhere. Figures have not as yet been gathered regarding arrest statistics. Additional Essexfields releases have been apprehended for new offenses, but have not been committed to a correctional institution. An analysis of these data will be forthcoming; but present indications seem to imply that even when Essexfields releases do get into trouble again, the nature of their offense is less severe than was their original offense. The above findings will, of course, be compared with the control groups so as to ascertain the true effectiveness of the Essexfields approach.

REFERENCES

Aichhorn, A. *Wayward youth.* New York: Viking, 1935.

Breckenridge, S. P., & Abbott, Edith. *The delinquent child and the home.* New York: Russell Sage Foundation, 1912.

Cloward, R. A., & Ohlin, L. E. *Delinquency and opportunity.* New York: Free Press, 1960.

Healy, W., & Bronner, Augusta. *New light on delinquency and its treatment.* New Haven: Yale Univ. Press, 1936.

McCorkle, L. W., Elias, A., & Bixby, F. L. *The Highfields story.* New York: Holt, Rinehart & Winston, Inc., 1958.

McCorkle, L. W., & Korn, R. Resocialization within walls. *Annals*; May, 1954, 293, 88–89.

Mannheim, Hermann. *Group problems in crime and punishment.* New York: Humanities Press, 1955. P. 24.

Ohlin, L. E., & Lawrence, W. Social interaction among clients as a treatment problem. *Soc. Work,* April, 1959, 4.

Redl, F., & Wineman, *D. Children who hate.* New York: Free Press, 1951.

Shaw, C. R., & McKay, H. D. *Social factors in juvenile delinquency.* Washington, D. C.: Government Printing Office, 1931.

Slavson, S. *Re-educating the delinquent.* New York: Crowell-Collier-Macmillan, 1954.

Tannenbaum, F. *Crime and the community.* Boston: Ginn, 1938. P. 16.

SUGGESTED ADDITIONAL READINGS

Al-Anon Family Group Headquarters, Inc. *Al-Anon faces alcoholism.* New York: Al-Anon Family Group Headquarters, Inc., 1965.

Bales, R. F. The therapeutic role of Alcoholics Anonymous as seen by a sociologist. *Quarterly Journal of Studies on Alcohol*, 1944, Vol. 5, 267–278.

Bales, R. F. Social therapy for a social disorder—compulsive drinking. *Journal of Social Issues*, 1945, Vol. 1, No. 3, 14–22.

Benjamin, Judith G., Freedman, Marcia K., and Lynton, Edith F. *Pros and cons: New roles for nonprofessionals in Corrections.* United States Department of Health, Education, and Welfare, Office of Juvenile Delinquency and Youth Development. Washington, D. C.: Government Printing Office, 1966.

Berzon, Betty, Reisel, Jerome, and Davis, David P. Peer-planned experience for effective relating: An audio tape program for self-directed small groups. Unpublished paper, Western Behavioral Science Institute, LaJolla, California.

Berzon, Betty, and Solomon, Lawrence N. The self-directed therapeutic group: An exploratory study. *International Journal of Group Psychotherapy*, 1964, Vol. 14, 366–369.

Bierer, Joshua. The Marlborough experiment. In Bellak, Leopold (Ed.) *Handbook of Community Psychiatry.* New York: Grune and Stratton, 1964. Pp. 221–248.

Bijou, Sidney W. Experimental studies of child behavior, normal and deviant. In Krasner, Leonard, and Ullmann, Leonard P. (Eds.) *Research in behavior modification.* New York: Holt, Rinehart and Winston, Inc., 1965. Pp. 56–58.

Brown, William F. Student-to-student counseling for academic adjustment. *Personal and Guidance Journal*, 1965, Vol. 43, 811–817.

Casriel, Daniel. *So fair a house: The story of Synanon.* Englewood Cliffs, N. J.: Prentice Hall, Inc., 1963.

Cohen, F. Alcoholics Anonymous principles and the treatment of emotional illness. *Mental Hygiene*, 1964, Vol. 48, 621–626.

Cook, J. A., and Geis, G. Forum anonymous: The techniques of Alcoholics Anonymous applied to prison therapy. *Journal of Social Therapy*, 1957, Vol. 3, 9–13.

Drakeford, John W. The common denominators in groups that help people change. *The Discoverer*, Vol. 4, No. 4, October 1967. (Ed. Ken Marlin; 330 Gregory Hall, Urbana Ill., 61801.)

Egerton, John. Where they try to make winners out of men who have always lost. *Southern Education Report*, 1966, May/June.

Gelfand, Donna M., Gelfand, Sidney, and Dobson, William R. Unprogrammed reinforcement of patients' behavior in a mental hospital. *Behaviour Research & Therapy*, 1967, 5, 201–207.

Hartup, Williard W. Peers as agents of social reinforcement. *Young Children*, 1965, Vol. 20, No. 3, 176–184.

Holzinger, R. Synanon through the eyes of a visiting psychologist. *Quarterly Journal of Studies on Alcohol*, 1965, Vol. 26, 304–309.

Hubbard, Fred D. "The youth consultant project of the program for detached workers, Young Men's Christian Association of Metropolitan Chicago." In Spencer, Carol (Ed.) *Experiment in culture expansion.* Proceedings of a conference on "The use of products of a social problem in coping with the problem," held at the California Rehabilitation Center, Norco, California, July, 1963. Sponsored by the National Institute of Mental Health, United States Department of Health, Education, and Welfare.

Human Development Institute, Inc. *Improving communication in marriage.* Atlanta, Georgia: Human Development Institute, Inc., 1967.

Jackson, J. K. The adjustment of the family to the crisis of alcoholism. *Quarterly Journal of Studies on Alcohol*, 1954, Vol. 15, 562–586.

Jackson, Maurice P. *Their brother's keepers.* A directory of therapeutic self-help groups, intentional communities, and lay training centers, 1962. Berkeley Baptist Divinity School, Berkeley, California.

Latimer, R. The social worker and the Alcoholics Anonymous program in a state hospital. *Journal of Psychiatric Social Work*, 1953, 175–180.

Lippett, Robert, Fox, Robert, and Schmuck, Richard. Innovating classroom practices to support achievement motivation and ego development. In Bower, Eli M., and Hollister, William C. (Eds.) *Behavioral science frontiers in education.* New York: John Wiley & Sons, Inc., 1967, pp. 322–344.

MacDougall, A. A. Group therapy for alcoholic addicts. *British Journal of Addiction*, 1958, Vol. 54, 127–132.

Maxwell, M. A. Alcoholics Anonymous: An interpretation. In Pittman, D. J., and Snyder, C. R. (Eds.) *Society, culture, and drinking patterns.* New York: John Wiley & Sons, Inc., 1962, pp. 577–585.

McKee, John M. The Draper experiment: A programmed learning project. In Ofiesh, Gabriel D., & Meierhenry, Wesley C. (Eds.) *Trends in programmed instruction.* Washington, D. C.: National Education Association, Department of Audiovisual Instruction, 1964.

Needham, Walter E., White, Helen, and Fitzgerald, Bernard J. A patient-therapist program. *Hospital and Community Psychiatry*, 1966, Vol. 17, No. 3, 44–45.

Operation Alateen. *It's a teen age affair; My mother is an alcoholic; A guide for sponsors of Alateen groups.* New York: Operation Alateen, P. O. Box 182, Madison Square Station.

Pfeiffer, Eric. Patients as therapists. *American Journal of Psychiatry*, 1967, Vol. 123, No. 11, 1413–1418.

Pratt, Steve, & DeLange, Walter. Theragnostic admission groups: For the mental hospital, a psychotherapeutic treatment-of-choice. *Mental Hospitals*, 1963, 14, 222–224.

Ripley, H. S., and Jackson, J. K. Therapeutic factors in Alcoholics Anonymous. *American Journal of Psychiatry*, 1959, Vol. 116, 44–50.

Sanders, David H. Social innovation in treating mental illness: A community experiment. Paper presented at The Institute on Interagency Programming for Psychiatric Rehabilitation, Fort Logan Mental Health Center, Denver, Feb. 1967; which was sponsored by the Vocational Rehabilitation Administration.

Slack, Charles W. Score—A description. In Spencer, Carol (Ed.) *Experiment in culture expansion.* Proceedings of a conference on "The use of products of a social problem in coping with the problem," held at the California Rehabilitation Center, Norco, California, July, 1963. Sponsored by the National Institute of Mental Health, United States Department of Health, Education, and Welfare.

Slack, Charles W., and Schwitzgebel, Ralph. A handbook: Reducing adolescent crime in your community. 1960. Available from senior author.

Soden, E. W. How a municipal court helps alcoholics. *Federal Probation*, 1960, Vol. 24, No. 3, 45–48.

Solomon, Lawrence N., and Berzon, Betty. The self-directed group: A new direction in personal growth learning. In Hart, J. T., and Tomlinson, T. M. (Eds.) *New directions in client-centered therapy.* Boston: Houghton Mifflin Co., 1969.

Spencer, Carol, Ed. *Experiment in Culture Expansion.* Report of proceedings of a conference on "The use of products of a social problem in coping with the problem," held at the California Rehabilitation Center, Norco, California, July, 1963. Sponsored by the National Institute of Mental Health, United States Department of Health, Education, and Welfare.

Sulzer, Edward S. Reinforcement and the therapeutic contract. *Journal of Counseling Psychology*, 1962, Vol. 9, 271–276.

Thompson, C. E., and Kolb, W. P. Group psychotherapy in association with Alcoholics Anonymous. *American Journal of Psychiatry*, 1953, Vol. 110, 29–33.

Volkman, R., and Cressey, D. R. Differential association and the rehabilitation of drug addicts. *American Journal of Sociology*, 1963, Vol. 69, 129–142.

Wahler, R. G. Child-child interactions in free field settings: some experimental analyses. *Journal of Experimental Child Psychology*, 1967, Vol. 5, 278–293.

Weiner, Hyman J., and Brand, Morris S. Involving a labor union in the rehabilitation of the mentally ill. *American Journal of Orthopsychiatry*, 1965, Vol. 35, 598–600.

Yablonsky, Lewis. *The tunnel back: Synanon.* New York: The Macmillan, Company, 1965.

PART 5

Teachers as Therapeutic Agents

Introduction

THE authors of the article on the Essexfields Concept suggested that school systems have a vast unused therapeutic resource in the potential of students to interact therapeutically toward those in their midst who are in need of help. A second untapped reservoir for potential therapeutic manpower also exists in the school system: the teachers. Ogden Lindsley has pointed out that if each psychiatrist were to be assigned his share of all the children in the country to watch over, he would be assigned about 3,660 children. For psychologists and social workers, the figures for each professional would be about 2,300 and 1,050, respectively. The ratio of teachers to children, on the other hand, is one to every 26 children.[1] Does it not make a great deal of sense for professionals to try to supply teachers with much more information about identifying children in need of help for emotional problems? But more to the point, should not these teachers be used actually to *provide help* for such children?

Teachers are clearly symbionts vis-a-vis each of their students. Their every action or inaction has a meaning in the lives of all their students. With some variation from time to time and from child to child, and whether or not they are conscious of it, teachers are doing more than succeeding or failing to teach the child needed skills. For each child they continuously are providing a lesson in how adult authority figures behave,

[1]Workshop on "Procedures for Training Behavior Managers" presented by the Center for Behavior Modification, Philadelphia, April, 1967.

providing a model for the child's future behavior, and altering the child's self-concept for better or worse. Conversely, every action—or significant inaction—on the child's part affects the teacher's conception of his or her adequacy as a professional, which often then in turn affects the teacher's concept of himself or herself as a person. Certainly, the teacher's emotions and moods are affected day to day, and even minute by minute, by the behaviors of the children in the class. Also, the great majority of teachers maintain a high degree of motivation for helping pupils develop their potential, not only intellectually, but as human beings. Unfortunately, lack of specific guidelines and guidance as to how they may accomplish the latter purpose serves to weaken their resolve, and because of the resulting inability to handle disciplinary and other problems, often reduces their ability to fulfill their primary educational objectives as well.

Whatever the teachers have learned in the basic training about child psychology frequently evaporates in the heat created by classroom frictions. These frictions occur among the children themselves, between the children and the teacher, and among the various goals to which the teacher aspires for her children (for example, the conflict between self-expression and discipline). Teachers often rightly feel that what they learned about psychology from texts and college classes was out of context and of little present use. They need an opportunity to reconsider basic child psychology and to keep abreast of current theory in the context of the present day to day *realities* they face in the school setting. Most of all, from the point of view of meeting the psychosocial and educational needs of the children in their classrooms, particularly the children with problems, the teachers need an in-service program that is oriented not only toward study, but toward therapeutic *action* on their part. As a scientist tests his theories by changing variables and watching the effects in the laboratory, the teacher needs to test proferred psychological concepts by attempting to effect change and growth in students in the classroom; and also, at least at first, needs supervision in doing so.

A teacher need not be expected to be able to change the entire life style of a child—although in many instances the teacher may be able to do this as well as anyone else outside the child's family. Certainly, in many instances there are enough significant variables within the teacher's control to modify very important aspects of a child's psychological adjustment; and insofar as school adjustment is concerned, the teacher is probably in a better position than anyone else to bring about improvement. The great majority of teachers do not need more "motivation" to effect such changes, nor do they need first to become paragons of psychological adjustments themselves.

Because the teacher is a symbiont, many of the child's problems as they become manifest in the classroom are, in fact, also the teacher's problems.

In the case of acting-out children, this is easy to see—the child disrupts the class, disrupts the teacher's plans, arouses conflicts about authoritarianism and hostility, and generally raises the teacher's level of anxiety. The problem posed by the very withdrawn child is less obvious, but is evident to psychologists who have worked with teachers. The withdrawn child is often a source of concern in that the child represents a challenge to the teacher's professional skills, and therefore affects the teacher's self-concept. Thus, the symbiotic nature of the relationship very often provides built-in motivation. And, equally important, again because the teacher is a symbiont, alleviation of a child's problem brings immediate satisfaction and reinforcement to the teacher. To effect changes in children's adjustment, the teacher must have guidance about what needs to be changed in his or her own relationship to the child, and in the sociocultural structure of the classroom.

Ongoing projects in which I am actively involved convince me that a broad-based, high-leverage in-service program involving the use of teachers as psychotherapeutic agents is entirely reasonable. It is too early to report on these projects at this time except to say, on the basis of qualitative observations, that teachers as a group are highly enthusiastic about such programs; that with supervised practice they can learn to regulate and direct their interpersonal behavior toward children in accord with prearranged plans, whether these be client-centered or behavioristic in orientation; that the child-teacher relationship is deeply important to both parties; and that such training may influence classroom philosophy and general practices (modify the subculture) as well as affect individual children.

Programs which have reached the reporting stage and which are presented here are not as programmatic or broadly based as the type of in-service training program mentioned above. Rather, they are geared toward the use of the teacher as a therapeutic agent carrying out a one-time treatment plan designed for a specified child. Harris, Wolf, and Baer, for example, describe work with several children to eliminate inappropriate crawling, crying, isolation, and passivity; and Wolf, Risley, Johnston, Harris, and Allen's paper describes work with an autistic boy. Also, the cases described are generally pupils in special classes of one kind or another, rather than in regular public school classrooms. The behavior modification described by Zimmerman and Zimmerman, for example, took place in a residential treatment center.

In Part 7 of this book, devoted mainly to Research, the reader will find a report by Becker *et al.* which is rather broad in scope. In this part, only the selection by Andronico and Guerney attempts to outline a broad program that would use, in a systematic manner, and on a continuous basis, the inherent motivations of teachers and the inherent accessibility of teachers to children. This is only a proposal, however, and it is in the other articles where we find actual examples demonstrating that teachers already have been shown to be effective as therapeutic agents. It should also be remembered that in addition to having much value in their own right, treatment efforts aimed at individual children provide invaluable information and experience for broader programmatic efforts.

As may be inferred from our earlier comments on projects now in progress, the reader should not assume, from the fact that all the individual case presentations follow the behavior therapy model, that this is the only appropriate therapeutic model which teachers can understand and learn to apply. I'm convinced by my own experiences that teachers can profit from other therapeutic models as well, and that in practice—especially when we consider the impact such instruction has on general educational philosophy—teachers should be trained in a variety of therapeutic models so that they may apply them individually or in combination in ways that are consonant with their own personalities and philosophies and the specific needs and problems of the given child or type of child with whom they are dealing.

In-service training and supervision of teachers in social-psychological and psychotherapeutic principles may make it possible to achieve widespread changes in the educational and psychosocial adjustment of our children today, and thus the adults of tomorrow. Certainly, the idea deserves thorough trial and evaluation.

Effects of Adult Social Reinforcement on Child Behavior*

FLORENCE R. HARRIS
MONTROSE M. WOLF
DONALD M. BAER

In a recent issue of this Journal, *Horowitz (1963) reviewed the literature concerning social reinforcement effects on child behavior. Laboratory findings concerning those factors determining reinforcer effectiveness were summarized. Now, three research workers at the University of Washington present the results of their recent and provocative work demonstrating the effectiveness of carefully worked-out contingencies of adult attention in modifying certain "problem" behaviors of children within the nursery school itself. There are unmistakable and important implications in this research for nursery school practice even though the authors prudently point to the care needed in the nursery school setting to bring childrens' behavior under the control of social reinforcement. These efforts are also preliminary, but the painstaking persistence of the Washington researchers reaffirms belief in the infinite modifiability of behavior and the potential of the nursery school teacher in this endeavor.*

Willard W. Hartup, *Research Editor*

Reprinted with permission from *Young Children*, Vol. XX, No. 1, October 1964, 8–17, Copyright © 1964, National Association for the Education of Young Children, and with the permission of the authors.

*These studies were supported in part by research grants from the National Institute of Mental Health (MH–02208–07) and the University of Washington Graduate School Research Fund (11–1873). The authors are also indebted to Sidney W. Bijou for his general counsel and assistance.

There is general agreement among educators that one of the primary functions of a nursery school is to foster in each child social behaviors that contribute toward more pleasant and productive living for all. However, there is no similar consensus as to precisely how this objective is to be attained. Many writers subscribe to practices based on a combination of psychoanalytic theory and client-centered therapy principles, usually referred to as a mental hygiene approach. Yet there are considerable variation and vagueness in procedures recommended, particularly those dealing with such problem behaviors as the child's hitting people, breaking valuable things, or withdrawing from both people and things. Read (1955), for example, recommends accepting the child's feelings, verbalizing them for him, and draining them off through vigorous activities. Landreth (1942) advises keeping adult contacts with the child at a minimum based on his needs, backing up verbal suggestions by an implicit assumption that the suggestion will be carried out and, when in doubt, doing nothing unless the child's physical safety is involved. In addition to some of the above precepts, Taylor (1954) counsels parents and teachers to support both desirable and undesirable behaviors and to give nonemotional punishment. According to Standing (1959), Montessori advocates that teachers pursue a process of nonintervention, following careful preparation of a specified environment aimed at "canalizing the energy" and developing "inner command." Nonintervention does not preclude the "minimum dose" of instruction and correction.

Using some combination of such guidance precepts, teachers have reported success in helping some nursery school children who showed problem behaviors; but sometimes adherence to the same teaching principles has not been helpful in modifying the behavior of concern. Indeed, it is usually not at all clear what conditions and principles may or may not have been operative. All of these precepts have in common the adult behaviors of approaching and attending to a child. Therefore, it seemed to the staff of the Laboratory Preschool at the University of Washington that a first step in developing possible explicit criteria for judging when and when not to attend was to study the precise effects that adult attention can have on some problem behaviors.

This paper presents an account of the procedures and results of five such studies. Two groups of normal nursery school children provided the subjects studied. One group enrolled twelve three-year-olds and the other, sixteen four-year-olds. The two teachers of the younger group and the three teachers of the older group conducted the studies as they carried out their regular teaching duties. The general methodology of these studies was developed in the course of dealing with a particularly pressing problem behavior shown by one child at the beginning of the school year. It is worth considering this case before describing the procedures which evolved from it.

The study dealt with a three-year-old girl who had regressed to an excessive amount of crawling (Harris, Johnston, Kelley, and Wolf, 1964). By "excessive" is meant that after three weeks of school she was spending most of her morning crawling or in a crouched position with her face hidden. The parents reported that for some months the behavior had been occurring whenever they took her to visit or when friends came to their home. The teachers had used the conventional techniques, as outlined above, for building the child's "security."

Observations recorded in the third week at school showed, however, that more than 80% of the child's time was spent in off-feet positions. The records also showed that the crawling behavior frequently drew the attention of teachers. On-feet behaviors, such as standing and walking, which occurred infrequently, seldom drew such notice.

A program was instituted in which the teachers no longer attended to the child whenever she was crawling or crouching, but gave her continuous warm attention as long as she was engaging in behavior in which she was standing, running, or walking. Initially the only upright behaviors that the teachers were able to attend to occurred when the child pulled herself almost to her feet in order to hang up or take down her coat from her locker, and when she pulled herself up to wash her hands in the wash basin. Within a week of the initiation of the new attention-giving procedure, the child acquired a close-to-normal pattern of on-feet behavior.

In order to see whether the change from off- to on-feet behavior was related to the differential attention given by the teachers, they reversed their procedure, making attention once again contingent only upon crawling and other off-feet behavior. They waited for occasions of such off-feet behavior to "reinforce" with attention, while not attending to any on-feet behavior. By the second day the child had reverted to her old pattern of play and locomotion. The observational records showed the child was off her feet 80% of the class session.

To see whether on-feet behavior could be re-established, the teachers again reversed their procedure, giving attention to the child only when she was engaging in behaviors involving upright positions. On-feet behavior rose markedly during the first session. By the fourth day, the child again spent about 62% of the time on her feet.

Once the child was not spending the greater portion of her day crawling about, she quickly became a well-integrated member of the group. Evidently she already had well-developed social play skills.

As a result of this demonstration that either walking or crawling could be maintained and that the child's responses depended largely upon the teachers' attending behaviors, the teachers began a series of further experimental analyses of the relationship between teacher attention and nursery school child behavior.

PROCEDURES

A specified set of procedures common to the next studies was followed. First, a child showing problem behavior was selected and records were secured. An observer recorded all of the child's behavior, the environmental conditions under which it occurred, and its immediate consequences under conventional teacher guidance. This was done throughout the 2½-hour school session, daily, and for several days. The records gave detailed pictures of the behavior under study. In each case, it became apparent that the problem behavior almost always succeeded in attracting adult attention.

As soon as these records, technically termed "baseline" records, of the typical behavior of the child and teachers were obtained, teachers instituted a program of systematically giving differential attention to the child. When the undesired behavior occurred, they did not in any way attend to him, but remained absorbed in one of the many necessary activities of teachers with other children or with equipment. If the behavior occurred while a teacher was attending to the child, she at once turned to another child or task in a matter-of-fact and nonrejecting manner. Concurrently, teachers gave immediate attention to other behaviors of the child which were considered to be more desirable than the problem behavior. The net effect of these procedures was that the child could gain a great deal of adult attention if he refrained from engaging in "problem behavior." If under this regime of differential attention the problem behavior diminished to a stable low level at which it was no longer considered a problem, a second procedure was inaugurated to check out the functional relationship between changes in the child's behavior and the guidance procedures followed.

The second procedure was simply to reverse the first procedure. That is, when the problem behavior occurred, the teacher went immediately to the child and gave him her full, solicitous attention. If the behavior stopped, she turned to other children and tasks, remaining thus occupied until the behavior recurred. In effect, one sure way for the child to secure adult attention was to exhibit the problem behavior. This procedure was used to secure reasonably reliable information on whether the teachers' special program had indeed brought about the changes noted in the child's behavior. If adult attention was the critical factor in maintaining the behavior, the problem behavior should recur in stable form under these conditions. If it did so, this was evidence that adult attention was, technically speaking, a positive social reinforcer for the child's behavior.

The final stage of the study was, of course, to return to procedures in which attention was given at once and continuously for behaviors considered desirable. Concurrently, adult attention was again withheld or withdrawn as an immediate consequence of the problem behavior. As the problem disappeared and appropriate behaviors increased, the intense program of differential adult attention was gradually diminished until the child was receiving attention at times and in amounts normal for the teachers in the group. However, attention was given only on occasions of desirable behavior, and never (or very seldom) for the undesirable behavior.

CRYING AND WHINING

Following the above procedures, a study was conducted on a four-year-old boy who cried a great deal after mild frustrations (Hart, Allen, Buell, Harris, and Wolf, 1964). This child averaged about eight full-fledged crying episodes each school morning. The baseline observations showed that this crying behavior consistently brought attention from the teachers, in the form of going to him and showing solicitous concern. During the following days, this behavior was simply ignored. (The only exceptions to this were to have been incidents in which the child had hurt himself considerably and was judged to have genuine grounds for crying. Naturally, his hurts were to be attended to. Such incidents, however, did not occur.) Ten days of ignoring the outcries, but giving approving attention for verbal and self-help behaviors, produced a steady weakening of the crying response to a nearly zero level. In the final five days of the interval, only one crying response was recorded. The number of crying episodes on successive days is graphed in cumulative form in Fig. 1.

During the next ten days, crying was again reinforced whenever it occurred, the teachers attending to the boy on these occasions without fail. At first, it was necessary to give attention for mere grimaces that might follow a bump. The daily crying episodes quickly rose to a rate almost as high as formerly. A second ten-day period of ignoring the outcries again produced a quick weakening of the response to a near-zero level, as is apparent in the figure. Crying remained at this low level thereafter, according to the informal judgment of the teachers.

The same procedures were used in another study of "operant crying" of a four-year-old boy, with the same general results.

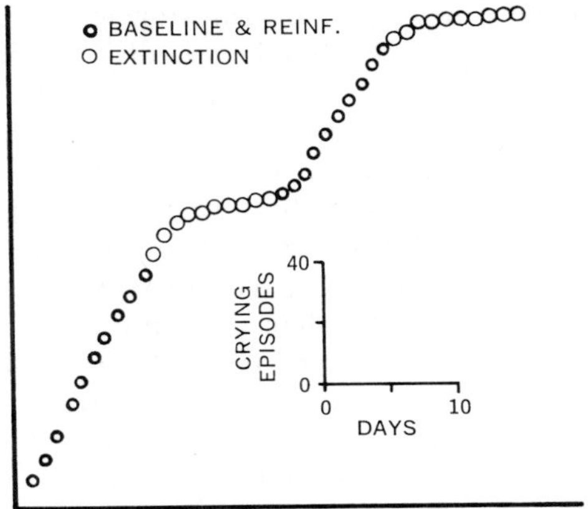

Fig. 1. Cumulative record of the daily number of crying episodes.

ISOLATE PLAY

Two studies involved children who exhibited markedly solitary play behavior. Extremely little of their morning at nursery school was spent in any interaction with other children. Instead, these children typically played alone in a quiet area of the school room or the play yard, or interacted only with the teachers. For present purposes, both of these response patterns will be called "isolate play." Systematic observation showed that isolate play usually attracted or maintained the attention of a teacher, whereas social play with other children did so comparatively seldom.

A plan was initiated in which the teacher was to attend regularly if the child approached other children and interacted with them. On the other hand, the teacher was not to attend to the child so long as he engaged in solitary play. To begin with, attention was given when the child merely stood nearby, watching other children; then, when he played beside another child; and finally, only when he interacted with the other child. Teachers had to take special precautions that their attending behaviors did not result in drawing the child away from children and into interaction solely with the teacher. Two techniques were found particularly effective. The teacher directed her looks and comments to the other child or children, including the subject only as a participant in the play project. For example, "That's a big building you three boys are making; Bill and Tom and Jim (subject) are all working hard." Accessory materials were also kept at hand so that the teacher could bring a relevant item for the subject to add to the play: "Here's another plate for your tea party, Ann."

In both isolate cases this new routine for giving adult attention produced the desired result: Isolate play declined markedly in strength while social play increased two- or threefold.

After about a week of the above procedure, the consequences of non-isolate and isolate play were reversed. The teachers no longer attended to the child's interactions with other children, but instead gave continuous attention to the child when he was alone. Within a week, or less, isolate play became the dominant form of activity in both cases.

The former contingencies were then reinstated: The teachers attended to social interactions by the child, and ignored isolate play as completely as they could. Again, isolate play declined sharply while social interaction increased as before. The results of one of these studies (Allen, Hart, Buell, Harris, and Wolf, 1964) are summarized in Fig. 2.

Figure 2 shows the changes in behavior of a 4½-year-old girl under the different guidance conditions. The graph shows the percentage of play time that she spent in interaction with other children and the percentage of time spent with an adult. The remainder of her time was spent alone. It is apparent that only about 15% of this child's play time was spent in social play as long as the teachers attended primarily to her solitary play. But interacting behaviors rose to about 60% of total play time when the teachers attended only to her social play. At the same time, her interactions solely with teachers, not being reinforced, fell from their usual 40% of the child's playtime to about 20%. These were considered reasonable percentages for this nursery school child. During Days 17 through 25 the schedule of adult reinforcement of social play was gradually reduced to the usual amount of attention, given at the usual irregular intervals. Nevertheless, the social behavior maintained its strength, evidently becoming largely self-maintaining.

After Day 25, the teachers took care not to attend too often to the child when she was alone, but otherwise planned no special contingencies for attending. Four checks were made at later dates to see if the pattern of social behavior persisted. It is apparent (Fig. 2, Post Checks) that the change was durable, at least until Day 51. Further checks were not possible because of the termination of the school year.

A parallel study, of a three-year-old isolate boy (Johnston, Kelley, Harris, Wolf, and Baer, unpub.) yielded similar results showing the same pattern of rapid behavioral change in response to changing contingencies for adult attention. In the case of this boy, postchecks were made on three days during the early months of the school following the summer vacation period. The data showed that on those days his interaction with children averaged 55% of his play time. Apparently his social play was well established. Teachers reported that throughout the remainder of the year he continued to develop ease and skills in playing with his peers.

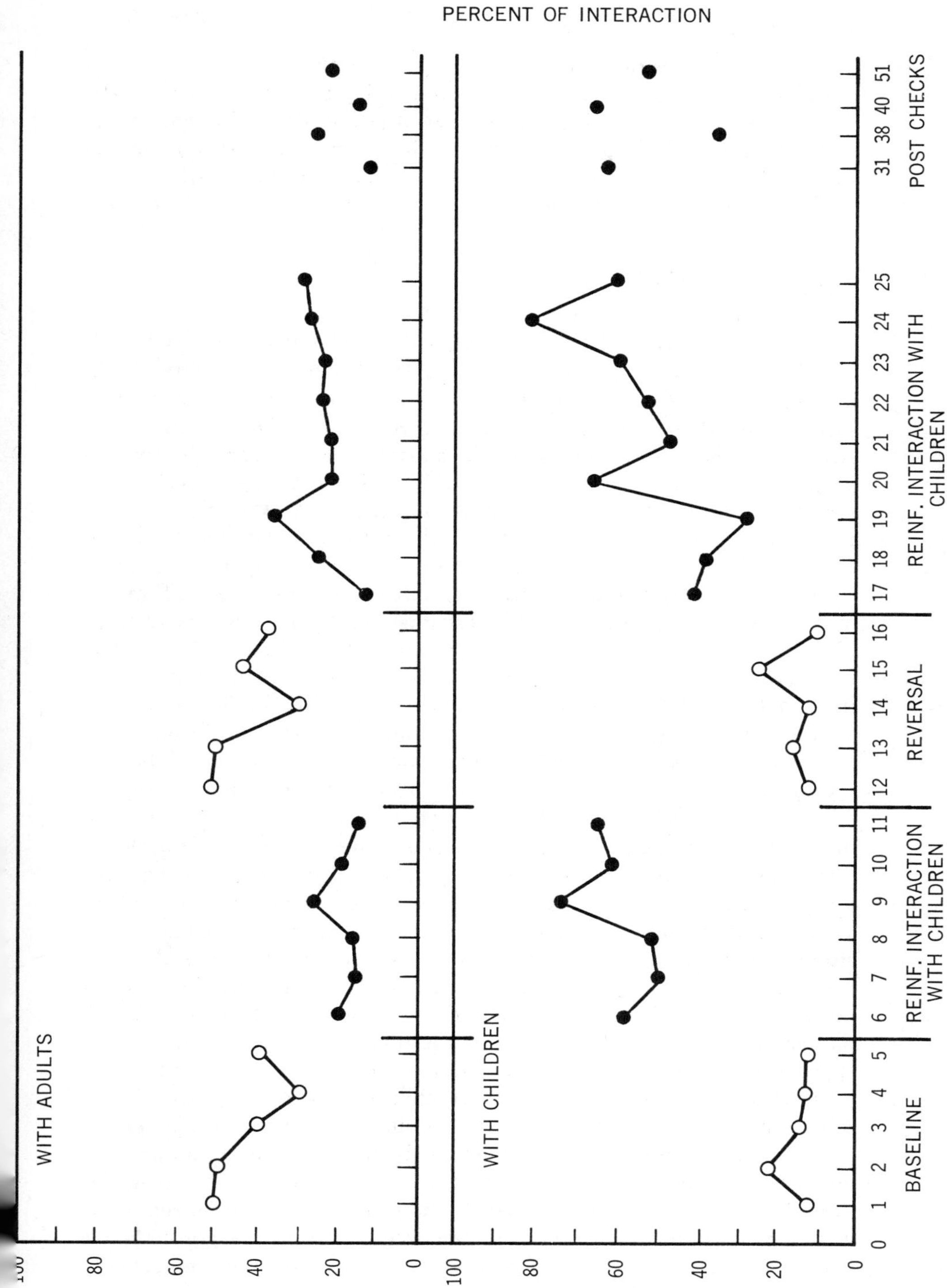

Fig. 2. Daily percentages of time spent in social interaction with adults and with children during approximately two hours of each morning session.

The immediate shifts in these children's play behavior may be partly due to the fact that they had already developed skills readily adapted to play with peers at school. Similar studies in progress are showing that, for some children, development of social play behaviors may require much longer periods of reinforcement.

EXCESSIVE PASSIVITY

A fifth case (Johnston, Kelley, Harris, and Wolf, unpub.) involved a boy noted for his thoroughgoing lack of any sort of vigorous play activity. The teachers reported that this child consistently stood quietly about the play yard while other children ran, rode tricycles, and climbed on special climbing frames, trees, fences, and playhouses. Teachers also reported that they frequently attempted to encourage him, through suggestions or invitations, to engage in the more vigorous forms of play available. Teachers expressed concern over his apparent lack of strength and motor skills. It was decided to select a particular form of active play to attempt to strengthen. A wooden frame with ladders and platforms, called a climbing frame, was chosen as the vehicle for establishing this activity. The teachers attended at first to the child's mere proximity to the frame. As he came closer, they progressed to attending only to his touching it, climbing up a little, and finally to extensive climbing. Technically, this was reinforcement of successive approximations to climbing behavior. Fig. 3 shows the results of nine days of this procedure, compared to a baseline of the preceding nine days. In this figure, black bars represent climbing on the climbing frame and white bars represent climbing on any other equipment in the play yard. The height of the bars shows the percentage of the child's play time spent in such activities. It is clear that during the baseline period less than 10% of the child's time was spent in any sort of climbing activity, but that during the course of reinforcement with pleased adult attention for climbing on the frame, this behavior greatly increased, finally exceeding 50% of the child's morning. (Climbing on other objects was not scored during this period.) There then followed five days during which the teachers ignored any climbing on the frame, but attended to all other appropriate activities. The rate of climbing on the frame promptly fell virtually to zero, though the child climbed on other apparatus and was consistently given attention for this. Another five days of reinforcement of use of the climbing frame immediately restored the climbing-frame behavior to a high stable level, always in excess of 40% of the boy's play time. After this, the teachers began an intermittent program of reinforcement for climbing on any other suitable objects, as well as vigorous active play of all sorts, in an effort to generalize the increased vigorous activity.

Frame-climbing weakened considerably, being largely replaced by other climbing activities, which were now scored again as data. Activities such as tricycle-riding and running were not systematically recorded due to difficulties in reliably scoring them. It is clear from the data obtained, however, that climbing activities were thoroughly generalized by this final procedure. Checks made the following school year in another play yard indicated that vigorous climbing had become a stable part of his behavior repertoire.

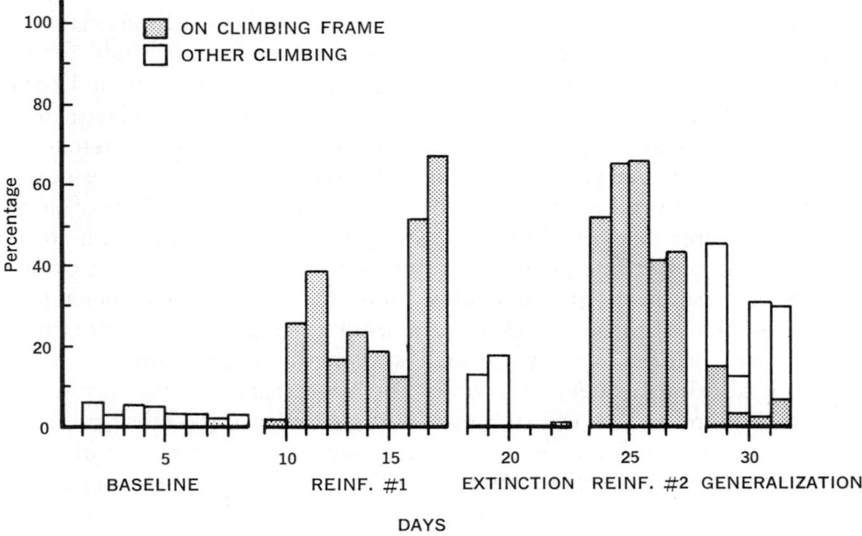

Fig. 3. Daily percentages of time spent in using a climbing-frame apparatus. Open bars indicate time spent in climbing on other equipment.

SUMMARY AND DISCUSSION

The above studies systematically examined effects of adult attention on some problem behaviors of normal preschool children. The findings in each case clearly indicated that for these children adult attention was a strong positive reinforcer. That is, the behavior which was immediately followed by a teacher's giving the child attention rose rapidly to a high rate, and the rate fell markedly when adult attention was withheld from that behavior and concurrently given to an incompatible behavior. While it seems reasonable that for most young children adult attention may be a positive reinforcer, it is also conceivable that for some children adult attention may be a negative reinforcer. That is, the rate of a behavior may decrease when it is immediately followed by the attention of an adult, and rise again as soon as the adult withdraws. Actually, for a few children observed at the preschool, it has been thought that adult attention was a negative reinforcer. This seemed to be true, for instance, in the case of the climbing-frame child. Before the study was initiated, the teachers spent several weeks attempting to make themselves positively reinforcing to the child. This they did by staying at a little distance from him and avoiding attending directly to him until he came to them for something. At first, his approaches were only for routine help, such as buttoning his coat. On each of these occasions they took care to be smilingly friendly and helpful. In time, he began making approaches of other kinds, for instance, to show a toy. Finally, when a teacher approached him and commented with interest on what he was doing, he continued his play instead of stopping, hitting out, or running off. However, since his play remained lethargic and sedentary, it was decided that special measures were necessary to help him progress more rapidly. It was the use and effects of these special measures that constituted the study. Clearly, however, adult attention must be or become positively reinforcing to a child before it can be successfully used to help him achieve more desirably effective behaviors.

Studies such as those reported here seem to imply that teachers may help many children rapidly through systematic programming of their adult social reinforcements. However, further research in this area seems necessary. Some of our own studies now in progress suggest that guidance on the basis of reinforcement principles may perhaps bring rapidly into use only behaviors which are already available within the repertory of the child. If the desired behavior requires skills not yet in the child's repertory, then the process of developing those skills from such behaviors as the child has may require weeks or months. For example, a four-year-old child who could verbalize but who very rarely spoke was helped to speak freely within several days. On the other hand, a child of the same age who had never verbalized required a lengthy shaping process that involved reinforcing first any vocalization, and then gradually more appropriate sounds and combinations of sounds. The latter study was still incomplete at the close of a year of work. The time required to develop social behaviors in isolate children has likewise varied considerably, presumably for the same reasons.

Although the teachers conducted these studies in the course of carrying out their regular teaching duties, personnel in excess of the usual number were necessary. The laboratory school was staffed with one teacher to no more than six children, making it possible to assign to one teacher the role of principal "reinforcer teacher" in a study. This teacher was responsible for giving the child immediate attention whenever he behaved in specified ways. In addition, observers were hired and trained to record the behavior of each child studied. Each observer kept a record in ten-second intervals of his subject's behavior throughout each morning at school. Only with such staffing could reinforcement contingencies be precisely and consistently administered and their effects recorded.

Unless the effects are recorded, it is easy to make incorrect judgments about them. Two instances illustrate such fallibility. A boy in the laboratory preschool frequently pinched adults. Attempts by the teachers to ignore the behavior proved ineffective, since the pinches were hard enough to produce at least an involuntary startle. Teachers next decided to try to develop a substitute behavior. They selected patting as a logical substitute. Whenever the child reached toward a teacher, she attempted to forestall a pinch by saying, "Pat, Davey," sometimes adding, "Not pinch," and then strongly approving his patting, when it occurred. Patting behavior increased rapidly to a high level. The teachers agreed that they had indeed succeeded in reducing the pinching behavior through substituting patting. Then they were shown the recorded data. It showed clearly that although patting behavior was indeed high, pinching behavior continued at the previous level. Apparently, the teachers were so focused on the rise in patting behavior that, without the objective data, they would have erroneously concluded that development of a substitute behavior was in this case a successful technique. A second example illustrates a different, but equally undesirable, kind of erroneous assumption. A preschool child who had to wear glasses (Wolf, Risley, and Mees, 1964) developed a pattern of throwing them two or three times per day. Since this proved expensive, it was decided that the attendants should put him in his room for ten minutes following each glasses-throw. When the attendants were asked a few days later how the procedure was working, they said that the glasses-throwing had not diminished at all. A check of the records, however, showed that there was actually a marked decrease. The throwing dropped to zero within five days. Presumably, the additional effort involved in carrying out the procedure had given the attendants an exaggerated impression of the rate of the behavior. Recorded data, therefore, seem essential to accurate objective assessments of what has occurred.

The findings in the studies presented here accord generally with results of laboratory research on social development reviewed in this journal by Horowitz (1963). The importance of social reinforcement was also noted by Bandura (1963) in his investigations of imitation. Gallwey (1964) has replicated the study of an isolate child discussed here, with results "clearly confirmatory of the effectiveness of the technique." Further studies in school situations that can combine the function of research with that of service seem highly desirable.

REFERENCES

Allen, K. Eileen, Hart, Betty M., Buell, Joan S., Harris, Florence R., & Wolf, M. M. Effects of social reinforcement on isolate behavior of a nursery school child. *Child. Develop.,* 1964, 35, 511–518.

Bandura, Albert. The role of imitation in personality development. *J. Nursery Ed.,* 1963, 18, 207–215.

Gallwey, Mary, Director of the Nursery School, Washington State University, Pullman, Wash., 1964. Personal communication.

Harris, Florence R., Johnston, Margaret K., Kelley, C. Susan, & Wolf, M. M. Effects of positive social reinforcement on regressed crawling of a nursery school child. *J. Ed. Psychol.,* 1964, 55, 35–41.

Hart, Betty M., Allen, K. Eileen, Buell, Joan S., Harris, Florence R., & Wolf, M. M. Effects of social reinforcement on operant crying. *J. Exp. Child Psychol.* In press.

Horowitz, Frances Degen. Social reinforcement effects on child behavior. *J. Nursery Ed.,* 1963, 18, 276–284.

Johnston, Margaret K., Kelley, C. Susan, Harris, Florence R., Wolf, M. M., & Baer, D. M. Effects of positive social reinforcement on isolate behavior of a nursery school child. Unpublished manuscript.

Johnston, Margaret K., Kelley, C. Susan, Harris, Florence R., & Wolf, M. M. An application of reinforcement principles to development of motor skills of a young child. Unpublished manuscript.

Landreth, Catherine. *Education of the Young Child.* New York: Wiley, 1942.

Read, Katherine H. *The Nursery School* (2nd ed.). Philadelphia: Saunders, 1955.

Standing, E. M. *Maria Montessori, Her Life and Work.* Fresno: American Library Guild, 1959.

Taylor, Katherine W. *Parents Cooperative Nursery Schools.* New York: Teachers College, Columbia University, 1954.

Wolf, Montrose M., Risley, T. R., & Mees, H. L. Application of operant conditioning procedures to the behavior problems of an autistic child. *Behav. Res. Ther.,* 1964, 1, 305–312.

Application of Operant Conditioning Procedures to the Behavior Problems of an Autistic Child: A Follow-Up and Extension*

MONTROSE WOLF
TODD RISLEY
MARGARET JOHNSTON
FLORENCE HARRIS
K. EILEEN ALLEN

The modification of an autistic boy's behavior in a nursery school setting is described. The procedures used to deal with his problem behaviors such as tantrums, pinching and toilet training are discussed.

INTRODUCTION

Recently, we (Wolf, Risley and Mees, 1964) described an application of operant behavior modification procedures to the behavior problems of an autistic preschool-age boy. In the present paper we describe further observations and modifications of this child's behavior carried out in a university nursery school setting. But first, a summary is presented of the history of the child's behavior problems and their earlier treatment.

Dicky was three-and-a-half years old when the previously reported study began. From hospital records, it appeared that Dicky progressed

Reprinted from *Behavior Research & Therapy* (in Press) with the permission of the Pergamon Press, Inc. and the authors.

*This research was supported in part by a grant (M-2232) from National Institutes of Health, United States Public Health Service. The authors are indebted to Jo Ann Bevers, Susan Kelly and Thelma Turbitt for their assistance with the study and to Sidney W. Bijou, Donald M. Baer, and Jay S. Birnbrauer for their frequent consultation. The major portion of this paper was presented at the Annual Convention of the Western Psychological Association, Portland, Oregon, April, 1964.

normally until his ninth month, when cataracts were discovered in the lenses of both eyes. At that time severe temper tantrums and sleeping problems began to develop. During his second year he had a series of eye operations which culminated with a removal of his occluded lenses. This made glasses-wearing necessary. For more than a year his parents tried, and failed, to make Dicky wear glasses. During this time Dicky was seen by a variety of specialists who diagnosed him, variously, as profoundly mentally retarded, diffuse and locally brain-damaged, and psychotic. One recommendation was that he be placed in an institution for the retarded since his prognosis was so poor.

Dicky did not eat normally and lacked normal social and verbal repertoires. His tantrums included self-destructive behaviors such as head-banging, face-slapping, hair-pulling, and face-scratching. His mother reported that after a severe tantrum "he was a mess, all black and blue and bleeding." He would not sleep at night, forcing one or both parents to remain by his bed. Sedatives, tranquilizers, and restraints were tried, without success.

He was admitted to a children's mental hospital with the diagnosis of childhood schizophrenia at the age of three. After three months' hospitalization the terminal report stated that there had been some improvement in his schizophrenic condition but no progress in glasses-wearing. A few months later his ophthalmologist predicted that unless Dicky began wearing glasses within the next six months he would permanently lose his macular vision. At that point the first and second authors were invited in as consultants by the hospital staff for the purpose of training Dicky to wear glasses.

On our recommendation, Dicky was readmitted to the hospital. By modifying the consequences of several of Dicky's problem behaviors, methods were developed which diminished the tantrums, sleeping and eating problems and established glasses-wearing and some appropriate verbal and social behavior.

The tantrums were dealt with by a combination of extinction and mild punishment. Dicky was sent immediately to "his room" (a bedroom containing a bed, chair, table, window, etc.) by his hospital attendant contingent upon each tantrum, the door remaining closed until the tantrum behavior declined. A few of the initial tantrums were quite violent, one lasting more than three-quarters of an hour.

The more severe self-destructive behaviors like head-banging, face-scratching, and hair-pulling almost completely disappeared in about two and one-half months. Crying, screaming, and face-slapping were almost nonexistent after about five and one-half months.

The bedtime problems were handled in a similar manner to the tantrums. Dicky was prepared for bed, cuddled and tucked in bed with the bedroom door left open. If he got out of bed, he was told to return to bed or his door would be shut. This procedure produced a series of tantrums for five consecutive nights. On the sixth night, Dicky was tucked in and went right to sleep. Bedtime was seldom a problem again.

Glasses-wearing was brought about by the method of successive approximations (shaping). Bites of the child's meals were used as reinforcers. Later, less manipulable reinforcers such as walks, rides, play, snacks, and so forth were used to maintain glasses-wearing. Once it was shaped, it increased gradually from only a few minutes a day to about twelve hours a day throughout the month preceding Dicky's release from the hospital.

The procedure used for generating a verbal repertoire was similar to that used to teach glasses-wearing. Dicky's verbal behavior was originally limited to occasional echolalic responses and what appeared to be self-stimulatory responses, such as songs. These verbal responses, however, were well-articulated and some were rather lengthy and complex. Using bits of his meals as reinforcers the attendant first reinforced Dicky for mimicking her as she named a series of five pictures one at a time. After several days the attendant gradually omitted saying the word first, and Dicky would usually say the word in the presence of each picture without a prompt. In three weeks he did this in the presence of about ten pictures. He then progressed to picture books, common household objects, and finally to temporally remote events.

After almost seven months in the hospital under our direction, Dicky was released. It was our feeling that since he was wearing his glasses, having almost no tantrums or bedtime problems, and was developing a rudimentary verbal and social repertoire, the hospital environment was less beneficial than would be his home.

Before Dicky was discharged from the hospital the parents were trained by the attendants to deal with the problems described above, should they arise again. Telephone interviews held soon after Dicky's release indicated that all was well and that Dicky was continuing to make progress.

Several months after Dicky returned home, we again interviewed his father. The father stated that there had been no recurrence of the severe problem behaviors. He expressed contentment with Dicky's rate of progress and described the pleasure he and his wife had found in the boy. But Dicky was then nearly five years old and when we considered his only moderate rate of development in the social areas and also the slow solving of his additional problems, like toilet training, we were not at all certain he would be ready for public school special education classes at the proper time, two years hence, around age seven.

The parents lived at an inconvenient distance from Seattle; but upon our recommendation, they enrolled Dicky in the Preschool Laboratory at the Developmental Psychology Laboratory on the University of Washington campus.

PROCEDURES AND RESULTS

Each weekday morning for two years, Dicky regularly attended a two-and-a-half hour class, the first year with normal three-year-old children and the second with normal four-year-olds. The nursery school staff consisted of experienced nursery school teachers with a thorough understanding of behavior modification principles. For the preceding year they had been carrying out a series of experimental analyses of the role of teacher attention as related to some relatively mild behavior problems of *normal* nursery school children (Harris, Wolf, and Baer, 1965). It was in the context of this behaviorally and experimentally oriented nursery school that we attempted to deal with a few more of Dicky's behavior problems. Our hope was to eventually prepare him for public school special education class.

Data Recording

Throughout the first year and during a portion of the second year observers recorded the occurrence of several of Dicky's behaviors during the nursery school class sessions using a recording form and notation system perfected in earlier studies (Allen, Hart, Buell, Harris, & Wolf, 1964). For behaviors which were quite discrete, each instance was noted, for example, urinating in the toilet. For other responses where an absolute number of events was difficult or meaningless to record, their presence during successive 10-second intervals was recorded. Examples of such behaviors were self-slapping, and pinching others, both of which occured in bursts. The observer had a specially-prepared recording sheet which was broken into squares representing successive 10-second intervals. The observer placed in a square one or more symbols representing the responses which occurred during that 10-second interval. A watch with a sweep second hand provided the 10-second temporal stimulus.

Self-slapping

In the interview with the father, noted above, we inquired about the parents' progress in teaching Dicky constructive skills such as the use of advanced toys. We were not very encouraged by the description of Dicky's development in this area. The father explained that attempts to instruct Dicky often led to his becoming "fussy", a condition which had preceded the temper tantrums prior to his hospitalization. When left to himself there was no difficulty, but when it was firmly suggested that he do something out of the ordinary he showed the preliminary stages of his old tantrum behavior, although there had been no return of the earlier self-destructive episodes. Unfortunately, this "fussiness" had been effective in suppressing his parents' attempts to establish further self-help and play skills.

In the nursery school, Dicky showed much the same pattern. During the first two weeks of school he was allowed to do much as he pleased. He spent most of his time lying on the floor, turning a small object in his hand or wandering about the room or play yard. Left alone he created no problem. However, when the teachers began guiding him firmly through activities of offering him play objects he began to whine. The teachers would persist and Dicky would react more vigorously. In a few days, he began crying and slapping himself, a return to his old temper tantrum pattern. The teachers attempted to disregard the outbursts. At the same time, they tried *not* to let the outbursts terminate the instruction period, since it was felt that such a contingency only would serve to maintain the tantrums. However, the energetic, loud, and self-destructive tantrums were very difficult to ignore, and during their occurrence it was impossible to engage him in an instructional activity or game. After several days it seemed apparent that the tantrums and slapping behavior were not going to diminish rapidly as a result of the ignoring condition; in fact, they appeared to be increasing in severity.

The tantrum problem previously had been dealt with in the hospital by sending Dicky to "his room" contingent upon each tantrum. It was decided to arrange a room in the nursery school for Dicky. During the 23rd class session, as designated by the first arrow in Figure 1, he was taken to "his room" consequent to a severe outburst. He remained in the room for

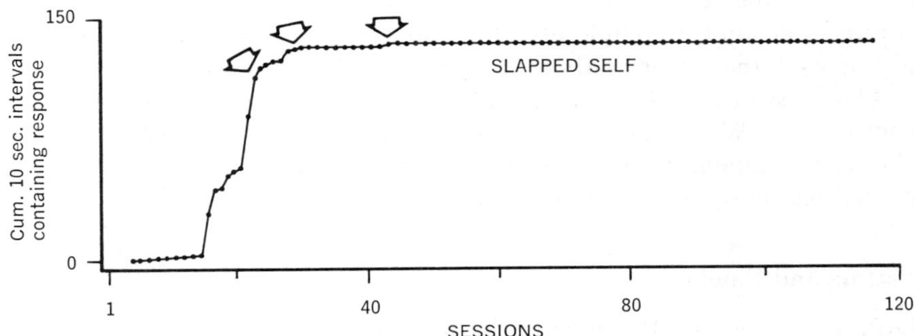

Figure 1. Self-slapping was recorded in cumulative ten-second intervals during the first year in nursery school. Each dot represents the total number of ten-second intervals containing one or more instances of the response during a nursery school class session. Each day's total was added cumulatively to those of the preceding class sessions. The arrows represent occasions when Dicky was sent to his room contingent upon self-slapping.

about 30 minutes, until the behavior had subsided. A significant reduction in tantrum behavior was observed during the next several days although there were a few self slaps. Again, during the 29th class session, after slapping himself, he was taken to his room. This time the tantrum subsided in 12 minutes. Except for one more self slap and a 9-minute stay in his room on day 43, the rate remained at zero for the remaining 63 class sessions.

In the hospital approximately 100 trips to "his room" had been necessary to sufficiently reduce the tantrum rate. In the nursery school only three trips were required to eliminate entirely the behavior in the new setting.

Pinching

Soon after Dicky began school, he developed a high rate of pinching the other children and the teachers. Painful pinching also was a behavior which was effective in disrupting the teachers' attempts to instruct him as well as in reducing the chance of social interaction by driving away the other children. The teachers ignored it as best they could, but again no change in rate was seen as a result of the ignoring condition.

There was a temporary decrease in the rate of pinching correlated with the decline in tantrum rate (see a, in Fig. 2) but the pinching soon recovered. But, since the room contingency had been successful in modifying the tantrums it was decided to apply it to pinching as well. After 31 class sessions, almost all of which contained several pinching instances, Dicky was sent to "his room" contingent upon pinching. This step was taken after the self-slapping had significantly diminished. The first room contingency almost completely eliminated the behavior. As can be seen in Figure 2, there were only four more pinching instances over the next 74 class sessions. Each of the later instances was also followed by a room contingency. When the rate was suddenly reduced, some of the other children commented that "Dicky doesn't pinch any more" and they appeared less hesitant to have Dicky approach them.

Patting and Pinching

During class session 19, when Dicky was pinching another child, a teacher showed Dicky how to "pat". The "patting" can best be described as a combination of patting and stroking. The teachers encouraged and praised Dicky for "patting instead of pinching". The observer began recording patting during session 24. As shown in Figure 3 patting behavior stabilized at a moderate rate within a few sessions.

Between sessions 19 and 32 (the dotted lines) the teachers reported a

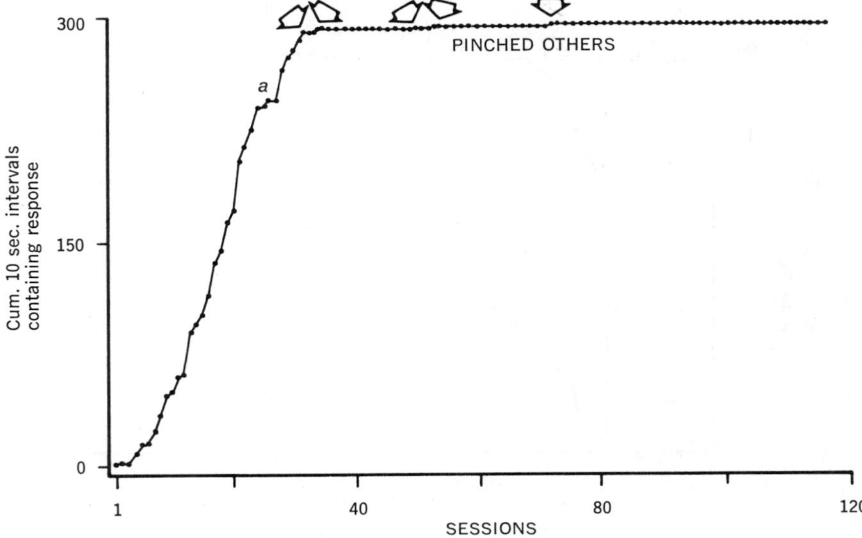

Figure 2. Pinching of teachers and other children was recorded in cumulative ten-second intervals. Each dot represents the total number of ten-second intervals containing one or more instances of the response during one nursery school class session. Each day's total was added cumulatively to those of the preceding class sessions. The arrows represent the occasions when Dicky was sent to his room contingent upon pinching.

decrease in pinching as patting was shaped and maintained. However, the observer's records showed no decrease in pinching until the room contingency was imposed directly for pinching. Without the more objective observer records the teachers would have erroneously concluded that the development of a substitute behavior was in this case a successful technique for decreasing an undesirable response.[2]

When pinching was suppressed there seemed to be no effect on the rate of patting which suggests that these behaviors were independent, although their topographies were somewhat similar. Several sessions later the rate of patting did decline, apparently as a function of teacher extinction since they were no longer concerned with substituting the response. In order to investigate this speculation a probe experiment was carried

[2]The development of substitute responses frequently has been suggested as a method of "siphoning repressed emotions off into socially acceptable patterns of behavior" (Hurlock, 1964).

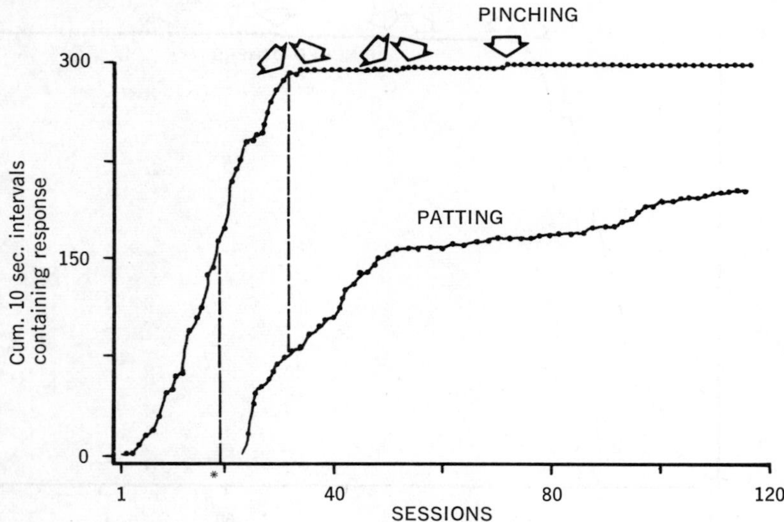

Figure 3. Ten-second intervals containing patting as well as pinching behavior were recorded. The asterisk indicated the session during which patting behavior was originally developed by the teacher. The vertical dashed lines enclose the period during which the teachers reported a substitution of pinching behavior by the patting response, a conclusion which was not substantiated by the more objective records of the observer.

out later in the year. An attempt was made to increase the rate of patting by making praise contingent upon patting behavior for a few weeks period. As can be seen in Fig. 3 there was a slight rise in the patting rate which corresponded to this period.

Toilet Training

Dicky had received no systematic toilet training and had no appropriate skills in the area, wearing diapers constantly. As noted earlier Dicky's parents were hesitant to pursue training which provoked any reaction similar to the earlier severe tantrum behavior; toilet training was no exception. Beginning with the first class session, the teachers set about teaching Dicky the use of the toilet.

In the nursery school there were toilets in a room directly off the classroom. These were always accessible. In addition, as part of the mid-morning routine all the children were taken into the bathroom and given the opportunity to use the toilet. Dicky mastered this regimen in a few days. With some guidance he would go up to the toilet, pull down his pants, and wait for a period. However, he usually lacked the crucial response.

Dicky was also occasionally taken to the toilet room and guided through the routine at times when it appeared he might be about to urinate (holding himself, "wiggling", etc.). These trials lasted as long as 20 minutes. When he did wet himself he was taken to the toilet room and his pants changed. On those occasions he also was told to go through the toilet routine on the chance that he might produce an additional trace.

As can be seen from the cumulative record in Figure 4, he wet his pants four times during the first three weeks of school. On the other days he did not urinate during the morning. After three of these instances he produced a trace in the toilet. For each trace he was given an M & M candy.

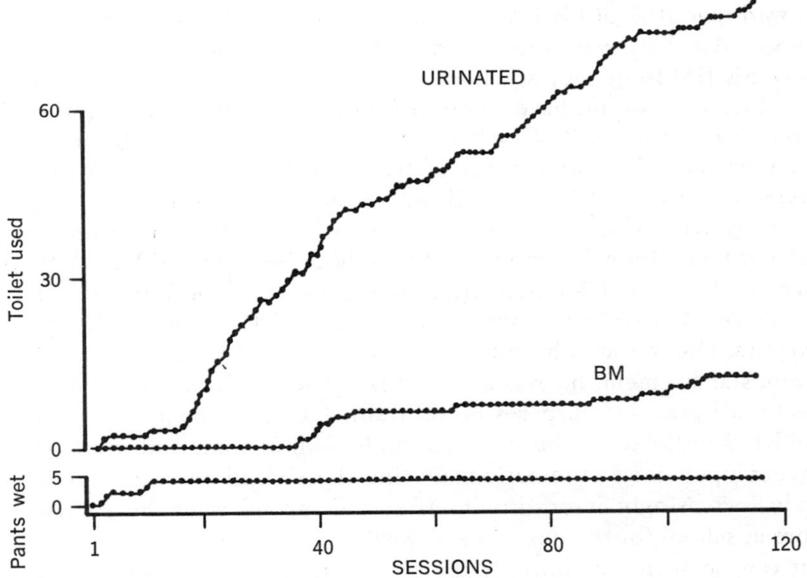

Figure 4. Cumulative instances of wet pants, toilet urination and toilet BM's.

One morning during the fourth week, Dicky was taken to the toilet room when he gave signs of being about to wet his pants. He produced a trace in the toilet and got an M & M. That day after school another attempt was made and he again produced a trace. The teachers kept him at the toilet a while longer. Soon he gave a slightly larger trace and received another M & M and a bite of ice cream. After additional waiting a short stream occurred; a few minutes later another short stream. He then appeared to relax and he voided completely. Each response had resulted in a bite of ice cream or an M & M. The complete series of events had taken about 25 minutes.

The following day he urinated twice at school when taken to the toilet.

The latencies were much shorter. The next day he urinated on the ferry coming to school and again after school with almost no delay. That same afternoon he urinated in the toilet at home for the first time. For a few days, he was given candy reinforcers both at home and at school for each use of the toilet. By the end of the first week candy was discontinued. However, a successful urination continued to evoke warm praise from teachers and parents. The parents reported only a few further instances of wet pants at home. As shown in Figure 4, there were no more at school.

After proper urination behavior was strongly established bowel training was begun. At the beginning of school the parents were asked to note down the time each day that Dicky soiled his pants. A plot of these times showed that 50% of his BM's occurred between 3:00 and 5:00 in the afternoon. After six weeks he had had only one BM soiling during school. Since his BM frequency at school was so low it was clear that most of the bowel training would have to be carried out at home by the mother. For several days at the end of each school session, the teachers trained Dicky to sit on the toilet for periods of from five to ten minutes. Sitting and "trying to have a BM" were followed with a bite of candy or ice cream. After two days of such training the mother began having Dicky sit on the toilet at home for a few minutes of each hour between 3:00 and 5:00 p.m. Each of the 5- to 10-minute trials was maintained only by parental approval. About 7 o'clock in the evening of the 14th day of the BM training program, Dicky stated he was going to have a BM in the "potty". To his parent's amazement, he was as good as his word. From that time on, he was for all practical purposes bowel trained. During the first week that he had BM's in the toilet, he received candy both at home and at school contingent upon each elimination. During the second week the candy was made increasingly intermittent. After the second week he received no more at school for the next several weeks and only rarely at home. In Fig. 4 it can be seen that initially there were frequent BM's in the toilet at school; however, there was a decrease to an almost zero rate correlated with the termination of the candy reinforcement contingency. Several weeks later the candy contingency was reinstated for a few weeks period which brought about only a slight increase in the BM rate at school. It was exactly a month before his parents reported BM-soiled pants and during the remainder of the year he had only five such recurrences.

Autisms

Two behaviors frequently were noted in Dicky which have been reported in autistic children. One consisted of a rhythmic twisting of the head and shoulders. Another, which we called "fiddling", involved a rapid flexing of his fingers and hands, often while touching toys, objects or people.

The twisting slowly decreased throughout the first year. The fiddling increased and then declined. The decline was correlated with the teacher's telling Dicky to keep his hands still. During the second year of nursery school both of these behaviors continued to decrease in frequency.

Social Behavior

Dicky's recorded rate of high-level, social interaction (verbalization, physical contact, shared play materials) with his nursery school classmates remained near zero throughout the first year. Systematic attempts were made to shape social behavior. Neither contingent teacher attention (Allen, et al., 1964) nor contingent edibles significantly increased Dicky's interaction with the other children that year. However, 24 days of data taken in January of his second year in nursery school showed that on the average (median) he spent 15% of his day in high-level, social interaction and 42% in close proximity (within three feet) to other children.

When we began working with Dicky in the hospital, his verbal behavior was almost completely non-social. Although it still had not reached a level which was normal for his age, it developed steadily during his two years of nursery school. His verbal repertoire came to include questions, comments on his environment, the reading and spelling out of words and signs and almost no inappropriate mimicking.[3]

The following year he attended a special education class in the public school, where, according to his parents, he made a good adjustment and learned to read at the primary level quite well.[4]

CONCLUSION

After three years' intensive application of operant behavior modification techniques, Dicky progressed from "hopeless" to the point that he was able to take advantage of a public school education program. Perhaps, through the continued efforts of his parents and teachers he may develop into a productive citizen.

[3]A large portion of Dicky's most recent verbal progress was due to a program of verbal development directed by Donald M. Baer, carried out during Dicky's second year in nursery school.

[4]Subsequent to our work with this child, the procedures for establishing verbal behavior and toilet training were replicated, with some revisions, with other children. For a discussion of these procedures see; Risley and Wolf, 1967, and Giles and Wolf, 1966.

REFERENCES

Allen, K. Eileen, Hart, Betty M., Buell, Joan S., Harris, Florence R., & Wolf, M. M. Effects of social reinforcement on isolate behavior of a nursery school child. *Child Develpm.*, 1964, 35, 511–518.

Giles, D. K. and Wolf, M. M. Toilet training institutionalized, severe retardates: an application of operant behavior modification techniques. *Amer. J. Ment. Def.*, 1966, 5, 766–780.

Harris, Florence R., Wolf, M. M., & Baer, D. M. Effects of adult social reinforcement on child behavior. *Young Child.*, 1964, 20–1, 8–17.

Risley, T. R. and Wolf, M. M. Establishing functional speech in echolalic children. *Behav. Res. Ther.*, in press.

Wolf, M. M., Risley, T. R., & Mees, H. L. Application of operant conditioning procedures to the behavior problems of an autistic child. *Behav. Res. Ther.*, 1964, 1, 305–312.

The Alteration of Behavior in a Special Classroom Situation

ELAINE H. ZIMMERMAN
J. ZIMMERMAN

Unproductive classroom behavior was eliminated in two emotionally disturbed boys by removing social consequences of the behavior. Behavior which was more adequate and efficient with respect to social and scholastic adjustment was shaped and maintained with social reinforcers.

The classroom behavior of two emotionally disturbed boys was altered by arranging and manipulating its consequences.

The boys, in-patients in a residential treatment center (LaRue D. Carter Memorial Hospital), attended the first author's English class daily for 1 hr as part of an educational therapy program. There were three boys in the class, each receiving individual attention.

CASE I

Subject 1 (S-1) was 11 years old. He appeared to have no organic disorder and was of normal intelligence. In early class sessions, whenever S-1 was called upon to spell a word which had previously been studied and drilled, he would pause for several seconds, screw up his face, and mutter

Reprinted with permission from the *Journal of the Experimental Analysis of Behavior*, 1962, Vol. 5, No. 1, 59–60, Copyright 1962 by the Society for the Experimental Analysis of Behavior, Inc., and with the permission of the authors.

letters unrelated to the word. Following this, the instructor *(E)* consistently asked him to sound out the word, often giving him the first letter and other cues, encouraging him to spell the word correctly. Only after *E* had spent considerable time and attention would the boy emit a correct response. The procedure was inefficient and profitless for improving the boy's spelling behavior. In fact, it may have been maintaining the undesirable pattern, since over the first 10 or 15 class sessions, consistently more time and attention were required of *E* to obtain a correct spelling response.

While "studying" in class, S-1 would obtain sheets of paper, wrinkle them, and throw them away, laughing as he caught *E*'s eye or that of one of the other students.

The Change in Approach

After several weeks in class, S-1 was quizzed via paper-and-pencil test on a lesson based on 10 spelling words, with time allotted for study and review. He handed in a paper with a muddled combination of barely legible letters. Immediately, *E* asked him to go to the blackboard. Her instructions were simply: "We will now have a quiz. I will read a word and you will spell it correctly on the board." She read the first word, and the subject misspelled it 10 or more times on the board. During this time, *E* sat at her desk, ignoring S-1, apparently busy reading or writing. Each time S-1 misspelled the word, he glanced at *E*; but she did not respond. The boy erased the word and tried again, several times repeating "I can't spell it," or "I can't remember how," etc. Although ignored, the boy made no effort to sit down or leave the room. After approximately 10 min, he spelled the word correctly; *E* looked up at him immediately, smiled, and said, "Good, now we can go on." She read a second word; and after a similar series of errors and verbal responses, S-1 spelled the word correctly. With each successive word (through 10 words), the number of inappropriate (unreinforced) responses decreased, as did the latency of the correct response. At the end of the quiz, *E* took the boy's spelling chart, wrote an "A" on it, and praised him. She then asked the subject to help her color some Easter baskets. They sat down together, and chatted and worked.

Thereafter, attention in the form of smiling, chatting, and physical proximity was given only immediately after the emission of desired classroom behavior or some approximation of it in the desired direction. Undesirable behavior was consistently ignored. As a result of a month of this treatment, the frequency of bizarre spelling responses and other undesirable responses declined to a level close to zero per class session. At the conclusion of this study, the boy was working more efficiently, and was making adequate academic progress.

CASE II

Subject S-2 was an 11-year-old boy, who, like S-1, had no apparent organic disorder and was also of normal intelligence. In initial class Sessions, S-2 emitted behavior considered undesirable in the classroom context with high frequency. He displayed temper tantrums (kicking, screaming, etc.), spoke baby-talk, and incessantly made irrelevant comments or posed irrelevant questions.

Several times a week, attendants dragged this boy down the hall to one of his classes as the boy screamed and buckled his knees. On several of these occasions, the boy threw himself on the floor in front of a classroom door. A crowd of staff members inevitably gathered around him. The group usually watched and commented as the boy sat or lay on the floor, kicking and screaming. Some members of the group hypothesized that such behavior seemed to appear after the boy was teased or frustrated in some way. However, the only observable in the situation was the consistent consequence of the behavior in terms of the formation of a group of staff members around the boy.

Observing one such situation which occurred before *E*'s class, *E* asked the attendent to put the boy in the classroom at his desk and to leave the room. Then *E* closed the door. The boy sat at his desk, kicking and screaming; *E* proceeded to her desk and worked there, ignoring S-2. After 2 or 3 min, the boy, crying softly, looked up at *E*. Then *E* announced that she would be ready to work with him as soon as he indicated that he was ready to work. He continued to cry and scream with diminishing loudness for the next 4 or 5 min. Finally, he lifted his head and stated that he was ready. Immediately, *E* looked up at him, smiled, went to his desk, and said, "Good, now let's get to work." The boy worked quietly and cooperatively with *E* for the remainder of the class period.

The Handling of Tantrums, Irrelevent Verbal Behavior, and Baby-talk

Each time a tantrum occurred, *E* consistently ignored S-2. When tantrum behavior was terminated, *E* conversed with the boy, placed herself in his proximity, or initiated an activity which was appealing to him. After several weeks, class tantrums disappeared entirely. Because the consequence of tantrum behavior varied in other situations, no generalization to situations outside the classroom has been observed.

Furthermore the frequency of irrelevant verbal behavior and of baby-talk declined almost to the point of elimination following the procedure of withholding attention after the emission of such behavior. On the other hand, when S-2 worked quietly or emitted desirable classroom behavior, *E* addressed him cordially and permitted some verbal interchange for several seconds. When a lesson was being presented to the class at large and S-2 listened attentively, *E* reinforced him by asking him a question he could answer or by looking at him, smiling at him, etc. The reinforcement was delivered intermittently rather than continuously because: (a) reinforcing every desired response of one student was impossible since *E*'s time was parcelled out among several students; and (b) intermittent reinforcement would probably be more effective than continuous reinforcement in terms of later resistance of the desired behavior to extinction. Like S-1, at the conclusion of the study this boy was working more efficiently in class and was making good progress. His speech was more generally characterized by relevancy and maturity.

The Potential Application of Filial Therapy to the School Situation[1]

MICHAEL P. ANDRONICO
BERNARD G. GUERNEY, JR.

Filial therapy is a method of treating emotionally disturbed children under ten years of age (Guerney, 1964; Fidler, Guerney, Andronico, & Guerney, 1964; Guerney, Guerney, & Andronico, 1966; Andronico, Fidler, Guerney, & Guerney, 1967). As presently conducted, filial therapy is not intended for children who are mentally retarded, perceptually or neurologically impaired, or psychotic. Also excluded are parents who appear to be pre-psychotic or suicidal. By virtue of circumstances rather than design, a truly lower class population has not yet been represented to a significant degree.

The children are not directly given therapy by a professional. Rather, parents are relied upon to effect changes in their children as well as themselves. The technique involves training the parents to play with their own children at home for prescribed periods of time, and under observation at the Clinic.

Training is conducted with groups of six to eight parents. The role that the parents are taught to take in the special play sessions is modeled after that of the client-centered play therapist. The importance of attempting to achieve genuine empathic understanding and acceptance of the child's

Reprinted from *Journal of School Psychology*, 1967, Vol. VI, No. 1, 2–7, with the permission of the Journal of School Psychology, Inc. and the authors. Brief biographies of the authors have been omitted.

[1]The preparation of this article was facilitated by Public Health Services grants MH 11975 and MH 02506, National Institute of Mental Health.

needs and feelings during the play sessions is stressed. The goals of the sessions are as follows: (a) to help the child change his perceptions or misperceptions of the parent's feelings, attitudes, and behavior; (b) to allow the child—mainly through the medium of play—to communicate thoughts, needs, and feelings to his parents that he had previously kept from awareness, thereby helping to resolve anxiety-producing internalized conflicts; and, finally, (c) to bring the child a greater feeling of self-respect, self-worth, and confidence.

Following the explanation of the rationale underlying the treatment, the parents observe the therapist demonstrating the technique in individual sessions with their children. Interspersed with these demonstrations over the course of training, the parents themselves conduct play sessions at the Clinic under the supervision of the therapist and under observation by the other group members. The parents thus have an opportunity to observe the therapist, be observed by other members of the group, and to observe the rest of the group and their children, all under similar play conditions.

After the training period, which lasts for about eight weeks, the parents begin play sessions at home. The specified time (initially 30 minutes, later 45 minutes) is set aside, and the parents engage the children in these play periods at home on a weekly basis. The parents continue their own group sessions throughout the course of the therapy, discussing the previous week's play periods with the therapist and the other group members. Also, from time to time throughout the therapy, sessions are again conducted at the Clinic under the group's observation.

In the beginning, the orientation of the parents' weekly group meetings, which continue for a year or more, is toward learning the method, and is so oriented partly in order to maximize motivation and minimize resistance. No pressure is put on the parent to apply the therapeutic principles outside of the sessions; he is allowed to make such generalizations when ready to do so. While technique remains a pertinent area for discussion for the duration of the parents' sessions, the emphasis may later move more in the direction of exploring the parents' own emotions, attitudes, and problems in relation to their children (especially as these are illuminated by their reactions and observations of the children's actions in the play sessions) and toward other significant persons in their lives.

Although filial therapy has so far been conducted only in the Psychological Clinic of Rutgers University and in the Hunterdon Medical Center, there is no reason apparent to the writers that it should not be tried out by qualified school psychologists in the public schools. Certainly the magnitude of the mental health problem as it makes itself apparent in the schools presents a challenge that invites, even demands, innovation. School psychologists are a group who, because of their present small numbers, can hope to become a truly effective force in bringing about change on a broad scale only if they drastically change (a) their number, (b) their role, by concentrating very heavily on research, and/or (c) their impact, by training and using others as extensions of themselves. The last of these alternatives is being focused upon here.

The small number of school psychologists, the heavy diagnostic load they typically must bear, and even the shortage of physical space, pose severe obstacles to the school psychologist who contemplates undertaking therapeutic action. Because of these obstacles, one-to-one therapeutic sessions on a broad scale obviously are impossible. Group methods offer some economy of time, space, and facility. Filial therapy offers the potential of still greater economy in these respects. It can be termed a "high leverage" treatment method—high leverage in this sense: by imparting to others who are significant figures in the life of the child those skills that are most relevant to a given type of problem, and supervising the application of those skills, the psychologist increases his power—he multiplies the force of his action. Through the use of such intermediaries, a given expenditure of the professional's time is multiplied in its application to a given individual, and/or affects more individuals. In filial therapy, in addition to having more time in therapeutically oriented play sessions with his parent than a school psychologist could give him, the child has the benefit of any generalizations the parent can make from what he has learned about therapeutic approaches to problems arising between them in everyday living. Considering the needs versus the resources in the mental health field in general, and the schools in particular, any technique offering such leverage should not go untried. Trial is especially indicated in additional settings when initial experience elsewhere suggests that a method is effective. This is the case with filial therapy, since experience to date with 12 groups in clinic settings has been quite encouraging.

An additional advantage that might be expected in adopting a filial therapy program in school would be the increased motivation of many parents to undertake and stay with a therapeutic program for their children. Frequently, parents' reactions to a recommendation for therapeutic action is negative. They tend to blame the school for the problems that the children are having. One of the reasons that this is so is that they have feelings of helplessness about their ability to help the child to adjust better in school. The schools themselves encounter frustration along these lines, since often they have problems in offering concrete suggestions to parents other than to say, "Go to the local child guidance clinic."

It has been our experience that parents who become involved in filial therapy generally maintain high motivation and a positive attitude toward treatment. Possibly one reason for this is the implicit and explicit attitude toward parents that is involved in the filial therapy approach that differs from attitudes implicit in traditional methods. Conventional approaches take the child away from the parent to treat him, with the underlying implication that the parent cannot deal with the child effectively, and that the child must thus be taken away from the parent for a certain period of time each week in order to be helped. Another implication is that not only must the child be taken away from the parent in order to be helped, but that the parents themselves have been directly responsible for the child's problems, and therefore also need to be treated. The filial therapy approach, on the other hand, explicitly states that the therapy is proceeding with the indispensable help of the parents; that the parents are necessary and directly involved in the treatment of their children. This factor may similarly enhance the motivation of parents to communicate more closely with schools, rather than to avoid schools and the anxieties involved with their children's having difficulties in school.

The hypotheses that are being put forth here are as follows: Filial therapy, with its clearly structured approach to helping the parents, will enable the school and the parents to help the children modify their behaviors, and the parents will thus see themselves as being a vital part of the child's treatment. This will presumably increase the parents' motivation to continue contact with the school, and will put the parents in a position to accept more readily discussions with school personnel, since, being collaborators with school personnel, they will be less likely to feel threatened by school authorities.

The preventative aspect of this approach is also noteworthy. Some "problem families" in the making may well be prevented from becoming problem families through this method. That is, a parent with a problem child, say, in the second or third grade is also encouraged to work with the younger children in filial therapy. This may eliminate or reduce some potential school problems that might develop in the younger children had the problems in the family gone unchecked, or had the family concentrated on the problems of only one child. It has been our experience that in some families the child who is initially referred for treatment is later thought by the parents to be less of a problem than another child in the family. The inclusion of all children within the age range appropriate for play techniques, therefore, can be conceived of as a corrective or preventative method in family mental health. Also, the group meetings always get around to discussing child rearing and attitudes toward children. These discussions modify parental viewpoints and help create better child-parent relationships for all children in the family.

In addition to the direct adoption of the filial therapy technique with groups of parents within a school setting, filial therapy principles have a possible application to teachers. The use of parents as therapeutic agents is based upon the belief in the efficacy of significant figures in the child's life in bringing about attitudinal and behavioral change. This means that, *given the skill to do so*, people who are already, by the nature of their everyday roles, important in a child's life are in a better position to bring about change than an outsider who is seen only an hour a week, even if that person is a trained therapist. Thus, *given the skill*, parents, who are the most important figures in a child's life, have more opportunity to make significant improvements in their child's mental health than anyone else. Similarly, teachers who are with children for a large part of the children's week—again, given the skill to do so—are also in a position to make very important contributions to a child's mental health.

Starting with the most direct application of filial therapy, it might be helpful to have some teachers learn the nondirective play techniques of filial therapy and give play sessions to one or two problem children in a class on some regular basis. Time and scheduling considerations would, of course, be a problem here, and would have to be worked out. The appropriately trained school psychologist would be able to teach and supervise groups of interested teachers in the same fashion as filial therapists do with parents. We would anticipate little difficulty in obtaining parental consent for extra time spent with teachers, as compared with the difficulty encountered in convincing parents to undertake and maintain clinic contacts. This would involve not only the increased ability of the special services team to reach many more children than they themselves could see directly, but would also enable the teachers to see continuing numbers of children in subsequent years. That is, one group of eight teachers might be seeing 16 children during one year. In subsequent years, they would be able to see similar numbers of children, and therefore increase the total number of children who are seen. Once these teachers had sufficiently mastered the attitudes and technique, supervision might be done on less than a weekly basis. After the first year, for example, supervision might be altered to an every other week schedule, and eventually to a monthly one, allowing the school psychologist to see many more groups of teachers.

Added to the direct help that the problem child would receive from the teacher is the importance of the therapeutic, empathic skills that would be conveyed to these teachers. The teachers will have been taught specific techniques for enhancing the child's self-concepts and for increasing their own ability to understand situations from a given child's viewpoint. The technique of clarifying children's feelings while at the same time firmly enforcing certain limits on behavior will have been another important technique practiced and learned. We would add here that other psychological principles and techniques appropriate for the classroom per se might be taught in addition to those having to do with the play sessions; for example, reinforcement principles, and techniques for applying them in the classroom setting.

It has been the authors' experience that in filial therapy, parents tend to generalize certain appropriate attitudes and methods from the limited situation of the play period to situations and events outside these sessions. If and when teachers do this, they will also tend to apply those principles that are relevant and appropriate to all their students, thus increasing the mental health milieu of the school. Although most teachers have encountered these principles in one form or another during their formal education, the presentation proposed here would be on a far deeper and more intensive level, with supervised practice; and thus, hopefully, would be more meaningful and realistic to them than their prior tutorial experiences.

As with parents, teachers' true willingness to communicate and cooperate with the school psychologist often leaves something to be desired. Again, as with parents, the training and use of teachers as direct therapeutic agents might increase their desire and ability to cooperate and communicate more fully with the psychologist. That is, teachers may become more favorably disposed to discuss freely some of the problems they have with children, and feel more directly involved with problem children they encounter, and have fewer feelings of frustration and helplessness. This might arise not only by virtue of the acquired skills themselves and the greater mutual understanding because of shared vocabulary and concepts, but also, most importantly, because of the implied trust and collaborative nature of the filial training process.

Another, less intensive application of filial training than that in which teachers work to help individual children would be to have teachers engaged in special, limited, individual sessions with children *only* for training purposes. The goal here would be limited to helping them to see how certain similar techniques could be employed in their day-to-day classroom interaction with children. Controlled empirical research in filial therapy has demonstrated that parents can learn the required role with their own children quite satisfactorily in the time allotted to training, and suggests that therapists who themselves have more experience in conducting client-centered play therapy with young children, and conducting filial groups, will be more effective in training parents (Stover, 1966).[2]

Qualitative observation of teachers now receiving similar training suggests that they are at least as adept in mastering the required role as are parents, despite the initial handicap of an almost "reflexive" teaching response to children.

Empirical research is currently under way exploring parent and child

[2]Naturally, any psychologist undertaking the role of filial therapist should himself first have studied, practiced, and received supervision in client-centered play therapy. Knowledge of group therapy principles would also be valuable.

personality variables, process variables, and outcome variables in filial therapy.

In summary, attempts have been made to spell out some of the ways in which approaches based on the assumptions and principles employed in filial therapy might be applied in a school setting. These attempts include a direct transfer of conventional filial therapy from the clinic to the school under the auspices of the school psychologist, using parents as therapeutic agents, the utilization of teachers as direct therapeutic agents, and the training of teachers to help them apply therapeutic principles in the classroom. The possible advantages of these applications in terms of increased parental and teacher motivation for helping children and collaborating with the psychologist were also discussed.

REFERENCES

Guerney, B., Jr. Filial therapy: description and rationale. *J. consult. Psychol.*, 1964, *28*, 304–310.

Fidler, J.W., Guerney, B., Jr., Andronico, M.P., & Guerney, Louise. Filial therapy as a logical extension of current trends in psychotherapy. Paper presented at Sixth International Congress of Psychotherapy. London, August, 1964.

Guerney, B.G., Jr., Guerney, Louise F., & Andronico, M.P. Filial therapy. *Yale Scientific Magazine*, March, 1966.

Stover, Lillian. Efficacy of training procedures for mothers in filial therapy. Unpublished doctoral dissertation, Rutgers, The State University, 1966.

Andronico, M.P., Fidler, J., Guerney, B., Jr., & Guerney, Louise. The combination of didactic and dynamic elements in filial therapy. *Internatl. J. Group Psychother.*, 1967, *17*, 10–17.

SUGGESTED ADDITIONAL READINGS

Allen, K. Eileen, Hart, Betty M., Buell, Joan S., Harris, Florence R., and Wolf, Montrose M. Effects of social reinforcement on isolate behavior of a nursery school child. *Child Development*, 1964, Vol. 35, 511–518. Also reprinted in Ullmann, Leonard P., and Krasner, Leonard (Eds.) *Case studies in behavior modification*, New York: Holt, Rinehart and Winston, Inc., 1966, 307–312.

Baer, Donald M., and Wolf, Montrose M. The reinforcement contingency in preschool and remedial education. Mimeographed document. Department of Human Development, Bureau of Child Research, University of Kansas, Lawrence, Kansas.

Becker, W. C., Madsen, Jr., C. H., Arnold, Carole R., and Thomas, D. R. The contingent use of teacher attention and praise in reducing classroom behavior problems. *Journal of Special Education*, 1967, Vol. 1, 287–307.

Hall, R. Vance, Lund, Diane, and Jackson, Delores. Effects of teacher attention on study behavior. *Journal of Applied Behavior Analysis*, 1968, Vol. 1, 1–12.

Hall, R. Vance, and Neubert, Marsha. Behavior changes in brain-injured children through social reinforcement. *Journal of Experimental Child Psychology*, in press.

Haring, Norris G. and Whelen, Richard J. Experimental methods in education and management. In Long, Nicholas J., Morse, William C., and Newman, Ruth G. (Eds.) *Conflict in the classroom.* Belmont, California: Wadsworth Publishing Co., Inc., 1965.

Harris, Florence R., Johnston, Margaret K., Kelley, C. Susan, and Wolf, Montrose M. Effects of positive social reinforcement on regressed crawling of a nursery school child. *Journal of Educational Psychology*, 1964, Vol. 55, No. 1, 35–41. Also reprinted in Ullmann, Leonard P., and Krasner, Leonard (Eds.) *Case studies in behavior modification.* New York: Holt, Rinehart and Winston, Inc., 1966, 313–319.

Hart, Betty M., Allen, K. Eileen, Buell, Joan S., Harris, Florence R., and Wolf, Montrose M. Effects of social reinforcement on operant crying. *Journal of Experimental Child Psychology*, 1964, Vol. 1, 145–153. Also reprinted in Ullmann, Leonard P., and Krasner, Leonard (Eds.) *Case studies in behavior modification.* New York: Holt, Rinehart and Winston, Inc., 1965, 320–325.

Lippett, Robert, Fox, Robert, and Schmuck, Richard. Innovating classroom practices to support achievement motivation and ego development. In Bower, Eli M., and Hollister, William C. (Eds.) *Behavioral science frontiers in education.* New York: John Wiley & Sons, Inc., 1967, Pp. 322–344.

Love, Leonore R. Information feedback as a method of clinical intervention. Paper presented at symposium, "Communication patterns in the family and the school as related to child adjustment," by Jacques Kaswan, Daphne Bugental, Armand A. Alkire, and Leonore R. Love, University of California, Los Angeles, at the Annual Meeting of the American Psychological Association, New York, Sept., 1966.

Margolin, Joseph B. An experimental approach to reading therapy. In Long, Nicholas J., Morse, William C., and Newman, Ruth G. (Eds.) *Conflict in the classroom.* Belmont, California: Wadsworth Publishing Co., Inc., 1965.

Patterson, Gerald R. A learning theory approach to the treatment of the school phobic child. In Ullmann, Leonard P., and Krasner, Leonard (Eds.) *Case studies in behavior modification.* New York: Holt, Rinehart and Winston, Inc., 1965. Pp. 279–285.

Phillips, E. Lakin. The use of the teacher as an adjunct therapist in child guidance. *Psychiatry: Journal for the Study of Interpersonal Processes,* 1957, Vol. 20, No. 4, 407–410.

Phillips, E. Lakin. Behavior change among children through use of adults as change agents. Paper presented at the Annual Meeting of the Eastern Psychological Association, Boston, 1967.

Thomas, Don R., Becker, Wesley C., and Armstrong, Marianne. Production and elimination of disruptive classroom behavior by systematically varying teacher's behavior. *Journal of Applied Behavior Analysis*, 1968, Vol. 1, 35–45.

Wolf, Montrose, Birnbrauer, Jay, Lawler, Julia, and Williams, Thomas. The operant extinction, reinstatement and re-extinction of vomiting behavior in a retarded child. Unpublished manuscript.

Wolf, Montrose M., Giles, David K., and Hall, R. Vance. Experiments with token reinforcement in a remedial classroom. Unpublished manuscript.

PART 6

Parents as Therapeutic Agents

Introduction

THE view was presented in the Introduction that the increased acceptance of treatment techniques which are relatively ahistorical and straightforward, as opposed to the genetic and complex methodology of psychoanalysis, has been a major underlying factor in the current movement toward the use of therapeutic agents. Nevertheless, if it seemed feasible or necessary for particular reasons, psychoanalysts also have used parents as psychotherapeutic agents.[1] In fact, as is so often the case in the field of psychotherapy, the trailblazer was none other than Sigmund Freud. He was the first to conduct psychotherapy almost entirely through the use of a therapeutic agent. The agent was the father of Little Hans, the boy whose treatment was reported in 1909 in the very famous "Analysis of a Phobia of a Five-Year-Old Boy" (1959). Freud indicated in that report that the father was responsible for the actual treatment, under his direction, and that the special nature of the relationship between father and son, and the father's special knowledge of the child, were "indispensable" to the treatment.

Freud's report has not been included here for several reasons. It is already widely known and widely available in collections of Freud's works. But perhaps more important is the fact that the emphasis in psychoanalytic case reports, including the one on Little Hans, tends to be on under-

[1]All references cited here may be found in the Suggested Additional Readings list at the end of this part.

standing the *psychodynamics* of the particular case, and, where possible, drawing theoretical conclusions or generalizations from these psychodynamics. Such reports, relative to their length, offer very little detailed and generalizable information about the *treatment process* itself. With a limited amount of space, such a report, in competition with other possible selections, would not sufficiently implement the treatment-oriented purpose of this book. The same consideration also led to the omission of some other extremely interesting reports as to the use of parents in the treatment of young children by orthodox psychoanalysts and analytically-oriented psychotherapists. It seems worthwhile at this point to review briefly these psychoanalytic reports even though they are not included in this book.

The role which the parent is asked to play by analytic therapists varies from a very ambiguous one, as a generally passive observer of the treatment process conducted in the therapist's office, to one in which—as in the case of Little Hans—the parent is himself solely responsible for carrying out treatment under the instructions of the analyst.

Several psychoanalytic reports describe the beneficial effects for the child of the mother's presence during treatment, even though the mother primarily plays the role of observer, and is apparently only occasionally called upon to interact directly with the child being treated. Hedy Schwarz (1950) in "The Mother in the Consulting Room" cites several advantages afforded by this approach, which she used with two three-and-a-half-year-old children. She writes:

> I had invited the mother . . . only to help the mother make up her mind about Mary's having treatment. Only as the treatment went on did I realize the dynamic value of this miniature group formation: how the mother was influenced indirectly by my analytic approach, which so patently respected the child's self-expression; how her patient interest as she watched the child's sessions, so different from her usual haste and bustle, had in itself therapeutic effect on the child; and how I for my part learned to formulate my interpretations more clearly so that they could be understood by both mother and child.
>
> It is one of the great advantages of mother and child being together in the treatment that in the child's mind there is no clash of loyalty towards analyst and mother and that the child patient does not, as so often happens in child analysis, need to feel guilty for trusting the analyst or confiding his secrets to her. Neither can the child have the impression that there are two sets of standards, one which the mother approves, one which the analyst approves. . . . . For the young child the physical presence of the mother during the treatment is a constant and much stronger proof of her tolerance and understanding of the analytic work than any verbal declaration.
>
> . . . At this stage of the child's behavioral development, the mother can absorb a great deal of knowledge about the child's libidinal as well as the aggressive impulses, even though they are directed against her. . . . The mother of a young child is so grateful for being allowed to take part in her child's treatment and so relieved that the child is not taken from her, that she forms to

> the analyst a very positive relationship which later on weathers many restrictions or frustrations posed by the child's needs (p. 346f).*

Among the other advantages to this procedure described by Schwarz are that it tends to allow the parent's expectations to be geared more realistically to the treatment process, and that the knowledge gained by the parent is helpful not only to the child in treatment, but to other children in the family as well.

Schwarz approached the idea of including the parent in the treatment process with trepidation, and was then pleased to find how many advantages it afforded. This is typical of psychoanalysts' reports on this subject. It is also typical that they see these advantages as limited to very young children, without presenting reasons as to why the advantages should be restricted only to this age group.

Erna Furman, in her "Treatment of Under-Fives by Way of Their Parents," speaks of a "uniquely" close bond between mothers and young children, which makes the mother capable of "recognizing many of her unconscious feelings, thoughts, and defenses, and of using them with insight to help him" (p. 251). Granted, children become progressively more independent from the time they begin school—but it seems unlikely that these capacities, or the benefits to their inclusion in the child's treatment process, should be entirely lost when the child reaches six, or even sixteen. Furman describes her approach as having been tried previously on children who are generally progressing adequately for their age and whose disturbance is between themselves and their environment, or, if partly internalized, was of recent origin or not rigidly defended. She contrasts her approach to direct educational methods and to reliance solely upon treating the mother to bring about changes for the child, indicating that her approach aims at keeping the focus of the work centered on the child, sometimes using direct advice, but mainly relying upon the " . . . child's material, and the mother's unconscious closeness to it, in order to give her some insight into herself as a mother and into the nature of her interaction with the child" (p. 251).**

Harold Kolansky (1960) is another psychoanalyst who has incorporated the parent into the treatment process, bringing the mother into the playroom with her daughter on a daily basis. He discusses the issue as follows: "In the intensive treatment of very young children it is extremely important to enlist the active participation of the mother." He quotes

*Quotations from Hedy Schwarz, The Mother in the Consulting Room: Notes on the Psychoanalytic Treatment of Two Young Children, *The Psychoanalytic Study of the Child*, Vol. 5, Copyright 1950 by International Universities Press, Inc., are used with their permission.

**Quotations from Erna Furman, Treatment of Under-fives by Way of Their Parents, *The Psychoanalytic Study of the Child*, Vol. XII, Copyright 1957 by International Universities Press, Inc., are used with their permission.

Burlingham's (1935) statement that "To maintain the sympathy and cooperation of the parents throughout the entire analysis of a child is a difficult and trying problem; and yet if one does not succeed in this, the analysis moves inevitably to an abrupt and premature interruption." Kolansky continues, "It seems to me that the mother's presence in the room had a doubly beneficial impact. On the one hand, as already stated, it gave full support to the treatment in the child's eyes. On the other hand, it had a direct impact on the mother who was visibly moved when she witnessed the emergence of the child's unconscious fears and wishes. Being faced with the child's unconscious motivations and conflicts caused her to become aware of some of her own conflicts, which she then attempted to handle differently. Therefore, her presence in the therapy room had a direct beneficial effect both on the child and on the mother" (p. 283f).*

As Kolansky points out, Berta Bornstein (1935) included the child's mother in treatment, and Steff Bornstein (1935), treating a three-year-old, also drew the mother into the analytic sessions. Kenneth Gordon, Jr. (1963) and Paula Elkisch (1935) are other psychoanalytically oriented therapists who have treated children in a parent's presence. Both reported treatments of very young children in autistic-symbiotic relationships with their parents. Gordon, whose general emphasis is on the appropriateness of this type of treatment for children with this particular type of disorder, writes:

> The most striking phenomenon observed during simultaneous treatment is the emotional impact of insight manifested by amazement on the part of the mother. This could be called an "insight jolt" which is most dramatic and appears to have a profound therapeutic force . . . . Once mother and child become aware of what is going on, they usually bring constructive efforts into play to create a better living relationship (p. 720f).

Elkisch distinguishes her inclusion of the parent from the work of Schwarz on the grounds that she, Elkisch, treated the *relationship* between mother and child, whereas Schwarz "merely had the mother present" (p. 109). She also says, however, that "During our sessions of three, I tacitly focused all my attention on the child" (p. 111). This apparent contradiction may be partly resolved by the fact that Elkisch: (a) relied upon imitation, or what would now be called "modeling," and (b) relied upon the changed behavior of the child in the play situation—reciprocal to the mother's changed behavior—bringing about further relationship changes. She says, "It seems possible in certain cases to establish a treatment situation in which the mother may be exposed to the experience of forming a different relationship to her child through the presence and emotional

*Quotations from Harold Kolansky, Treatment of a Three-year-old Girl's Severe Infantile Neurosis: Stammering and Insect Phobia, *The Psychoanalytic Study of the Child*, Vol. XV, Copyright 1960 by International Universities Press, Inc., are used with their permission.

participation of a therapist; at the same time, the child can be made to react in a new way to the changed and changing relationship of the mother toward him" (p. 109f).

The reliance upon the mother modeling herself after the therapist is further seen in Elkisch's comments on what she regards as the necessity of conducting individual sessions with the mother preceding the joint mother-child sessions. She says that after several of these sessions, " . . . it could be assumed that Mrs. L. would soon want to imitate my handling of the child—and not merely 'imitate,' but want to participate in my unconditional acceptance of George, to which she was exposed. . . ." (Another interesting parallel to current behavioral conceptions of treatment is the fact that, like mothers of children in some types of behavior therapy, George's mother kept careful records of his "speaking performance," noting and counting the words he spoke at home.)

It is apparent from this review that there are no inviolable prohibitions in psychoanalytic theory to prevent the analyst from incorporating the parents of young children directly in the treatment process.

In addition to the analytic tradition, examples may be found among those belonging to a client-centered orientation and those employing a behavior therapy approach. The former approach is represented by Louise and Bernard Guerney, Jr. (1961), who report on the successful treatment of a severely disturbed nine-year-old girl with a procedure wherein the mother's presence during the child's client-centered play therapy sessions was a very important aspect of the treatment. Straughan (1964) followed a similar procedure in treating an eight-year-old girl who was friendless, unhappy, and prone to lie. He explains his positive results in terms of learning theory. Thus, adherents of three broad major theoretical orientations in the field of psychotherapy—psychoanalytic, client-centered, and behavioristic—have all reported successful experiences with the procedure of allowing the parent to enter the therapeutic process as a relatively passive observer.

There are several studies which go a step further than simply having the parent present as an observer. Such studies are not included in this section because the techniques described do not go so far as to directly teach general therapeutic principles, provide training in role behaviors appropriate to those principles, nor directly encourage their application by the parent under supervision. They will be reviewed, however, because these techniques appear useful in their own right, and could provide an experiential base for therapists who may wish to approach the use of parents as therapeutic agents in an attenuated or gradual manner.

Ruben and Thomas, in their article, "Home Training of Instincts and Emotions" (1947), discuss how they treat certain problems of young children through interpreting the nature and meaning of the child's difficulties to the mothers and have them make the appropriate psychoanalytic interpretations. They write, "Instead . . . of directing our attention to possible faulty approaches which the parent may have made because of her own difficulties, we prefer to attempt to show her the child as an entity with a personality of his own . . . thus improving her relationship to him" (p. 124). They state that their experiences along these lines with the problems of 130 children, including feeding and sleeping disturbances, temper, severe jealousy, and stuttering, have shown that "the mother can frequently accept interpretations about the child's instinctual wishes which she would have difficulty in accepting about her own and that sometimes, having accepted them for the child, she is more able to accept them for herself" (p. 124). They further find that, "The mother usually answers with a sigh of relief our suggestion that she should herself convey to the child the knowledge and insight we provide. In this way, she is imbued with confidence in her own educational ability, and at the same time an atmosphere of mutual appreciation is established between herself and the advisers" (p. 123).

In "A Short Communication on a Traumatic Episode in a Child of Two Years and Seven Months," Elizabeth Gero-Heymann (1955) reports on the psychoanalytic treatment of the child's phobia by having the mother make up songs and draw pictures to elicit and show acceptance of the child's anger toward her mother. Lawrence Kubie (1937) has reported on the resolution of a traffic phobia through conversations between a father and son.

Rangell (1952) has reported on the successful psychoanalytic treatment of nightmares in a seven-year-old boy. Describing the case, he says, "Clearly, there was a neurotic symptom present which by its content, intensity and direction demanded analytic treatment . . . referral to a child analyst was in order. This simple move, however, as is so often the case, was ruled out promptly for economical reasons. Treatment in a clinic was the next logical thought, but previous experience made me dubious about the prospect of securing adequate analytically-oriented treatment this way" (p. 364). Rangell therefore decided to treat the boy solely through his parents, whom he knew personally—instructing them by letter. In discussing the use of parents as therapeutic agents Rangell wrote, "The reversal of the pathologic process, and the redirecting of instinctual energy does not take place via the intervention of a new object, with a new type of relationship which is then transferred back to the parents, but rather by a direct alteration in the attitudes and responses of the very persons who provoked the original repression and displacements. The child is subjected to a new and therapeutic experience in living within the familiar arena of his own life, '*in situ*,' so to speak, or '*in vivo*,' rather than to a comparatively artificial and laboratory-like analytic relationship" (p. 387).*

It was noted in the main introduction that the use of significant others, and especially symbionts, may become an important component in mental health's "third revolution," which involves a movement toward public health practices. It is therefore highly interesting to note that "the first recorded case of nationally provided psychoanalytic therapy" was that of a four-and-a-half-year-old child whose treatment was carried out mainly by his mother. The case is presented at length by Augusta Bonnard (1950) in "The Mother as Therapist, in a Case of Obsessional Neurosis." She concluded that when feasible, analytic treatment by the parent affords significant advantages: great economy of the analyst's, and the child's time, and the fact that the parent also learns truths, the spreading effects of which are invaluable. She points out that when a parent acts as the therapist, the child receives twenty-four-hour help.

The client-centered theoretical orientation also is represented among those reports which describe the use of parents as therapeutic agents. Natalie Rogers Fuchs (1957) under the guidance of her father, Dr. Carl Rogers himself, acted a psychotherapeutic role in successfully treating a serious problem of constipation in her one-and-a-half-year-old daughter. In England, B. M. Pechey (1955) reported on seven cases ranging from 3 to 10 years of age, using the following technique: After a few nondirective interviews with a mother, the therapist observed the parent playing with her child in a playroom, under instructions to play just as she would at home. After each session, the therapist discussed what he observed with the mother. "The interview is directed naturally to those areas of the play which reveal interpersonal tensions, over-acceptance, excessive demands, etc., and a full, free ventilation of ideas and feelings follows." After two to twelve such observations and discussions, the cases were terminated generally with success. He also writes that "since these original seven cases were treated, about 100 children in all have had one or more sessions of this type, and the value of the method has been confirmed." The technique is somewhat similar to Guerney's filial therapy when filial therapy is conducted on an individual rather than a group basis. (Individual filial therapy is sometimes conducted in the process of training therapists in the technique.) There also exists a similarity to what takes place during the group sessions in filial therapy when parents and therapist discuss the play sessions conducted at home or in the clinic's observation facilities. The chief difference, aside from the group versus individual procedures, is that in Pechey's technique, the play sessions are

*Quotations from Leo Rangell, A Treatment of Nightmares in a Seven-year-old Boy, *The Psychoanalytic Study of the Child*, Vol. V, Copyright 1950 by International Universities Press, Inc., are used with their permission.

used more as a diagnostic tool to provide information useful to therapist and parent; while in filial therapy the parent is asked to play a specified type of therapeutic role and given instructions and supervision in doing so; he actually is acting as a therapeutic agent.

This is also the nature of a major difference between the types of therapy presented in this section and family therapy. Before elaborating on this difference, we will mention the similarities. One is that the methods described in this part and family therapy approaches both attempt to deal directly with *relationship* factors in addition to intrapsychic phenomena. Another similarity is that actual examples of important relationship phenomena occur in the natural course of treatment. These interactions are observed by the therapist and parents alike, and serve as meaningful raw material for examination. As earlier suggested, the major difference is that in family therapy the family members—be they children or parents—are not given planned, specific, supervised instructions and practices in behaving toward one another in more helpful ways than is habitual for them. Instead, the way they *do* behave is analyzed and discussed and feelings are expressed and explored, and out of this, plus an identification and imitation of the model provided by the therapist, it is expected that new and more constructive relationship patterns will emerge. Operational formulation of more desirable patterns of interaction, and their deliberate rehearsal and practice under the observation and supervision of the therapist generally are absent.

There appears to be no inherent reason that this should continue to be so. It is hoped that studies will emerge in the near future which explore the feasibility of family members, as a group, acting as therapeutic agents for one another. As of now, it is only possible to call the reader's attention to the references under Suggested Additional Readings which may represent significant steps in this direction.

Rachel A. Levine (1964), in the approach she describes in "Treatment in the Home," places somewhat greater emphasis than is often found in reports on family therapy on the therapist as a demonstrator of technique employed with children, which the parents are encouraged to adopt in their own interaction with the children. In the "Multiple Impact Therapy with Families" (MacGregor, *et al.*, 1964), a great deal of reliance is placed on the continuation of therapeutic patterns after termination of the brief but very intensive type of family therapy they employ. The Information Feedback technique (Love, 1966) involves the kind of careful study and comparison of specific behavioral characteristics of family members which could provide a basis for practiced role changes by family members vis-a-vis one another. Finally, Salvador Minuchin, in "Conflict Resolution Therapy" (1965), actually has begun to make some direct use of family members as therapeutic agents. When using this method, he selects one member to observe other family members interacting through a one-way screen, and then sends him back into the family with specific instructions to try to change an ongoing interaction pattern.

In the selections which *have* been included in this part, one or more of the following apply: the parents receive instruction in the general principle underlying the therapeutic interactions they are asked to undertake with their children; they are given specific examples of the kinds of interpersonal behaviors expected of them, sometimes through actual demonstrations, and given an opportunity to discuss the principles and examples; they are asked to rehearse or practice the required behaviors; and they are given feedback or supervision in their attempts to put into practice what they have learned.

As explained in the main introduction, the two psychotherapeutic orientations most likely to foster such an approach are found in Skinner's work in reinforcement and in Carl Rogers' client-centered therapy. In preference to commenting on the specific selections, I will limit my comments in this introduction to these two general orientations as they apply to the use of parents as therapeutic agents.

A major difference between them stems largely from an orientation on the part of the behavior therapist to pay almost exclusive attention to behavior, as opposed to making inferences about feelings; while the Rogerian is inclined, conversely, to pay attention almost exclusively to feeling rather than overt behavior. The behavior therapist's motto might be, "If feelings are to be altered (that is, if they are even worth discussing), it will follow upon alteration of one's behavior." Whereas the Rogerian's might be, "If behavior is to be altered (that is, if it is even worth discussing), it will follow upon altered perception of one's feelings."

That is the impression sometimes conveyed in publications, in which authors strive for brevity and maximal theoretical consistency. In practice, however, in the present writer's observations, most client-centered therapists are also very much concerned with the behavior of their clients when it comes to evaluating the effectiveness of their efforts, and most behavior therapists are quite unlike "social reinforcement machines," being sensitive and concerned about the feelings of the people whom they treat.

Another difference between the behavior modification and client-centered orientations seems to stem from the fact that the behavior modification therapist views the parent as his client, while the client-centered therapist working with a child views both child and parent as clients. Walder (1966) says, "We view the parent as our subject (or client); therefore we try to help the parent with *his* client, the child" (p. 5). The emphasis is on helping the parent to train the child to suit the *parent's* needs. In the client-centered approach, as represented by filial therapy, a great deal of effort is expended in trying to get the parent to fulfill certain needs of the *child*, whether or not the parent is aware that the child was not getting those needs fulfilled when the parent first brought him for treatment.

But it is all too easy to exaggerate differences and forget that varying methods can often accomplish the same ends, even if their avowed goals are different. Thus, in filial therapy, as the parent begins to understand and show acceptance of the child's feelings and viewpoint, the child becomes more interested in pleasing the parent and winning his praise—and the filial therapist need not refrain from pointing out the ways and means by which praise reinforces behavior and may be used constructively in everyday living. Indeed, the therapist has already pointed out the effects of praise as a reinforcer in asking the parent to *avoid* it in the *playroom*. In reinforcement therapy, as the child is trained to become less obnoxious to the parent, the parent becomes more interested in pleasing and understanding the child, and it does not seem unreasonable for the behavior therapist to encourage and enhance the parent's aptitude for such empathic behavior.

In short, to use a currently popular phrase, the reader is urged not to get too hung-up in these differences, but to view the alternate approaches as potentially compatible in large measure. After all, do behavior therapists never try to act empathically toward their own children? Do client-centered therapists refrain from praising the behaviors of their own children which meet their approval? The reader should continue to evaluate research evidence, and to consider each method in terms of his own philosophical and theoretical views; his own personality; the particular needs, strengths, and weaknesses of the general population with which he works; and most of all, of the individual case or family he is attempting to help.

In closing this introduction, it seems appropriate also to point to a common goal shared by many of those working with parents as therapeutic agents regardless of theoretical orientation: the education and training of parents as a way of *preventing* psychological difficulties, not merely alleviating them once they arise. In a paper on utilizing parents as therapeutic agents (1966), I pointed out that a major advantage of doing so is that it helps one acquire the type of information and knowledge that will be necessary to launch an effective program aimed at primary prevention of emotional disturbances; and Walder has said, "We sometimes wonder what the effect on society would be if all parents-to-be had learned the principle of behavior modification before the children arrived" (1966, p. 6).

Behavior Therapy in the Home: Amelioration of Problem Parent-Child Relations with the Parent in a Therapeutic Role[1]

ROBERT P. HAWKINS
ROBERT F. PETERSON
EDDA SCHWEID
SIDNEY W. BIJOU

The experimental modification of a problem mother-child relationship is described. The child, a four-year-old boy, was extremely difficult to manage and control. Treatment was carried out in the home with the mother as the therapist. The child's objectionable behaviors were observed to change in frequency and topography as a consequence of the treatment and appeared to generalize from the experimental hour to the remaining hours of the day. Nearly a month later, these changes were still in evidence.

In recognition of the important part parents play in the behavioral (or personality) development of the child, various agencies dealing with child behavior problems have often utilized techniques whose goal is to modify parent-child relationships. For example, the parent of a child who exhibits deviant behavior may, himself, be given psychotherapy in order to change his behavior toward the child. Alternatively, the parent may merely be given advice as to how he should react differently toward the child, or both parent and child may be given psychotherapy and/or counseling. The technique employed is likely to depend on the type of therapist consulted and the therapist's theoretical orientation. A general discussion of therapeutic techniques with children has been presented by Bijou and Sloane (in press).

Reprinted with permission from *Journal of Experimental Child Psychology*, 1966, Vol. 4, No. 1, 99–107, Copyright 1966 by Academic Press Inc., and with the permission of the authors.

[1]This research was supported in part by a grant from National Institute of Mental Health (MH-2232), U. S. Public Health Service.

Traditional types of therapy have a number of deficiencies. First, the child's behavior is seldom observed by the therapist, leaving definition of the problem and description of the child's behavior totally up to the parent. Second, the behavior of the parent toward the child is seldom observed. Thus considerable reliance is placed on the verbal report of the parent and child and on the imagination of the therapist. Third, when "practical suggestions" are made by the therapist, they may be so general or technical that it is difficult for the parent to translate them into specific behavior. Fourth, since no objective record is kept of behavior changes over short intervals (e.g., minutes, hours, days) it is difficult to judge the effectiveness of the treatment.

Wahler, Winkel, Peterson, and Morrison (1965) have developed a technique for effectively altering mother-child relationships in a laboratory setting, with objective records being kept of the behavior of both mother and child. The present study was an investigation of the feasibility of treatment in the natural setting where the child's behavior problem appeared—the home. As in the Wahler *et al.* studies, the mother served as the therapeutic agent. She received explicit instructions on when and how to interact with the child. The behaviors of both the mother and the child were directly observed and recorded.

METHOD

Subject

The child in this study was a four-year-old boy, Peter S. He is the third of four children in a middle-class family. Peter had been brought to a university clinic because he was extremely difficult to manage and control. His mother stated she was helpless in dealing with his frequent tantrums and disobedience. Peter often kicked objects or people, removed or tore his clothing, called people rude names, annoyed his younger sister, made a variety of threats, hit himself, and became very angry at the slightest frustration. He demanded attention almost constantly, and seldom cooperated with Mrs. S. In addition, Peter was not toilet trained and did not always speak clearly. Neither of these latter problems was dealt with in the study.

Peter had been evaluated at a clinic for retarded children when he was three years old and again when he was four and a half. His scores on the Stanford Binet, form L-M were 72 and 80, respectively. He was described as having borderline intelligence, as being hyperactive, and possibly brain-damaged.

Procedure

The experimenters (*Es*), observing the mother and child in the home, noted that many of Peter's undesirable behaviors appeared to be maintained by attention from his mother. When Peter behaved objectionably, she would often try to explain why he sould not act thus; or she would try to interest him in some new activity by offering toys or food. (This "distraction" method is often put forth by teachers as a preferred technique for dealing with undesirable behavior. Behavior theory suggests, however, that while distraction may be temporarily effective in dealing with such behaviors, repeated employment of such a procedure may increase the frequency of the unwanted set of responses.) Peter was occasionally punished by the withdrawal of a misused toy or other object, but he was often able to persuade his mother to return the item almost immediately. He was also punished by being placed on a high-chair and forced to remain there for short periods. Considerable tantrum behavior usually followed such disciplinary measures and was quite effective in maintaining mother's attention, largely in the form of verbal persuasion or argument.

Prior to the study, the child's difficulties were discussed thoroughly with his mother. She was told that therapy might take several months, was of an experimental nature, and would require her participation. She readily agreed to cooperate.

Treatment consisted of two to three sessions per week, each approximately 1 hour in length. Peter's mother was instructed to go about her usual activities during these sessions. His younger sister was allowed to be present and to interact with him in her usual way. Peter was allowed to move freely through the main part of the house—the recreation room, laundry room, dinette, kitchen, and living room—because the wide openings between these areas made it possible to observe his activity with a minimum of movement on the *Es*' part. The *Es* never responded to Peter or his sister. When the children asked questions about them or spoke to them, they were told by the mother to "leave them alone; they are doing their work."

Initial observations showed that the following responses made up a large portion of Peter's repertory of undesirable behavior: (1) biting his shirt or arm, (2) sticking out his tongue, (3) kicking or hitting himself, others or objects, (4) calling someone or something a derogatory name, (5) removing or threatening to remove his clothing, (6) saying "No!" loudly and vigorously, (7) threatening to damage objects or persons, (8) throwing objects, and (9) pushing his sister. These nine responses were collectively termed "Objectionable behavior" (O behavior), and their frequency of occurrence was measured by recording, for each successive 10-second interval, whether or not an O behavior occurred. This same method was used to obtain a record of the frequency of all verbalizations Peter directed to his mother and of the frequency of her verbalizations to him.

In order to assess interobserver reliability, two *E*s were employed as observers on eight occasions and three *E*s on one occasion. Since it was sometimes possible for an observer to detect when another observer had scored a response, the obtained reliability scores may be overestimated. For every session of observation each observer obtained total frequency scores for the O behaviors, the child's verbalizations, and the mother's verbalizations. When two observers were employed, proportion of agreement, in any one of these three classes of behavior, was calculated by dividing the smaller score by the larger. When three observers were employed, the three proportions for a class of behavior were averaged to obtain mean proportion of agreement. Agreement on O behaviors ranged from .70 to 1.00, with a mean of .88. Agreement on mother's verbalizations to Peter ranged from .82 to .98, with a mean of .94. Agreement on Peter's verbalizations to his mother ranged from .90 to .99, with a mean of .96.

Treatment was divided into five stages: the first baseline period, the first experimental period, the second baseline period, the second experimental period, and a follow-up period.

First Baseline Period. During this period Peter and his mother interacted in their usual way. Their behaviors were recorded by the *Es* and after some 16 sessions, when an adequate estimate of the pretreatment rate of O behavior had been obtained, the next stage was begun.

First Experimental Period. Prior to the beginning of this period, the mother was informed of the nine objectionable behaviors which would be treated. She was shown three gestural signals which indicated how she was to behave toward Peter. Signal "A" meant she was to tell Peter to stop whatever O behavior he was emitting. Signal "B" indicated she was immediately to place Peter in his room and lock the door. When signal "C" was presented, she was to give him attention, praise, and affectionate physical contact. Thus, every time Peter emitted an O behavior, Mrs. S. was either signaled to tell him to stop or to put him in his room. On the first occurrence of a particular O behavior during the experimental session, Mrs. S. was merely signaled to tell Peter to stop; but if he repeated the same response at any subsequent time during that session, she was signaled to place him in his room. (This isolation period may be viewed as a period of "time out" from stimuli associated with positive reinforcement. See Ferster and Appel, 1961.) Occasionally, when *E* noticed that Peter was playing in a particularly desirable way, Signal "C" was given and his mother responded to him with attention and approval. Mrs. S. was asked to restrict the application of these new behavioral contingencies to the experimental hour. She was told to behave in her usual way at all other times.

The period of Peter's isolation was not counted as part of the experimental hour, so each session consisted of 1 hour of observation in the main living area of the house. When placed in his room, Peter was required to remain there a minimum of 5 minutes. In addition, he had to be quiet for a short period before he was allowed to come out (a technique employed by Wolf, Risley, and Mees, 1964). Since all objects likely to serve as playthings had been previously removed from the room, he had little opportunity to amuse himself. Neither Mrs. S. nor Peter's sister interacted with him during "time out." On two occasions, however, it was necessary to deviate from his procedure. These deviations occurred when Peter broke windows in his room and called out that he had cut himself. The first time Mrs. S. entered his room, swept up the glass, reprimanded him for breaking the window, noted the (minor) nature of his injury and left. The second time she bandaged a small cut and left immediately. Peter broke a window on one other occasion but since no injury was apparent, the act was ignored.

Second Baseline Period. When, after six experimental sessions, the frequency of O behaviors appeared stable, contingencies were returned to those of the earlier baseline period. Mrs. S. was told to interact with Peter just as she had during previous (nonexperimental) observation sessions. This second baseline period consisted of 14 sessions.

Second Experimental Period. After the second baseline period, the experimental procedure was reintroduced and continued for six sessions. Contingencies were identical to those of the first experimental period except that special attention for desirable play was excluded, save one accidental instance.

Follow-up. For 24 days after the second experimental period there was no contact between the *E*s and the S. family. Mrs. S. was given complete freedom to use any techniques with Peter that she felt were warranted, including "time out," but she was given no specific instructions. After this 24-day interval (whose length was limited by the impending departure of one *E*) a three-session, posttreatment check was made to determine whether the improvements effected during treatment were still evident. These 1 hour follow-up sessions were comparable to earlier baseline periods in that Mrs. S. was instructed to behave in her usual manner toward Peter.

RESULTS AND DISCUSSION

The frequency of Peter's O behaviors in each treatment condition is shown in Fig. 1. Asterisks mark sessions in which observer reliability was assessed. These nine reliability sessions are plotted in terms of the mean of the frequencies obtained by the different observers. During the first baseline period, the rate of O behavior varied between 18 and 113 per session. A sharp decrease occurred in the first experimental period; the rate ranged from one to eight per session. In the course of this period, Peter was isolated a total of four times, twice in session 17, once in session 18, and again in session 22. He received special attention twice in session 17, six times in session 18, and once each in sessions 20 and 21.

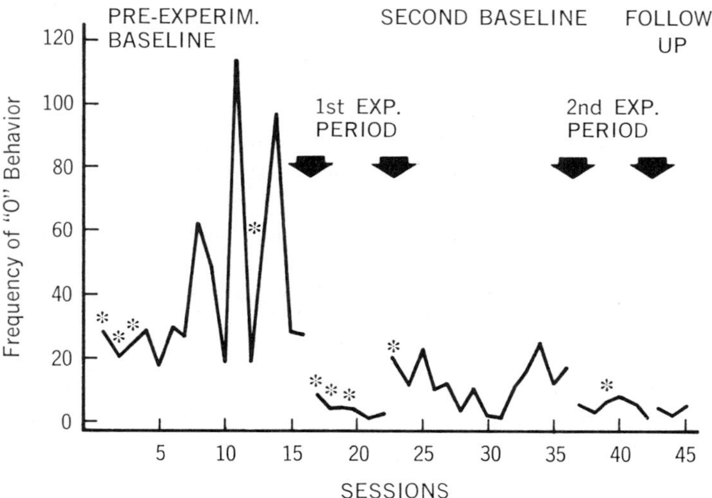

Fig. 1. Number of 10-second intervals, per 1-hour session, in which O behavior occurred. Asterisks indicate sessions in which reliability was tested.

During the second baseline period, the rate of O behaviors varied between 2 and 24 per session. Although this was an increase over the previous experimental period, the frequency of response did not match that of the first baseline period. This failure to return to earlier levels may have occurred for several reasons. For example, midway through the second baseline, Mrs. S. reported considerable difficulty in responding to Peter as she had during the first baseline period. She stated she felt more "sure of herself" and could not remember how she had previously behaved toward her son. It was apparent that Mrs. S. now gave Peter firm commands when she wanted him to do something and did not "give in" after denying him a request. The *E*s also noted that Peter was receiving more affection from his mother. This increased affection, however, seemed to be due to a change in Peter's behavior rather than his mother's, since Peter had recently begun to approach her with affectionate overtures.

The rate of O behaviors in the second experimental period was comparable to that of the first experimental period, from two to eight per session. Special attention was (accidentally) given once in session 38.

Data obtained during the Follow-up period show that Peter's O behaviors remained low in rate after the passage of a 24-day interval. Mrs. S. reported that Peter was well behaved and much less demanding than he had previously been. She stated that she had been using the time out procedure approximately once a week. (It was the *E*'s impression that not only the quantity but also the quality, i.e., topography, of O behaviors had changed. As early as the second baseline period it had been observed that O behaviors frequently lacked components which had been present earlier, such as facial expressions, voice qualities, and vigor or movement that typically constitute "angry" behavior.) Thus, it would appear that not only were the treatment effects maintained in the absence of the *E*s and the experimental procedures, but they had generalized from the treatment hour to the remaining hours of the day. These developments were being maintained by the use of occasional isolation (contingent, of course, on the occurrence of an Objectionable behavior) and other alterations in the mother's behavior.

Evidence that Mrs. S.'s behavior toward her child did change during the course of treatment is presented in Fig. 2 which shows the verbal interaction between Peter and his mother. It can be seen by comparing Figs. 1 and 2 that the frequency of O behavior and the frequency of the mother's verbalizations to Peter sometimes covaried. A positive correlation is particularly evident during the second baseline period; and a negative correlation during the follow-up. The correlation between O behavior and mother verbalization was determined for each of the five stages of the experiment. During the first and second baseline periods the correlations were .17 and .47, respectively, while for the experimental and follow-up periods they were −.41, −.20, and −.71 in that order. None of these correlations differ significantly from zero. Combining these figures into nontreatment (baseline periods) and treatment (experimental and follow-up periods) yields correlations of .39 for the former and −.41 for the latter. These coefficients were found to be significantly different from one another ($z = 2.48$, $p = .007$). This finding may indicate that Mrs. S., when left to her usual way of interbehaving with Peter, attended to (and thus maintained through social reinforcement) his undesirable behaviors while ignoring (extinguishing) desirable (non-O) responses. A number of studies (Allen, Hart, Buell, Harris, and Wolf, 1964; Harris, Johnston, and Kelley, 1964; Hart, Allen, Buell, Harris, and Wolf, 1964; Wahler *et al.*, 1965) have demonstrated that social reinforcement in the form of adult attention can influence the behavior of the young child. It is interesting to note that Mrs. S.'s proclivity to respond to Peter's O behaviors was reversed during the two experimental periods and thereafter.

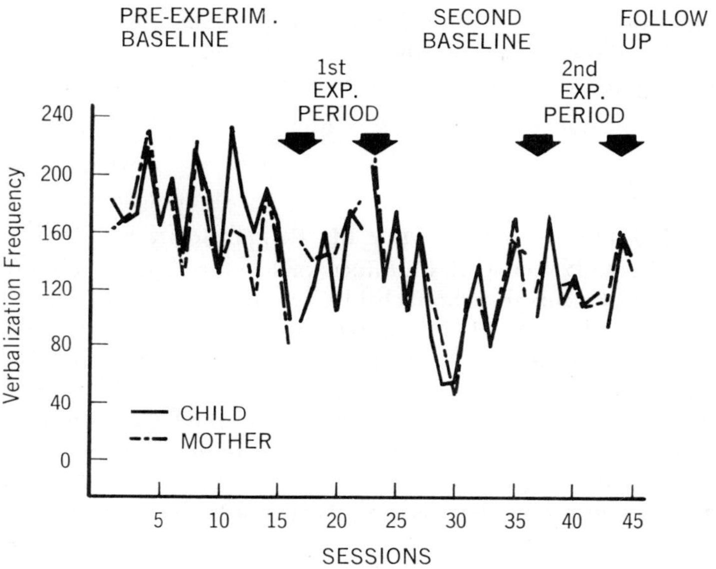

Fig. 2. Number of 10-second intervals, per 1-hour session, in which Peter spoke to his mother or the mother spoke to Peter.

Besides showing a relationship between the mother's verbalizations and Peter's O behaviors, a comparison of Figs. 1 and 2 also shows that the time-out procedure operated in a selective manner. Even though the isolation technique reduced the rate of undesirable responses, other classes of behavior such as verbalizations were not affected. This is evidenced by the fact that Peter's verbalization rate during the combined treatment periods did not differ significantly from his rate during nontreatment periods ($F = 2.24$; $df = 1, 43$; $.25 > p > .10$).

The results of this study show that it is possible to treat behavioral problems in the home, with the parent as a therapeutic agent. Home treatment may, in some cases, be more effective than treatment in the clinic, particularly when the undesirable responses have a low probability of occurrence in settings other than the home. Since it is widely held that many of a child's problems originate in the home environment, direct modification of this environment (including the behavior of other family members) may arrest the difficulty at its source. One limitation of this type of study, however, is the requirement of a cooperative parent. If this requirement can be met, the use of the parent as therapist can not only free the professional for other duties, but the parent, in learning to use techniques of behavioral control, may become generally more skillful in dealing with the responses of the developing child and more capable in handling any future difficulties that may occur.

REFERENCES

ALLEN, K. EILEEN, HART, BETTY M., BUELL, JOAN S., HARRIS, FLORENCE R., AND WOLF, M. M. Effects of social reinforcement on isolate behavior of a nursery school child. *Child Develpm.*, 1964, **35**, 511–518.

BIJOU, S. W., SLOANE, H. N. Therapeutic techniques with children. In L. A. Pennington and I. A. Berg (Eds.). *An introduction to clinical psychology* (3rd ed.). New York: Ronald.

FERSTER, C. B., AND APPEL, J. B. Punishment of S^{Δ} responding in matching to sample by time-out from positive reinforcement. *J. Exp. Anal. Behav.,* 1961, **4**, 45–56.

HARRIS, FLORENCE R., JOHNSTON, MARGARET, K., KELLY, C. SUSAN, AND WOLF, M. M. Effects of positive social reinforcement on regressed crawling of a nursery school child. *J. Educ. Psychol.,* 1964, **55**, 35–41.

HART, BETTY M., ALLEN, K. EILEEN, BUELL, JOAN S., HARRIS, FLORENCE R., AND WOLFE, M. M. Effects of social reinforcement on operant crying. *J. Exp. Child Psychol.,* 1964, **1**, 145–153.

WAHLER, R. G., WINKEL, G. H., PETERSON, R. F., AND MORRISON, D. C. Mothers as behavior therapists for their own children. *Behav. Res. Ther.*, 1965, **3**, 113–124.

WOLF, M., RISLEY, T., AND MEES, H. Application of operant conditioning procedures to the behaviour problems of an autistic child. *Behav. Res. Ther.,* 1964, **1**, 305–312.

Training and Utilizing A Mother As the Therapist For Her Child

SALEEM A. SHAH

Recent estimates concerning the vast extent of psychological distress in the population, and the concurrent acute scarcity of mental health manpower, indicate a pressing need for short-term and more efficient therapeutic techniques, for better conceptualization of deviant behavior leading to improved prevention and treatment, and also for innovative and far-reaching methods of manpower utilization. During the past few years increased attention has been given to the use of various non-professional "change agents" capable of functioning in a variety of treatment situations. Such "change agents" have included school teachers, nurses, psychiatric aides and attendants, parents and others.

The active involvement of parents in the treatment of their disturbed children certainly is not new. However, it is maintained that in many instances the focus of therapeutic efforts could more appropriately be upon the parents; they can then be helped to function as effective "change agents" for their children. A considerable amount of literature—both clinical and experimental—has accumulated testifying to the effectiveness of such procedures in a variety of situations.

Since the manner in which maladaptive behavior is conceptualized determines to a large extent the treatment approaches used, the conceptualization inherent in the present therapeutic procedures needs to be made explicit. Behavior is viewed as involving a relationship or an interaction

This paper was presented at the Eastern Psychological Association Meeting, Boston, 1967 and is reprinted with the permission of the author.

between an individual and a particular environment. Behavior is neither fixed nor absolute, and neither can it be viewed as an emergent quality of the individual. Since behavior represents an interaction between the individual and the physical and social environment, efforts at its modification may be directed at the individual and also to alterations of the environment. That is, efforts are made to establish functional relationships between the behavior and the environmental and other variables maintaining and otherwise influencing such behavior. Once such relationships have been established, systematic manipulation of the independent variables will be expected to result in changes in the behavior of concern.

While the above behavior modification approach has been used in a number of cases, this presentation will describe the treatment of a four-year-old child as part of treatment for the mother. The mother—herself rather emotionally disturbed—was used as the primary "change agent" for the child. The therapist had no direct contact with the child.

Initially, Mrs. Smith had been seen for collateral interviews in connection with her husband's treatment. The husband had been referred for therapy for a longstanding homosexual problem—dating back to about age nine—which recently had come to light, and also for various marital and other difficulties. The couple had been married five years and had three children: Mary, the oldest, was four, and two boys, ages two years and eight months. Mrs. Smith was a 23-year-old high school graduate with a very insecure, dependent, and emotionally labile personality, and a history of *grand mal* epileptic seizures. She had experienced five *grand mal* seizures in her life and was on medication (phenobarbital) which had effectively controlled the seizures. Electroencephalographic examinations had revealed definite abnormality indicating organicity consistent with the diagnosis of epilepsy. The wife was prone to periods of depression and irritability during her menses, and also had periodic episodes of impulsive and violent outbursts in response evidently to stresses and provocations in the home.

Mr. Smith had voiced increasing concern about his wife's outbursts of rage—most of them directed at four-year-old Mary. He also told of receiving frequent telephone calls from his wife demanding and begging that he return home from work lest she seriously harm Mary and the other children. Concern about the safety and welfare of the children, and also about Mrs. Smith's serious problems, led to her involvement in treatment. It had been learned that the mother would often beat Mary rather severely—sometimes using a ruler or a stick; at times she would throw objects at the child—ashtrays, spoons, shoes, etc. On a couple of occasions the wife had slashed at the furniture with a knife during such outbursts. Mrs. Smith confirmed the above information and stated that such outbursts seemed to make her feel better—even though later she would experience much guilt about them, especially regarding her beating of Mary. The mother had consulted the family physician several times but the tranquilizing medication prescribed had not been of any help.

Mary was described as a bright and alert child who, even though completely trained at age two, had during the past couple of months become enuretic. Much of this enuresis was diurnal, would occur about three or four days a week, and sometimes there would be as many as four or even five incidents of diurnal enuresis on a single day. There were also other behavior problems: sassing, disobedience and defiance, going into the parents' bedroom—an 'off-limits' area—and using the mother's make-up on the walls, floor and furniture, taking mother's jewelry, playing with it, breaking it, and managing to lose much of it, etc. Despite numerous beatings Mary would repeat such misbehavior as though deliberately inviting harsh punishment from the mother.

A sample from the mother's behavioral notes kept for the therapist will provide an idea as to the kind of interaction to which the mother-daughter relationship had deteriorated:

> " . . . . I woke up to Mary screaming and sassing Nellie (mother's sister), so I jumped out of bed, immediately hateful, and beat Mary with a hairbrush until it broke in half. All the while I was screaming at her. Her little legs and bottom are all bruised. I came downstairs and sat at the kitchen table trying to shut out everything because it hurt so badly and I was afraid. Mary and Billy (four-year-old nephew) began yelling and fighting and I ran into the living room and threw Mary on the sofa. I was choking her when I realized what I was doing. . . . . I had to call Tom (husband) at work and tell him to come home because it was only 11 o'clock and I was afraid to trust myself all day. He wouldn't let me hurt Mary, and I really don't want to—I don't know why I do."

Information obtained from the mother, and corroborative details obtained independently from Mr. Smith, confirmed the impression that Mary's behavior did not involve any serious pathology. The main problem by far was the mother's behavior and the distinct possibility of serious harm to the child. It was, therefore, decided to focus attention upon the mother and, as part of her therapy, to use her as the "change agent" for her daughter. The mother's pronounced guilt about her behavior, her pleas for help, and her general intelligence, indicated her ability to carry out the procedures recommended.

The mother was asked to keep daily behavioral notes describing in detail various incidents with Mary—how they started, how she (the mother) responded to them, Mary's reactions, etc. Mrs. Smith was also questioned about her own daily schedule, her moods, feelings, etc., and she was asked to include *all* such information in her notes. It had been planned to obtain base-line data for a period of two weeks prior to initiating therapeutic interventions. In view, however, of the seriousness of the physical assaults upon Mary and the severity of the mother's own problems, it was decided to implement therapeutic interventions immediately upon receipt of the first week's notes.

It was urgently indicated that fairly prompt *behavior control* had to be achieved to prevent harm to Mary while other efforts at behavior modification proceeded. A variety of procedures were utilized to prevent and otherwise control situations leading to the beatings. In addition, specific instructions were given to Mrs. Smith that physical punishment was no longer to be used in view of its many deleterious effects. A number of specific alternatives were suggested for disciplining Mary.

Treatment was complicated by several disrupting features in the family which seemed to place considerable emotional pressure on the mother. In addition to problems created by knowledge of her husband's homosexuality, the previously poor state of the marital relationship had undergone further deterioration. Also, Mrs. Smith's sister—illegitimately pregnant for the second time—had been living with them in the small three bedroom house with her four-year-old son (also an illegitimate child). In addition to all this, the distraught mother had been experiencing difficulties with the use of birth control pills. It was only later discovered to what extent the use of the pills had complicated Mrs. Smith's problems.

Careful analysis of the information obtained from Mrs. Smith revealed various operant patterns and contingencies unwittingly exerted by the mother and Mary to influence each other's behavior. For example, episodes of severe beatings seemed to relate, in part, to the following variables: mother's agitated mood, erratic sleep schedule, sleeping late and waking up tired and irritable, being unable to cope with initial provocations from Mary, increased intensity of and accumulating pressures exerted by the child's continued misbehavior culminating in the mother's outburst and the beatings. It became obvious that the child was able to exert remarkably strong aversive control over the mother through the misbehavior. Such behaviors demanded and received mother's attention, often resulted in severe beatings, and would end with a guilt and sorrow-ridden mother tearfully hugging and kissing the child, apologizing profusely for her behavior, and pleading that both try harder to avoid such episodes. As will doubtless have been noticed, such a pattern of responses by the mother was almost perfectly programmed to shape "masochistic" behavior in the child.

The aforementioned contingencies, functional relationships, and some basic operant principles were explained to Mrs. Smith. In step-by-step fashion a detailed program was outlined for the handling of Mary, for regulating the mother's own behavior, and for establishing control in regard to various aspects of their interaction. The importance of consistent and conscientious application of these procedures was emphasized and the detailed behavioral notes were to be maintained. Mrs. Smith was forewarned that initially there might not appear to be much progress and that there may even be some increase in the misbehavior, but that the program outlined had to be diligently followed. During this period the mother was seen twice a week and was also asked to contact the therapist by telephone in the event of any complications or unforeseen developments.

Among the procedures utilized were the following: the mother was urged to get to bed earlier, to use progressive relaxation to sleep and to alleviate tension at other times, and to wake up with the children in the mornings; physical punishment of Mary was to be stopped and prompt use of physical isolation was to be used early in the behavioral chain, viz., Mary was to be confined to her room for a period of time; almost any positive behavior by the child, or cessation for a while of misbehavior, e.g., diurnal enuresis, was to be promptly reinforced; instead of through frequent punishments, the child's behavior was to be influenced by a variety of positive reinforcers—suckers, candy, pennies, shopping trips, helping mother, playing games with mother, obtaining verbal praise and individual attention from mother, and other forms of affectionate behavior. In contrast, misbehavior was to receive no response other than confinement of Mary to her room and deprivation of the aforementioned reinforcements. The above reinforcements were carefully regulated to provide an almost optimal schedule for modifying Mary's behavior. Extinction procedures were used to eliminate the child's aversive control over the mother. These procedures were modified in light of feedback obtained from the mother in order to most effectively accomplish the therapeutic objectives.

Distinct improvements began to be noticed by the second week and there were no incidents of severe beating in the months following. These changes were indicated by Mrs. Smith's detailed behavioral notes and were independently corroborated by the husband. A couple of samples from the behavioral notes four and five weeks after treatment was started are provided:

> 3/12—Mary was being provocative in egging on the other children, the patient wrote, ". . . but before I exploded, I realized that all I had to do to keep peace was to get rid of the trouble-maker. So Mary was sent to her room till lunch time and everything calmed down."
>
> 3/15—"Mary seems to have changed overnight! Still her pants have been dry without a reminder and she couldn't possibly be a better child. She's so agreeable lately; she's a pleasure to be with."

The improvements continued and a very positive and warm relationship between mother and child was stabilized by the end of the second month of treatment. Mrs. Smith noted early in the treatment program that periodic fluctuations in Mary's behavior seemed to relate to her own behavior and to her inconsistency in adhering to the procedures recommended. Obviously, changes in Mary's behavior followed certain changes which the mother *first* had to make in regard to her own behavior. Thus, in order to help her daughter, Mrs. Smith in a real sense had to help herself and develop better regulation of her own behavior. Progress has continued and Mrs. Smith reports that she has on her own been able to apply the procedures learned with her other children.

The following is an excerpt from the mother's follow-up note about two years later:

> ". . . Of course, for a while Mary wasn't quite sure what to think of the sudden change in me and as a result she challenged me quite a bit. In fact, she succeeded in making me awfully angry at times. Whenever this happened I 'calmly' got rid of her (before I blew my cool) by sending her to her room and she was saved a real clobbering! . . . It only took a few months to untangle us completely and during this time Mary and I were growing closer and closer together. She began acting happier and more sure of herself and most important, sure of me. Mary was about four—that's all—when she climbed on my lap one day and said, 'Oh Mommy, I love you! I love you and I *like* you too!' So young and yet old enough to voice the whole difference in us. Now we *liked* each other too."

This therapeutic illustration adds to the literature indicating the general usefulness and efficiency of behavior modification procedures, and the many situations where utilization of parents as primary "change agents" is both possible and desirable. The basic principles involved in such treatment approaches are explicit, they can fairly easily be communicated, they can be applied under direction by persons not having very much formal education, and the focus upon behavior allows rather accurate monitoring and evaluation. The results of numerous clinical and experimental programs not only provide evidence of the effectiveness of such approaches, but have important implications for training and for developing strategies for skillful use of available mental health manpower.

REFERENCES

1. Bijou, S.W. & Baer, D.M. *Child development.* Vol. I. New York: Appleton-Centuy-Crofts, 1961.
2. Bijou, S.W. & Baer, D.M. *Child development.* Vol. II. New York: Appleton-Century-Crofts, 1965.
3. Ferster, C.B., Nernberger, J.E. & Levitt, E.B. The control of eating. In Staats, A.W. (Ed.) *Human learning: studies extending conditioning principles to complex behavior.* New York: Holt, Rinehart & Winston, Inc., 1964.
4. Ferster, C.B. & Simons, J. Behavior therapy with children. *Psychol. Record,* 1966, 16, 65–71.

5. Gewirtz, J. L. & Baer, D. M. The effect of brief social deprivation on behaviors for a social reinforcer. *J. Abn. Soc. Psychol.*, 1958, 56, 49–56.
6. Goldiamond, I. Self-control procedures in personal behavior problems. *Psychol. Reps.*, 1965, 17, 851–868.
7. Patterson, G.R. et al. A behavior modification technique for the hyperactive child. *Beh. Res. Ther.*, 1965, 2, 217–226.
8. Patterson, G.R. & Ebner, M.J. Application of learning principles to the treatment of deviant children. Paper presented at American Psychological Assoc., Chicago, Sept. 1965.
9. Phillips, E.L. Parent-child psychotherapy: a follow-up study comparing two techniques. *J.Psychol.*, 1960, 4, 195–202.
10. Shah, S.A. Behavior therapy and psychotherapy with offenders. Paper presented at American Psychological Assoc., Atlantic City, April 1965.
11. Shah, S.A. Treatment of offenders: some behavioral concepts, principles and approaches. *Federal Probation*, June 1966.
12. Ullmann, L.H. & Krasner, L. (Eds.) *Case studies in behavior modification.* New York: Holt, Rinehart & Winston, Inc., 1965.

Modification of a Deviant Sibling Interaction Pattern in the Home

K. DANIEL O'LEARY
SUSAN O'LEARY
WESLEY C. BECKER

The experimental modification of a sibling interaction is described. A 6-yr-old boy and his 3-yr-old brother frequently engaged in assaultive and destructive behavior. Treatment was carried out in the home using the experimenter and later the mother as the therapist. The children's undesirable behavior changed markedly as a result of a token reinforcement system and a time-out from reinforcement procedure. According to parental and teacher reports, the behavior reinforced during the experimental hour did generalize to other times and situations.

INTRODUCTION

There have been many demonstrations in clinic settings of the application of a functional analysis of behavior to children's disorders (Ferster, 1967a, 1967b; Lovaas *et al.*, 1965; Wahler *et al.* 1965; Wolf *et al.*, 1964). However, applications of behavioral principles in the home have been limited (Hawkins *et al.*, 1966; Williams, 1959). With the increasing emphasis on the diagnosis and modification of behavior *in situ*, it is probable that in the future, behavior therapists will concentrate on the stimulus situations in which the problem behavior is most likely to be emitted. Ultimately it is the parental environment which must maintain the child's be-

Reprinted with permission from *Behavior Research & Therapy*, 1967, Vol. 5, 113–120, Copyright 1967, Pergamon Press, Inc., and with the permission of the authors.

havior, and behavior reinforced in the clinic will be extinguished if parents do not provide the contingencies to maintain them. On the other hand, if behavior extinguished in the clinic receives parental attention, it is likely that the problem behavior will be quickly reinstated. Therefore, direct modification of children's behavior by parents under a clinician's guidance would seem to be a very useful approach.

This case study demonstrates the application of a set of procedures selected to produce efficiently behavior change in two deviant siblings. The procedures combined prompting, shaping, and instructions to increase cooperative behavior. This behavior was reinforced initially by M & M candies and later by points which could be exchanged for small toys. In the latter half of the study, time out from positive reinforcement (TO) was used to weaken some deviant behavior which was not reduced by the reinforcement of the incompatible cooperative behavior. TO was in the form of an isolation period (Hawkins *et al.*, 1966; Wolf *et al.*, 1964). Because of the exploratory nature of the application of these procedures in the home, the interactive behavior of two boys was first brought under control by the experimenter. Later this control was transferred to the boys' mother.

SUBJECTS

A 6-year-old boy, Barry A., and his 3-year-old brother, Jeff, were the two subjects in this study. Both parents are university faculty members, and they have a third son who is a 2-year-old.

Psychiatric History

Barry had been under psychiatric treatment for 2 years and was described by his psychiatrist as "seriously disturbed." He was reported to be extremely hyperactive, aggressive, and destructive. His EEG was symmetric and within normal limits. Although it was not possible to give him an intelligence test, the psychiatrist felt that his intelligence was within normal limits. He was diagnosed as an "immature, braindamaged child with a superimposed neurosis," although the nature and cause of his brain damage could not be specified.

Parental Report

According to Mr. and Mrs. A., Barry fought with his brother whenever they were alone. He damaged toys and furniture. He had temper tantrums and failed to follow parental instructions. Shortly before Barry was referred to our research unit, he had thrown a rock through a neighbor's window. He roamed away from home, and he would occasionally enter strangers' houses.

Mrs. A. reported that the boys angered her by screaming, yelling, and hurting each other when they were alone in the basement playroom. Consequently, an observer and the experimenter watched the interaction of the two boys when they played in the basement. From these observations it was quickly learned that there was a great deal of commanding behavior by Barry. If Jeff did not follow these commands, he would be coerced physically and often thrown on the floor. They would break each other's toys or constructions, and this would lead to further fighting. From the experimenter's observations in the home it appeared that parental attention was largely contingent upon high intensity undesirable responses. Since Mrs. A. usually remained upstairs while the boys were in the basement playroom, only the screaming, yelling, and fighting which could be heard easily received any attention.

On the basis of initial impressions made from the home observations it was decided to focus on the frequency of three general classes of behavior: deviant, cooperative, and isolate. The deviant behavior consisted of kicking, hitting, pushing, name-calling, and throwing objects at each other. The cooperative behavior was asking for a toy, requesting the other's help, conversation, and playing within 3 ft. of one another. Isolate behavior was designated as the absence of verbal, physical, or visual interaction between the boys.

PROCEDURES AND RESULTS

The treatment was divided into four stages: the first baseline period, the first experimental period, the second baseline period, and a second experimental period. Observation and treatment occurred approximately three times per week extending from November to March (sickness and vacàtions precluded some observations).

Base Period I

In order to assess inter-observer reliability, the observer and the experimenter made observations on five occasions during the baseline period. The observer and the experimenter sat 3 ft apart so that it was not possible for one observer to detect the symbols recorded by the other. Observations were made on a 20-sec rate, 10-sec-rest basis. Total observation time was approximately 30 min each day. The reliabilities were calculated by dividing the number of perfect agreements by the number of different responses observed. A perfect agreement was the presence of the same observed behavior for both raters in a 20-sec interval. The average reliability calculated thus was .78. Using two raters, the proportion of agreement in the three general classes of behavior can also be calculated by dividing the smaller score by the larger (Hawkins *et al.*, 1966). Calculated thus, agreement on deviant responses ranged from 0.92 to 1.00 with a mean of 0.95. Agreement on cooperative responses ranged from 0.85 to 1.00 with a mean of 0.92. Agreement on isolate behavior was 1.00.

The experimental arrangement and the absence of a third trained observer made it difficult to obtain reliability checks after the first baseline period. While the failure to obtain reliability checks somewhat weakens the value of these data, the high level of initial reliabilities clearly demonstrates that the coding system could be objectively applied. The reported data are all based on the observations of the same observer.

Base period observations were made only when Mrs. A. was not in the playroom. She was, however, allowed to come down to the playroom to discipline the children as she saw fit, since the observers did not talk or interact with the children. Such times were simply excluded from the observations.

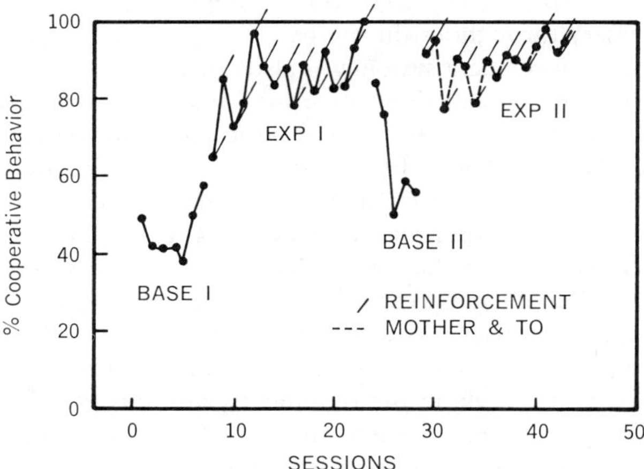

Fig. 1. Percentage of cooperative behavior divided by the percentage of deviant and cooperative behavior.

During the first baseline period (Fig. 1), the frequency of cooperative behavior divided by the total frequency of cooperative and deviant behavior yielded percentages ranging from 39 to 57 per cent with a mean of 46 per cent. Although the percentage of cooperative behavior on the graph shows a slight rise, the percentage of cooperative behavior calculated on the basis of cooperative, deviant, and isolate behavior was actually declining. However, it was decided to graph only cooperative behavior as a percentage of cooperative behavior plus deviant behavior because our experimental operations were aimed at changing the topography of whatever interaction occurred, and isolate behavior is not an interaction.

Experimental Period I

During the first 2 days of the experimental period, cooperative responses emitted by either child were continually reinforced by the experimenter who put an M & M candy in the child's mouth and simultaneously said "Good". The cooperative responses which were reinforced were any instance of verbal utterances such as asking for a toy, requesting the other's help, and saying "Please" and "Thank you." On the third and fourth day the experimenter alternately reinforced approximately every second or fourth cooperative response. On the fifth day the boys were instructed that they would receive an M & M if they asked each other for things, if they said "Please" and "Thank you," if they answered each other's questions, and if they played nicely together, e.g. building things together, pulling each other in the wagon, taking turns, and carrying out a request. These instructions were repeated on all succeeding days of the experimental periods, and the children were prompted by the experimenter as he felt necessary throughout the study.

The token reinforcement system was also introduced on the fifth day. The boys were told that in addition to getting M & M's, checks would be put on the blackboard for cooperative behavior and removed for deviant behavior. The blackboard was divided in half by a chalk line to designate separately the checks for Barry and Jeff. When a check was received for one or both boys the experimenter would tell them who was receiving a check. Checks could be exchanged for back-up reinforcers, which consisted of candy bars, bubble gum, caps, kites, comic books, puzzles, and other small toys. Frequent discussions were held with the boys' parents in order to ensure that the toys would indeed serve as reinforcers. The total cost of the token system throughout the treatment procedure was $10.67.

A procedure was used for each child in which the number of checks needed to receive the reinforcer was continually increased. On the twelfth day of the token system the use of M & M's was discontinued, but a back-up reinforcer was always present. However, there were some days when one or the other of the boys did not receive enough checks to obtain a back-up reinforcer. Initially, when the boys did not receive a reinforcer, they cried, screamed, and had violent temper tantrums. The experimenter simply ignored this behavior and instructed Mrs. A. to do likewise. The purpose of increasing the number of checks to receive a reinforcer was to permit transition to greater delay of reinforcement without disruption and in order to maintain the high percentage of cooperative behavior.

The amount of cooperative play was greatly increased during this period (Figure 1). As contrasted with the mean percentage of cooperative play during the first baseline of 46 per cent, the mean percentage of cooperative play during the first experimental period was 85 per cent.

Base Period II

During the second base period, in which the experimenter was absent and only the observer present, the amount of cooperative play gradually declined to a level similar to that of the first baseline (50 per cent). This drop in the percentage of cooperative responses demonstrates that the experimenter could utilize instructions, prompts, and a token reinforcement system to control the children's behavior. As in the first base period, mother could intervene as she thought necessary.

Experimental Period II

With the reinstatement of the experimental procedures the amount of cooperative behavior increased markedly. Two days after the second experimental period started, when the boys had resumed their prior percentage of cooperative responding, Mrs. A. was instructed to run the token system exactly as the experimenter had done with two additional features. On the second day a punishment procedure TO was made contingent upon kicking, hitting, pushing, name-calling, and throwing objects at each other. On the sixth day, a stretch out of the token system was begun, requiring points to be earned over several days for pay off. As can be seen in Figure 1, when the second experimental period was terminated the delay of reinforcement was 3 days.

To assist Mrs. A. in learning what to do, two hand signals were used by the experimenter to indicate when Mrs. A. was to administer token reinforcers or the punishment procedure. During the second experimental period, the experimenter gradually faded into the background so that Mrs. A. was able to execute the procedures without signals from the experimenter.

Although the percentage of deviant behavior was relatively low during the first experimental period, occasional fights which ended in yelling and screaming occurred and were very disruptive. Since giving and removing checks was not powerful enough to eliminate all of the deviant behavior, a punishment procedure called time out from positive reinforcement (TO) was instituted (Ferster and Appel, 1961). The TO procedure consisted of isolating either of the children in the bathroom for the deviant behavior listed above. Everything which could easily be removed was taken from the bathroom so that the boys had little opportunity to amuse themselves. After some initial resistance upon being taken to the bathroom, both boys accepted the TO without much argument. They had to remain in the bathroom for at least 5 min. In addition, they had to be quiet for a period of 3 min before they were allowed to come out. This latter requirement ensured that termination of TO was contingent upon behavior which the mother wished to strengthen (being quiet on request) and permitted TO to function both as a punisher for behavior which led to TO and a negative reinforcer for behavior which terminated TO.

During the first 3 days of the TO procedure, TO was used approximately once a day for each child. It was used at most four times a day, and during the last 4 days of the experimental period it was used only once for Jeff. The decreasing frequency of the need for TO is indicated in the cumulative record of Figure 2.

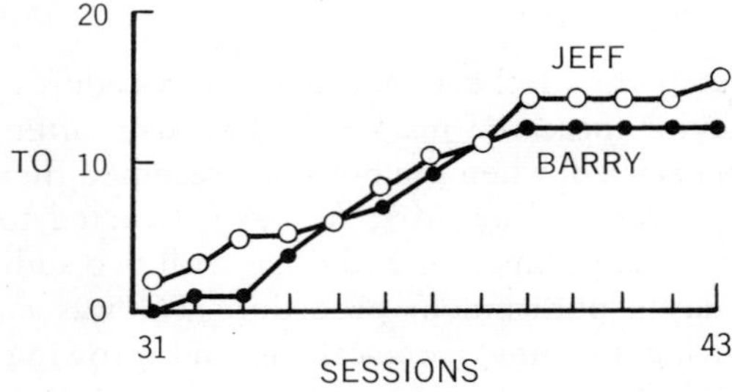

Fig. 2. Cumulative frequency of TO.

As can be seen in Figure 1, this combination of procedures under mother's control produced high cooperative behavior (90 per cent) during the second experimental period.

The application of the TO procedure was restricted to the experimental hour initially, but following the ninth session of the second experimental period (session 40) when the percentage of cooperative play seemed relatively stable, Mrs. A. was allowed to use TO at other times. In addition, following session 40 the minimum amount of time the children had to stay in the bathroom was increased to 8 min. The number of times TO was used outside the experimental session fell from three times per day to less than one time every other day over approximately one month. As can be seen in Fig. 2, TO was not needed in the experimental session after day 40.

DISCUSSION

As mentioned previously, cooperative behavior was represented as a percentage of deviant plus cooperative since our manipulations were aimed at changing the topography of whatever interactions occurred. From a graph of isolate behavior as a percentage of isolate, cooperative and deviant behavior (Figure 3), it can be seen that the changes produced during the first experimental period were not due to a change in the amount of isolate play. That is, the experimental manipulations did not greatly reduce all interactions at the same time that cooperative interactions were made stronger.

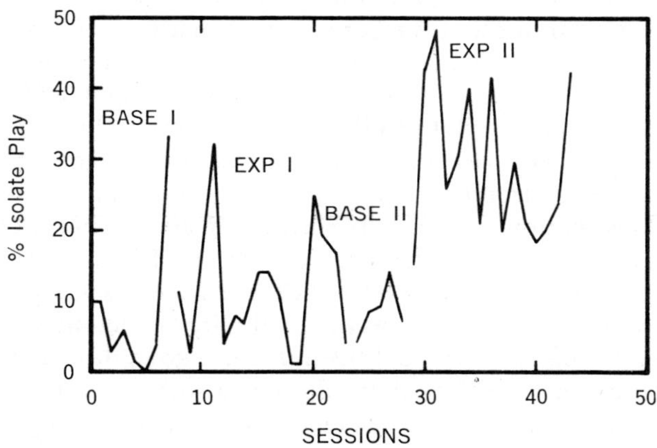

Fig. 3. Percentage of isolate behavior divided by the percentage of deviant, cooperative, and isolate behavior.

The rise in isolate play during the second experimental period was probably the result of fewer prompts being used by Mrs. A. than by the experimenter. This increase in isolate play was not interpreted as a particularly undesirable outcome because the topography of their interactions had changed markedly. Our aim was to reduce the frequency of the hitting, kicking, pushing, name-calling, and throwing objects and to increase cooperative interactions. Had we been concerned about a decrease in the frequency of interactions *per se,* we could have manipulated the contingencies in order to maintain a high level of interaction.

The drop in cooperative play during the second baseline could be attributed to the discontinuance of the token reinforcement system, the instructions, or the prompts. The physical absence of the experimenter during the second baseline period may also have been related to the changes in the behavior observed. Because of the severity of the boys' problems and parental concerns, it was impossible to introduce the experimenter, instructions, prompts, token and back-up reinforcers systematically. Consequently, the relative contributions of each aspect of the treatment cannot be here assessed. Furthermore, Jeff's increasing verbal repertoire probably helped maintain cooperative play as the study progressed. Other equally unknown factors may have accounted for the behavioral changes observed. Thus, this study represents a demonstration rather than an experimental analysis.

It should be made clear that the application of the set of procedures used in this study did not eliminate all deviant behavior. Barry sporadically emitted rough behavior at school and because of his disruptive outbursts at school, he will be placed in a behavior modification class. Nonetheless, Barry's parents and teacher reported that he progressed markedly during the year. The incidents of hitting and kicking were greatly reduced. He will now ask for things rather than grab them and an anecdotal report indicates that he plays well with a neighbor's child.

The experimental phase of this study was not designed to reprogram the boys' entire environment, but reprogramming could be accomplished in many ways. Following the experimental phase of our work, Mr. and Mrs. A. were instructed to continue the use of TO for hitting, kicking, and pushing. Some of Barry's other behavior, such as his infrequent but repetitive head turning and occasional wild arm swinging, were simply to be ignored. Formerly, Barry had been under a great deal of aversive control and the parents were strongly advised to stop spanking Barry.

As mentioned previously, it was evident from parental report and home observation that many of Barry's low intensity responses had been extinguished by his parents. However, disruptive behavior of high intensity received attention from both parents and this attention likely reinforced such behavior. In order to reverse this condition, both parents were advised to respond to the children when they were behaving appropriately, not only when they were misbehaving. The importance of praise and affection in maintaining appropriate behavior was repeatedly emphasized. In order to establish and reinforce more appropriate behaviors, Barry now receives a penny each time he makes his bed, and he has been saving this money for small toys.

Barry's eneuretic problem was eliminated with the use of a commercially produced alarm device. The alarm is connected to a bed pad, and the alarm rings whenever the child urinates on the pad. Barry had worn diapers every night prior to the use of the alarm device, and he had a long history of failures in attempting to arrest the bedwetting. Consequently, both Barry and his mother were given as much understanding of the treatment process as possible, a realistic appreciation of the possibility of cure and of the demands which the treatment procedures would place upon them.

Following Lovibond's account (1964), it was emphasized that about one-third of children whose bedwetting is arrested, start wetting again and have to use the device a second time. Thus complete treatment was thought of as requiring the use of the device on two occasions. Records of the treatment were kept, and within 7 weeks of starting the treatment Barry was completely dry. A three month follow-up indicated that there was no relapse.

The fact that this boy, who had been diagnosed "brain damaged," could behave as well as he did astonished his parents. Such evidence should make one very hesitant to use such labels as "brain damaged." Like autism and mental retardation, the label "brain damaged" implies concepts and assumptions which generate attitudes of futility. Bijou's (1965) comment with regard to autism and retardation seems equally important concerning brain damage.

> "These disturbances, like other forms of psychological behaviors, are undoubtedly determined by multiple conditions—social, physical, and organismic—and, as such, call for not a dismissing label but a challenge for analysis."

The need for further exploration of behavior therapy techniques with children is great. It has been demonstrated that reinforcement techniques are effective in shaping cooperative responses in both normal and schizophrenic children (Azrin and Lindsley, 1956; Hingten *et al.*, 1965). However, the study reported here is one of the few demonstrations of behavior modification in the home, and our techniques were devised to meet clinical and research needs as the study progressed. It is evident, however, that the principles of behavior modification can be utilized readily by a parent to change a child's behavior.

REFERENCES

AZRIN H. H. and LINDSLEY O. R. (1956) The reinforcement of cooperation between children. *J. Abnorm. Soc. Psychol.* **52**, 100–102.

BIJOU S. W. (1965) Experimental studies of child behavior, normal and deviant. In *Research in Behavior Modification* (Eds. Krasner L. and Ullmann L. P.) Holt, Rinehart & Winston, Inc., New York.

FERSTER C. B. An operant reinforcement analysis of infantile autism. *Am. J. Psychother.* (In press.)

FERSTER C. B. Operant reinforcement in the natural milieu. *Exceptional Children.* In Press.

FERSTER C. B. and APPEL J. B. (1961) Punishment of Ss responding in matching to sample by time out from positive reinforcement. *J. Exp. Analysis. Behav.* **4**, 45–56.

HAWKINS R. P., PETERSON R. F., SCHWEID E. and BIJOU S. W. (1966) Behavior therapy in the home: amelioration of problem parent-child relations with the parent in a therapeutic role. *J. Exp. Child Psychol.* **4**, 99–107.

HINGTGEN J. N., SANDERS B. J. and DEMYER M. K. (1965) Shaping cooperative responses in early childhood schizophrenics. In *Case Studies in Behavior Modification* (Eds. ULLMANN L. P. and KRASNER L.). Holt, Rinehart & Winston, Inc., New York.

LOVAAS I., SCHAEFFER B. and SIMMONS J. (1965) Experimental studies in childhood schizophrenia: building social behaviors in autistic children using electric shock. *J. Exp. Study Personality* **1**, 99–109.

LOVIBOND S. H. (1964) *Conditioning and Enuresis.* Crowell-Collier-Macmillan, New York.

WAHLER R. G., WINKEL G. H., PETERSON R. F. and MORRISON D. C. (1965) Mothers as behavior therapists for their own children. *Behav. Res. & Therapy* **3**, 113–124.

WILLIAMS C. D. (1959) The elimination of tantrum behavior by extinction procedures. *J. Abnorm. Soc. Psychol.* **59**, 269.

WOLF, M. M., RISLEY T. and MEES H. (1964) Application of operant conditioning procedures to the behavior problems of an autistic child. *Behav. Res. & Therapy* **1**, 305–312.

A Behaviour Modification Programme For A Child With Multiple Problem Behaviours*

G. R. PATTERSON
G. BRODSKY

INTRODUCTION

Even now, in its infancy, the behaviour modification movement has its full quota of prophets, critics and Don Quixotes (on both sides of the windmill). However, the present report is directed less to either crusaders or infidels, and more toward clinical psychologists who are in the process of deciding whether there may be something in behaviour modification technology which is of practical value in changing the behaviour of deviant children.

In considering this question, it seems to the present writers that there are at least three respects in which the behaviour modification literature is deficient. The data which will be presented in the present report are a modest attempt to rectify some of these deficiencies.

In general, the literature has been deficient in reports which present *"hard"* data, describing *successful* treatment of children who have *multiple* sets of problem behaviour. All three deficiencies will have to be met be-

Reprinted with permission from *Journal of Child Psychology and Psychiatry*, 1966, Vol. 7, 277–295, Copyright 1966, Pergamon Press, Inc., and with the permission of the authors.

*This project was financed by USPH grant MH 08009-03. The writers gratefully acknowledge the co-operation of the nursery school teacher, Mrs. Ann Bradwell, who permitted these procedures to be carried out in her classroom and to the parents of Karl who generously gave their permission for the publication of this report.

fore behaviour modification technology can occupy a respectable position. These deficiencies are illustrated in sources such as the excellent review by Grossberg (1964) or the presentation of cases in the edited volume by Ullmann and Krasner (1965). In some of the studies the data collected were excellent, and describe dramatic changes, but the behaviour studied represents only "mild" or single classes of deviance. Illustrations of such investigations are to be found in the classic study by Jones (1924) on children's fears; Williams (1959) on tantrum behaviours; Harris, *et al.* (1964) on crawling; and Jones' (1960) review of the literature on the treatment of enuresis. These studies perform the necessary function of establishing the *possibility* that principles from learning theories do have practical implications for the treatment of deviant children. The fact is, however, that most children referred to clinics have four or five problem behaviours. There have been attempts to deal with children displaying multiple problems or highly aversive behaviour, but these attempts have been limited in several important respects. In some studies of this kind the investigators unfortunately have followed the clinical tradition and provided only general descriptions, by the therapist or parent, of behaviour change. The reports by Lazarus and Abramowitz (1962) and Patterson (1965a) are examples of studies which do not provide adequate criterion data. Lacking these, it is not possible to evaluate the effectiveness of the treatment. In a movement that is less than 10 years of age, it is perhaps to be expected that the earlier studies will show many defects. However, it is to be hoped that contemporary studies will not continue to make the same errors. It is of critical importance that we provide criterion data we can use to evaluate the effect of our efforts.

Another group of investigators provide an example of the second style of deficiency. This group has dealt with the behaviour patterns of the extremely aversive child, and they have provided excellent data describing the effects of their treatment programs. However, these researchers have not as yet been *successful* in producing a remission of deviant behaviours in their subjects. This latter group of investigators have attempted to deal with "autistic" children; Ferster and DeMeyer (1961), Wolf, Mees and Risley (1963), Lovaas, Schaeffer and Simmons (1964), Bricker (1965), and Hingtgen, Sanders and DeMeyer (1965). When compared to the results produced by traditional treatment programmes, the efforts of the behaviour modifiers are dramatic indeed. In spite of the fact that the data from these studies are of high quality and attest to significant changes in the behaviour of these children, the primary patterns of deviant behaviour persist for these subjects. If we hold to a rigorous definition of the term "successful" we cannot claim as an example the efforts of the behaviour modifiers with autistic children.

The present report describes a set of conditioning programmes for the treatment of a pre-school boy who was referred for several behaviour problems. The procedures are adaptations derived from the writings of Skinner (1958); in these procedures, both social and non-social reinforcers were used to shape the adaptive behaviours. The problem behaviours were "severe" in the sense that they were highly aversive to adults and to other children. In all respects he represented a typical case referred to child guidance clinics. In the study, an attempt was made to provide observation data showing the effect of the conditioning programmes for each set of deviant behaviours. In an effort to maximize the generalization and persistence of treatment effects, most of the conditioning procedures were introduced in the schoolroom and the home. For the same reason, much of the effort was directed toward re-programming the peer culture and the parents.

METHODS

The Child

Karl was a 5-year-old boy whose parents had been asked to remove him from kindergarten. From the parent's report, it seemed that Karl was characterized by a multitude of deviant behaviour. For example, when separated from his mother, he became intensely aggressive, biting, kicking, throwing toys, screaming and crying. The teacher's legs were a mass of black and blue marks; on several occasions he had tried to throttle her. The mother also reported sporadic enuresis. His speech pattern was immature, showing several minor articulation defects. There was a general negativism in his interaction with adults; for example, it was extremely difficult to get him to dress or feed himself. The mother thought he might be retarded, but his I.Q. tested at the end of the study was well within the normal range. The mother felt that the behaviour pattern exhibited by Karl was so extreme and had persisted for such a period of time that it was extremely unlikely that he would change. As she said, Karl was very "strong headed". She was especially concerned about the behaviour he exhibited when he was brought to school in the mornings. For example, on the previous week he had actually held on to her dress with his teeth in an effort to keep her at the school. At age 2 years, Karl was hospitalized for a few days' diagnostic study for suspected leukemia. The results of the diagnostic studies were negative; however, following the hospitalization it was increasingly difficult to leave him with baby-sitters.

At the close of the first interview, the mother smiled ruefully and said that she did not think that the programme we outlined would help Karl. However, his behaviour was so aversive to her that she agreed to participate in it.

His play interaction with other children was limited in frequency and rather primitive in quality. Much of the time he ignored the other children. When he did interact with them, there was an awkward and frequently aggressive quality to his behaviour which led the teacher to be concerned about their safety. As a result, much of the time he was followed about the room by an adult.

When presenting a report of a single case in which multiple problems are evident, it is very difficult to provide an adequate means for specifying the conditions under which replication could occur. By keeping the description of the child somewhat vague, the present writers could always claim that unsuccessful replication attempts by other investigators were involved with subjects that were "really" not like the one described by the writer. For this reason some effort was made to provide a careful description of the child; a procedure for doing this has been outlined by Patterson (1964). Karl was observed during the occasion of his first visit to the clinic for the presence, or absence, of 149 behavioural items. These behavioural items, plus the report of the parent and teacher as to "symptoms", constituted the description of Karl.

The behavioural items and symptom list had been previously used with a sample of one-hundred deviant boys to determine the factor structure which characterized this matrix. This analysis produced five oblique factors. The distribution of scores for each of the five factors had been transformed into deviation scores; and the distributions were normalized by the use of McCall's (1922) T score. The factor profile resulting from the combination of behavioural observation in Karl's first hour at the clinic, and the report by parents and teachers of his "symptoms", is shown (Fig. 1).

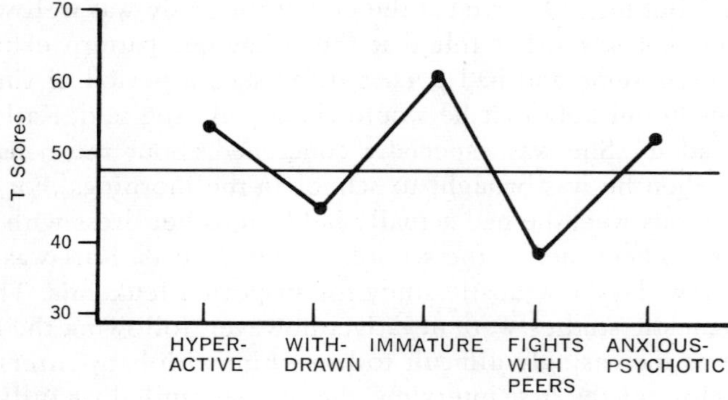

Fig. 1. The profile of factor scores describing Karl

To summarize the description, Karl would be characterized as high on the Immaturity factor, and moderately high on the Hyperactivity and Anxiety-Psychotic factors. This profile was very similar to the mean profile for a class of deviant children obtained by Patterson (1964).* The similarity of Karl's profile to that of the group indicated that he was a member of a class of patients that is often referred to clinics for treatment. As suggested earlier, these profile scores can serve as a basis of subject-comparison in attempts which might be made to replicate the present study.

The Parents

Karl's mother was an attractive woman, 30 years of age. She dressed appropriately and showed herself to be a reasonably well organized housekeeper and mother. She had received an eleventh grade education. A cursory investigation of her background and behaviour did not reveal any marked psychopathology; this was in keeping with her MMPI profile of −97.

Karl's father was a husky, assertive man, 31 years of age. He had received a tenth grade education. A semi-skilled laborer, he was away from home much of the time. It was our impression that there was no obvious psychopathology characterizing the father; this was also corroborated by his MMPI profile of 13′ 427−09. Both the parents agreed in stating that the father had better control over Karl's behaviour than did the mother. They believed that the improved control was due to Karl's fear of the physical punishment which the father used on occasion.

Formulation

A paradigm such as the one currently being used by behaviour modifiers may generate statements which lead to successful outcomes of treatment programmes. The fact that the data support statements about treatment outcomes does *not* necessarily lend support to other statements, made from the same paradigm, which purport to "explain" the *antecedents* for the deviant behaviour. These are two separate sets of statements, and each require their own set of verification data. However, such tests will not be made until behaviour modifiers explicate their "speculations" about

*The mean factor scores for this group were: Hyperactive 53; Withdrawn 39·5; Immature 65·0; Fights with Peers 38·0; and Anxious-Psychotic 59·3. In the earlier study four out of a hundred deviant boys had profiles of this kind. This group of four boys were highly homogeneous as evidenced by Haggard's *R* (1958), coefficient of profile similarity, of 0·73. The intraclass correlation took into account variations in level, scatter, and ranking of profiles for the group.

probable antecedents for various classes of deviant behaviours. It is our intention to provide here a set of testable speculations about the antecedents for behaviours of the kind displayed by Karl.

After our initial observations in the school, we outlined the following formulation for the temper tantrum behaviours displayed at school.

Being left at school was a stimulus associated in the past with deprivation state. This deprivation state, and cues associated with it, elicit an emotional state. This emotional state was labelled "separation anxiety". The eliciting cues (S) and the anxiety state produce high amplitude behaviours which are reinforced in two ways. (1) These behaviours frequently terminate the presence of the aversive stimuli and (2) they are also maintained by positive social reinforcers.

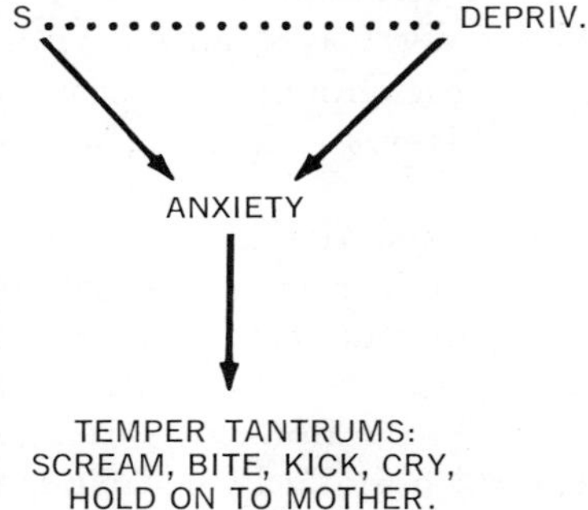

The key concept in this formulation was the use of a deprivation paradigm to explain the presence of anxiety in Karl. Such an approach is based upon the assumption that deprivation of social reinforcers creates an emotional state.* We assume that such deprivation must occur frequently in the lives of most children but that it is most likely to produce an intense emotional reaction in those children that we have labelled as "selective responders". Such a child has been conditioned to respond to social rein-

*The existence of such a state, and the appropriateness of the label "anxiety" is attested to by a series of laboratory studies. A series of instrumental conditioning studies have shown that children who have been deprived of social contact for a time are more responsive to social reinforcers, Walters and Roy (1960), Walters and Karol (1960), Erickson (1962), Gewirtz and Baer (1958). There are also data showing the relation between deprivation of social reinforcers and physiological measures of anxiety. Unpublished data from our own laboratories showed that social deprivation produced a significant increase in "anxiety" as measured by skin conductance. A group of fifteen first and second grade girls were isolated while they responded to the apparatus (without being reinforced). There was a significant increase in skin conductance from the first to the second half of the trial ($P = 0.03$ level).

forcers dispensed by only a limited number of social agents.† The main result of selective responding is that the absence of the mother (parents) signifies that social reinforcers are no longer forthcoming. Thus when left at school or with a babysitter, he is, in effect, placed in an immediate deprivation state. The stimuli associated with the onset of this deprivation constitute a set of eliciting stimuli for the emotional state which typically accompanies this kind of deprivation. This complex of eliciting stimuli, deprivation and accompanying emotional state are usually labelled as anxiety.‡

It would seem to be the case that not all deprivations led to anxiety states for Karl. For example, he could play by himself in the yard for extensive periods of time. We assume that the stimuli associated with some deprivation states would be more aversive than others. For Karl, it seemed to be the case that he was most anxious in deprivation conditions that he could not terminate upon demand. For example, being left at school was a stimulus associated with long periods of social deprivation; in addition, he had no control over the length of time which he was to be deprived. His playing in the yard by himself was a deprivation state which he could terminate at any time by simply going into the house. In summary, it was postulated that there was a relationship between deprivation of social reinforcers and anxiety; a relation between selective responsiveness and anxiety; and a relation between control over the period of deprivation and level of anxiety.

Karl has learned to avoid the onset of this anxiety by throwing temper tantrums, kicking, biting, etc. This behaviour was reinforced either when the mother remained at the kindergarten in an attempt to comfort her son; or when the teacher interacted with Karl and attempted to quiet him by holding him or reading to him, etc. Thus, Karl's behaviour was being maintained both by the presentation of these positive reinforcers and by the avoidance of the deprivation state. It is important in this respect to

†Karl seemed to be a good example of the hypothesized relation between selective responding and deviant behaviour outlined by Patterson and Fagot (1966). Their laboratory findings showed that some boys were responsive to social reinforcers dispensed by only one or two of the three major classes of social agents (mother, father, or peer). Such boys were more likely to be described as deviant when rated by teachers. In the present case we believe that Karl was responsive to social reinforcers dispensed by only a few people, e.g. his mother and his father. By and large, his behaviour was not under the control of reinforcers dispensed by peers. Quite possibly this lack of control was due to the fact that Karl was raised in the country and had little opportunity to learn to be responsive to peers.

‡The data reported in the Patterson and Fagot publication offered some support for these speculations. Boys who were shown to be responsive to social reinforcers dispensed by mothers, fathers, and by peers were described by teachers as being the most anxiety-free. On the other hand, boys who were selectively responsive to only one or two of these agents were also rated as being more anxious.

note that we assumed Karl to be responsive to the teacher. Observations of Karl suggested that this was so; it also seemed to be the case that the presence of other children in the room making demands upon the teacher created a situation in which Karl was being minimally deprived most of the time.

In planning a treatment programme, it was assumed that the intense destructive behaviour owed at least part of their amplitude to the presence of the emotion, anxiety. One of our behaviour modification programmes must then deal with anxiety. However, reducing the anxiety will *not* necessarily extinguish the destructive behaviours; it may, for example, only reduce their level of intensity. For this reason, a second major component of the treatment programme involved the strengthening of socially adaptive behaviours which would compete with the occurrence of the behaviours associated with temper tantrums and other atavisms. Presumably relatively permanent elimination of deviant behaviours may best be achieved by programmes that include the conditioning of socially adaptive behaviours which compete with their occurrence. This second point of focus involved the training of both the peer group and the parent to respond positively to socially adaptive behaviours displayed by Karl. In Karl's case, we suspected that the parents were using negative reinforcers to control his behaviour and that there were few positive reinforcers dispensed by peers for socially adaptive behaviours. Most of the peer group seemed to find Karl's behaviour quite aversive and avoided him as much as possible.

In addition to the temper tantrums, there was another class of deviant behaviour which was of interest. The label used to characterize this second, broad class of responses was "negativism". Karl seemed to precede many of the dramatic temper displays, both at kindergarten and at the clinic, with a verbal warning. For example, he would state that he was going to kick the experimenter or the teacher. On many occasions he would refuse to comply with any requests with a flat "No". Frequently such behaviours would be reinforced by the behaviour of the adult. When faced with such "warnings", the adults would withdraw their requests. Perhaps the mother learned that such "warnings" were stimuli preceding subsequent temper tantrums. Mother could avoid what was most certainly, for her, a negative reinforcer, by withdrawing her request of Karl. In this way, Karl was being reinforced in a variety of settings each day for a complex of behaviours which we have labelled as "negativistic".

It is clear that an effective treatment programme will require several different conditioning procedures. It will be necessary to condition a new set of responses to the cues eliciting the anxiety reaction. It also will be necessary to extinguish the destructive behaviours and teach him some alternative mode of responding. We also must increase the frequency of the few socially adaptive behaviours he does demonstrate. The peers in turn must be re-programmed to provide more social reinforcers for Karl, particularly for the occurrence of his socially adaptive behaviours. The latter set of procedures is pivotal, for it partially insures the persistence of any change in Karl's behaviour produced by our intervention. Finally an effective way must be found of altering the set of contingencies provided by the parents of Karl's anxiety responses, his temper tantrums, his immature behaviours, and his negativistic behaviours.

Treatment Procedures

There were four conditioning programmes used in the study. The procedures were as follows: (A) an extinction-counter conditioning programme for the temper tantrum behaviours; (B) an extinction-counter conditioning programme for the anxiety reactions elicited when being separated from mother; (C) a positive reinforcement programme to increase the frequency of positive initiations between Karl and the peer group; (D) and finally, a programme to change the schedule of reinforcements used by the parents to maintain negativistic and immature behaviours. As some of these programmes were used simultaneously, confusion will be minimized by outlining the development of each of these procedures on a day-to-day basis.

October 5. Programme A (Temper Tantrums). Karl was brought to the door of the mobile laboratory to obtain a laboratory measure of his responsiveness to social reinforcers. He looked frightened (his pupils were dilated), and refused to come. When carried into the laboratory, he kicked the experimenter, screamed, cried, and attempted to destroy the equipment. The experimenter brought him into one of the cubicles, closed the door and pinned Karl to the floor by the ankles. While Karl screamed, bit, and threw objects, *E* made every effort to prevent Karl from injuring him, and sat looking as bored as circumstances would permit. *E* looked at Karl and talked to him only when he was reasonably calm. Karl was told he could leave as soon as he quieted down. The episode lasted about 30 min.

Programme D (Re-train the Parents). We had not planned beforehand to begin re-programming the parent in this session. However, when Karl displayed his tantrum behaviours, the mother was brought to an adjoining room and observed the interaction through a one-way glass. A second experimenter explained to her that we were introducing a "time-out" procedure for Karl. As long as the destructive behaviour lasted, he would be pinned down and effectively removed from all of the usual sources of positive reinforcement. The mother was told that such adult behaviours as "the mother stays in the classroom", "the teacher hugs him", "the teacher looks frightened or reads him stories" were powerful reinforcers for temper tantrums. The behaviour of the experimenter with Karl served as a model for behaviours which the mother was to imitate.

October 6. Programme A (Temper Tantrums). The mother had to drag Karl to the clinic today. Once inside, he refused to accompany *E* to play room and was picked up (kicking, clawing, screaming and crying). In the play room he was pinned to the floor by his ankles and cried for 30 sec. As soon as he stopped the tantrum behaviours, he was released.

Programme B (*Anxiety*). Patterson (1965a) described a technique in which dolls were used to represent situations in which a child would be separated from his mother. A similar procedure was used with Karl. After being presented with a situation in which the mother (doll) was separated from the boy (doll), Karl was asked if "the doll" would be afraid. If he said "No", he was reinforced with an M & M chocolate candy. He was also reinforced whenever he described behaviours which would compete with the occurrence of fear or temper tantrums, i.e. "I would play". The dropping of his M & M in his cup was preceded by an auditory signal coming from his "Karl Box". The "Karl Box" contained an electric counter, light, and a rather loud bell. Any one, or all, of these could be activated by *E*.

During this first session (15 min), Karl participated in a series of six doll sequences and received a total of thirty M & Ms.

Programme D (Re-training the Parents). The mother and the second *E* observed Karl's play room behaviour through an observation window. During the temper tantrum, the mother was shown the non-reinforcing (and non-punitive) behaviour of the *E* holding Karl. She, in turn, was encouraged, to leave him quickly at school and thus reinforce the tantrum behaviours as little as possible. Mother was impressed with the fact that temper tantrums lasted only a few minutes today.

After the session in the play room, the two experimenters, Karl and the mother talked for 10 min. Mother was instructed to reinforce him on those occasions in which he did not act in a frightened way when being separated from her, when he was co-operative, and when he behaved in a grown-up fashion. She was instructed to bring in notes describing four occasions on which she had reinforced Karl for any of these following behaviours: for not being afraid, for being co-operative, for being "grown up". Karl listened to this interchange with some interest.

Programme C (Programme to Increase Positive Interaction between Karl and Peers). The "Karl Box" was used during the recess period at Kindergarten. Karl was told that the buzzer would sound each time that he "played with another kid without hurting him". If Karl were within range, *E* dispensed social reinforcers for appropriate initiations, i.e. "That is good, Karl". He was also informed that the candy which he earned would be divided among all the children and distributed during snack time. He earned seventy M & Ms in a 10-min period; during this time he displayed no aversive behaviours.

October 7. Programme A (Temper Tantrums). The same tantrum behaviours were observed at the clinic. The same procedures were applied as described for the previous day. However, today the behaviour terminated as soon as Karl was carried into the play room.

Programme B (Anxiety). The same doll play procedure was used as described for the previous day; the session lasted about 20 min. Karl earned thirty M & Ms and a plastic ship. (The latter we "traded" in for ten M & Ms.) All of the reinforcers were delivered immediately and accompanied by the sound of the bell in the "Karl Box".

Programme D (Re-train the Parents). The mother observed Karl's behaviour in the play room. She was told of the necessity for reinforcing appropriate behaviour immediately. She was also reminded of the importance of *not* reinforcing maladaptive behaviours, such as non-co-operation, temper tantrums or immature behaviours. The interactions of the experimenter and Karl were used to illustrate these points.

During the "group" interview which followed, the mother reported with pride that Karl was co-operative several times yesterday. Karl was very pleased with her remarks. She gave the following written examples of her efforts to reinforce him.

1) Karl put away his clothes for me and I told him that he was a good boy and hugged him.
2) Karl got a diaper for me and I told him how nice he was to help me take care of his baby brother.
3) Karl went to bed without any argument and didn't wet the bed and I told him how grown-up he was getting.
4) Karl picked up walnuts for me and I told him he was really getting to be such a big boy and kissed him.

Programme C (Interaction of Karl and Peers). The other children had received their M & Ms from Karl's previous day's work and were curious when *E* again appeared with the box. They asked *E* what it was, and *E* told them that it was a "Karl Box". They asked, "What is a Karl Box?" *E* said, "It is a box that makes a noise, and gives candy whenever you talk to Karl". Immediately several children said "Hi Karl" to the box. *E* said, "No, you must say it to Karl, not to the box". The peers then received 150 reinforcers for initiating social contacts with Karl. He in turn was reinforced for responding appropriately and for initiating contacts of his own. The conditioning session lasted only about 10 min. The M & M bonanza was again distributed to all of the children.

October 8. Programme A (Temper Tantrum). Karl began to whimper as soon as he saw the experimenter's reception room and ran and hid. He then kicked and clawed as he was picked up and began to cry loudly. He was told that he could earn M & Ms by walking up the stairs himself.

He was placed at the bottom of the stairs; but he refused to move. The experimenter commented that Karl was not screaming, kicking or hurting people even though he was a little afraid. At this point the buzzer sounded on the "Karl Box". After a few seconds Karl was again asked to place his foot on the bottom step; but he refused. After a moment, the experimenter said, "Too bad, the next time the box went off you were going to earn one of these plastic boats. Guess I'll just have to keep the boat and carry you up the stairs again." There was a moment of silence at which point Karl said, "Suppose you touch my hand and see what happens". The experimenter touched Karl's hand. Karl immediately placed his feet on the stairs. The buzzer sounded and Karl was handed the plastic boat. At this point, he walked up the stairs and was reinforced by the bell for each step into the play room.

Programme B (Anxiety). Karl and experimenter sat in the doorway of the play room. The mother was instructed to say "Goodbye, Karl", and Karl in turn was told to say goodbye to the mother while she walked across the room. As Karl said "Goodbye", he was reinforced by the bell and by the *E* saying "Very good, Karl". Karl was asked if he was afraid. He said that he was. *E* said "But you did sit there. You didn't run after her, and you didn't scream or kick. That is very good." (Bell sounded.) This was repeated several times with the mother moving further away each time until she walked across the lawn as Karl waved goodbye from the second-story window.

Programme D. (Re-training the Parents). Mother reported that Karl was making good progress both in being able to tolerate her leaving him at school, and also in his increasingly co-operative and mature behaviour at home. Both the *E*s and the mother praised Karl, who was obviously very pleased. Mother brought her "homework" with examples of how she had reinforced Karl for these behaviours on the previous day.

1) Karl took his bath without any argument at all and I told him how proud I was of him and let him sit in my lap in the rocking chair for a while.
2) Karl went to bed and I told him how big he was for it and kissed him.
3) Karl got into the car to come to the University without arguing and I told him how nice he was.

We pointed out to the mother that she still found herself doing for Karl things which he could do for himself; e.g. tying his shoes, buttering his bread. We practised breaking such a behaviour down into small steps and providing reinforcement for *any kind of progress* rather than waiting for terminal behaviour before reinforcing. We also set up a point system so that each time Karl co-operated in one of these new behaviours he received a point, which mother recorded as part of her homework. When he had earned ten points, Karl could select any one of the plastic toys from our display.

Programme C (Peer and Karl Interactions). The school period was highly structured today. It was not possible to condition for peer interaction without disrupting the group. We left shortly; Karl was obviously disappointed, but remained in the group.

October 11. Programmes A and B (Temper Tantrums and Anxiety). Karl walked up to the play room to the accompaniment of the bell and much praise from his parents and both *E*'s. He said that now he only felt a little bit afraid when leaving his parents. We all agreed that he would no longer have to come to the clinic.

Programme D (Training the Parents). The father, who had been absent from home during the past week, had returned. The procedures were reviewed for him in the clinic with mother and Karl present. Arrangements were made for the remainder of the work with parents to take place in the home.

Programme C (Peer Interaction). Neither experimenter was able to go to the school today.

October 12. Programme D (Training Parents). One of the *E*s went to Karl's home along with an observer. Karl was extremely co-operative in following his parents' requests. *E* followed the mother around, offering suggestions on the best way to interact with Karl. When mother was slow in reinforcing him, *E* again explained the importance of the immediacy of reinforcement. In addition, the mother was again shown the principles of shaping successive approximations to a desired behaviour. As an example, she asked Karl to comb his hair which he had not done before. She was then instructed to reinforce him for the *attempt* (which was actually a fairly good job). After several such successes it was explained to her that she was to reinforce Karl tomorrow only when he had done a better job. A similar procedure was begun in shaping the behaviours involved in tying his shoes.

Programme C (Peer-Karl Interaction). The previous programme was continued. M & Ms were made contingent upon Karl's initiating social contacts and peers initiating contacts to Karl.

October 13. Programme D (Re-train the Parents). Karl was again observed at home. He showed no deviant behaviour. Mother reported that she had reinforced Karl for improving in tying his shoes, and for hair combing. *E* reviewed for mother the general principles underlying the approach with Karl and explained how she might adapt them to use in future situations, such as leaving Karl alone in the evenings with a babysitter. Mother reiterated that Karl was like a new boy and they were delighted with his progress.

Programme C (Peer-Karl Interaction). Today there was no conditioning in the classroom.

October 14. Programme B, C and D. The mother came to the school and operated the "Karl Box". She was instructed to reinforce Karl for playing with other children, or any socially appropriate behaviours which resulted in his staying away from the immediate vicinity of his mother.

Mother, teacher, and Karl agreed that there was no reason for continuing the programmes as there were no further behaviours that anyone believed should be changed. It was arranged with the parents, and the teacher, to follow up the effects of the programme by observing Karl in the school for several weeks following the study.

Procedures for Collecting Data

All of the observation data used in testing the effectiveness of the treatment programmes were collected in the classroom setting. In the first introduction to this setting, two observers, seated in the classroom, dictated narrative accounts of Karl's behaviour, and the reactions of the teachers and the peer group. These initial impressions provided a basis for constructing a check list that was introduced during the second day's observation. Using the check list, observers tabulated the occurrence of the following behaviours: (1) the frequency of positive initiations, i.e. talking to another child, smiling, by peers to Karl. (2) the frequency of his positive initiations to peers. (3) the occurrence of withdrawal or isolation from the group, e.g. sitting 3 or 4 feet away from the group and not attending to or participating in the group activities. (4) the occurrence of negativistic behaviours, e.g. when asked to join the group, play a game, come into the room, etc., his behaviour indicated non-compliance. (5) temper tantrums; when being left by parent behaviours occurred such as: cry, scream, kick, bite and hit.

The observations were made during periods ranging in length from 20 min to 60 min per day. The behaviours were tabulated by 14 sec intervals. To reduce the variability somewhat, the observations were collected during the same 60-min period each day (12.30 to 1.30). The data were collected each day during the time immediately prior to the conditioning procedures introduced in the classroom.*

During the study, the data were collected by three different observers, but chiefly by one. On several occasions she was accompanied by an untrained observer. On the first such occasion 300 separate events were recorded; but the two observers agreed only 61 per cent of the time. On the

*It required 3 days of trial and error to construct the check list; at this point we had intended to collect a week's baseline data for each of the deviant responses. However, on the third day of our being in the classroom, the teacher informed us that she would have to drop him from the class unless he improved. It seemed to us that her toleration of these behaviors for 3 weeks had already been above and beyond the call of duty; consequently, we initiated our conditioning procedures. Being Good Samaritans, however, resulted in our obtaining only one day's baseline observation data.

second occasion, 264 events were noted and the two observers agreed 84 per cent of the time. This suggests that with a minimum of training, comparatively unskilled observers can be used to collect these kinds of data.

RESULTS

Each day the observers in the school provided an estimate of the duration of Karl's temper tantrum; this information was combined with the data from his behaviour at the clinic to form a "total" score for the day. A tantrum was said to have stopped when Karl had ceased to cry, kick, or scream for at least half a minute. During the 3 weeks previous to the study, the teacher told us that Karl had averaged about 30 min at the beginning of each school session. The data showing the effect of the programme on temper tantrum behaviours are presented in Fig. 2.

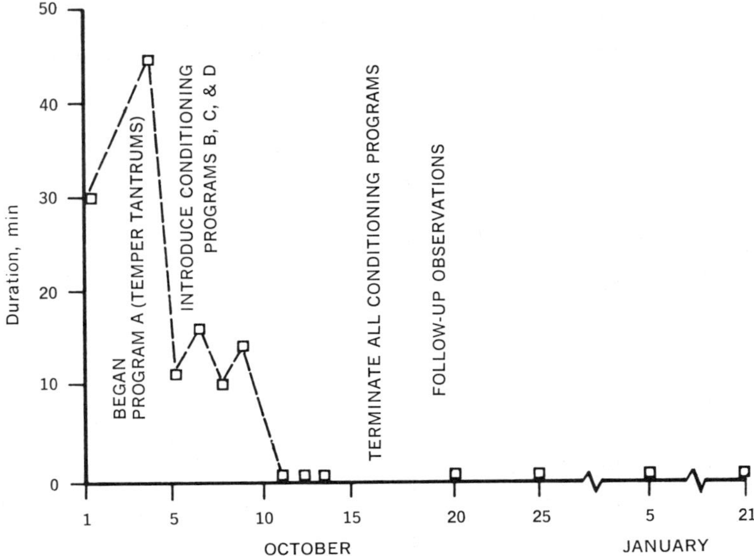

Fig. 2. Duration of temper tantrums.

In many respects, both the data and the procedure are similar to those described by Williams (1959) in which tantrum behaviours were controlled by the withdrawal of positive social reinforcers. As shown in Figure 2, there was a marked reduction in the duration of the temper tantrums by the second day of the programme. After the initial, dramatic reduction in duration, they were being emitted at a reasonably steady rate for a period of about 4 days. During this "plateau", he displayed a total of about 10 min of tantrums per day. Most of these were occurring in the classroom on the occasion of the mother's leaving him with the teacher. In this setting, both of the adults were providing him with a good deal of reinforcement for tantrums. However, by the sixth day of the programme procedure, the adults no longer provided reinforcers for them and they terminated. They did not recur during the 3-month follow-up.

The second set of data showed the change in frequency of occurrence of two classes of behaviours observed in the nursery school. The first category, "isolated", was defined by such behaviours as sitting several feet apart from the group.

Most of the time the children were engaged in a series of organized games, storytelling and group singing. These provided an occasion in which the teacher frequently made suggestions or demands to each of the children. Non-compliance with such demands was coded as "negativism".

If either of the behaviours occurred during a 15-sec time interval, it would receive one entry on the data sheet. The ordinate in Fig. 3 indicates the per cent of the 15-sec intervals in which they were observed to occur.

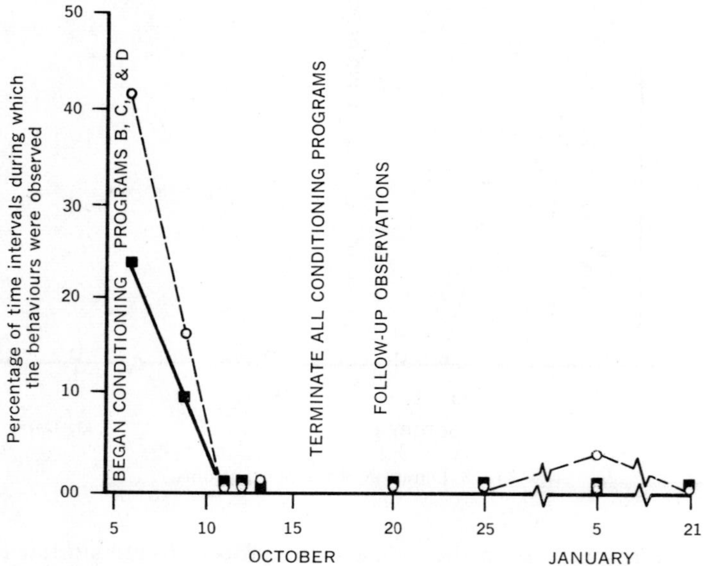

Fig. 3. Frequency of occurrence of negativistic and isolated behaviours.
■Frequency of negativistic behaviours.
○Frequency of isolated behaviours.

The data showed that by the second day of conditioning there was a dramatic drop in the occurrence for both classes of deviant behaviour. In both cases, the rate of occurrence dropped to almost zero and stayed there during the remainder of the 3-month follow-up period.

In observing Karl, the baseline data showed that the other children tended to avoid him, probably as a result of the aversive quality of much of his behaviour (pushing, elbowing, kicking, throttling, pinching). The prediction was that if Karl's aversive behaviours decreased in rate the peer group would increase the frequency of their social reinforcers. Data presented in the report by Patterson and Ebner (1965) showed that when the aversive behaviours were decreased for two hyperactive children in different classrooms, the change was accompanied by a marked increase in the amount of social reinforcers provided (by peers) for one of the subjects *but not for the other subject.* This would suggest that the effect of a reduction in aversive behaviours is somewhat a function of the social group in which it occurs. To the extent that these variables are not understood, the final outcome of our treatment programme is determined in large part by chance factors. However, it should be possible to directly reprogramme the schedule of reinforcement provided by the peer group, and the procedures innovated in the present study represented such an approach. If successful, the programme should result in an increase in the frequency of social initiations by peers and a corresponding increase in their use of positive social reinforcers contingent upon Karl's behaviours. The data to be presented here represented only a partial test of the hypothesis because the data were collected only for the occurrence of social *initiations* by peers to Karl. It was predicted that the conditioning programme would result in an increase in the frequency of initiations of positive social contacts made by the peer group to Karl and a corresponding increase in the frequency of positive initiations made by Karl to the peer group. The data for the frequency of social initiations consisted of such responses as: talking, smiling, playing, and touching. These events were also recorded by 15-sec intervals (Fig. 4).

Early in the conditioning period, the frequency of occurrence of positive initiations by peers increased nine- or ten-fold. It should be kept in mind that these data were collected each day in the period immediately prior to the conditioning sessions; these data then reflect generalization, or transfer of conditioning effects.

There was a significant increase in frequency of social initiations by peers to Karl; there was also a significant increase in the frequency of positive social initiations by Karl to the peers. Both sets of initiations were at least doubled during conditioning. However, 2 months after the termination of the study it is clear that some of these earlier, more dramatic gains have been lost. The data from the end of the follow-up period show that the overall gain was only two- or three-fold for both sets of behaviours.

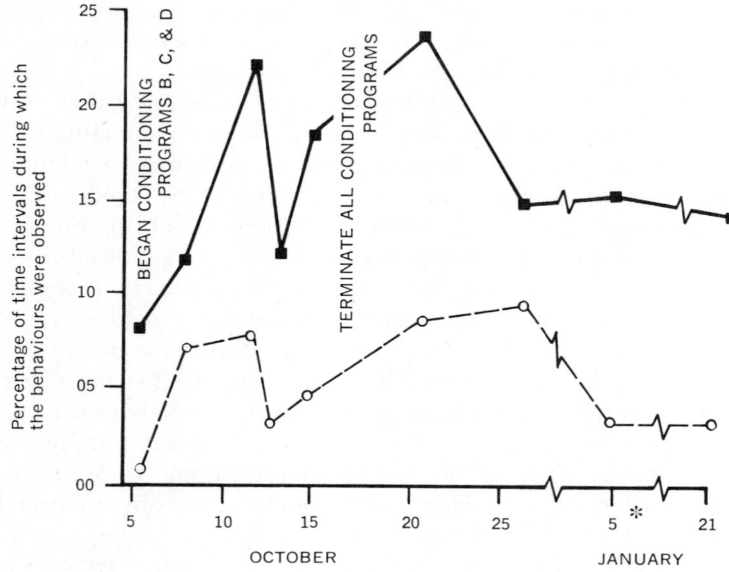

Fig. 4. Changes in the interaction between Karl and his peers.
■Frequency of positive initiations by Karl.
○Frequency of positive initiations by peers.
*Based upon only 20 min of observation; the remainder of the period was too highly structured to permit social initiations.

Discussions with both parents and with the teacher during the follow-up period indicate that Karl is "a changed boy". The casual observer in the classroom would have no reason to select Karl as showing particularly deviant behaviour. His behaviour is characterized by less avoidance of social contacts and increased responsiveness to social reinforcers. Although still somewhat impulsive, Karl no longer displayed temper tantrums, nor did he isolate himself. During the baseline period, Karl would clutch a child by the arm and say such things to him as "I like you". He would then continue to hold the child's arm as he stared intently into the other child's face for a good 10 sec.* These primitive interactions no longer occurred. By any reasonable criteria, the changes in Karl constituted "successful treatment".

*This latter set of behaviour was of particular concern to the writers because of its similarities to atavistic behaviours of this kind occasionally observed in schizophrenic children. Following the study, Karl was examined by an ophthalmologist who prescribed glasses. These "primitive" behaviours disappeared.

DISCUSSION

In some respects, data of the kind presented in this report are becoming commonplace. They show that manipulation of reinforcement contingencies has a significant impact upon behaviour; these findings in turn have practical implications for the treatment of children with deviant behaviour problems. The first "rush" of data collecting activity served both to reiterate our faith in the Law of Effect, and also to definitely place the promissory note proffered by the behaviour modifier in a place of prominence. However, at this point in the development of the field, we should be able to raise questions which are more sophisticated than those which characterized the earlier investigations. There is one set of questions which have been encountered repeatedly in attempts to carry out behaviour modification studies in the laboratories here at Oregon. The general question concerns statements about the variables which determine the persistence and generality of treatment effects. In our first studies we were impressed by the fact that we were obtaining dramatic generalization of conditioning effects (Patterson, 1965a, 1965b). In one of these studies the control over hyperactive behaviours quickly generalized from the conditioning periods to occasions in which the child was not directly under the control of the apparatus. We assumed that the generalization occurred because of the similarity in stimulus components present during conditioning and those present during the remainder of the day. In fact, our procedures had been constructed in an effort to maximize just such transfer of effects. For example, in the series of studies using hyperactive children as subjects, the conditioning was carried out in the classroom setting on occasions when the subject was engaged in routine classroom activities (Patterson, 1965b). The observation data obtained in this series of studies showed that not only did the conditioning effects generalize, but they persisted over extended periods of time. The data presented by Patterson and Ebner (1965) showed that a drop in the rate of production of deviant behaviour can produce an effect on the social environment. In *some* groups, when the subject becomes less deviant, the peers began to dispense more positive social reinforcers. Presumably, these reinforcers are contingent upon social behaviours which would compete with the occurrence of the deviant behaviours. However, as yet there are no data available which show that this latter hypothesis is indeed the case.

Our assumption is that the effect of the conditioning (or any successful treatment) produces a re-programming of the social environment; the altered programme of positive and negative reinforcers maintains the effect of the initial behaviour modification. The fact that the peer group now responds by dispensing more social reinforcers also means that the effect would "generalize" to any social setting in which one would find members of this peer group. In effect the term "stimulus generalization" is an oversimplification. For this reason, in our own discussions about the process, we use the phrase "re-programming the social environment" rather than "stimulus generalization".

There are several implications which follow from such a reformulation. For example, if the social environment does not increase the frequency of social reinforcers for socially adaptive behaviours, then any "improvement" occurring from a treatment programme will be of short duration. *Or*, if the social environment continues to "pay off" for the deviant behaviour at a very high rate, the likely outcome would be very little "improvement". An example of the latter would be the attempt to shape some socially adaptive behaviours in an institutional setting which is programmed to pay off heavily for deviant behaviours; e.g. institutions for delinquent adolescents have been shown to provide 70 per cent positive reinforcement for deviant behaviours (Patterson, 1963; Furniss, 1964).

Taken together, the implications of these trends in the data are quite clear. The major focus of the behaviour modifier should be upon the task of directly manipulating the reinforcement programmes being provided by the social environment, rather than upon the behaviour of the individual subject. In effect, we are accusing the behaviour modifier of following too closely the medical model. In the medical model, the behaviour modifier would remove the "tumour" (change the deviant behaviour) and then terminate his treatment programme. It is reasonable to believe that changing deviant behaviour is simply not good enough; the goals for the behaviour modifier must *also* be that of re-programming the social environment in which the subject finds himself.

Attempts to re-programme the social environment are only just beginning. The programme described by Birnbrauer (1965) and by C. Hanf (personal communication) are extremely provocative. In these attempts, the parent and child are observed interacting under relatively controlled laboratory conditions. The parent is reinforced for appropriately reinforcing the child. In our own laboratories, we have recently completed the development of a programmed teaching manual for use by parents and teachers. The main programme consisted of 120 frames which describe the concepts of social reinforcers, extinction, negative reinforcers, latency of reinforcement, and accidental reinforcement of deviant child behaviours. For each of the families which we are now investigating, the observation data in the home and the school are used to develop a branching programme for use by other mothers who have children with similar problems. For example, based upon our experience with Karl, we now have a fifty frame programme on separation phobia and temper tantrum behaviours in children. These programmes will be used in conjunction with our attempts to develop conditioning procedures to be used in re-training the parents *in the home.* This would mean devising new techniques to insure that the change in the programme of social reinforcers is provided both by adults and by peers. For example, it may be necessary to change our thinking about confining deviant children to groups in which they are mutually reinforcing each other's deviant behaviours. It is also necessary for us to re-consider the traditional clinical models which present the 1 to 1 relationship as *the* basis for behaviour change. Our speculations lead us to believe that rather than improving the technology for changing behaviour on a 1 to 1 basis, procedures in the future may rather completely differ from techniques for directly changing the behaviour of the child and focus instead upon a technology which will re-programme the social environment.

This is one further point which should be made in setting behaviour modification procedures in proper perspective. We might take the changes observed in Karl's behaviour as a case in point. Presumably, the conditioning procedures strengthened socially adaptive behaviours which competed with the occurrence of deviant behaviour. However, we do *not* believe that the conditioning procedures *shaped new* classes of socially adaptive behaviours, nor do we believe that the classes of deviant behaviours have been *extinguished.* In the present context, the terms "shaping", "conditioning", or "extinction" refer only to the fact that rankings have been changed in the hierarchy of response probabilities. The term extinction does not imply that such behaviours as "negativism" have vanished. By the same token, such socially adaptive behaviours as "smiling at a peer" are not in any sense completely novel to the child's repertoire. "Conditioning" as it is used here implies only that a member of the class of responses such as "smiling at a peer" are more likely to occur. In a sense, we see the effect of most modification or treatment programmes as consisting of the re-arranging of social behaviours *within already existing hierarchies.*

In this perspective, the "therapist's" main function is to *initiate* the first link in a chain reaction. Such a chain reaction could *not* occur unless the child had been previously conditioned for socially adaptive behaviours. Also, the major changes occur outside the conditioning trials as the social environment begins to respond differently to the child who is being treated. It is the social environment which supports (or sabotages) the changes produced in treatment. In some cases this change in the schedule of positive social reinforcements results in the increased visibility of a whole spectrum of social behaviours which had previously been at very low strength. This latter phenomenon is familiar to both behaviour modifiers and to traditional therapists.

SUMMARY

The report described a series of behaviour modification programmes for altering hyperaggressive, fearful, negativistic behaviours in a 5-year-old child who had been rejected by his peer group. The parents, teachers, peer group *and* the experimenters served as treatment agents. One programme counter conditioned the fear reactions; a "time out" procedure was used to alter the assaultive behaviour, and an operant conditioning technique was used to increase co-operative behaviours. Finally, a conditioning programme was initiated which altered the interaction between child and his peers. Observation data were collected prior to, during, and following the experimental programme to provide a basis for evaluating the outcomes.

REFERENCES

BIRNBRAUER, J. S., BIJOU, S. W., WOLF, M. M., and KIDDER, J. D. (1965) Programmed instruction in the classroom. In *Case Studies in Behaviour Modifications.* (Edited by . Ullmann and L Krasner). Holt, Rinehart & Winston, Inc., New York, pp. 358–363.

BRICKER, W. A. Speech training with autistic and mentally retarded children. Paper read at the Society for Research in Child Development Convention, Minneapolis, 1965.

ERICKSON, MARILYN T. (1962) Effects of social deprivation and satiation on verbal conditioning in children. *J. Comp. Physiol. Psychol.,* **55**, 953–957.

EYSENCK, H. J. (1960) *Behaviour Therapy and the Neurosis.* Pergamon Press, Oxford.

FERSTER, C. B., and DEMYER, MARLAN K. (1961) The development of performances in autistic children in an automatically controlled environment. *J. Chron. Dis.,* **13**, 312–345.

FURNISS, JEAN M., 1964. Peer reinforcement of behaviour in an institution for delinquent girls. Unpub. M. A. thesis, Oregon State University, Corvallis, Oregon.

GEWIRTZ, J. AND BAER, D. (1958) Deprivation and satiation of social reinforcers as drive conditions. *J. Abnorm Soc. Psychol.,* **57**, 165–172.

GROSSBERG, J. M. (1964) Behaviour therapy: a review. *Psychol. Bull.,* **62**, 73–88.

HAGGARD, E. A. (1958) *Intra Class Correlations and the Analysis of Variance.* Dryden, New York.

HARRIS, FLORENCE, JOHNSTON, MARGARET, KELLY, SUSAN, and WOLF, M. (1964) Effects of positive social reinforcement on regressed crawling of a nursery school child. *J. Educ. Psychol.*, **55**, 35–41.

HINGTGEN, J. N., SANDERS, B., and DEMYER, MARION (1965) Shaping co-operative responses in early childhood schizophrenia. In *Case Studies in Behaviour Modification.* (Edited by L. Ullmann and L. Krasner). Holt, Rinehart & Winston, Inc., New York.

JONES, H. G. (1960) The behavioural treatment of enuresis nocturn. In *Behaviour Therapy and the Neurosis.* (Edited by Eysenck, H. J.). Pergamon Press, Oxford, pp. 377–403.

JONES, MARY C. (1924) A laboratory study of fear: The case of Peter. *Pedag. Semin.*, **31**, 308–315.

KANFER, F. H., and PHILLIPS, JEANNE (1965) Behaviour therapy: A panacea for all ills or a passing fancy? Mimeo paper, Univ. of Oregon Medical School, Portland, Oregon.

LAZARUS, H. A., and ABRAMOWITZ, A. (1962) The use of "motive images" in the treatment of children's phobias. *J. Ment. Sci.*, **108**, 191–195.

LOVAAS, I., SCHAEFFER, B., and SIMMONS, J. (1964) Experimental studies in childhood schizophrenia: Building social behaviours using electric shock. Paper read at *Am. Psychol. Ass.*, Los Angeles.

MCCALL, W. A. (1922) *How to Measure in Education.* Crowell-Collier-Macmillan, New York.

PATTERSON, G. R. (1963) State Institutions as teaching machines for delinquent behaviour. Unpublished mimeo paper, Child Study Center, University of Oregon.

PATTERSON, G. R. (1964) An empirical approach to the classification of disturbed children. *J. Clin. Psychol.*, **20**, 326–337.

PATTERSON, G. R. (1965a) A learning theory approach to the treatment of the school phobic child. In *Case Studies in Behaviour Modification.* (Edited by L. Ullmann and L. Krasner). Holt, Rinehart and Winston, Inc., New York.

PATTERSON, G. R. (1965b) The modification of hyperactive behaviour in children. Paper read at *Soc. Res. Child Dev.*, Minneapolis, Minn.

PATTERSON, G. R., and EBNER, M. (1965) Applications of learning principles to the treatment of deviant children. Paper read at *Am. Psychol. Conv.*, Chicago, Ill.

PATTERSON, G. R., and FAGOT, BEVERLY (1966) Children's responsiveness to multiple agents in a social reinforcement task. Mimeo paper, Child Study Center, University of Oregon, Eugene, Oregon.

SKINNER, B. F. (1958) *Science of Human Behaviour.* Crowell-Collier-Macmillan, New York.

ULLMANN, L. and KRASNER, L. (Eds.) (1965) *Case Studies in Behaviour Modification.* Holt, Rinehart and Winston, Inc., New York.

WALTERS, R. H., and KAROL, PEARL (1960) Social deprivation and verbal behaviour. *J. Personality,* **28,** 89–107.

WALTERS, R. H., and ROY, E. (1960) Anxiety, social isolation and reinforcer effectiveness. *J. Personality,* **28,** 358–367.

WILLIAMS, C. D. (1959) The elimination of tantrum behaviour by extinction procedures. *J. Abnorm. Soc. Psychol.,* **59,** 269.

WOLF, M., RISLEY, T., and MEES, H. (1963) Application of operant conditioning procedures to the behaviour problems of an autistic child. Paper read at *Western Psychol. Ass.,* Santa Monica, Calif. (mimeo).

WOLFE, J. (1958) *Psychotherapy by Reciprocal Inhibition.* Stanford University Press, Stanford.

Teaching Behavioral Principles to Parents of Disturbed Children

LEOPOLD O. WALDER
SHLOMO I. COHEN
DENNIS E. BREITER
PAUL G. DASTON
IRWIN S. HIRSCH
J. MICHAEL LEIBOWITZ

The major purpose of the applied research described below is to explore and develop procedures for training parents to be effective behavior therapists for their own disturbed children. One goal of our work has been to write manuals of procedure in order to make our methods objective and generally available.

Our research is based on the assumptions that the behavior of the child is a function of his environment and that the person responsible for the child's environment is the appropriate change agent. The parents are typically responsible for the child's environment; therefore, we attempt to give the parents technical information and consultation to help them control that environment more effectively. We apply principles and techniques from the experimental psychology of learning to accomplish this goal.

Treatments we have utilized and continue to develop include (1) having educational group meetings with parents, (2) consulting with individual pairs of parents, and (3) structuring a more controlled laboratory-like environment within the home. As part of our research program different families are exposed to all, one, or some combination of these educational techniques.

We typically work with the parents of children who are labelled schizo-

This is a revision of a paper read at the Eastern Psychological Association Meeting, Boston, 1967 and is printed with the permission of the authors.

phrenic, autistic, brain damaged, or retarded. Currently, 19 families all with behaviorally disturbed children are involved in three projects.

Fifteen mothers are participating in Project H (Hirsch, 1967). These mothers are being exposed to the *group education only* treatment. An additional 15 mothers are on a waiting list to serve in future research with the group only treatment.

In Project B (Breiter, 1967) one set of parents has been exposed to intensive consultation in their home. Under the supervision of the consultant, each parent is also required to individually demonstrate the skills they have acquired by altering specific undesirable behaviors of their child in a controlled environment within the home.

Three families participate in the third project. The three pairs of parents are exposed to all three treatments. These parents attend a series of individual consultative interviews which are coordinated with the educational meetings. Each set of parents is advised by the individual behavior consultant to structure a laboratory-like environment for teaching the child in their home. The remainder of the present discussion is largely concerned with the three treatments (group meeting, individual consulting, and use of controlled environments in the home) as applied to the group of three families.

One evening a week for 16 weeks the three pairs of parents come to our facilities. During these weeks the six parents and two staff members meet together for a one-hour group educational session. During the last 12 of the 16 weeks, each pair of parents remains for an hour after the group meeting to meet with one or two staff members for a one-hour individual consultative session. We shall describe, in turn, these group and individual sessions.

THE EDUCATIONAL GROUP

The educational group is composed of the three pairs of parents, a group leader who is a member of our staff, and a second staff member who is a passive observer of group leader behaviors. The purposes of the group are to teach the parents general principles of learning and to teach them to perform a functional analysis of behavior. Admission to the group is contingent upon the parents' completion of a weekly written homework assignment. These assignments usually consist of the parents' reading short behavioral vignettes which describe specific behavior problems. Written answers to questions which follow the vignettes are the parents' ticket of admission to the subsequent group session. The written answers to the problems presented in the vignettes provide data relevant to observing changes in the parents' verbal sophistication in behavior control techniques during the 16 weeks of parent participation in the project. To try to define the educational techniques in the group, observations have been made on such group leader behaviors as the use of operant concepts, praising parents, punishing parents and the use of other accepted learning techniques.

To achieve our group educational goals we have developed a program with four major steps. The first of these steps is *to teach the parents how to accurately observe behavior and record data.* We have allotted four weeks to achieve this first step. During these first four weekly sessions, the parents hear brief lectures on the importance of accurately observing and recording behavior and are taught techniques to accomplish these goals. Following each of these lectures, the parents are required to actually engage in the behavior of observing and recording by viewing short two-person interactions through a one-way mirror. The parents' observations are the basis for discussing problems encountered in the accurate observation of behavior. In this way the parents are gradually shaped to be objective recorders of behavior rather than subjective interpreters. They are taught to accurately observe behavior and record data so that a behavioral problem can be precisely defined. We view precise specification of the behaviors involved as essential to the functional analysis of the problem behaviors.

In addition to practicing observation and answering questions about the behavioral vignettes, the parents are instructed to observe their child in the home for a short period every day and to hand in these observations at the following group meeting. The parents are also required to rank order the five most undesirable behaviors to be decreased. As the first four weeks continue, the parents refine these lists in clear behavioral terms. For example, a parent may initially list "negativism" as an undesirable behavior. By the fourth week, the behavior referred to may be more accurately described as "Johnny doesn't go to sleep when I tell him to".

At week 5 we start the consultative interviews (to be described below) and the second step in the educational program. During this phase we introduce contrived contingencies into the observed behavioral interactions and teach the parents to *identify these contingencies.* A short lecture about the ABC's of behavior—*A*ntecedent events, *B*ehaviors, and *C*onsequent events—introduces this phase of the program. Behavior-environment interactions are discussed and examples are given. A Greenspoonian situation is also observed in which one person says "uh-huh" or "yes" following each statement of self-reference made by a second person. In the discussion subsequent to this observation session, the operations of reinforcement and extinction are discussed and clarified. Prepared materials about these topics written by members of our staff, and relevant studies from the professional literature are required reading for the parents. Questions on all the materials are distributed and written answers to the questions comprise the homework to be handed in at the following session. Session 6 is used to demonstrate the importance of the immediacy of reinforcement. Written materials on shaping are distributed at this meeting together with questions to be answered.

The third step in the program is focussed on *allowing parents to practice shaping.* We have allotted 8 weeks to achieve this goal, since shaping is the primary skill required for dealing with the child who exhibits severe behavioral deficits. In session 7, written educational materials and questions on shaping are discussed. Following this discussion, the group leader demonstrates important principles by shaping a behavior of one of the parents, while the remaining parents observe the demonstration. In this session a shaping switch is used which operates a short tone and a counter, both of which have proved to be reinforcers. Parents being shaped are instructed to earn as many points as possible.

In week 8, a movie on "Reinforcement Therapy" is shown. Parents are instructed to observe things in the film related to past discussions in the group sessions. In the subsequent two sessions (9 and 10) while the other parents observe, each parent in turn is given the opportunity to shape a behavior of another parent by using the tone as a reinforcer for a desired behavior. All of the sessions conclude with a discussion about what occurs during the shaping sessions. Then, for four sessions (11 – 14) the parents are given the opportunity to shape two behaviors (bar pressing and rearing) in food-deprived rats and to study the effects of intermittent reinforcement on responding in extinction. We use the animal laboratory facilities for this aspect of the educational program.

The last step in the group educational program is *to review the principles and procedures of behavior control and see how they have been applied by the parents.* We achieve this step in the final two sessions (15 and 16) when parents make case presentations to the group of some of the procedures they instituted in their homes.

INDIVIDUAL CONSULTATION

The second technique to be described here is consultation with individual pairs of parents. *Individual consultation* starts for the three families on week 5 and overlaps with the remaining 12 weeks of the group educational series. After each of the last 12 group meetings there is a short break. Each pair of parents then enters one of three consultation rooms with their behavior consultant. Ideally the consultant has prepared an agenda for that meeting. What occurs is described in three ways. (1) Observers on the other side of one-way mirrors count occurrences of predetermined categories of consultant behaviors; (2) the consultant takes notes and dictates a report after the parents have left; and (3) the consultant records the session with an audio tape recorder. Copies of the agenda are given to the observers and to the parents at the start of the session.

The agenda first lists the assignments due from the previous consultative meeting. If the parents have not fulfilled the assignment, the session ends immediately after the assignments have been discussed and clarified and the parents are asked to return when the assignment is completed. The assignment may consist of a written progress report by the parents or a tally of the frequency of some behaviors of the child and how the parent responded. If the parents have completed the assignment, the complete agenda is followed. During later interviews parents may be asked to prepare and bring in a program describing changes in the way they will respond to one of the child's behaviors. At the end of each individual session the parents are given another assignment. Early in the series of interviews the consultant takes more responsibility for devising the assignment, but the parents are progressively given more and more responsibility in planning subsequent procedures. An example from one of our current cases may be useful here.

In order to get first-hand data on a mother-child interaction about which the parents complained, the consultant rode along in the car as the mother drove somewhere with two of her children. It became clear to the consultant that the mother responded to her children when their playing in the car interfered with her driving safely. She did not respond to them when they were not bothering her. It seemed to the consultant that the mother was supporting the very behaviors that bothered her. In fact the complaints of the parents related only to negative behaviors which they wanted to decrease. Based on these observations the parents were told that they would also have to specify the child behaviors to be increased so that they could more efficiently use the techniques they were being taught. Completion of the assignment was, of course, their ticket of admission for future consultation. Once they had defined the behaviors to be increased they were admitted to the following consultative session. In that session they were told how to count the occurrences of the negative (to be decreased) and positive (to be increased) behaviors in order to establish baselines. The parents were given increasingly more responsibility in planning the manipulation of the child's environment in the car to change the child's behavior in the desired direction.

The individual consultation aspects of our program most resemble conventional psychotherapy or counseling. The two parents of the child meet weekly with a behavior consultant (and occasionally with a co-consultant). They talk together in an office for up to 60 minutes with the discussion focussing on helping the parents to deal with their child by advising them in the application of the principles of behavior control.

After the parents leave, the consultants meet as a group to receive feedback from the observers. In addition, consultants are praised if they are described as behaving within the specified limits of an operant framework. Some of the consultants' behaviors which are praised are: teaching and advising parents; using operant concepts; selectively reinforcing desired parental behaviors; working to reduce the parents' discomfort by helping them gain relevant skills; shaping parental competence in behavior modification; and in general providing the parents with a model for them to imitate. In this feedback session, we not only describe our form of behavioral consultation, we also attempt to control the behaviors of the consultants.

CONTROLLED LEARNING ENVIRONMENT

The third technique to be described is the *controlled learning environment.* The use of operant techniques for the control of behavior requires that one have control of the environment in which the behavior is emitted. Investigators who have utilized behavior modification techniques in institutions (Ayllon, 1963) have programmed the environment to respond selectively to specified response classes and have controlled the supply of reinforcers. The situation in the home is usually much different. Home environments maintain parental behaviors which are often incompatible with the behaviors necessary for effecting positive changes in the child. One example of this is the frequent difficulty experienced in getting mothers to deprive their children of food. Other difficulties arise because the home environment also supports child behaviors which compete with the behaviors that parents may wish to instate. When a parent is attempting to shape some behavior, the situation is usually aversive to the child and his attempts to escape to another area of the home are intermittently reinforced. Unless some changes in the home environment are accomplished, attempts to modify behaviors will be only partially successful. The establishment of a controlled environment is a step in this direction.

Our experience with establishing controlled learning environments in the homes of the three families we have been discussing is still limited. We shall use as an example the family in Project B which is being given only individual consultation in their home. There the consultant helped the parents establish two controlled environments, one for an hour each afternoon with the mother as experimenter and the other for an hour each evening with the father as experimenter. In these settings the interactions between the child and a parent are recorded as the parent attempts to teach the child some skill. On the basis of these records, changes in parent responding are suggested. Remarkable improvements in the child's behavior in those restricted learning environments have followed. In addition the parents are learning to treat the child differently outside of the experimental session, and gratifying changes in the child's behavior are becoming apparent.

Our plans with this technique include helping other families set up learning laboratories in their homes and introducing token economies. Such a controlled therapeutic environment in the home may be what is needed to more efficiently modify extreme behavior patterns.

To sum up, we have described a research and development program. We are building new techniques, we are objectifying the techniques we have built, and we are evaluating these techniques. The evaluation of these techniques involves improving the quality of data and designing studies with adequate controls and comparisons. We have not had time in the present discussion to detail all of our efforts to achieve these purposes, but our goal is to deliver to the clinical community therapeutic skills which are teachable and have demonstrated effectiveness.

REFERENCES

Ayllon, Teodoro. Intensive treatment of psychotic behavior by stimulus situations & food reinforcement. *Behavior Research and Therapy,* 1963, *1*, 53–61.

Breiter, D. E. The analysis of deviant child behaviors in the home. Unpublished doctoral dissertation, University of Maryland, 1967.

Hirsch, I. S. Training mothers in groups as reinforcement therapist for their own children. Unpublished doctoral dissertation, University of Maryland, 1967.

Filial Therapy: Description and Rationale[1]

BERNARD GUERNEY, JR.[2]

Filial Therapy involves training parents, in groups of 6 to 8, to conduct play sessions with their emotionally disturbed young children, using an orientation and methodology modeled after client-centered play therapy. After training, the parents conduct their play sessions at home while continuing their weekly group meetings. Parents' sessions with their therapist begin with discussion of the play sessions, but may extend to any other areas that are emotionally relevant. Preliminary experience with 2 groups suggests that this type of method is deserving of further exploration as a method of increasing leverage of professional resources, and as a tool for gaining further insight into children's fantasy and parent-child relationships.

The great and growing need for combating emotional problems demands that much research be done to increase the leverage of professionals' time in effective psychotherapy. New methods should be explored to combat emotional problems early in life. Once such problems become

Reprinted with permission from *Journal of Consulting Psychology*, 1964, Vol. 28, No. 4, 304–310, Copyright 1964 by the American Psychological Association, and with the permission of the author.

[1]This research was supported, in part, by a grant from the University Research Council of Rutgers State University and, in part, by Public Health Service grant MH-08653–01 from the National Institute of Mental Health.

[2]The author is very grateful to Louise F. Guerney and Michael Andronico for their counsel, and their services as Filial Therapists; and to Lillian Stover, Thomas Steinberg, and Louise Clempner for their assistance in organizing and screening the Filial Therapy groups.

relatively fixed, even massive expenditures of professional time often later fail to be of use. Hobbs (1963), speaking of plans for the development of clinical psychology, states that,

> clinical psychology should now reclaim its birthright and devote itself primarily to problems of children. Fully one-half of our resources for the conduct of research and the provision of services should be invested in people under the age of twenty. Another one-fourth of our resources for research and service should be invested in adults who are identified primarily through their relationships with children [p. 3].

Also, there should be attempts to develop new methods which allow each hour of professional time (and each square foot of physical facility, if you will) to help more individuals, and help them as effectively or more effectively than traditional methods have been able to do. We again quote Hobbs (1963):

> Much of the practice of clinical psychology as well as psychiatry is obsolete. A profession that is built on a fifty minute hour of a one-to-one relationship between therapist and client . . . is living on borrowed time. The only substantial justification for investing the time of a highly trained professional person in the practice of psychotherapy as we know it is the possibility of discovering new and more efficient ways of working with people who are in trouble [p. 3].

The filial psychotherapy proposed here represents an attempt to develop a new method incorporating both these goals. (In addition, taking a long-range view, the method may have potential as a preventative measure and as a method of building a foundation in childhood for better mental health and self-realization in adulthood.)

The technique uses parents as therapeutic agents with their own children. While the approach outlined here is new, there are encouraging precursors to employing parents in this capacity. Freud (1959) states in *Analysis of a Phobia in a Five-Year-Old Boy,*

> the treatment itself was carried out by the child's father. . . . No one else could possibly have prevailed on the child to make such avowals; the special knowledge by means of which he was able to interpret the remarks made by his . . . son was indispensable [p. 149].

Another precedent is reported by Moustakas (1959). He suggests that "play therapy" sessions be conducted in the home by parents of relatively normal children, and he describes the very positive experiences of some mothers and children in such "relationship therapy." One such experience is reported separately by Natalie Fuchs (1957). With the encouragement of her father, Carl Rogers, she undertook home play therapy sessions with her daughter, and achieved impressive results in overcoming a toilet-training problem. A third major precedent is the view, supported by illustrative material, of Dorothy Baruch (1949) that play sessions at home offer a way of fostering good parent-child relationships. The home play techniques recommended by Moustakas and Baruch are in the same Rogerian tradition as those used in Filial Therapy. The parents to which they refer were not necessarily dealing with children who were emotionally disturbed in the clinical sense, but neither did the parents have continued close instruction, supervision, and the opportunity to discuss the process in a group therapy situation, as is the case in Filial Therapy. Thus, we regard their favorable experiences as encouraging with respect to Filial Therapy.

NATURE OF FILIAL THERAPY

Filial Therapy involves the training of parents of young children (in groups of six to eight) to conduct play sessions with their own children in a very specific way. After training, parents continue to meet weekly with the therapist to discuss results, conclusions, and inferences about their children and themselves. The sessions between the parents and child take place at home. The parent begins the play sessions at 30 minutes once weekly. This may later be increased, as desired, up to 45 minutes and two or more times a week.

The manner in which the child's play sessions are to be conducted is intended first to break the child's perception or misperception of the parent's feelings, attitudes, or behavior toward him. Second, they are intended to allow the child to communicate thoughts, needs, and feelings to his parents which he has previously kept from them, and often from his own awareness. (This communication is mainly through the medium of play.) The children's sessions with their parents are thus meant to lift repressions and resolve anxiety-producing internalized conflicts. Third, they are intended to bring the child—via incorporation of newly perceived attitudes on the part of his parents—a greater feeling of self-respect, self-worth, and confidence. The techniques or methods to be employed by the parents to accomplish this are modeled as closely as possible after therapy techniques in the Rogerian tradition, as exemplified by the writing, for example, of Dorfman (Rogers, 1951, Ch. 6) and Moustakas (1953).

Parent groups consist of mothers and fathers, about equally divided, who are not spouses. Because of the unique problems presented by the approach, flexibility of the group therapist's approach is necessary. Instructional techniques are used, including demonstration play sessions conducted by the therapist, and role-playing techniques. But when exploration of parental feelings and attitudes is involved in the instruction and later discussions, the group therapist is relatively client centered. Intensive probing and interpretation are generally not used.

The therapy may be described in terms of three general stages:

Stage 1. The first part of Stage 1 consists of an explanation, in as simple and personally meaningful terms as possible, of the benefits to be derived for the child and for parent-child relationships from the period of free expression and self-direction described. This is described in terms of release from tension-producing inner conflict, freer communication processes from child to parent, giving the child a greater sense of self-direction, self-respect, and self-confidence. The goals of the sessions are interwoven with discussion of the specific techniques to be employed. Full attention is paid to the parents' feelings and reactions, rather than employing a straight didactic approach. The goals of the sessions are explained to the parents as follows:

1. The encouragement of complete determination of the activities of the child by the child, within certain specified, definite limits, such as no destruction of nonplay material, and no activities which would be physically painful to child or parent.
2. The development of empathic understanding on the part of the parent as to the basic needs and feelings the child is trying to communicate and express through his play.
3. The immediate communication back to the child that these needs and feelings are understood, and that he as an individual is fully accepted, whatever his feelings or thoughts may be.
4. The need of the child to learn to see and accept responsibility for his actions. This is represented in the sessions by an understanding, but completely firm, enforcement of the "limits," mentioned earlier, under which the sessions are run. In other words, the child is expected to learn that he and his feelings are accepted, but that certain overt acts are not tolerated, and when the child performs them he will immediately, and invariably, suffer the undesirable consequence. In the context of the sessions, this consequence is the termination of the particular session.

It is emphasized to the parent that specific techniques will be meaningless, or worse, if they are applied only mechanically and not as a reflection of a genuine attempt at empathy. However, specific techniques to aid them in accomplishing the above goals are taught. These are the traditional techniques of Rogerian therapy: structuring, restatement of content, and, with major emphasis, clarification of feeling. Several demonstration sessions by the therapist are conducted, with the parents behind a one-way screen. Normal children and the children of the parents in the group are used for the demonstrations.

In the second part of Stage 1, the parents attempt to play their session role with either another parent's child or their own before beginning at home. The therapist's and parents' observed sessions are discussed by the group to enhance the group's understanding of the role, and their mastery of it. The orientation at the beginning is a completely task-oriented one, designed to maximize motivation and minimize resistance. The therapist clearly differentiates the parent's general role from the session role, and parents are not especially encouraged to attempt any of these techniques outside the session. But the questions concerning this possibility are discussed. (It is felt that much of that kind of generalization which is desirable could take place without direct encouragement from the therapist.)

Stage 2. The second stage begins after about six to eight sessions. When the parents and the therapist feel they are ready, the parents begin their sessions at home with their own children. Each parent has been provided, usually at their expense, with about $25 worth of standard play therapy equipment, including a family of Flagg dolls, a "house" made out of a corrugated box with lines painted on it to delineate "rooms," a "Joe Palooka" puncho bag, rubber knife, clay, crayons, paper, tea set, etc. They conduct the play session in a room suitable for play activities, and arrange things so that they will be uninterrupted for the preset time of the session. Parents take notes following the sessions, according to a prescribed outline. When available, tape recordings of the sessions that the parents may make at home can also be used as a starting point for discussion.

Techniques always remain a pertinent area for discussion in the group sessions themselves, and the therapist is always willing to revert to methodological and, therefore, task-oriented discussion. However, at this point, the therapist endeavors to focus the parents' attention on their own emotional reactions in the sessions, as well as those of their children.

Final Stage. As the therapy succeeds sufficiently to suggest to the parent that there is no longer a need for help, this is discussed by the group, and the parent, of course, is free to terminate. If and when a group gets down to three or four people for this reason, or because parents drop out for other reasons, a group may be merged with another similarly diminished group.

RATIONALE FOR FILIAL THERAPY

The question may rightly be asked: "How can parents who presumably contributed heavily to the creation of the problem be agents who are now expected to make a major contribution to its solution? Will not asking these parents to interact with their children in emotionally laden, conflicted areas only worsen the problem?" We would reply first that parents interact heavily with their children under any circumstances. What we are training them to try to do during their session is to accept and understand their problems better, and in the process to *avoid* interpreting their behavior to them, avoid punitive action, etc. It is hard to see how this can worsen the child's predicament. And, should the sessions not directly help the child, they may still serve a very valuable purpose as catalysts to meaningful discussion in the parents' group therapy sessions.

To further clarify the issues, the theoretical views and propositions underlying this approach are briefly summarized below:

1. With young children living with their families, the primary source of maladjustment can presumably be traced directly or indirectly to interpersonal relationships, past and present, within the family, and to the patterns of deprivation, conflict, and defense that these relationships have engendered.

2. Two complementary, traditional paths for resolving the difficulties of the child are: (*a*) a therapist working with the child individually, fulfilling deprived needs and resolving conflicts, and (*b*) a therapist working with the parent toward changing the network of family relationships that support and reinforce the child's maladjustment.

3. In 2*a* above, the child's therapist, using traditional play therapy techniques, is presumably effective for three primary, interrelated reasons: *(a)* because the therapist delivers affective supplies needed by the child, and revises the child's self-concept via his respect and concern for the child; *(b)* because the therapist, by permissiveness and understanding, can extinguish the anxiety associated with certain feelings and thoughts, thereby relaxing defenses and allowing for the working through of conflicts and previously repressed feelings; a process which, to complete the circle, further reduces overdeveloped defensive patterns; *(c)* because the therapist serves, through all his interactions with the child, to correct the distortions (or, in terms of learning theory, overgeneralizations) that the child carries with him in his perceptions of other people. These distortions were based on his experiences within the family, and had served to perpetuate and reinforce his intrapsychic and interpersonal difficulties. (Note that from the point of view presented in 3*a*, *b*, and *c*, the therapist's permissiveness and understanding are paramount. Detailed knowledge of intrapsychic dynamics is viewed as playing a very secondary role; rather, permissiveness, understanding, interest, and concern create the climate under which the individual can work through and resolve his problems, see Hobbs, 1962).

4. In the method proposed, the parent's intimate involvement in the specific plan to help the child will mobilize the parent's motivation to be helped and, perhaps more important, to be *of* help. It is anticipated that

this will eliminate much of the resistance that is encountered where the parent is not quite sure exactly what is going on in the treatment of the child; or worse, when despite reassurances to the contrary, the parent emotionally interprets the treatment plan as meaning that he has done something wrong and the only way to aid his child is to yield up the child to a therapist who will try to correct the damage he has done. Under these circumstances, the parent sometimes unconsciously fears that the child's therapist is a rival. Many such parents probably never begin treatment. If they do, there is the danger—of which all child therapists are aware—of a parent terminating therapy at precisely the point where progress has begun with the child, because of this rivalry. The present approach, on the other hand, may be expected to give the parents the feeling that they are not necessarily a destructive force in the child's life, but that, in fact, their help is vital in aiding the child. It is expected that this will have the effect of enhancing motivation to undertake and continue treatment.

5. With very few exceptions, parents of nonpsychotic, young, emotionally troubled children, given a very *clearly defined* role to play for a *clearly limited* time of day, and given *corrective feedback* by the therapist and by other parents attempting to learn the same thing, may be expected to learn to play that role with the child reasonably successfully.

6. A parent's very difficulties in learning to play such a role may prove to be a valuable source of material for re-examination and eventual insight. Such difficulties may enable the Filial Therapist, other parents in the group, and the particular parent himself to quickly bring to the fore the particular values he adheres to in child rearing, his conception of the good parent, his areas of inflexibility and of inability to respond to the needs of the child. It is anticipated that this will be a catalytic force for group therapy of parents that will be of significant value.

7. The fact that the parent is experimenting regularly, even for short spans of time, with a new role, could well have the effect of weakening habitual negative patterns of interaction with the child. It may do so by making it apparent that behavior which previously seemed the only possible kind of response to a given behavior on the part of the child is but one of several alternatives. (For example, recognition of the child's feeling, accompanied by firm setting of limits, as an alternative to punitive remarks and actions.) It is expected that this will facilitate the parent's ability to change negative patterns of interaction with the child.

8. By attentively observing the child with the child's needs uppermost in mind, and by the child's increased freedom in expressing himself during the sessions, the parent is in a position to gain greater understanding of the child, from which the parent can in turn gain more realistic expectations and attitudes.

9. The degree of voluntary attention and devotion to the child's needs

on the part of the parent should prove to be therapeutic, even if there is a degree of failure in fulfilling the exact requirements of the prescribed role that is greater than is anticipated. This is expected by virtue of the fact that the interest and attention will at least be there; which could lead to an increased sense of security, improved self-concept, and a reduction of hostility on the part of the child.

10. Every bit of success the parent achieves in successfully filling the prescribed role should have an effect many times more powerful than that of a therapist doing the same thing. Referring back to points *3a, b,* and *c* above: *(a)* a relatively small amount of affection, attention, interest, etc., from the parent, directly, can be expected to be more therapeutic to the child than a large amount from a therapist or parent surrogate; *(b)* assuming some success in the parent's learning of the permissive and understanding role, anxiety should be much more easily extinguished in the presence of the precise stimulus (parent) under which it was originally induced than in the presence of a stimulus which only resembles it (therapist); the child should therefore proceed to lift repression and work through conflicts more quickly; *(c)* when discriminations are established by the child to the effect that the parent himself differs in behavior according to circumstances, overgeneralizations can be corrected at the source; moreover, the whole image of the parent can be reformulated in a much more positive way, allowing the child to make positive rather than negative generalizations toward other people.

11. To a greater extent than in any other form of therapy, with the possible exception of Family Group Therapy, this technique offers the parents an opportunity to learn attitudes and interpersonal techniques which can serve them in consolidating their gains after formal therapy has ended. Further, it may extend their ability to help all their children fulfill their potentials as persons maximally, rather than simply improve negative aspects of their personalities.

PRESENT STATUS OF RESEARCH IN FILIAL THERAPY

At the Rutgers University Psychological Clinic, two Filial Therapy groups are being conducted. One has been going for 10 months and the other for 8 months. A third recently has been started at the Hunterdon Medical Center. Thus, there is not enough evidence at the present time for any quantitative report of results. However, it seems appropriate to present certain qualitative observations, even at this time.

Without evidence to the contrary, one might predict that the play sessions would be emotionally barren and devoid of socially undesirable reference to members of the family. Such a view would be based on the assumption that the parent's presence would inhibit expression of such material, or that the parent-as-therapist would subtly steer the child away from such material. One might also assume that parents could not maintain objectivity and would react negatively in the play sessions to signs of their child's hostility toward them, and be more or less ashamed to discuss such material with one another.

Our experience does not support these assumptions as being generally valid in the context of the Filial Therapy situation. On the contrary, the parent's presence seems often to be a stimulus to "threatening" family-related content, particularly aggression, rather than an inhibiting factor; such themes seem to begin at least as quickly as in ordinary play therapy—frequently in the first or second session. And the parents—trained to assume some of the important attitudes and goals of therapists—welcome the opportunity to present socially unacceptable themes enacted by their children, especially when such themes involve family members. Although attempts to ignore or minimize *implications* of such material are not uncommon, some of the messages are clearly perceived, giving the parent a fuller understanding of the depth of the child's feelings and his own unique view of the world. (One mother, for example, said she and her husband had often commented on the absence of hostility in their daughter, but lately recognized that such hostility had been there all along, when the girl called the "bop bag" she was punching "mother" and then "father.") The excerpt given below from a mother's report of home sessions is presented not as being typical, but to illustrate the above points, and to show that it is not unreasonable to attribute therapeutic potential to the play session itself, in addition to the group therapy experience per se of the parents' therapy sessions.

The boy, Fred, is 7 years old. It must be noted first that his presenting symptoms were the antithesis of overt aggression, and the mother's behavior completely opposite that of a client-centered therapist. As described in the psychological report before therapy began:

> Fred complains frequently of headaches . . . is a nervous child, eats poorly, is enuretic, bites his nails . . . has nightmares . . . is a persistent throat clearer, unhappy, quiet, easily offended, and has no real friends. He is afraid of physical aggression, generally complaining about this sort of behavior from his peers. He denies competition and hostility in himself. . . . Testing and interviewing indicate a directing, assertive mother always controlling and guiding, warning and protecting.

Notes written on the interpretive interview with the mother and father at about the same time stated,

> Mrs. S. seems cold and rigid . . . she said she "flares up" about psychological matters—her worst arguments with her husband come when he tries to im-

> part some psychological insight to her about the children. She also said playing with children runs against her grain and it is something she would like to avoid. . . . Mrs. S. literally winced at the recognition that she would have to spend one hour a week playing with her child.

Nevertheless, in response to the argument that such feelings were all the more reason that she should undertake the task, Mrs. S. agreed to do so, and is one of those who now reports marked improvement in her ability to relate to the child and in the child's behavior.

The excerpt, from a tape recording of the group session, is Mrs. S's report to the group of two consecutive play sessions at about the eighth month of therapy:

> He punched the "bop bag" on the head and said, "That's Sally [his 8 year old sister] . . . I have to kill her. Look how the blood rushes out of her head." I said, "Yes, it is really messy." . . . He said, "Look at her cute belly button." He was almost imitating people who admire Sally's looks. I run into this constantly; people always admiring Sally and nobody saying "Boo" about him. . . . [In the next session] he said to me "I will call out the spiders and tell them to put you in a web; the spiders are my mean friends . . . better yet, I'll get the ghosts to hang you! They will close your eyes and shut your mouth!" I said, "You want my mouth shut; you think I talk too much." He said, "Yes, you boss too much!" After a few minutes of this, he called me "Dad"; it was a Freudian slip—he was doing that all day today, too, oddly enough. . . . This ghost business, I just realized . . . it has come up once or twice before. He does want a light in the hall when he goes to sleep. Yet he has never directly said he is afraid of ghosts. . . . Do you think his Freudian slip was important? I think it was. I think he is angry at both of us.

The tone in which this was said was obviously not hostile, but reflected simple acceptance and understanding. She then went on to question how she could best clarify the feelings underlying the fact that when Fred pretends to stab her with the play knife he always turns the knife back upon himself.

In general, it can be said that parents' motivation is high, most play their session role remarkably well, the children are responding with significant emotional release, including dynamic material, and a number of parents have reported great improvement. Thus, our experience has encouraged us to plan for quantitative studies of the Filial method. It has also prompted the present paper, since it has been demonstrated to our satisfaction that this method, or such variations of it as others may devise, is worthy of thorough exploration—exploration not only with the aim of increasing the leverage of professional persons and the physical resources at their disposal, but as another tool for increasing knowledge about the emotional and fantasy life of children, especially as it relates to parent-child interaction.

REFERENCES

BARUCH, DOROTHY W. *New ways in discipline.* New York: McGraw-Hill, 1949, Pp. 161–175.

FREUD, S. Analysis of a phobia in a five-year-old boy. In, *Collected papers.* New York: Basic Books, 1959. Pp. 149–289.

FUCHS, NATALIE R. Play therapy at home. *Merrill-Palmer Quart.,* 1957, 3, 89–95.

HOBBS, N. Sources of gain in psychotherapy. *Amer. Psychologist,* 1962, 17, 741–747.

HOBBS, N. Strategies for the development of clinical psychology. *Amer. Psychol. Ass. Div. Clin. Psychol. Newsltr.,* 1963, **16**(2), 3–5.

MOUSTAKAS, C. W. *Children in play therapy.* New York: McGraw-Hill, 1953.

MOUSTAKAS, C. W. *Psychotherapy with children.* New York: Harper & Row, 1959.

ROGERS, C. R. *Client-centered therapy.* Boston: Houghton Mifflin, 1951.

Filial Therapy: A Case Illustration

BERNARD G. GUERNEY, JR.
LOUISE F. GUERNEY
MICHAEL P. ANDRONICO

The particular case to be presented was chosen for several reasons. The obvious ones are that it proceeded according to our expectations, was successful, and rather dramatic in content; which, of course, is not always the case. But, in addition, it is particularly interesting because the mother, who was the parent selected to be trained to work with the child, was regarded—to quote from summaries of the diagnostic and interpretive interviews before therapy began—as "a challenge to the limits and capacity of filial therapy to motivate parents . . . ." This guarded assessment of the mother's capacity for conforming to the required role was based partly on her personality, and also on her strongly expressed feeling that "the idea of interacting with the child in a play situation is emotionally repulsive." Further, Mrs. S's (the name and initial are fictitious) attitude toward psychology and psychiatry was quite negative. Because of a previous brush with someone in an allied field, she regarded persons in these professional areas as meddlers who are looking for things to criticize, under the guise of presenting an individual with insight about himself.

Her boy, Fred, was a seven-year-old referred to the Rutgers Psychological Clinic by the county mental health clinic. It was reported that he was a nervous child, had frequent headaches, ate poorly, was enuretic, had nightmares, masturbated excessively, bit his nails, and manifested tic-like

This is an excerpt from the article Filial Therapy, *Yale Scientific Magazine*, 1966, Vol. 40, No. 6, p. 6ff., and is reprinted here with the permission of the Yale Scientific Magazine and the authors.

throat clearing. Socially, he was quiet, easily offended, with no friends. He feared physical aggression, and took flight from play with peers when games of this sort were introduced.

Tests of personality revealed that he perceived his home life as highly uncomfortable. He perceived his mother as directing and assertive, always guiding, warning, and protecting, in a most unwelcome way. Father was seen as a hostile figure. There was some indication that the mother was regarded as the more threatening figure "behind the scene," but Fred refused to acknowledge hostility in himself or his mother. The examiner's summary pictured Fred as a bright, anxious child, developing compulsive behavior and manifesting many nervous symptoms. Fear of physical aggression and some hypochondriacal behavior were also present.

Mrs. S. was a very bright, well-read woman in her late thirties. She was rigid and controlling in all phases of her life. She injected herself into all phases of Fred's existence, demanding appreciation for all that she did. She constantly instructed and moralized. She was in awe of authority figures she respected, very scornful toward those she did not. Because of space limitations, we will not discuss the father's personality, except to say that it was relatively bland.

MOTHER'S REACTION TO THE GROUP

Mrs. S. initially reacted against the idea of being a member of a group. She found the other members' comments rather worthless, and felt that only the psychologist's statements had any real meaning. She particularly disliked one group member and attacked her from time to time in terms of how people like her made the group idea a poor one. Mrs. S's criticisms were handled as reflective of her personality rather than a realistic appraisal of the group approach. Ultimately, Mrs. S. confessed to the group that she did, after all, see value in a group approach, because she felt that she had gained as a person in learning to be more accepting of antagonistic views, in contrast to her previous need to attack them. She regarded the behavior of the therapist, which served as a model in this respect, as inducing this change in herself. Toward the end, more than once, she led the group in relating how the group discussions had benefited them.

THE PLAY SESSIONS

With respect to the play session technique, Mrs. S. asked meaningful questions from the beginning. She doubted the wisdom of simply reflecting the child's own feelings, and felt that directing and interpreting his behavior would be more productive. However, she was willing to give the approach a try, and learned to play the role required in the play periods very well. Her biggest problem was in refraining from asking leading questions, which she did control for the most part. While she did not achieve the ultimate in empathic attitude, she became fairly warm and relaxed, and even had a genuinely good time during the play periods—joining in play, as requested by her boy, in a good-natured manner with no airs of adult superiority. Fred accepted the sessions with enthusiasm, and kept up a high level of interest in them until close to the end, when he could take them or leave them. (When problems diminish, motivation to work on them generally lessens as well.) Some of his play periods read like textbook sessions. He expressed, and apparently worked through, Oedipal feelings, castration fears, ambivalence toward his parents and himself, conflict over aggressive feelings, and self-destructive impulses; and, in the end, genuine positive feelings toward himself and his family emerged.

Fred entered into the play situations eagerly, and centered most of his activity for the initial sessions around the Joe Palooka "bop bag" (which bounces back and allows the subject to feel he is really fighting). He commented that he did not want to try to make anything with the Tinkertoy for fear that it would turn out badly. Until Session 4, his mother's special role did not fall under scrutiny. At Session 4, he seemed to be annoyed by the style of her comments and made various critical remarks about them. This abated after a few weeks, when he apparently realized she was not going to change her behavior, and because she handled these remarks by reflecting and accepting his annoyance. Thus, he learned that his mother could tolerate his criticisms—and aggression—and in turn respond uncritically, and even sympathetically.

By Session 6, Fred was able to assemble Tinkertoy objects without fear of making mistakes, and used them quite creatively. However, in quantity and dynamic quality of play, Joe Palooka continued to remain the focus. In the course of the sessions, this punching bag was at times labeled with his father's nickname and soundly beaten. As Father, Palooka had his penis cut off with a rubber knife (no penis actually appears on the figure). As Mother, it was beaten, stabbed, shot, hugged, and told, Fred loved it. As Sister, it was killed, "with blood gushing from its head."

Early in the sessions, Fred had accidently hit Mother with the punching bag. He then received a warning that hitting mother in any form would not be permitted, and would cause the session to end. A few weeks later he did it again; the session was ended. The next week, Fred asked Mother to be sure to tell him when he had one minute left. Mother did, and Fred immediately walloped her with the punching bag. She pointed out that he seemed to have been wanting to do that all of the session (as indicated by various remarks), but that he had waited until the end. He explained that this way he lost only one minute and was still able to hit her. This system he devised continued from this until Session 45. After that, on the rare occasions when Joe Palooka or some other object hit her, it seemed to be truly an accident.

In puppet play, his family was wiped out by crocodiles, storms, huge monsters, Nazis, etc. Father was always first to go—with the son looking after mother, usually until the last minute, when everyone was killed.

At about Session 40, a different tone began to emerge in Fred's play. He included Mother in more activities, wanted her to join him in beating up Palooka, help him by giving him clay bombs to throw, play cards with him, and the like. More often Joe Palooka was Mother, whom he hugged, kissed, and said to, "I adore you." However, there was an increase also in the hostility directed toward her. As Palooka, Mother's nipples were bitten off after he sucked them. He named her the daughter of Frankenstein, made Palooka into his daughter, and bombed her with clay bombs. He drew war pictures with swastikas, which he knew from experience outside the session she did not like, sat on her lap like a baby, and then stuck his tongue out at her. She came into focus as the main figure of interest, and great conflict about her was revealed. He loved her, wanted her, needed her, etc., but could not do so unconditionally. Strong negative feelings were present as well, and feeling of anxiety about his aggressive feelings toward her.

Toward the end, the sessions were calmer and less emotional in content. More of them were devoted to simple play-poker, target games, etc. However, Palooka was still important. Fred usually played the role of world champ and beat him up soundly. (At this point, he started wrestling with father in real life.) Finally, after it was announced to Fred that sessions would end after two more, he had a very symbolic session where he staged "pretend temper tantrums" and then assumed his normal voice and laughed. Mrs. S. remarked that "Big Fred is laughing at Baby Fred," and he agreed. He seemed to be exorcising the babyish element in himself in this way, bidding it goodbye goodhumoredly, because he was ready to do so.

RESULTS

In addition to providing catharsis for the child, this play made it possible for the mother to see that he reacted to her with a variety of feelings, depending on his anxiety level, most pressing emotional needs, etc. It was easier to see why in real life she did not see consistent devotion, obedience, etc., but these positive feelings were actually present. She was able to adjust her expectation of his emotional commitment to her to more realistic levels, saving herself from disappointment when he was not all "love." This, combined with newfound ability to resist being manipulated by him in the hope of "buying his appreciation" made their relationship much more satisfying to both.

By the time 55 home play sessions were held, all symptoms were completely removed or greatly diminished. After 11 more sessions, Mrs. S. decided that though he was still somewhat introverted she could accept this degree of introversion, and therapy was terminated.

SUGGESTED ADDITIONAL READINGS

Allen, K. Eileen, and Harris, Florence R. Elimination of a child's excessive scratching by training the mother in reinforcement procedures. *Behaviour Research & Therapy,* 1966, Vol. 4, 79–84.

Bachrach, Arthur J., Erwin, William J., and Mohr, Jay P. The control of eating behavior in an anorexic by operant conditioning techniques. In Ullmann, Leonard P., and Krasner, Leonard (Eds.) *Case studies in behavior modification.* New York: Holt, Rinehart and Winston, Inc., 1965. Pp. 153–164.

Baruch, Dorothy W. *New ways in discipline.* New York: McGraw-Hill Book Company, Inc., 1949.

Bentler, Peter M. An infant's phobia treated with reciprocal inhibition therapy. *Journal of Child Psychology and Psychiatry,* 1962, Vol. 3, 185–189. Also reprinted in Ullmann, Leonard P., and Krasner, Leonard (Eds.) *Case studies in behavior modification.* New York: Holt, Rinehart and Winston, Inc., 1965. Pp. 297–300.

Bijou, Sidney W. Experimental studies of child behavior, normal and deviant. In Krasner, Leonard, and Ullmann, Leonard P. (Eds.) *Research in behavior modification.* New York: Holt, Rinehart and Winston, Inc., 1965. Pp. 56–58.

Bonnard, Augusta. The mother as therapist, in a case of obsessional neurosis. In *The psychoanalytic study of the child*, Vol. V. New York: International Universities Press, 1950. Pp. 391–408.

Bornstein, Berta. Phobia in a two-and-a-half-year-old child. *Psychoanalytic Quarterly,* 1935, Vol. 4, 93–119.

Bornstein, Steff. A child analysis. *Psychoanalytic Quarterly,* 1935, Vol. 4, 190–225.

Borstelmann, L. J. Missionaries or educators? Parent education with poverty families. Paper presented at Consultation Conference in Washington, D. C., December, 1964, sponsored by Interdepartmental Committee on Children and Youth and revised under the auspices of the Durham Education Improvement Program, funded by the Ford Foundation.

Burlingham, Dorothy T. Child analysis and the mother. *Psychoanalytic Quarterly,* 1935, Vol. 4, 69–92.

Elkisch, Paula. Simultaneous treatment of a child and his mother. *American Journal of Psychotherapy,* 1953, Vol. 7, 105–130.

Freud, Sigmund. Analysis of a phobia in a five-year-old boy. *Collected papers,* Vol. 3. New York: Basic Books, 1959. P. 149f. (First published in *Jahrbuch, fur psychoanalytische und psychopathologische Forschungen,* Bd. 8, 1909.)

Fries, Margaret E. The child's ego development and the training of adults in his environment. In *The psychoanalytic study of the child,* Vol. II. New York: International Universities Press, 1946. Pp. 85–112.

Fuchs, Natalie Rogers. Play therapy at home. *The Merrill-Palmer Quarterly,* 1960, Vol. 3, No. 2, 89–95.

Furman, Erna. Treatment of under-fives by way of their parents. In *The psychoanalytic study of the child,* Vol. XII. New York: International Universities Press, 1957. Pp. 250–262.

Gero-Heymann, Elizabeth. A short communication on a traumatic episode in a child of two years and seven months. In *The psychoanalytic study of the child,* Vol. X. New York: International Universities Press, 1955. Pp. 376–380.

Gordon, Kenneth. An approach to childhood psychosis: simultaneous treatment of mother and child. *Journal of American Academy of Child Psychiatry,* 1963, Vol. 2, 711–724.

Graziano, Anthony M. Programmed psychotherapy: a behavioral approach to emotionally disturbed children. Paper presented at the 38th Annual Meeting of the Eastern Psychological Association, Boston, 1967.

Guerney, Jr., Bernard G. The use of parents as therapeutic agents. Paper presented at the Annual Meeting of the American Psychological Association, New York, 1966.

Guerney, Jr., Bernard G., Stover, Lillian, and Andronico, Michael P. On educating disadvantaged parents to motivate children for learning: A filial approach. *Community Mental Health Journal,* 1967, Vol. 3, No. 1, 66–72.

Guerney, Jr., Bernard G. On educating parents to motivate their underprivileged children for academic performance: A pilot project. Unpublished report.

Hall, R. Vance, and Broden, Marcia. Behavior changes in brain-injured children through social reinforcement. *Journal of Experimental Child Psychology,* 1967, Vol. 5, No. 4, 463–479.

Jacobs, Lydia. Methods used in the education of mothers: A contribution to the handling and treatment of developmental difficulties in children under five years of age. In *The psychoanalytic study of the child,* Vol. III/IV. New York: International Universities Press, 1949. Pp. 409–422.

Jensen, Gordon D., and Womack, Mariette G. Operant conditioning techniques applied in the treatment of an autistic child. *American Journal of Orthopsychiatry,* 1967, Vol. 37, 30–34.

Kolansky, Harold. Treatment of a three-year-old girl's severe infantile neurosis: Stammering and insect phobia. In *The psychoanalytic study of the child,* Vol. XV. New York: International Universities Press, 1960. Pp. 261–285.

Kubie, Lawrence S. Resolution of a traffic phobia in conversations between a father and son. *Psychoanalytic Quarterly,* 1937, Vol. 6, 223–226.

Levenstein, Phyllis, and Sunley, Robert. An effect of stimulating verbal interaction between mothers and children around play materials. Paper presented at the 44th Annual Meeting of the American Orthopsychiatric Association, Washington, D.C., 1967.

Levine, Rachel A. Treatment in the home. *Social Work*, 1964, Vol. 9, 19–28.

Lindsley, Ogden R. An experiment with parents handling behavior at home. *Johnstone Bulletin,* 1966, Vol. IX, No. 1, 27–36. Edward R. Johnstone Training and Research Center, Bordentown, N.J.

Love, Leonore R. Information feedback as a method of clinical intervention. Paper presented at the Annual Meeting of the American Psychological Association, New York, 1966.

MacGregor, Robert, Ritchie, Agnes M., Serrano, Alberto C., and Shuster, Jr., Franklin P., under the direction of McDanald Jr., Eugene C., and Goolishian, Harold A. *Multiple impact therapy with families.* New York: McGraw-Hill Book Company, Inc., 1964.

Minuchin, Salvador. Conflict-resolution family therapy. *Psychiatry,* 1965, Vol. 28, No. 3, 278–286. Also reprinted in Stollak, Gary E., Guerney, Jr., Bernard G., and Rothberg, Meyer (Eds.) *Psychotherapy research: Selected readings.* Chicago: Rand McNally & Company, 1966. Pp. 608–617.

Patterson, Gerald R. A learning theory approach to the treatment of the school phobic child. In Ullmann, Leonard P., and Krasner, Leonard (Eds.) *Case studies in behavior modification.* New York: Holt, Rinehart and Winston, Inc., 1965. Pp. 279–285.

Patterson, G. R., McNeal, Shirley, Hawkins, Nancy, and Phelps, Richard. Reprogramming the social environment. *Journal of Child Psychology and Psychiatry,* in press.

Pechey, B. M. The direct analysis of the mother-child relationship in the treatment of maladjusted children. *British Journal of Medicine and Psychology*, 1955, Vol. 28, 101–112.

Peterson, Donald R., and London, Perry. A role for cognition in the behavioral treatment of a child's eliminative disturbance. In Ullmann, Leonard P., and Krasner, Leonard (Eds.) *Case studies in behavior modification.* New York: Holt, Rinehart and Winston, Inc., 1965. Pp. 289–295.

Prince, G. Stewart. A clinical approach to parent-child interaction. *Journal of Child Psychology and Psychiatry*, 1961, Vol. 2, 169–184.

Phillips, E. Lakin. Behavior change among children through use of adults as change agents. Paper presented at the Annual Meeting of the Eastern Psychological Association, Boston, 1967.

Rangell, Leo. A treatment of nightmares in a seven-year-old boy. In *The psychoanalytic study of the child*, Vol. V. New York: International Universities Press, 1950. Pp. 358–390.

Rickard, Henry C., and Mundy, Martha B. Direct manipulation of stuttering behavior: An experimental-clinical approach. In Ullmann, Leonard P., and Krasner, Leonard (Eds.) *Case studies in behavior modification.* New York: Holt, Rinehart and Winston, Inc., 1965. Pp. 268–274.

Risley, Todd, and Wolf, Montrose. Establishing functional speech in echolalic children. *Behaviour Research and Therapy.* 1967, Vol. 5, No. 2, 73–88.

Ruben, Margaret, and Thomas, Ruth. Home training of instincts and emotions. *Health Education Journal*, 1947, Vol. 5, 119–124.

Russo, Salvatore. Adaptations in behavioural therapy with children. *Behaviour Research and Therapy*, 1964, Vol. 2, 43–47.

Schwarz, Hedy. The mother in the consulting room: Notes on the psychoanalytic treatment of two young children. In *The psychoananalytic study of the child*, Vol. 5. New York: International Universities Press, 1950. Pp. 343–357.

Straughan, James H. Treatment with child and mother in the playroom. *Behaviour Research and Therapy*, 1964, Vol. 2, 37–41.

Wahler, Robert G. Behavior therapy with oppositional children: Attempts to increase their parent's reinforcement value. Paper presented at meeting of Southeastern Psychological Association, 1967.

Walder, Leopold O., in collaboration with Breiter, Dennis E., Cohen, Shlomo, Daston, Paul G., Forbes, James A., and McIntire, Roger W. Teaching parents to modify the behaviors of their autistic children. Paper presented at Annual Meeting of the American Psychological Association, New York, 1966.

Waldstein, Daniel. Environmental structuring in child treatment. Paper presented at the Eastern Psychological Association Convention, New York, 1966.

Wetzel, Ralph J., Baker, Jean, Roney, Marcia, and Martin, Marian. Outpatient treatment of autistic behavior. *Behaviour Research and Therapy, 1966, Vol. 4, 169*–177.

Williams, C. D. The elimination of tantrum behavior by extinction procedures. *Journal of Abnormal and Social Psychology*, 1959, Vol. 59, 269. Also reprinted in Ullmann, Leonard P., and Krasner, Leonard (Eds.) *Case studies in behavior modification.* New York: Holt, Rinehart and Winston, Inc., 1965. Pp. 295–296.

Wolf, Montrose, and Risley, Todd. Application of operant conditioning procedures to the behaviour problems of an autistic child. *Behaviour Research and Therapy*, 1964, Vol. 1, 305–312.

Zeilberger, Jane, Sampen, Sue E., and Sloane, Jr., H. N. Modification of a child's problem behaviors in the home with the mother as therapist. *Journal of Applied Behavior Analysis*, 1968, Vol. 1, 47–53.

PART 7

Research on the Use of Symbionts and Nonprofessionals

Introduction

THE use of symbionts and nonprofessionals as psychotherapeutic agents for children and adults departs from many assumptions long held by professional practitioners of psychotherapy. This departure is certainly open to legitimate doubts concerning feasibility and validity. In part, such questions eventually will be answered via the *qualitative* judgments of practitioners in the field. One of the secondary advantages of the use of nonprofessionals and symbionts as therapeutic agents, however, is the fact that it affords the professional a great opportunity for conducting *empirical* research. It does so because of the economy of time it affords the clinician-researcher and because it allows him to increase the number of cases he can treat and study within a reasonable span of time. Because of this—and doubtless also because innovators tend to be research-minded and because they feel the same ethical need to question their methods as do their critics—the clinical efforts of the pioneers in the use of nonprofessional therapeutic agents in many instances have been conducted almost from inception within the framework of empirical research.

This fusion of clinical practice with research made it difficult to decide in some instances whether a given article belonged in a more clinically oriented section or in this one. In the end, those which were chosen for this section were studies which went beyond the study of a single case, and which emphasized the empirical findings as opposed to descriptions of clinical methodology.

As a group, the findings of the research reports on grown-ups working with children suggest that teachers (as in the study by Becker, *et al.*), parents, and at least one group of nonprofessionals (the college student volunteers in Stollak's study) can be trained in a relatively short period of time to alter their behavior in directions deemed therapeutically desirable. Such changes may be in the direction of paying greater attention to feeling and the avoidance of directive behavior on the one hand, as in the Stover and Guerney study, or on the other hand, ignoring emotional behaviors previously responded to in order selectively to reinforce different behaviors, as reported in the selection by Wahler, *et al.* The findings further suggest that such modification by the adult affects the situational behavior of children in a relatively short period of time. Finally, what very little information there is on the subject suggests that professionals may fare second best to parents as attitude and behavior modifiers: in the Brookover, *et al.* study, parents with some guidance and instruction seemed more effective in modifying students' self-concept and achievement than experts or counselors.

The NIMH project reported by Rioch, *et al.* draws upon the "goldmine of psychological talent" to be found among women of about forty years of age who are looking for constructive activities outside the home, and represents a milestone in the movement toward the use of nonprofessionals. From the point of view of the trainees, professionals, and the clients involved, the results of the intensive training program in psychotherapeutic skills were generally positive.

In their article evaluating an integrated didactic and experiential approach, Carkhuff and Truax offer evidence that with appropriate intensive training methods, it apparently is possible to obtain a reasonably high level of certain psychotherapeutic behaviors in a shorter period of time and with personnel far less elite than in the NIMH training study. The view that this success in training is therapeutically relevant is supported by the next selection by these authors, which showed that lay hospital personnel trained by these methods were able to effect improvement in ward behavior of mental patients.

Poser's research suggests that the "naive enthusiasm" and lack of "professional stance" of untrained lay therapists, even without professional supervision, may lead to results (with chronic schizophrenics) which are actually slightly better than results achieved by professional therapists. (It also yields a bit of support for the helper-therapy principle in that two patient-therapists seemed to show enhanced mental health as a result of their helper roles.)

Of course, the findings of all these initial studies must be regarded as only tentative. (For some negative results see Suggested Additional Readings: Sines, *et al.*, 1961.) Not only do the findings demand replication of the studies, but, like most research studies, these raise more questions than they answer. If the early indications are confirmed, that under certain circumstances and with certain types of cases nonprofessionals are more effective than professionals, it will certainly stimulate new thinking about the relative importance of the various components of the therapeutic process, about the characteristics and abilities of therapists which are conducive to success in therapy, and about the ways in which the type of problem the client presents should be matched to the type of therapy he is offered.

What can be regarded as the one certain conclusion from the research conducted to date is a very familiar one: much more research is needed. In this instance not only scientists but, though they may not be aware of it, large segments of the population—including hundreds of thousands of emotionally troubled children—are awaiting further results.

The Contingent Use of Teacher Attention and Praise In Reducing Classroom Behavior Problems[1]

WESLEY C. BECKER
CHARLES H. MADSEN, JR.
CAROLE REVELLE ARNOLD
DON R. THOMAS

The influence of the teacher's attention, praise, nearness and other social stimuli in maintaining deviant as well as positive social behavior in children has been repeatedly demonstrated with pre-school children (e.g., Allen, Hart, Buell, Harris & Wolf, 1964; Harris, Johnston, Kelley & Wolf, 1964). The expectancy that attention in almost any form may maintain deviant behaviors lies in the high probability that attentional responses from adults will be repeatedly followed by relief from aversive stimulation or the presentation of positive reinforcers in the history of most children. With such a history, stimuli produced by attentional responses are likely to become positive conditioned reinforcers which function to strengthen responses that are followed by such attentional stimuli. An essentially similar process is involved in the establishment of the effectiveness of praise comments such as "good boy," "that's fine," "you're doing great," which acquire conditioned reinforcement value through their repeated pairing with positively reinforcing stimuli.

Reprinted from *Journal of Special Education*, 1967, Vol. 1, No. 3, 287–307, with the permission of the Journal of Special Education and the authors.

[1]We are extremely indebted to the principal of Hays School, Urbana, Ill., John M. Bustard, for his complete support of our work and to the teachers who made this research possible: Connie Carlson, Barbara Creinin, Joan Gusinow, Ozella Kelker and Mary Thomas. We also wish to acknowledge the assistance and support of Dr. Lowell M. Johnson, Director of Elementary Education, Urbana School District, Unit #116. This study was supported by grant HD-00881-04 from the National Institute of Child Health and Human Development.

Various forms of attention by nursery school teachers have been used to modify such behaviors as "regressive" crawling, isolate behavior, excessive orientation to adults, "aggressive" rather than cooperative peer interactions, and lethargy or passivity, among others. In addition, a similar procedure has been used to train mothers to modify the demanding-aggressive behavior of their children (Hawkins, Peterson, Schweid & Bijou, 1966). There is little question in the face of the extensive research by Sidney Bijou, Donald Baer and their students that a powerful principle for influencing the development of social behaviors has been isolated.

The group of studies to be reported here demonstrate how the selective use of teacher attention and praise can be effectively applied in managing behavior problems in elementary classrooms; the studies also explore methods of training teachers to be more effective in this regard.

THE SETTING

The studies were carried out in Urbana, Illinois, in an elementary school whose population was 95% Negro. Our research group was invited into the school because it was believed that we could provide a service and they would provide us with a research laboratory. Seven teachers (half of those invited) agreed to participate in a workshop and seminar on the application of behavioral principles in the classroom. This report covers studies involving five of these teachers carried out between February and June, 1966.

The conduct of our research was guided to some extent by the necessity of establishing good relationships within the school system. Even though we had been invited by the school administration to see what we could do, there was still a need to convince teachers to participate, to keep them participating and to help them feel comfortable with observers in their classrooms. The comments of one of our teachers express better than we can the background into which the research had to be adapted.

> At one time few teachers wanted to work at our school, and only those who could not find a better position would teach. Suddenly the school found itself qualified under Title I of the Elementary and Secondary School Act to receive Federal aid. A large percent of its population was termed "culturally deprived" or perhaps more aptly, "deprived of middle-class culture." The school was bombarded with specialists, aides, volunteers, and experimental groups from the University of Illinois, all wanting to borrow the children or to help the children. By planning carefully, class interruptions were held to a minimum, but even then planning was done around a music teacher, an art teacher, a language teacher, special small group speech classes and language classes. With all of this going on, plus many other items I shall leave unmen-

> tioned, it became increasingly more difficult to develop a continuous daily program. A self-contained classroom was a thing of the past. My attitude began to become very negative. I am not capable of judging the merits or demerits of this program; only time will measure this. I am merely attempting to describe briefly the setting, from my vantage point, into which a class in "behavior modification" was introduced. The enthusiasm held by some for the possibilities of behavior modification did not particularly excite me. The observing would interrupt my class and make it very difficult for me to function comfortably. The plan of the experiment was a bit nebulous, since too much knowledge of what was to be done would affect the results. To add to all this, these people were *psychologists!* My reinforcement history of working with psychologists need not be discussed here. I will simply state my relationship with them was inconsequential and negative; their reports were read carefully for some new information, but, finding none usually, the reports were filed as useless.
>
> I vacillated for days on whether to take part in the class or not, finally deciding, despite my anxiety about the observation, that the only way to make educational psychology practical was to allow psychologists into the classroom to observe for themselves the classroom situation and problems.

Because of the need to sell ourselves to the teachers and maintain close contact with them, the seminar-workshop was initiated at the beginning of the second semester. At the same time we began to train observers, select target children and make baseline recordings of the children's behavior. This sequence of events is not ideal, since even though instructed otherwise the teachers were likely to try out the procedures they were learning in the workshop before we wished them to do so. The fact that they did this is suggested by an occasional decreasing baseline of problem behavior for a target child. Most changes, however, were dramatic enough that this potential loss in demonstrating an experimental effect did not grossly distort possible conclusions.

Most work in this area has used designs of the ABAB type. After baseline (A) an experimental effect is introduced (B), withdrawn (A), and reintroduced (B). We did not use this design (though we had an accidental counterpart to it in one room where the second (A) condition was provided by a student teacher) because: (a) we were afraid it might jeopardize the teacher's support; (b) the values of the experimental processes involved have been repeatedly confirmed; (c) "accidental" influences which might have produced changes in behavior would be unlikely to happen to ten children at the same time in five different classrooms; (d) we are unimpressed by arguments that Hawthorne effects, time alone or other "uncontrolled" variables such as the "weather" are causative in view of (b) and (c) above. By electing not to use an ABAB design we were also able to show the persistence of effects maintained by conditioned reinforcers over a longer period of time (nine weeks) than is usually the case. As a result of our caution and our success, we are now in a position where teachers and administrators in other schools are permitting us to establish controlled designs in return for our helping them with their problem children.

PROCEDURES

Selection of Target Children. The authors began by observing in the classrooms of the teachers who had volunteered for the project, and then discussing possible problem children with them. After tentative selection of two children in each class, explicit behavior coding categories were evolved and tested. The final selection was contingent upon demonstration that problem behavior did occur frequently enough to constitute a problem and could be reliably rated.

Rating Categories. During the first four weeks the rating categories were repeatedly revised as reliability data demanded. Where it was not possible to get rater agreement for a category above 80%, a new definition was sought or a category abandoned. For example, in three classes (A, B & C) inappropriate talking and vocal noise were rated as separate categories (see Table 1). In two classes (D and E) the behavior patterns made it difficult to discriminate between these behaviors, so they were combined. The general rules followed in establishing categories were as follows:

1. They should reflect behaviors which interfered with classroom learning (time on task), and/or,
2. They should involve behaviors which violated the rules for permissible behavior established by the teacher and/or,
3. They should reflect particular behaviors a teacher wanted to change (e.g., thumbsucking).
4. The classes should be constituted of behaviors which were topographically similar in some important way.
5. The classes should be mutually exclusive.
6. The definitions must refer to observables and not involve inferences.
7. The number of classes should not exceed ten.

As Table 1 indicates, some codes were usable with all ten target children; others were devised especially for a particular child. For convenience we will speak of the Categories A and B in Table 1 as "deviant behaviors."

Observer Training and Reliabilities. Observers were obtained from undergraduate classes in psychology and education and were paid $1.50 an hour. Initially they worked in pairs, often in conjunction with one of the authors. After each rating session of 40 minutes, ratings were compared and discussed and reliability examined by category. Definitions were clarified and changes made when necessary. Reliabilities were above 80%

TABLE 1

Coding Categories for Children with Teachers A, B and C

SYMBOLS	CLASS LABEL	CLASS DEFINITIONS
A. Behaviors Incompatible with Learning: General Categories		
X	Gross Motor Behaviors	Getting out of seat; standing up; running; hopping; skipping; jumping; walking around; rocking in chair; disruptive movement without noise; moving chair to neighbor.
N	Disruptive noise with objects	Tapping pencil or other objects; clapping; tapping feet; rattling or tearing paper. *Be conservative, only rate if could hear noise with eyes closed. Do not include accidental dropping of objects or noise made while performing X above.*
A	Disturbing others directly and aggression	Grabbing objects or work; knocking neighbor's book off desk; destroying another's property; hitting; kicking; shoving; pinching; slapping; striking with object; throwing object at another person; poking with object; attempting to strike; biting; pulling hair.
O	Orienting responses	Turning head or head and body to look at another person, showing objects to another child, attending to another child. *Must be of 4 seconds duration to be rated. Not rated unless seated.*
!	Blurting Out, Commenting and Vocal Noise	Answering teacher without raising hand or without being called on; making comments or calling out remarks when no question has been asked; calling teacher's name to get her attention; crying; screaming; singing; whistling; laughing loudly; coughing loudly. *Must be undirected to another particular child, but may be directed to teacher.*
T	Talking	Carrying on conversations with other children when it is not permitted. *Must be directed to a particular child or children.*
//	Other	Ignoring teacher's question or command; doing something different from that directed to do (includes minor motor behavior such as playing with pencil when supposed to be writing). *To be rated only when other ratings not appropriate.*
B. Special Categories for Children with Teachers A, B, and C (to be Rated Only for Children Indicated)		
+	Improper position Carole and Alice	Not sitting with body and head oriented toward the front with feet on the floor, e.g., sitting on feet; standing at desk rather than sitting; sitting with body sideways but head facing front. *Do not rate if chair sideways but head and body oriented toward the front with feet on the floor.*
S	Sucking Alice and Betty	Sucking fingers or other objects.

Symbols	Class Label	Class Definitions
B	Bossing Carole	Reading story out loud to self or other children (*do not rate! in this case*); acting as teacher to other children, as showing flash cards.
//	Ignoring Charley	This category expanded to include playing with scissors, pencils, or crayons instead of doing something more constructive during free time.
C. Relevant Behavior		
—	Relevant Behavior	Time on task, e.g., answers question, listening, raises hand, writing assignment. *Must include whole 20 seconds except for orienting responses of less than 4 seconds duration.*

before the baseline period was begun. Several reliability checks were made each week throughout baseline and periodically thereafter. As indicated in Figures 1 to 5, reliability only occasionally fell below 80% when calculated by dividing the smaller estimate by the larger.

The observers were carefully trained not to respond to the children in the classes. They were to "fade into the walls." This procedure quickly extinguished the children's responses to the observers. Several incidents were reported where children were surprised to see the observers respond to a request from the teacher to move. After a while it was possible for other visitors to come into the class without distracting the children as they had in the past.

Rating Procedure. Except for a few occasional absences, target children were observed for 20 minutes a day, four days a week. In the experimental phase of the study frequency of reliability checks were reduced so that ratings of teacher behavior could also be obtained. Each observer had a clipboard with a stop watch taped to it. Observers would start their watches together and check for synchronization every five minutes (end of a row). They would observe for 20 seconds and then take ten seconds to record the classes of behavior which occurred during the 20-second period. All data are reported in terms of the percentages of the time intervals during which deviant behavior was observed to occur. The activities in which the children were involved varied considerably from day to day and contributed to daily fluctuation. For this reason only weekly averages are reported.

Ratings of Teacher Behavior. At the beginning of the experimental phase for four teachers, and for a week prior to the experimental phase for teacher E, a 20-minute sample of the teacher's behavior was also obtained. The rating categories are given in Table 2. The main purpose of the ratings was to insure that the experimental program was being followed.

Experimental Phase Instructions. Following a five-week baseline period (for most children) teachers were given instructions to follow for the nine-week experimental period. In all classes the teachers were given general rules for classroom management as follows (typed on a 5″ x 8″ card to be kept on their desks):

General Rules for Teachers

1. Make explicit rules as to what is expected of children for each period. (Remind of rules when needed.)
2. *Ignore* (do not attend to) behaviors which interfere with learning or teaching, unless a child is being hurt by another. Use punishment which seems appropriate, preferably withdrawal of some positive reinforcement.
3. Give *praise* and *attention* to behaviors which facilitate learning. Tell child

TABLE 2

Teacher Coding Categories

SYMBOLS	CLASS LABEL	CLASS DEFINITIONS
C	Positive Contact	Positive physical contact must be included—such behaviors as embracing, kissing, patting (on head), holding arm, taking hand, sitting on lap, etc.
P	Verbal Praise	This category includes paying attention to appropriate behavior with verbal comments indicating approval, commendation or achievement such as: "That's good." "You're studying well." "Fine job." "I like you."
R	Recognition in Academic Sense	Calling on child when hand is raised. (Do not rate if child calls teacher's name or makes noises to get her attention.)
F	Facial Attention	Looking at child when smiling. (Teacher might nod her head or give other indication of approval—while smiling.)
A	Attention to Undesirable Behavior	This category includes the teacher's verbally calling attention to undesirable behavior and may be of high intensity (yelling, screaming, scolding or raising the voice) or of low intensity ("Go to the office." "You know what you are supposed to be doing." Etc.) Calling the child to the desk to talk things over should also be included, as well as threats of consequences. Score the following responses to deviant behavior separately:
L	Lights	Turning off the lights to achieve control.
W	Withdrawal of Positive Reinforcement	Keeping in for recess, sending to office, depriving child in the classroom.
/	Physical Restraint	Includes holding the child, pulling out into hall, grabbing, hitting, pushing, shaking.

what he is being praised for. Try to reinforce behaviors incompatible with those you wish to decrease.
Examples of how to praise: "I like the way you're working quietly." "That's the way I like to see you work." "Good job, you are doing fine."
Transition period. "I see Johnny is ready to work." "I'm calling on you because you raised your hand." "I wish everyone were working as nicely as X," etc. Use variety and expression.

In general, give praise for achievement, prosocial behavior and following the group rules.

In addition to these general rules, teachers in classes A to D were given specific instructions with respect to their target children. An example follows:

Special Rules for Alice

Attempt to follow the general rules above, but try to give extra attention to Alice for the behavior noted below, but try not to overdo it to the extent that she is singled out by other children. Spread your attention around.

1. Praise sitting straight in chair with both feet and chair legs on floor and concentrating on own work.
2. Praise using hands for things other than sucking.
3. Praise attention to directions given by teacher or talks made by students.
4. Specify behavior you expect from her at beginning of day and new activity, such as sitting in chair facing front with feet on floor, attention to teacher and class members where appropriate, what she may do after assigned work is finished, raising hand to answer questions or get your attention.

The fifth teacher was given the general rules only and instructed not to give the target children any more special attention than was given the rest of the class. This procedure was decided upon because our observers felt that general classroom management was a problem for Mrs. E. She relied heavily on negative control procedures, and the general level of disruptive behaviors in the room was high. In view of this, we decided to see if the two target children in her class might not be used as barometers of a more general effect on the class of a change in control procedures.

When we first initiated the experimental phase of the study, we attempted to give the teachers hand signals to help them learn when to ignore and when to praise. This procedure was abandoned after the first week in favor of explicit instructions, as given above, and daily feedback on their progress. While hand signals and lights have been found to be effective in helping parents learn to discriminate when to respond or ignore (Hawkins, Peterson, Schweid & Bijou, 1966), the procedure is too disruptive when the teacher is in the middle of a lesson and is consequently placed in conflict about which response should come next.

At this point, the seminar was used to discuss and practice various ways of delivering positive comments. For some teachers, delivery of positive comments was difficult, and their initial attempts came out in stilted, stereotyped form. With time, even our most negative teacher was smiling and more spontaneous in her praise (and enjoying her class more). Shortly after the experimental phase began, one teacher commented, "I have at least 15 minutes more every morning and afternoon in which to do other things."

The experimental phase was initiated March 30th and ended May 27th. A breakdown in the heating plant in part of the building for the week of April 8th (Week 7) accounts for the loss of data for some children that week.

RESULTS

The main results are presented in Figures 1 to 5. The average "deviant" behavior for ten children in five classes was 62.13% during baseline and 29.19% during the experimental period. The *t*-test for the differences between correlated means was significant well beyond the .001 level. All children showed less deviant behavior during the experimental phase. However, differential teacher attention and praise were not very effective with Carole and did not produce much change in Dan until his reading skills were improved. Each child and class will be discussed in more detail and a breakdown of the behaviors which changed will be examined.

Teacher A

Mrs. A is an anxious, sensitive person who expressed many doubts about her ability to learn to use "the approach" and about whether it would work with her middle-primary adjustment class. Both of the children on whom data were collected (Figure 1) changed remarkably, as did Mrs. A and other members of her class. The teachers' views of what happened to themselves and to members of their classes are very instructive and will be presented elsewhere.

Albert (age 7-8) tested average on the Stanford-Binet, but was still on first-grade materials during his second year in school. He was selected because he showed many behaviors which made learning difficult. He talked, made other noises, did not attend to teacher and got in and out of his seat a lot. He loved to be "cute" and arouse laughter. In Mrs. A's words:

> He was a very noisy, disruptive child. He fought with others, blurted out, could not stay in his seat, and did very little required work. I had to check constantly to see that the minimum work was finished. He sulked and responded negatively to everything suggested to him. In addition, he was certain that he could not read. If I had planned it, I could not have reinforced

> this negative behavior more, for I caught him in every deviant act possible and often before it occurred. I lectured him and, as might be expected, was making only backward motion. In November Albert came to me to tell me something and I was shocked by the intensity of his stuttering. He simply could not express his thought because his stuttering was so bad. I declared an "I like Albert Week." I gave him a great deal of attention, bragged about his efforts and was beginning to make some progress. This turned out to be the basis upon which an "ignore and praise" technique could be established. When the class began, I could see quickly what had happened to my relationship with Albert and had to fight to keep up my negative remarks until the baseline was established. Finally, I was free to use the technique. He quickly responded and his deviant behavior decreased to 10%, the lowest recorded. Along with the praising and ignoring, I attempted to establish a calmer atmosphere in which to work, and carefully reviewed class behavior rules. A good technique with Albert was to have him repeat the rule because "he was following it."

During Weeks 8 and 9 Albert showed less than 12% deviant behavior on the average. His worst performance out of seven observation days was 18.77% and he was under 5% deviant four out of seven days. Then an unplanned experimental reversal occurred.

Mrs. A relates what happened:

> As my student teacher gradually assumed more and more of the teaching load, the deviant behavior increased again. She made the same mistakes that I had. I deliberately planned her work so that I would be working with Albert most of the time. She felt the efficiency of the direct command, but she also realized that this was not modifying Albert's behavior in a lasting way. Gradually, she accepted the positive approach and in the last week or two of her work the deviant behavior began again to decrease. She had learned that with so negative a child as Albert, only building rapport by using positive reinforcement would succeed.
>
> Albert has improved delightfully. He still blurts out, but makes an effort to stop this. He is often seen holding his hand in the air, biting his lips. He completes his work on time, and it is done well. Often, when he has to re-do a paper, he takes it cheerfully and says, "I can do this myself." No sulking. He still finds it difficult to sit for a long period of time, but time on task has increased. He works very hard on his reading and has stated that he can read. His stuttering has decreased almost to zero. When the observers were questioned concerning this, they had detected little, if any stuttering. Most important to me, Albert has become a delightful child and an enthusiastic member of our class who feels his ideas are accepted and have merit.

Examination of the separate categories of behavior for Albert only serves to confirm the teacher's reports about which behaviors were most frequent and which changed the most.

The record of Mrs. A's behavior showed that she attended to and praised positive behaviors more than 90% of the time during the experimental period. Similar effective following of procedures was demonstrated for all five teachers.

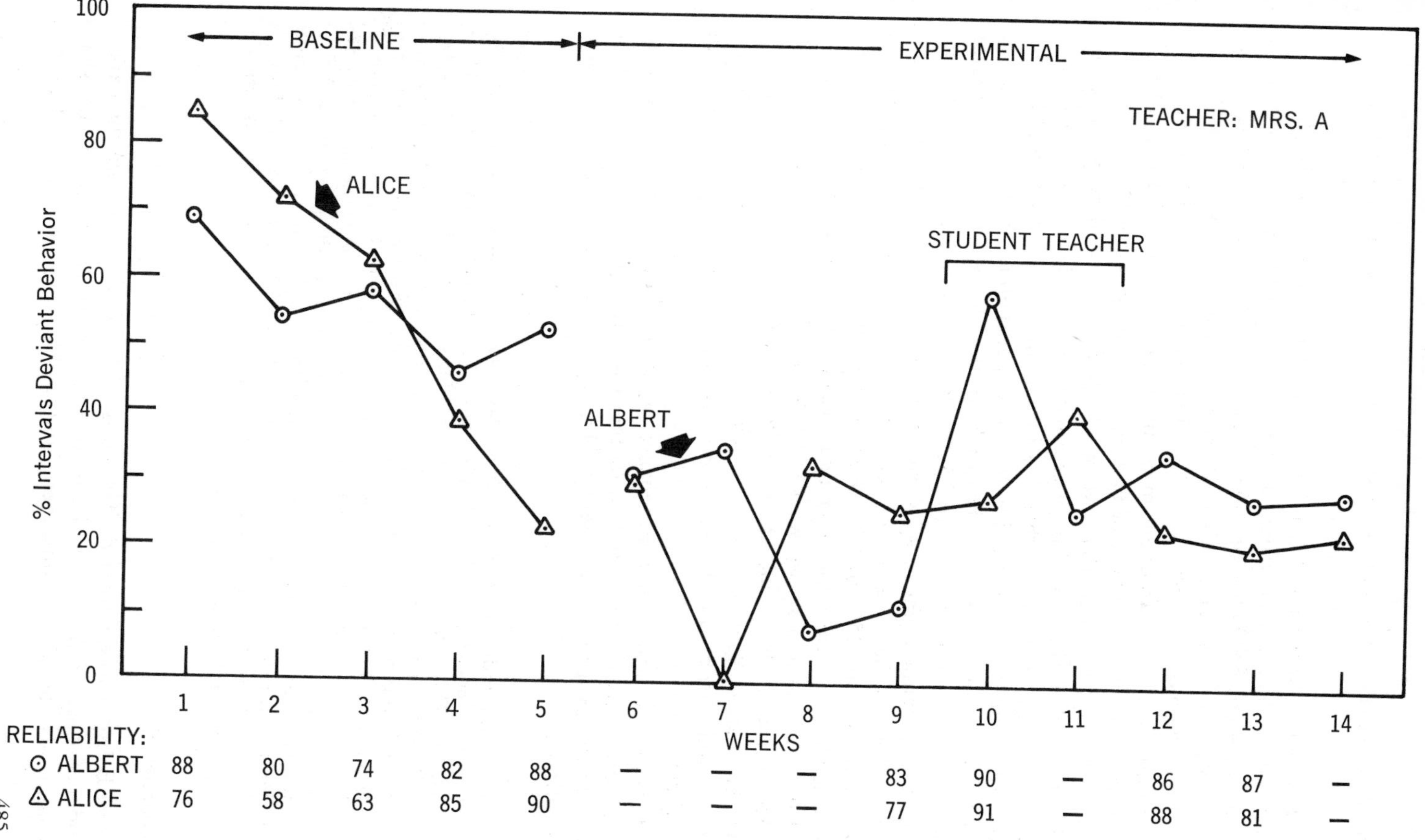

Figure 1. Percentages of deviant behavior for two children in Class A.

Alice (age 7-8) scored 90 on the Stanford-Binet and was doing low first grade work. The data on Alice are less clear than those for Albert since her average deviant behavior showed a decline prior to the experimental phase. Mrs. A considered Alice a "sulking child." She would withdraw at times and not talk. She would sit inappropriately in her chair, suck her thumb, and make frequent movements of her hands and legs. Mrs. A said that Alice would report headaches after being scolded.

Mrs. A also indicated that two weeks before the end of baseline she told Alice that she was "disgusted with your sulking and would you please stop it." Mrs. A felt that this instruction in part accounted for the drop in deviant behavior prior to the experimental phase. Analysis of Alice's separate classes of behavior indicates, however, that the motor category declined from 45% to 25% to 8% the first three weeks of baseline and remained under 12% the rest of the experiment. Following this decline in "getting out of seat," frequency of odd sitting positions went from 0% to 25% to 18% over the first three weeks of baseline and declined to zero over the next two weeks. There was also a decline in talking during the first two weeks of baseline. In other words Mrs. A got Alice to stay in her seat, sit properly and talk less prior to the experimental change. The behaviors which show a correlation with the experimental change are decreases in *orienting, sucking* and *other* (ignoring teacher) response categories.

It is probable that the maintenance of Alice's improvement, except for the short lapse when the student teacher took over the class, can be attributed to the experimental program. Mrs. A reported at the end of the year as follows:

> Alice is a responsible, hard-working student who now smiles, makes jokes, and plays with others. When a bad day comes, or when she doesn't get her way and chooses to sulk, I simply ignore her until she shows signs of pleasantness. Through Alice I have learned a far simpler method of working with sulking behavior, the one most disagreeable kind of behavior to me. Alice is a child who responds well to physical contact. Often a squeeze, a pat, or an arm around her would keep her working for a long while. This is not enough, however. Alice is very anxious about problems at home. She must have opportunity to discuss these problems. Again through the class suggestions, I found it more profitable to discuss what she could do to improve her problems than to dwell on what went wrong. Alice's behavior is a good example of the effects of a calm, secure environment. Her time on task has lengthened and her academic work has improved.

Teacher B

Mrs. B had a lower intermediate class of 26 children. Before the experimental phase of the study, she tended to control her class through sharp commands, physical punishment and withholding privileges. The two children on whom observations were made (Figure 2) showed considerable change over the period of the experiment. Observers' comments indicate that Mrs. B was very effective in following the instructions of the experimental program. Only occasionally did she revert to a sharp command or a hand slap.

Betty (age 9-7) scored average on various assessments of intelligence and was doing middle third-grade work. Her initial problem behaviors included "pestering" other children, blurting out, sucking her thumb, making noises. She also occasionally hit other children. Often she said or did things that evoked laughter from others. As Figure 2 shows, many of her problem behaviors showed a reduction during the baseline period (as happened with Alice), but thumbsucking did not. The experimental program brought thumbsucking under control for a while, but it increased markedly the last week of the experiment. Betty's other problem behaviors showed continued improvement over the experimental period and remained at a level far below baseline for the last five weeks of the experimental period.

Boyd (age 9-7) was of average IQ. His achievement test placements varied between second- and third-grade levels. During baseline he was high on getting out of his seat and making other gross movements, talking out of turn and making noises. Mrs. B also reported that Boyd had difficulty "saying words he knows," giggled a lot and would not try to do things alone. He very much liked to be praised and tried not to do things which led to scolding. During this period Boyd was getting a great deal of teacher attention, but much of the attention was for the very behaviors Mrs. B wished to eliminate. Through a gradual shaping process Boyd learned to sit in his seat for longer periods of time working on task. He has learned to work longer by himself before asking for help. Mrs. B reports that he is less anxious and emotional, although we have no measure of this. Blurting out was not stopped entirely, but now he usually raises his hand and waits to be called on in full class activities and waits for his turn in reading.

Teacher C

Our biggest failure occurred in Mrs. C's middle primary class of about 20 children. Mrs. C was one of our most positive teachers, and we underestimated the severity of the many problems she was facing. With our present knowledge, we would likely have gone directly to a more potent token economy system for the whole class (see O'Leary & Becker, 1967). The above misjudgment notwithstanding, the experiment reported below is still of considerable value in pointing to one of the limits of "the approach," as our teachers came to call it. Besides focusing on Carole and

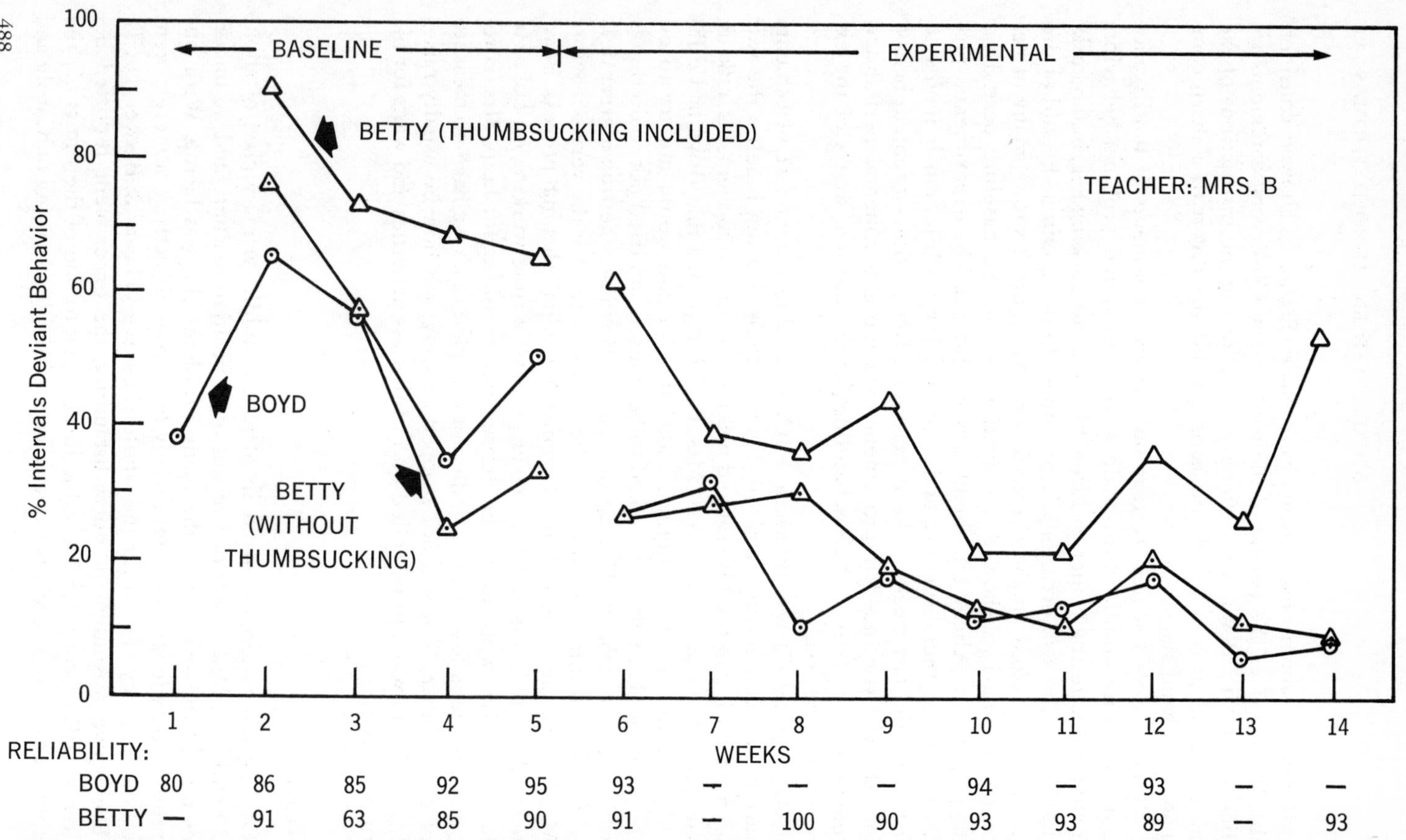

Figure 2. Percentages of deviant behavior for two children in Class B.

Charley, as described below, we assisted Mrs. C in extinguishing tantrums in Donna (beginning Week 8), and in reducing swearing and hitting by Hope. The work with Donna was very successful.

Carole (age 7-5) scored from 78 to 106 on various intelligence tests. She was working at the mid first-grade level. Carole is an incessant beehive of activity. She scored high on response categories which indicate that she spent much time talking out of turn, turning in her seat, getting out of her seat, bossing other children and hitting others. Her most frequent behavior was talking when she should have been quiet. She was very responsive to peer attention. At times she would stand at the back of the room and read out loud to everyone. She liked to play teacher. She was also described as good at lying, cheating, stealing and smoking. Like most of the children in the study, Carole came from a deprived, unstable home. Descriptions of home backgrounds for most of the children in this study consist of sequences of tragic events (see Mrs. D).

The experimental phase of the program reduced Carole's average deviant behavior from about 75% during baseline to 55% for Weeks 7 to 9. A detailed analysis of Carole's responses shows that talking out of turn and blurting out still constituted over 30% of her deviant responses during Weeks 7 to 9. However Carole was in her seat more, sitting properly, responding more relevantly to teacher, and was on task 50% of the time. We were not satisfied with her improvement and felt that Charley (our other target child) while doing well, could also do better.

On April 25th (Week 9) we instituted a program in which ten cent notebooks were taped to Carole and Charley's desks. Mrs. C told the children that every 30 minutes she would put from one to ten points in their notebooks, depending on how hard they worked and how well they followed the class rules. At the end of the day if they had a certain number of points they could exchange the points for a treat. The initial reinforcer was candy. During this phase the rest of the class could earn a candy treat by helping Carole and Charley earn points. In this way they were not left out. The number of points required was based on a shifting criterion geared to Carole and Charley's progress. As noted below and in Figure 3, Charley responded well to this added incentive and was gradually shifted to saving points over two, then three, then five days to earn puzzles. Carole still resisted. She worked for points for several days, but on May 3rd (Week 10) she announced she was not going to work for points today, and she didn't. She was a hellion all day. Over the following two weeks Carole worked for a ring and then the components of a make-up kit. We were seeking stronger reinforcers and were stretching the delay of reinforcement.

On May 17th Mrs. C reported that Carole had earned points for three days in a row and was entitled to a component of the make-up kit. The

20% deviant behavior of that week showed that Carole could behave and work. The last week of May, Carole was back to talking and blurting out again. While some of our reinforcers were effective, Carole still needs a classroom where the structure would require her to depend on the teacher for praise and attention and where peer attention to her deviant behavior could be controlled.

Charley was presumed to be age 8 years and 2 months at the start of the study, but in fact was two years older. His IQ was given as 91, but with a proper CA was 73. He was doing mid-first-grade work in most subjects. Charley picked on the girls, hit other boys and bullied them (he was larger), got loud and angry if reprimanded, and at times he sulked and withdrew. No one was going to force him to do anything. Our ratings showed him highest in categories labeled *motor activities* (out of seat), *ignoring* teacher's requests, *turning in seat* and *talking* to peers.

Initially Charley responded very effectively to rules and praise. He loved to receive praise from Mrs. C. However, praise was not enough to keep him on task. Also he was still fighting with Donna at recess. As noted above, a point system was initiated April 25th (Week 9) which worked well for the rest of the semester, while the delay of reinforcement was gradually extended to five days. On April 25th Charley was also informed that further fighting with Donna would lead to a loss of the following recess.

Comments on May 10th: "Charley is great. He ignores others who bother him as well as keeping busy all the time." May 26th: "Charley seems much more interested in school work and has been getting help with reading from his sister at home."

It is not possible to evaluate whether the point system was necessary for Charley. At best we know that social reinforcement helped considerably and that the point system did help to maintain good classroom behavior.

Teacher D

Mrs. D teaches a lower intermediate class of about 25 children. One group of her children had been in a slow class where the teacher allowed them "to do what they wanted." A brighter group had been taught by a strict teacher who enforced her rules. Since September the class has been divided and subdivided six times and has had seven different teachers.

Mrs. D describes the families of her two target children as follows:

> Don has average ability and achieves below the average of the class. The father works late afternoons and evenings. The mother, a possible alcoholic, has been known to do some petty shoplifting. She is frequently away from home in the evening. One older brother drowned at the age of seven. An

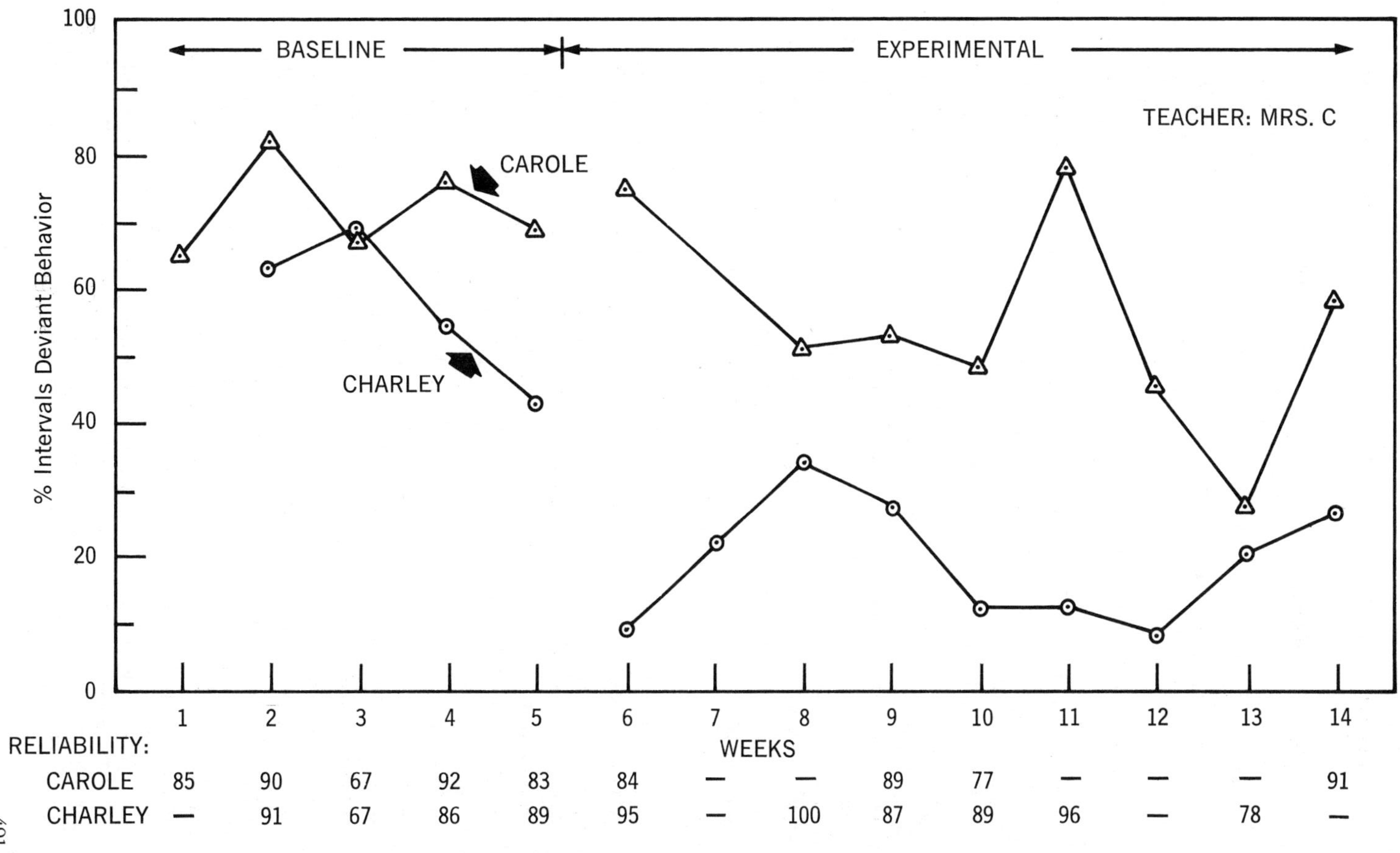

Figure 3. Percentages of deviant behavior for two children in Class C.

> older sister with above average ability left home at the age of fifteen. She later married. Her husband was killed this spring in an automobile accident. Another older sister lost an arm at a very early age and is an unwed mother at the age of fourteen. Another sister attends Junior High School.
>
> Dan's mother is of mixed parentage and has been in the hospital this year. The mother is divorced. The father remarried and it appears that there is a good relationship between the two families; however, the father has been in prison because of "dope."

Mrs. D was initially quite bothered about being observed, but quickly learned to look more carefully at the way in which her behavior affected that of her class.

Don was 10 years and 4 months old at the start of the study. In April of 1961 he was recommended for EMH placement. Since kindergarten his performance on intelligence tests had risen from 75 to 102. He was obviously of at least average ability. His level of school achievement was between grades two and three, except for arithmetic reasoning (4.3). Observations revealed a high frequency of moving around the room and talking when he should have been working. He was called "hyperactive" and said to have poor "attention." His talking to other children was quite annoying to his teacher and interfered with classwork. Don appeared to respond to teacher attention, but obtained such attention most often when he was acting up.

The experimental procedures quickly brought Don's level of deviant behavior down from about 40% to under 20%. He was particularly good at working when the task was specifically assigned. When he was left to his own devices (no stimulus control) he would start to play around. These observations suggest that Don would greatly profit from more individualized programming of activities. He was reported to show improved behavior in his afternoon classes involving several different teachers.

Danny was age 10 years, 6 months at the start of the study. He measured near 85 on several IQ tests. His classroom behavior was described as being generally disruptive and aggressive. During baseline he scored high on *motor, talking, orienting, ignoring* and *noise.* By all standards Danny was a serious behavior problem. He seldom completed work assignments and was in the slowest reading group. Because of the severity of his behavior and difficulty staying on task, an educational diagnosis was requested during the early part of baseline. The staffing at Week 2 indicated a two-year reading deficit and a one-year arithmetic deficit. The following comments from the psychological report which followed the staffing are of interest:

> Danny's lack of conscience development and other intrinsic controls still present a serious problem in controlling his behavior. His immediate impulsive aggressive reaction to threatening situations may hamper any educational remediation efforts. The evidence presented still suggests that Danny, in

> light of increasing accumulation of family difficulties, lack of consistent masculine identification, his irascible and changeable nature, and educational pressures will have a difficult time adjusting to the educational situation.
>
> It is our opinion that unless further action is implemented, i.e., school officials should attempt to refer this boy to an appropriate agency (Mental Health, Institute for Juvenile Research) for additional help and correction, he is likely to become a potentially serious acting out youngster.

The data on Danny presented in Figure 4 are most interesting. They show a small improvement in his behavior the first two weeks of the experimental phase. Generally the observers felt the whole class was quieter and better behaved. Danny especially stayed in his seat more of the time. However, a most dramatic change occurs when tutoring sessions in reading were begun (Week 8 to 9). It would appear that unless the child is capable of following the assigned activity, social reinforcement for "on task" behavior is not enough. In Danny's data this point is supported by an analysis of the kinds of activities where he showed the most improvement. Dan was averaging 80% deviant behavior when the activity was workbook assignments related to reading and language. In the reading group, where the teacher was there to help and direct activity, he averaged only 40% deviant behaviors. By early May (Week 11) the amount of deviant behavior during "seat work" activities had dropped to an average of 15%, with only an occasional bad day.

Well into April, Danny had not shown much improvement in his afternoon classes (with teachers not in our program). Several observations suggested that he would still show high rates of deviant behaviors on days when he was otherwise on task, if the activity shifted to something he could not do. For example, May 5th showed 25% deviant behavior during a period of seat work *(reading)*, 30% during *spelling*, and 55% an hour later during *grammar* and *composition*. Danny was just beginning to move in reading, but was not ready for composition. The increase during Week 13 is due to one day where he was rated 40% off task. The rater comments indicate the basis for the "deviant" rating: "Danny should have been sitting quietly after doing his work, but, instead of just waiting for the next assignment, he was playing with clay with another child. However, he was very quiet." Comments from May 9th and 10th give some flavor of the changes which occurred.

> May 9th: Mrs. D reported that Danny, after he finished reading, immediately started on spelling. This is a highly unusual occurrence. Until now Danny has avoided spelling activities until made to work on them.
>
> May 10th: Danny completely surprised the observer when he was on task the whole observation period, except for one minor talking to neighbor.

In view of the rather dramatic changes Danny has made in classroom behavior through a combination of remediation and social reinforcement,

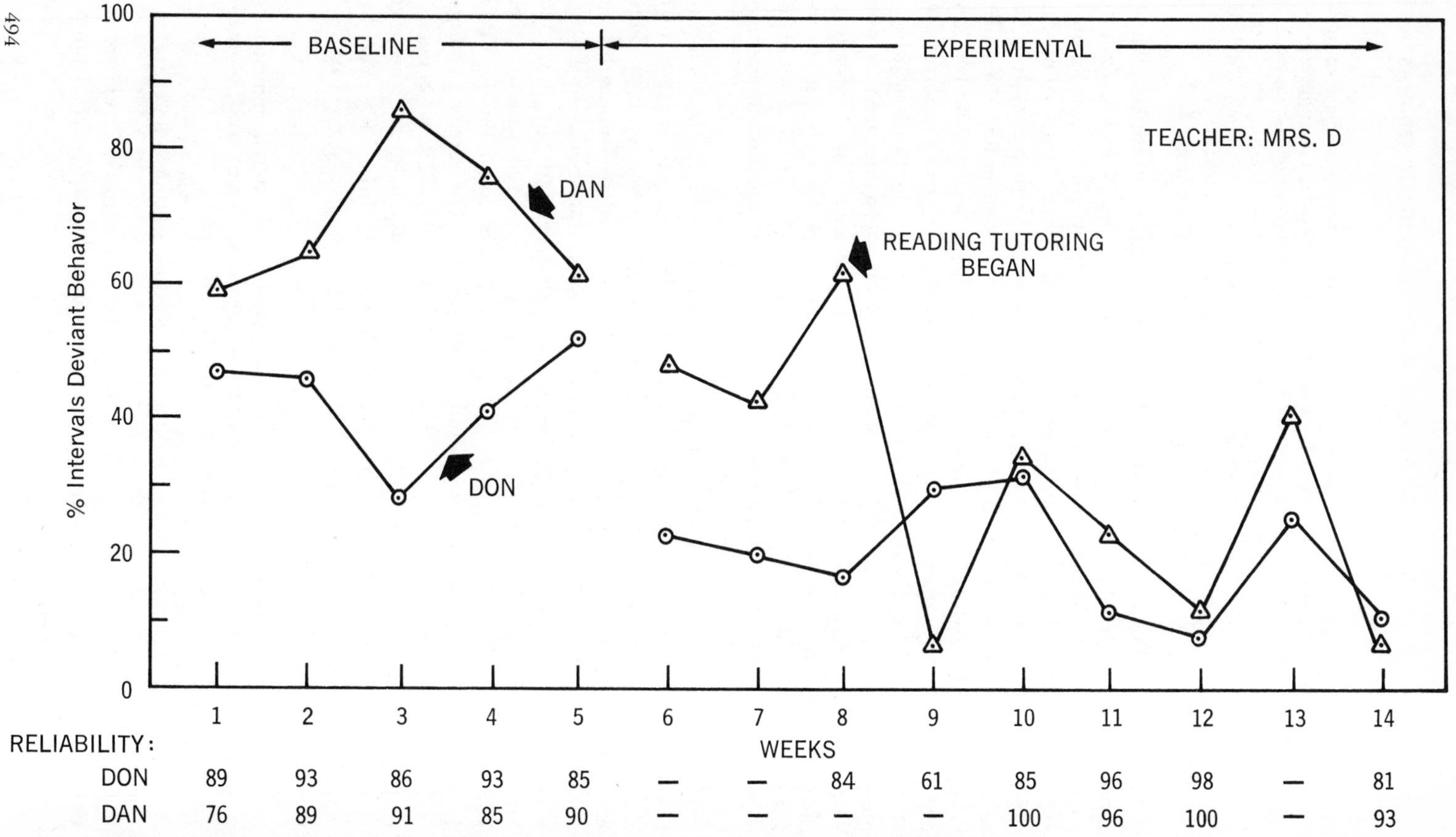
BASELINE
EXPERIMENTAL
TEACHER: MRS. D
DAN
DON
READING TUTORING BEGAN
% Intervals Deviant Behavior
100
80
60
40
20
0
1
2
3
4
5
6
7
8
9
10
11
12
13
14
WEEKS
RELIABILITY:
DON 89 93 86 93 85 — — 84 61 85 96 98 — 81
DAN 76 89 91 85 90 — — — — 100 96 100 — 93

Figure 4. Percentages of deviant behavior for two children in Class D.

perhaps it is necessary to question the assumptions implicit in the quotation from Danny's psychological report given earlier. It should be noted that no attempt was made to work on family problems, his conscience, his masculine identification, or his "irascible nature" in changing his adjustment to school.

Teacher E

We have saved until last the most dramatic of all the changes produced in teachers and children. Mrs. E had a lower primary class of 23 children.

Observation of February 1, 1966:

> Six children were in a reading group and 15 were working on individual projects. The noise level for the entire classroom was extremely high and went higher just before recess. Some behaviors noted included whistling, running around the room (5 occasions), yelling at another child (many times), loud incessant talk, hitting other children (7 times), pushing, shoving, and getting in front of each other in recess line. Mrs. E would re-establish quiet by counting to 10, after giving a threat.

Observations suggested that control was obtained mainly by shouting, scolding and the like in an attempt to suppress unwanted behaviors. This approach would work for a while, but there was then a gradual build up in noise until quiet was again demanded. Figure 5 shows that Mrs. E's responses on three days prior to a shift to positive reinforcement contained very few positive statements. Essentially, there was nothing to maintain appropriate classroom behaviors. The focus was on what not to do rather than what to do. There is a good possibility that the attention given deviant behavior in fact served to reinforce it.

Edward and **Elmer** were selected as barometers which might reflect changes for the whole class. Mrs. E was given the general instructions presented above but no special instructions for Edward and Elmer. They were not to receive more attention than other members of the class. She was to make her rules clear, repeat them as needed, ignore deviant behavior and give praise and attention to behavior which facilitated learning. We wanted to see if a general approach to classroom management would be effective with children showing a high level of deviant behavior. The rating of Mrs. E's behavior before and after the change clearly shows an effect of the experimental instructions and training on her behavior.

Edward (age 6-8) tested 95 on the Stanford-Binet. Mrs. E considered him to be "distractible," to have poor work habits, show poor attention and not to comprehend what he read. He never finished assignments. He could sight read and spell first grade words. The baseline observations showed a high incidence of wandering about the room, turning around in his seat, talking at the wrong time and making odd noises. He also showed little peer play.

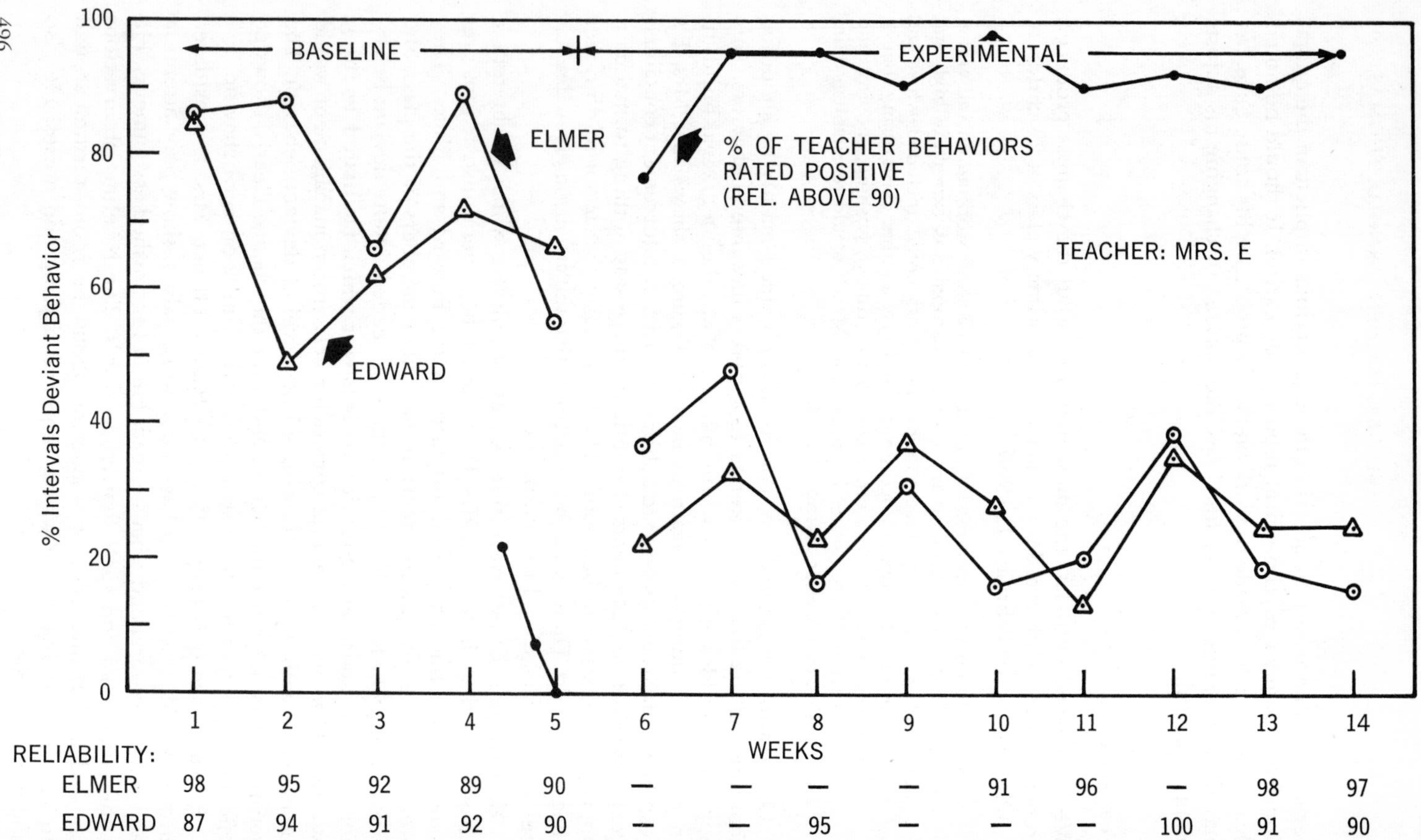

Figure 5. Percentages of deviant behavior for two children in Class E, and change in

A psychological examination in January of 1966 stressed Edward's poor social history (his parents had not talked to each other for three years), his lack of enthusiasm and emotional responsiveness, the apparent restriction on his peer interaction by his mother and his need for better listening and language skills. Edward received speech therapy while in kindergarten. Throughout the baseline and experimental phase of this study, Edward was seen by a social worker and continued in speech therapy. In view of the fact that his (and Elmer's) behavioral changes are found to be directly associated with the change in classroom procedures, rather than time per se, these other treatments do not offer convincing alernative explanations for the data.

Edward greatly reduced the time he spent in aimless wandering, twisting in his seat and talking. He responded well to praise in both the reading group and class activities. Mrs. E reports that he began to complete assignments. He also showed better give and take with his peers, and would laugh, cry and make jokes. While still "distractible," he has learned to work independently for longer periods of time.

Elmer (6 years, 10 months) scored 97 on a group IQ test. He apparently started out the school year working well, but his work deteriorated. He seemed "nervous," hyperactive and would not work. He threw several tantrums and would cry if his work was criticized. His twin sister was also in the class and was doing well. By comparison Elmer often lost out. The parents expected as much of Elmer as of his sister. During baseline he was rated as showing inappropriate gross motor behaviors as much as 70% of the time. *Talking* was as high as 50% at times. *Noise* and *turning* in seat were at about 10% each. Initially our observers thought he was brain damaged.

Elmer's rapid response to positive reinforcement and a better structured classroom made it possible for him to stay on task longer. However, he did not improve greatly in his reading group. When the children were silently reading, he would at times clown and make noises. More work on reading will be necessary for academic progress.

Elmer's father came to work as a teacher's aid in one of our other classes just after the shift off baseline. His work with Mrs. C and changes in Elmer led slowly to his accepting the value of a positive rather than a punitive approach. Very likely father's attempt to be more rewarding with Elmer contributed to the maintenance of Elmer's improved classroom behavior. More to the point, however, is the fact that Elmer's improved classroom behavior (we showed father the graph during Week 9) served to reinforce father's acceptance of a positive approach.

In her report at the end of the semester Mrs. E felt that 12 of 23 children in her class definitely profited from her change in behavior, that six children were unchanged, three somewhat improved and two more deviant. The children who were reported unchanged tended to be the quiet and submissive ones who escaped Mrs. E's attention much of the time. From her own comments, it is likely that those reported to be more deviant seem so only because they stand out from the group more now that Elmer and Edward are not such big problems.

IMPLICATIONS

The results of these investigations demonstrate that quite different kinds of teachers can learn to apply behavioral principles effectively to modify the behavior of problem children. These results extend to the elementary classroom, with normal teacher-pupil ratios, the importance of *differential* social reinforcement in developing effective social behaviors in children Work now in progress suggests that rules alone do nothing and that simply ignoring deviant behavior actually increases such behavior The combination of ignoring deviant behavior and reinforcing an incompatible behavior seems critical. Nearly all of our teachers found that the technique of praising a child who was showing an incompatible appropriate behavior, when another child was misbehaving, was especially effective This action keeps the teacher from attending to the deviant act and at the same time provides vicarious reinforcement for an incompatible behavior. In the future we hope to bring together a group of techniques which various teachers found effective in implementing the general strategy of this project.

These findings add support to the proposition that much can be done by the classroom teacher to eliminate behaviors which interfere with learning without extensive changes in the home, or intensive therapy.

REFERENCES

Allen, K. E., Hart, B. M., Buell, J. S., Harris, F. R., & Wolf, M. M. Effects of social reinforcement on isolate behavior of a nursery school child. *Child Development*, 1964, 35, 511–518.

Harris, F. R., Johnston, M. K., Kelley, C. S., & Wolf, M. M. Effects of positive social reinforcement on regressed crawling of a nursery school child. *Journal of Educational Psychology*, 1964, 55, 35–41.

Hawkins, R. P., Peterson, R. F., Schweid, E., & Bijou, S. W. Behavior therapy in the home: Amelioration of problem parent-child relations with the parent in a therapeutic role. *Journal of Experimental Child Psychology*, 1966, 4, 99–107.

O'Leary, K. D., & Becker, W. C. Behavior modification in an adjustment class: A token reinforcement program. *Exceptional Children*, 1967, in press.

Wahler, R. G., Winkel, G. H., Peterson, R. E., & Morrison, D. C. Mothers as behavior therapists for their own children. *Behaviour Research and Therapy*, 1965, 3, 2, 113–124.

Self-Concept of Ability and School Achievement

W. B. BROOKOVER
EDSEL ERICKSON
DON HAMACHEK
LEE JOINER
JEAN LEPERE
ANN PATERSON
SHAILER THOMAS

The challenge of educating the youth of today is of vital concern to adults faced with the intellectual demands of an increasingly complex era. The intellectual revolution of the past century has produced a vast body of knowledge and skills which require a greater proportion of individuals who are more highly educated. The responsibility for assisting all individuals to develop and utilize those skills in creative and imaginative ways is of prime concern in meeting the ever-changing demands of a space-oriented society.

Current discussion of the need for higher levels of training and education to meet the advanced technological complexity of our society has encountered an obstacle in a basic assumption of the field of educational testing and placement.[1] In view of an increasing need for persons with high levels of training, it is essential that there be an increase in the supply of persons who are considered able to attain such proficiency. The traditional search has been for "talented" individuals, seemingly endowed

This paper was presented at the Sixth World Congress of the International Sociological Association in Evian, France, September, 1966. It is printed with the permission of the authors. Research was partially supported by U.S. Office of Education Cooperative Research Projects 845 and 1636.

[1]See Wilbur B. Brookover, "A Social Psychological Conception of Classroom Learning," *School and Society,* LXXXVII (1959), 84–87; Ronald G. Corwin, "An Alternative to the Search for Talent," mimeographed paper delivered at the Ohio State University Counseling and Guidance Training Institute, 1962; Robert J. Havighurst, *American Higher Education in the 1960's* (Columbus, Ohio: Ohio State University, 1960).

with a "gift." Basic to this search is the assumption that only a relatively small and constant proportion of the population is capable of superior achievement. James B. Conant, for example, assumes that only 15 to 25 percent of the high school youth in the United States can profit by higher education in mathematics, science, and foreign languages.[2]

When it is assumed that only one-fifth to one-fourth of our students have the talent necessary for high achievement and that little can be done for the others, the nation's collective achievement and development have been limited unnecessarily. As a result, our society is greatly handicapped in competing with other societies which assume that nearly all students have the ability to achieve at high levels. The basic assumption of this study, that achievement for most students can be raised by self-concept enhancement, implies that a narrow conception of fixed limits in student potential or capacity is invalid.

THE PROBLEM AND GENERAL THEORY

Perceptual psychologists such as Combs and Snygg[3] and others have for some time emphasized the importance of the individual's perception in what has been identified as intelligence or ability to learn. While the theoretical orientation of the experimental approach reported here is compatible with this theory, it is more directly derived from the symbolic-interactionist theory of George Herbert Mead.[4]

The general hypothesis derived from this theory is that the functional limits of one's ability are in part set by one's self-conception of ability to achieve in academic tasks relative to others. This self-concept of ability is acquired in interaction with significant others.

> "In this context, the self is the intervening variable between the normative patterns of the social group or the role expectations held by significant others, on one hand, and the learning of the individual, on the other. We hypothesize that, for the expectations of others to be functional in a particular individual's behavior, they must be internalized and become a part of the person's conception of himself. Although we recognize the relevance of self in all aspects of human behavior, our interest at this point is in a particular aspect of self as it functions in the school learning situation. We postulate that the child acquires, by taking the role of the other, a perception of his

[2]James B. Conant, *The American High School Today* (New York: McGraw-Hill, 1959), p. 20.

[3]Arthur W. Combs and Donald Snygg, *Individual Behavior* (2nd Edition, New York: Harper & Row, 1959).

[4]George H. Mead, *Mind, Self and Society* (Chicago: University of Chicago Press, 1934). The authors have also been influenced by the theoretical work of John W. Kinch, "A Formalized Theory of the Self-Concept," *The American Journal of Sociology,* LXVIII (1963), 481–486; Combs and Snygg, *op. cit.;* and Harry S. Sullivan, *Conceptions of Modern Psychiatry* (Washington, D.C.: William Alanson White Psychiatric Foundation, 1947).

> own ability as a learner of the various types of skills and subjects which constitute the school curriculum. *If* the child perceives that he is unable to learn mathematics or some other area of behavior, this self-concept of his ability becomes the functionally limiting factor of his school achievement. "Functional limit" is the term used to emphasize that we are speaking not of genetic organic limits on learning but rather of those perceptions of what is appropriate, desirable, and possible for the individual to learn. We postulate the latter as the limits that actually operate, within broader organic limits, in determining the nature or extent of the particular behavior learned."[5]

This research project is dedicated to the discovery of strategies for enhancing the self-concepts of students who are impeded in their performance by low self-evaluations of academic ability.

Prior investigations by the authors[6] have clearly indicated that many students are impeded in their academic performance by low self-concepts of ability to achieve in academic tasks. Furthermore, these investigations have shown that self-concept of ability functions independently of measured intelligence in predicting school achievement. Additional findings have shown that a student's self-concept of academic ability is associated with the evaluations which he perceives significant others such as parents, teachers, and friends hold of his academic ability.

There were two main aspects of the investigation.[7] The first involved an experiment designed to enable study of the effect of systematically induced changes in the perceived evaluations and expectations held by a student's significant others on his self-concept of ability and academic achievement. The second was a longitudinal study (grades 7 – 10) of the 463 subjects who were not included in the experiment. Both of these aspects provide data for U. S. Office of Education Cooperative Research Project No. 2831. This portion of the study follows these students through the remainder of their high school careers.

OBJECTIVES

The overall objective of the experiment was to explore methods for developing talent among junior high school students through the enhance-

[5]Wilbur B. Brookover and David Gottlieb, *A Sociology of Education* (2nd Edition, New York: American Book Company, 1964), p. 469.

[6]Wilbur B. Brookover, Ann Paterson, and Shailer Thomas, "Self-Concept of Abilities and School Achievement," Cooperative Research Project No. 845, U. S. Office of Education, East Lansing, Office of Research and Publications, Michigan State University, 1962.

[7]Wilbur B. Brookover, Jean M. LePere, Don E. Hamachek, Shailer Thomas, and Edsel Erickson, "Self-Concept of Ability and School Achievement, II," Cooperative Research Project No. 1636, U. S. Office of Education, East Lansing, Bureau of Educational Research Services, Michigan State University, October, 1965.

ment of the student's self-concept of academic ability. Experimental objectives derived from the underlying theoretical orientation were:

1. To enhance the self-concepts of academic ability of low-achieving students and thereby enhance their academic achievement;
2. To explore the effects of three different treatments designed to modify self-concepts of ability;
3. To offer some basis for deciding which of three methods may be effective in enhancing self-concept of academic ability;
4. To test the basic hypothesis of symbolic interaction theory that changes in self-concept will be associated with changes in behavior;
5. To determine relationships, trends, and constancy of relationship of self-concept of ability to other relevant variables (academic achievement, the evaluation of significant others, and self-attitudes toward achievement) over a longitudinal period.

The main objective of the longitudinal study was to clarify the theoretical propositions that self-concepts of ability derive primarily from the perceived evaluations of significant others, and that self-concept of ability is a "functionally limiting factor" in school achievement. Further objectives included:

1. To determine whether change in the perceived evaluations of significant others is a *necessary but not sufficient* condition for bringing about change in self-concept of ability;
2. To determine whether change in self-concept of ability is a *necessary but not sufficient* condition for the occurrence of a particular academic performance;
3. To gain information concerning the reciprocal-role relationships of students with significant others over a longitudinal period;
4. To determine what patterns, if any, are apparent in the perceptions of parents, friends, and teachers over the longitudinal period.

PROCEDURES

Experimental Designs: Three experimental designs were used to evaluate three different methods of self-concept enhancement and any resulting influence on academic achievement. Each experiment was carried out in a separate junior high school in order to avoid contamination of treatments. All subjects were Caucasian students who were in the ninth grade during the 1962–63 academic year in an urban school system and had achieved below the mean GPA (computed on the four subjects of math, English, social studies, and science) for the previous two semesters. The treatment period covered the school year.

Parent Experiment: Three groups of students who met the above criteria were randomly selected and placed in an experimental group, a placebo group to control for a possible "Hawthorne Effect," or a control group. Parents of the experimental subjects who were unwilling to cooperate were placed in the control group and the experimental group was then filled by willing subjects from the control group. Thus, although an attempt was made to maintain each group as a random sample, this was not entirely possible. Parents of the experimental group were instructed to communicate to their children in various ways that they thought their children were capable and that they ought to achieve at a higher level. The parents were told not to inform their children that the parents were participating in any program pertinent to the children. Neither the students nor their teachers were aware that a program was being carried on which involved them.

The parents of the placebo subjects were given essentially the same treatment as the experimental group parents except that no mention was made of their children's ability. The parents of the control group were not contacted.

Expert Experiment: Low-achieving students defined in the same manner as above were randomly assigned to an experimental group, a placebo group and a control group. A person from the University meeting with the experimental group subjects communicated high evaluations and expectations of them. With the placebo subjects school problems were discussed in a non-directive manner. The control group subjects were not contacted.

Counselor Experiment: Other considerations were involved in the selection of groups for the Counselor Experiment. In addition to achieving below the mean for their class during both semesters of the eighth grade, students had to be below the class average on the self-concept of ability scale and perceive their parents as holding low (below the mean of the class) evaluations of their ability. Also, these students had to have been in the school system since fourth grade and have complete school records. From this population an experimental group and a control group were randomly drawn. No placebo group was used in this experiment.

Longitudinal Study: There were 463 subjects, including 204 males and 259 females in the longitudinal population. This population included all of the Caucasian students in an urban school system on whom complete data was available and who were not participating in a special education program or in studies designed to enhance self-concept.

Analysis was made of the stability of student responses on each of the variables and on associations between the variables. A study was made of both magnitude and proportion of association and change. In addition, the constancy of associations between the relevant variables was examined in order to determine: (1) the extent of these associations under varying times and conditions during the longitudinal period; (2) patterns of association; and, (3) discernible trends.

RESULTS

Parent Experiment: There was no significant change in either self-concept of ability or achievement for students in the placebo or the control group over the nine-month period. The experimental group revealed, however, a significant increase in both self-concept of ability and grade point average.

There were significant changes in the experimental group parents as well. They viewed their children and their children's teachers more positively.

Expert Experiment: Analysis revealed that none of the three groups improved significantly in self-concept or achievement over the treatment period.

Counselor Experiment: Test analysis revealed that there had been no significant change in either self-concept of ability or on GPA at the end of the treatment period.

Longitudinal Study: Analysis led to an acceptance of the following statements:

1. The perceived evaluations of significant others are a major factor in self-concept of academic ability at each grade level, eight through ten.
2. The perceived parental evaluation of females showed a higher relationship to their self-concept of academic ability than was apparent for the males. No between sex differences were observed for the perceived evaluations of friends and teachers.
3. An increasing congruency appears to develop between the perceived evaluations of parents, friends, and teachers from the seventh through the tenth grades.
4. Changes in the perceived evaluations of others are associated with changes in self, more than with changes in achievement. This was expected.
5. Self-concept of ability was a significant factor in achievement at all levels.
6. There were no consistent sex differences in the relationships of self-concept of ability and achievement.
7. Changes or stability in self-concept of ability are associated with changes or stability in both perceived evaluations of others and in

achievement. The associated change in achievement is noted, however, only over long periods of time (three years).

8. Specific self-concepts in subject matter areas are less stable in predicting achievement than are general self-concepts of ability.

9. The relationship of self-concept to achievement is not associated with differences in school attended.

10. Socio-economic class has a low relationship to self-concept of ability and achievement.

11. Self-concept is not merely a reflection of memory of past performance.

12. Self-concept of ability is not merely a reflection of past achievement.

13. Parents are academic significant others for most students at all grade levels, seven through ten.

14. Changes in the association of major variables over the longitudinal period are not accounted for by group changes in response to the measures of these variables at any grade level (e.g. changes in grading standards). The student body tends to distribute the same on each of the major variables at all grade levels.

CONCLUSIONS

Though the experiments were not designed to make statistical comparisons, certain comparative statements are in order. The findings that the expert and counseling treatments failed to induce significant changes in either self-concept or achievement suggest that working through an already established significant other is more likely to be effective than developing a new significant other for students. It was found that not only can improvement of self-concept of ability be effected by working with parents who are academic significant others to their children, but that this improvement in self-concept also reflects itself in improved academic performance. Furthermore, analysis of data for the students of placebo group parents indicates that mere attention to parents and an involvement in discussion of general school and adolescent problems does not result in their communicating anything to their children with reference to perceptions of self in relation to school achievement. To be most effective, it is suggested, one should overtly and specifically deal with self-concept.

Finally, this study found no reason for rejecting, and considerable evidence for accepting, the theoretical propositions that (1) self-concepts of academic ability derive primarily from the perceived evaluations of significant others, usually parents, and that (2) for most low achieving students, self-concept of ability is a functionally limiting factor in their academic performance.

BIBLIOGRAPHY OF PAPERS, ARTICLES, AND DISSERTATIONS BASED ON SELF-CONCEPT OF ABILITY AND SCHOOL ACHIEVEMENT PROJECT

Brookover, Wilbur B., LePere, Jean M., Erickson, Edsel L., Thomas, Shailer. "Definitions of Others, Self-Concept, and Academic Achievement: A Longitudinal Study," paper presented at the American Sociological Association at Chicago, Illinois, 1965.

Brookover, Wilbur B., LePere, Jean M., Hamachek, Don, Erickson, Edsel. "The Effects of Three Treatment Conditions on Changing Self-Concept and Achievement," paper presented at the Ohio Valley Sociological Meetings, April 30, 1964.

Brookover, Wilbur B., Paterson, Ann, and Thomas, Shailer. "Self-Concept of Ability and School Achievement," U. S. Office of Education *Cooperative Research Project No. 845*, (East Lansing: Office of Research and Publications, Michigan State University, 1962).

Brookover, Wilbur B., LePere, Jean M., Erickson, Edsel L., Thomas, Shailer. "Definitions of Others, Self-Concept, and Academic Achieve-Achievement II," U. S. Office of Education *Cooperative Research Project No. 1636*, (East Lansing: Bureau of Educational Research Services, Michigan State University, 1965).

Brookover, Wilbur B., Thomas, Shailer, and Paterson, Ann. "Self-Concept of Ability and School Achievement," *Sociology of Education*, XXXVII (1964), 271–278.

Erickson, Edsel L. "Implications of Self-Concept Enhancement and Academic Achievement for Educational Theory and Practice," paper presented at meetings of the American Educational Research Association at Chicago, Illinois, 1964.

Erickson, Edsel L. "Introduction: Symposium on Self-Concept and Its Relationship to Academic Achievement: A Longitudinal Analysis," paper presented at meetings of the American Educational Research Association at Chicago, Illinois, 1965.

Erickson, Edsel L., and Thomas, Shailer. "The Normative Influence of Parents and Friends Upon School Achievement," paper presented at meetings of the American Educational Research Association, Chicago, Illinois, 1965.

Erickson, Edsel L., Brookover, Wilbur B., Joiner, Lee M., Towne, Richard C. "A Social-Psychological Study of the Educable Mentally Retarded:

An Educational Application of Symbolic Interactionism," paper presented at 1965 national meeting of the Council for Exceptional Children, Portland, Oregon.

Erickson, Edsel L., Brookover, Wilbur B., and Joiner, Lee M. "Educational Plans, Aspirations, and Achievement: A Longitudinal Study," unpublished manuscript, Bureau of Educational Research Services, Michigan State University, East Lansing, 1965.

Erickson, Edsel L. *A Study of the Normative Influence of Parents and Friends Upon Academic Achievement*, Ed. D. Thesis, Michigan State University, 1965.

Hamachek, Don E. "Characteristics of Low-Achieving, Low Self-Concept Junior High School Students and the Impact of Small Group and Individual Counseling on Self-Concept Enhancement and Achievement," paper presented at meetings of the American Educational Research Association at Chicago, Illinois, 1964.

Hamachek, Don E. "Abstract—The Role of Counselor as a Significant Other in Self-Concept Enhancement," paper presented at meetings of the American Educational Research Association at Chicago, Illinois, 1965.

Haarer, David L. *A Comparative Study of Self-Concept of Ability Between Institutionalized Delinquent Boys and Non-Delinquent Boys Enrolled in Public Schools*, Ph.D. Thesis, Michigan State University, 1964.

Joiner, Lee M., Erickson, Edsel L., Brookover, Wilbur B., Krugh, Corwin A., Sproull, Natalie. "Student Definitions of the Educational Expectations of Others and the Development of Educational Plans: A Longitudinal Study of High School Males," paper presented at meetings of the American Educational Research Association, Chicago, Illinois, 1966.

LePere, Jean M. "A Study of the Impact of the Parent on the Child's Concept of Self as it Relates to Academic Achievement," paper presented at meetings of the American Educational Research Association at Chicago, Illinois, 1964.

LePere, Jean M. "A Longitudinal Analysis of the Relationship of Self-Concept and Academic Achievement of Students from Seventh through Tenth Grades," paper presented at the meetings of the American Educational Research Association at Chicago, Illinois, 1965.

Morse, Richard J. "Self-Concept of Ability, Significant Others and School Achievement of Eighth-Grade Students: A Comparative Investigation of Negro and Caucasian Students," unpublished M.A. Thesis, Michigan State University, 1963.

Sandeen, Carl. *Aspirations for College Among Male Secondary School Students from Seventh to Tenth Grade*, Ph.D. Thesis, Michigan State University, 1964.

Thomas, Shailer, and Paterson, Ann. "An Empirical Investigation of Self-Concept in a Learning Situation," paper presented at meetings of the Ohio Valley Sociological Society at East Lansing, Michigan, 1962.

Thomas, Shailer. "An Experimental Approach: The Enhancement of Self-Concept of Junior High School Students Through Large Group Sessions," paper presented at meetings of the American Educational Research Association at Chicago, Illinois, 1964.

Thomas, Shailer. *A Study to Enhance Self-Concept of Ability and Raise School Achievement Among Low-Achieving Ninth Grade Students*, Ph.D. Thesis, Michigan State University, 1964.

The Experimental Effects of Training College Students As Play Therapists[1,2]

GARY E. STOLLAK[3]

The need for "innovative and imaginative development of new manpower sources" (Gamin, 1966) to overcome the shortages of mental health personnel has been well-documented and emphasized (Gamin, 1966; Guerney, 1964; Schofield, 1964; Rioch, 1966). Mike Gamin and others such as Margaret Rioch and Bernard Guerney have further noted "the growing recognition that individuals possessing less than complete professional training can serve an important role in helping persons who are experiencing emotional distress and mental disabilities. In other words individuals with different levels of training can provide important services to people in need of help" (Gamin, 1966). Only until very recently, though, has there been research or systematic attempts to develop either "innovative and imaginative programs" or in using subprofessionals, or minimally trained individuals, as therapists.

The work of Margaret Rioch is well known (Rioch et al., 1963). She and her colleagues trained mature women to act as therapists. More recently, Carkhuff and Truax (1965) and Poser (1966) reported on their training a group of five lay hospital personnel and eleven undergraduates, respectively, to work with groups of chronic hospitalized adults. Davison

[1]This paper was presented at the 1967 annual meeting of the Midwestern Psychological Association in Chicago, Illinois. It is printed with the permission of the author.

[2]The research was supported by an All University grant from Michigan State University.

[3]The author would like to thank James Lurie and James Love who acted as coders and Michelle Ferguson for her statistical and computational aid.

(1966) has attempted to train undergraduates to act as social reinforcers for autistic children. The nurse, too, has been used in attempts to modify the behavior of hospitalized adults (Ayllon and Michael, 1959; Bachrach, Erwin, and Mohr, 1966).

A major trend in the research literature has been the attempts to use parents as therapeutic agents or behavior modifiers for their children. Ullmann and Krasner's "Case studies in behavior modification" (1966) has papers by Patterson, Peterson and London, Williams, Madsen and others in which parents played an important role in selecting, reinforcing, and changing behavior such as bed-wetting, temper tantrums, and phobias.

Guerney and his co-workers (1964; 1966; Guerney, Guerney and Andronico, 1966) have developed a technique they call "filial therapy" in which parents are trained in groups of 6–8 to employ principles and techniques used in client-centered play therapy in play sessions in the clinic and at home with their own children under ten years of age. In a recent doctoral dissertation Stover (1966) found that as a result of training in filial therapy parents were able to play the required role and their children by the third session showed a significant increment, as compared to the control group, in aggressive responses and expression of negative feeling. To determine the factors accounting for the possible varying degrees of success in filial therapy Guerney[4] is presently studying the effects of (1) the parent's personality, (2) the ability of the parent to master the required role, (3) the type of problem presented by the child, and (4) the occurrence or lack of occurrence of certain patterns of events in the course of the child's play sessions.

The present study attempted to use the procedures and techniques that Guerney developed in filial therapy to train college undergraduates as play therapists with emotionally disturbed children under ten. It was hypothesized that the students would increase their use of reflective statements from the first to tenth sessions and that the children seen by these students would, during this time, (a) increase their expression of leadership behavior, (b) decrease their expression of dependency behavior, and (c) increase their expression of aggression and other negative feelings.

METHOD

A notice was read to several sophomore and junior level psychology classes at Michigan State University requesting volunteers to learn play therapy. All who would volunteer were asked to make a commitment for two years to the project. Approximately seventy-five volunteers were

[4]Personal communication.

administered Smith's Sensitivity-to-People test[5] as a pilot attempt to study possible differences between students on training and performance. The five males and five females with the lowest scores were designated Low Potential Therapists (LPT) and the five males and five females with the highest scores on the test were designated High Potential Therapists (HPT). The twenty students were randomly assigned to three groups. Two volunteers dropped out at this point for academic and other personal reasons.

The three groups of six students each met separately during a ten week training program. As in Guerney's training of parents, the first two group sessions of one-hour each were devoted to explaining the nature and purpose of the role that they would be asked to play in the weekly sessions they would be having with their child. The student's role is modeled as closely as possible after that taken by a client-centered play therapist. The basic task is: "(a) to be empathic with the child during the sessions—to make every effort to understand how the child is viewing himself and his world at the moment and what his feelings of the moment are; (b) to be fully understanding and accepting of the child—i.e., his feelings and thoughts, whatever their nature; (c) to leave the direction that the play sessions take (within certain clearly defined limits . . .) completely to the child; and (d) most of all, to *convey* this understanding and acceptance to the child." (Guerney, Guerney and Andronico, 1966). The rationale and value of such an approach was emphasized including possible explanations of behavioral change in the child caused by the student's behavior.

The preceding was taught through examples of possible situations they would encounter and didactic lectures. However, group discussion was stimulated and promoted.

During the third through fifth training sessions, I demonstrated play therapy techniques with "normal" children (kindly provided by colleagues in the psychology department) for one-half hour each session. The students observed through a one-way mirror and were asked to keep detailed notes of the interaction of the author and child. After the session with the child, there was an hour or more group discussion of what exactly went on, the rationale for my actions, and the doubts, fears, and concerns of the students about acting in such a manner. Examples and possible problems they would encounter were again emphasized and discussed.

During the sixth through tenth training sessions, each student played with a normal child. During each one-half hour session, two students would see the child (fifteen minutes per student). The other members of the group would observe through the one-way mirror. Again, group dis-

[5]Write to Henry Clay Smith—Department of Psychology, Michigan State University, East Lansing, Michigan 48823, for copies of this test.

cussions followed the play sessions with the child. These centered especially around the differences between the students, between the students and myself, and on their feelings about and difficulties in acting in the client-centered manner.

At the end of the tenth session each student was assigned a child between the ages of four and ten, obtained from the waiting lists of the Lansing Child Guidance Clinic or the Psychological Clinic at Michigan State University.[6] Only children who were diagnosed as brain damaged, mentally retarded, or severely disturbed were excluded from selection. Each parent was called by or called the author and informed of the availability of service. When they stated they were desirous of service for their child, they were told that a student clinician from Michigan State University would be calling them shortly. Assignment of children to students was made randomly. Each student made the contact with the parent, set up an appointment time, and began regular weekly one-half hour contacts.

I and other trained personnel observed the first two sessions of each student watching for gross incompetency on the part of the student, and possible bizarre behavior on the part of the child that would require more "professional" attention. No student or child had to be removed from the project because of these reasons.

Each student was required to keep a detailed report of his interaction with the child and parent before, during, and after the play sessions which was and continues to be discussed at one-hour weekly meetings and handed in to me.

Children's Behavior During the Sessions

The first, fifth, and tenth sessions were observed by trained coders through a one-way mirror. Children's aggressive behavior was coded every 15 seconds during the session on an intensity continuum devised by Siegel (1965). The categories included: the child having shown no aggression (0), mild or playful aggression (1), stronger and more forceful aggression (2), or intense aggression in which the child seemed highly involved (3). A reliability study between coders during the training phase of the project yielded a correlation between total intensity ratings from 3 sessions of .92. The coders were unaware either of the research hypotheses or which students were in the HPT or LPT groups.

During each 15 second interval in the first, fifth, and tenth session, leadership, dependency, and negative feelings were coded following a system devised by Guerney et al. (1965). *Leadership* was scored when the child

[6]The author is grateful to Gilbert DeRath and Hilda Parker for their aid in obtaining children at their respective clinics.

suggested, instructed, directed, gave ideas, guidance and otherwise asserted himself with the student. *Dependency* was scored when the child requested evaluation or praise, instruction, direction, ideas, guidance, or leadership from the student, and *Negative Feeling* was scored when the child expressed annoyance, anger, or dislike toward an object or person (including accusation, cursing, and disparaging remarks).

Correlations between the two coders for each of these variables during the three training sessions were: Leadership, .86; Dependency, .82; and Negative Feeling, .87. During any 15-second interval more than one category could be scored but no category was scored more than once during that interval.

Student Therapist Behavior During the Sessions

All sessions were taped. For each fifteen seconds of the tapes of the first, fifth, and tenth sessions of each student, trained coders, uninformed of the number of the session and, again, the characteristics of the students, coded for Reflection of Content and Clarification of Feeling (after Ashby, Ford, Guerney and Guerney, 1957). Interrater reliability for each category was above .80. Stover (1966) found that the category primarily responsible for the significant differences obtained between experimental and control groups over three sessions was reflection or restatement of content. She felt that clarification of feeling, presumably a more therapeutically meaningful type of response, is more difficult to master. She suggested that probably only when they become less concerned with what *not* to do and more concerned with what *to* do would therapists in training increase their use of clarification of feelings. Observation of the undergraduates in the present study suggested early use of clarification of feeling statements.

RESULTS

Two student therapists left school for emotional and academic reasons and four cases were terminated by parents, prior to the completion of ten sessions. Although the four students were assigned new cases, the old or new case data was not included in the analysis below. The data below include those obtained from the twelve students who completed ten sessions with their child.

Student's Behavior

The mean number of intervals in which reflective statements were made in the first, fifth, and tenth sessions are shown in Table 1.

TABLE 1

Mean Number of Intervals Student's Statements Were Reflective (Maximum Is 120)

	High Potential Therapists (n = 5)		Low Potential Therapists (n = 7)	
	Reflection of Content	Clarification of Feeling	Reflection of Content	Clarification of Feeling
First Session	58	12	51	8
Fifth Session	62	26	59	27
Tenth Session	69	21	65	26

As can be seen in Table 1, for both the HPT's and LPT's the mean number of intervals in which they made reflection of content statements increased over the ten sessions. Clarification of feeling statements also increased from the first to fifth then dropped slightly from the fifth to tenth. Analyses of variance for groups with unequal means (Winer, 1962) was applied to the data. The obtained F's were highly significant (p. < .01). A planned set of orthogonal comparisons (Hays, 1963, p. 468) was performed. The results indicated that between the first and fifth sessions, there was, for the HPT's a significant increase in clarification of feeling statements but not in reflection of content. Likewise for the LPT's. Also for both the LPT's and HPT's, there is a significant increase in reflection of content from the first to tenth and in clarification of feeling. There were no significant differences between fifth and tenth sessions in either category and no significant difference between HPT's and LPT's on any category at any session.

Children's Behavior

The mean number of intervals the children expressed negative feelings, leadership, and dependency behaviors, and the mean intensity of aggression scores for the first, fifth, and tenth sessions can be seen in Table 2. The data for the children were combined due to the lack of significant differences between HPT's and LPT's.

As can be seen in Table 2, there is little change in the aggression scores over the three sessions. An analysis of variance indicated that there was no significant change in the aggression scores. Statistical tests on the other three behaviors over sessions indicated that expression of negative feelings increased significantly from the first to tenth (however not from first to fifth or fifth to tenth), leadership behavior increased from first through

TABLE 2

Mean Intensity of Aggression Scores (Maximum Is 360) and Mean Number of Intervals Children Expressed Negative Feelings, Leadership, and Dependency Behavior (Maximum Is 120) (N = 12)

	AGGRESSION	NEGATIVE FEELING	LEADERSHIP	DEPENDENCY
First Session	2.7	.5	3.7	2.4
Fifth Session	2.1	1.7	10.6	1.9
Tenth Session	3.4	2.9	12.7	2.6

fifth (but not from fifth to tenth). No significant changes in dependency behaviors were obtained over the three sessions.

DISCUSSION

Although the present study did not evaluate the children's behavior outside the play sessions, several interesting findings were obtained concerning in-session behavior. Undergraduate students *do* significantly change their behavior during the sessions, increasing their reflection of content and clarification of feeling statements. These changes were not only statistically significant, but also seemed to be of sufficient magnitude to have possibly effected an increase in the expression of negative feelings and leadership behavior of the children. However, the lack of control groups necessitates qualification of any conclusion that it was the particular behaviors and changes in the students' behaviors that produced such changes in the children's behavior. Further research is planned with appropriate control groups. Along with the possibility of the personality test used being inappropriate for our purposes, the lack of significant differences between HPT's and LPT's could also be a result of the training phase of the project. Such training may have washed out the effects of personality differences. Future research is planned to study personality differences obtained on several measures before and during training as well as during the actual play therapy sessions.

I feel more confident now than I did at the beginning of the study that college students would be able to play the prescribed role with the children. There are many incidents in which the students demonstrated a sensitivity and empathy equal to or exceeding that of many advanced graduate students I have supervised. Their youth and malleability, their openness to suggestion, and their eagerness to learn are obvious positive characteristics. These undergraduates seemed not only to give "support" to these children which Rosenbaum (1966) felt was all college students could offer, but I feel were acting maturely and competently, and in the fullest sense of the word as "therapists" attempting to bring about "change". Whether college students can be trained to bring about change in the behaviors of adolescents or adults, or with more disturbed children and individuals is for research to determine. The probability that many of them can be trained to work with less seriously disturbed children is high, and that they can be seen as a potential source of personnel in child guidance clinics and possibly in the schools, is clear. The potential is there. Will we tap it? As others have pointed out (Rioch, 1966) it will not be until we get over *our* need for security, prestige, and status, and begin to redefine our own tasks as clinical psychologists and therapists, that the training and use of sub-professionals will become part of our profession.

In summary, as Rioch (1966) has recently commented: "More important even than saving of traditional professional time, these new workers have a double advantage. They bring fresh points of view, flexible attitudes, and sometimes new methods into the field. They also solve their problems in helping to solve the problems of others. They become constructive, better integrated citizens themselves, which is the most important thing of all, for in doing so they add to the community's pool of good will, rather than to its pool of discontent and suspicion" (p. 291).

REFERENCES

Ashby, J.D., Ford, D.H., Guerney, B.G., Jr., and Guerney, Louise. Effects on clients of a reflective and a leading type of psychotherapy, *Psychological Monographs*, 1957, 71, No. 24.

Ayllon, T., and Michael, J. The psychiatric nurse as a behavioral engineer, *Journal of the Experimental Analysis of Behavior*, 1959, 2, 323–334.

Bachrach, A.J., Erwin, W.J., and Mohr, J.P. The control of eating behavior in an anorexic by operant conditioning techniques, in L. Ullmann & L. Krasner (Eds.) *Case studies in behavior modification*, Holt, Rinehart & Winston, Inc., N.Y., 1966, 153–163.

Carkhuff, R.R., and Truax, C.B. Lay mental health counseling. The effects of lay group counseling, *Journal of Consulting Psychology*, 1965, 29, 426–431.

Davison, G.C. The training of undergraduates as social reinforcers for autistic children, in L. Ullmann & L. Krasner (Eds.) *Case studies in behavior modification*, Holt, Rinehart & Winston, Inc., N.Y., 1966, 146–148.

Gamin, M. *The critical need for additional mental health manpower.* State of Washington Conference on Mental Health Training Needs —Dec. 3, 1966.

Guerney, B.G. Jr. Filial therapy: description and rationale, *Journal of Consulting Psychology*, 1964, 28, 304–310.

Guerney, B.G. Jr. The utilization of parents as therapeutic agents, Paper presented at the 1966 American Psychological Association convention.

Guerney, B.G. Jr., Burton, Jean, Silverberg, Dana, & Shapiro, Ellen, Use of adult responses to codify childrens' behavior in a play situation. *Perceptual and Motor Skills*, 1965, 20, 614–615.

Guerney, B.G. Jr., Guerney, Louise, and Andronico, M. Filial Therapy, *Yale Scientific Magazine*, 1966, 40, 6–14.

Hays, W.L. *Statistics for psychologists*, Holt, Rinehart, & Winston, Inc., N.Y., 1963.

Poser, E.G. The effect of therapist's training on group therapeutic outcome. *Journal of Consulting Psychology*, 1966, 30, 283–289.

Rioch, Margaret J. Changing concepts in the training of therapists, *Journal of Consulting Psychology*, 1966, 30, 290–292.

Rioch, M.J., Elkes, C., Flint, A.A., Usdansky, B.S., Newman, R.G. and Silber, E. National Institute of Mental Health pilot study in training mental health couselors, *American Journal of Orthopsychiatry*, 1963, 33, 678–689.

Rosenbaum, M. Some comments on the use of untrained therapists. *Journal of Consulting Psychology*, 1966, 30, 292–294.

Schofield, W. *Psychotherapy: the purchase of friendship*, Prentice-Hall: N.Y., 1964.

Siegel, Alberta. Film-mediated fantasy aggression and strength of aggressive drive, *Child Development*, 1956, 27, 365–378.

Stover, Lillian. *The efficacy of training procedures for mothers in filial therapy*, unpublished doctoral dissertation, Rutgers-The State University, 1966.

Ullmann, L., and Krasner, L. *Case studies in behavior modification*, Holt, Rinehart & Winston, Inc., N.Y., 1966.

Winer, B.J. *Statistical principles in experimental design*, McGraw-Hill: N.Y., 1962.

Mothers as Behavior Therapists for Their Own Children

ROBERT G. WAHLER
GARY H. WINKEL
ROBERT F. PETERSON
DELMONT C. MORRISON

An attempt was made to modify the deviant behavior of three children by producing specific changes in the behavior of their mothers. It was demonstrated that a mother's social behavior may function as a powerful class of reinforcers for her child's deviant as well as normal behavior. It was also demonstrated that a mother's reactions to her child's behavior may be systematically modified, at least within the confines of an experimental setting, and these modifications may produce marked changes in her child's deviant behavior.

Two reviews of the literature on behavior therapy (Bandura, 1961; Grossberg, 1964) reveal a large number of systematic attempts to apply principles of learning theory to psychotherapy. It would appear that many investigators, working within the conceptual frameworks of respondent and operant learning, have produced practical changes in the deviant behavior of both adults and children.

Typically, these investigators have implied that stimuli making up the adult's or child's natural environments are responsible for development and maintenance of the deviant behaviors involved. That is, through unfortunate contingencies between stimuli, or between stimuli and behavior, deviant behavior is produced and maintained. However, while most investigators have assumed that this is true, few have accepted the full

Reprinted with permission from *Behaviour Research & Therapy*, 1965, Vol. 3, 113–124, Copyright 1965, Pergamon Press, Inc., and with the permission of the authors.

implications of this position. Instead of changing "faulty" contingencies involving the natural environment, most research therapists have placed their subjects in artificial environments, designed to modify the deviant behavior through extinction, punishment, and/or reinforcement of responses which are incompatible with the deviant behavior. Although these techniques have produced some remarkable changes in the deviant behavior within the artificial environments—and in some cases within the natural environments—one wonders about the effect that the unmodified natural environments would eventually have on the behavior changes; logically, it would be expected that the deviant behavior would again be strengthened, and behavior developed in the artificial environments would be weakened.

From the standpoint of methodology there is good reason for the behavior therapists' failure to deal with the natural environment. Since the efficacy of their techniques depends upon control of specific contingencies between stimuli, or between stimuli and behavior, they have typically chosen to work in settings that are highly contrived. However, the extent of this methodological problem is, in large part, correlated with the patient's age. Undoubtedly, the natural environment of the young child is far less complex than that of an adolescent or an adult, and it therefore should present fewer difficulties in systematic control. One might conclude that attempts to develop therapeutic techniques for the control of natural environments should initially utilize children as patient-subjects.

Most psychotherapists assume that a child's parents compose the most influential part of his natural environment. It is likely, from a learning theory viewpoint, that their behaviors serve a large variety of stimulus functions, controlling both the respondent and operant behaviors of their children. It then follows that if some of the child's behavior is considered to be deviant at a particular time in his early years, his parents are probably the source of eliciting stimuli and reinforcers which have produced, and are currently maintaining this behavior. A logical procedure for the modification of the child's deviant behavior would involve changing the parents' behavior. These changes would be aimed at training them both to eliminate the contingencies which currently support their child's deviant behavior, and to provide new contingencies to produce and maintain more normal behaviors which would compete with the deviant behavior.

Techniques of parent-child psychotherapy have been investigated by several researchers (Prince, 1961; Russo, 1964; Straughan, 1964). However, the procedures used in these studies did not permit assessment of variables which were maintaining the children's deviant behavior, nor did they permit analyses of those variables which were responsible for changing the deviant behavior. While the investigators concluded that changes in the children's deviant behavior were probably a function of changes in the parents' behavior, these conclusions could not be clearly supported.

Thus, in the further study of parent-child therapeutic techniques it would be of value to utilize procedures which will provide information concerning those stimulus events provided by the parents which function to maintain deviant classes of the child's behavior. Once these controlling stimulus events are detected, it might prove feasible to modify the occurrence of these events in ways which will produce predictable and clinically significant changes in the child's behavior.

The present experiment was an attempt to modify the deviant behavior of three children by producing specific changes in the behavior of their mothers. The major purposes of the study were: (1) to experimentally analyze the mother-child interbehaviors in an effort to specify those variables (i.e. reinforcement contingencies) which may function to maintain the deviant behavior of the children; (2) to eliminate these variables in an effort to modify the children's deviant behavior. Therefore, the focus of the study was not on producing long term changes in the children, but rather to discover how their deviant behavior is maintained and how appropriate changes may be brought about.

METHOD

Subjects and Apparatus

Subjects were three boys varying in age from four to six years and their respective mothers. While the children's behavior problems would probably be considered moderate by most clinical standards, all had exhibited behavior which was sufficiently deviant to motivate their parents to seek psychological help. More detailed information on the children and their mothers will be presented in a later section.

The apparatus was located in the Gatzert Child Development Clinic of the University of Washington. The equipment consisted of a playroom with two adjoining observation rooms which were equipped for visual and auditory monitoring of behavior in the playroom. Each observation room contained a panel with three microswitches which were connected to a Gerbrand six-channel event recorder; depression of the microswitches by observers activated selected channels of the event recorder. In addition, the playroom was equipped with a signal light which could be illuminated by the experimenter in one of the observation rooms.

General Procedure

Prior to the behavior therapy sessions, the parents of each child were seen in interviews aimed at obtaining descriptions of the behavior which created problems at home and/or at school. The interviewer also asked the parents to describe their typical reactions to these behavior patterns whenever they occurred.

All mother-child cases were seen separately for approximately twenty-minute sessions, held once or twice weekly in the playroom. The mother and her child were always the sole occupants of the playroom.

Classification of Mother-Child Interbehavior. For the first two sessions, the mother was instructed, "Just play with——as you might at home". These instructions were modified for one of the cases when a later analysis of the data revealed little or no evidence of what the parents had earlier described as deviant behavior. In this case the mother was given other instructions, based on her description of her typical behavior at home.

During these sessions, two observers, working in separate observation rooms, obtained complete written records of the child's and the mother's behavior. Analysis of these records began with a selection of the child's deviant behavior. This selection was based upon similarities between the recorded behavior and the behavior which the parents reported to create problems at home. A second classification of the child's behavior was made to establish a class of behavior which the experimenter regarded as incompatible with the deviant behavior. Later, strengthening of this class was used in eliminating the deviant behavior.

A second analysis of the written records involved a description of the mother's ways of reacting to her child's deviant behavior, and to his incompatible behavior. Essentially, this analysis provided a description of possible reinforcers provided by the mother for the two classes of the child's behavior.

Observer Reliability and Baseline Measures of Behavior. Following the classification sessions, instructions to the mother were the same; however, the observers now recorded only three classes of behavior—two for the child (deviant behavior and incompatible behavior) and one for the mother (her reactions to her child's behavior classes). This was done by depressing selected microswitches every five seconds for any of the previously classified deviant or incompatible behavior patterns which occurred during the five-second intervals. Another microswitch was reserved for any behavior of the mother's which occurred immediately after the child's two classes of behavior. Essentially, this system was a time-saving device which eliminated the laborious procedure of writing down behavior and then classifying it. Thus, once the child's deviant and incompatible behaviors, and the mother's reactions to them were defined and labeled by the experimenter, the observers' attention in further sessions was focused only on these behavior patterns.

The observational records obtained from the above sessions were also analysed for observer reliability. For each behavior class an agreement or disagreement was tallied for every five-second interval. The percentage of agreements for observers was then computed for each behavior class, for each session. Observer agreement of ninety per cent or better was considered to be adequate; once this agreement was obtained on all behavior classes the baseline sessions were begun. Essentially, the baseline sessions provided a measure of the strength or rate of occurrence of the child's deviant or incompatible behavior, and a measure of how frequently the mother responded to them. These sessions were continued until both mother and child showed fairly stable behavioral rates.

Before the baseline sessions were begun, one of the observers was arbitrarily chosen to record the data, and the other observer served only as a reliability check. In all cases reliability checks showed observer agreement of ninety per cent or better.

Behavior Modification Procedures. Following the baseline sessions, E made systematic attempts to change the mother's reactions to her child's behavior. These attempts involved the use of instructions to the mother before and after the playroom sessions, plus signal light communications to her during the sessions. During initial sessions, E used the signal light as a cueing system, essentially to tell the mother when and how to behave in response to her child's behavior. As the mother improved in her ability to follow instructions, E eventually changed the function of the signal light from cueing system to reinforcement system. The mother was now required to discriminate and respond appropriately to her child's behavior without E's cueing. E used the signal light to provide immediate feedback to the mother concerning her correct and incorrect discriminations, thus teaching her appropriate discrimination responses.

Instructions and the coded significance of the signal light were determined from the baseline data and principles of operant learning theory. In general, the aim was to eliminate possible reinforcers provided by the mother for her child's deviant behavior, but to have her produce them following the child's incompatible behavior. It was thus hoped to train the mother to weaken her child's deviant behavior through a combination of extinction, and by reinforcement of behavior which would compete with the deviant behavior. To accomplish these goals, the mother was first shown the baseline data and given a complete explanation of it; she was also given numerous examples of her child's deviant behavior and his incompatible behavior. She was then told that in further sessions she must completely ignore her child's deviant behavior and respond in any approving way only to his incompatible behavior. The signal light was described to her as an aid which would help her to carry out the instructions. She was told to keep an eye on the light and to respond to her child *only* if it was illuminated; otherwise she was to sit in a chair, ostensibly reading a book and make no verbal or non-verbal contact with her child. E, of course, illuminated the light only following the child's incompatible behavior. In one case, where the child's deviant behavior proved to be unusually resistant to extinction, the mother was trained in the use of a punishment technique as well as the differential reinforcement procedure.

When the observational data revealed that the mother was responding appropriately to the signal light, she was told that in later sessions she must make her own decisions to respond or not respond to her child. She was again told to keep an eye on the light, since it would now be illuminated following her correct decisions.

Experimental Demonstration of Mother's Control. As later results will indicate, the behavior modification procedures appeared to be effective in producing expected changes in the behavior of the mothers and their children. However, there yet remained the task of demonstrating that modification of the child's behavior was solely a function of the mother's ways of reacting to him. In further sessions the mother was instructed to react to her child as she had done during the baseline sessions; that is, to again be responsive to the deviant behavior. If the mother's reactions to her child during the behavior modification sessions had been responsible for weakening his deviant behavior, one would expect that this procedure would strengthen the deviant behavior. Once this test for control had been made, the mother was instructed to again make her reinforcement contingent only upon the incompatible behavior, thus resuming her "therapeutic" ways of reacting to him.

RESULTS

Case Number One

Danny was a six-year-old boy who was brought to the Child Development Clinic by his parents, because of his frequent attempts to force them to comply with his wishes. According to the parents, he virtually determined his own bedtime, foods he would eat, when the parents would play with him, and other household activities. In addition, he frequently attempted, with less success, to manipulate his teacher and peers. His parents reported they were simply "unable" to refuse his demands, and had rarely attempted to ignore or punish him. On the few occasions when they had refused him, they quickly relented when he began to shout or cry.

During the classification and baseline sessions, Danny's mother reported that she was extremely uncomfortable, because of Danny's behavior and her knowledge that she was being observed. Figure 1 shows cumulative records of Danny's deviant and incompatible behaviors during all therapy sessions. His deviant behavior was labelled as "commanding be-

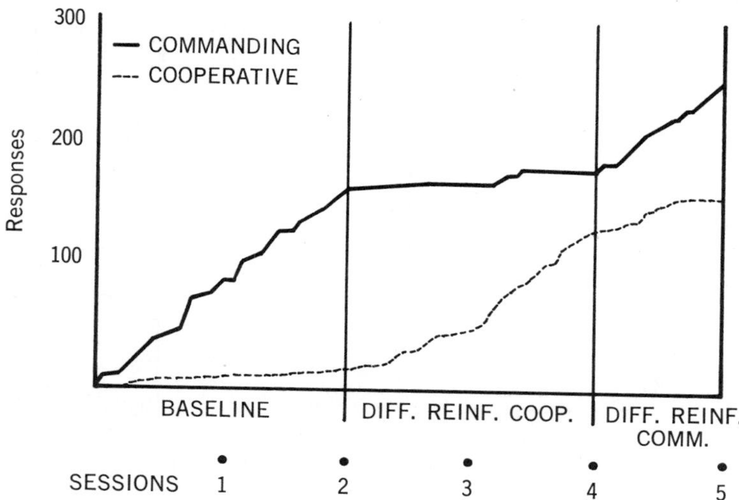

Fig. 1. Rate measures of Danny's commanding and cooperative behavior over baseline and therapy sessions.

havior" during the classification sessions, and was defined as any verbal or non-verbal instructions to his mother (e.g. pushes his mother into a chair; "Now we'll play this;" "You go over there and I'll stay here;" "No, that's wrong. Do it this way."). The incompatible behavior, labelled as "cooperative behavior", was defined as non-imperative statements or actions or by questions. Note the marked difference in rate between the deviant and incompatible behaviors during the two baseline sessions. Figure 2 shows cumulative records of the mother's general reactions to Danny's two behavior classes during the therapy sessions. Her reactions usually consisted of following Danny's instructions and such verbal comments as "Okay, if that's what you think; am I doing it right now?"

Following the baseline sessions the mother was instructed to be responsive to Danny's cooperative behavior but to completely ignore his commanding behavior. Reference to Fig. 2 indicates that she was successful in following these instructions. During the first two differential reinforcement sessions her rate of response to his commanding behavior dropped to zero, while her response to his cooperative behavior increased steadily in rate. (Use of the signal light as a cueing system was discontinued for the second differential reinforcement session.) Danny's behavior during the differential reinforcement sessions is shown in Fig. 1. Note that his rate of commanding behavior dropped considerably compared to the baseline sessions, while his cooperative behavior increased sharply in rate. Interestingly enough, Danny's mother reported that she was much more comfortable with him during the last of these sessions.

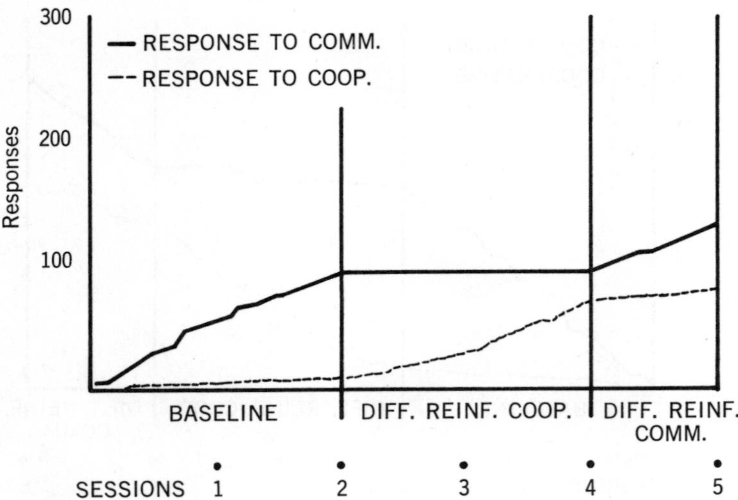

Fig. 2. Rate measures of Mother's general responses to Danny's commanding and cooperative behavior over baseline and therapy sessions.

The test of Mother's control was performed following the first two differential reinforcement sessions. This one session demonstration involved instructing the mother to behave as she had done during the baseline sessions. As the rate of response curves in Figs. 1 and 2 indicate, change in the mother's behavior was again correlated with the expected change in Danny's behavior; his rate of commanding behavior increased compared to the previous two sessions, and his cooperative behavior declined in rate. Thus, the finding that Danny's commanding and cooperative behaviors could be weakened when his mother's reactions to these classes were eliminated, and strengthened when they were replaced, points with some certainty to the fact that her behavior changes were responsible for the changes in Danny's behavior.

Further sessions were planned to reinstate the contingencies of the first differential reinforcement sessions. Again the mother was instructed to reinforce only the cooperative behavior; unfortunately, administrative problems made it necessary to terminate this case before the sessions could be conducted.

Case Number Two

Johnny, age four, was brought to the Clinic by his parents because of what they termed "very dependent" behavior. In addition, they were concerned about a nursery-school teacher's report that he frequently hit or kicked his peers and teacher when they were inattentive to him. According to his mother, Johnny rarely showed this behavior at home, but instead tended to follow her around the house much of the day, asking questions and requesting her help for various tasks. She, in turn, tended to be very responsive to this behavior and also tended to interrupt him when he played alone or with his peers. When asked why she behaved in these ways, she reported that she was quite concerned about the possibility that he might break things in the house or get into trouble with his playmates; she felt much more comfortable when he was at her side or at least within sight.

Johnny's teachers felt that his aggressive behavior in nursery school was related to his "dependence on others for direction and support". They stated that if he was told what to do, or if a teacher watched him or played with him, the hitting and kicking was not likely to occur. However, it was also apparent from the teacher's report that, inadvertently, they may have been providing social reinforcement for his aggressive behavior.

Following an analysis of the classification session, two classes of Johnny's behavior were defined; the deviant class was labeled "dependent behavior," which included such behavior as questions and non-verbal requests for help (e.g. bringing a toy to her following a request for her to play with it or to show him how it works). Aggressive behavior, such as hitting or kicking did not occur. Behavior considered incompatible with the deviant class was labeled "independent behavior." This class included any behavior in which he played alone, with no verbal comment to his mother.

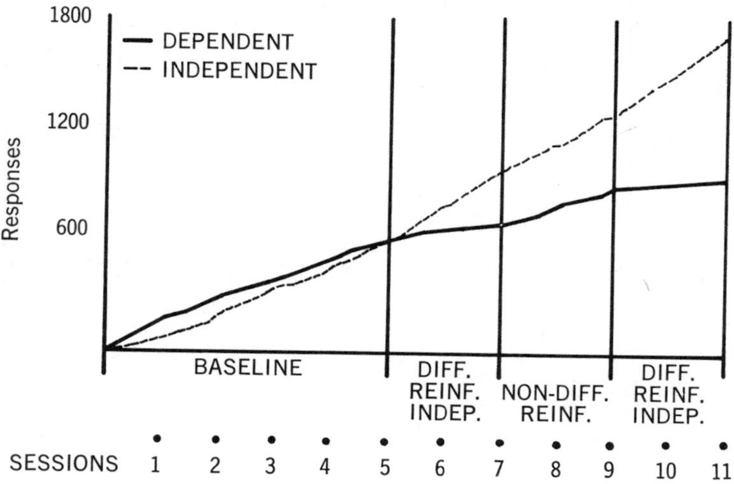

Fig. 3. Rate measures of Johnny's dependent and independent behavior over baseline and therapy sessions.

Figure 3 shows cumulative records of Johnny's dependent and independent behaviors during all therapy sessions. Note that the response rates for his two behavior classes during the baseline sessions are roughly comparable. Figure 4 shows cumulative records of mother's general reactions to Johnny's two behavior classes during the therapy sessions. Her reactions to his dependent behavior usually involved answering his questions or granting his requests for help. Consistent with her self observations, Mother's reactions to Johnny's independent behavior almost always involved interrupting his play with imperative statements or non-verbal interference such as taking a toy away from him.

During the differential reinforcement sessions, Johnny's mother was instructed to ignore his dependency behavior and respond approvingly to his independent behavior. Reference to the differential reinforcement sessions shown in Fig. 4 indicate that she was successful in following these instructions, even following elimination of the cueing system after the first session. As the rate of response curves show, her rate of response to his independent behavior increased, and for his dependent behavior it dropped to zero. Correlated with his mother's behavior changes, Johnny's behavior changed in the expected ways. The rate of response curve for his dependent behavior, seen in Fig. 3, dropped compared to the baseline sessions, while his independent behavior increased in rate.

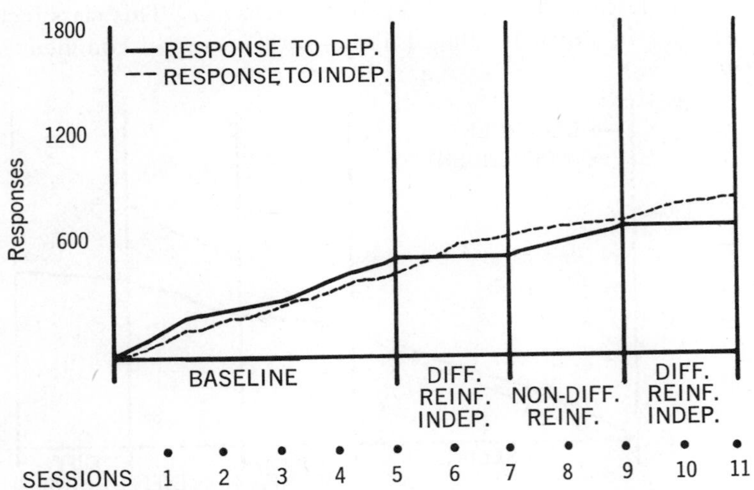

Fig. 4. Rate measures of Mother's general responses to Johnny's dependent and independent behavior over baseline and therapy sessions.

Following the two differential reinforcement sessions, the test of mother's control was performed. She was now instructed to resume her baseline behavior, and as the data indicate, she was successful in following these instructions; her response rates shown in the non-differential reinforcement sessions in Fig. 4, were roughly similar, and comparable to her baseline rates.

Again, correlated with these changes in Mother's behavior, Johnny's behavior changed in the expected ways. Reference to the non-differential reinforcement sessions of Fig. 3 shows that his response rates for the two behavior classes are comparable to his baseline rates.

The final two sessions involved reinstatement of Mother's differential reinforcement contingencies without use of the cueing system. The response rates shown in the last two sessions of Figs. 3 and 4 indicate that this procedure was effective. Therefore, as was true in case number one, the finding that Johnny's deviant and incompatible behavior patterns could be weakened when his mother's reactions to these classes were eliminated, and strengthened when they were replaced, supports the contention that her behavior changes were responsible for the changes in Johnny's behavior.

Case Number Three

Eddie, age four, was brought to the Clinic because of what his parents referred to as "extreme stubbornness." According to the parents, this behavior occurred only in the presence of Eddie's mother. Essentially, this "stubbornness" involved ignoring her commands and requests or doing the opposite of what he was told or asked to do.

She reported that her reactions to this behavior usually involved pleas, threats, and spankings, none of which appeared to be effective. It also became clear that most of her interactions with him were restricted to his oppositional behavior; she rarely played games with him, read to him, or talked to him. She did however, attempt to respond approvingly to his infrequent cooperative behavior. When asked why she was so selective in her interactions with him, she reported that because of his opposition, she felt "frustrated with him" and "angry with him" most of the time. She was convinced that he opposed her because he "liked" to get her angry.

During the classification sessions it became necessary to modify the instructions to Eddie's mother. Initially she was told to "just play with Eddie as you would at home." However, as might have been expected, mother and child ignored each other. The instructions were then changed to require mother to ask Eddie to play with a different toy every sixty seconds. These instructions were in effect throughout all therapy sessions. Eddie's behavior was classified as either oppositional (not complying with mother's request) or cooperative (complying).

Figure 5 shows cumulative records of Eddie's oppositional and cooperative behaviors during all therapy sessions. Note that his rate of opposi-

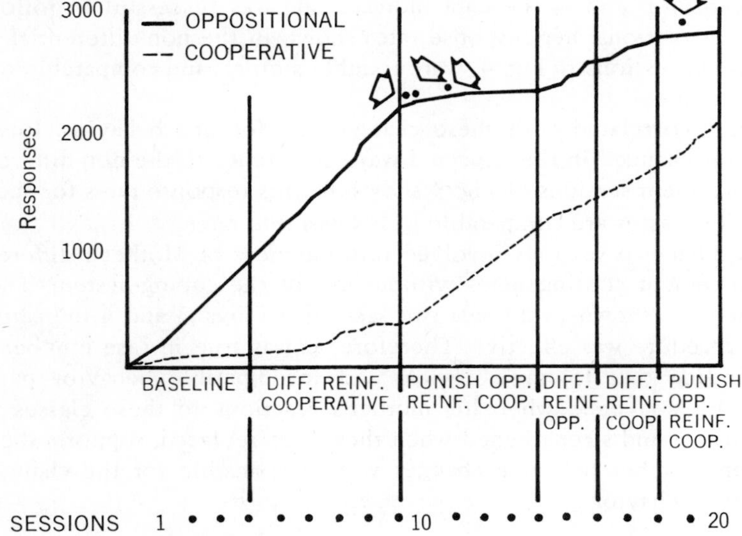

Fig. 5. Rate measures of Eddie's oppositional and cooperative behavior over baseline and therapy sessions.

tional behavior during the baseline sessions is far greater than his rate of cooperative behavior. Figure 6 shows cumulative records of Mother's general reactions to Eddie's two behavior classes. Her reactions to his oppositional behavior almost always involved threats or repetition of her request. Following his few cooperative responses, she either ignored him or stated her approval in a low voice without smiling.

During the differential reinforcement sessions, Eddie's mother was instructed to ignore his oppositional behavior and respond enthusiastically and with a smile to his cooperative behavior. As the differential reinforcement sessions shown in Fig. 6 indicate, she was successful in following the instructions and use of the cueing system was discontinued after the second session. Reference to the same sessions in Figure 5 indicates that the expected changes in Eddie's behavior occurred gradually as the sessions progressed. However, note that the increase in his rate of cooperative behavior was not marked, and it declined during the fourth and fifth differential reinforcement sessions. Because of this problem, E decided to instruct Mother in the use of a punishment procedure which could be combined with the differential reinforcement technique. She was instructed to isolate Eddie in an empty room (adjacent to the playroom) immediately following any of his oppositional responses. She was also told to leave him alone in this room for five minutes, unless he exhibited other undesirable behavior such as temper tantrums; if this type of behavior occurred, he remained in the room until it terminated.

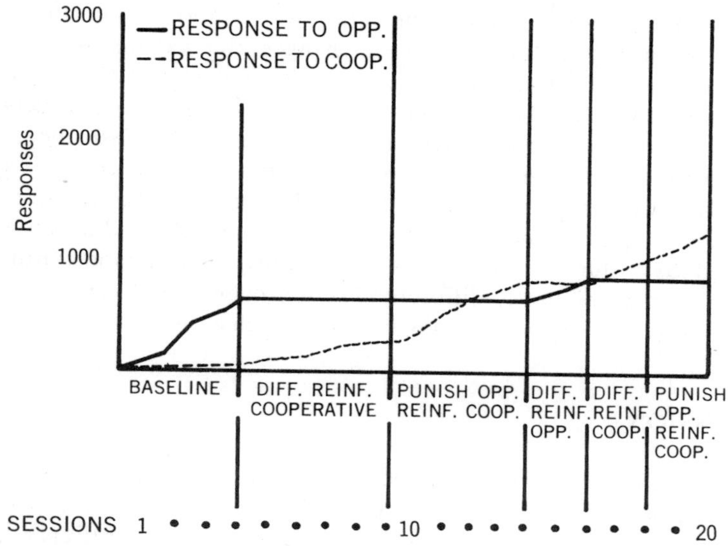

Fig. 6. Rate measures of Mother's general responses to Eddie's oppositional and cooperative behavior over baseline and therapy sessions.

Eddie's behavior during the punishment-reinforcement sessions is shown in Fig. 5. The arrows indicate those instances in which Mother was signaled via the cueing system, to initiate the punishment procedure. Note the marked change in Eddie's oppositional and cooperative behavior; his oppositional behavior declined sharply in rate while his rate of cooperative behavior increased markedly. As these records also indicate, modifications in Eddie's behavior were maintained during the last two punishment-reinforcement sessions by Mother's use of differential reinforcement alone. Interestingly enough, Eddie's mother reported, following one of these latter sessions, that she "actually enjoyed being with him".

The test of Mother's control of Eddie's behavior was complicated by the fact that she had used two procedures in the course of the therapy sessions. As a result, two questions had to be answered: (1) Was Mother responsible for the changes in Eddie's behavior? (2) Was one of her procedures more important than the other in producing these changes? To answer these questions, Mother was first instructed to respond only to Eddie's oppositional behavior. The differential-reinforcement-oppositional sessions of Fig. 6 revealed that she was successful in following these instructions. Correlated with these changes in Mother's behavior, Eddie's oppositional behavior (Fig. 5) increased in rate, while his cooperative behavior declined in rate. Thus, it seemed certain that Mother was responsible for the earlier changes in Eddie's behavior. To determine whether Mother's differential reinforcement or differential reinforcement *plus* punishment had produced these changes, she was instructed in one set of sessions to resume her differential reinforcement of Eddie's cooperative behavior; in another set of sessions she was instructed to differentially reinforce the cooperative behavior and punish the oppositional behavior. Mother's success in following these instructions is shown in the last two sessions of Fig. 6 and by the arrow in the last session of Fig. 5. As Fig. 5 also indicates, the expected changes in Eddie's behavior occurred only during the last set of sessions, thus demonstrating that Mother's combined use of differential reinforcement and punishment was responsible for the modifications in Eddie's behavior.

DISCUSSION

The data from two of the cases reported in this study indicate that a mother's social behavior may function as a powerful class of positive reinforcers for her child's deviant as well as his normal behavior. Experimental analysis of case number one revealed that Danny's mother was maintaining his commanding and cooperative behavior patterns through her reactions to these two response classes. A similar experimental analysis of case number two showed that Johnny's mother was maintaining his dependent and independent behavior through her reactions to these response classes. In both of these cases the response rates of the children's deviant and incompatible behavior patterns were weakened when their mothers' contingent behavior was eliminated, and strengthened when they were replaced. It would thus seem beyond a reasonable possibility of coincidence that the children's behavior classes were under the control of their respective mothers. However, this conclusion could not be supported by the data from case number three. It will be recalled that little rate change occurred in Eddie's oppositional and cooperative behavior following manipulation of the contingencies between these response classes and his mother's behavior; not until his mother utilized a punishment procedure did dramatic rate changes occur. Thus, little can be said concerning variables in Eddie's natural environment which were responsible for maintaining his deviant and incompatible behavior.

The data reported in this study are also of interest in terms of the modification of deviant child behavior. In all cases it proved possible to train the mothers in the effective use of behavior modification techniques based upon principles of operant learning theory. In two of the cases (Danny and Johnny) the techniques simply involved instructing the mothers to change the usual contingencies between their behavior and their children's deviant and incompatible behavior. Since it had been experimentally demonstrated with these cases that the mothers were providing social reinforcement for their children's deviant behavior, the next logical step would involve training the mothers to ignore these behavior patterns and to provide their reinforcers for behavior which was incompatible with the deviant behavior. As the data indicate, this differential reinforcement procedure was quite effective within the confines of the experimental setting.

Selection of the behavior modification technique used for the third case (Eddie) required more reliance on past research findings than on information gained from an analysis of mother-child interbehavior. Since E was unable after five sessions to determine the source of control of Eddie's deviant behavior, it was decided to stop the search for controlling stimulus events and concentrate on finding the most practical means of eliminating his deviant behavior. Past research (Wolf *et al.*, 1964) has shown that social isolation may function as a highly effective punishment technique for deviant child behavior. As the data indicate, Eddie's mother made very effective use of this technique.

The design of this study did not permit assessment of the generality of the changes in the children's behavior. One would expect that since the mothers were responsible for the changes which were produced, the question of generality would in part be a question of how well the mothers' "therapeutic" behaviors were maintained outside the experimental setting. That is, were their newly learned reactions to their children effective in obtaining reinforcement from the natural environment as well as from the experimental setting? Further research is planned to provide answers to this question.

REFERENCES

Bandura A. (1961) Psychotherapy as a learning process. *Psychol. Bull.*58, 143–149.

Grossberg J. M. (1964) Behavior therapy: A review. *Psychol. Bull.* 62, 73–88.

Prince G. S. (1961) A clinical approach to parent-child interaction. *J. Child Psychol. Psychiat.* 2, 169–184.

Russo S. (1964) Adaptations in behavioral therapy with children. *Behav. Res. Ther.* 2, 43–47.

Straughan J. H. (1964) Treatment with child and mother in the playroom. *Behav. Res. Ther.* 2, 37–41.

Wolf M. M., Risley T. and Mees H. (1964) Application of operant conditioning procedures to the behavior problems of an autistic child. *Behav. Res. Ther.* 1, 305–312.

The Efficacy of Training Procedures for Mothers in Filial Therapy[1]

LILLIAN STOVER
BERNARD G. GUERNEY, JR.

Filial therapy is a new psychotherapeutic method that extends specific Rogerian approaches to the training of parents for treatment of their own young emotionally disturbed children (Guerney, 1964). Parents are trained in groups of six to eight to employ principles and techniques used in client-centered play therapy in play sessions in the Clinic and at home with their own children. The rationale underlying this approach is that if the parent could be taught to execute the essentials of the role usually taken by the therapists, the parent would conceivably be more effective than a professional, on the basis that "(a) the parent has more emotional significance to the child, (b) anxieties learned in the presence of, or by the influence of, parental attitude could be more effectively unlearned, or extinguished, under similar conditions, and (c) interpersonal mis-expectations should be efficiently corrected if appropriate delineations were made clear to the child by the parent himself as to what is, and what is

Reprinted from *Psychotherapy: Theory, Research and Practice*, 1967, Vol. 4, No. 3, 110–115 with the permission of Psychologists Interested in The Advancement of Psychotherapy, and the authors.

[1]This research was made possible by Public Health Research Grant MHI 1975, and a grant from The Center for Computer and Information Services. The authors wish to acknowledge the assistance of Dr. Michael Andronico, who served as one of the therapists, and Drs. Nelson Hanawalt, Milton H. Schwartz, Jack I. Bardon, Charles E. Cress, Herbert Gerjuoy, and Mrs. Adele Borrus, Ellen Shapiro and Eleanor Epner.

not, appropriate behavior according to time, place, and circumstances" (Guerney, Guerney, & Andronico, 1966).

Further, in filial therapy one can hope for a more parsimonious utilization of the professional therapist's time by extending portions of his role to a nonprofessional with the further advantages of: (a) avoidance of fears and rivalry that develop in the parent as the child decreases dependency and develops affection for the therapist, (b) reduction of guilt and feelings of helplessness that often arise when the parent is obliged to abandon the problem to the expert for resolution, and (c) avoidance of the problems that otherwise could be aroused when the parent does not develop appropriate new responses to new behavioral patterns of the child.

Precedents to the use of parents as therapeutic agents with their own children may be found in Freud (1959) and Bonnard (1950), using psychoanalytic principles, and (with a young child with a very limited problem) Fuchs (1957), using Rogerian techniques. Play sessions at home between parents and children not clinically deviant have been recommended by Baruch (1949) and by Moustakas (1959) as a means of facilitating freer expression on the part of the child and improving parent-child relationships.

The question is whether parents of emotionally disturbed children can develop behaviors that will contribute to the solution of interpersonal problems that the parents presumably helped create.

The present research was designed to assess the feasibility of training mothers for the desired reflective, empathic role in conducting weekly one-half hour play sessions with their own children. It was hypothesized that the mothers in the Experimental (trained) group, relative to the Control (untrained) group, would increase their percentage of reflective statements and decrease their percentage of directive statements.

A secondary purpose was to see whether the children's behavior would reflect such a change in role behavior even as early as in the first few training sessions that were under investigation. An increase in negative attitudes prior to the increase in positive attitudes on the part of the child has been found to be related to the climate of permissive acceptance and respect for the child's feeling engendered by the client-centered therapist (Landisberg and Snyder, 1946; Moustakas, 1955). Reflection and clarification of feeling are also expected to help the child take the lead in initiating activity, and to decrease his dependency on the therapist for direction during the play sessions (Dorfman, 1951). Thus, the specific hypotheses tested were: by the fourth play session the children in the Experimental group, relative to the Control group, would be expected to move in the direction of: (a) increase in percentage of leadership statements, (b) decrease in percentage of dependency statements, (c) increase in percentage of aggressive acts, and (d) increase in percentage of negative feeling statements. Any positive results at all, with respect to *children's* behavior in this early stage of parent training, would be regarded as highly encouraging.

METHOD

Subjects

Two Control (*C*) and two Experimental (*E*) groups of six to eight mothers were formed by random assignment from those applying for psychological services at the Psychological Clinic of Rutgers University. The children—18 boys and 10 girls—ranged in age from 5½ to 10 years (average age: 7 years, 8 months).

The children were diagnosed as emotionally maladjusted. Children who had been diagnosed as neurologically impaired, intellectually retarded, or psychotic were excluded. The IQ's ranged from 98 to 160, with a mean score of 115. The parents were typically from the middle class, with incomes ranging from \$5,000 to \$15,000. All but one mother had completed high school and some had college education. Fathers were generally in professional or semi-professional occupations. They were thus characterized by Socio-economic Positions 2 and 3 (Hollingshead, 1957).

Procedures

Group Assignment and Socio-economic Status. The mothers were assigned to either the *C* or *E* group, following the interpretive interview, when they accepted the Clinic's recommendation for filial therapy. The groups were formed entirely by random selection techniques. However, after assignment, an analysis was made of the composition of each group in terms of characteristics that might influence the outcome measures. The groups were found not significantly different on eight of the nine characteristics studied. The eight variables were: child's chronological age, child's IQ, number of siblings, father's age, mother's age, father's education, mother's education, father's occupation.

The two groups did differ in a measure *combining* two of those just mentioned. This was an Index of Social Position (*SP*), a weighted score based on fathers' occupational levels and their years of education (Hollingshead, 1957). The *E* group was divided into High (*SP* 1 and 2) and Low (*SP* 3 and 4), and mothers' change scores on proportion of reflective statements were compared. A two-tailed t-test proved nonsignificant. Change scores for the *C* group were also compared for high and low status, and the difference was again nonsignificant. Therefore, the change toward reflective verbal behavior was not affected by socio-economic status within the range represented here.

Structuring for Mothers. As part of the diagnostic process, the mothers were asked to participate with their child in an observed, tape-recorded, one-half hour play session in a play room with one-way viewing mirror. Standardized instructions were presented to the mother as follows: "We would like to observe you in a play situation with your child for one-half hour in this play room. Please feel free to use any or all of the play materials and do whatever you would do at home."

Following the diagnosis, the parents were interviewed again and informed of the Clinic's recommendations. A brief description of the filial therapy process was given at that time. Mothers who accepted the recommendation for filial therapy were assigned to either the *C* or the *E* group as previously described. They were aware that research was a function of this Clinic and that they would be involved, but they knew nothing about the specific hypotheses being investigated. All conditions were described in identical terms to the two groups except for the following:

The *C* group mothers were told that there would be a waiting period of 13 to 16 weeks, during which time they would be called in with their children for three more observed play sessions.

The *E* group mothers were advised that they might begin group training sessions in filial therapy within three to six weeks, or as soon as a group of six to eight mothers could be formed for one meeting day a week. They were also informed that as part of the training procedures they would be asked to bring their child in for three more observed play sessions.

Experimental Treatment—The Training Sessions. The specific procedures for the indoctrination of parents tested in a pilot project (Guerney, 1964) were applied in the study. The techniques to be employed by the parents were closely modeled after Rogerian client-centered play therapy, with emphasis on developing an empathic relationship with the child.

The first step was to discuss the possible benefits to be derived for the child, and for parent-child relationships, that might be expected to accrue from the application of the method of filial therapy. The mothers in the *E* group then observed demonstrations through a one-way screen, and were encouraged to model their behavior after that of the group leader, a psychologist who demonstrated the process of following the child's lead in the initiation and direction of activities. The mothers were encouraged to attempt not only specific techniques, but to seek to express a genuine empathy with the child. Following three to five such demonstrations with non-clinic children, the mothers each demonstrated with their own child, and received comments on their techniques by the other group members and the trainer. Mothers' feelings about accepting their reflective role were explored in the group meeting, with a view to developing insight into their relations with their children. Their reactions to the demonstrated play sessions, and a growing awareness of their child's needs, formed the basis of subsequent weekly mothers' group meetings. The therapist was reflective, also, and sought to provide an empathic understanding of their feelings, much as they were being expected to provide in play sessions with their children.

The training groups met at the Clinic for ten one-and-a-half-hour sessions of discussion and observation. (*C* groups were trained and both groups went on to receive filial therapy after the experiment was completed.)

Control Group Treatment. The *C* groups received no training in the course of this experiment. They served to reveal the effect of time and the experience of play sessions in the Clinic play therapy room, as well as whatever behavioral changes might occur merely through anticipation of help or taking the step toward clinic diagnosis. They had the same number of play sessions with their own children, under observation at the Clinic, as the *E* group. Contact with the Clinic staff during these visits was minimal. Generally, only the arrangements for the succeeding sessions and the schedule for the ensuing group meetings were discussed.

Dependent Measures—Reflective and Directive Verbal Behavior. These behaviors were measured via codings of magnetic tapes of their training play sessions, after a coding system developed by Ashby, Ford, Guerney, and Guerney (1957). The *Reflective* category included all of the following: Reflective Leads; Restatement of Content; Clarification of Feeling; Reflective Structuring. The other category: *Directive* statements included: Directive Leads; Unsolicited Suggestion, Advice, Information or Persuasion; Approval, Encouragement or Reassurance; Criticism, Disagreement or Sarcasm; Directive Structuring; Interpretation.

High reliability was established by Ashby, *et al.* (1957) in that three out of four of their judges agreed 92% of the time on the response categories. A slight modification was developed for this study in terms of the specialized role taken in play sessions with children. Three subcategories involving role play behavior were added: Solicited Role Play, Clarification of Feeling Through Role Play (included as Reflective Behavior) and Unsolicited Role Playing (included as Directive Behavior). To assess the reliability of the revised coding procedure, eleven tapes were independently coded by two undergraduate students after approximately eight hours of training and practice. Interrater reliabilities (Pearson Product Moment formula) for each of the 13 subcategories ranged from .67 to .99.

Generally, fourth sessions (third training session) were compared with the first (diagnostic or base-line) sessions, but mechanical breakdowns caused the loss of eight first or fourth session tapes out of the 56 recorded. Second or third session tapes were substituted in those instances. Comparability between the *C* and *E* groups was maintained in terms of number of interim sessions. Also, the average time elapsed between pre- and post-sessions was virtually the same for the two groups (*E*, 87 days and *C*, 82 days).

Children's Behavior in the Sessions. Following Guerney, *et al.* (1966), children's verbal statements were coded as follows: *Leadership*: The child suggests, instructs, directs, gives ideas, guidance, or otherwise asserts himself with the adult. *Dependency*: The child requests evaluation or praise, instruction, direction, ideas, guidance or leadership from the adult. *Negative Feeling*: The child expresses annoyance, anger, or dislike toward an object or person (including accusations, cursing, and disparaging remarks).

To establish reliability the same two undergraduate college students independently coded eleven randomly selected first and fourth session tapes. The two coders listened to the tapes simultaneously; but they discussed only the audibility of the recording. Pearson Product Moment correlations were: Negative Feeling, .93; Dependency, .88; Leadership, .66.

Active aggression or nonverbal aggression was defined as overt hostile behavior toward a toy or the mother. This included any act of aggression such as hitting, kicking, punching, poking, slapping, or aiming a toy knife or gun in the direction of any toy doll, puppet, punching bag, or the mother. (Aggression toward the mother was, of course, almost totally on a symbolic rather than a physical level.) This expressive, aggressive behavior is usually seen in client-centered play therapy, and is regarded as typical of an effective treatment process. It tends to increase in the early phases of client-centered play therapy and to decrease in the later phases (Moustakas, 1955).

Children's nonverbal aggressive behavior was observed (without sound) and coded in units of 15-second intervals: from no aggression (0), mild or playful aggression (1), stronger or more forceful aggression (2), to intense aggression in which the child seemed highly involved (3).

This coding system was devised by Siegel (1956) (who did, however, also use sound cues). In the present study, replication of her reliability study on 19 sessions provided a Pearson correlation of .99.

The coders were unaware of the research hypotheses and of which children came from the *E* and *C* groups.

Experimental Therapists. The training of the *E* group mothers was conducted by two therapists. The male therapist (E_2) had previously conducted four filial therapy groups and had experience with 25 youngsters in individual Rogerian client-centered play therapy and 36 youngsters in group therapy. The female therapist (E_1) had participated as an observer in one filial therapy group and had previously conducted play therapy with eight youngsters.

RESULTS AND DISCUSSION

Mother's Behavior

The percentages of Reflective statements for each group in the early and later play sessions are shown on Table 1.

TABLE 1

Group Means: Percentage of Mothers' Total Statements that Were Reflective

	C (N=14)	E_1 (N=8)	E_2 (N=6)
Early Session	.44	.43	.37
Later Session	.41	.58	.95
Mean Gain	−.03	.15	.58

Comparability of the three groups in their early session with respect to percentage of Reflective statements was remarkably good. Inspection of the later session proportions reveals a very clear cut difference between the two experimental subgroups—each trained by different clinicians. E_1 effected a mean gain of 15 percent while E_2 effected a 58 percent increase. There was no change in the control group.

The proportions per individual subject were transformed into arcsin ratios (Steel and Torrie, 1960) and a simple one-way analysis of variance for groups with unequal means (Winer, 1962) was applied to the three groups. The obtained $F = 19.59$ ($df = 2,25$) is highly significant ($p < .001$).

A planned set of orthogonal comparisons (Hays, 1963, p. 468) was performed. Table 2 shows the mean differences and t-ratios. Although the two *E* groups differed from each other in this respect, each of them produced a significantly greater increase in Reflective behavior compared with the *C* group.

The *C* group experienced a drop (20%) in total verbal behavior, but little change in the proportion of Directive and Reflective comments, or in any one sub-category. The E_1 group showed a sharp decrease (62%) in all responses, primarily by inhibiting their Directive responses. The E_2 group decreased 29% in total response. Evidently, the movement away from Directive behavior involved a very great increase in Reflective statements in E_2 and a drop in Directive statements in both E_1 and E_2.

In each of these comparisons it is evident that the training sessions proved effective in changing mothers' verbal statements in the hypothesized direction.

TABLE 2

Planned Comparisons of Mothers' Reflective Behavior Following Analysis of Variance

COMPARISON	MEAN DIFFERENCE	t	P
1. C vs. E_1	9.564	2.41	<.02*
2. C vs. E_2	41.730	10.25	<.001*
3. E_1 vs. E_2	32.166	13.75	<.001**
4. C vs. $E_{1+2/2}$	51.294	6.67	<.001*

*One-tailed test. **Two-tailed test.

When teaching mothers about attempting empathic understanding in the play sessions with their youngsters, the more experienced therapist probably provided higher levels of this dimension in his relationship to the mothers themselves in the weekly group meetings. This enabled a mother to explore her own feelings in a therapeutic climate much like the one she was learning to provide for her youngster in the play session. Thus, while a mother was being taught reflective techniques, she was experiencing them herself in the group meetings.

In light of current interest in studying interaction among family members for the purpose of studying family dynamics (Drechsler and Shapiro, 1961; Wynne and Singer, 1963; Cheek, 1964; Haley, 1964) and family therapy (Elbert, Rosman, Minuchin, and Guerney, 1964), the sub-category distribution of maternal responses to their children was studied in the present investigations. In all three groups, the highest number of mean responses in the first (spontaneous) play sessions fell in the category of Unsolicited Suggestions, Advice, Information, Persuasion (168). Following this in frequency were the following trio of response categories: Reflective Leads (197), Directive Leads (68), and Solicited Role Playing (60). Four categories were used infrequently: Restatement of Content (30), Approval-Encouragement-Reassurance (27), Reflection of Feeling Through Role Play (17), and Criticism, Disagreement, Sarcasm (16). The following categories were used seldom or not at all: Unsolicited Role Playing (2), Clarification of Feeling (2), Reflective Structuring (1), Directive Structuring (0), and Interpretation (0).

None of the sub-categories showed shifts with training that would be unexpected on the basis of the overall results.

However, it is important to note the following: Despite the fact that the sub-category Clarification of Feeling rose from no responses to the second most frequent response (after Restatement of Content) in the E_2 group, it was not frequent in either *E* group after training.

The category primarily responsible for the significant change observed was Restatement of Content. Clarification of Feeling is a more empathic, subtle, and presumably therapeutically meaningful type of response, and one that is more difficult to master. That this type of response was not extensively used in the early stage of training is not surprising, or different (in the writers' experience) from that found in training graduate students at such an early stage of their training and experience. Experience with filial therapy suggests that parents later become less cautious, less concerned with what *not* to do (lead, interpret), and more concerned with what *to* do (empathize, clarify feeling).

Children's Behavior

The four variables of the children's behavior were thought to be intercorrelated. The measures were taken in the same one-half hour time segments and so, as one increased, another necessarily decreased. Thus, multivariate analysis of variance, a procedure for the simultaneous analysis of two or more intercorrelated variables (Cooley and Lohnes, 1962) was applied to these data (Table 3).

TABLE 3

Mean Changes in Intensity of Active Aggression and Number of Children's Statements from Early to Later Session for Control vs. Experimental Groups

	C	C vs. E_{1+2}		C vs. E_1		C vs. E_2	
		E_{1+2}	$t_{(df=26)}$	E_1	$t_{(df=20)}$	E_2	$t_{(df=18)}$
Active Aggression	−9.29	23.14	2.85**	20.88	2.30*	26.17	3.23**
Verbal Negative Feeling	−1.43	6.50	1.81*	1.88	1.10	12.67	2.41**
Verbal Dependency	−4.57	−1.36	.74	1.75	1.20	−5.50	−.21
Verbal Leadership	1.43	−.86	−.31	0.00	−1.66	−2.00	−.41

*$p<.05$, one-tailed test. **$p<.01$, one-tailed test.

Children's nonverbal aggression increased in both the *E* groups and decreased in the *C* groups, the differences between groups reaching statistical significance. The E_2 group children also revealed significantly more verbal negative feeling than the *C* group children. Although the change in the E_1 group did not reach statistical significance, it did increase on this dimension rather than decrease as did the *C* group. There was virtually no change in children's verbal leadership either in the *C* or *E* groups and no statistical difference on the verbal dependency dimension.

Thus, while there were only four play sessions included in the comparison of children's behavior, some trends were beginning to emerge. The changes in mothers' behavior appear to have been not only statistically significant, but also of sufficient magnitude to have effected some concomitant behavior of their children (aggression) even during the initial training phase of filial therapy.

The question of whether parents can learn to modify their pattern of interaction with their own emotionally disturbed children in the direction of the role behavior of client-centered therapists has been answered affirmatively. Also, in some significant aspects of their behavior in the play situation, children respond quickly to this change in mother's behavior. The questions now indicated for future empirical research include those of how this process continues over time in the play sessions and what bearing it, and the entire process of filial therapy, have on the overall relationship between parent and child, and the child's general emotional adjustment.

REFERENCES

ASHBY, J. D., FORD, D. H., GUERNEY, JR., B. G., & GUERNEY, LOUISE. Effects on clients of a reflective and a leading type of psychotherapy. *Psychol. Monog.*, 1957, **71** (24).

BARUCH, DOROTHY. *New ways in discipline.* New York: McGraw-Hill, 1949.

BONNARD, AUGUSTA. The mother as therapist, in a case of obsessional neurosis, in *The psychoan. study of the child V.* New York: Intl. Univ. Press, 1950, 391–408.

CHEEK, FRANCES E. The "schizophrenogenic mother" in word and deed. *Family Process,* 1964, **3**, 155–177.

COOLEY, W. W., & LOHNES, P. R. *Multivariate procedures for the behavioral sciences.* New York: John Wiley, 1962, Pp. 60–71.

DORFMAN, ELAINE. Play therapy. Chapter 4 in Rogers, C. R. *Client-centered therapy.* Boston: Houghton Mifflin, 1951, Pp. 235–277.

DRECHSLER, R. J., & SHAPIRO, M. I. A procedure for the direct observation of family interaction in a child guidance clinic. *Psychiatry,* 1961, 24 (2), 163–170.

ELBERT, SHIRLEY, ROSMAN, BERNICE, MINUCHIN, S., & GUERNEY, B. A method for the clinical study of family interaction. *Am. J. Orthopsychiat.,* 1964, **34**, 885–894.

FREUD, S. Analysis of a phobia in a five-year old boy. In, *Collected papers.* New York: Basic Books, 1959. Pp. 149–289.

FUCHS, NATALIE ROGERS. Play therapy at home. *The Merrill-Palmer Quart.,* 1957, **3**, 89–95.

GUERNEY, JR., B. G. Filial therapy: description and rationale. *J. Consult. Psychol.*, 1964, **28**, 304–310.

GUERNEY, JR., B. G., BURTON, JEAN, SILVERBERG, DANA, & SHAPIRO, ELLEN. Use of adult responses to codify children's behavior in a play situation. *Perceptual and Motor Skills*, 1965, **20**, 614–615.

GUERNEY, JR., B. G., GUERNEY, LOUISE, & ANDRONICO, M. Filial therapy. *Yale Scientific Magazine*, 1966, **40**, 6–14.

HALEY, JAY. Research on family patterns: an instrument of measurement. *Family Process*, 1964, **3**, 41–65.

HAYS, W. L. *Statistics for psychologists.* New York: Holt, Rinehart and Winston, Inc., 1963.

HOLLINGSHEAD, A. B. *Two factor index of social position.* New Haven: August B. Hollingshead, 1957.

LANDISBERG, SELMA, & SNYDER, W. U. Nondirective play therapy. *J. Clin. Psychol.*, 1946, **2**, 203–213.

MOUSTAKAS, C. E. The frequency and intensity of negative attitudes expressed in play therapy: a comparison of well-adjusted and disturbed young children. *J. Genet. Psychol.*, 1955, **86**, 309–325.

MOUSTAKAS, C. E. *Psychotherapy with children.* New York: Harper & Row, 1959.

SIEGEL, ALBERTA. Film-mediated fantasy aggression and strength of aggressive drive. *Child Develpm.* 1956, **27**, 365–378.

STEEL, R. G. D., & TORRIE, J. G. *Principles and procedures of statistics.* New York: MacGraw-Hill, 1960, Pp. 448–449.

WINER, B. J. *Statistical principles in experimental design.* New York: McGraw-Hill, 1962.

WYNNE, L. C., & SINGER, MARGARET. Thought disorder and family relations of schizophrenics. *Arch. Con. Psychiat.*, 1963, **9**, 191–198 and 199–206.

National Institute of Mental Health Pilot Study in Training Mental Health Counselors

MARGARET J. RIOCH
CHARMIAN ELKES
ARDEN A. FLINT
BLANCHE SWEET USDANSKY
RUTH G. NEWMAN
EARLE SILBER

The paper describes the first year's work in an experiment to test the hypothesis that carefully selected mature people can be trained within two years to do psychotherapy under limited conditions. Eight 40-year-old married women with children were trained in a very practical program. The results were positive.

In the spring of 1960 a pilot study was begun in the Adult Psychiatry Branch of the National Institute of Mental Health to explore one means of alleviating the shortage of trained workers in the mental health field and of filling some of the community's needs for lowcost psychotherapy. The idea behind the experiment is that, even as the Public Health nurse can perform many duties with and for patients, thereby freeing the medical officer for tasks requiring greater training, so also a corps of workers could be trained in the mental health field, thereby freeing a significant amount of the psychiatrist's time.

One of the best reservoirs of people gifted for this kind of work consists of married women of about 40 who are looking for a constructive activity outside the home to take the place of the job of child rearing. To exploit this gold mine of psychological talent would be to kill two birds

Reprinted with permission from *American Journal of Orthopsychiatry*, 1963, Vol. XXXIII, No. 4, 678–689, Copyright, 1963, American Orthopsychiatric Association, Inc., and with the permission of the authors.

with one stone: The need for low-cost therapy could be alleviated and the mature woman's need to be useful could in some cases be filled. This latter would not be a salvage operation for neurotic middle-aged ladies, but rather the appropriate deployment of people who have performed successfully in one phase of life and who are now passing to another. These women have an inestimable advantage over the usual beginning psychotherapist; they have resided for a considerably longer time on this planet and have been engaged in the highly complex interpersonal training ground of child rearing and family living. By virtue of this they are less self-absorbed than their more youthful counterparts and have a larger pool of experience from which to draw.

The objective of this study is in line with the recommendation of the Report of the Joint Commission on Mental Health and Illness "that nonmedical mental health workers with aptitude, sound training, practical experience and demonstrable competence should be permitted to do general, short-term psychotherapy—namely, the treating of persons by objective, permissive, nondirective techniques of listening to their troubles and helping them resolve these troubles in an individually insightful and socially useful way."

The experiment can be divided into four phases. The first two, Recruitment and Selection, have been completed. The third, Training, is in process. The fourth, Evaluation, has been accomplished for the first year's work, and will be repeated with variations for the second year, in June 1962. A follow-up study is being planned for the years following the experiment itself.

The hypothesis, which was tested in the recruitment stage, was that there is a large unexploited reservoir of talent among middle-aged women, waiting and eager to be used. This was amply demonstrated, at least for the Washington area.

The recruitment lasted approximately six weeks. During this short period by means of 60 telephone calls and six short public speeches, 80 women became sufficiently interested to request application blanks. Forty-nine applications were returned filled out. No blank was sent out before a 10-minute telephone conversation had taken place with the applicant, explaining the program and emphasizing its experimental character. Applicants were told that there would be no financial recompense during the two-year training period, and that there was no guarantee of success, or of future employment. The insecurity that we were obliged to emphasize with regard to our experimental program limited its appeal to people who could and would take a risk. They were all from the middle class and most of them had been to college. We thought the program might well appeal to many from the lunatic fringe, but, of the 42 women who came to the NIH for the selection procedures, at most three might be thought to fall into this category: Even including these, all were capable people whose services could and should be used in some form in the community.

We began the selection phase by asking for an autobiography of about 1,500 words from each applicant. The 42 women who complied with this request were invited to come to the National Institutes of Health in groups of approximately eight for a day of group procedures, including tests and discussions. On the basis of these, the Committee on Selection* chose 20 who were given individual interviews and tests and from whom eight were finally chosen as the successful candidates. Their median age was 40–44. One was widowed; all the others were living with their husbands. All had children, the average number being 2.4. Their husbands were all either professionals or executives. They were all college graduates; three had advanced degrees. Of their undergraduate majors, four were in the behavioral sciences, three in the humanities, one in biology. Six had held paying jobs at a professional level. Four had been psychoanalyzed.

The hypothesis to be tested by this phase was that, by the various group and individual procedures used, a number of candidates could be selected who would have good general intelligence, perceptiveness, integrity and sufficient emotional maturity to be able to operate effectively together and to cope with the stresses of psychotherapeutic work. To be complete, this hypothesis should include the statement that the selectors were for the most part the teachers in the Training Program.

This hypothesis has proved correct at least to the extent that all eight of the selected candidates have remained in the program and intend to continue in this field.† Further, the staff has not wished to recommend dismissal of any one of them. It cannot, of course, be claimed that the procedures used selected the best of the applicants. We have no way of knowing how much better some of the rejectees may have been than the selected candidates.

The training began in September, 1960, and is to run officially for four semesters. Actually, from what we know of the eight women in this experiment, they will continue their training indefinitely in one form or another. The two years we are offering them constitute only a beginning of their awareness of themselves as therapeutic instruments. This report will deal with the two semesters completed in June, 1961.

In planning our program, we had to decide at the start whether we were training professionals or technicians. In other words, should we expose our students to a variety of theories and practices with the intention of

*The Committee consisted of Drs. Margaret Rioch, Chairman, Charmian Elkes, Arden Flint, Nathene Loveland, David Hamberg, Beatrix Hamburg.

†One was absent from the city during the second semester, which she had told us might occur. She has returned for the second year.

helping them gradually to find their own way, or should we teach them to follow directions according to a set method? We agreed on the former course. The statement was made explicitly to the students that there is no one "right way" to do therapy but that each person develops his own style, which is right for him because it is an integral function of his own personality. The instructors, including the consultants, are people with a variety of backgrounds: Some are psychoanalysts, some psychiatrists, some psychologists. All of them hold a broad, more or less eclectic point of view with regard to theory and practice. We are unable to make a sharp distinction between counseling and therapy. Our students are called Mental Health Counselors for lack of a better term. What they do in their interviews varies a great deal from one to another, from one phase of their development to another, and from one patient to another. Sometimes they listen sympathetically and supportively; sometimes they "represent reality" or give common-sense advice; sometimes they engage in a process of exploration of the patient's feeling and attitudes with a view to a better understanding of them; and occasionally they are able to draw out into the open some aspect of a patient to which he had previously been blind, and to help him become more aware and accepting of this aspect. In our teaching we have emphasized that the patient's problem has something to do with distorted perceptions of himself and others and that he would be able to see more clearly if the anxiety in these areas were reduced. We have also emphasized the need to listen to the patient on more than one level, to hear the unspoken messages and to respond to them as well as to the spoken ones. And we have stressed above all the importance of self-awareness.

Our training is narrow but intensive; it is sharply focused on psychotherapy, and only on psychotherapy. This differentiates it from training for social work, psychology and psychiatry. Members of all three of these professions engage in psychotherapy, but their education includes many other things. Our hypothesis is that the intensive training offered to carefully selected applicants can produce in a relatively short time people qualified to do this particular task for which the need is so great.

In setting up our program we tried to allow ourselves maximum flexibility, but we did have certain notions about how it would be structured. One was that the students should be thoroughly and frequently supervised and supported in their work; a second was that they should be given a broad, undogmatic point of view with as little jargon as possible. A third was that the work would be primarily practical, on-the-job training, and only secondarily theoretical. These have all been carried out.

We had some other intentions, however, which have been modified. First, we planned that the training would be 20 hours a week, or half time for two years. But the students have worked so hard that they have turned it into what is now practically a full-time program. Second, we thought that we would limit the type of patient to be seen, so that the training would be more intensive in one area. We chose college students partly because of the already existing interest in the Adult Psychiatry Branch; partly because we thought they would be easy to treat and by and large not so very sick, and thus appropriate for a first experiment; and partly because, from the general mental health point of view, this seemed like a good age for preventive psychiatry. For practical reasons having to do chiefly with geography and transportation, we were unable to carry out this intention. Not enough college students were available to the outpatient service at the NIH, so we included high school students and their parents. Then other adults came seeking help, bringing the age range of our patients to between 15 and 55. There has been a preponderance of adolescents and their parents, however, and we have emphasized in our course work the problems of this developmental phase.

Third, we intended to have our students see patients with relatively minor disturbances. This intention has gone the way of unrealistic expectations, since practically none of the patients who have sought out our services has been really easy to treat. We think that in general it is best to screen out those patients who are schizophrenic, those who act out a great deal and those who would probably develop a very demanding and possessive sort of transference relationship. In some cases we have taken a calculated risk because there was no other possibility for treatment. In some cases in which our screening was faulty, the trainee performed the useful service of helping the patient and his family, through a series of introductory interviews, to accept more intensive and experienced therapy than we could offer.

Fourth, we intended to screen all patients for the trainees. While this still occurs consistently at NIH, initial interviewing is now being done by some of the trainees in their community placements.

The training covered the following five areas:

1. The first was practical work at NIH. This consisted of interviewing normal subjects and patients, group therapy for adolescents and their parents, individual and group supervision including listening to the playback of the trainees' own tape-recorded interviews. This was the most important part of the work.

The trainees began by interviewing the normal control subjects who live at the Clinical Center of the NIH and are studied by the various institutes. Most of them were college students. It was a great advantage to have this resource in the initial period, especially in an untried pilot program. Since a number of these "normal" people had very serious problems, we became aware that our trainees were able to cope with a greater degree of emotional disturbance than we had originally intended to have them handle. Before the end of the first semester each trainee had been assigned at least one real patient.

From the very beginning all the interviews were tape-recorded. Each trainee listened to her own interviews, not only by herself and with a supervisor, but with the whole group. One of the remarkable aspects of the first year's work was the way in which an atmosphere of mutual support developed among the students, making it possible for them to expose their floundering and blundering to each other without essential loss of self-esteem.

The supervision took place at scheduled times both individually and in groups of four or eight. In addition, it was made clear that the supervisors were always available to their students in case of need. The need might be a matter of supporting the trainee in dealing with a demanding patient, answering a practical question of how to refer a patient's relative to a psychiatrist, or sitting down for an extra session with the tape recording and working through the anxiety about a given situation. It is fair to say that the trainees felt confident that they could rely upon their supervisors for prompt assistance in a crisis and for a generally benign attitude in dealing with their difficulties. This does not imply that the supervisors were uncritical or that the process of supervision was anxiety-free. It does imply that we had a fair measure of success in establishing what might reasonably be called a therapeutic environment, although no formal therapy (group or individual) of the trainees was ever undertaken in the program. It should be mentioned here, however, that during this first year one trainee continued until late winter her previously begun analysis. Two returned to therapists with whom they had earlier terminated. One began therapy for the first time. This indicates that the program stirred up considerable anxiety. It is our opinion that this was by and large constructive in that it led the trainees to work through problems that would otherwise have limited their effectiveness as therapists. Those who were or had been in therapy learned at first hand what it is like to be a patient. If the students had been unable, for financial or other reasons, to arrange treatment for themselves when needed, it would have been advisable to proceed differently. Group therapy could be made part of the regular schedule, or the program could be maintained at a lower level of anxiety. In the latter case there might be some loss in effectiveness.

2. The second area of training was observation of group, family and individual therapy.

3. The third consisted of lectures and seminar discussions.

4. The fourth was outside reading and report writing.

5. And the fifth was community placements. These were arranged partly to broaden the experience of the trainees and partly to open doors that might lead to future employment. This was the beginning of a feeling-out process to see how the community would react to the trainees and how

the trainees would fit and function in the community. We met with a remarkably open-hearted and open-minded welcome on the part of most, though not all, of the agencies with which we had contact. Only two of the ten agencies we approached declined to accept any trainees. The placements for the first year were in one federal probation office, two juvenile courts, three clinics, one university counseling center and one social service agency. The trainees were especially warmly welcomed and well thought of in the probation office, the juvenile courts, and two of the clinics. In one clinic the attitudes of the staff were mixed and shifting. The university was very warmly hospitable but not enthusiastic about future employment. The social service agency turned out to be an unsuitable placement. For the second year we have trainees placed in seven clinics, two public high schools, one public junior college, two universities and one college.

The evaluation phase of the work will not, of course, be complete until the second year of training is over. The follow-up study will, we hope, present additional material. The results of the first year's evaluation are being presented now as part of a progress report.

We are aware that there is no recognized standard method of measuring the amount learned in this field or the degree of competence of a psychotherapist or the success of anyone's therapeutic endeavors. We have tried to approach the problem in five different ways.

1. In an effort to obtain an objective judgment of the trainees' work, uncolored by the personal investment of the teachers in the project, we obtained the services of four raters from outside the Washington area who, without knowing anything about the program or the background of the trainees, agreed to do blind ratings of tape-recorded therapeutic interviews.* After listening to and rating each tape, the rater was to open a sealed envelope containing an autocriticism of the interview by the trainee. This also was to be rated on several criteria, as well as on global impression. The results of this procedure are summarized in TABLES 1, 2 and 3. Two ratings on each of two interviews are not enough to represent a valid judgment of any one interviewer, but the average of 28 judgments is a reasonable assessment of the group of trainees as a whole.†

The average rating on the global impression of all the interviews was 3.0, that is, in the middle range of the scale. The average rating on the global impression of the autocriticisms was 3.6. Since no one's average

*We are indebted to Drs. Roy R. Grinker, Jr., LeRoy P. Levitt, Melvin N. Seglin from the Michael Reese Hospital, Chicago, and to Miss Nea Norton, Assistant Professor of Psychiatry, Yale University, for their help in this part of the evaluation.

Since one trainee was absent for the second semester, the evaluation of the first year's work is based on the accomplishments of the other seven.

†We owe the clear formulation of this idea to a personal communication from Dr. Roy Grinker.

TABLE 1* Rating of Interview

Name of rater: ____________ Code no. of interview: ________

	EXCELLENT 5	GOOD 4	SATISFACTORY 3	PASSABLE 2	POOR 1
1. Global impression of interview	3	5	12	4	4
2. Respect for the patient	2	15	8	1	2
3. Interest ,in the patient	4	14	7	3	0
4. Understanding of the patient	4	4	9	8	3
5. Success in drawing out affect	2	5	6	11	3
6. Beginning of interview	1	3	7	10	4
7. End of interview	1	7	2	10	4
8. Professional attitude	3	18	4	3	0
9. Skill in using patient's cues	1	7	4	10	6
	VERY EASY	EASY	MEDIUM	DIFFICULT	VERY DIFFICULT
Patient's accessibility to therapy (i.e., an easy or difficult patient)	2	3	7	14	1

Remarks:

TABLE 2* Rating of Autocriticism

Name of rater: ____________ Code no. of interview: ________

	EXCELLENT 5	GOOD 4	SATISFACTORY 3	PASSABLE 2	POOR 1
1. Global impression	5	10	10	2	1
2. Shows awareness of major weakness or weaknesses	5	6	9	5	2
3. Shows awareness of the main points at which communication broke down	7	4	8	6	2
4. Shows awareness of how and where communication was facilitated	3	10	6	5	3
5. Shows awareness of her own "inner workings"	4	12	5	5	2

Remarks:

*Tables 1 and 2 are reproductions of the rating blanks sent to the raters. The numbers in each box represent the number of times a rating was assigned to that box. Totals are not always the same because occasionally a rater did not rate, if the recording was not clear enough to allow him to form a judgment.

TABLE 3*

	AVERAGE SCORE
Rating of Interviews	
1. Global impression of interview	3.4
2. Respect for the patient	4.0
3. Interest in the patient	4.0
4. Understanding of the patient	3.4
5. Success in drawing out affect	3.2
6. Beginning of interview	2.7
7. End of interview	2.9
8. Professional attitude	4.2
9. Skill in using patient's cues	3.0
Rating of Patient's Accessibility to Therapy	
(i.e., an easy or difficult patient)	3.2
5—very easy	
4—easy	
3—medium	
2—difficult	
1—very difficult	
Rating of Autocriticism	
1. Global impression	4.0
2. Shows awareness of major weakness or weakness	3.7
3. Shows awareness of main points at which communication broke down	3.7
4. Shows awareness of how and where communication was facilitated	3.6
5. Shows awareness of her own "inner workings"	3.8

*Table 3 shows the average scores on the blind ratings, first year: 5—excellent; 4—good; 3—satisfactory; 2—passable; and 1—poor.

It is important to remember that the "reference interview" done by a professional therapist was given an average rating of 3 by six judges.

rating was below 2, or passable, and since 3, or the middle range of the scale, represents satisfactory performance this part of our evaluation procedure has shown positive results.

2. We have tried to assess the changes that took place in the patients seen by the trainees at NIH, considering at the same time the kind of patient and the degree of difficulty of the treatment. TABLE 4 (page 554) summarizes the work. As in all such assessments of change under therapy, there is no way of knowing how much of this might have occurred without any intervention whatsoever.

There were in all 49 patients—18 males, 31 females, 21 adolescents, 28 adults. Each trainee saw an average of seven patients once a week. The diagnoses were distributed as follows: 20 personality trait disorder, 12 neurotic reaction, 6 schizoid or borderline schizophrenic, 5 immature or unstable personality, 4 adjustment reaction of adolescence, 2 diagnosis doubtful. None of these patients changed for the worse. In 19 there was

TABLE 4

Over-all Summary of Work with NIH Patients by All Seven Trainees

	N	
Number of patients		
Males	18	
Females	31	
Young adolescents (ages 15–16)	7	
Older adolescents (ages 17–19)	14	
Young adults (ages 20–25)	5	
Mature adults (ages 30–55)	23	
Average no. of patients per trainee	7	
Total number of patients	49	
Number of interviews		
Average no. of interviews by each trainee	77	
Range of no. of interviews with a single patient	1 to 26	
Average no. of interviews with a single patient	10	
Total no. of interviews	539	
Diagnoses of patients		
Personality trait disorders (14 of these were patients who came for help ostensibly because of their children)	20	
Neurotic reaction	12	
Schizoid or borderline schizophrenic	6	
Immature or unstable personalities	5	
Adjustment reaction of adolescence	4	
Diagnosis doubtful	2	
Rating of patients' improvement or nonimprovement in the course of therapy		%
Marked improvement	3	6
Moderate improvement	10	20
Slight improvement	17	35
No change	19	39
Rating of patients according to difficulty of treatment.		
Very difficult	13	
Difficult	21	
Medium	10	
Easy	5	
Very easy	0	

no change. Thirty, or 61 per cent, showed some change. Seventeen showed a slight improvement; ten showed a moderate improvement; three, marked improvement. In evaluating the results it is important to remember that 69 per cent of the patients were "difficult or very difficult to treat," and that the length of treatment at the time of our evaluation was in no case more than six months, and, on the average, ten weeks. That the patients themselves were favorably impressed is demonstrated by the fact that of those who came asking for help, only one dropped out of therapy.

3. We asked the supervisors in ten community placements to rate the trainees who worked with them. The ratings are shown in TABLE 5. The general results here are highly favorable. The average rating is "good," and none is lower than "satisfactory."

TABLE 5*

Name of agency: ______________ Name of trainee: ______________	EXCELLENT 5	GOOD 4	SATISFACTORY 3	PASSABLE 2	POOR 1	INSUFFICIENT INFORMATION	AVERAGE SCORE
The trainee did the work assigned to her in a way which was: (Please use other students in training as a yardstick)	4	4	1				4.3
The trainee fitted into this agency in a way which was:	4	4	1				4.3
The trainee made progress during the time she was with this agency in a way which was:	4	1	4				3.9
Comments:							
			Signature: ______________				

*This table reproduces the blank sent to the supervisors in the various agencies, except that the last column on the right has been added to represent an average rating. The numbers in each box represent the number of times it was checked by a supervisor with regard to one trainee. One supervisor placed no check marks giving as the reason: "Assignments for direct service were so limited (due to limitations in time she was available and suitable assignments for a beginning trainee) that I feel it impossible to make an appraisal of patterns of her relating to families, staff and supervisor."

The table is incomplete since one supervisor has not yet returned his rating. Some trainees had more than one placement during the year.

4. We asked the trainees themselves to evaluate the program. There was general agreement on their part that it had been important to have one systematic, very well-given background course in personality development. There was general appreciation of a "human" attitude on the part of instructors who were willing to expose their own fears and failings, especially in their therapeutic work. They liked it particularly when theory and practice were brought close together, as in a course on family interaction patterns that was integrated with the group therapy for adolescents and their parents. The practical work was considered the "guts" of the program and wishes were expressed for more opportunities to listen with the supervisors to selected tapes of their own interviews and to observe more interviews by experienced therapists. Some of the placements were considered useful; some, more or less time wasting.

For all of the trainees the program has been an important step in their lives. Although they were warned *ad nauseam* that it is an experiment with no guarantee of success or future employment, they are, without exception, looking forward to using this training in serious work. They have raised the question whether a degree or certificate of some kind might be obtained that would enable them to identify themselves in any community in which they might live as being equipped to do the kind of work for which they have been trained. For all of them, the program supplied something they needed in that it filled satisfyingly a vacuum left by their children's growing up.

5. The teachers in the program have reported their impressions. Not all of the instructors are in a position to pass judgment on the clinical competence of all the trainees, but there has been a consensus on the part of those who have worked with them that they are a responsive, intelligent, conscientious group of people. During the first semester, comments were made several times to the effect that their "receptors" were good although the "broadcasting" was often awkward. From the beginning they impressed observers with their perceptiveness. One of the consultants observed with pleased surprise that when he asked for a description of a patient he really got it, in full detail.

As therapists they have all performed some useful services to patients during this past year, and none of them has done anyone any harm. They have improved considerably since the beginning of the course in their ability to draw out troublesome material and to respond appropriately to patients' cues.

Their greatest fault has been a tendency to follow the dictates of polite society. In other words, they pleasantly reassure, protect and sympathize when it would be better to question more deeply and seriously. A second fault is a tendency to try to deal on a surface, common-sense level with problems that are soluble only by eliciting unconscious conflicts.

We do not contend that the work of the trainees with their patients was highly skillful. Some of it was skillful; some was adequate; some was awkward. The fact of the matter is that favorable change sometimes occurred in spite of awkward, blundering work.

It is, of course, not yet possible to form a judgment about the degree of usefulness these women will demonstrate when they have finished the two-year course and are away from the protection of the group and their familiar teachers. Their future employment is uncertain and the quality of their performance will no doubt depend upon the kind of settings in which they find themselves, as well as upon what they will take with them at the end of the course. We hope to arrange a weekly seminar for them for the years following the training, not only for the purpose of continuing education, but also because it will be important from the point of view of morale so long as their identity in the field is an uncertain one.

What, now, are the implications of this pilot study for the general field of mental health?

First, there is a potential reservoir of workers in the age group we have tapped that is not presently being exploited. There may well be others, such as retired persons, who could also be used in various ways.

Second, we have anecdotal evidence to the effect that the 40-year-old married woman with children is reluctant to embark upon the regular training programs set up for young graduate students, and in some cases she is not welcomed in them. She does respond eagerly to a program tailored flexibly to her situation.

Third, there is the large and complex question of whether there is need and space for a new profession in the field of mental health. Many people have been concerned that the training for psychotherapy as a major professional activity is not optimally served in psychiatry, psychology or social work.* The present study is not by any means an attempt to prepare doctors of psychotherapy who would be licensed to practice independently. Our goal is a far more modest one. If such people as our trainees can perform useful services to patients—and in their first year of training they have done just that—then it should be possible for departments of psychiatry, psychology or social work to offer a subcurriculum something like this one, with emphasis upon practical work, which would train people in psychotherapy. The students in such curricula would no doubt arrive at varying levels of competence, ranging from listening sympathetically and giving commonsense advice, to skillful therapeutic interviewing with optimal use of unverbalized messages, and so on. They could be employed in settings in which they need not work above or beyond the limits of their competence. There will, of course, be no rigorous proof that this NIH pilot project can be replicated unless and until it is tried elsewhere. But there is no essential element in our program that could not be reproduced in other centers with good universities and clinics. A double purpose would be served if this could occur: More patients could be seen and more people could find a constructive use for their talents.

*See L. S. Kubie, "The Pros and Cons of a New Profession: A Doctorate in Medical Psychology," *Texas Reports on Biology and Medicine*, 12(3): 125–170.

Training in Counseling and Psychotherapy: An Evaluation of an Integrated Didactic and Experiential Approach[1]

ROBERT R. CARKHUFF[2]
CHARLES B. TRUAX[3]

An approach to training in counseling and psychotherapy integrating the didactic-intellectual approach which emphasizes the shaping of therapist behavior with the experiential approach which focuses upon therapist development and growth was successfully implemented with both a group of graduate students in clinical psychology and a group of lay hospital personnel, including 3 attendants, a volunteer worker, and an industrial therapist. The program relied heavily upon scales which in previous and extensive research had been predictive of positive patient outcome in estimating levels of therapist empathy, positive regard, and congruence and patient depth of self-exploration. It was found that the trainees could be brought to function at levels of effective therapy quite commensurate to those of more experienced therapists in less than 100 hours of training.

A recent attempt (Truax, Carkhuff, & Douds, 1964) was made to implement a view of training in counseling and psychotherapy that would inte-

Reprinted with permission from *Journal of Consulting Psychology*, 1965, Vol. 29, No. 4, 333–336, Copyright 1965 by the American Psychological Association, and with the permission of the authors.

[1]The authors wish to acknowledge the critical technical contributions of Edward P. Williams to the training program and data analyses and the cooperative efforts of John Corcella, Robert DeBurger, and Logan Gragg.

[2]Robert Carkhuff's work was supported by Public Health postdoctoral research fellowship number 7 F[2]MH-19,912-02, and the program was supported by Research and Development Grant No. 906-PM to the authors from the Vocational Rehabilitation Administration.

[3]Psychotherapy Research Group.

grate the didactic-intellectual approach which emphasizes the shaping of therapist behavior with the experiential approach which focuses upon therapist development and growth. Briefly, the approach set forth involves the supervisor's didactically teaching the trainee the former's accumulated research and clinical learnings concerning effective therapeutic dimensions in the context of a relationship which provides the trainee with experiences which the research and clinical learnings suggest are essential for constructive change or positive therapeutic outcome. For example, the teacher-supervisor might teach about high levels of empathic understanding while himself attempting to provide high levels of this dimension in his relationships to the trainees. Supervision is itself viewed as a therapeutic process: a learning or relearning process which takes place in the context of a particular kind of interpersonal relationship which is free of threat and facilitative of trainee self-exploration.

This integrated approach has grown out of programs of research into the processes of individual and group counseling and psychotherapy which appear to have identified at least four critical process variables in effective therapeutic processes. The dimensions include: (*a*) therapist accurate empathic understanding; (*b*) therapist warmth or positive regard; (*c*) therapist genuineness or self-congruence; and (*d*) patient depth of self-exploration. There is extensive evidence to indicate that the three therapist-offered conditions predictably relate to the patient process variable of intrapersonal exploration, and all four dimensions have been shown to relate significantly to a variety of positive patient personality and behavioral change indexes (Barrett-Lennard, 1962; Bergin & Solomon, 1963; Braaten, 1961; Halkides, 1958; Rogers, 1962; Tomlinson & Hart, 1962; Truax, 1961; Truax & Carkhuff, 1964a, 1964b; Wagstaff, Rice, & Butler, 1960).

A central part of the training program involves the application of research scales which have been predictive of positive patient outcome in researching these dimensions. With the help of the scales which had successfully measured or estimated the levels of the therapeutic conditions in previous research, the trainees are didactically taught the therapeutic conditions involved. The beginning counselors are then exposed to tape-recorded samples of counseling or psychotherapy rated at various levels of therapist-offered conditions and client-process involvement. The trainees get practice at discriminating levels of therapist and client conditions. Further, the trainees receive empathy training in which the trainee listens to patient statements and then is asked to formulate his response in terms of the feeling and content of the communication. The trainees then role-play, and finally their initial clinical interviews with hospitalized patients are recorded and then rated so as to give them immediate and concrete informational feedback on how well they are learning to put into operation the concepts involved.

Two separate, but essentially identical, training programs have been successfully implemented. The first program involved 12 advanced graduate students, ranging in age from the 20's to the 30's, in a regular university graduate course in "Individual Psychotherapy." The second and simultaneously run program involved five volunteer but otherwise unselected lay hospital personnel, ranging in age from the 30's to the 50's. These five volunteers consisted of three aides, a volunteer worker, and an industrial therapist. Only the industrial therapist had a college education. The programs lasted one semester of 16 weeks. The classes met twice a week for 2 hours on each occasion. In addition, the trainees spent approximately two additional hours per week listening on their own to recorded therapy.

METHODOLOGY

During the last week of the semester of training, each trainee had a single clinical interview with each of three hospitalized patients. From the three tapes of each trainee, six 4-minute excerpts were randomly selected, two excerpts from each tape. For purposes of comparison, excerpts of therapy interviews were similarly selected from the recordings of sessions in which 11 patients from a similar patient population were seen by experienced therapists in the Schizophrenic Project of the Wisconsin Psychiatric Institute. In addition, random excerpts were obtained from the publicly dispered tapes of therapy interviews of four prominent therapists. The combined experienced therapists included the following: Albert Ellis, William Fey, Eugene T. Gendlen, Rollo May, Allyn Roberts, Carl R. Rogers, Jack Teplinsky, Charles B. Truax, Julius Seeman, Al Wellner, and Carl Whitaker. The experienced therapists ranged in age from the 30's to the 60's.

Following the pattern of rating upon which much of the extensive body or research in support of the four dimensions has been built, undergraduate students who were not psychology majors and who were naive concerning therapeutic practices were trained on the particular individual scales involved to a degree of intrarater reliability of not less than .50 in order to insure that the ratings were not random. While .50 was the cut-off level, in most cases the rate-rerate reliabilities hovered in the 70's and 80's. In the rater training, the prospective raters were exposed to therapy excerpts selected because of a high degree of rating agreement by a variety of raters, including experienced therapists, at the various levels of the scales involved in order to insure a spread in the therapy process levels which the prospective raters were to rate. In the Wisconsin Schizophrenic Project and the Kentucky Group Therapy Project and in the analyses of data from other resources such as Chicago and Stanford, the therapy process ratings of undergraduate students trained on these particular individual scales successfully predicted therapeutic outcome (Rogers, 1962; Truax & Carkhuff, 1964a, 1964b). Four raters were trained to rate the therapist accurate empathy scale; four different raters rated patient depth of self-exploration; two other raters rated therapist positive regard; and two still different raters rated therapist congruence.

The therapist accurate empathy (AE) scale is a 9-point scale attempting to specify stages along a continuum. At the lowest stage, for example, ". . . the therapist seems completely unaware of even the most conspicuous of the client's feelings. . . ." At the highest stage, Stage 9, the therapist ". . . unerringly responds to the client's full range of feelings in their exact intensity . . . ." The product moment correlations between the four raters employed on the AE training data ranged in the .40's and .50's with one correlation falling to .24.[4]

The scale measuring therapist unconditional positive regard (UPR) is a 5-point scale running from the lowest point where ". . .the therapist is actively offering advice or giving clear negative regard. . . ." to the highest point where ". . . the therapist communicates unconditional positive reward without restriction. . . ." The product-moment correlation between the two raters employed was .48.[4]

Therapist self-congruence (TSC) is estimated by a 7-point scale where Stage 1 is indicated by a ". . . striking evidence of contradiction between the therapist's experiencing and his current verbalization. . . ." and Stage 7 is noted when ". . . the therapist is freely and deeply himself in the relationship. . . ." The correlation between the two raters employed was .62.[4]

Client depth of self-exploration (DX) is measured by a 9-point scale running from the lowest stages where ". . . the patient actively evades personally relevant material. . . ." to the highest stages where ". . . the patient is deeply exploring and being himself. . . ." The product-moment correlations between the four raters employed on the DX training data ranged in the .50's and .60's with only one correlation falling below .47.[4]

RESULTS

The results appear in Tables 1 and 2. It can be readily seen that, with the notable exception of the critical DX variable, where the lay therapists' mean scores were approximately equal to those of the students and the experienced therapists, the groups consistently performed in the following rank order: (*a*) the experienced therapists; (*b*) the graduate students;

TABLE 1

Mean Scale Values of Therapy Process Variables for Groups of Trainees and Experienced Therapists

SCALE	NUMBER OF POINTS	LAY[a] ($n = 5$)	*SD*	STUDENTS[a] ($n = 12$)	*SD*	EXPERIENCED ($n = 15$)	*SD*
AE	(9)	4.58	.30	5.14	.69	5.22	.84
UPR	(5)	2.82	.62	3.05	.32	3.16	.40
TSC	(7)	4.86	.35	5.23	.48	5.51	.45
DX	(9)	4.66	.30	4.56	.60	4.86	.56

[a]Personnel involved in training program.

[4]All intercorrelations for the ratings on all scales were significant beyond the .01 level.

TABLE 2

t Tests for Significant Differences of Therapy Process Variables for Groups of Trainees and Experienced Therapists

Scale	Students versus Lay	Students versus Experienced	Lay versus Experienced
AE	1.750	.267	1.641
UPR	1.045	.786	1.417
TSC	.487	1.556	2.955*
DX	.357	1.304	.741

*Significant at the .01 level.

and (*c*) the lay personnel. While a hierarchy of performance was established, the experienced therapists did not effect significantly better process levels than the graduate students on any dimensions, and the latter were not significantly higher than the lay group on any indexes. The only significant difference was found in the comparison of the experienced and the lay groups on the therapist self-congruence dimension.

DISCUSSION

The results suggest that in a relatively short training period, i.e., approximately 100 hours, both graduate students and lay hospital personnel can be brought to function at levels of therapy nearly commensurate with those of experienced therapists.

It is notable that on the empathy dimension all of the groups functioned near Stage 5, which is characterized by the ". . . therapist accurately respond[ing] to all of the client's more readily discernible feelings. . . ." All groups hovered around Stage 3 of the unconditional positive regard scale where ". . . the therapist indicates a positive caring for the patient or client but it is a semipossessive caring. . . ." On the therapist self-congruence scale all groups functioned near Level 5 where ". . . there are no negative cues suggesting any discrepancy between what he says and what he feels, and there are some positive cues indicating genuine response to the patient. . . ." The patients of all the groups of therapists are engaged in the therapeutic process of self-exploration at Levels 4 and 5 where ". . . personally relevant material is discussed . . ." and frequently, ". . . either with feeling indicating emotional proximity, or with spontaneity. . . ." To sum: it may be said that the trainees, both students and lay personnel, engaged almost as well as the more experienced therapists in what would commonly be characterized as *effective psychotherapy*.

For purposes of comparison, there is Bergin and Solomon's (1963) analysis of six different supervisory groups of postinternship fourth-year graduate students from a more didactically and psychoanalytically oriented clinical training program of a school of some repute in the field on an expanded version of the empathy scale. By inserting a stage between Levels 2 and 3 of the present scale, the authors obtained the following average ratings, with many of the ratings between Levels 2 and 3 and all of those above Stage 3 tending to be inflated if compared to assessments employing the 9-point empathy scale: Group A, 2.14; Group B, 3.84; Group C, 3.20; Group D, 2.02; Group E, 1.91; Group F, 2.08. It should be noted here that Bergin and Solomon also found empathy to be positively related to outcome. While we have only empathy ratings for comparison, it can easily be seen that the highest of these levels of functioning on empathic understanding is nowhere near those produced by the integrated program described here.

That the experienced therapists are significantly higher than the lay personnel, as well as relatively higher than the graduate students, on the self-congruence dimension, suggests that with experience the therapists come to be more freely, easily, and deeply themselves in the therapeutic encounter. In this regard, one handicap with which the lay personnel may have been operating is the lack of any real theroretical orientation to indicate to them where they were going in their encounters. The very notion that counseling and therapy may take place devoid of any theoretical knowledge is currently being assessed in a lay group counseling treatment study. While the present program did not emphasize outside readings, the graduate sudents tended to glean from other sources some direction for themselves and their activities.

It is perhaps noteworthy that the lay personnel, consistently the lowest on all scales assessing the level of therapist-offered conditions, engage their patients in a depth of intrapersonal exploration commensurate with that of the experienced therapists and the students. The suggestion is that other dimensions come into play in effecting patient self-exploration which, in turn, is so highly correlated with patient outcome criteria. Perhaps the oft-noted social class variables are relevant here in the sense that lower socio-educational class therapists are in some way more facilitative in engaging their patient counterparts in the therapeutic process.

REFERENCES

BARRETT-LENNARD, G. T. Dimensions of therapist response as causal factors in therapeutic change. *Psychological Monographs*, 1962, 76 (43, Whole No. 562).

BERGIN, A. E., & SOLOMON, SANDRA. Personality and performance correlates of empathic understanding in psychotherapy. *American Psychologist,* 1963, **18**, 393.

BRAATEN, L. J. The movement of non-self to self in client-centered psychotherapy. *Journal of Counseling Psychology*, 1961, **8**, 20–24.

HALKIDES, GALATIA. An investigation of therapeutic success as a function of four variables. Unpublished doctoral dissertation, University of Chicago, 1958.

ROGERS, C. R. The interpersonal relationship: The core of guidance. *Harvard Educational Review*, 1962, **32**, 416–429.

TOMLINSON, T. M., & HART, J. T., JR. A validation study of the process scale. *Journal of Consulting Psychology*, 1962, **26**, 74–78.

TRUAX, C. B. The process of group psychotherapy. *Psychological Monographs*, 1961, **75** (14, Whole No. 511).

TRUAX C. B., & CARKHUFF, R. R. For better or for worse: The process of psychotherapeutic personality change. Chapter in Blossom T. Wigdor (Ed.), *Recent advances in behavior change.* Montreal, Canada: McGill Univer. Press, 1964. (a)

TRUAX C. B., & CARKHUFF, R. R. Significant developments in psychotherapy research. Chapter in L. Abt and B. F. Riess (Eds.), *Progress in clinical psychology*, Vol. VI. New York: Grune & Stratton, 1964. (b)

TRUAX, C. B., CARKHUFF, R. R., & DOUDS, J. Toward an integration of the didactic and experiential approaches to training in counseling and psychotherapy. *Journal of Counseling Psychology*, 1964, **11**, 240–247.

WAGSTAFF, A. K., RICE, L. N., & BUTLER, J. M. Factors in client verbal participation in therapy. *Counseling center discussion papers*, University of Chicago, 1960, **6** (9), 1–14.

Lay Mental Health Counseling: The Effects of Lay Group Counseling[1]

ROBERT R. CARKHUFF
CHARLES B. TRUAX[2]

8 therapeutic groups of 10 hospitalized mental patients each were seen twice a week for a total of 24 sessions by 5 trained lay hospital personnel. 70 patients served as controls. The lay personnel, primarily attendants, had been trained by an approach integrating the didactic approach which emphasizes the shaping of therapist behavior with the experiential approach which focuses upon therapist development and "growth." Heavy training emphasis was placed upon research scales assessing process variables, which had been predictive of positive patient outcome, rather than any particular theoretical orientation. At the end of the 3-month period, significant improvement was noted in the ward behavior of the treatment group when compared to the control group.

Since the introduction of effective tranquilizers and other psychomimetic compounds, a very large percentage of the nation's hospitalized mental

Reprinted with permission from *Journal of Consulting Psychology*, 1965, Vol. 29, No. 5, 426–431, Copyright 1965 by the American Psychological Association, and with the permission of the authors.

[1]The research was supported in part by Research and Development Grant 906-PM from the Vocational Rehabilitation Administration to the authors. R. R. Carkhuff's work was supported by Public Health Fellowship 7 F2 MH-19, 912-02 from the National Institute of Mental Health, United States Public Health Service.

[2]The authors gratefully acknowledge the critical technical contributions of Edward P. Williams to the data analyses and the training program and the co-operative efforts of John Corcella, Robert DeBurger, and Logan Gragg.

patients have become susceptible to psychotherapeutic intervention. Further, psychotherapeutic approaches to facilitating constructive personality change are being widely used in the treatment of neurotic and emotionally disturbed persons. Essentially psychotherapeutic approaches are used in present-day counseling programs in schools, industries, and rehabilitation programs throughout the nation. It has become strikingly clear, however, that available and projected manpower at the disciplines currently practicing psychotherapy fall severely short of the available and projected demand.

Further, recent research identifying certain specifiable elements of effective psychotherapy has opened new avenues for the specific training of therapists. It has been suggested (Truax & Carkhuff, 1964a; 1964b) that the research measuring instruments which have successfully discriminated between specific behaviors of effective therapy and noneffective or psychonoxious therapy[3]could be applied directly to training programs. Thus, tape-recorded samples of psychotherapy rated very high in the known elements of effective psychotherapy could be selected to provide concrete examples for the beginning therapists. More specifically, the measuring scales such as the accurate empathy scale could be used to rate samples drawn from a trainee's own early therapeutic interviews and thus give the trainee immediate and concrete informational feedback about his own performance. Such an approach would mark a very radical departure from current training practices which heavily emphasize intellectual learning, too often perhaps at the expense of learning the art of operationalizing the concepts involved in effective psychotherapy.

Also, since the training of a therapist in a clear sense involves the personality change of the trainee, it might be expected that variables in effective psychotherapy should logically be applied to the training of the therapists. This implies, for example, that the teacher-supervisor should provide the conditions of accurate empathy, unconditional positive regard, and self-congruence or genuineness for the trainee during supervisory sessions. The continuing use of such therapeutic conditions in a supervisory trainee program not only would be expected to contribute to the trainee's personality change directly, but also to provide the trainee with a clear and observable model of a therapist to be imitated. A training program dealing in this fashion with recent research evidence identifying some of the effective elements in psychotherapy has been described (Truax, Carkhuff & Douds, 1964). The program involves both concrete didactic and more molar experiential aspects including a quasi group-therapy experience for the trainees. This training program has been implemented both with lay hospital personnel and with postgraduate clini-

[3]This term has been coined by Haim Ginott in a personal communication to describe therapists who provide the kind of relationship in which patient deterioration is observed.

cal psychology students. An analysis of the findings (Carkhuff & Truax, 1964) indicated that after a training program involving less than 100 hours, both lay personnel and clinical psychology trainees did not differ markedly from a group of highly experienced psychotherapists in the process measures of the psychotherapeutic interviews they produced. On at least one dimension from the only study (Bergin & Solomon, 1963) which was available for purposes of comparison, empathic understanding, the lay personnel performed at levels significantly higher than postinternship graduate students. The present study is an attempt to evaluate the effectiveness of the lay personnel involved in the program by comparing the improvements observed in groups of hospitalized mental patients seen by them in group psychotherapy with equivalent control groups not receiving lay group counseling.

Recent reported evidence suggests the potential therapeutic effectiveness of minimally trained nonprofessional personnel. Thus, Appleby (1963) demonstrated significant improvement in chronic schizophrenics who were treated by hospital aides functioning in effect as lay therapists. Mendel and Rapport (1963) have also shown the value of lay personnel over a 51-month period of observation in helping chronic patients remain outside of the hospital with only periodic supportive interviews.

The present program differs quite markedly from the training program reported by Rioch (1963), who clearly demonstrated that specially selected, bright, sophisticated, and educated housewives could learn from very intensive and long-term training (similar to that involved in graduate schools with good practicum programs) and could be as well regarded by their supervisors as those trained in regular graduate schools. The program described by Rioch, while important as a demonstration, would be extremely difficult to replicate elsewhere and in general would be as expensive to duplicate as it would be to pay for graduate school (which of course has the advantage of professional status).

By contrast, the counseling or psychotherapy training program described here, since it involves less than 100 hours of training (and less than 65 hours of supervisor time), is not more expensive to implement than a great many hospital aide training programs. Further, since it relies heavily upon research instruments and training tapes it is more readily replicable.

The present training program is also of theoretical significance. A number of studies (Barrett-Lennard, 1962; Bergin & Solomon, 1963; Braaten, 1961; Halkides, 1958; Rogers, 1962; Tomlinson & Hart, 1962; Truax, 1961; Truax & Carkhuff, 1964a, 1964b; Wagstaff, Rice, & Butler, 1960) have now amassed evidence suggesting that three therapist-offered conditions and one critical dimension of patient behavior are significantly associated with constructive personality change in a variety of hospitalized and nonhospitalized patients: (*a*) therapist accurate empathic understanding, (*b*) therapist communication of warmth or unconditioned positive regard, (*c*) therapist genuineness or self-congruence, and (*d*) patient depth of self-exploration. These studies have been conducted with trained and relatively experienced therapists so that the variables studied operated in the context of a thorough knowledge of patient psychopathology and dynamics. It could very well be that these four elements of effective psychotherapy are in fact effective only in the context of a thorough knowledge of psychopathology and dynamics. Since the training program with the lay personnel involved no training in psychopathology and personality dynamics, an evaluation of their effectiveness would throw some light upon the necessity or value of training in psychopathology and personality dynamics.

METHODOLOGY

Five volunteer but otherwise unselected hospital personnel[4] from Eastern State Hospital, Lexington, Kentucky, were involved in the training program. These volunteers consisted of three aides, a volunteer worker, and an industrial therapist. Only the industrial therapist had a college education. The hospital personnel ranged in age from 32 to 50 (*M*, 41.40; *SD*, 7.42).

Briefly, the training involved the supervisor didactically teaching the trainee about effective therapeutic dimensions in the context of a relationship providing the trainee the experiential base of these dimensions. Research scales which had successfully measured the levels of therapeutic conditions of tape-recorded therapy in research predictive of therapy outcome were employed in teaching the trainees to discriminate levels of the four conditions involved. The trainee then received empathy training in which they listened to patient statements and then were asked to formulate their responses in terms of the feeling and content of the communication. The trainees role-played and finally had initial clinical interviews with hospitalized patients. All phases of training were recorded for purposes of rating within the class so as to give the trainees immediate and concrete informational feedback on how well they were learning to operationalize the concepts involved.

Three of the lay personnel were assigned to two groups each of 10 patients in each group. Due to limitations in the population available, the two remaining counselors were assigned only one group each of 10 patients. With the exception that 10 less patients were represented in the control groups, the patients were divided into groups according to the years institutionalized and randomly assigned to treatment groups. In total, then, 150 Eastern State Hospital patients were involved, with 80 in the treatment groups and 70 in control groups. Three of the treatment groups were females ($N = 30$), and 24 members of the control groups were females.

Criteria for patient selection included the following: patients who were

[4]The lay hospital personnel who gave so much of themselves to the training program are Jean Dansby, Julia Hardy, Gene Lee, Mary Washington, and Polly White.

not expected to be discharged within a 3-month period, patients who were not currently being seen in any form of psychotherapeutic treatment, and patients who were not diagnosed to be mentally retarded or to have organicity. The patient population involved the typical multiplicity of diagnostic categories not only among various patients but also within the clinical histories of the individual patients. The variety of current diagnosis included manic-depressive reactions of the manic and depressive types, psychotic-depressive reactions and schizophrenic reactions, simple catatonic and schizoaffective types, with the great majority of all patients diagnosed as hebephrenic, paranoid, or chronic undifferentiated types. One patient fell into each of the following categories: psychoneurotic anxiety reaction, sociopathic personality disturbance, passive-aggressive personality trait disturbance, and transient adult situational personality disturbance.

The treatment group ranged in age from 24 to 64 with an *M* of 50.03 years (*SD*, 11.14). These patients had had an average of 7.44 (*SD*, 3.65) years of education, with some patients having had no schooling and some having college degrees. The number of hospital admissions, including their present stay, ran from the first admission to the fourth and averaged 1.96 (*SD*, .92), and the length of stay during the present hospitalization ranged from 1 to 36 years with an *M* of 13.62 (*SD*, 11.23).

The control group members varied in age from 20 to 66 (*M*, 46.96; *SD*, 11.47) and schooling from 0 to 16 grades or college (*M*, 7.51; *SD*, 3.36). The average number of hospital admissions was 2.09 (*SD*, 1.04) range again from 1 to 4, while the years of the present hospitalization varied from 1 to 34 with an *M* of 10.03 (*SD*, 8.19).

In summary, the population was essentially an older chronic one with an average of two admissions. While the sample was a severely disabled one, it represented the great bulk of the hospital population which is usually not serviced by the professional staff and thus provided a testing ground for the usefulness of lay treatment.

The patients were seen twice a week for a total of 24 sessions over a period of approximately 3 months in time-limited group counseling. There was no problem-oriented or personnel-oriented basis for group assignment. Patients were simply randomly assigned to the individual treatment and the control groups. The sessions were recorded for the purposes of supervision and any subsequent analyses. The lay counselors continued to meet as a group for purposes of being supervised twice a week for an hour each time.

In the treatment process, the lay counselors were oriented only toward providing high levels of therapeutic conditions. They had no cognitive map of where they were going except to attempt to elicit a degree of self-exploration relating to the problems and concerns which the patients brought to the session. The therapist's role was to communicate a warm and genuine concern and depth of understanding. There was no special focus for discussion; no topics were forbidden; and in general as the sessions evolved, they included discussions of the usual range of emotion-laden or intellectualized topics from sexual material to concerns regarding autonomy and more immediate and pragmatic concerns like the method for "getting out" of the hospital, or even "staying in."

Outcome criteria to be assessed included hospital discharge rates and pre- and posttreatment ratings of ward behavior by the nurses and ward attendants of the particular wards from which the patients came. In all, seven wards were involved, so the nurses and ward attendants of these seven wards were involved in the rating. An attempt was made to give pre- and posttesting using a battery of psychological tests including the MMPI, the *Q* sort for Self and Ideal Self, and an Anxiety scale. Unfortunately, because of the degree of chronicity and pathology as well as the general low level of educational attainment, less than 30% of both groups or 18 members of the treatment group and 16 members of the control group proved testable, so that the evaluation of patient change was based upon changes in ward behavior.

RESULTS

Of the 80 patients who were seen in counseling, 6 dropped out, all within the first six sessions. Eleven of the remaining 74 patients who continued with some great degree of regularity were discharged after 2 or more months of therapeutic treatment. Of the 70 control patients, 6 were discharged within the 3-month period of time. While the direction and absolute values are meaningful, a chi-square of 1.42 did not yield statistically significant differences.

All of the patients were rated before and after treatment on the short-form "Gross Ratings of Patient Behavior" (Carkhuff & DeBurger, 1964), a series of four nine-point scales where 9 represents the highest value in the positive direction and 1 represents the lowest value in the negative direction. The scales assessed four critical areas: (*a*) "degree of psychological disturbance"; (*b*) "degree of constructive interpersonal concern"; (*c*) "degree of constructive intrapersonal concern," and perhaps most important, (*d*) the "degree of overall improvement over the past 3 months," for which only postratings were obtained. The posttreatment ratings were available for all treatment and control group members. Twenty of the preratings necessary to assess the first three indexes of ward behavior of the control group were, however, lost or misplaced. Analysis of the posttreatment "overall improvement" ratings indicates that the 20 patients whose preratings were misplaced tended to be rated slightly worse than the control group in general, thus suggesting that the differences between treatment and control groups on the three other scales are conservative. Five of the 20 were rated improved; 5, deteriorated; and 10, no change. As can be seen from Table 1, all scale differences between treatment and control groups were statistically significant by chi-square. It is notable that only one of the treatment group patients was rated as deteriorated in his overall behavior over the previous 3 months, while 38 were judged improved. Twelve of the control-group members were rated behaviorally deteriorated overall, while 19 were rated improved. Furthermore, it is clear from the other scale values that control group members tended to remain unchanged, while there was a greater variability in the treatment group ratings.

TABLE 1

Direction of Changes of Gross Ratings of Patient Behavior by Ward Personnel

	Patient groups		
Overall improvement (Postratings only)	$(N = 74)$		$(N = 70)$
Improved	38		19
Deteriorated	1	$\chi^2 = 21.47$***	12
Unchanged	35		39
Psychological disturbance (Pre- and postratings)	$(N = 74)$		$(N = 50)$
Improved	28		8
Deteriorated	19	$\chi^2 = 17.28$***	5
Unchanged	27		37
Interpersonal concerns (Pre- and postratings)	$(N = 74)$		$(N = 50)$
Improved	33		16
Deteriorated	14	$\chi^2 = 11.23$**	2
Unchanged	27		32
Intrapersonal concerns (Pre- and postratings)	$(N = 74)$		$(N = 50)$
Improved	28		15
Deteriorated	16	$\chi^2 = 6.79$*	4
Unchanged	30		31

*Significant at the .05 level.
**Significant at the .01 level.
***Significant at the .001 level.

DISCUSSION AND IMPLICATIONS

The evidence points to uniformly significant improvement in the patients treated by lay group counseling when compared to control patients. The suggestion is that a specific but relatively brief training program, devoid of specific training in psychopathology, personality dynamics, or psychotherapy theory, can produce relatively effective lay mental health counselors. It is significant that three of the five lay counselors in the present study had only a high-school education or less, two had attended college, and only one had completed college. In view of the relatively brief training, it would seem feasible to train a large percentage of currently existing hospital aide staff, *at no extra cost*, and thus provide regular lay group counseling to almost all hospitalized patients.

It is of significance that the patient population used in the present evaluation was an unselected one, by and large involving a preponderance of chronic hospitalized patients. A recent study by Spitzer, Lee, Carnahan, and Fleiss (1964) has indicated that the Kentucky Hospital population is significantly more pathological and less communicative, perhaps due to a lower socioeducational status, than patient populations in similar institutions in northern and more urbanized states. Thus, lay group counseling produced significant improvement in patients who on the average had spent an average of 13½ years in their current hospitalization, had had one previous hospitalization, had a seventh-grade education, and who were already 50 years of age.

Since pre- and postratings of ward behavior were used as the basic measure of change, biased reports from the ward staff should be considered. We have long been somewhat suspicious of reported improvements when the ward doctor treated patients and asked the ward staff to evaluate his effectiveness. The lay counselors had no direct connection with any of the wards involved. It should be noted also that in the present case the ward staff and the hospital personnel in general were initially resistant to the idea that hospital attendants should even be allowed to conduct group counseling. The lay therapist did not initially enjoy high status. The admitted and outspoken bias of the ward personnel involved in the behavioral ratings was against rather than for lay group counseling: the expectation of the ward personnel initially was that the lay group counseling would upset the patients and that therapy with nonprofessional therapists would be harmful rather than helpful.

The "attention factor" in relation to the patients themselves should, however, be considered. Most of the patients had received no special treatment, especially no psychotherapeutic treatment during their many years of hospitalization. There was in fact great difficulty initially in getting patients to attend the group sessions, although most attended regularly after the first few weeks, many looking forward to this special form of attention which they were receiving. Although present resources did not allow for such a control, future replication should incorporate a second control group of patients attending "sessions" conducted by untrained lay personnel.

The evidence that the treatment group produced greater variability in outcome compared to the control group parallels equivalent findings in psychotherapy (Barron & Leary, 1955; Cartwright & Vogel, 1960; Shlien, Mosak, & Dreikurs, 1960). It is perhaps of some significance that only one treated patient was judged deteriorated in overall behavior. This compared most favorably with reported effects of professional group psychotherapy with even less chronic hospitalized patients.

In addition, the absolute number of treatment group members getting out, while not statistically significant due to the patient *N* involved, and, while always qualified by what goes into the process of patient discharge, nearly doubled those of the control group.

In summary, the present research has demonstrated the effectiveness of time-limited lay group counseling, evolving from a short-term integrated didactic and experiential approach to training. It is felt that the results indicate great promise for the possibly critical role which lay personnel might play in coping with our evergrowing mental health concerns. The results point to the need for further and continued search and research into this potentially vast and untapped resource.

REFERENCES

APPLEBY, L. Evaluation of treatment methods for chronic schizophrenia. *Archives of General Psychiatry*, 1963, **8**, 8–21.

BARRETT-LENNARD, G. T. Dimensions of therapist response as causal factors in therapeutic change. *Psychological Monographs,* 1962, **76**(43, Whole No. 562).

BARRON, F., & LEARY, T. Changes in psychoneurotic patients with and without psychotherapy. *Journal of Consulting Psychology,* 1955, **19**, 239–245.

BERGIN, A. E., & SOLOMON, SANDRA. Personality and performance correlates of empathic understanding in psychotherapy. Paper read at American Psychological Association, Philadelphia, September 1963.

BRAATEN, L. J. The movement from non-self to self in client-centered psychotherapy. *Journal of Counseling Psychology,* 1961, 8, 20–24.

CARKHUFF, R. R., & DEBURGER, R. Gross ratings of patient behavior. University of Massachusetts, 1964. (Mimeo)

CARKHUFF, R. R., & TRUAX, C. B. Training in counseling and psychotherapy: An evaluation of an intregrated didactic and experiential approach. Paper submitted, *Journal of Consulting Psychology,* 1964.

CARTWRIGHT, ROSALIND D., & VOGEL, J. L. A comparison of changes in psychoneurotic patients during matched periods of therapy and no therapy. *Journal of Consulting Psychology,* 1960, **24**, 121–127.

HALKIDES, GALATIA. An investigation of therapeutic success as a function of four variables. Unpublished doctoral dissertation, University of Chicago, 1958.

MENDEL, W. M., & RAPPORT, S. Outpatient treatment for chronic schizophrenic patients: Therapeutic consequences of an existential view. *Archives of General Psychiatry,* 1963, **8**, 190–196.

RIOCH, MARGARET. Unpublished United States Public Health Services Progress Report, Washington School of Psychiatry, Washington, D. C., 1963.

SHLIEN, J. M., MOSAK, H. H., & DREIKURS, R. Effect of time limits: A comparison of client-centered and Adlerian psychotherapy. *American Psychologist,* 1960, **15**, 415 (Abstract).

SPITZER, R., LEE, JOAN, CARNAHAN, W., & FLEISS, J. A comparison of rural and urban schizophrenics in differing state institutions. Paper presented at American Psychiatric Association, Los Angeles, Calif., May 1964.

TOMLINSON, T. M., & HART, J. T., JR. A validation study of the process scale. *Journal of Consulting Psychology,* 1962, 26, 74–78.

TRUAX, C. B. The process of group psychotherapy. *Psychological Monographs,* 1961, 75(14, Whole No. 511).

TRUAX, C. B., CARKHUFF, R. R. For better or for worse: The process of psychotherapeutic personality change. In *Recent advances in behavior change.* Montreal, Canada: McGill Univer. Press, 1964. Pp. 118–163.

TRUAX, C. B., & CARKHUFF, R. R. Significant developments in psychotherapy research. In Abt and Reiss (Eds.), *Progress in clinical psychology,* Vol. VI. New York: Grune & Stratton, 1964. (b)

TRUAX, C. B., CARKHUFF, R. R., & DOUBS, J. Toward an integration of the didactic and experientail approaches to counseling and psychotherapy. *Journal of Counseling Psychology,* 1964, 11, 240–247.

WAGSTAFF, A. K., RICE, L. N., & BUTLER, J. M. Factors in client verbal participation in therapy. *Counseling center discussion papers,* University of Chicago, 1960, 6(9), 1–14.

The Effect of Therapists' Training on Group Therapeutic Outcome[1]

ERNEST G. POSER

The outcome of group therapy for psychotic patients was used as the dependent variable in assessing the comparative efficacy of trained and untrained therapists. The latter were undergraduate students with no training or experience in psychotherapy. For this reason, their role in psychotherapy was viewed as analogous to that of a placebo in studies assessing drug effects. Changes in psychological test performance of 295 patients before and after 5 months of group therapy served as the criterion of therapeutic behavior change. By comparison to an untreated control group the lay therapists achieved slightly better results than psychiatrists and psychiatric social workers doing group therapy with similar patients. Caution was urged in extending the implications of these results beyond group therapy with schizophrenic patients.

The present manpower shortage in the mental health professions has given new impetus to investigations concerned with therapist variables in studies of therapeutic outcome. Hence, it is not surprising that recent work in this field, notably by Anker and Walsh (1961), Beck, Kantor, and Gelineau (1963), Rioch, Elkes, Flint, Usdansky, Newman, & Silber (1963), and Schofield (1964) should have focused attention on what appear to be

Reprinted with permission from *Journal of Consulting Psychology*, 1966, Vol. 30, No. 4, 283–289, Copyright 1966 by the American Psychological Association, and with the permission of the author.

[1]This project was supported by Canadian Dominion-Provincial Mental Health Research Grant No. 604-5-73. Special thanks are due to C. A. Roberts and H. E. Lehmann of Douglas Hospital for their part in making this study possible.

the active therapeutic ingredients of the patient-therapist interaction. All of these authors suggest that effective therapy can be carried out by personnel without professional training, and most of them provide objective evidence in support of this view.

Truax (1963) and his associates also drew attention to nonacademic qualifications of therapists by their ingenious demonstration that those rated high with respect to certain human qualities, such as "accurate empathy," tend to improve the psychological functioning of schizophrenics, while therapists rated low in empathy actually impair the clinical status of their patients. The therapist's personality attributes with which Truax is concerned are essentially those previously elaborated by Rogers (1957), who does not feel that special intellectual professional knowledge —psychological, psychiatric, medical, or religious—is required of the therapist. In this context he observes that "intellectual training and the acquiring of information has, I believe, many valuable results—but becoming a therapist is not one of those results [p. 101]." This view is consistent with the speculation that nonprofessional workers, possibly selected in accordance with Truax's criteria, could do effective therapy, at least with certain types of patients.

There is urgent need for studies seeking to define those aspects of the treatment process which crucially affect therapeutic outcome. Without such information, it is difficult to distinguish between the necessary and the superfluous conditions of therapeutic personality change. But it may be misleading to think of the variance accounting for therapeutic outcome only in terms of active versus inactive ingredients, if the term "active" is meant to imply the deliberate application of some theory or procedure to the conduct of psychotherapy. There may be a third source of therapeutic change related to the familiar placebo effect operative in most other forms of medical and psychiatric treatment. Because, strictly speaking, there is no such thing as "inert" psychotherapy in the sense that placebos are pharmacologically inert, the term "placeboid" might serve to describe this effect in psychotherapy.

Rosenthal and Frank (1956) have dealt with the placebo phenomenon in some detail and conclude that

> . . . improvement under a special form of psychotherapy cannot be taken as evidence for: (*a*) correctness of the theory on which it is based; or (*b*) efficacy of the specific technique used, unless improvement can be shown to be greater than, or qualitatively different from that produced by the patients' faith in the efficacy of the therapist and his technique—"the placebo effect" [p. 300].

More recently, Frank, Nash, Stone, and Imber (1963) have shown that some psychiatric patients recover simply as a result of attending a clinic or receiving placebo, without psychotherapy or other treatment being given.

Such studies, however, do not bear on the crucial problem of placeboid effects in the psychotherapeutic interaction itself. They do not tell us whether some of the supposedly active ingredients of therapy, such as the theoretical training or experience of the therapist, for instance, are or are not relevant to therapeutic outcome. Could it be that such behavior change as does occur posttherapeutically is due to other factors not hitherto considered to be necessary antecedents of therapeutic change? Fiedler (1950) and others have already shown that adherents of widely disparate theoretical persuasions achieve much the same results in psychotherapy, and more recently similar findings have been reported by Gelder, Marks, Sakinofsky, and Wolff (1964) with respect to the comparative outcome of psychotherapy and behavior therapy. Though rich in implication, none of these studies were specifically designed to test for placeboid effects in therapeutic outcome. To do so, according to Rosenthal and Frank (1956), requires, in addition to the therapy under study, the application of

> another form of therapy in which patients had equal faith, so that the placebo effect operated equally in both, but which would not be expected by the theory of therapy being studied to produce the same effects [p. 300].

The present study constitutes an attempt to provide a controlled experiment in line with the above suggestion.

The therapeutic technique under study was group therapy with chronic schizophrenics. The fact that such therapy is most often carried out by psychiatrists, social workers, occupational therapists, and psychologists (Poser, 1965) suggests that training in one of these professions is commonly regarded as an appropriate, if not essential, prerequisite for the successful group therapist. To test the validity of this assumption three treatment conditions were compared in this investigation.

In the first, group therapy was conducted by highly trained psychiatrists, social workers, and occupational therapists. In the second condition all therapists were undergraduate students without previous training or experience relevant to the care of mental patients. Because a comparison of two treatments in terms of their effectiveness would be meaningless without first demonstrating the validity of the outcome criterion to be applied, a control group of untreated patients was also included.

In terms of Rosenthal and Frank's statement cited above, the untrained therapists in the present investigation were thought to provide a form of treatment which, by virtue of their lacking professional sophistication, would prove to be less effective than that offered by trained personnel. This, at least, would be the prediction if it is true that training and experience are relevant to therapeutic outcome. At the same time, there was no reason to believe that the patients had more faith in the trained than the untrained therapists, since they were in the main unaware of this distinction. Hence placeboid effects, if any, could operate equally in both therapeutic situations. In fact, the untrained therapists are here conceptualized as contributing nothing but placeboid effect, much as the pharmacologically inert substance does in a placebo-controlled drug study. By corollary, the theoretical sophistication and past experience of a trained therapist is, for the purpose of this study, viewed as the active ingredient in the therapeutic process. In other words, it is proposed that such therapeutic effectiveness as untrained therapists do attain is attributable to nonspecific aspects of the helping relationship, such as activation, sympathy, opportunity for verbal ventilation, regularity of attendance, and the like. These would appear to be formally comparable to the nonspecific factors thought to underlie placebo responses as, for instance, attention giving, expectation inducing, pill ingestion, and many other situational variables familiar to the drug therapist. Many of these variables are highly effective in the treatment of certain physical disabilities, as placebo studies of patients with headaches (Jellinek, 1946) or the common cold (Diehl, Baker, and Cowan, 1940) have abundantly shown. A similar phenomenon may operate in psychotherapy, which would account for the near-ubiquitous two-thirds improvement rate consequent upon most forms of psychotherapy.

METHOD

Subjects. A total of 343 male chronic schizophrenics was studied. They represent almost the entire male schizophrenic population of a 1,500-bed hospital, only assaultive patients and those suffering from known organic brain damage having been excluded. Their median age was 47 years (range 20–73). All of them had been hospitalized uninterruptedly for at least 3 years. Their median length of hospitalization was 14 years, with a range from 3 to 44 years.

The vast majority of these patients were receiving phenothiazine medication at the time of the study. This was continued throughout, and only in emergencies was medication changed during the course of the project.

Therapists. The untrained therapists consisted of 11 young women between the ages of 18 and 25. All were undergraduate students in one of Montreal's universities, and most had never had a course in psychology. None intended to enter a mental health profession, nor had any of them ever visited a mental hospital. No attempt was made to select a particular type of applicant. Anyone who expressed interest in the project and accepted the terms of employment was enrolled. They were paid at the standard rate for summer employment at that time and were asked to consent to the taking of numerous psychological tests which were to be used for a subsequent investigation. As an additional control, two inpatients—one an alcoholic and the other suffering from hysteria—were asked to act as untrained therapists.

The professional therapists were seven psychiatrists, six psychiatric social workers, and two occupational therapists. In addition to their formal professional qualifications, that is, certification in psychiatry, all the psychiatrists had had from 5 to 17 years of professional experience. All but one had previously done group psychotherapy, and three were specialized in this area. Their ages ranged from 35 to 50, and all were male.

All social workers had had postgraduate professional training leading to a degree and at least 5 years' professional experience. Two were specialized in group work, and all but two had had previous experience doing case or group work with psychotic patients. Their ages ranged from 36 to 43, and two out of the six were male.

The two occupational therapists had professional experience of 5 and 7 years' duration, respectively, and this included some mental hospital work. Both were female, one aged 27 and the other 30.

None of the therapists taking part in this project were on the staff of the hospital where this work was done, nor were any of the patients known to the therapists prior to the start of the project. All were paid at the rate appropriate to their profession.

Tests. Selection of these was guided by three considerations. First, the performance required had to be within the behavioral repertoire of chronic schizophrenic patients. Second, preference was given to tests which had previously been demonstrated to differentiate normals from psychotics. Since a large number of patients were involved, the third criterion was purely practical—those tests were chosen which could be administered in a relatively short space of time.

The final test battery consisted of two psychomotor, two perceptual, and two verbal tests, in addition to the Palo Alto Hospital Adjustment Scale (McReynolds & Ferguson, 1946), intended to provide a quantitative estimate of the patients' adjustment in the hospital. The tests were:

1. Speed of tapping (TAP). (The number of taps on a reaction key in 10 seconds.)
2. A test of visual reaction-time (RT) involving choice.
3. The Digit-Symbol test (DS) of the Wechsler-Bellevue Scale I.
4. A color-word conflict test (Stroop), in which the score reflects the time taken by the patient to read 100 color names under three conditions of increasing difficulty (Thurstone & Mellinger, 1953).
5. Verbal fluency (VF). (The number of different animals named in 1 minute.)
6. The Verdun Association List (VAL), a 20-item word-association test devised by Sigal (1956) to discriminate between working and nonworking mental hospital patients.

All of these tests were individually administered immediately before or after therapy. Occasionally a patient was found untestable before or after therapy. Such patients were seen by another examiner, so that no patient was given a zero score on any test unless he had been given two opportunities to take it from a different examiner on each occasion

Procedure. The 343 patients were selected for this project by the psychiatric staff of the hospital. Each patient was assigned to a group in such a way that every unit of 10 patients would be matched as closely as possible with every other unit in terms of the patients' age, severity of illness, and length of hospitalization. Following this, the groups were compared with respect to their mean test performance prior to therapy. Where major disparities between groups were noted, individual patients were exchanged, so that all groups were roughly comparable with respect to age, clinical status, length of hospitalization, and test performance prior to therapy.

At this stage six groups (one of them composed of 13 patients) were picked at random to serve as untreated controls. Patients in these groups received the usual hospital care, but were excluded from all forms of group treatment other than routine occupational therapy. The remaining 28 groups were each assigned to a therapist picked at random from among the project staff available at the time. The project extended over three periods of 5 months. In the first of these, 11 untrained therapists took part; in the second, seven professional and one untrained therapist; and in the final period, eight professional and one untrained therapist.

Each therapist met his or her group during 1 hour daily 5 days a week for a period of 5 months. A special attendant saw to it that patients would join their groups at the appropriate time and place. Even so, one or two patients in almost every group refused to attend regularly. Their absences were recorded, and only those patients who attended at least two-thirds of all available sessions were reevaluated at the end of the 5-month period. This reduced the total number of patients included in the study from 343 to 295. At the time of the posttherapy retest no group had less than six members who met the attendance criterion.

Both the trained and untrained therapists were quite free to conduct their therapy sessions in any way they wished. Wherever possible, the materials or facilities they required were provided by the hospital, but at no time did the project director offer suggestions for procedure or in any way facilitate communication among therapists while the project was under way. To get some idea of each therapist's approach, a few sessions of every group were attended by an observer. Also, each therapist was asked to keep a daily record of his group's activities. Some therapists used only verbal communication during therapy; others arranged activities ranging from party games and dancing to "communal" painting and public speaking. All stressed interaction among members of their group.

RESULTS

The pre- and posttherapy test scores of all patients were subjected to covariance analysis. The covariance adjusted posttherapy scores of the untreated control group were then compared to those of the patients treated by lay therapists (Table 1) and those of the professional therapists (Table 2), respectively. This was done for each of the six tests separately. On all tests, with the exception of the Stroop, a high score indicates better performance than a low score.[2]

Similar comparisons were made between the posttherapy scores of pa-

[2]The reversal of direction in the Stroop test scores arises from the raw score's being expressed as a ratio.

tients receiving lay therapy and those treated by professionals (Table 3). Finally, in Table 4, interprofessional comparisons are made between the posttherapy test behavior of patients treated by social workers and psychiatrists.

TABLE 1

Covariance Adjusted Posttherapy Scores of Untreated Patients and Those Treated by Lay Therapists

TREATMENT		TAP	VF	VAL	DS	RT	STROOP
Untreated controls	Mean	45.763	11.699	26.218	20.428	.169	2.508
(N = 63)	*SD*	9.772	4.449	6.580	7.204	.054	.768
Treated by lay therapists	Mean	49.735	12.600	28.786	24.135	.197	1.025
(N = 87)	*SD*	10.222	4.370	8.264	6.812	.063	.698
	t	2.308**	1.295	1.801*	2.922****	2.613	2.336***

* $p < .10$.
** $p < .05$.
*** $p < .02$.
**** $p < .01$.

TABLE 2

Covariance Adjusted Posttherapy Scores of Untreated Patients and Those Treated by Professional Therapists

TREATMENT		TAP	VF	VAL	DS	RT	STROOP
Untreated controls	Mean	45.763	11.699	26.218	20.428	.169	2.508
(N = 63)	*SD*	9.772	4.449	6.580	7.204	.054	.768
Treated by professional therapists	Mean	46.372	10.948	28.104	23.187	.154	.835
(N = 145)	*SD*	9.894	3.061	6.950	5.612	.049	.579
	t	.387	1.148	1.427	2.313***	1.688	2.903****

***$p < .02$.
****$p < .01$.

It appears from these tables that the largest number of significant differences in test behavior occur between the untreated group and those groups treated by lay therapists. Four out of the six tests reflect significantly better performance by the patients of lay therapists. The VAL approaches significance in the expected direction.

On comparing the test behavior of the untreated with that of patients treated by professionals, only two out of six tests show significant superiority of the latter group (Table 2).

A direct comparison of patients treated by lay and professional therapists reveals a significantly better performance on the part of those treated by the former on three of the six tests (Table 3). It is of interest to note that the standard deviation on every test is smaller for the group of patients treated by professional therapists.

Table 4 suggests that there is no significant difference between post-therapeutic test performance of patients treated by social workers and the performance of those treated by psychiatrists.

TABLE 3

Covariance Adjusted Posttherapy Scores of Patients Treated by Lay and Professional Therapists

TREATMENT		TAP	VF	VAL	DS	RT	STROOP
Treated by lay therapists	Mean	49.735	12.600	28.786	24.135	.197	1.025
(N = 87)	*SD*	10.222	4.370	8.264	6.812	.063	.698
Treated by professional therapists	Mean	46.372	10.948	28.104	23.187	.154	.835
(N = 145)	*SD*	9.894	3.061	6.950	5.612	.049	.579
	t	2.331**	2.899****	.588	.930	4.998*****	.356

** $p < .05$.
**** $p < .01$.
***** $p < .001$.

TABLE 4

Covariance Adjusted Posttherapy Scores for Patients Treated by Social Workers and Psychiatrists

TREATMENT		TAP	VF	VAL	DS	RT	STROOP
Treated by social workers	Mean	47.332	10.613	27.687	22.324	.154	1.025
(N = 53)	*SD*	10.222	3.05	6.618	6.603	.063	.656
Treated by psychiatrists	Mean	46.252	11.212	28.011	23.307	.151	.755
(N = 60)	*SD*	8.978	3.162	7.899	5.459	.040	.561
	t	.564	.743	.203	.688	.249	.321

Because the study began with patients treated by lay therapists, it was possible before the end of the project to retest some of the patients and most of the untreated controls who took part in that first phase of the investigation. These scores, obtainable from 61 patients, constitute a 3-year follow-up and are presented in Table 5. To save time, only four of the original six tests were given in this part of the study, and a t test for correlated means was used to evaluate the difference between the two test sessions, separated by 3 years. Table 5 shows that test performance after 3

TABLE 5

Three-Year Follow-up of Schizophrenics
Treated by Lay Therapists
($N = 61$)

STAGE		TAP	VF	RT	VAL
Before treatment	Mean	38.84	9.02	326.24	19.08
	SD	19.63	5.50	405.09	14.07
Three years later	Mean	48.15	10.52	183.07	24.20
	SD	17.50	6.43	320.04	14.53
	t	4.22*****	2.58***	3.61*****	3.32****

*** $p < .02$.
**** $p < .01$.
***** $p < .001$.

years was still significantly better than it was before treatment on all of the tests used. That this result was not a function of greater familiarity with the tests at follow-up—by which time each patient had taken them twice before—is indicated by the result of retesting 23 untreated controls after 3 years. Only on the tapping test did they show significantly better performance on follow-up, much as they had done on the first retest after 5 months.

In an effort to get some measure of change in the patients' ward behavior, the Hospital Adjustment Scale was administered to 80 patients, all of whom had been treated by lay therapists. The scale was administered before treatment, and again after 5 months. On each occasion it was completed both by the nursing supervisor and an attendant familiar with the patients. The supervisor's ratings showed significant improvement between test and retest, but the attendants' ratings did not. It was felt that this equivocal result reflected little more than the greater ego-involvement of the supervisors, whose wish to see the project succeed might well have influenced their ratings.

Unfortunately it was not possible to have the scale completed by personnel sufficiently familiar with the patients to assess their behavior and yet unaware of their participation in the project. For this reason and also because of the ward staff's strong resistance to the time consuming task of filling out the scale it was not administered to subsequent therapy groups.

DISCUSSION

The objection may be made that changes in psychological test performance, as employed in this study, do not constitute a relevant criterion of therapeutic outcome. The usual alternatives are rating scales, questionnaires, or the comparison of discharge rates before and after therapy. None of these seemed appropriate for the present patient population, consisting as it did of schizophrenics with many years of hospitalization. The behavioral repertoire of such patients is so limited that rating scales are difficult to complete, as our own attempt at using the Hospital Adjustment Scale clearly showed. For the same reason, questionnaires completed by the patients would be hard to interpret. Discharge rates during and after therapy were compared, but showed no significant difference between treated and untreated groups. Nor would this be expected in the light of previous findings, such as those of Beck et al. (1963). Their study showed that in a sample of 120 psychotics, those who were discharged during the Harvard undergraduate volunteer program had, on the average, been hospitalized for 4.7 years, whereas the undischarged patients had been hospitalized for 12.4 years. This is consistent with earlier studies, suggesting that after 4 years of hospitalization only 3% of patients are likely to be discharged.

With one exception (Stroop) the verbal and performance tests employed in the present investigation were known from earlier work to discriminate effectively between psychotics and normals. It therefore seems justified to interpret significant incremental change in the treated groups' test behavior as reflecting therapeutic gain. This conclusion is validated by the absence of such change in the untreated control group on five out of the six tests. That the TAP did show significant improvement on retest of the control group may reflect the greater emphasis placed on activity programs for mental patients in recent years. On the other hand, since tapping was the first test to be administered to each patient, initial performance on it may have been impaired by apparatus stress or the novelty effect of the test situation.

Why lay therapists should have done somewhat better than professional therapists in facilitating the test behavior of their patients remains a matter of conjecture. It seems likely that the naïve enthusiasm they brought to the therapeutic enterprise, as well as their lack of "professional stance" permitted them to respond more freely to their patients' mood swings from day to day. Certainly, the activities in which they engaged their patients had a less stereotyped character than that offered by their professional counterparts. On the other hand, the greater standard deviation in the test behavior of those treated by lay therapists suggests that they may have helped some of their patients at the expense of others. Professional therapy, by contrast, seems to have had a more even effect on all participants.

The 3-year follow-up data for the untrained group are highly encouraging and support the conclusion that the therapy given achieved more than transient activation. It is planned to carry out similar follow-up studies on the patients treated by professional therapists.

The groups treated by fellow patients were too small to make quantitative assessment very meaningful. Their results were, however, treated separately in the covariance analysis and showed no significant difference from patients treated by lay or professional therapists. They received excellent cooperation from their fellows, as evidenced by their group attendance record, which showed full attendance in one group and 8 out of 10 in the other. Those who knew the patient-therapists clinically agreed that participation in the project had enhanced their mental health. Both are now discharged after prolonged hospitalization.

To extend the conclusions from this study beyond its present context, that is, the outcome of group therapy with chronic schizophrenics, would clearly be premature. When viewed in relation to the literature reviewed at the outset of this paper, the present findings do, however, support the conclusion that traditional training in the mental health professions may be neither optimal nor even necessary for the promotion of therapeutic behavior change in mental hospital patients.

REFERENCES

ANKER, J. M., & WALSH, R. P. Group psychotherapy, a special activity program, and group structure in the treatment of chronic schizophrenics. *Journal of Consulting Psychology*, 1961, **25**, 476–481.

BECK, J. C., KANTOR, D., & GELINEAU, V. A. Follow-up study of chronic psychotic patients "treated" by college case-aide volunteers. *American Journal of Psychiatry*, 1963, **120**, 269–271.

DIEHL, H. S., BAKER, A. B., & COWAN, D. W. Cold vaccines, further evaluation. *Journal of the American Medical Association*, 1940, **115**, 593–594.

FIEDLER, F. E. A comparison of therapeutic relationships in psychoanalytic, non-directive and Adlerian therapy. *Journal of Consulting Psychology*, 1950, **14**, 436–445.

FRANK, J. D., NASH, E. H., STONE, A. R., & IMBER, S. D. Immediate and long-term symptomatic course of psychiatric outpatients. *American Journal of Psychiatry*, 1963, **120**, 429–439.

GELDER, M. G., MARKS, I. M., SAKINOFSKY, I., & WOLFF, H. H. Behavior therapy and psychotherapy for phobic disorders: Alternative or complementary procedures? Paper presented at the 6th International Congress of Psychotherapy, London, 1964.

JELLINEK, E. M. Clinical tests on comparative effectiveness of analgesic drugs. *Biometrics Bulletin*. 1946, **2**, 87.

McREYNOLDS, P., & FERGUSON, J. T. *Clinical manual for the Hospital Adjustment Scale.* Palo Alto: Consulting Psychologists Press, 1946.

POSER, E. G. Group therapy in Canada: A national survey. *Canadian Psychiatric Association Journal,* 1966, 11, 20–25.

RIOCH, M. J., ELKES, C., FLINT, A. A., USDANSKY, B. S., NEWMAN, R. G., & SILBER, E. National Institute of Mental Health pilot study in training mental health counselors. *American Journal of Orthopsychiatry,* 1963, 33, 678–689.

ROGERS, C. R. The necessary and sufficient conditions of therapeutic personality change. *Journal of Consulting Psychology,* 1957, 21, 95–103.

ROSENTHAL, D., & FRANK, J. D. Psychotherapy and the placebo effect. *Psychological Bulletin,* 1956, 53, 294–302.

SCHOFIELD, W. *Psychotherapy: The purchase of friendship.* Englewood Cliffs, N. J.: Prentice-Hall, 1964.

SIGAL, J. The Verdun Association List. Unpublished doctoral dissertation, University of Montreal, 1956.

THURSTONE, L. L., & MELLINGER, J. J. *The Stroop test.* University of North Carolina, The Psychometric Laboratory, 1953.

TRUAX, C. B. Effective ingredients in psychotherapy: An approach to unraveling the patient-therapist interactions. *Journal of Counseling Psychology,* 1963, 10, 256–263.

SUGGESTED ADDITIONAL READINGS

Anker, James M., and Walsh, Richard P. Group psychotherapy, a special activity program, and group structure in the treatment of chronic schizophrenics. *Journal of Consulting Psychology*, 1961, Vol. 25, No. 6, 476–481.

Appleby, Lawrence. Evaluation of treatment methods for chronic schizophrenia. *Archives of General Psychiatry*, 1963, Vol. 8, 8–21.

Beck, J. C., Kantor, D., and Gelineau, V. A. Follow-up study of chronic psychotic patients "treated" by college case-aide volunteers. *American Journal of Psychiatry*, 1963, Vol. 120, 269–271.

Berenson, Bernard G., Carkhuff, Robert R., and Myrus, Pamela. The interpersonal functioning and training of college students. *Journal of Counseling Psychology*, 1966, Vol. 13, No. 4, 441–446.

Berkowitz, Samuel. Acquisition and maintenance of generalized imitative repertoires of profoundly retarded children with retarded peers functioning as models and reinforcing agents. Unpublished doctoral dissertation, University of Maryland, 1968.

Berzon, Betty, & Solomon, Lawrence N. The self-directed therapeutic group: Three studies. *Journal of Counseling Psychology*, 1966, Vol. 13, No. 4, 491–497.

Brown, Paul, and Elliott, Rogers. Control of aggression in a nursery school class. *Journal of Experimental Child Psychology*, 1965, Vol. 2, 103–107.

Gelfand, Donna M., Gelfand, Sidney, and Dobson, William R. Unprogrammed reinforcement of patients' behaviour in a mental hospital. *Behaviour Research and Therapy*, 1967, Vol. 5, 201–207.

Holzberg, Jules D., Gerwitz, Herbert, and Ebner, Eugene. Changes in moral judgment and self-acceptance in college students as a function of companionship with hospitalized mental patients. *Journal of Consulting Psychology*, 1964, Vol. 28, No. 4, 299–303.

Holzberg, Jules D., and Knapp, Robert H. The social interaction of college students and chronically ill mental patients. *American Journal of Orthopsychiatry*, 1965, Vol. 35, 487–492.

Holzberg, Jules D., Knapp, Robert H., and Turner, John L. Companionship with the mentally ill: Effects on the personalities of college student volunteers. *Psychiatry*, 1966, Vol. 29, No. 4, 395–405.

Levenstein, Phyllis, and Sunley, Robert. An effect of stimulating verbal interaction between mothers and children around play materials. Paper presented at the 44th Annual Meeting of the American Orthopsychiatric Association, Washington, D. C., 1967.

Linden, James I., and Stollak, Gary E. The training of undergraduates in play techniques. *Journal of Clinical Psychology*, in press.

Magoon, Thomas M., and Golann, Stuart E. Nontraditionally trained women as mental health counselors/psychotherapists. *Personnel and Guidance Journal*, 1966, Vol. 44, 788–792.

May, Dorothy C. Use of volunteers in conjunction with psychotherapy. Masters thesis, Smith College School for Social Work, 1949.

McGinnis, C. A. The effect of group therapy on the ego-strength scale scores of alcoholic patients. *Journal of Clinical Psychology*, 1963, Vol. 19, 346–347.

Mendel, Werner M., and Rapport, Samuel. Outpatient treatment for chronic schizophrenic patients: Therapeutic consequences of an existential view. *Archives of General Psychiatry*, 1963, Vol. 8, 190–196.

Rappaport, Julian, and Chinsky, Jack M. Non-professionals as mental health workers in a state hospital setting: A preliminary report. Paper presented at the 39th Annual Meeting of the Eastern Psychological Association, Washington, D. C., April, 1968.

Rosenbaum, Max. Some comments on the use of untrained therapists. *Journal of Consulting Psychology*, 1966, Vol. 30, No. 4, 292–294.

Schiffer, Allan L. The effectiveness of group play therapy as assessed by specific changes in a child's peer relations. Paper presented at the meeting of the American Orthopsychiatric Association, Washington, D. C., 1967.

Sines, Lloyd K., Silver, Reuben J., and Lucero, Rubel J. The effect of therapeutic intervention by untrained "therapists." *Journal of Clinical Psychology*, 1961, Vol. 17, No. 4, 394–396.

Truax, Charles B. The use of supportive personnel in rehabilitation counseling: Process and outcome. Mimeographed document. The Rehabilitation Research and Training Center, University of Arkansas, Fayetteville, Arkansas.

Wahler, Robert G. Behavior therapy for oppositional children: Love is not enough. Paper presented at the 39th Annual Meeting of the Eastern Psychological Association, Washington, D. C., April, 1968.

Ward, Michael H., and Baker, Bruce L. Reinforcement therapy in the classroom. Paper presented at the 39th Annual Meeting of the Eastern Psychological Association, Washington, D. C., April, 1968.

Wolf, Montrose M., Giles, David K., and Hall, R. Vance. Experiments with token reinforcement in a remedial classroom. Unpublished manuscript.

Zunker, Vernon G., and Brown, William F. Comparative effectiveness of student and professional counselors. *Personnel and Guidance Journal*, 1966, Vol. 44, 738–743.

Name Index

Subject Index